Readings in Medieval History

Volume II

Readings in Medieval History

Volume II

second edition

edited by
Patrick J. Geary

broadview press

Canadian Cataloguing in Publication Data

Main entry under title:

Readings in medieval history

2nd ed.
ISBN 1-55111-211-6 (v. 2)

1. Middle Ages – History – Sources. I. Geary, Patrick J., 1948–

D113.R42 1998   940.1   C98-930375-6

Broadview Press
Post Office Box 1243, Peterborough, Ontario, Canada K9J 7H5

in the United States of America:
3576 California Road, Orchard Park, NY 14127

in the United Kingdom:
B.R.A.D. Book Representation & Distribution Ltd., 244A, London Road, Hadleigh, Essex SS7 2DE

Broadview Press gratefully acknowledges the support of the Canada Council, the Ontario Arts Council, and the Ministry of Canadian Heritage.

Typesetting and assembly: True to Type Inc., Mississauga, Canada.

PRINTED IN CANADA

Preface

"History is merely the applied utilization of documents." This old dictum of the positivist-historicist tradition, rightly criticized by generations of historians reacting against a mechanical, pseudo-objective approach to history, nevertheless contains a deep and abiding truth. History is after all done with documents — primary sources are at the heart of the historical enterprise. But the dictum should be qualified in two ways. First, we must remember how much this "applied utilization," far from being an objective and naturally imposed process, is rather one of creativity and interpretation. Second, "document" must be understood in a broad sense to denote not just written texts but every echo of the past, written, oral, physical, mental. In this sense every historian must begin with documents, and every student of history must be exposed to these documents in order to understand the creative elaborations that are what historians of every stripe make of them. A healthy introduction to such primary sources is not only vital to the development of historical understanding, but it is also the source of the greatest pleasure to historians, the creative pursuit of meaning in the past, and thus a pleasure which should not be denied students.

It is the modest intention of this volume to place at the disposal of students beginning their exploration of medieval history some of these documents so that they can actually participate in the continuing process of interpretation and debate which is at the heart of the historical enterprise. I hope that these documents will bring them more than merely a deeper knowledge of the received tradition of medieval history. May the recognition of the fragmentary and ambiguous nature of the documentation with which historians have reconstructed the past inspire in students a healthy scepticism toward these syntheses and engender an impatience to acquire the necessary skills to do their own medieval history and to do it better.

Since this volume intends neither to argue for any particular interpretation of medieval history nor to serve as mere illustration of currently fashionable historical theses, four principles have guided the selection of the documents it contains.

First, entire documents or long excerpts have been included whenever possible, since truncated and severely abridged texts do not allow students to understand the form and context of historical sources or to attempt their own analyses of them. The result is a volume containing fewer texts than might be desired, but students and instructors should be able to do more with those that are included. The editor particularly regrets that, with the exception of the Old High German *Song of Hildebrand*, literary texts have been excluded. The reason is that excellent inexpensive translations of the classics of medieval literature are generally available for students and should be included in any history syllabus.

Second, rather than selecting widely different texts to illustrate particular issues, some texts are grouped to form a dossier in which the individual documents relate to each other. This is of course what the practicing historian attempts to compile and examine. These examples, such as the series of documents concerning land holding from Cluny, three contradictory treatises on the eternality of the world, and a group of Florentine catasto filings from the Alberti family, provide students with the opportunity to examine historical questions from a variety of differing documents and perspectives. Likewise, it should be possible for students to make valid connections among documents across units. Thus, for example, the selection from the Theodosian code can be related to texts from the Salic law, Anglo-Saxon law, and twelfth-century Italian marriage contracts. Guibert of Nogent's autobiography can be compared with that of the emperor Charles IV and the *Book of Margery Kempe*.

Third, wherever possible the documents presented here have been selected because they have been the object of significant scholarship available in English. Nothing is more frustrating for a student beginning to develop an interest in medieval history than to find the issues he or she raises in relationship to a particular text have been discussed only in Continental languages. Thus, for example, one reason for the selection of the book of the miracles of St. Foy rather than other hagiographic texts is that it has been the subject of a number of recent studies in English from a variety of perspectives. The example of an inquisitorial dossier comes from Montaillou, brilliantly if controversially studied by Emmanuel Le Roy Ladurie.

Finally, although I have my own prejudices and preferences in terms of how one does history, I have made a sincere effort to provide the raw material for many types of historical investigations. There is no one exercise that can be done with each document, no single way that an instructor can make use of them, nor is there one point of view toward which the selection of documents tacitly points. They can be used equally by the political historian, the cultural historian, the social historian or the historian of mentalities.

Of course, every historical enterprise is limited by the perspective and competence of the investigator, and this volume is no exception. One could easily compile an equally valuable alternative list of readings to this one, and one could validly object to the geographical limitations from which the sources are taken. I have tried to take into account the range of documents my colleagues are currently using by surveying medievalists and by examining syllabi and other source books. I have then selected accurate translations or made new ones. Finally, I have included a number of hitherto untranslated texts in order to provide the sorts of documents representative of the types of sources to which medievalists are turning in contemporary research. I sincerely hope that my colleagues will feel free to send me suggestions for additions and deletions so that future editions of the volume may be even more responsive to their needs.

Don LePan, President of Broadview Press, who suggested that a new medieval reader was needed and encouraged me to undertake it, deserves much of the credit for this book. I would like to thank as well Barbara Rosenwein, Susanna Foster Baxandall, George Beech, and Jonathan M. Elukin for their contributions. I owe a lasting debt of gratitude to John William Rooney, Jr., who first introduced me to the joy of reading the sources of medieval history. Wolter Braamhorst and Anne Picard spent many hours assisting me in finding appropriate translations and editions. J. Patout Burns and Richard Kay provided many useful suggestions for revisions.

I have been gratified by the positive response that greeted the first edition of *Readings in Medieval History*. Clearly the book has proven useful to many teachers and students over the past seven years. In preparing a second edition, Don Le Pan, the editor of Broadview Press, and I took advantage of the many written comments that we have received through the years from users. Many instructors urged that certain texts be added or omitted, although no clear consensus emerged that particular basic and essential documents were absent or that others were superficial. We determined therefore to eliminate very little (only the selection from Martinus Capella's *Marriage of Philology and Mercury*) but to add in one particular area that was frequently cited as under-represented: the voices of women in the medieval world. Thus, in addition to the *Passion of Saint Perpetua*, the *Testament of Clare of Assisi*, the testimony of Beatrice of Planissoles before the inquisition of Jacques Fournier, and the *Book of Margery Kempe*, and the 1427 catasto reports of the women of the Alberti family of Florence already in the first edition, we have added the *Life of Queen Batildis*, written by a nun of the monastery of Chelles in the seventh century, a long selection from the trial of Joan of Arc, and sections from the *Dialogues of Catherine of Siena*.

There was much greater consensus on other issues. The first edition contained a number of typographical and other similar errors. Students and instructors alike found the pages too crowded to annotate passages as they went along. With the able assistance of Ronald Finucane the vast majority of these have been corrected. We have also enlarged the format of the book so that students can use the wider margins for note taking. We hope that the result is a more attractive and useful book and one that will continue to open a world of excitement and wonder to students of the middle ages into the new millennium.

Patrick J. Geary

For my students and especially in memory of

Bridget Bernadette Phillips

1966–1989

whose tragic death cut short a career of great promise.

Contents

MIRACLES OF SAINT FOY

SAINT FOY (FAITH) WAS TRADITIONALLY REPUTED TO HAVE BEEN A girl of twelve martyred at Agen in 303. In the ninth century monks from the monastery of Conques stole her relics and brought them to their monastery where they became the object of a major pilgrimage from the tenth century. The body of the saint was kept in a case reliquary while the head was venerated in a golden statue which represented the young woman seated in glory.

Bernard of Angers, a student of Fulbert of Chartres (ca. 960-1028) and later director of the episcopal school in Angers, made three pilgrimages to Conques and, although at first skeptical of the cult, was entirely won over to the saint. His book of her miracles helped to spread the cult of Saint Foy across Europe and also served as a model for hagiographical dossiers for other cults.

Source: A. Bouillet, ed. *Liber miraculorum Sancte Fidis* (Paris: Alphonse Picard, 1897).

Concerning Vuitbert whose eyes, having been gouged out, were restored by Saint Foy

In the region of Rodez where reposes the blessed virgin Foy, in the vicus of Conques, there lived a priest named Gerald, who is still alive. He had a godson who was attached to him both by kinship and by episcopal confirmation named Vuitbert, who was his domestic servant and a competent administrator of his property. Once this Vuitbert went to Conques to celebrate the feast. When the solemn vigil was completed the next morning, that is the very day of the feast, as he was returning home, by bad fortune he encountered his lord who had been moved against him by an inexplicable evil zeal. This priest, when he saw him in the garb of a pilgrim, began with words of peace, but then was roused to aggressive abuse: "Well, Vuitbert, I see you have become a Roman." (This was the way the people of the area called pilgrims). He answered, "Yes, master, I am returning from the feast of Saint Foy." Then after speaking amicably of various things, the priest gave him permission to depart. But after he had gone on a little way, looking over his back this priest of the Jewish treason, if one can call one contaminated by such a sacrilege a priest, ordered his servant to wait a bit for him. Vuitbert complied and suddenly the priest ordered him to be encircled and held by his men.

When he saw this, shaking with fear, he asked of what crime he was accused, but the evil man gave only this response: "You did me wrong and are planning even worse things. This is why I want for reparations nothing less than your own eyes," and would not describe any more openly the nature of the offense as if from modesty. It is unjust for a priest to make judgment based on his own jealousy since the cause of this evil had arisen from the suspicion of debauchery with women. Vuitbert, since he was ignorant of the affair, confidently offered to vindicate himself of all culpability. "My lord," he said, "if you would openly indicate all the crimes of which you suspect me, I am prepared to refute them legally. I am unable to determine by what law I ought to incur your wrath and that of your followers." The priest replied, "Enough, enough, of your superficial excuses; the sentence has been pronounced: your eyes will be torn out."

But Vuitbert, seeing the priest stand firm in his gladiatorial resolve and seeing the hour of his irreparable destruction imminent, and discerning no other opportunity of defending himself but prayer, although despairing of his safety, made this plea: "Lord, pardon me! If not for my innocence, at least for the love of God and of Saint Foy for the love of whom I am now wearing the holy habit of a pilgrim."

At these words the wild monster, not taking

seriously either God or his saint, contorted by rage, vomited forth the poison of blasphemy which he had in his heart: "Neither God not Saint Foy will save you today! You will not be able to escape my hands by invoking them. And don't expect that out of reverence for the habit of a pilgrim I would consider you worthy and inviolable since you have so evilly harmed me." This said, he ordered the man be thrown down and that his eyes be torn out. But when he could force none of his three men whose names we omit because of the horror of this barbarity, to carry out such a deed, ordering them at least to hold him down and descending from his horse, he tore out the eyes of his godson with the same fingers which were consecrated to holding the body of Christ and tossed them away.

These things did not happen without the presence of the heavenly power, which does not abandon men who call upon divine assistance and is always near those calling on it in truth and which passes judgment for those enduring injury. Those who were present immediately saw a snow white dove, or as the doer of this evil deed claimed, a magpie. This magpie or dove took up the bloody eyes of the poor unfortunate and rising high above the earth carried them toward Conques.

Nor should one wonder if God entrusted magpies with the task of protecting the eyes in this desert of a place since he had preserved the life of Elias in the desert by means of ravens. Or by chance, as the divinity wished, unknown birds may have come, which could be thought of neither as magpies nor as doves. In truth there is no ambiguity between the two types of birds since the servants saw a white dove, but the priest was unable to see anything but a pie which is distinctive by its black and white. But because God shows himself terrible to the evildoer and mild to the just, it may be that for the innocent and for those grieving with a clear conscience at the sight of such evil a white species of bird was seen while it appeared mixed to the evil doer. Nevertheless when the wicked priest saw this, he was overcome with remorse and began to cry profusely, at which one of his companions told him that it was too late and in vain to act in such a way. After he departed, he never again celebrated

the mass either because he did not dare to do so having perpetrated such a crime or, as is more likely, because he altogether neglected it because of worldly concerns.

The mother of this Gerald, profoundly upset by the great wrong done to an innocent person, received Vuitbert into her home and provided for everything he needed with great charity until he was well. For during this same time he had gone before her, not on the order of his lord but rather to show her the more severe than usual atrocity which on her word her son had caused, by which false zeal she felt wounded in her heart. Once he was well in the same year he sought his food in the art of a public entertainer and so well accepted his injury that as he was accustomed to say he did not worry about not having eyes, so much did the desire for gain and the pleasure of amusing delight him.

A year passed. The day before the vigil of Saint Foy, he had fallen to sleep when he saw before him a young girl of indescribable beauty. Her appearance was like that of an angel. Her face shone and appeared with droplets of rose and scarlet. Her expression surpassed all human beauty. Her size was as had been read that it was in the time of her passion, that of an adolescent, not yet of mature age. She wore majestic clothing entirely brocaded of gold and surrounded by a variety of subtle colors. Her wide sleeves, carefully pleated, fell to her feet. She wore on her head a diadem decorated with four gems from which radiated extraordinary light. The smallness of her body seems to me to have signified nothing more than that at the time of her passion, as we have said, one reads that she had been a youth.

The beauty of her mouth, in so far as it was given to the one to which this vision appeared to see, and her marvelous clothing, were not, I believe, without cause, for these were in themselves glorious symbols. We can see that the so to speak too large clothes represented the armour or protection of overflowing faith. The golden radiance properly represents the illumination of spiritual grace. What could the delicacy of the colors and the pleated sleeves mean unless they offered the trace of divine wisdom? On the most important part of the body, that is the head, were seen four gems, which remind us of the four principal virtues, prudence, fortitude, justice and temperance. Since Saint Foy had the knowledge and perfection of these virtues and, deeply filled with the Holy Spirit she cultivated in the depths of her loving heart those other virtues derived from these, she was altogether pleasing to the Most-High. Moreover, not ignorant of the greatest good she offered herself to holy martyrdom as a willing and pure sacrifice to Christ. There remains the beauty of her face. We mentioned it first according to the order of our account, reserving its mystery for the end because it presents us with the culmination and the end of all life, that is, charity. It is right that charity be represented by white which surpasses all the colors by its brilliance. It is right to understand charity, the most perfect of virtues, which we place before the ruddiness which suggests martyrdom. This is not absurd because no one obtains the grace of martyrdom without the eminence of charity. Saint Foy heroically protected this virtue when for His love she faced with bravery a horrible death.

Thus the saint, leaning on the bedpost, softly touched the right cheek of the sleeper and whispered to him, "Vuitbert, are you asleep?" He answered, "Who is there?" "I am Saint Foy," she replied. "My lady, why have you come to me?" "Simply to see you." Vuitbert thanked her, and Saint Foy replied, "Do you know me?" He recognized her as if he had already seen her and answered, "Yes, I see you well, my lady, and I recognize you perfectly." "Tell me how you are and how your affairs are doing." "Very well, my Lady, and all is going very well. Everything succeeds for me by the grace of God." "What," she said, "how can all be going well when you cannot see the light of the heavens?" But he, as happens in dreams, thought that he could see although he could not. This last question reminded him of his torn out eyes. "How could I see," he asked, "when, last year, while returning from your feast, alas, I lost my eyes by the brutality of an unjust master?" The saint said, "He offended God too much and raised the anger of the Creator, he who harmed you so seriously in your body without your having merited it. But if tomorrow, on the vigil of my martyrdom, you go to Conques, and you buy two candles and place one before the

altar of the Holy Savior, the other before the altar where my bodily clay is placed, you will merit to enjoy the complete restoration of your eyes. For with a great supplication concerning the injury done you I moved the piety of the divine Judge to mercy. I bothered God by my incessant prayers until I obtained for you this cure." After these words she still insisted and urged him to go to Conques and encouraged him because he hesitated before the expense. "A thousand people, whom you have never before seen," she said, "will give to you. Besides, so that you can easily complete the present business, go quickly at dawn to the church of this parish, (this was the parish of he who had deprived him of his eyes which since ancient times was called Espeyrac) and hear Mass there, and you will receive six pence." He thanked her as a benefactor deserved and the celestial power left him.

He awoke immediately and went to the church where he told his vision. People thought that he was delirious. But not at all discouraged, he went through the crowd asking each in order to obtain twelve pence. Finally a certain Hugo, moving apart from the others, opened his purse and offered him six pence and one obole, that is, a little more than the vision had announced. This first success increased his confidence. What more can I say? He arrived at Conques, told his vision to the monks, bought the candles, presented them to the altar, and started the vigil before the golden statue of the holy martyr.

Around midnight it seemed to him that he could see as though two small glowing berries, no larger than the fruit of a laurel, came from above and buried themselves deeply into his gouged eye sockets. At the shock, his thoughts became muddled and he fell asleep. But at the hour of lauds the chanting of the psalms awoke him and he seemed to see spots of light and the silhouettes of people moving about, but he had an unbelievable headache and only half conscious he thought that he was dreaming. Gradually coming out of his stupor, he began to distinguish more clearly forms and finally himself again he recalled the vision he had seen. He raised his hands to his eyes and touched those windows of his flesh returned to the light and entirely reconstituted. He went to tell his neighbors and broke forth in praises for the immeasurable magnificence of Christ. This caused an indescribable rejoicing. Each person asked himself if he was dreaming or if he had actually seen an extraordinary miracle. The most amazed were those who had known him the longest.

Among these things something ridiculous and worthy of applause happened. Since he was a man of the purest simplicity, the fear entered his heart that perhaps that Gerald who had torn out his eyes might come to the public feast and again if he should by chance encounter him he might once more by the force of his hand remove the glory of his eyes in his wrath. Therefore amongst the confusion of the common crowd he attempted to slip away unseen. Since he was not yet certain of the gift of recovering his sight a great bewilderment took over him when by chance hurrying with the tightly packed crowd to the church he came opposite an ass which he saw as clear as day. When he had admired it, rebuking its owner with severity, he said, "You, whoever you are, you fool, move your ass so that you do not block travellers." When the former was absolutely certain of what had happened, he withdrew quickly and hurried to find a certain knight known to him whose city (castle) was situated on a high cliff whence it was protected by nature such that it appeared inaccessible to all sorts of siege machines, not further from Conques than sixteen miles. After he had fled to this castle because of the protection of its impregnable valleys, with difficulty he at last returned (to Conques) because of the many entreaties and promises of security made by the monks. When many people coming from far and near hurried there desiring to see him because of this unheard-of miracle, as they left rejoicing they gave him many gifts. And this is what Saint Foy had said to him in the vision as we said, "A thousand men whom you have never seen will give to you," naming a finite number, as is customary in the Scriptures, for an infinite one.

Next, so that he might be better known and established in the place, abbot Arlaldus of happy memory who has recently died, with the common agreement of the brothers, gave him the task of selling wax which was extremely abundant here by the hand of God. From whence, when he had gathered together with many complaints he began, as is the nature of men, to become swollen with pride, and when there appeared in his soul the desire of a woman, he immediately forgot the dignity of the miracle worked in him. But in order that this might not be borne unavenged, suddenly the revenge of the holy virgin caused the misfortune that one of the man's eyes was blinded, not totally, and when he was led to the remedy of penance, she entirely restored his vision. Later on he again and again fell into the habit of wallowing in lust, and pursued by divine vengeance, he lost the vision of one eye, and recovered it when he repented. We could write as many chapters of miracles as often as this happened, were our purpose not to avoid excess. At last, when this had happened to him without cease, he lost the use of both his eyes. For this reason, in order to do more perfect penance, after cutting his beard and receiving the tonsure, he bound himself over to the clerical order. Although this ignorant and illiterate layman did this, nevertheless it was founded in love of God and thus he merited to recover his eyesight. Thus finally after so many lashings of correction, the impatience of his lust which could be said to have heaped up filth in him, was not punished corporally any further. Now this old man, reduced by evil actions to the lowest value and poverty, now is nourished by the public alms of the brothers, and he is content with his diminished condition and for the most part the support offered him in his twilight years. He rejoices in the fame of such a restoration, altogether secure from the fickleness of frivolity.

Thus I, a witness of the truth of divine providence, have painted without any falsification, as is contained in this writing, what I received from the mouth of this Vuitbert. Nor did I add anything for a more decorative effect nor do I think that I can escape unpunished if I think to celebrate in a lying style this eternal friend and beloved of God Saint Foy, who it is known suffered the deadly sentence of martyrdom for truth which is Christ. Finally, since many whose authority is sufficiently accepted have accepted prodigious things even though they happened much before their own time only based on the testimony of those who were not present at the events and who were intent to describe them in the most elegant manner, why should I allow things which took place in my own time and which I saw with my own eyes, and concerning which the people of the Auvergne, Rouergue, the Toulousin, and other regions present indisputable testimony, which pertain to our duty of teaching, disappear from memory? Especially since this thing which we have just finished describing with such little adornment almost violently forces such an insignificant person as myself to presume to present a subject so dangerous and arduous.

In this region there are few people trained in writing, I do not know whether by sloth or ignorance (since there are many who glory in the profession of learning who never show themselves learned by their works), but these writers, ungrateful for their gifts, have either wilfully neglected these great events or been entirely ignorant of them. Therefore I declare that it is better to be accused of audacity than to incur the guilt of negligence provided that I attempt to write down in letters what by no means he can do if writing for posterity is to be served without having the reproach of doubt or the condemnation of truth. So that there should be no doubt that this above mentioned Vuitbert was not immediately cured by divine mercy there, but in truth as was said above lost his eyes, he was without health for a whole year. Moreover he showed the taking of his eyes by evil means to many of his neighbors and when this had been recognized by all He cured him at last. Thus this miracle was no less than that of the man born blind in the Gospel possibly even more astonishing. But we recall what the Truth had promised: "He who believes in me, the works which I do he too will do, and he will even do greater things because I go to the Father."

XI Concerning those who, robbing St. Foy, suddenly perished in the collapse of a roof

There was another miracle of divine vengeance, but in a time before my arrival, which encourages the ecclesiastics and those devotedly serving the divine cult in the house of God and which terrified those who violently rob the goods of the holy

church of God or who claim the inheritance of the saints as their own right. For in this time there are many whom we can justly term antichrists, who are so blinded by ambition that they dare to invade church rights, that they not only do not revere the offices of sacred ministry but they even attack them not only with invective and with beatings, but even afflict them with death. We have seen canons, monks and abbots despoiled of their honor and deprived of their goods and destroyed by death. We have seen bishops, some condemned by proscription, others expelled from their bishopric without cause, others cut down with the sword, and even burned by Christians in terrible flames for the defense of ecclesiastical rights, if in truth one can call those people Christians, who attack the order of Christian religion, they who stand opposed to Christ and to truth in all things. Because these undergo no punishment in the present life, they are not terrified by celestial vengeance. Rather they hope that there will never be any vengeance and there are even those who do not believe in a future judgment because in doing evil they have always enjoyed success and in following their own wills they have always escaped punishment. They have never experienced any hint of vengeance and therefore what they hear about vengeance of Christ they consider to be fables. Therefore it is necessary that the divine avenger punish some of them even in this world, lest they becomes so elated by their impunity that it appear a trivial thing to irritate God. It is also needed so that prowling folly, which rejects the sweet yoke of Christ and disdains the warnings of holy correction might be so bridled by the suffering of present punishments so that it will impose a limit on its own malice lest it be more severely punished or that it might repent altogether and return to health. Then those who prepared their soul similarly for a like deed might be terrified by such an example and might repent of their intended evil, and might hurry in penance to the society of the sons of light. But having spoken about these things first, let us come now to that end toward which we hurry.

There was in the region of Cahors a noble woman, Doda, lord of Castelnau on the Dordogne. She had unjustly occupied an estate of

Saint Foy which is called Alans. At the moment of her death, concerned about the salvation of her soul, she returned this property to the monastery of Conques. Hildegar, the son of her daughter, succeeded her, rich in the abundance of wealth as well as in the honor of office. He ruled from this famous castle in the territory of Albi called Penne, and he again dared to invade once more the same property and to take it from the monastery of Conques. For this reason the monks, in order to recover their property through the justice of the divine judge from the hand of this most violent robber, as was their custom, decided to go to in procession with the populace carrying as was the custom, the venerable effigy of the holy virgin. I shall explain later my feelings about this image, which might appear to be an object of superstition. There it happened that a knight of Hildegar (the grandson of Doda), whose name we forget and right now we are not able to return to Conques in order to ask for it, was reveling on Christmas, was dining in the midst of splendid knights and a succession of servants. Having consumed more wine than he was accustomed, among other things bodily abused the servants of Saint Foy, called them vile manure, protesting that he was amused to see the monks carrying their statue, a mask or sham worthy of ridicule and spittle, onto the contested estate. He would not be scared away by this nor would he defend his lord's rights any less violently and strenuously. Rather it seemed simple if he were to show how altogether vile this statue was by trampling it under foot. It would be tedious to tell how many times, three and four or more, he repeated such insults and laughter, when suddenly, the terrible sound of a divine storm was heard. It suddenly destroyed the balcony, the structure of the upper story collapsed, and all of the roof fell in. However, of the whole multitude who were present, only the blasphemer, his wife, and his five servants were killed. And so that no one might think that the house collapsed and that these men were killed by chance; the seven bodies were found thrown far out of the windows. Their remains lie in the cemetery of Saint-Antoin in the region of Albi.

Listen, robbers and devastators of Christian estates: the punishments of God are ineluctable and just are his judgments. His vengeance cedes place to no power; if it hold back for a time, it will strike with more force in the future. If you escape it in the present, a harsher punishment awaits you: that of eternal fire.

XII The processions of Saint Foy

There are many and undeniable indications that divine justice exercises a terrible judgment upon those who speak against Saint Foy. We will tell about one most extraordinary event when we speak about the image of the holy martyr. It is an ancient custom in all of Auvergne, Rodez, Toulouse and the neighboring regions that the local saint has a statue of gold, silver, or some other metal according to their means. This statue serves as a reliquary for the head of the saint or for a part of his body. The learned might see in this a superstition and a vestige of the cult of demons, and I myself who am but an ignoramus had the same impression the first time that I saw the statue of Saint Gerard enthroned on the altar resplendent with gold and stones, with an expression so human that the simple people sense that they are being watched by the gaze of an inquisitor and they pretend that it winks at pilgrims whose prayers it answers. I admit to my shame that turning to my friend Bernerius and laughing I whispered to him in Latin, "What do you think of the idol? Wouldn't Jupiter or Mars be happy with it?" And Bernerius was inspired to add rather ingenuous pleasantries and to revile the statue. We were not wrong: when one adores the true God, it is inappropriate and absurd to make images of plaster, wood or bronze except for the image of the Lord crucified that Christian piety makes with love to celebrate the memory of the passion of the Lord and which all of the holy Church has adopted. As for saints, it is sufficient that the truthful books or frescoes on walls recall their memory. For we do not tolerate statues of saints for any reason, unless as an ancient abuse and an eradicable and inborn custom of the ignorant. In certain regions these images take on such an importance that if, for example, I had the misfortune to express my reflections on the image of St. Gerard out loud, I would have had to pay dearly for my crime.

Three days later we arrived at Saint Foy. At the moment that we entered the monastery it happened by chance that the back of the sanctuary where the holy image is kept was open. We approached but the crowd was such that we could not prostrate ourselves like so many others already lying on the floor. Unhappy, I remained standing, fixing my view on the image and murmuring this prayer, "Saint Foy, you whose relics rest in this sham, come to my assistance on the day of judgment." And this time again I looked at my companion the scholastic Bernerius from out of the corner because I found it outrageous that all of these rational beings should be praying to a mute and inanimate object. My idle talk or little understanding nevertheless did not come from a clean conscience, because I should not have disrespectfully called a sacred image, which is not consulted for divination by means of sacrifices like an idol but is rather for revering the memory of a martyr in honor of the highest God, a sham like those of Venus of Diana. Later I greatly regretted to have acted so stupidly toward the saint of God. This was because among other miracles Don Adalgerius, at that time dean and later as I have heard, abbot (of Conques and Figeac), told me a remarkable account of a cleric named Oldaric. One day when the venerable image had to be taken to another place, because he thought himself smarter than the others, his heart was so twisted that he restrained the crowd from bringing offerings and he insulted and belittled the image of the saint with various insults. The next night, a lady of imposing severity appeared to him: "You," she said, "how dare you insult my image?" Having said this, she flogged her enemy with a staff which she was seen to carry in her right hand. He survived only long enough to tell the vision in the morning.

Thus there is no place left for arguing whether the effigy of Saint Foy ought to be venerated since it is clear that he who reproached the holy martyr nevertheless retracted his reproach, nor is it a spurious idol where nefarious rites of sacrifice or of divination are conducted, but rather a plus memorial of the holy virgin before which great numbers of faithful decently and eloquently implore her efficacious intercession for their sins. And what is more wisely to be recognized,

the container of the relics of the saints was made as a votive offering of the craftsman in the form of that person and is by far a more precious treasure than the ark of the covenant was of old. In the statue of Saint Foy her whole head is preserved, which is surely one of the most noble pearls of the celestial Jerusalem. Out of consideration of her merits, the divine goodness effects such prodigies that I have never heard the like concerning any other saint in our time. Therefore the image of Saint Foy is not something which ought to be destroyed or vituperated, especially since it has never led anyone to fall back into the error of paganism nor has it lessened the virtues of the saints nor caused the slightest harm to religion.

XXVIII That Saint Foy performs great miracles at synods and concerning the boy in whom a fourfold miracle was worked

Nor do I think it should be omitted that among the many bodies of saints which are carried to councils as is the custom of the region, Saint Foy, holding as it were the first place, shows forth the glory of miracles. Among the many of these there are two which we do not think tedious to recount in this book. The most reverend Arnaldus, bishop of Rodez (1025-1031) convoked a synod in his dioceses to which the various bodies of the saints were carried from the various communities of monks and canons. The battle lines of the saints were arranged in tents and pavilions in the field of St. Felix which is about one mile from the town. The golden majesty of Saint Amantius, likewise confessor and bishop, the golden reliquary of Saint Saturninus, martyr, and the golden image of Mary, the mother of God, and the golden majesty of Saint Foy especially adorned the field. There was present in addition many relics of the saints whose number will not be estimated in the present writing. Here one famous and miraculous event was chosen by the All-powerful to glorify his faithful follower. A boy born blind and lame, deaf and mute, was carried by his kinsmen and placed below the image which occupied the sublime position of honor. After remaining here for about one hour, he merited divine medicine. And made entirely well by the gift of grace, he rose up speaking, hearing, seeing and happily walking about on his feet without difficulty. When the cries of the vulgar masses went up at such a wonder, the lords in attendance at the council, who were deliberating a bit removed, began to ask each other saying, "What does this cry from the people mean?" The countless Bertilda (of Rouergue d. ca. 1015)

answered them, "What else could this be, unless it is Saint Foy joking around as usual." Then, when the event had been investigated, filled with wonder and joy, everyone urged the whole assembly to the praise of God, contemplating frequently with great joy that the venerable lady had said that Saint Foy was playing.

ANSELM

Proslogion

ANSELM OF CANTERBURY (CA. 1033/34-1109) WAS BORN TO AOSTA, but came to the Norman monastery of Bec to study with his fellow country-man Lanfranc. He succeeded his teacher in 1063 as abbot and then, in 1093 as archbishop of Canterbury. He was the outstanding teacher and writer in the tradition of what has been termed the "old scholasticism," that is, the pursuit of a rational foundation to Augustinian theology based on elementary dialectics. His *Proslogion* is his attempt to prove the existence of God using the "ontological argument," a proof based entirely on the concept of being.

Source: S.N. Deane, *Anselm: Basic Writings* (La Salle: Open Court Publishing Company, 1962).

Preface

After I had published, at the solicitous entreaties of certain brethren, a brief work (the *Monologium*) as an example of meditation on the grounds of faith, in the person of one who investigates, in a course of silent reasoning with himself, matters of which he is ignorant; considering that this book was knit together by the linking of many arguments, I began to ask myself whether there might be found a single argument which would require no other for its proof than itself alone; and alone would suffice to demonstrate that God truly exists, and that there is a supreme good requiring nothing else, which all other things require for their existence and well-being; and whatever we believe regarding the divine Being.

Although I often and earnestly directed my thought to this end, and at times that which I sought seemed to be just within my reach, while again it wholly evaded my mental vision, at last in despair I was about to cease, as if from the search for a thing which could not be found. But when I wished to exclude this thought altogether, lest, by busying my mind to no purpose, it should keep me from other thoughts, in which I might be successful; then more and more, though I was unwilling and shunned it, it began to force itself upon me, with a kind of importunity. So, one day, when I was exceedingly wearied with resisting its importunity, in the very conflict of my thoughts, the proof of which I had despaired offered itself, so that I eagerly embraced the thoughts which I was strenuously repelling.

Thinking, therefore, that what I rejoiced to have found, would, if put in writing, be welcome to some readers, of this very matter, and of some others, I have written the following treatise, in the person of one who strives to lift his mind to the contemplation of God, and seeks to understand what he believes. In my judgment, neither this work nor the other, which I mentioned above, deserved to be called a book, or to bear the name of an author; and yet I thought they ought not to be sent forth without some title by which they might, in some sort, invite one into whose hands they fell to their perusal. I accordingly gave each a title, that the first might be known as, An Example of Meditation on the Grounds of Faith, and its sequel as, Faith Seeking Understanding. But after both had been copied by many under these titles, many urged me, and especially Hugo, the reverend Archbishop of Lyons, who discharges the apostolic office in Gaul, who instructed me to this effect on his apostolic authority—to prefix my name to these writings. And that this might be done more fitly, I named the first, *Monologium*, that is, A Soliloquy; but the second, *Proslogium*, that is, A Discourse.

Chapter I.

Exhortation of the mind to the contemplation of God.—It casts aside cares, and excludes all thoughts save that of God, that it may seek Him. Man was created to see God. Man by sin lost the blessedness for which he was made, and found the misery for which he was not made. He did not keep this good when he could keep it easily. Without God it is ill with us. Our labors and attempts are in vain without God. Man cannot seek God, unless God himself teaches him; nor find him, unless he reveals himself. God created man in his image, that he might be mindful of him, think of him, and love him. The believer does not seek to understand, that he may believe, but he believes that he may understand; for unless he believed he would not understand.

Up now, slight man! flee, for a little while, thy occupations; hide thyself, for a time, from thy disturbing thoughts. Cast aside, now, thy burdensome cares, and put away thy toilsome business. Yield room for some little time to God; and rest for a little time in him. Enter the inner chamber of thy mind; shut out all thoughts save that of God, and such as can aid thee in seeking him; close thy door and seek him. Speak now, my whole heart! speak now to God, saying, I seek thy face; thy face, Lord, will I seek (Psalms xxvii. 8). And come thou now, O Lord my God, teach my heart where and how it may seek thee, where and how it may find thee.

Lord, if thou art not here, where shall I seek thee, being absent? But if thou art everywhere, why do I not see thee present? Truly thou dwellest in unapproachable light. But where is unapproachable light, or how shall I come into it? Or who shall lead me to that light and into it, that I may see thee in it? Again, by what marks, under what form, shall I seek thee? I have never seen thee, O Lord, my God; I do not know thy form. What, O most high Lord, shall this man do, an exile far from thee? What shall thy servant do, anxious in his love of thee, and cast out afar from thy face? He pants to see thee, and thy face is too far from him. He longs to come to thee, and thy dwelling-place is inaccessible. He is eager to find thee, and knows not thy place. He desires to seek thee, and does not know thy face. Lord, thou art my God, and thou art my Lord, and never have I seen thee. It is thou that hast made me, and hast made me anew, and hast bestowed upon me all the blessings I enjoy; and not yet do I know thee. Finally, I was created to see thee, and not yet have I done that for which I was made.

O wretched lot of man, when he hath lost that for which he was made! O hard and terrible fate! Alas, what has he lost, and what has he found? What has departed, and what remains? He has lost the blessedness for which he was made, and has found the misery for which he was not made. That has departed without which nothing is happy, and that remains which, in itself, is only miserable. Man once did eat the bread of angels, for which he hungers now; he eateth now the bread of sorrows, of which he knew not then. Alas! for the mourning of all mankind, for the universal lamentation of the sons of Hades! He choked with satiety, we sigh with hunger. He bounded, we beg. He possessed in happiness, and miserably forsook his possession; we suffer want in unhappiness, and feel a miserable longing, and alas! we remain empty.

Why did he not keep up for us, when he could so easily, that whose lack we feel so heavily? Why did he shut us away from the light, and cover us over with darkness? With what purpose did he rob us of life, and inflict death upon us? Wretches that we are, whence have we been driven out; whither are we driven on? Whence hurled? Whither consigned to ruin? From a native country into exile, from the vision of God into our present blindness, from the joy of immortality into the bitterness and horror of death. Miserable exchange of how great a good, for how great an evil! Heavy loss, heavy grief, heavy all our fate!

But alas! wretched that I am, one of the sons of Eve, far removed from God! What have I undertaken? What have I accomplished? Whither was I striving? How far have I come? To what did I aspire? Amid what thoughts am I sighing? I sought blessings, and lo! confusion. I strove towards God, and I stumbled on myself. I sought calm in privacy, and I found tribulation and grief, in my inmost thoughts. I wished to smile in the joy of my mind, and I am compelled to frown by the sorrow of my heart. Gladness was hoped for, and lo! a source of frequent sighs!

And thou too, O Lord, how long? How long, O Lord, dost thou forget us; how long dost thou turn thy face from us? When wilt thou look upon us, and hear us? When wilt thou enlighten our eyes, and show us thy face? When wilt thou restore thyself to us? Look upon us, Lord; hear us, enlighten us, reveal thyself to us. Restore thyself to us, that it may be well for us,—thyself, without whom it is so ill with us. Pity our toilings and strivings toward thee, since we can do nothing without thee. Thou dost invite us; do thou help us. I beseech thee, O Lord, that I may not lose hope in sighs, but may breathe anew in hope. Lord, my heart is made bitter by its desolation; sweeten thou it, I beseech thee, with thy consolation. Lord, in hunger I began to seek thee; I beseech thee that I may not cease to hunger for thee. In hunger I have come to thee; let me not go unfed. I have come in poverty to the Rich, in misery to the Compassionate; let me not return empty and despised. And if, before I eat, I sigh, grant, even after sighs, that which I may eat. Lord, I am bowed down and can only look downward; raise me up that I may look upward. My iniquities have gone over my head; they overwhelm me; and, like a heavy load, they weigh me down. Free me from them; unburden me, that the pit of iniquities may not close over me.

Be it mine to look up to thy light, even from afar, even from the depths. Teach me to seek thee, and reveal thyself to me, when I seek thee, for I cannot seek thee, except thou teach me, nor find thee, except thou reveal thyself. Let me seek thee in longing, let me long for thee in seeking; let me find thee in love, and love thee in finding. Lord, I acknowledge and I thank thee that thou hast created me in this thine image, in order that I may be mindful of thee, may conceive of thee, and love thee; but that image has been so consumed and wasted away by vices, and obscured by the smoke of wrong-doing, that it cannot achieve that for which it was made, except thou renew it, and create it anew. I do not endeavor, O Lord, to penetrate thy sublimity, for in no wise do I compare my understanding with that; but I long to understand in some degree thy truth, which my heart believes and loves. For I do not seek to understand that I may believe, but I believe in order to understand. For this also I believe,—that unless I believed, I should not understand.

Chapter II.

Truly there is a God, although the fool hath said in his heart, There is no God.

And so, Lord, do thou, who dost give understanding to faith, give me, so far as thou knowest it to be profitable, to understand that thou art as we believe; and that thou art that which we believe. And, indeed we believe that thou art a being than which nothing greater can be conceived. Or is there no such nature, since the fool hath said in his heart, there is no God? (Psalms xiv. 1). But, at any rate, this very fool, when he hears of this being of which I speak—a being than which nothing greater can be conceived—understands what he hears, and what he understands is in his understanding; although he does not understand it to exist.

For, it is one thing for an object to be in the understanding, and another to understand that the object exists. When a painter first conceives of what he will afterwards perform, he has it in his understanding, but he does not yet understand it to be, because he has not yet performed it. But after he has made the painting, he both has it in his understanding, and he understands that it exists, because he has made it.

Hence, even the fool is convinced that something exists in the understanding, at least, than which nothing greater can be conceived. For, when he hears of this, he understands it. And whatever is understood, exists in the understanding. And assuredly that, than which nothing greater can be conceived, cannot exist in the understanding alone. For, suppose it exists in the understanding alone: then it can be conceived to exist in reality; which is greater.

Therefore, if that, than which nothing greater can be conceived, exists in the understanding alone, the very being, than which nothing greater can be conceived, is one, than which a greater can be conceived. But obviously this is impossible. Hence, there is no doubt that there exists a being, than which nothing greater can be conceived, and it exists both in the understanding and in reality.

Chapter III.

God cannot be conceived not to exist.—God is that, than which nothing greater can be conceived.—That which can be conceived not to exist is not God.

And it assuredly exists so truly, that it cannot be conceived not to exist. For, it is possible to conceive of a being which cannot be conceived not to exist; and this is greater than one which can be conceived not to exist. Hence, if that, than which nothing greater can be conceived, can be conceived not to exist, it is not that, than which nothing greater can be conceived. But this is an irreconcilable contradiction. There is, then, so truly a being than which nothing greater can be conceived to exist, that it cannot even be conceived not to exist; and this being thou art, O Lord, our God.

So truly, therefore, dost thou exist, O Lord, my God, that thou canst not be conceived not to exist; and rightly. For, if a mind could conceive of a being better than thee, the creature would rise above the Creator; and this is most absurd. And, indeed, whatever else there is, except thee alone, can be conceived not to exist. To thee alone, therefore, it belongs to exist more truly than all other beings, and hence in a higher degree than all others. For, whatever else exists does not exist so truly , and hence in a less degree it belongs to it to exist. Why, then, has the fool said in his heart, there is no God (Psalms xiv. 1), since it is so evident, to a rational mind, that thou dost exist in the highest degree of all? Why, except that he is dull and a fool?

Chapter IV.

How the fool has said in his heart what cannot be conceived.—A thing may be conceived in two ways: (1) when the word signifying it is conceived; (2) when the thing itself is understood. As far as the word goes, God can be conceived not to exist; in reality he cannot.

But how has the fool said in his heart what he could not conceive; or how is it that he could not conceive what he said in his heart? since it is the same to say in the heart, and to conceive.

But, if really, nay, since really, he both conceived, because he said in his heart; and did not say in his heart, because he could not conceive; there is more than one way in which a thing is said in the heart or conceived. For, in one sense, an object is conceived, when the word signifying is conceived; and in another, when the very entity, which the object is, is understood.

In the former sense, then, God can be conceived not to exist; but in the latter, not at all. For no one who understands what fire and water are can conceive fire to be water, in accordance with the nature of the facts themselves, although this is possible according to the words. So, then, no one who understands what God is can conceive that God does not exist; although he says these words in his heart, either without any, or with some foreign, signification. For, God is that than which a greater cannot be conceived. And he who thoroughly understands this, assuredly understands that this being so truly exists, that not even in concept can it be non-existent. Therefore, he who understands that God so exists, cannot conceive that he does not exist.

I thank thee, gracious Lord, I thank thee; because what I formerly believed by thy bounty, I now so understand by thine illumination, that if I were unwilling to believe that thou dost exist, I should not be able not to understand this to be true.

Chapter V.

God is whatever it is better to be than not to be; and he, as the only self-existent being, creates all things from nothing.

What art thou, then, Lord God, than whom nothing greater can be conceived? But what art thou, except that which, as the highest of all beings, alone exists through itself, and creates all other things from nothing? For, whatever is not this is less than a thing which can be conceived of. But this cannot be conceived of thee. What good, therefore, does the supreme Good lack, through which every good is? Therefore, thou art just, truthful, blessed, and whatever it is better to be than not to be. For it is better to be just than not just; better to be blessed than not blessed.

Chapter VI.

How God is sensible (*sensibilis*) although he is not a body.—God is sensible, omnipotent, compassionate, passionless; for it is better to be these than not be. He who in any way knows, is not improperly said in some sort to feel.

But, although it is better for thee to be sensible, omnipotent, compassionate, passionless, than not to be these things; how art thou sensible, if thou art not a body; or omnipotent, if thou hast not all powers; or at once compassionate and passionless? For, if only corporeal things are sensible, since the senses encompass a body and are in a body, how art thou sensible, although thou art not a body, but a supreme Spirit, who is superior to body? But, if feeling is only cognition, or for the sake of cognition,—for he who feels obtains knowledge in accordance with the proper functions of his senses; as through sight, of colors; through taste, of flavors,—whatever in any way cognises is not inappropriately said, in some sort, to feel.

Therefore, O Lord, although though art not a body, yet thou art truly sensible in the highest degree in respect of this, that thou dost cognise all things in the highest degree; and not as an animal cognises, through a corporeal sense.

Chapter VII.

How he is omnipotent, although there are many things of which he is not capable.—To be capable of being corrupted, or of lying, is not power, but impotence. God can do nothing by virtue of impotence, and nothing has power against him.

But how art thou omnipotent, if thou art not capable of all things? Or, if thou canst not be corrupted, and canst not lie, nor make what is true, false—as, for example, if thou shouldest make what has been done not to have been done, and the like—how art thou capable of all things? Or

else to be capable of these things is not power, but impotence. For, he who is capable of these things is capable of what is not for his good, and of what he ought not to do; and the more capable of them he is, the more power have adversity and perversity against him; and the less has he himself against these.

He, then, who is thus capable is so not by power, but by impotence. For, he is said to be able because he is able of himself, but because his impotence gives something else power over him. Or, by a figure of speech, just as many words are improperly applied, as when we use "to be" for "not to be," and "to do" for what is really "not to do," or "to do nothing." For, often we say to a man who denies the existence of something: "It is as you say it to be," though it might seem more proper to say, "It is not, as you say it is not." In the same way, we say: "This man sits just as that man does," or, "This man rests just as that man does"; although to sit is not to do anything, and to rest is to do nothing.

So, then, when one is said to have the power of doing or experiencing what is not for his good, or what he ought not to do, impotence is understood in the word power. For, the more he possesses this power, the more powerful are adversity and perversity against him, and the more powerless is he against them.

Therefore, O Lord, our God, the more truly art thou omnipotent, since thou art capable of nothing through impotence, and nothing has power against thee.

Chapter VIII.

How he is compassionate and passionless. God is compassionate, in terms of our experience, because we experience the effect of compassion. God is not compassionate, in terms of his own being, because he does not experience the feeling (*affectus*) of compassion.

But how art thou compassionate, and, at the same time, passionless? For, if thou art passionless, thou dost not feel sympathy; and if thou dost not feel sympathy, thy heart is not wretched from sympathy for the wretched; but this it is to be compassionate. But if thou art not compassionate, whence cometh so great consolation to the wretched? How, then, art thou compassionate and not compassionate, O Lord, unless because thou art compassionate in terms of our own experience, and not compassionate in terms of thy being.

Truly, thou art so in terms of our experience, but thou art not so in terms of thine own. For, when thou beholdest us in our wretchedness, we experience the effect of compassion, but thou dost not experience the feeling. Therefore, thou art both compassionate, because thou dost save the wretched, and spare those who sin against thee; and not compassionate, because thou art affected by no sympathy for wretchedness.

Chapter IX.

How the all-just and supremely just God spares the wicked, and justly pities the wicked. He is better who is good to the righteous and the wicked than he who is good to the righteous alone. Although God is supremely just, the source of his compassion is hidden. God is supremely compassionate, because he is supremely just. He saveth the just, because justice goes with them; he frees sinners by the authority of justice. God spares the wicked out of justice; for it is just that God, than whom none is better or more powerful, should be good even to the wicked, and should make the wicked good. If God ought not to pity, he pities unjustly. But this it is impious to suppose. Therefore, God justly pities.

But how dost thou spare the wicked, if thou art all just and supremely just? For how, being all just and supremely just, dost thou augur that it is not just? Or, what justice is that to give him who merits eternal death everlasting life? How, then, gracious Lord, good to the righteous and the wicked, canst thou save the wicked, if this is not just, and thou dost not aught that is not just? Or, since thy goodness is incomprehensible, is this hidden in the unapproachable light wherein thou dwellest? Truly, in the deepest and most secret parts of thy goodness is hidden the fountain whence the stream of thy compassion flows.

For thou art all just and supremely just, yet thou art kind even to the wicked, even because thou art all supremely good. For thou wouldst be less good if thou wert not kind to any wicked being. For, he who is good, both to the righteous and the wicked, is better than he who is good to be good alone; and he who is good to the wicked, both by punishing and sparing them, is better than he who is good by punishing them alone. Therefore, thou art compassionate, because thou art all supremely good. And, although it appears why thou dost reward the good with goods and the evil with evils; yet this, at least, is most wonderful, why thou, the all and supremely just, who lackest nothing, bestoweth goods on the wicked and on those who are guilty toward thee.

The depth of thy goodness, O God! The source of thy compassion appears, and yet is not clearly seen! We see whence the river flows, but the spring whence it arises is not seen. For, it is from the abundance of thy goodness that thou art good to those who sin against thee; and in the depth of thy goodness is hidden the reason for this kindness.

For, although thou dost reward the good with goods and the evil with evils, out of goodness, yet this the concept of justice seems to demand. But, when thou dost bestow goods on the evil, and it is known that the supremely Good hath willed to do this, we wonder why the supremely Just has been able to will this.

O compassion, from what abundant sweetness and what sweet abundance dost thou well forth to us! O boundless goodness of God, how passionately should sinners love thee! For thou savest the just, because justice goeth with them; but sinners thou dost free by the authority of justice. Those by the help of their deserts; these, although their deserts oppose. Those by acknowledging the goods thou hast granted; these by pardoning the evils thou hatest. O boundless goodness, which dost so exceed all understanding, let that compassion come upon me, which proceeds from thy so great abundance! Let it flow upon me, for it wells forth from thee. Spare, in mercy; avenge not, in justice.

For, though it is hard to understand how thy compassion is not inconsistent with thy justice; yet we must believe that it does not oppose justice at all, because it flows from goodness, which is no goodness without justice; nay, that it is in true harmony with justice. For, if thou art compassionate only because thou art supremely good, and supremely good only because thou art supremely just, truly thou art compassionate even because thou art supremely just. Help me, just and compassionate God, whose light I seek; help me to understand what I say.

Truly, then, thou art compassionate even because thou art just. Is, then, thy compassion born of thy justice? And dost thou spare the wicked, therefore, out of justice? If this is true, my Lord, if this is true, teach me how it is. Is it because it is just, that thou shouldst be so good that thou canst not be conceived better; and that thou shouldst work so powerfully that thou canst not be conceived more powerful? For what can be more just than this? Assuredly it could not be that thou shouldst be good only by requiting (*retribuendo*) and not by sparing, and that thou shouldst make good only those who are not good, and not the wicked also. In this way, therefore, it is just that thou shouldst spare the wicked, and make good souls of evil.

Finally, what is not done justly ought not to be done; and what ought not to be done is done unjustly. If, then, thou dost not justly pity the wicked, thou oughtest not to pity them. And, if thou oughtest not to pity them, thou pityest them unjustly. And if it is impious to suppose this, it is right to believe that thou justly pityest the wicked.

Chapter X.

How he justly punishes and justly spares the wicked.—God, in sparing the wicked, is just, according to his own nature, because he does what is consistent with his goodness; but he is not just, according to our nature, because he does not inflict the punishment deserved.

But it is also just that thou shouldst punish the wicked. For what is more just than that the good should receive goods, and the evil, evils? How, then, is it just that thou shouldst punish the wicked, and, at the same time, spare the wicked? Or, in one way, dost thou justly punish, and in another, justly spare them? For, when thou punishest the wicked, it is just, because it is consistent

with their deserts; and when, on the other hand, thou sparest the wicked, it is just, not because it is compatible with their deserts, but because it is compatible with thy goodness.

For, in sparing the wicked, thou art just, according to thy nature, but not according to ours, as thou art compassionate, according to our nature, and not according to thine; seeing that, as in saving us, whom it would be just for thee to destroy, thou art compassionate, not because thou feelest an affection (*affectum*), but because we feel the effect (*effectum*); so thou art just, not because thou requitest us as we deserve, but because thou dost that which becomes thee as the supremely good Being. In this way, therefore, without contradiction thou dost justly punish and justly spare.

Chapter XI.

How all the ways of God are compassion and truth; and yet God is just in all his ways. We cannot comprehend why, of the wicked, he saves these rather than those, through his supreme goodness; and condemns those rather than these through his supreme justice.

But, is there any reason why it is not also just, according to thy nature, O Lord, that thou shouldst punish the wicked? Surely it is just that thou shouldst be so just that thou canst not be conceived more just; and this thou wouldst in no wise be if thou didst only render goods to the good, and not evils to the evil. For, he who requiteth both good and evil according to their deserts is more just than he who so requites the good alone. It is, therefore, just, according to thy nature, O just and gracious God, both when thou dost punish and when thou sparest.

Truly, then, all the paths of the Lord are mercy and truth (Psalms xxv. 10); and yet the Lord is righteous in all his ways (Psalms cxlv. 17). And assuredly without inconsistency: For, it is not just that those whom thou dost will to punish should be saved, and that those whom thou dost will to spare should be condemned. For that alone is just which thou dost will; and that alone unjust which thou dost not will. So, then, thy compassion is born of thy justice.

For it is just that thou shouldst be so good that thou art good in sparing also; and this may be the reason why the supremely Just can will goods for the evil. But if it can be comprehended in any way why thou canst will to save the wicked, yet by no consideration can we comprehend why, of those who are alike wicked, thou savest some rather than others, through supreme goodness; and why thou dost condemn the latter rather than the former, through supreme justice.

So, then, thou art truly sensible (*sensibilis*), omnipotent, compassionate, and passionless, as thou art living, wise, good, blessed, eternal: and whatever it is better to be than not to be.

Chapter XII.

God is the very life whereby he lives; and so of other like attributes.

But undoubtedly, whatever thou art, thou art through nothing else than thyself. Therefore, thou art the very life whereby thou livest; and the wisdom wherewith thou art wise; and the very goodness whereby thou art good to the righteous and the wicked; and so of other like attributes.

Chapter XIII.

How he alone is uncircumscribed and eternal, although other spirits are uncircumscribed and eternal.—No place and time contain God. But he is himself everywhere and always. He alone not only does not cease to be, but also does not begin to be.

But everything that is in any way bounded by place or time is less than that which no law of place or time limits. Since, then, nothing is greater than thou, no place or time contains thee; but thou art everywhere and always. And since this can be said of thee alone, thou alone art uncircumscribed and eternal. How is it, then, that other spirits also are said to be uncircumscribed and eternal?

Assuredly thou art alone eternal; for thou alone among all beings not only dost not cease to be, but also dost not begin to be.

But how art thou alone uncircumscribed? Is it

that a created spirit, when compared with thee, is circumscribed, but when compared with matter, uncircumscribed? For altogether uncircumscribed is that which, when it is wholly in one place, cannot at the same time be in another. And this is seen to be true of corporeal things alone. But uncircumscribed is that which is, as a whole, at the same time everywhere. And this is understood to be true of thee alone. But circumscribed, and, at the same time, uncircumscribed is that which, when it is anywhere as a whole, can at the same time be somewhere else as a whole, and yet not everywhere. And this is recognised as true of created spirits. For, if the soul were not as a whole in the separate members of the body, it would not feel as a whole in the separate members.

Therefore, thou, Lord, art peculiarly uncircumscribed and eternal; and yet other spirits also are uncircumscribed and eternal.

Chapter XIV.

Hast thou found what thou didst seek, my soul? Thou didst seek God. Thou hast found him to be a being which is the highest of all beings, a being than which nothing better can be conceived; that this being is life itself, light, wisdom, goodness, eternal blessedness and blessed eternity; and that it is everywhere and always.

For, if thou hast not found thy God, how is he this being which thou hast found, and which thou hast conceived him to be, with so certain truth and so true certainty? But, if thou hast found him, why is it that thou dost not feel thou hast found him? Why, O Lord, our God, does not my soul feel thee, if it hath found thee? Or, has it not found him whom it found to be light and truth? Or, could it understand anything at all of thee, except through thy light and thy truth?

Hence, if it has seen light and truth, it has seen thee; if it has not seen thee, it has not seen light and truth. Or, is what it has seen both light and truth; and still it has not yet seen thee, because it has seen thee only in part, but has not seen thee as thou art? Lord my God, my creator and renewer, speak to the desire of my soul, what thou art other than it hath seen, that it may clearly see what it desires. It strains to see thee more; and sees nothing beyond this which it hath seen, except darkness. Nay, it does not see that it cannot see farther, because of its own darkness.

Why is this, Lord, why is this? Is the eye of the soul darkened by its infirmity, or dazzled by thy glory? Surely it is both darkened in itself, and dazzled by thee. Doubtless it is both obscured by its own insignificance, and overwhelmed by thy infinity. Truly, it is both contracted by its own narrowness and overcome by thy greatness.

For how great is that light from which shines every truth that gives light to the rational mind? How great is that truth in which is everything that is true, and outside which is only nothingness and the false? How boundless is the truth which sees at one glance whatsoever has been made, and by whom, and through whom, and how it has been made from nothing? What purity, what certainty, what splendor where it is? Assuredly more than a creature can conceive.

Chapter XV.

He is greater than can be conceived.

Therefore, O Lord, thou art not only that than which a greater cannot be conceived, but thou art a being greater than can be conceived. For, since it can be conceived that there is such a being, if thou art not this very being, a greater than thou can be conceived. But this is impossible.

Chapter XVI.

Thus is the unapproachable light wherein he dwells.

Truly, O Lord, this is the unapproachable light in which thou dwellest; for truly there is nothing else which can penetrate this light, that it may see thee there. Truly, I see it not, because it is too bright for me. And yet, whatsoever I see, I see through it, as the weak eye sees what it sees through the light of the sun, which in the sun itself it cannot look upon. My understanding cannot reach that light, for it shines too bright. It does not comprehend it, nor does the eye of the soul endure to gaze upon it long. It is dazzled by the brightness, it is overcome by the greatness, it

is overwhelmed by the infinity, it is dazed by the largeness, of the light.

O supreme and unapproachable light! O whole and blessed truth, how far art thou from me, who am so near to thee! How far removed art thou from my vision, though I am so near to thine! Everywhere thou art wholly present, and I see thee not. In thee I move, and in thee I have my being; and I cannot come to thee. Thou art within me, and about me, and I feel thee not.

Chapter XVII.

In God is harmony, fragrance, sweetness, pleasantness to the touch, beauty, after his ineffable manner.

Still thou art hidden, O Lord, from my soul in thy light and thy blessedness; and therefore my soul still walks in its darkness and wretchedness. For it looks, and does not see thy beauty. It hearkens, and does not hear thy harmony. It smells, and does not perceive thy fragrance. It tastes, and does not recognize thy sweetness. It touches, and does not feel thy pleasantness. For thou hast these attributes in thyself, Lord God, after thine ineffable manner, who hast given them to objects created by thee, after their sensible manner; but the sinful senses of my soul have grown rigid and dull, and have been obstructed by their long listlessness.

Chapter XVIII.

God is life, wisdom, eternity, and every true good.—Whatever is composed of parts is not wholly one; it is capable, either in fact or in concept, of dissolution. In God wisdom, eternity, etc., are not parts, but one, and the very whole which God is, or unity itself, not even in concept divisible.

And lo, again confusion; lo, again grief and mourning meet him who seeks for joy and gladness. My soul now hoped for satisfaction; and lo, again it is overwhelmed with need. I desired now to feast, and lo, I hunger more. I tried to rise to the light of God, and I have fallen back into my darkness. Nay, not only have I fallen into it, but I feel that I am enveloped in it. I fell before my mother conceived me. Truly, in darkness I was conceived, and in the cover of darkness I was born. Truly, in him we all fell, in whom we all sinned. In him we all lost, who kept easily, and wickedly lost to himself and to us that which when we wish to seek it, we do not find; when we find, it is not that which we seek.

Do thou help me for thy goodness' sake! Lord, I sought thy face; thy face, Lord, will I seek; hide not thy face far from me (Psalms xxvii. 8). Free me from myself toward thee. Cleanse, heal, sharpen, enlighten the eye of my mind, that it may behold thee. Let my soul recover its strength, and with all its understanding let it strive toward thee, O Lord. What art thou, Lord, what art thou? What shall my heart conceive thee to be?

Assuredly thou art life, thou art wisdom, thou art truth, thou art goodness, thou art blessedness, thou art eternity, and thou art every true good. Many are these attributes: my straitened understanding cannot see so many at one view, that it may be gladdened by all at once. How, then, O Lord, art thou all these things? Are they parts of thee, or is each one of these rather the whole, which thou art? For, whatever is composed of parts is not altogether one, but is in some sort plural, and diverse from itself; and either in fact or in contempt is capable of dissolution.

But these things are alien to thee, than whom nothing better can be conceived of. Hence, there are no parts in thee, Lord, nor art thou more than one. But thou art so truly a unitary being, and so identical with thyself; rather thou art unity itself, indivisible by any conception. Therefore, life and wisdom and the rest are not parts of thee, but all are one; and each of these is the whole, which thou art, and which all the rest are.

In this way, then, it appears that thou hast no parts, and that thy eternity, which thou art, is nowhere and never a part of thee or of thy eternity. But everywhere thou art as a whole, and thy eternity exists as a whole forever.

Chapter XIX.

He does not exist in place or time, but all things exist in him.

But if through thine eternity thou hast been, and art, and wilt be; and to have been is not to be destined to be; and to be is not to have been, or to be destined to be; how does thine eternity exist as a whole forever? Or is it true that nothing of thy eternity passes away, so that it is not now; and that nothing of it is destined to be, as if it were not yet?

Thou wast not, then, yesterday, nor wilt thou be to-morrow; but yesterday and to-day and to-morrow thou art; or, rather, neither yesterday nor to-day nor to-morrow thou art; but simply, thou art, outside all time. For yesterday and to-day and to-morrow have no existence, except in time; but thou, although nothing exists without thee, nevertheless dost not exist in space or time, but all things exist in thee. For nothing contains thee, but thou containest all.

Chapter XX.

He exists before all things and transcends all things, even the eternal things.—The eternity of God is present as a whole with him; while other things have not yet that part of their eternity which is still to be, and have no longer that part which is past.

Hence, thou dost permeate and embrace all things. Thou art before all, and dost transcend all. And, of a surety, thou art before all; for before they were made, thou art. But how dost thou transcend all? In what way dost thou transcend those beings which will have no end? Is it because they cannot exist at all without thee; while thou art in no wise less, if they should return to nothingness? For so, in a certain sense, thou dost transcend them. Or, is it also because they can be conceived to have an end; but thou by no means? For so they actually have an end, in a certain sense; but thou, in no sense. And certainly, what in no sense has an end transcends what is ended in any sense. Or, in this way also dost thou transcend all things, even the eternal, because thy eternity and theirs is present as a whole with thee; while they have not yet that part of their eternity which is to come, just as they no longer have that part which is past? For so thou dost ever transcend them, since thou art ever present with thyself, and since that to which they have not yet come is ever present with thee.

Chapter XXI.

Is this the age of the age, or ages of ages?—The eternity of God contains the ages of time themselves, and can be called the age of the age or ages of ages.

Is this, then, the age of the age, or ages of ages? For, as an age of time contains all temporal things, so thy eternity contains even the ages of time themselves. And these are indeed an age, because of their indivisible unity; but ages, because of their endless immeasurability. And, although thou art so great, O Lord, that all things are full of thee, and exist in thee; yet thou art without all space, that neither midst, nor half, nor any part, is in thee.

Chapter XXII.

He alone is what he is and who he is.—All things need God for their being and their well-being.

Therefore, thou alone, O Lord, art what thou art; and thou art he who thou art. For, what is one thing in the whole and another in the parts, and in which there is any mutable element, is not altogether what it is. And what begins from non-existence, and can be conceived not to exist, and unless it subsists through something else, returns to non-existence; and what has a past existence, which is no longer, or a future existence, which is not yet,—this does not properly and absolutely exist.

But thou art what thou art, because, whatever thou art at any time, or in any way, thou art as a whole and forever. And thou art he who thou art, properly and simply; for thou hast neither a past existence nor a future, but only a present existence; nor canst thou be conceived as at any time non-existent. But thou art life, and light, and wisdom, and blessedness, and many goods of this nature. And yet thou art only one supreme good; thou art all-sufficient to thyself, and needest none; and thou art he whom all things need for their existence and well-being.

Chapter XXIII.

This good is equally Father, and Son, and Holy Spirit. And this is a single, necessary Being, which is every good, and wholly good, and the only good.—Since the Word is true, and is truth itself, there is nothing in the Father, who utters it, which is not accomplished in the Word by which he expresses himself. Neither is the love which proceeds from the Father and Son unequal to the Father or the Son, for Father and Son love themselves and one another in the same degree in which what they are is good. Of supreme simplicity nothing can be born, and from it nothing can proceed except that which is this, of which it is born, or from which it proceeds.

This good thou art, thou, God the Father; this is thy Word, that is, thy Son. For nothing, other than what thou art, or greater or less than thou, can be in thy Word by which thou dost express thyself; for thy Word is true, as thou art faithful. And hence it is truth itself, just as thou art; no other truth than thou; and thou art of so simple a nature, that of thee nothing can be born other than what thou art. This very good is the one love common to thee and to thy Son, that is, the Holy Spirit proceeding from both. For this love is not unequal to thee or to thy Son; seeing that thou dost love thyself and him, and he, thee and himself, to the whole extent of thy being and his. Nor is there aught else proceeding from thee and from him, which is not unequal to thee and to him. Nor can anything proceed from the supreme simplicity, other than what this, from which it proceeds, is.

But what each is, separately, this is all the Trinity at once, Father, Son, and Holy Spirit; seeing that each separately is none other than the supremely simple unity, and the supremely unitary simplicity, which can neither be multiplied nor varied. Moreover, there is a single necessary Being. Now, this is that single, necessary Being, in which is every good; nay, which is every good, and a single entire good, and the only good.

Chapter XXIV.

Conjecture as to the character and the magnitude of this good.—If the created life is good, how good is the creative life!

And now, my soul, arouse and lift up all thy understanding, and conceive, so far as thou canst, of what character and how great is that good. For, if individual goods are delectable, conceive in earnestness how delectable is that good which contains the pleasantness of all goods; and not such as we have experienced in created objects, but as different as the Creator from the creature. For, if the created life is good, how good is the creative life! If the salvation given is delightful, how delightful is the salvation which has given all salvation! If wisdom in the knowledge of the created world is lovely, how lovely is the wisdom which has created all things from nothing! Finally, if there are many great delights in delectable things, what and how great is the delight in him who has made these delectable things.

Chapter XXV.

What goods, and how great, belong to those who enjoy this good.—Joy is multiplied in the blessed from the blessedness and joy of others.

Who shall enjoy this good? And what shall belong to him, and what shall not belong to him? At any rate, whatever he shall wish shall be his, and whatever he shall not wish shall not be his. For, these goods of body and soul will be such as eye hath not seen nor ear heard, neither has the heart of man conceived (Isaiah lxiv. 4; 1 Corinthians ii. 9).

Why, then, dost thou wander abroad, slight man, in thy search for the goods of thy soul and thy body? Love the one good in which are all goods, and it sufficeth. Desire the simple good which is every good, and it is enough. For, what dost thou love, my flesh? What dost thou desire, my soul? There, there is whatever ye love, whatever ye desire.

If beauty delights thee, there shall the righteous shine forth as the sun (Matthew xiii. 43). If swiftness or endurance, or freedom of body, which naught can withstand, delight thee, they shall be angels of God,—because it is sown a natural body; it is raised a spiritual body (1 Corinthians xv. 44)—in power certainly, though not in nature. If it is a long and sound life that pleases thee, there a healthful eternity is, and an eternal health. For the righteous shall live forever (Wisdom v. 15), and the salvation of the righteous is of the Lord (Psalms xxxvii. 39). If it is satisfaction of hunger, they shall be satisfied when the glory of the Lord hath appeared (Psalms xvii. 15). If it is quenching of thirst, they shall be abundantly satisfied with the fatness of thy house (Psalms xxxvi. 8). If it is melody, there the choirs of angels sing forever, before God. If it is any not impure, but pure, pleasure, thou shalt make them drink of the river of thy pleasures, O God (Psalms xxxvi. 8).

If it is wisdom that delights thee, the very wisdom of God will reveal itself to them. If friendship, they shall love God more than themselves, and one another as themselves. And God shall love them more than they themselves; for they love him, and themselves, and one another, through him, and he, himself and them, through himself. If concord, they shall all have a single will.

If power, they shall have all power to fulfil their will, as God to fulfil his. For, as God will have power to do what he wills, through himself, so they will have power, through him, to do what they will. For, as they will not will aught else than he, he shall will whatever they will; and what he shall will cannot fail to be. If honor and riches, God shall make his good and faithful servants rulers over many things (Luke xii. 42); nay, they shall be called sons of God, and gods; and where his Son shall be, there they shall be also, heirs indeed of God, and joint-heirs with Christ (Romans viii. 17).

If true security delights thee, undoubtedly they shall be as sure that those goods, or rather that good, will never and in no wise fail them; as they shall be sure that they will not lose it of their own accord; and that God, who loves them, will not take it away from those who love him against their will; and that nothing more powerful than God will separate him from them against his will and theirs.

But what, or how great, is the joy, where such and so great is the good! Heart of man, needy heart, heart acquainted with sorrows, nay, over-whelmed with sorrows, how greatly wouldst thou rejoice, if thou didst abound in all these things! Ask thy inmost mind whether it could contain its joy over so great a blessedness of its own.

Yet assuredly, if any other whom thou didst love altogether as thyself possessed the same blessedness, thy joy would be doubled, because thou wouldst rejoice not less for him than for thy-self. But, if two, or three, or many more, had the same joy, thou wouldst rejoice as much for each one as for thyself, if thou didst love each as thy-self. Hence, in that perfect love of innumerable blessed angels and sainted men, where none shall love each other less than himself, every one shall rejoice for each of the others as for himself.

If, then, the heart of man will scarce contain his joy over his own so great good, how shall it con-tain so many and so great joys? And doubtless, seeing that every one loves another so far as he rejoices in the other's good, and as, in that perfect felicity, each one should love God beyond com-pare, more than himself and all the others with him; so he will rejoice beyond reckoning in the felicity of God, more than in his own and that of all the others with him.

But if they shall so love God with all their heart, and all their mind, and all their soul, that still all the heart, and all the mind, and all the soul shall not suffice for the worthiness of this love; doubtless they will so rejoice with all their heart, and all their mind, and all their soul, that all the heart, and all the mind, and all the soul shall not suffice for the fullness of their joy.

Chapter XXVI.

Is this joy which the Lord promises made full?—The blessed shall rejoice according as they shall love; and they shall love according as they shall know.

My God and my Lord, my hope and the joy of my heart, speak unto my soul and tell me whether this is the joy of which thou tellest us through thy Son: Ask and ye shall receive, that your joy may be made full (John xvi. 24). For I have found a joy that is full, and more than full. For when heart, and mind, and soul, and all the man, are full of that joy, joy beyond measure will still remain. Hence, not all of that joy shall enter into those who rejoice; but they who rejoice shall wholly enter into that joy.

Show me, O Lord, show thy servant in his heart whether this is the joy into which thy servants shall enter, who shall enter into the joy of their Lord. But that joy, surely, with which thy chosen ones shall rejoice, eye hath not seen nor ear heard, neither has it entered into the heart of man (Isaiah lxiv. 4; 1 Corinthians ii. 9). Not yet, then, have I told or conceived, O Lord, how greatly those blessed ones of thine shall rejoice. Doubtless they shall rejoice according as they shall love; and they shall love according as they shall know. How far they will know thee, Lord, then! and how much they will love thee! Truly, eye hath not seen, nor ear heard, neither has it entered into the heart of man in this life, how far they shall know thee, and how much they shall love thee in that life.

I pray, O God, to know thee, to love thee, that I may rejoice in thee. And if I cannot attain to full joy in this life, may I at least advance from day to day, until that joy shall come to the full. Let the knowledge of thee advance in me here, and there be made full. Let the love of thee increase, and there let it be full, that here my joy may be great in hope, and there full in truth. Lord, through thy Son thou dost command, nay, thou dost counsel us to ask; and thou dost promise that we shall receive, that our joy may be full. I ask, O Lord, as thou dost counsel through our wonderful Coun-sellor. I will receive what thou dost promise by virtue of thy truth, that my joy may be full. Faith-ful God, I ask. I will receive, that my joy may be full. Meanwhile, let my heart meditate upon it; let my tongue speak of it. Let my heart love it; let my mouth talk of it. Let my soul hunger for it; let my flesh thirst for it; let my whole being desire it, until I enter into thy joy, O Lord, who art the Three and the One God, blessed for ever and ever. Amen.

BERNARD OF CLAIRVAUX

Sermons on the Song of Songs

BERNARD OF CLAIRVAUX (CA. 1090-1153) WAS THE DOMINANT personality of the first half of the twelfth century. As abbot of the Cistercian monastery of Clairvaux, which he founded, he was constantly involved in the political, religious, and philosophical issues of his time. His intellectual productions represent the tradition of monastic spirituality and he was a sharp and constant critic of the new philosophical movements based on Aristotelian logic. In his *Sermons on Song of Songs* one sees the allegorical method of scriptural exegesis applied to the most beloved book of the Bible in the monastic tradition.

Source: Kilian Walsh, OCSO, *The Works of Bernard of Clairvaux* vol. 2 *Song of Songs I* (Kalamazoo: Kalamazoo Publications Inc., 1981).

Sermon 1: On The Title Of The Book

The instructions that I address to you, my brothers, will differ from those I should deliver to people in the world, at least the manner will be different. The preacher who desires to follow St Paul's method of teaching will give them milk to drink rather than solid food, and will serve a more nourishing diet to those who are spiritually enlightened: "We teach," he said, "not in the way philosophy is taught, but in the way that the Spirit teaches us: we teach spiritual things spiritually." And again: "We have a wisdom to offer those who have reached maturity," in whose company, I feel assured, you are to be found, unless in vain have you prolonged your study of divine teaching, mortified your senses, and meditated day and night on God's law. Be ready then to feed on bread rather than milk. Solomon has bread to give that is splendid and delicious, the bread of that book called the Song of Songs. Let us bring it forth then if you please, and break it.

2. Now, unless I am mistaken, by the grace of God you have understood quite well from the book of Ecclesiastes how to recognize and have done with the false promise of this world. And then the book of Proverbs—has not your life and your conduct been sufficiently amended and enlightened by the doctrine it inculcates? These are two loaves of which it has been your pleasure to taste, loaves you have welcomed as coming from the cupboard of a friend. Now approach for this third loaf that, if possible, you may always recognize what is best. Since there are two evils that comprise the only, or at least the main, enemies of the soul: a misguided love of the world and an excessive love of self, the two books previously mentioned can provide an antidote to each of these infections. One uproots pernicious habits of mind and body with the hoe of self-control. The other, by the use of enlightened reason, quickly perceives a delusive tinge in all that the world holds glorious, truly distinguishing between it and deeper truth. Moreover, it causes the fear of God and the observance of his commandments to be preferred to all human pursuits and worldly desires. And rightly so, for the former is the beginning of wisdom, the latter its culmination, for there is no true and consummate wisdom other than the avoidance of evil and the doing of good, no one can successfully shun evil without the fear of God, and no work is good without the observance of the commandments.

3. Taking it then that these two evils have been warded off by the reading of those books, we may suitably proceed with this holy and contemplative discourse which, as the fruit of the other

two, may be delivered only to well prepared ears and minds.

II.

Before the flesh has been tamed and the spirit set free by zeal for truth, before the world's glamour and entanglements have been firmly repudiated, it is a rash enterprise on any man's part to presume to study spiritual doctrines. Just as a light is flashed in vain on closed or sightless eyes, so "an unspiritual person cannot accept anything of the Spirit of God." For "the Holy Spirit of instruction shuns what is false," and that is what the life of the intemperate man is. Nor will he ever have a part with the pretensions of the world, since he is the Spirit of Truth. How can there be harmony between the wisdom that comes down from above and the wisdom of the world, which is foolishness to God, or the wisdom of the flesh which is at enmity with God? I am sure that the friend who comes to us on his travels will have no reason to murmur against us after he has shared in this third loaf.

4.   But who is going to divide this loaf? The Master of the house is present, it is the Lord you must see in the breaking of the bread. For who else could more fittingly do it? It is a task that I would not dare to arrogate to myself. So look upon me as one from whom you look for nothing. For I myself am one of the seekers, one who begs along with you for the food of my soul, the nourishment of my spirit. Poor and needy, I knock at that door of his which, "when he opens, nobody can close," that I may find light on the profound mystery to which this discourse leads. Patiently all creatures look to you, O Lord. "Little children go begging for bread; no one spares a scrap for them;" they await it from your merciful love. O God most kind, break your bread for this hungering flock, through my hands if it should please you, but with an efficacy that is all your own.

III.

5.   Tell us, I beg you, by whom, about whom and to whom it is said: "Let him kiss me with the kiss

of his mouth." How shall I explain so abrupt a beginning, this sudden irruption as from a speech in mid-course? For the words spring upon us as if indicating one speaker to whom another is replying as she demands a kiss—whoever she may be. But if she asks for or demands a kiss from somebody, why does she distinctly and expressly say *with the mouth*, and even with *his own* mouth, as if lovers should kiss by means other than the mouth, or with mouths other than their own? But yet she does not say: "Let him kiss me *with his mouth;*" what she says is still more intimate: "with the kiss of his mouth." How delightful a ploy of speech this, prompted into life by the kiss, with Scripture's own engaging countenance inspiring the reader and enticing him on, that he may find pleasure even in the laborious pursuit of what lies hidden, with a fascinating theme to sweeten the fatigue of research. Surely this mode of beginning that is not a beginning, this novelty of diction in a book so old, cannot but increase the reader's attention. It must follow too that this work was composed, not by any human skill but by the artistry of the Spirit, difficult to understand indeed but yet enticing one to investigate.

IV.

6.   So now what shall we do? Shall we by-pass the title? No, not even one iota may be omitted, since we are commanded to gather up the tiniest fragments lest they be lost. The title runs: "The beginning of Solomon's Song of Songs." First of all take note of the appropriateness of the name "Peaceful," that is, Solomon, at the head of a book which opens with the token of peace, with a kiss. Take note too that by this kind of opening only men of peaceful minds, men who can achieve mastery over the turmoil of the passions and the distracting burden of daily chores, are invited to the study of this book.

7.   Again, the title is not simply the word "Song," but "Song of Songs," a detail not without significance. For though I have read many songs in the Scriptures, I cannot recall any that bear such a name. Israel chanted a song to Yahweh celebrating his escape from the sword and the tyran-

ny of Pharoah, and the twofold good fortune that simultaneously liberated and avenged him in the Red Sea. Yet even though chanted, this has not been called a "Song of Songs"; Scripture, if my memory serves me right, introduces it with the words: "Israel sang this song in honor of Yahweh." Song poured from the lips of Deborah, of Judith, of the mother of Samuel, of several of the prophets, yet none of these songs is styled a "Song of Songs." You will find that all of them, as far as I can see, were inspired to song because of favors to themselves or to their people, songs for a victory won, for an escape from danger or the gaining of a boon long sought. They would not be found ungrateful for the divine beneficence, so all sang for reasons proper to each, in accord with the Psalmist's words: "He gives thanks to you, O God, for blessing him." But King Solomon himself, unique as he was in wisdom, renowned above all men, abounding in wealth, secure in his peace, stood in no need of any particular benefit that would have inspired him to sing those songs. Nor does Scripture in any place attribute such a motive to him.

8. We must conclude then it was a special divine impulse that inspired these songs of his that now celebrate the praises of Christ and his Church, the gift of holy love, the sacrament of endless union with God. Here too are expressed the mounting desires of the soul, its marriage song, an exultation of spirit poured forth in figurative language pregnant with delight. It is no wonder that like Moses he put a veil on his face, equally resplendent as it must have been in this encounter, because in those days few if any could sustain the bright vision of God's glory. Accordingly, because of its excellence, I consider this nuptial song to be well deserving of the title that so remarkably designates it, the Song of Songs, just as he in whose honor it is sung is uniquely proclaimed King of kings and Lord of lords.

V.

9. Furthermore if you look back on your own experience, is it not in the victory by which your faith overcomes the world, in "your exit from the horrible pit and out of the slough of the marsh,"

that you yourselves sing a new song to the Lord for all the marvels he has performed? Again, when he purposed to "settle your feet on a rock and to direct your steps," then too, I feel certain, a new song was sounding on your lips, a song to our God for his gracious renewal of your life. When you repented that he not only forgave your sins but even promised rewards, so that rejoicing in the hope of benefits to come, you sing of the Lord's ways: how great is the glory of the Lord! And when, as happens, texts of Scripture hitherto dark and impenetrable at last become bright with meaning for you, then, in gratitude for this nurturing bread of heaven you must charm the ears of God with a voice of exultation and praise, a festal song. In the daily trials and arising from the flesh, the world and the devil, that are never wanting to those who live devout lives in Christ, you learn by what you experience that man's life on earth is a ceaseless warfare, and are impelled to repeat your songs day after day for every victory won. As often as temptation is overcome, an immoral habit brought under control, an impending danger shunned, the trap of the seducer detected, when a passion long indulged is finally and perfectly allayed, or a virtue persistently desired and repeatedly sought is ultimately obtained by God's gift; so often, in the words of the prophet, let thanksgiving and joy resound. For every benefit conferred, God is to be praised in his gifts. Otherwise when the time of judgment comes, that man will be punished as an ingrate who cannot say to God: "Your statutes were my song in the land of exile."

10. Again I think that your own experience reveals to you the meaning of those psalms, which are called not Song of Songs but Song of the Steps, in that each one, at whatever stage of growth he be, in accord with the upward movements of his heart may choose one of these songs to praise and give glory to him who empowers you to advance. I don't know how else these words could be true: "There are shouts of joy and victory in the tents of the just." And still more that beautiful and salutary exhortation of the Apostle: "With psalms and hymns and spiritual canticles, singing and chanting to the Lord in your hearts."

VI.

11. But there is that other song which, by its unique dignity and sweetness, excels all those I have mentioned and any others there might be; hence by every right do I acclaim it as the Song of Songs. It stands at a point where all the others culminate. Only the touch of the Spirit can inspire a song like this, and only personal experience can unfold its meaning. Let those who are versed in the mystery revel in it; let all others burn with desire rather to attain to this experience than merely to learn about it. For it is not a melody that resounds abroad but the very music of the heart, not a trilling on the lips but an inward pulsing of delight, a harmony not of voices but of wills. It is a tune you will not hear in the streets, these notes do not sound where crowds assemble; only the singer hears it and the one to whom he sings—the lover and the beloved. It is pre-eminently a marriage song telling of chaste souls in loving embrace, of their wills in sweet concord, of the mutual exchange of the heart's affections.

12. The novices, the immature, those but recently converted from a worldly life, do not normally sing this song or hear it sung. Only the mind disciplined by persevering study, only the man whose efforts have borne fruit under God's inspiration, the man whose years, as it were, make him ripe for marriage—years measured out not in time but in merits—only he is truly prepared for nuptial union with the divine partner, a union we shall describe more fully in due course. But the hour has come when both our rule and the poverty of our state demand that we go out to work. Tomorrow,[1] with God's help, we shall continue to speak about the kiss, because today's discourse on the title sets us free to resume where we had begun.

Sermon 2: Various Meanings Of The Kiss

During my frequent ponderings on the burning desire with which the patriarchs longed for the incarnation of Christ, I am stung with sorrow and shame. Even now I can scarcely restrain my tears, so filled with shame am I by the lukewarmness, the frigid unconcern of these miserable times. For which of us does the consummation of that event fill with as much joy as the mere promise of it inflamed the desires of the holy men of pre-christian times? Very soon now there will be great rejoicing as we celebrate the feast of Christ's birth.[2] But how I wish it were inspired by his birth! All the more therefore do I pray that the intense longings of those men of old, their heartfelt expectation, may be enkindled in me by these words: "Let him kiss me with the kiss of his mouth." Many an upright man in those far-off times sense within himself how profuse the graciousness that would be poured upon those lips. And intense desire springing from that perception impelled him to utter: "Let him kiss me with the kiss of his mouth," hoping with every fiber of his being that he might not be deprived of a share in a pleasure so great.

2. The conscientious man of those days might repeat to himself: "Of what use to me the wordy effusions of the prophets? Rather let him who is the most handsome of the sons of men, let him kiss me with the kiss of his mouth. No longer am I satisfied to listen to Moses, for he is a slow speaker and not able to speak well. Isaiah is 'a man of unclean lips,' Jeremiah does not know how to speak, he is a child; not one of the prophets makes an impact on me with his words. But he, the one whom they proclaim, let him speak to me, 'let him kiss me with the kiss of his mouth.' I have no desire that he should approach me in their person, or address me with their words, for they are 'a watery darkness, a dense cloud'; rather in his own person, 'let him kiss me with the kiss of his mouth'; let him whose presence is full of love, from whom exquisite doctrines flow in streams, let him become 'a spring inside me, welling up to eternal life.' Shall I not receive a richer infusion of grace from him whom the Father has anointed with the oil of gladness above all his rivals, provided that he will bestow on me the kiss of his mouth? For his living, active word is to me a kiss, not indeed an adhering of the lips that can sometimes belie a union of hearts, but an unreserved infusion of joys, a revealing of mysteries, a marvellous and indistinguishable mingling of the divine light with the enlightened mind, which, joined in truth to God,

is one spirit with him. With good reason then I avoid trucking with visions and dreams; I want no part with parables and figures of speech; even the very beauty of the angels can only leave me wearied. For my Jesus utterly surpasses these in his majesty and splendor. Therefore I ask of him what I ask of neither man nor angel: that he kiss me with the kiss of his mouth.

II.

Note how I do not presume that it is with his mouth I shall be kissed, for that constitutes the unique felicity and singular privilege of the human nature he assumed. No, in the consciousness of my lowliness I ask to be kissed with the kiss of his mouth, an experience shared by all who are in a position to say: 'Indeed from his fullness we have, all of us, received.' "

3. I must ask you to try to give your whole attention here. The mouth that kisses signifies the Word who assumes human nature; the nature assumed receives the kiss; the kiss however, that takes its being both from the giver and the receiver, is a person that is formed by both, none other than "the one mediator between God and mankind, himself a man, Christ Jesus." It is for this reason that none of the saints dared say: "let him kiss me with his mouth," but rather, "with the kiss of his mouth." In this way they paid tribute to that prerogative of Christ, on whom uniquely and in one sole instance the mouth of the Word was pressed, that moment when the fullness of the divinity yielded itself to him, as the life of his body. A fertile kiss therefore, a marvel of stupendous self-abasement that is not a mere pressing of mouth upon mouth; it is the uniting of God with man. Normally the touch of lip on lip is the sign of the loving embrace of hearts, but this conjoining of natures brings together the human and divine, shows God reconciling "to himself all things, whether on earth or in heaven." "For he is the peace between us, and he has made the two into one." This was the kiss for which just men yearned under the old dispensation, foreseeing as they did that in him they would "find happiness and a crown of rejoicing," because in him were hidden "all the

jewels of wisdom and knowledge." Hence their longing to taste that fullness of his.

4. You seem to be in agreement with this explanation, but I should like you to listen to another.

III.

Even the holy men who lived before the coming of Christ understood that God had in mind plans of peace for the human race. "Surely the Lord God does nothing without revealing his secret to his servants, the prophets." What he did reveal however was obscure to many. For in those days faith was a rare thing on the earth, and hope but a faint impulse in the heart even of many of those who looked forward to the deliverance of Israel. Those indeed who foreknew also proclaimed that Christ would come as man, and with him, peace. One of them actually said: "He himself will be peace in our land when he comes." Enlightened from above they confidently spread abroad the message that through him men would be restored to the favor of God. John, the fore-runner of the Lord, recognizing the fulfillment of that prophecy in his own time, declared: "Grace and truth have come through Christ Jesus." In our time every Christian can discover by experience that this is true.

5. In those far-off days however, while the prophets continued to foretell the covenant, and its author continued to delay his coming, the faith of the people never ceased to waver because there was no one who could redeem or save. Hence men grumbled at the postponements of the coming of the Prince of Peace so often proclaimed by the mouth of his holy prophets from ancient times. As doubts about the fulfillment of the prophecies began to recur, all the more eagerly did they make demands for the kiss, the sign of the promised reconcilement. It was as if a voice from among the people would challenge the prophets of peace: "How much longer are you going to keep us in suspense? You are always foretelling a peace that is never realized; you promise a world of good but trouble on trouble comes. At various times in the past and in various different ways this same hope was fostered

by angels among our ancestors, who in turn have passed the tidings on to us. 'Peace! Peace!' they say, 'but there is no peace.' If God desires to convince me of that benevolent will of his, so often vouched for by the prophets but not yet revealed by the event, then let him kiss me with the kiss of his mouth, and so by this token of peace make my peace secure. For how shall I any longer put my trust in mere words? It is necessary now that words be vindicated by action. If those men are God's envoys let him prove the truth of their words by his own advent, so often the keynote of their predictions, because unless he comes they can do nothing. He sent his servant bearing a staff, but neither voice nor life is forthcoming. I do not rise up, I am not awakened, I am not shaken out of the dust, nor do I breathe in hope, if the Prophet himself does not come down and kiss me with the kiss of his mouth."

6.   Here we must add that he who professes to be our mediator with God is God's own Son, and he is God. But what is man that he should take notice of him, the son of man that he should be concerned about him? Where shall such as I am find the confidence, the daring, to entrust myself to him who is so majestic? How shall I, mere dust and ashes, presume that God takes an interest in me? He is entirely taken up with loving his Father, he has no need of me nor of what I possess. How then shall I find assurance that if he is my mediator he will never fail me? If it be really true, as you prophets have said, that God has determined to show mercy, to reveal himself in a more favorable light, let him establish a covenant of peace, an everlasting covenant with me by the kiss of his mouth. If he will not revoke his given word, let him empty himself, let him humble himself, let him bend to me and kiss me with the kiss of his mouth. If the mediator is to be acceptable to both parties, equally dependable in the eyes of both, then let him who is God's Son become man, let him become the Son of Man, and fill me with assurance by this kiss of his mouth. When I come to recognize that he is truly mine, then I shall feel secure in welcoming the Son of God as mediator. Not even a shadow of mistrust can then exist, for after all he is my brother, and my own flesh. It is impossible that I should be

spurned by him who is bone from my bones, and flesh from my flesh.

7.   We should by now have come to an understanding how the discontent of our ancestors displayed a need for this sacrosanct kiss, that is, the mystery of the incarnate Word, for faith, hard-pressed throughout the ages with trouble upon trouble, was ever on the point of failing, and a fickle people, yielding to encouragement, murmured against the promises of God. Is this a mere improvisation on my part? I suggest that you will find it to be the teaching of the Scriptures: for instance, consider the burden of complaint and murmuring in those words: "Order on order, order on order, rule on rule, rule on rule, a little here, a little there." Or those prayerful exclamations, troubled yet loyal: "Give those who wait for you their reward, and let your prophets be proved worthy of belief." Again: "Bring about what has been prophesied in your name." There too you will find those soothing promises, full of consolation: "Behold the Lord will appear and he will not lie. If he seems slow, wait for him, for he will surely come and he will not delay." Likewise: "His time is close at hand when he will come and his days will not be prolonged." Speaking in the name of him who is promised the prophet announces: "Behold I am coming towards you like a river of peace, and like a stream in spate with the glory of the nations." In all these statements there is evidence both of the urgency of the preachers and of the distrust of those who listened to them. The people murmured, their faith wavered, and in the words of Isaiah: "the ambassadors of peace weep bitterly." Therefore because Christ was late in coming, and the whole human race in danger of being lost in despair, so convinced was it that human weakness was an object of contempt with no hope of the reconciliation with God through a grace so frequently promised, those good men whose faith remained strong eagerly longed for the more powerful assurance that only his human presence could convey. They prayed intensely for a sign that the covenant was about to be restored for the sake of a spiritless, faithless people.

8.   Oh root of Jesse, that stands as a signal to the

peoples, how many prophets and kings wanted to see what you see, and never saw it!

IV.

Happy above them all is Simeon, by God's mercy still bearing fruit in old age! He rejoiced to think that he would see the long-desired sign. He saw it and was glad; and having received the kiss of peace he is allowed to go in peace, but not before he had told his audience that Jesus was born to be a sign that would be rejected. Time proved how true this was. No sooner had the sign of peace arisen than it was opposed, by those, that is, who hated peace; for his peace is with men of good-will, but for the evil-minded he is "a stone to stumble over, a rock to bring men down." Herod accordingly was perturbed, and so was the whole of Jerusalem. Christ "came to his own domain, and his own people did not accept him." Those shepherds, however, who kept watch over their flocks by night, were fortunate for they were gladdened by a vision of this sign. Even in those early days he was hiding these things from the learned and the clever, and revealing them to mere children. Herod, as you know, desired to see him, but because his motive was not genuine he did not succeed. The sign of peace was given only to men of good-will, hence to Herod and others like him was given the sign of the prophet Jonah. The angel said to the shepherds: "Here is a sign for you," you who are humble, obedient, not given to haughtiness, faithful to prayer and meditating day and night on God's law. "This is a sign for you," he said. What sign? The sign promised by the angels, sought after by the people, foretold by the prophets; this is the sign that the Lord Jesus has now brought into existence and revealed to you, a sign by which the incredulous are made believers, the dispirited are made hopeful and the fervent achieve security. This therefore is the sign for you. But as a sign what does it signify? It reveals mercy, grace, peace, the peace that has no end. And finally, the sign is this: "You will find a baby, wrapped in swaddling clothes and lying in a manger." God himself, however, is in this baby, reconciling the world to himself. He will be put to death for your sins and raised to life to justify you, so that made righteous by faith

you may be at peace with God. This was the sign of peace that the Prophet once urged King Achez to ask of the Lord his God, "either from the depths of Sheol or from the heights above." But the ungodly king refused. His wretched state blinded him to the belief that in this sign the highest things above would be joined to the lowest things below in peace. This was achieved when Christ, descending into Sheol, saluted its dwellers with a holy kiss, the pledge of peace, and then going up to heaven, enabled the spirits there to share in the same pledge in joy without end.

9. I must end this sermon. But let me sum up briefly the points we have raised. It would seem that this holy kiss was of necessity bestowed on the world for two reasons. Without it the faith of those who wavered would not have been strengthened, nor the desires of the fervent appeased. Moreover, this kiss is no other than the Mediator between God and man, himself a man, Christ Jesus, who with the Father and Holy Spirit lives and reigns as God for ever and ever. Amen.

Sermon 3: The Kiss Of The Lord's Feet, Hands And Mouth

Today the text we are to study is the book of our own experience. You must therefore turn your attention inwards, each one must take note of his own particular awareness of the things I am about to discuss. I am attempting to discover if any of you has been privileged to say from his heart: "Let him kiss me with the kiss of his mouth." Those to whom it is given to utter these words sincerely are comparatively few, but any one who has received this mystical kiss from the mouth of Christ at least once, seeks again that intimate experience, and eagerly looks for its frequent renewal. I think that nobody can grasp what it is except the one who receives it. For it is "a hidden manna," and only he who eats it still hungers for more. It is "a sealed fountain" to which no stranger has access; only he who drinks still thirsts for more. Listen to one who has had the experience, how urgently he demands: "Be my savior again, renew my joy." But a soul like mine, burdened with sins, still subject to carnal passions, devoid of any knowledge of spiritual delights, may not presume to make such a request, almost totally unacquainted as it is with the joys of the supernatural life.

2.   I should like however to point out to persons like this that there is an appropriate place for them on the way of salvation. They may not rashly aspire to the lips of a most benign Bridegroom, but let them prostrate with me in fear at the feet of a most severe Lord. Like the publican full of misgiving, they must turn their eyes to the earth rather than up to heaven. Eyes that are accustomed only to darkness will be dazzled by the brightness of the spiritual world, overpowered by its splendor, repulsed by its peerless radiance and whelmed again in a gloom more dense than before. All you who are conscious of sin, do not regard as unworthy and despicable that position where the holy sinner laid down her sins, and put on the garment of holiness. There the Ethiopian changed her skin, and, cleansed to a new brightness, could confidently and legitimately respond to those who insulted her: "I am black but lovely, daughters of Jerusalem." You may ask what skill enabled her to accomplish this change, or on what grounds did she merit it? I can tell you in a few words. She wept bitterly, she sighed deeply from her heart, she sobbed with a repentance that shook her very being, till the evil that inflamed her passions was cleansed away. The heavenly physician came with speed to her aid, because "his word runs swiftly." Perhaps you think the Word of God is not a medicine? Surely it is, a medicine strong and pungent, testing the mind and the heart. "The Word of God is something alive and active. It cuts like any double-edged sword but more finely. It can slip through the place where the soul is divided from the spirit, or the joints from the marrow: it can judge the secret thoughts." It is up to you, wretched sinner, to humble yourself as this happy penitent did so that you may be rid of your wretchedness. Prostrate yourself on the ground, take hold of his feet, soothe them with kisses, sprinkle them with your tears and so wash not them but yourself. Thus you will become one of the "flock of shorn ewes as they come up from the washing." But even

then you may not dare to lift up a face suffused with shame and grief, until you hear the sentence: "Your sins are forgiven," to be followed by the summons: "Awake, awake, captive daughter of Sion, awake, shake off the dust."

II.

3.   Though you have made a beginning by kissing the feet, you may not presume to rise at once by impulse to the kiss of the mouth; there is a step to be surmounted in between, an intervening kiss on the hand for which I offer the following explanation. If Jesus says to me: "Your sins are forgiven," what will it profit me if I do not cease from sinning? I have taken off my tunic, am I to put in on again? And if I do, what have I gained? If I soil my feet again after washing them, is the washing of any benefit? Long did I lie in the slough of the marsh, filthy with all kinds of vices; if I return to it again I shall be worse than when I first wallowed in it. On top of that I recall that he who healed me said to me as he exercised his mercy: "Now you are well again, be sure not to sin any more, or something worse may happen to you." He, however, who gave me the grace to repent, must also give me the power to persevere, lest by repeating my sins I should end up by being worse than I was before. Woe to me then, repentant though I be, if he without whom I can do nothing should suddenly withdraw his supporting hand. I really mean nothing; of myself I can achieve neither repentance nor perseverance, and for that reason I pay heed to the Wise Man's advice: "Do not repeat yourself at your prayers." The Judge's threat to the tree that did not yield good fruit is another thing that makes me fearful. For these various reasons I must confess that I am not entirely satisfied with the first grace by which I am enabled to repent of my sins; I must have the second as well, and so bear fruits that befit repentance, that I may not return like the dog to its vomit.

4.   I am now able to see what I must seek for and receive before I may hope to attain to a higher and holier state. I do not wish to be suddenly on the heights, my desire is to advance by degrees. The impudence of the sinner displeases God as

much as the modesty of the penitent gives him pleasure. You will please him more readily if you live within the limits proper to you, and do not set your sights at things beyond you. It is a long and formidable leap from the foot to the mouth, a manner of approach that is not commendable. Consider for a moment: still tarnished as you are with the dust of sin, would you dare touch those sacred lips? Yesterday you were lifted from the mud, today you wish to encounter the glory of his face? No, his hand must be your guide to that end. First it must cleanse your stains, then it must raise you up. How raise you? By giving you the grace to dare to aspire. You wonder what this may be. I see it as the grace of the beauty of temperance and the fruits that befit repentance, the works of the religious man. These are the instruments that will lift you from the dunghill and cause your hopes to soar. On receiving such a grace then, you must kiss his hand, that is, you must give glory to his name, not to yourself. First of all you must glorify him because he has forgiven your sins, secondly because he has adorned you with virtues. Otherwise you will need a bold front to face reproaches such as these: "What do you have that was not given to you? And if it was given, how can you boast as though it were not?"

III.

5.   Once you have had this twofold experience of God's benevolence in these two kisses, you need no longer feel abashed in aspiring to a holier intimacy. Growth in grace brings expansion of confidence. You will love with greater ardour, and knock on the door with greater assurance, in order to gain what you perceive to be still wanting to you. "The one who knocks will always have the door opened to him." It is my belief that to a person so disposed, God will not refuse that most intimate kiss of all, a mystery of supreme generosity and ineffable sweetness. You have seen the way that we must follow, the order of procedure: first, we cast ourselves at his feet, we weep before the Lord who made us, deploring the evil we have done. Then we reach out for the

hand that will lift us up, that will steady our trembling knees. And finally, when we shall have obtained these favors through many prayers and tears, we humbly dare to raise our eyes to his mouth, so divinely beautiful, not merely to gaze upon it, but—I say it with fear and trembling—to receive its kiss. "Christ the Lord is a Spirit before our face," and he who is joined to him in a holy kiss becomes through his good pleasure, one spirit with him.

6.   To you, Lord Jesus, how truly my heart has said: "My face looks to you. Lord, I do seek your face." In the dawn you brought me proof of your love, in my first approach to kiss your revered feet you forgave my evil ways as I lay in the dust. With the advancement of the day you gave your servant reason to rejoice when, in the kiss of the hand, you imparted the grace to live rightly. And now what remains, O good Jesus, except that suffused as I am with the fullness of your light, and while my spirit is fervent, you would graciously bestow on me the kiss of your mouth, and give me unbounded joy in your presence. Serenely lovable above all others, tell me where will you lead your flock to graze, where will you rest it at noon? Dear brothers, surely it is wonderful for us to be here, but the burden of the day calls us elsewhere. These guests, whose arrival has just now been announced to us, compel me to break off rather than to conclude a talk that I enjoy so much. So I go to meet the guests, to make sure that the duty of charity, of which we have been speaking, may not suffer neglect, that we may not hear it said of us: "They do not practice what they preach." Do you pray in the meantime that God may accept the homage of my lips for your spiritual welfare, and for the praise and glory of his name.

Notes

1   The early Cistercians gathered daily in chapter after prime to receive instruction from the Abbot.
2   Bernard places this Sermon in the context of Advent, whose liturgy has undoubtedly influenced its thought.

GUIBERT OF NOGENT

Memoirs

GUIBERT OF NOGENT (CA. 1064-1121), CAME FROM A FAMILY OF minor nobility in Picardy. He entered the monastery of Flay and in 1104 became abbot of Nogent. His writings include a history of the first crusade, a treatise critical of the veneration of relics, and various theological and exegetical works. His autobiography, modeled in part on Augustine's *Confessions*, is the first full autobiography in the Middle Ages and contains revealing information on Guibert, his family, and monastic mentality.

Source: C.C. Swinton Bland, revised by John F. Benton, *Self and Society in Medieval France: The Memoirs of Abbot Guibert of Nogent* (New York: Harper and Row, 1970).

Book 1

CHAPTER 1

I confess to Thy Majesty, O God, my endless wanderings from Thy paths, and my turning back so often to the bosom of Thy Mercy, directed by Thee in spite of all. I confess the wickedness I did in childhood and in youth, wickedness that yet boils up in my mature years, and my ingrained love of crookedness, which still lives on in the sluggishness of my worn body. Whenever I call to mind my persistence in unclean things, O Lord, and how Thou didst always grant remorse for them, I am amazed at the long-suffering of Thy compassion, which is beyond all that man can conceive. If repentance and a prayerful mind cannot exist without the entrance of Thy Spirit, how dost Thou so graciously suffer them to creep into the hearts of sinners, how dost Thou grant so much favor to those who turn away from Thee, indeed, even to those who provoke Thee to wrath? Thou knowest, Almighty Father, how stubbornly we set our hearts against those who incur our anger and with how much difficulty we forgive those who have offended us often or even once, either by a look or a word.

But Thou art not only good but truly goodness itself, even its very source. And since Thy aid goes out to all in general, shalt Thou not be able also to succor each single being? Why not? When the world lay in ignorance of God, when it was wrapped in darkness and the shadow of death, when, as night went on its course, a universal silence prevailed, by whose merit, by whose cry could Thy Almighty Word be summoned to come forth from Thy royal seat? When all mankind gave no heed to Thee, Thou couldst not even then be turned from pity on them; no wonder that Thou shouldst show Thy compassion on one single sinner, great sinner though he be! It is not for me to say that Thou art merciful more readily to individual men than to men in general, for in either case there is no halting in Thy willingness, because there is nothing more willing than Thee. Since Thou art the fountain, and since Thou owest to all what flows forth from Thee, manifestly Thou dost not withhold from any what belongs to all.

I am forever sinning, and between sins ever returning to Thee, fleeing from goodness and forsaking it. When I turn back to goodness, will goodness lose its essence and, overwhelmed by manifold offenses, will it then be different? Is it not said of Thee that Thou wilt not "in Thy anger shut up Thy mercies"? The same psalmist sings that this mercy shall abide both now and forever. Thou knowest that I do not sin because I see that Thou art merciful, but I do confidently avow that Thou art called merciful because Thou art at hand for all who seek Thy indulgence. I am not abusing Thy mercy whenever I am driven to sin by the necessity of sinning, but it would indeed be an impious abuse if I ever took delight in the waywardness of sin because the return to Thee after sinning is so easy. I sin, it is true, but when reason returns, I repent that I yielded to the lust of my heart and that my soul, with unwilling heaviness, bedded itself in baskets full of dung.

In the midst of these daily afflictions of a fall followed by a sort of resurrection, what was I to do? Is it not far wiser to struggle toward Thee for a time, to take breath in Thee even for a moment, than to forget all healing and to despair of Thy grace? And in what does despair consist, if not in throwing oneself deliberately into the pigsty of every outrageous lust? For when the spirit no longer resists the flesh, the very substance of the unhappy soul is wasted in the profligacy of pleasure. As a man who is drowning in a tempest of waters is sucked down into the deep, so one's judgment is drawn down from the mouth of the pit to the depths of evil.

Holy God, while my wits, recovering from the drunkenness of my inner being, come back to Thee, although at other times I do not go forward, yet at least meanwhile I am not turning from knowledge of myself. How could I catch even a glimpse of Thee if my eyes were blind to see myself? If, as Jeremiah says, "I am the man that sees my poverty," it surely follows that I should shrewdly search for those things by which my lacks may be supplied. And on the contrary, if I do not understand what is good, how shall I be able to know evil, much less to forswear it? If I know beauty, I shall never be frightened by foulness. Both matters are therefore apparent, that I should seek knowledge of myself, and, enjoying that, I should consequently not fail in self-knowledge. It is a worthy act and singularly for my soul's good that through these confessions the darkness of my understanding should be dispersed by the searching rays Thy light often casts upon it, by which, being lastingly illuminated, it may forever know itself.

CHAPTER 2

The first thing to do is to acknowledge Thee the benefits Thou hast conferred on me, O God, that Thy servants who shall read of them may weigh exactly the cruelty of my ingratitude. For hadst Thou bestowed on me only what Thou dost allot

to other men, wouldst Thou not have exceeded all that I merit? But Thou didst add many more things that redound to Thy praise and not at all to mine, and still other things about which I think I should remain silent. For if my birth, wealth, and appearance, to mention no other things (if there are any), are the gifts of Thy hand, O Lord, good men do not praise them, except when those to whom Thou hast given them guard under the rule of honor; otherwise they are regarded as utterly contemptible because they are subject to the flaw of changeableness. What have I to do with those things which only serve the interests of lust and pride with their outward show and reputation? They are of such a neutral nature that according to the quality of the mind they may be turned to good or evil, and the more changeable they are, the more suspect their inconstancy renders them. If no other reason could be found, it is sufficient to observe that no one achieves by his own efforts his parentage or good looks, and of these things in particular all that he has was a gift to him.

Human effort may play a part in the acquisition of some other things, such as wealth and skill; as Solomon testifies, "When the iron be blunt, with much labour it shall be sharpened." Yet even all that is confuted by the ready answer that unless the "light which enlighteneth every man that cometh into this world" be shed on him, and unless Christ shall open to him the doors of learning with the key of knowledge, there is no doubt that every teacher shall spend himself in vain or dull ears. Therefore any sensible man would be foolish to claim anything as his own except his sin.

But, leaving these matters, let us return to the subject with which we began. I said, O Good and Holy One, that I thanked Thee for Thy gifts. First and above all, I render thanks to Thee because Thou didst bestow on me a mother who was beautiful, yet chaste, modest, and steeped in the fear of the Lord. Without doubt I would have proclaimed her beauty in a worldly and foolish fashion if I had not austerely declared beauty to be but an empty show. Still, just as the obligatory fasting of the utterly poor is less praiseworthy, since they cannot choose their food, while the abstinence of rich men takes its value from their abundance, in the same way beauty has the higher title to praise of every sort the more desirable it is, so long as it hardens itself against the temptations of lust. If Sallust Crispus had not thought beauty devoid of morality worthy to be praised, he would never have said of Aurelia Orestilla, "In whom good men never found aught to praise except her beauty." If he declares that her good looks alone were to be praised by the good, but that in all else she was foul, I confidently affirm that this was Sallust's meaning: it is as if he had said that she was deservedly approved for a gift of nature from God, although it appears that she was defiled by added impurities. In the same way, we praise beauty in an idol which is justly proportioned, and although, where faith is concerned, an idol is called "nothing" by the Apostle, and nothing more profane could be imagined, yet it is not unreasonable to commend the true modeling of its members.[1]

Certainly however transitory may be the nature of beauty, which is liable to change through the instability of the blood, yet following the usual standard of symbolic goodness, it cannot be denied to be good. For if whatever has been eternally established by God is beautiful, then all that is temporarily fair is, as it were, the reflection of that eternal beauty. "The invisible things of God are clearly seen, being understood by the things that are made," says the Apostle. Angels have always presented countenances of shining beauty when they appear to men. Hence, the wife of Manue says, "There came a man of God to me having the countenance of an angel." On the contrary, according to the first Peter, devils are "reserved in a mist" till the day of the great judgment; they usually appear in an extremely ugly form, except when they deceitfully "transform themselves into angels of light." And not unjustly so, since they have revolted from the splendor of their noble peers.

Furthermore, we are told that the bodies of the elect ought to conform to the glory of the body of Christ, so that the vileness that is contracted by accident or natural decay is amended to the pattern of the Son of God as transfigured on the Mount. If their internal models are beautiful and good, those who manifest their image, especially if they do not depart from their measure, are beautiful, and hence they are good. Augustine himself, in his book *On Christian Doctrine*, if I am not mistaken, is known to have said, "He who has a beautiful body and an ugly soul is less to be mourned than if he had an ugly body, too." If therefore a blemished exterior is rightly a matter for sorrow, without any doubt a thing is good which can be spoiled by combination with something bad, or improved by a quality of respectability.

Thanks to Thee, O God, that Thou didst infuse her beauty with virtue. The seriousness of her manner was such as to make evident her scorn for all vanity; the gravity of her eyes, the restraint of her speech, and the modesty of her expression gave no encouragement to light looks. Thou knowest, Almighty God, Thou didst put into her in earliest youth the fear of Thy name and into her heart rebellion against the allurements of the flesh. Take note that never or hardly ever was she to be found in the company of women who made much of themselves, and just as she kept Thy gift unto herself, so she was sparing in blame of those who were incontinent, and when sometimes a scandalous tale was circulated by strangers or those of her own household, she would turn away and take no part in it, and she was as much annoyed by such whisperings as if she had been slandered in her own person. God of Truth, Thou knowest it is not something personal, such as my love for my mother, that prompts me to say these things. The power of my words should have the more force, since the rest of my race are in truth mere animals ignorant of God, or brutal fighters and murderers, who must surely become outcast from Thee unless Thou shouldst with the greatness of Thy accustomed mercy pity them. But a better opportunity will occur in this work to speak of her. Let us now turn to my own life.

CHAPTER 3

To this woman, as I hope and believe truest to me of all whom she bore, Thou granted that this worst sinner should be born. In two senses I was her last child, for while the others have passed away with the hope of a better life, I am left with a life of utter despair. Yet, through her merit next to Jesus and His Mother and the Saints, while I still live in this evil world there remains to me the hope of that salvation which is open to all. Certainly I know, and it is wrong to disbelieve, that, as in the world she showed me a greater love and brought me up in greater distinction (with a mother's special affection for her last-born), she remembers me the more now that she is in the presence of God. From her youth she was full of God's fire in Zion, since the concern she had for me in her heart did not cease whether she was asleep or awake. And now that she is dead, the wall of her flesh being broken away, I know that in Jerusalem that furnace burns with greater heat than words can express, the more that, being filled there with the Spirit of God, she is not ignorant of the miseries in which I am entangled, and, blessed as she is, she bewails my wanderings when she sees my feet go astray from the paths of goodness marked out by her recurrent warnings.

O Father and Lord God, Who didst give being to me (I who am bad in such manner and measure as Thou knowest) from her so truly and really good, Thou didst also grant me hope in her merit, a hope which I should not dare to have at all if I were not for a little near Thee relieved of the fear of my sins. Likewise Thou didst bring into my wretched heart perhaps not hope so much as the shadow of hope, in that Thou didst vouchsafe to me birth, and rebirth also, on the day that is the highest of all days and best-loved by Christian people. My mother had passed almost the whole of Good Friday in excessive pain of childbirth (in what anguish, too, did she linger, when I wandered from the way and followed slippery paths!) when at last came Holy Saturday, the day before Easter.

Racked by pains long-endured, and her tortures increasing as her hour drew near, when she thought I had at last in natural course come to birth, instead I was returned within the womb. By this time my father, friends, and kinsfolk, were crushed with dismal sorrowing for both of us, for while the child was hastening the death of the mother, and she her child's in denying him deliverance, all had reason for compassion. It was a day on which, with the exception of that solemn office which is celebrated exclusively and at its special time, the regular services for the household were not taking place. And so they asked counsel in their need and fled for help to the altar of the Lady Mary, and to her (the only Virgin that ever was or would be to bear a child) this vow was made, and in the place of an offering this gift laid upon the gracious Lady's altar: that should a male child be born, he should be given up to the religious life in the service of God and the Lady, and if one of the inferior sex, she should be handed over to the corresponding calling. At once a weak little being, almost an abortion, was born, and at that timely birth there was rejoicing only for my mother's deliverance, the child being such a miserable object. In that poor mite just born, there was such a pitiful meagerness that he had the corpse-like look of a premature baby; so much so that when reeds (which in that region are very slender when they come up—it being then the middle of April—) were placed in my little fingers, they seemed stouter in comparison. On that very day when I was put into the baptismal font—as I was so often told as a joke in boyhood and even in youth—a certain woman tossed me from hand to hand. "Look at this thing," she said. "Do you think such a child can live, whom nature by a mistake has made almost without limbs, giving him something more like an outline than a body?"

All these things, my Creator, were signs of the state in which I seem now to live. Could truth in Thy service be found in me, O Lord? I have shown no firmness toward Thee, no constancy. If to the eye any work of mine has appeared good, many times crooked motives have made it slight. God of supreme love, I have said that Thou gavest me hope, or a faint likeness of some little hope, out of the promise of that joyous day on which I was born and reborn and offered, too, to her who is Queen of all next to God. O Lord God, I do not realize with what reason Thou hast given me that the day of birth brings nothing better than the day of death to those who live an unprofitable life? It is denied beyond dispute that no merits can exist prior to the day we are born but can exist on the day of our death; if it should be our chance not to live in goodness, then I confess that famous days, whether for birth or death, can do us no good.

For if it is true that He made me, and not I myself, and that I did not fix the day, and had no right to the choice of it, its bestowal on me by God affords me neither hope for honor unless my life, imitating the holiness of the day, justifies its promise. Certainly my birthday would then be brightened by the joyous character of the season if the purpose of my life were controlled by virtue searching for uprightness; and the glory of a man's entry into the world would appear a favor granted to his merit if his spirit continuing in righteousness should glorify his end. Whether I be named Peter or Paul, whether Remi or Nicolas, I shall not profit, in the words of the poet, "by the name that has been derived from great Iulus" unless I carefully copy the examples of those whom Providence or fortune has made my namesakes. Behold, O God, how my swelling heart puffs up again, how a feather's weight will be magnified into a matter of pride!

O Lady who rules Earth and Heaven after thy only Son, how good was the thought of those who placed me under bondage to thee! And how much better would my thoughts have been if in later years I had bent my heart to that vow's resolve! Behold, I declare that I was given to be especially thy own, nor do I deny that sacrilegiously and knowingly I took myself from thee. Did I not rob thee of myself when I preferred my stinking willfulness to thy sweet odour? But although many times by such deceit I stole myself away from thee, yet to thee, and through thee to God the Father and the only Son, I returned more fearlessly when I contemplated that offering. And when, recurring a thousand times to my sins, I pined again, then out of thy never-failing compassion my sureness was born again, and I was encouraged to hope by the gift of thy earlier mercy. But why that word "earlier"? I have so often known, and continue to know daily, the constancy of thy mercy, I have escaped so often from the prison of my fall when thou didst set me free, that on those old matters I would gladly keep utter silence when such a wealth of freedom rules. As often as the repetition of sin begets in me a cruel hardening of the heart, then my resort to thee, as by a natural instinct, softens it again; and after looking at myself, after considering my misfortunes, when I come close to fainting in despair, almost involuntarily I feel springing up in my unhappy soul a

certainty of recovery in thee. It lies so close to my thought that in whatever ills I am entangled, thou canst not, if I dare to say it, be a defaulter in my need. To thee in particular shall I lay the due cause of my ruin if thou hast no regard in his perversity for him who was taken straight from the womb to thee, and if thou givest him no welcome when he turns to thee again. Since clearly the power is thine at will, and the authority of the Son is known to overflow to the mother, from whom may I rather demand salvation than from thee to whom I cry out "I am thine" by right of the bondage that began at my birth? At another time how gladly will I reflect upon these things with thee! But first let us touch upon other matters.

CHAPTER 4

After birth I had scarcely learned to cherish my rattle when Thou, Gracious Lord, henceforth my Father, didst make me an orphan. For when about eight months had passed, the father of my flesh died. Great thanks are due to Thee that Thou didst allow that man to depart in a Christian state. If he had lived, he would undoubtedly have endangered the provision Thou hadst made for me. Because my young body and a certain natural quickness for one of such tender age seemed to fit me for worldly pursuits, no one doubted that when the proper time had come for beginning my education, he would have broken the vow which he had made for me. O Gracious Provider, for the well-being of us both Thou didst determine that I should not miss the beginning of instruction in Thy discipline and that he should not break his solemn promise for me.

And so with great care that widow, truly Thine, brought me up, and at last she chose the day of the festival of the Blessed Gregory for putting me in school. She had heard that that servant of Thine, O Lord, had been eminent for his wonderful understanding and had abounded in extraordinary wisdom. Therefore she strove with bountiful almsgiving to win the good word of Thy Confessor, that he to whom Thou hadst granted understanding might make me zealous in the pursuit of knowledge. Put to my book, I had learned the shapes of the letters, but hardly yet to join them into syllables, when my good mother, eager for my instruction, arranged to place me under a schoolmaster.

There was a little before that time, and in a measure there was still in my youth, such a scarcity of teachers that hardly any could be found in the towns, and in the cities there were very few, and those who by good chance could be discovered had but slight knowledge and could not be compared with the wandering scholars of these days. The man in whose charge my mother decided to put me had begun to learn grammar late in life, and he was the more unskilled in the art through having imbibed little of it when he was young. Yet he was of such character that what he lacked in letters he made up for in honesty.

Through the chaplains who conducted the divine services in her house, my mother approached this teacher, who was in charge of the education of a young cousin of mine and was closely bound to some of my relatives, at whose court he had been raised. He took into consideration the woman's earnest request and was favorably impressed by her honorable and virtuous character, but he was afraid to give offense to those kinsmen of mine and was in doubt whether to come into her house. While thus undecided, he was persuaded by the following vision:

At night when he was sleeping in his room, where I remember he conducted all the instruction in our town, the figure of a white-headed old man, of very dignified appearance, seemed to lead me in by the hand through the door of the room. Halting within hearing, while the other looked on, he pointed out his bed to me and said, "Go to him, for he will love you very much." When he dropped my hand and let me go, I ran to the man, and as I kissed him again and again on the face, he awoke and conceived such an affection for me that putting aside all hesitation, and shaking off all fear for my kinsfolk, on whom not only he but everything that belonged to him was dependent, he agreed to go to my mother and live in her house.

Now, that boy whom he had been educating so far was handsome and of good birth, but he was so eager to avoid proper studies and unsteady under all instruction, a liar and a thief, as far as

his age would allow, that he never could be found in productive activity and hardly ever in school, but almost every day played truant in the vineyards. Since my mother's friendly advances were made to him at the moment when the man was tired of the boy's childish folly, and the meaning of the vision fixed still deeper in his heart what he had already desired, he gave up his companionship of the boy and left the noble family to which he was attached. He would not have done this with impunity, however, if their respect for my mother, as well as her power, had not protected him.

CHAPTER 5

Placed under him, I was taught with such purity and checked with such honesty from the vices which commonly spring up in youth that I was kept from ordinary games and never allowed to leave my master's company, or to eat anywhere else than at home, or to accept gifts from anyone without his leave; in everything I had to show self-control in word, look, and deed, so that he seemed to require of me the conduct of a monk rather than a clerk. While others of my age wandered everywhere at will and were unchecked in the indulgence of such inclinations as were natural at their age, I, hedged in with constant restraints and dressed in my clerical garb,[2] would sit and look at the troops of players like a beast awaiting sacrifice. Even on Sundays and saints' days I had to submit to the severity of school exercises. At hardly any time, and never for a whole day, was I allowed to take a holiday; in fact, in every way and at all times I was driven to study. Moreover, he devoted himself exclusively to my education, since he was allowed to have no other pupil.

He worked me hard, and anyone observing us might have thought that my little mind was being exceedingly sharpened by such perseverance, but the hopes of all were disappointed. He was, in fact, utterly unskilled in prose and verse composition. Meanwhile I was pelted almost every day with a hail of blows and harsh words while he was forcing me to learn what he could not teach.

In this fruitless struggle I passed nearly six

years with him, but got no reward worth the time it took. Yet otherwise, in all that is supposed to count for good training, he devoted himself completely to my improvement. Most faithfully and lovingly he instilled in me all that was temperate and modest and outwardly refined. But I clearly perceived that he had no consideration or restraint in the trial he put me to, urging me on without intermission and with great pain under the pretense of teaching me. By the strain of undue application, the natural powers of grown men, as well as of boys, are blunted, and the hotter the fire of their mental activity in unremitting study, the sooner is the strength of their understanding weakened and chilled by excess, and its energy turned to apathy.

It is therefore necessary to treat the mind with greater moderation while it is still burdened with its bodily covering. If there is to be silence in heaven for half an hour, so that while it continues the unremitting activity of contemplation cannot exist, in the same way what I may call perseverance will not stay fresh while struggling with some problem. Hence we believe that when the mind has been fixed exclusively on one subject, we ought to give it relaxation from its intensity, so that after dealing in turn with different subjects we may with renewed energy, as after a holiday, fasten upon that one with which our minds are most engaged. In short, let wearied nature be refreshed at times by varying its work. Let us remember that God did not make the world without variety, but in day and night, spring and summer, winter and autumn, He has delighted us by temporal change. Let everyone who has the name of master see in what manner he may moderate the teaching of boys and youths, since such men think their students should be treated like old men who are completely serious.

Now, my teacher had a harsh love for me, for he showed excessive severity in his unjust floggings, and yet the great care with which he guarded me was evident in his acts. Clearly I did not deserve to be beaten, for if he had the skill in teaching which he professed, it is certain that I, though a boy, would have been well able to grasp anything that he taught. But because he stated his thoughts poorly and what he strove to express was not at all clear to him, his talk rolled ineffec-

tively on and on in a banal but by no means obvious circle, which could not be brought to any conclusion, much less understood. He was so uninstructed that he retained incorrectly, as I have said before, what he had once learned badly late in life, and if he let anything slip out (incautiously, as it were), he maintained and defended it with blows, regarding all his own opinions as firmly established. I think he certainly should have avoided such folly, for indeed, a learned man says, "before one's nature has absorbed knowledge, it is less praiseworthy to say what you know than to keep silent about what you do not know."

While he took cruel vengeance on me for not knowing what he did not know himself, he ought certainly to have considered that it was very wrong to demand from a weak little mind what he had not put into it. For as the words of madmen can be understood by the sane with difficulty or not at all, so the talk of those who are ignorant but say they know something and pass it on to others will be the more darkened by their own explanations. You will find nothing more difficult than trying to discourse on what you do not understand, so that your subject is obscure to the speaker and even more to the listener, making both look like blockheads. I say this, O my God, not to put a stigma on such a friend, but for every reader to understand that we should not attempt to teach as a certainty every assertion we make, and that we should not involve others in the mists of our own conjectures.

It has been my purpose here, in consideration of the poorness of my subject to give it some flavour by reasoning about things, so that if the one deserves to be reckoned of little value, the other may sometimes be regarded as worthwhile.

CHAPTER 6

Although he crushed me by such severity yet in other ways he made it quite plain that he loved me as well as he did himself. With such watchful care did he devote himself to me, with such foresight did he secure my welfare against the spite of others and teach me on what authority I should beware of the dissolute manners of some who paid court to me, and so long did he argue with my mother about the elaborate richness of my dress, that he was thought to guard me as a parent, not as a master, and not my body alone but my soul as well. As for me, considering the dull sensibility of my age and my littleness, I conceived much love for him in response, in spite of the many weals with which he furrowed my tender skin, so that not through fear, as is common in those of my age, but through a sort of love deeply implanted in the heart, I obeyed him in utter forgetfulness of his severity. Indeed, when my master and my mother saw me paying due respect to both alike, they tried by frequent tests to see whether I would dare to prefer one or the other.

At last, without any intention on the part of either, an opportunity occurred for a test which left no room for doubt. Once I had been beaten in school—the school being no other than the dining hall of our house, for he had given up the charge of others to take me alone, my mother having wisely required him to do this for a higher wage and a better position. When my studies, such as they were, had come to an end about the time of vespers, I went to my mother's knee after a more severe beating than I had deserved. And when, as often happened, she began to ask me repeatedly whether I had been whipped that day, I, not to appear a telltale, entirely denied it. Then against my will she threw off my inner garment (which is called a shirt or *chemise*) and saw my little arms blackened and the skin of my back everywhere puffed up with the cuts from the twigs. Grieved to the heart by the very savage punishment inflicted on my tender body, troubled, agitated, and weeping with sorrow, she said: "You shall never become a clerk, nor any more suffer so much to get an education." At that, looking at her with what reproach I could, I replied: "If I had to die on the spot, I would not give up studying my lessons and becoming a clerk." I should add that she had promised that if I wished to become a knight, when I reached the age for it she would give me the arms and equipment of knighthood.

When I had declined all these offers with a good deal of scorn, she, Thy servant, O Lord, accepted this rebuff so gladly, and was made so cheerful by my disdain of her proposal, that she repeated to my master the reply with which I had opposed her. Then both rejoiced that I had such an eager longing to fulfill my father's vow. I was eager to pursue my lessons more quickly, although I was poorly taught. Moreover, I did not shirk the church offices; indeed, when the hour sounded or there was occasion, I did not prefer even my meals to that place and time. That is how it was then: but Thou, O God, knowest how much I afterward fell away from that zeal, how reluctantly I went to divine services, hardly consenting even when driven to them by blows. Clearly, O Lord, the impulses that animated me then were not religious feelings begotten by thoughtfulness, but only a child's eagerness. But after adolescence had exhausted itself in bringing forth wickedness within me, I hastened toward the loss of all shame and that former zeal entirely faded away. Although for a brief space, my God, good resolve, seemed to shine forth, it came to pass that it soon vanished, overshadowed by the storm clouds of my evil imagination.

CHAPTER 7

At length my mother tried by every means to get me into a church living. Now, the first opportunity for placing me was not only badly but abominably chosen. My adolescent brother, a knight and defender of the castle of Clermont (which, I should say, is situated between Compiègne and Beauvais), was expecting some money from the lord of that stronghold, either as largess or as a moneyfief, I do not know which.[3] And when he deferred payment, probably through want of ready money, by the advice of some of my kinsmen it was suggested to him that he should give me a canonry, called a prebend, in the church of that place (which, contrary to canon law, was subject to his authority)[4] and that he should then cease to be troubled for what he owed.

At that time the Apostolic See was making a fresh attack on married priests; this led to an outburst of rage against them by people who were so zealous about the clergy that they angrily demanded that married priests should either be deprived of their benefices or should cease to perform their priestly duties. Thereupon a certain nephew of my father, a man conspicuous for his power and knowledge but so bestial in his debauchery that he had no respect for any woman's conjugal ties, now violently inveighed against the clergy because of this canon, as if exceptional purity of heart drove him to horror of such practices. A layman himself, he refused to be bound by a layman's laws, their very laxity making his abuse of them more shameful. The marriage net could not hold him; he never allowed himself to be entangled in its folds. Being everywhere in the worst odour through such conduct, but protected by the rank which his worldly power gave him, he was never prevented by the reproach of his own unchastity from thundering persistently against the holy clergy.

Having found a pretext by which I might profit at the expense of a priest with a benefice, he begged the lord of the castle, with whom, as one of his intimates, he had more than sufficient influence, to summon me and invest me with that canonry, on the ground that the cleric was an absentee and utterly unsuitable for the office. For, contrary to all ecclesiastical law and right, he held the office of abbot by permission of the bishop, and, not being under rule himself, he demanded obedience to rule from those who were.[5] At this time not only was it treated as a serious offense for the members of the higher orders[6] and the canons to be married, but it was also considered a crime to purchase ecclesiastical offices involving pastoral care, such as prebends and the offices of precentor, provost, etc., not to speak of the higher dignities. Consequently, those who were empowered to transact the affairs of the church, those who favored the side of the cleric who had lost his prebend, and many of my contemporaries began to stir up a whispering campaign about simony and excommunication, which recently the cleric had talked of publicly.

Now, married priest as he was, although he would not be separated from his wife by the suspension of his office, at least he had given up celebrating mass. Because he treated the divine mysteries as of less importance than his own body, he was rightly caught in that punishment which he thought to escape by the renunciation of the Sacrifice. And so, being stripped of his canonry, because there was no longer anything to restrain him, he now began freely to celebrate mass, while keeping his wife. Then a rumour grew that at this service he was daily repeating the excommunication of my mother and her family. My mother, always fearful in religious matters, dreading the punishment of her sins and therefore the giving of offense, thereupon surrendered the prebend which had been wickedly granted, and, in the expectation of some cleric's death, bargained with the lord of the castle for another for me. Thus "we flee from weapons of iron and fall before a bow of brass," for to grant something in anticipation of another's death is nothing else than a daily incentive to murder.

O Lord my God, at that time I was wrapped up in these evil hopes and in no wise occupied with waiting for Thy gifts, which I had not yet learned to know. This woman, Thy servant, did not yet understand the hope, the certainty, she ought to have of my sustenance in Thee and had not learned what benefits had already been won for me from Thee. Since while still in the world she had for a short time thoughts that were of the world, it is no wonder that she sought to obtain for me those things which she had chosen to get for herself, believing that I, too, would desire the things of the world. Later, however after perceiving the peril of her own soul, when she burdened the many secret places of her heart with sorrow for her past life, then she thought it the worst madness to practice for others what she scorned for herself, as though she had said, "What I do not wish to be done to me, I will not do to another," and what she had ceased to seek for herself, she thought it a wicked thing to desire for someone else, if he should be injured by it. Far different is the practice of many, whom we see with a show of poverty casting away their own advantages but too eager to secure the advancement of others not only of their own family, which is bad enough, but of those unrelated to them, which is worse.

CHAPTER 12

After these lengthy accounts I return to Thee, my God, to speak of the conversion of that good woman, my mother. When hardly of marriageable age, she was given to my father, a mere youth, by the provision of my grandfather, since she was of the nobility, had a very pretty face, and was naturally and most becomingly of sober mien. She had, however, conceived a fear of God's name at the very beginning of her childhood. She had learned to be terrified of sin, not from experience but from dread of some sort of blow from on high, and—as she often told me herself—this dread had so possessed her mind with the terror of sudden death that in later years she grieved because she no longer felt in her maturity the same stings of righteous fear as she had in her unformed and ignorant youth.

Now, it so happened that at the very beginning of that lawful union conjugal intercourse was made ineffective through the bewitchments of certain persons. It was said that their marriage drew upon them the envy of a stepmother, who had some nieces of great beauty and nobility and who was plotting to slip one of them into my father's bed. Meeting with no success in her designs, she is said to have used magical arts to prevent entirely the consummation of the marriage. His wife's virginity thus remained intact for three years, during which he endured his great misfortune in silence; at last, driven to it by those close to him, my father was the first to reveal the facts. In all sorts of ways, his kinsmen endeavored to bring about a divorce, and by their constant pressure upon my father, who was then young and dull-witted, they tried to induce him to become a monk, although at that time there was little talk of this order. They did not do this for his soul's good, however, but with the purpose of getting possession of his property.

When their suggestion produced no effect, they began to hound the girl herself, far away as she was from her kinsfolk and harassed by the violence of strangers, into voluntary flight out of sheer exhaustion under their insults, and without waiting for divorce. She endured all this, bearing with calmness the abuse that was aimed at her, and if out of this rose any strife, she pretended ignorance of it. Besides this, certain rich men, perceiving that she was not in fact a wife, began to assail the heart of the young girl; but Thou, O Lord, the builder of inward chastity, didst inspire her with purity stronger than her nature or her youth. Thy grace it was that saved her from burn-

ing, though set in the midst of flames, Thy doing that her weak soul was not hurt by the poison of evil talk, and that when enticements from without were added to those impulses common to our human nature, like oil poured upon the flames yet the young maiden's heart was always under her control and never won from her by any allurements. Are not such things solely Thy doing, O Lord? When she was in the heat of youth and continually engaged in wifely duties, yet for seven whole years[7] Thou didst keep her in such contenence that, in the words of a certain wise man, even "rumour dared not speak lies about her".

O God, Thou knowest how hard, how almost impossible it would be for women of the present time to keep such chastity as this; whereas there was in those days such modesty that hardly ever was the good name of a married woman sullied by evil rumour. Ah! how wretchedly have modesty and honor in the state of virginity declined from that time to this our present age, and both the reality and the show of a married woman's protection fallen to ruin. Therefore coarse mirth is all that may be noted in their manners and naught but jesting heard, with sly winks and ceaseless chatter. Wantonness shows in their gait, only silliness in their behaviour. So much does the extravagance of their dress depart from the old simplicity that in the enlargement of their sleeves, the tightness of their dresses, the distortion of their shoes of Cordovan leather with their curling toes, they seem to proclaim that everywhere modesty is a castaway. A lack of lovers to admire her is a woman's crown of woe, and on her crowds of thronging suitors rests her claim to nobility and courtly pride. There was at that time, I call God to witness, greater modesty in married men, who would have blushed to be seen in the company of such women, than there is now in brides. By such shameful conduct they turn men into greater braggarts and lovers of the market place and the public street.

What is the end of all this, Lord God, but that no one blushes for his own levity and licentiousness, because he knows that all are tarred with the same brush, and, seeing himself in the same case as all others, why then should he be ashamed of pursuits in which he knows all others engage? But why do I say "ashamed" when such men feel shame only if someone excels them as an example of lustfulness? A man's private boastfulness about the number of his loves or his choice of a beauty whom he has seduced is no reproach to him, nor is he scorned for vaunting his love affairs before Thee. Instead, his part in furthering the general corruption meets with the approval of all. Listen to the cheers when, with the inherent looseness of unbridled passions which deserve the doom of eternal silence, he shamelessly noises abroad what ought to have been hidden in shame, what should have burdened his soul with the guilt of ruined chastity and plunged him in the depths of despair. In this and similar ways, this modern age is corrupt and corrupting, distributing evil ideas to some, while the filth thereof, spreading to others, goes on increasing without end.

Holy God, scarcely any such thing was heard of in the time when Thy handmaid was behaving as she did; indeed, then shameful things were hidden under the cloak of sacred modesty and things of honor had their crown. In those seven years, O Lord, that virginity which Thou didst in wondrous fashion prolong in her was in agony under countless wrongs, as frequently they threatened to dissolve her marriage with my father and give her to another husband or to send her away to the remote houses of my distant relatives. Under such grievous treatment she suffered bitterly at times, but with Thy support, O God, she strove with wonderful self-control against the enticements of her own flesh and the inducements of others.

I do not say, gracious Lord, that she did this out of virtue, but that the virtue was Thine alone. For how could that be virtue that came of no conflict between body and spirit, no straining after God, but only from concern for outward honor and to avoid disgrace? No doubt a sense of shame has its use, if only to resist the approach of sin, but what is useful before a sin is committed is damnable afterward. What prostrates the self with the shame of propriety, holding it back from sinful deeds, is useful at the time, since the fear of God can bring aid, giving holy seasoning to shame's lack of savour, and can make that which was profitable at the time (that is, in the world)

useful not for a moment but eternally. But after a sin is committed a sense of shame which leads to vanity is the more deadly the more it obstinately resists the healing of holy confession. The desire of my mother, Thy servant, O Lord God, was to do nothing to hurt her worldly honor, yet following Thy Gregory, whom, however, she had never read or heard read, she did not maintain that desire, for afterward she surrendered all her desires into Thy sole keeping. It was therefore good for her at that time to be attached to her worldly reputation.

Since the bewitchment by which the bond of natural and lawful intercourse was broken lasted seven years and more, it is all too easy to believe that, just as by prestidigitation the faculty of sight may be deceived so that conjurers seem to produce something out of nothing, so to speak, and to make certain things out of others, so reproductive power and effort may be inhibited by much less art; and indeed it is now a common practice, understood even by ignorant people.[8] When that bewitchment was broken by a certain old woman, my mother submitted to the duties of a wife as faithfully as she had kept her virginity when she was assailed by so many attacks. In other ways she was truly fortunate, but she laid herself open not so much to endless misery as to mourning when she, whose goodness was ever growing, gave birth to an evil son who (in my own person) grew worse and worse. Yet Thou knowest, Almighty One, with what purity and holiness in obedience to Thee she raised me, how greatly she provided me with the care of nurses in infancy and of masters and teachers in boyhood, with no lack even of fine clothes for my little body, so that I seemed to equal the sons of kings and counts in indulgence.

And not only in my mother, O Lord, didst Thou put this love for me, but Thou didst inspire with it other, far richer persons, so that rather because of the grace Thou didst grant me than under the obligations of kinship, they lavished on me careful tending and nurture.

O God, Thou knowest what warnings, what prayers she daily poured into my ears not to listen to corrupting words from anyone. Whenever she had leisure from household cares, she taught me how and for what I ought to pray to Thee.

Thou alone knowest with what pains she labored so that the sound beginning of a happy and honorable childhood which Thou hadst granted might not be ruined by an unsound heart. Thou didst make it her desire that I should without ceasing burn with zeal for Thee, that above all Thou might add to my outward comeliness inner goodness and wisdom. Gracious God, Gracious Lord, if she had known in advance under what heaps of filth I should blot out the fair surface of Thy gifts, bestowed by Thee at her prayer, what would she have said? What would she have done? How hopeless the lamentations she would have uttered! How much anguish she would have suffered! Thanks to Thee, sweet and temperate Creator, "Who hath made our hearts." If, indeed, her vision had pierced the secret places of my heart, unworthy of her pure gaze, I wonder if she would not there and then have died.

CHAPTER 13

After introducing these comments by way of anticipation, let us return to what we left further back. I have learned that this woman had such a fear of God's name, even while she was serving the world, that in her obedience to the church, in almsgiving, in her offerings for masses, her conduct was such as to win respect from all. Full belief in my story will, I know, be made difficult by a natural suspicion that the partiality of a son has exaggerated her virtues. If to praise one's mother be thought a cautious, disingenuous way of glorifying oneself, I dare to call Thee to witness, O God, Who knowest her soul, in which Thou didst dwell, that I have truthfully asserted her surpassing merit. And indeed, since it is clearer than daylight that my life has strayed from the paths of the good and that my pursuits have always been an affront to any sensible person, of what avail will the reputation of my mother and father or ancestors be to me when all their grandeur will be squeezed out of their wretched offspring? I, who through lack of will and deed fail to make their behaviour live again, am riding posthaste to infamy if I claim their praise for myself.

While she was still a young married woman, something happened which gave no slight impulse to the amendment of her life. The French in the time of King Henri were fighting with great bitterness against the Normans and their Count William, who afterward conquered England and Scotland, and in that clash of the two nations it was my father's fate to be taken prisoner. It was the custom of this count never to hold prisoners for ransom, but to condemn them to captivity for life. When the news was brought to his wife (I put aside the name of mother, for I was not yet born, nor was I for a long time after), she was struck down half dead with wretched sorrow; she abstained from food and drink, and sleep was still more difficult through her despairing anxiety, the cause of this being not the amount of his ransom but the impossibility of his release.

In the dead of the night, as she lay in her bed full of deep anxiety, since it is the habit of the Devil to invade souls weakened with grief, suddenly, while she lay awake, the Enemy himself lay upon her and by the burden of his weight almost crushed the life out of her. As she choked in the agony of her spirit and lost all use of her limbs, she was unable to make a single sound; completely silenced but with her reason free, she awaited aid from God alone. Then suddenly from the head of her bed a spirit, without doubt a good one, began to cry out in loud and kindly tones, "Holy Mary, help her." After the spirit had spoken out in this fashion for a bit, and she had fully understood what he was saying and was aware that he was thoroughly outraged, he sallied forth burning with anger. Thereupon he who lay on her rose up, and the other met and seized him and by the strength of God overthrew him with a great crash, so that the room shook heavily with the shock of it, and the maidservants, who were fast asleep, were rudely awakened. When the Enemy had thus been driven out by divine power, the good spirit who had called upon Mary and routed the Devil turned to her whom he had rescued and said, "Take care to be a good woman." The attendants, alarmed by the sudden uproar, rose to see how their mistress was and found her half dead, with the blood drained from her face and all the strength crushed out of her body. They questioned her about the noise and heard about the causes of it from her, and they were scarcely able by their presence and talk and by the lighting of a lamp to revive her.

Those last words of her deliverer—nay, Thy words, O Lord God, through the mouth of Thy messenger—were stored up forever in the woman's memory and she stood ready to be guided to a greater love, if with God's help the opportunity should occur later. Now, after the death of my father, although the beauty of her face and form remain undimmed, and I, scarcely half a year old, gave her reason enough for anxiety, she resolved to continue in her widowhood. With what spirit she ruled herself and what an example of modesty she set may be gathered from the following event. When my father's kinsmen, eager for his fiefs and possessions, strove to take them all by excluding my mother, they fixed a day in court for advancing their claims. The day came and the barons were assembled to deliver justice. My mother withdrew into the church, away from the avaricious plotters, and was standing before the image of the crucified Lord, mindful of the prayers she owed. One of my father's kinsmen, who shared the views of the others and was sent by them, came to request her presence to hear their decision, as they were waiting for her. Whereupon she said, "I will take part in this matter only in the presence of my Lord." "Whose lord?" said he. Then, stretching out her hand toward the image of the crucified Lord, she replied, "This is my Lord, the advocate under whose protection I will plead." At that the man reddened and, not being very subtle, put on a wry smile to hide his evil intent and went off to tell his friends what he had heard. And they, too, were covered with confusion at such an answer, since they knew that in the face of her utter honesty they had no just grounds, and so they ceased to trouble her.

Shortly after that, one of the leading men of that place and province, my father's nephew, who was as greedy as he was powerful, addressed the woman in the following terms: "Madame," said he, "since you have sufficient youth and beauty, you ought to marry, so that your life in this world would be more pleasant, and the children of my uncle would come under my care to be brought up by me in a worthy fashion, and finally his possessions would devolve to my authority, as it is right they should."[9] She replied, however, "You know that your uncle was of very noble descent. Since God has taken him away, Hymen shall not repeat his rites over me, my lord, unless a marriage with some much greater noble shall offer itself." Now, the woman was quite crafty in speaking of marrying a greater noble, knowing that could hardly, if at all, come to pass. Consequently, since he bristled at her talk of a higher noble, she, who was wholly set against nobles and commoners alike, put an end to all expectation of a second marriage. When he set down to overweening pride her talk of a greater noble, she replied, "Certainly either a greater noble or no husband at all." Perceiving the resolution with which the lady spoke, he desisted from his designs, and never again sought anything of the kind from her.

In great fear of God and with no less love of all her kin and especially of the poor, this woman wisely ruled our household and our property. That loyalty which she had given her husband in his lifetime she kept unbroken and with double constancy to his spirit, since she did not break the ancient union of their bodies by a substitution of other flesh on his departure, and almost every day she endeavored to help him by the offering of her life-bringing Sacrifice. Friendly to all the poor in general, to some in her great pity she was generous and courtly to the full extent of her means. The sting of remembering her sins could not have been sharper if she had been given up to all kinds of wickedness and dreaded the punishment of every ill deed that is done. In plainness of living there was nothing else she could do, for her delicacy and her customary sumptuous diet did not accord with frugality. In other matters her behaviour was completely unexpected. I personally have both seen and made certain by touch that although on certain occasions she wore outer garments of rich material, next to her skin she was covered with the roughest haircloth. Although her delicate skin was completely unaccustomed to it, she wore this cloth throughout the day and even went to bed in it at night.

She never or hardly ever missed the night offices, while she regularly attended the assemblies of God's people in holy seasons, in such fashion that scarcely ever in her house was there rest from the singing of God's praises by her chaplains, who were always busy at their office. So constantly was her dead husband's name on her lips that her mind seemed to turn on no other subject, and in her prayers, in giving alms, even in the midst of ordinary business, she continually spoke of the man, because she could do nothing without thinking of him. For when the heart is full of love for someone, the mouth shapes his name whether one wants to or not.

CHAPTER 14

Passing over those matters in which she showed her goodness, but not her most admirable qualities, let us proceed with what is left. When I had passed about twelve years, as I was told, after my father's death, and his widow had managed her house and children while wearing a laywoman's clothes, she now made haste to bring to happy birth a resolve with which she had long been in labour. While she was still pondering this idea, discussing it with no one but that master and teacher of mine whom I discussed before, I heard a certain devil-possessed dependent of hers, who was rambling on under the Devil's influence about other matters, shouting out these words, "The priests have placed a cross in her loins." Nothing indeed could have been truer, although I did not then understand what he was intimating, for thereafter she submitted not to one but to many crosses. Soon afterward, while her intention was still unknown to anyone but the person I have mentioned, who was then a sort of steward in her house and who himself a little later followed her in her conversion by renouncing the world, she saw the following vision in a dream: she seemed to be marrying a man and celebrating her nuptials, much to the amazement and even stupefaction of her children, friends, and kinsfolk. The next day when my mother went into the country for a walk attended by the man who was my teacher and her steward, he explained what she had seen. My mother did not need to be a skilled interpreter in such matters. One look at my master's face, and without speech from him she knew that the vision pointed to the subject of their many conversations about the love of God, to Whom she longed to be united. Making haste

with what she had begun and overcome by the burning zeal within her, she withdrew from the life of the town in which she lived.

At the time of this withdrawal, she stayed with the owner's permission at a certain manor belonging to the lord of Beauvais, Bishop Guy. This Guy was a man of courtly manner and noble birth, in person well-fitted for the office he held. After conferring notable benefits on the church of Beauvais, such as laying the first stone of a church for regular canons dedicated to St. Quentin, he was charged before Archbishop Hugues of Lyon, the papal legate, with simony and other crimes by those who owed their training and advancement to him. Because he did not appear when summonsed, he was declared deposed by default, and, being at Cluny and afraid of the sentence pronounced against him, he retired into the monastery there. Since he seemed to cherish my mother and my family and loved me most of all with a special affection, as one who had received from him every sacrament of benediction except that of the priesthood, when members of my mother's household asked him to live for a while in his property adjoining the church of that place, he gladly consented. Now, this manor, named Catenoy, was about two miles distant from our town.

While staying there, she resolved to retire to the monastery of Fly. After my master had a little house built for her there near the church, she then came forth from the place where she was staying. She knew that I should be utterly an orphan with no one at all on whom to depend, for great as was my wealth of kinsfolk and connections, yet there was no one to give me the loving care a little child needs at such an age; though I did not lack for the necessities of food and clothing. I often suffered from the loss of that careful provision for the helplessness of tender years that only a woman can provide. As I said, although she knew that I would be condemned to such neglect, yet Thy love and fear, O God, hardened her heart. Still, when on the way to that monastery she passed below the stronghold where I remained, the sight of the castle gave intolerable anguish to her lacerated heart, stung with the bitter remembrance of what she had left behind. No wonder indeed if her limbs seemed to be torn from her body, since she knew for certain that she was a cruel and unnatural mother. Indeed, she heard this said aloud, as she had in this way cut off her heart and left bereft of succor such a fine child, made worthy, it was asserted, by so much affection, since I was held in high regard not only by our own family but by outsiders. And Thou, good and gracious God, didst by Thy sweetness and love marvelously harden her heart, the tenderest in all the world, that it might not be tender to her own soul's harm. For tenderness would then have been her ruin, if she, neglecting her God, in her worldly care for me had put me before her own salvation. But "her love was strong as death," for the closer her love for Thee, the greater her composure in breaking from those she loved before.

Coming to the cloister, she found an old woman in the habit of a nun whom she compelled to live with her, declaring that she would submit to her discipline, as she gave the appearance of great piety. "Compelled," I say, because once she had tested the woman's character, she exerted all her powers of persuasion to get her companionship. And so she began gradually to copy the severity of the older woman, to imitate her meager diet, to choose the plainest food, to give up the soft mattress to which she had been accustomed, to sleep in contentment with only straw and a sheet. And since she still had much beauty and showed no sign of age, she purposely strove to assume the appearance of age with an old woman's wrinkles and bowed form. Her long flowing locks, which usually serve as a woman's crowning beauty, were frequently cut short with the scissors; her dress was black and unpleasant-looking, its unfashionable width adorned with countless patches; her cloak was undyed and her shoes were pierced with many a hole past mending, for there was within her One whom she tried to please with such mean apparel.

Since she had learned the beginning of good deeds from the confession of her old sins, she repeated her confessions almost daily. Consequently, her mind was forever occupied in searching out her past deeds, what she had thought or done or said as a maiden of tender years, or in her married life, or as a widow with a wider range of activities, continually examining the seat of reason and bringing what she found to

the knowledge of a priest, or rather to God through him. Then you might have seen the woman praying with such sharp sighs, pining away with such anguish of spirit that as she worshiped, there was scarcely ever a pause in the heart-rending sobs that went with her entreaties. She had learned the seven penitential psalms from the old woman I mentioned before, not by sight but by ear, and day and night she turned them over in her mind, chewing them with such savour, one might say, that the sighs and groans of those sweet angel songs never ceased to echo in Thy ears, O Lord. But whenever assemblies of people from outside disturbed her beloved solitude—for all who were acquainted with her, especially men and women of noble rank, took pleasure in conversing with her because of her wondrous wit and forbearance—on their departure, every untrue, idle, or thoughtless word she had uttered during their talk begat in her soul indescribable anguish until she reached the familiar waters of penitence or confession.

Whatever the zeal and anxiety she showed in such matters, she could win for her soul no confidence, no composure to stay her unceasing lamentations, her earnest and tearful questionings whether she could ever earn pardon for her offenses. Thou knowest, O Lord, the extent of her sins, and I have some knowledge of it. How small was their whole sum compared with those of others who neither sorrow nor sigh! Thou knowest, O Lord, how well I was able to assess the condition of her thoughts, because I never saw her heart grow cold in the fear of punishment and in her love for Thee.

CHAPTER 15

Why go on? While she was divorcing herself from the world in the manner I have described, I was left without a mother, teacher, and master. For he who after my mother had so faithfully trained and taught me, fired by my mother's example, love, and counsel, himself entered the monastery of Fly. Possessing a perverted liberty, I began without any self-control to abuse my power, to mock at churches, to detest school, to try to gain the company of my young lay cousins devoted to knightly pursuits by cursing the appearance of a clerk, to promise remission of sins, and to indulge in sleep, in which formerly I was allowed little relaxation, so that by unaccustomed excess of it my body began to degenerate. Meanwhile my mother heard the agitating news of my doings and was struck half dead by what she heard, surmising my immediate ruin. For the fine clothing which I had for the church processions, provided by her in the hope that I might be the more eager for the clerk's life, I wore everywhere on wanton pursuits which my age did not permit; I emulated older boys in their juvenile rowdiness, and I was completely bereft of responsibility and discretion.

The more restrained and chastened I had been before, the worse my looseness, or even madness, now became. Unable to endure what she heard, my mother therefore went to the abbot and begged him and the brotherhood that my master might be allowed to resume my training. The abbot, brought up by my grandfather and under obligation for benefits received at his court, was amenable; he gave me a ready welcome and followed up his kind reception with still kinder treatment thereafter. I call Thee to witness, Holy God and my Provider, that from the moment I entered the monastery church and saw the monks sitting there, at that sight I was seized by a longing for the monk's life which never grew cold, and my spirit had no rest until its desire was fulfilled. Since I lived with them in the same cloister and observed their whole existence and condition, as the flame increases when fanned by the wind, so by contemplation of them my soul, yearning continually to be like them, could not but be on fire. Lastly, with redoubled entreaties the abbot of the place daily urged me to become a monk there, and although I passionately desired to do so, my tongue could not be loosened by any of the demands of those who desired me to make such a promise. Although now that I have grown older it would be very hard for me to keep silent with such a full heart, as a boy I was able to maintain that silence without much difficulty.

After some time I brought up the matter with my mother, and she, fearing the instability of boyhood, rejected my proposal with a great many arguments, which made me very sorry that I had revealed my intention. When I also told my master, he opposed it still more. Deeply annoyed at the opposition of both, I determined to turn my mind elsewhere; and so I began to act as if I had never had such a desire. After putting the matter off from the week of Pentecost until Christmas, and being both eager and anxious to bring the matter to an end, I was unable to bear Thy incitement within me, O Lord, and threw off my respect for my mother and my fear of my master. I went to the abbot, who greatly desired this to happen but had failed to draw any promise from me, and cast myself at his feet, tearfully imploring him, using these very words, to receive a sinner. He gladly granted my prayer and provided the necessary habit as soon as he could—that is, on the next day—and invested me with it while my mother watched in tears from afar, and he ordered that alms should be offered on that day.

Meanwhile my former master, who was unable to teach me any longer because of the stricter rule, at least took care to urge me to subject to close interrogation those holy books which I was reading, to reflect upon those discourses less known by more learned men, and to compose short pieces of prose and verse, warning me to apply myself the more closely because less care was being expended by others on my instruction. O Lord, True Light, I well remember the inestimable bounty Thou didst then bestow on me. For as soon as I had taken Thy habit at Thy invitation, a cloud seemed to be removed from the face of my understanding and I soon began to find my way through those things in which earlier I had wandered blindly and in error. Besides, I was suddenly inspired with such a love of learning that I yearned for it above all else and thought the day was lost on which I did not engage in some such work. How often they thought I was asleep and resting my little body under the coverlet when my mind was really concentrated on composition, or I was reading under a blanket, fearful of the rebuke of the others.

And Thou, Holy Jesus, didst know with what motive I did this, chiefly to win glory and so that greater honor in this present world might be thine. My friends were clearly my enemies, for although they gave me good advice, yet they

often plied me with talk of fame and literary distinction and, through these things, the winning of
high status and wealth. They put into my short-
sighted mind hopes worse than the eggs of asps,
and since I believed that all their promises would
quickly come to pass, they deceived me with the
vainest expectations. What they said might come
to pass in the fullness of age, I thought I would
surely attain in adolescence or early manhood.
They proclaimed my learning (which by Thy gift
was daily increasing) and good birth according to
worldly standards and good looks, but they did
not remember that by such steps a man "shall not
go up unto Thy altar, lest his nakedness be discovered." For he that "climbeth up another way,
the same is a thief and a robber," which is nakedness.

But in these beginnings of mine under Thy
inspiration, if it had any wisdom at all, my mind
ought to have been prepared for temptation. In
truth my wisdom at that time was to some degree
foolishness. Although I was moved by the childish emotions of joy or anger, would that I now, O
Lord, so hated my great sins as then I feared Thy
judgment and hated sins that were minor or
scarcely sins at all. Sensibly and with great eagerness, I imitated those whom I saw weeping bitterly for their sins, and whatever came from Thee
gave delight to my sight and hearing. And I who
now search the Scriptures for vocabulary and
matter for display, and even store in my mind the
disreputable sayings of pagan writers to make
mere babbling, in those days got from them tears
and matter for sorrow, and thought my reading
vain if I found in it no matter for meditation,
nothing leading to repentance. So, unknowingly,
I acted wisely.

But that old Foe, who has learned from ages of
experience how to deal with the varying conditions of heart and age, he, I say conceived new
conflicts for me, according to the measure of my
mind and little body. He presented to my gaze in
sleep many visions of dead men, especially those
whom I had seen or heard of as slain with swords
or by some such death, and by such sights he so
terrified my spirit when it was relaxed in sleep
that but for the watchful protection of that master
of mine, I could not have been kept in my bed at
night, or prevented from calling out, and I would

have nearly gone out of my mind. Although this
trouble may seem childish and ridiculous to
those who have not felt it, it is regarded as a great
calamity by those who are oppressed by it, so that
fear itself, which most men consider absurd, can
be held in check by no reasoning or counsel.
Although the sufferer himself cares not at all for
what he suffers, his spirit, when once for a brief
moment it is plunged in sleep, has no power to
shake off the horrid sights; indeed, the mind,
deeply disturbed by its terrors, dreads the return
of sleep itself. To this emotion, crowds or solitude
are the same, since the company of others is no
defense against such fear, and dwelling alone
either leaves it as bad as before or makes it worse.

My condition, Lord God, was then far different
from my present state. Then I clearly had great
respect for Thy law and unbounded loathing for
all sin, and I eagerly drank in all that could be
said or heard or known from Thee. I know, Heavenly Father, that by such childish application the
Devil was savagely enraged, although later he
was appeased by the surrender of all my pious
fervour. One night, in winter, I believe, kept
awake by my wretched anxiety, I was lying in my
bed, thinking I was safer with a lamp close by
that gave a bright light, when suddenly and
apparently close above my head there arose the
tumult of many voices, although it was the dead
of night. One voice uttered no words, but only a
howl of distress. Shaken by these nightmarish
events, I lost my senses and seemed to see a certain dead man who, someone cried out, had been
killed at the baths. Struck with the terror of the
phantasy, I leaped screaming from my bed, and,
looking around as I leaped, I saw the lamp extinguished and through the shadows of a high cloud
of darkness I saw standing near me a demon in
his own shape. At that horrible sight I should
have gone almost mad, had not my master, who
very frequently stayed on guard to control my
terrors, adroitly soothed my perturbed and ter-
ror-struck wits.

Even in the tender years of childhood, I was
aware that the desire for a good endeavor which
burned in my heart enraged the Devil in no small
measure to stir up wickedness in me. Gracious
God, what victories, what crowns for victories I
would deserve today if I had stood fast to the end

in that struggle! I have concluded from many tales I have heard that devils are most fiercely embittered against recent converts or those who continually aspire to this manner of life. I remember that in the time of Bishop Guy of Beauvais, whom I mentioned before, there was a certain young knight in his household whom the bishop cared more for than almost all his retainers. This man, repenting with horror of his vices, resolved at all costs to fly from contact with the world. While torn with anxious thoughts about this return to a pristine state, he was sleeping one night in the bishop's chamber along with the bishop and a God-fearing man named Ivo, a native of Saint-Quentin, I think, who was very famous for his writing and distinguished for his almost more famous eloquence, and who was a monk of Cluny who filled the office of prior there for a long time under Abbot Hugues of blessed memory. Some other men who were equally outstanding in the holy life were there as well. One of the chief nobles from a neighboring town, a very courtly and discreet man, kept watch while the rest slept in the dead of night. As his thoughts wandered at will and his eyes roved hither and thither, suddenly the figure of a chief devil with a small head and a hunched back appeared advancing toward the man, and, looking at each of the beds in turn, he proceeded to walk slowly around the room. When the great Deceiver came to the mattress of the young man whom I mentioned as being most beloved by the bishop, he halted and, turning his gaze on the sleeper, said: "This man troubles me bitterly and worst of all those who sleep here." After saying that, he headed for the door of the latrine and went in. The man who was looking on, while paying attention to all this, was oppressed with a burden which made speech or movement impossible. But when the Adversary went out, both faculties returned to him, and in the morning, on relating his vision to the wiser men and inquiring with them into the condition and disposition of the young man, he found that his heart was earnestly set on entering a holier life. If there is more joy in heaven over one sinner that is converted than over ninety just men who need not penance, then without doubt we may fully believe that the enemies of the human race are vexed with the most bitter hatred at the rescue of those who change for the better. And just as I, after a good beginning, have clearly followed a pestilent course, so he, after accepting the Devil's testimony, henceforward gradually fell away and grew cold, returning to his worldly interests. Still, one may believe how painfully that sudden stirring of our good intentions must sting the hearts of devils. And no wonder that the Devil is grieved by the sudden and transient emotions of any penitent, since even the shallow self-abasement of that wicked king Ahab brought him to the attention of God before that of men. Hence the Lord said to Elias, if I am not mistaken, "Hast thou not seen Ahab humbled before me? Therefore, because he has humbled himself for my sake, I will not bring the evil in his days."

CHAPTER 16

With the gradual growth of my young body, as the life of this world began to stir my itching heart with fleshly longings and lusts to suit my stature, my mind repeatedly fell to remembering and dwelling on what and how great I might have been in the world, in which my imaginings often traveled beyond the truth. These thoughts, Gracious God Who cares for all, Thou didst reveal to Thy servant, my mother. Whatever the state, healthy or diseased, to which my unstable heart changed, an image of it came to her in a vision of Thy will, O God. But since dreams are said to follow many cares, and that is indeed true, yet her cares were not aroused by the heat of greed, but were created by a real eagerness for inward holiness. Soon after the troubling vision was impressed on her most pious mind, as she was very subtle and clear-sighted in the interpretation of such matters, when she had perceived what trouble was betokened by her dream, she soon summoned me and in private questioned me about my activities, what I was doing, and how I was behaving. Since I was in such submission to her that my will was one with hers, I readily confessed all those things in which my mind seemed to grow slack, following the content of the dreams which I had feared, and after she had warned me to improve, with true affection I at once promised to do so.

O my God, she often spoke to me in enigmas concerning that state in which I now suffer, and what she believed I had done or should do in that state in which I was then, so that every day I now experience in the secret places of my heart the truth of her statements and contemplate their fulfillment. Since my master was also moved by an incessant and heartfelt solicitude, enlightened by Thee, he saw through many kinds of figures what was happening at the time and what might come to pass in the future. By God's gift, both foretold adversity and success, on the one hand terrifying me, on the other comforting me, so that whether I would or not, I abstained from hidden weaknesses, because by Thy wonder-working so much was revealed to those who loved me, and sometimes I rejoiced in the promise of a better hope.

At a time when I was swayed by a spirit of sullenness because of the envy which I suffered from my superiors and equals, I hoped with the aid of my relatives to be able to transfer to some other monastery. Some of our brotherhood, seeing me once far below them both in age and learning, in ability and understanding, and afterward perceiving that I equalled them, or, if I may say so, altogether surpassed them—since He Who is the key to all knowledge had by His gift alone stimulated in me a hunger for learning—raged against me with such burning and evil wrath that, wearied with everlasting disputes and quarrels, I often regretted I had ever seen or known letters. They so greatly disturbed my work and, when an occasion arose over some matter of learning, so often started disputes with their constant questions that they seemed to have as their sole object to make me change my resolve and to impede my talents. But as when oil is poured on a fire a livelier flame creeps forth from what was supposed to put it out, the more my ingenuity was overtaxed in such labors, the better it became, like an oven rendered stronger by its own heat. The questions by which they thought to crush me gave great keenness to my intelligence, and the difficulty of their objections, which required much pondering to find answers and the turning over of many books, brought about a strengthening of my wits and ability in debate. Although I was thus bitterly hated by them, yet Thou knowest, O Lord, how little, if at all, I hated them, and when they could not put any stigma on me, as they wished, in disparagement they told everyone that I was too proud of my little learning.

Although from difficulties of this sort abundant good was produced, yet my spirit grew weak, languishing under the endless torture of its thoughts and surrounded by these annoyances, which affected me bitterly. With a fearful heart and failing powers of reason, I did not consider what profit there was in hardship, but eagerly decided to seek the solution which the weakness of my flesh suggested. When I therefore proposed to leave the place, not so much with the kindly permission of my abbot as at the suggestion and demand of my kinsfolk, my mother gave her assent, too, believing that I was doing this from pious motives, for the place to which I wished to retire was considered very holy. Then the following vision appeared to her to witness to the good and evil in me.

She thought she was in the church of that monastery; that is, of Saint-Germer of Fly. When she looked at the church more closely, she saw it was foresaken in a most lonely fashion; the monks, too, were not only ragged and covered with cassocks huge beyond belief, but all alike were shortened to a cubit in height like those commonly called dwarfs. But since "where your treasure is, there is your heart, and where your gaze is turned, there is your love," she fixed a long look on me, and saw that I stood no higher than the rest and was covered with no better apparel. While she was mourning my plight and that of such a church, suddenly a woman of beauty and majesty beyond measure advanced through the midst of the church right up to the altar, followed by one like a young girl whose appearance was in its deference appropriate to her whom she followed. Being very curious to know who the lady was, my mother was told that she was the Lady of Chartres. At once she interpreted this to mean the Blessed Mother of God, whose name and relics at Chartres are venerated throughout almost all the Latin world. Going up to the altar, the lady knelt in prayer and the noble attendant who in the vision was following her did the same behind her. Then, rising and stretching out her hand with the appearance of great reproof, she said, "I founded this church. Why should I permit it to be deserted?" Then this standard-bearer of piety turned her tranquil gaze on me and, pointing with her shining hand, said, "I brought him here and made him a monk. By no means will I permit him to be taken away." After this the attendant repeated these same words in like fashion. No sooner had that powerful one spoken than in a moment all that ruin and waste was changed and appeared as it had before, and the dwarf stature of the rest and of myself, too, was amended and made normal by the power that attended her command. When my prudent mother had given me an orderly narrative of this dream, I received such a story with such remorse and tears, and, influenced by the meaning of so desirable a dream, I so restrained my indulgence in thoughts of wandering that I was never again drawn by a desire for another monastery.

O Lady, Mother of Heaven, this and other things like it gave me the opportunity to return to you, rising above the horror of my sins and the countless apostasies by which I rebelled from your love and service, while my heart prophesies that the wide bosom of Thy mercies cannot be closed against me even by mountains of my ill deeds. I shall always remember, too, Lady of Heaven, that when, as a boy, I was eager to put on this habit, one night in a vision I was in the church dedicated to you and I thought I was carried from it by two devils. And when they had taken me to the roof of the church, they fled away and let me go uninjured within the walls of that church. I often recall these things when I consider my incorrigibility, and the more often I repeat those sins, or rather add to them sins which get worse and worse, I turn back to you, most holy one, as a refugee from the peril of despair, abusing my little hope or faith.

Although I am forever sinning, compelled by my weakness and not through the willfulness of pride, yet I in no wise lose the hope of amendment. Clearly "a just man falls seven times and rises again." If the number seven here stands for an entirety, as it usually does, then no matter how many ways a man falls by sin and although his flesh is weak, if he resolves to rise again to righteousness, if he shows the grief of a penitent, he does not at all lose the name of a just man. Why

would we cry aloud to God to deliver us from our necessities if the corruption of our nature did not condemn us, whether we will or no, to the servitude of sin? "I see it," the Apostle says, "leading me captive in the law of sin, that is in my members; for I do not that good which I will; but the evil which I hate, that I do."

There is a depth of certain evils which a wicked man despises when he enters. Moreover, concerning certain other depths a cry is made to God, and the petitioner does not doubt that his voice is heard. There is a scorn of despair begotten by excess of sinning, which can be of this depth, where "there is no sure standing," in which misery does not stand. There is lastly the depth out of which Jeremiah was drawn by a rope of rags, and although that be deep, yet farther on it has a bottom; for despite the loosening of the understanding through much sinning, yet reason gives some little check, so that it is not swallowed up in the bottomless gulf without any knowledge of all its iniquity.

CHAPTER 17

After steeping my mind unduly in the study of versemaking, with the result that I put aside for such ridiculous vanities the matters of universal importance in the divine pages, I was so far guided by my folly as to give first place to Ovid and the pastoral poets and to aim at a lover's urbanity in distributions of types and in a series of letters. Forgetting proper severity and abandoning the modesty of a monk's calling, my mind was led away by these enticements of a poisonous license, and I considered only if I could render the conversation of the courts in the words of some poet, with no thought of how much the toil which I loved might hurt the aims of our holy profession. By love of it I was doubly taken captive, being snared both by the wantonness of the sweet words I took from the poets and by those which I poured forth myself, and I was caught by the unrestrained stirring of my flesh through thinking on these things and the like. Since my unstable mind, unaccustomed now to discipline, was grinding out these things, no sound could come from my lips but that which my thought prompted.

Hence it came to pass that, from the boiling over of the madness within me, I was carried along to words which were a bit obscene and composed some sort of little compositions, irresponsible and indiscreet, in fact bereft of all decency. When this came to the attention of the master I have mentioned, he took it very bitterly, and while he was provoked by his distaste, he fell asleep. As he slept, there appeared to him the following vision: an old man with beautiful white hair—in fact that very man, I dare say, who had brought me to him at the beginning and had promised his love for me in the future—appeared to him and said with great severity, "I wish you to give account to me for the writings that have been composed; however, the hand which wrote them is not his who wrote." When my master had related this to me, he and I gave much the same interpretation to the dream. We mourned and were joyful in Thy hope, on the one hand seeing Thy displeasure in that fatherly rebuke, and on the other thinking from the meaning of the vision that confidence in some amendment of my frivolity was to come. For when the hand that wrote the letters was said not to be his who write them, without doubt it meant that the hand would not continue in such shameful activity. It was mine and is not, as it is written, "Turn the wicked and they shall not be," and that which was mine in the practice of vice, when applied to the pursuit of virtue, lost all the efficacy of that utterly worthless ownership.

And yet Thou knowest, O Lord, and I confess, that at that time my life was chastened neither by fear of Thee, nor by shame, nor by respect for that holy vision. I put no check on that irreverence I had within me, and did not refrain from the vain jests of frivolous writers. I hammered out these verses in secret and dared to show them to no one, or at least only to a few like myself, but I often recited those which I could, inventing an author for them. I was delighted when those which I thought it inconvenient to acknowledge as mine were praised by those who shared such studies, and what did not produce the profit of any praise for their author still left him to enjoy the profit, or rather the shamefulness, of sin. But Thou didst punish these acts, O Father, in Thy own good time. Thou didst fence in my wander-ing soul with rising misfortune against me for such work and with great adversity, and Thou didst hold me down with bodily infirmity. Then "the sword reached even to the soul," and vexation touched my understanding.

When the punishment of sin had brought understanding to my hearing, then at last the folly of useless study withered away. Since I could not bear to be idle, as if by some necessity I rejected these fancies of mine, took up the spiritual life again, and turned to more appropriate exercises. All too late I began to pant for the knowledge that had repeatedly been distilled for me by many good scholars: to busy myself, that is, with commentaries on the Scriptures, to study frequently the works of Gregory, in which are to be found the best keys to that art, and, according to the rules of ancient writers, to treat the words of the prophets and the Gospels in their allegorical, their moral, and finally their anagogical meaning. In this work I had the special encouragement of Anselm, the abbot of Bec, afterward archbishop of Canterbury, who was born across the Alps in the region of Aosta, a man of sublime example and holiness of life. While he was still prior at Bec, he admitted me to his acquaintance, and though I was a mere child of most tender age and knowledge, he readily offered to teach me to manage the inner self, how to consult the laws of reason in the government of the body. Both before he became abbot and as abbot, he was a familiar visitor at the abbey of Fly where I was, welcomed for his piety and his teaching. He bestowed on me so assiduously the benefits of his learning and with such ardor labored at this that it seemed as if I alone were the unique and special reason for his frequent visits.

His teaching was to divide the mind in a three-fold or fourfold way, to treat the operations of the whole interior mystery under the headings of appetite, will, reason, and intellect. By a resolution, based on clear analyses, of what I and many others thought to be one, he showed that appetite and will are not identical, although it is established by evident assertions that in the presence of reason or intellect they are practically the same.[10] He discussed with me certain chapters of the Gospels on this principle, and most clearly explained the difference between willing and being subject to appetite; it was plain, however, that he did not originate this, but got it from books at hand which did not so explicitly deal with these matters. I then began to endeavor to equal his methods in similar commentaries, so far as I could, and to search carefully with all the keenness of my mind everywhere in the Scriptures to see if anything accorded on the moral level with these thoughts.

It came to pass that when I was traveling with my former abbot to a certain monastery in our province, I suggested to him as a man of great piety that on coming to the chapter meeting he should preach a sermon there. He turned over to me what he was asked to do, exhorting and ordering me to do it in his place. Now, the birth of Mary Magdalene is celebrated on that day. Taking the text of my sermon from the Book of Wisdom, I contented myself with that single word for the homily I was asked to give: "Wisdom," that is, "overcomes evil; she reaches therefore from end to end mightily, and orders all things sweetly." When I had explained this with such oratory as I could, and had pleased my audience with the suitability of these remarks, the prior of the church, who was no mean student of sacred literature within the limits of his understanding, in a friendly way asked me to write something which would give him the material for preparing sermons on any subject. Since I knew that my abbot, in whose presence I had said this, would be annoyed by my writings, I approached the man with caution and, acting as if I came on behalf of his friend and did not care much about it myself, I begged him to grant what I was asking for the sake of the prior, whom he professed to love. Supposing that I would write very briefly, he consented. When I had snatched his consent from his mouth, I began to work at what I had in mind.

I proposed to undertake a moral commentary on the beginning of Genesis, that is, the Six Days of Creation. To the commentary, I prefixed a treatise of moderate length showing how a sermon ought to be composed. I followed up this preface with a tropological[11] exposition at length of the Six Days, with poor eloquence but such as I was capable of. When my abbot saw that I was commenting on the first chapter of that sacred histo-ry, he no longer took a favorable view of the matter and warned me with great reproof to put an end to these writings.[12] I saw that such works only put thorns in his eyes, and by avoiding both his presence and that of anyone who might report it to him, I pursued my task in secret. For the composition and writing of this or my other works, I did not prepare a draft on the wax tablets, but committed them to the written page in their final form as I thought them out. In that abbot's time my studies were carried on in complete secrecy. But when he was gone, finding my opportunity when the pastoral office was vacant, at last I attacked and quickly finished my work. It consisted of ten books which followed the four activities of the inner man mentioned before, and I so carried out the moral treatment in all of them that they went from beginning to end with absolutely no change in the order of the passages. Whether in this little work I helped anyone, I do not know, although I have no doubt that most learned men were greatly pleased with it. This much is certain, that I gained no little profit from it myself, seeing that it saved me from idleness, that servant of vice.

Since then, I wrote a little book in chapters on various meanings in the Gospels and the prophets, including some things from the books of Numbers, Joshua, and Judges. I am putting off the completion of this because after finishing what I have in hand, I propose, if I am still alive and God prompts me, to engage at times in similar exercises. As I did in treating Genesis, I mostly followed the tropological approach, and the allegorical in a few instances. In Genesis, I therefore gave my attention chiefly to morals, not that there was wanting matter for thought on the allegorical level, had I equally worked that out, but because in my opinion moral meanings are in these times more useful than allegories, since faith is established unchanged by God but morals are almost universally debased by the many forms of vice, and because I had neither the freedom nor the wish to enlarge my book to excessive length.

CHAPTER 18

As much as my mother esteemed my success in

learning, she was greatly perturbed by her dread of the excesses of a dangerous time of life. How earnestly she begged me to follow her example! Although God had given her such great good looks, she thought little of that in her which won praise, as though she were unaware of her beauty, and she cherished her widowhood as if, unable to bear them, she had always loathed a wife's bedtime duties. Yet Thou knowest, O Lord, how much loyalty, how much love she rendered to her dead husband, how with almost daily masses, prayers, and tears, and much almsgiving, she strove without ceasing to release his soul, which she knew was fettered by his sins. By the wonderful dispensation of God, it came about that in frequent visions she saw in the clearest images what pains he endured in his purgation. Without doubt such visions come from God; for when no perverse sense of security is falsely caused by the assumption of the beauty of light,[13] but a stimulus is given to prayer and almsgiving by the sight of suffering and punishment, and when the remedies of the divine office are clearly demanded by the dead, or rather by the angels, who care for dead Christians, it is proof enough that these things come from God, because devils never seek the salvation of any man's soul. The anxious mind of that good woman was kindled again by these signs and was inflamed by the intimation of his soul's torments to constant efforts to intercede for her former husband.

One summer night, for instance, on a Sunday after matins, after she had stretched out on her narrow bench and had begun to sink into sleep, her soul seemed to leave her body without her losing her senses. After being led, as it were, through a certain gallery, at last she issued from it and began to approach the edge of a pit. After she was brought close to it, suddenly from the depth of that abyss men with the appearance of ghosts leaped forth, their hair seemingly eaten by worms, trying to seize her with their hands and to drag her inside. From behind the frightened woman, who was terribly distressed by their attack, suddenly a voice cried out to them, saying, "Touch her not." Compelled by that forbidding voice, they leaped back into the pit. Now, I forgot to say that as she passed through the gallery, as she knew she had left her mortal being,

her one prayer to God was to be allowed to return to her body. After she was rescued from the dwellers in the pit and was standing by its edge, suddenly she saw that my father was there, appearing as he did when he was young. When she looked hard at him and piteously asked of him whether he was called Evrard (for that had been his name), he denied that he was.

Now, it is no wonder that a spirit should refuse to be called by the name which he had as a man, for spirit should give no reply to a spirit which is inconsistent with its spiritual nature. Moreover, that spirits should recognize each other by their names is too absurd to be believed; otherwise in the next world it would be rare to know anyone except those close to us. Clearly it is not necessary for spirits to have names, since all their vision, or rather their knowledge of vision, is internal.

Although he denied that he was called by that name, and yet nonetheless she felt that it was he, she then asked him where he was staying. He indicated that the place was located not far away, and that he was detained there. She also asked how he was. Baring his arm and his side, he showed both of them so torn, so cut up with many wounds, that she felt great horror and emotional distress as she looked. The figure of a little child was also there, crying so bitterly that it troubled her greatly when she saw it. Moved by its cries, she said to him, "My lord, how can you endure the wailing of this child?" "Whether I like it or not," said he, "I endure it." Now, the crying of the child and the wounds on his arm and side have this meaning. When my father in his youth was separated from lawful intercourse with my mother through the witchcraft of certain persons, some evil counselors appealed to his youthful spirit with the vile advice to find out if he could have intercourse with other women. In youthful fashion he took their advice, and, having wickedly attempted intercourse with some loose woman unknown to me, he begat a child which at once died before baptism. The rending of his side is the breaking of his marriage vow; the cries of that distressed voice indicate the damnation of that evilly begotten child. Such, O Lord, O Inexhaustible Goodness, was Thy retribution on the soul of Thy sinner, who yet lives by faith. But let us return to the orderly narrative of the vision.

When she asked him whether prayer, almsgiving, or the mass gave him any relief (for he was aware that she frequently provided these things for him), he replied that they did, adding, "But among you there lives a certain Li(ea)gearde." My mother understood that he named this woman so that she would ask her what memory of him she had. This Li(ea)gearde was very poor in spirit, a woman who lived for God alone apart from the customs of the world.

Meanwhile, bringing her talk with my father to an end, my mother looked toward the pit, above which was a picture, and in the picture she saw a certain knight named Renaud, of no mean reputation among his countrymen. After dinner on that very day, which as I said before was a Sunday, this Renaud was treacherously killed at Beauvais by those close to him. In that picture he was kneeling with his neck bent down, puffing to blow up a fire in a heap of fuel. This vision was seen in the early morning, whereas he perished at midday, doomed to descend into those flames which he had kindled by his deserts. In the same picture she saw a brother of mine who was helping, but he died long afterward. He was taking a dreadful oath by the sacrament of God's body and blood. The significance of this is precisely that by false swearing and by taking the holy name of God and His sacred mysteries in vain, he earned both his punishment and the place of his punishment.

In the course of the same vision, she also saw that old woman who, as I said, lived with her at the beginning of her conversion, a woman who clearly was always mortifying her body with crosses on the outside, but, it was said, was not enough on her guard against a hunger for vainglory. She saw this woman carried off by two coal-black spirits, her form a mere shadow. Moreover, while that old woman was alive and the two were living together, when they were talking of the state of their souls and the coming of death, they once took a mutual pledge that the one who died first should, through the grace of God, appear to the survivor and make known to her the nature of her condition, whether good or bad. They confirmed this by prayer, earnestly beseeching God that after the death of either the other

should be allowed to discover by the revelation of some vision her happy or unhappy state. When the old woman was about to die, she had seen herself in a vision deprived of her body and going with others like her to a certain temple, and, as she went, she seemed to be carrying a cross on her shoulders. Coming to the temple with that company, she was compelled to stay outside, the doors being barred against her. Finally, after her death she appeared to someone else in the midst of a great stench to express her gratitude for giving prayers which had saved her from decay and pain. While the old woman was dying, at the foot of the bed she saw standing a horrible devil with eyes of dreadful and monstrous size. When she adjured him by the holy sacraments to flee in confusion from her and seek nothing of her, with that frightful charge she drove him off.

My mother drew her conclusions about the cries of the infant, of whose existence she had been aware, from the exact way in which the vision agreed with the facts, when she put them together, and from the immediate prophecy of the impending slaying of the knight, whom she had seen assigned to the place of punishment below. Having no doubt about these things, she devoted herself wholly to bringing help to my father. Setting like against like, she chose to take on the raising of a little child only a few months old that had lost its parents. But since the Devil hates good intentions no less than faithful actions, the baby so harassed my mother and all her servants by the madness of its wailing and crying at night—although by day it was very good, by turns playing and sleeping—that anyone in the same little room could get scarcely any sleep. I have heard the nurses whom she hired say that night after night they could not stop shaking the child's rattle, so naughty was he, not through his own fault, but made so by the Devil within, and that a woman's craft failed entirely to drive him out. The good woman was tormented by extreme pain; amid those shrill cries no contrivance relieved her aching brow, nor could any sleep steal over her sorely tried and exhausted head, since the frenzy of the child goaded from within and by the Enemy's presence caused continual disturbance. Although she passed her sleepless nights in this way, she never appeared listless at the performance of the night offices. Since she knew that these troubles were to purge away those of her husband, which she had seen in her vision, she bore them gladly, because she rightly thought that by sharing his suffering herself she was lessening the pains of the other sufferer. Yet she never shut the child out of her house, never appeared less careful of him. Indeed, the more she perceived that the Devil was cruelly blazing against her to destroy her resolve, the more she chose to submit with equanimity to any inconvenience rising from it; and the more she happened to experience the eagerness of the Devil in the irritation of the child, the more she was assured that his evil sway over the soul of her husband was being countered.

Notes

1 By idols, Guibert means classical statues.

2 Guibert here puns on *infulsa*, which in classical Latin sometimes means a woolen headdress worn by a victim about to be sacrificed.

3 The lord of Clermont-en-Beauvaisis was Renaud I, who fought at the battle of Mortemer in 1054 and was still alive in 1084. Guibert refers to his brother as *municeps*, an ambiguous word which probably means that he was one of the nobles of the castle.

4 The collegiate church attached to the castle of Clermont was consecrated to the Virgin and St. Arnoul, and came to be known as Notre-Dame-du-Chatel. Although church reformers of the late eleventh century condemned lay presentation to canonries and other ecclesiastical benefices, the practice remained common. While it would have been improper for a boy not yet twelve to be given a benefice, this abuse, too, was not uncommon.

5 That is, with the authorization of the bishop of Beauvais the lord of Clermont had the right of presentation and oversight over the canons of the church in his castle.

6 Priest, deacon, and subdeacon.

7 Since earlier in the chapter Guibert says that consummation was delayed for three years, this and the following reference to seven years may be figurative and intended to call to mind the seven-year periods Jacob served for Rachel.

8 Writing early in the eleventh century, Burchard of Worms proposed that priests hearing confessions might ask, "Hast thou done what some adulteresses are wont to do? When first they learn that their lovers wish to take legitimate wives, they thereupon by some trick of magic extinguish the male desire, so that they are impotent and cannot consummate their union with their legitimate wives. If thou hast done or taught others to do this, thou shouldst do penance for forty days on bread and water." See *Medieval Handbooks of Penance*, trans. John T. McNeill and Helena M. Gamer (New York, 1938), p. 340.

9 By the law of succession being applied here, if a widow remarried, her dower was held in trust by the family of her first husband to be administered for the children of that marriage.

10 Augustine described the three faculties of the soul as memory, intelligence, and will. Anselm's novelty was to replace memory with reason and add appetite or desire; this allowed him to argue that the will was always free, since appetite was a separate function. Under the control of reason, will and appetite could be one.

11 That is, an analysis on the moral level.

12 Origen and Jerome refer to a Hebrew tradition that no one under thirty should read the beginning of Genesis, the beginning and end of Ezekiel, and the Song of Songs.

13 That is, by the Devil.

FULBERT OF CHARTRES

Letter to William of Aquitaine

IN 1020 BISHOP FULBERT OF CHARTRES (CA. 960-1028) WROTE DUKE
William V of Aquitaine (ca. 960-1030) on the duties of lords and vassals. This
ideal image of feudal relations can be contrasted with the brutal realities in
the two documents which follow.

Source: *Recueil des historiens des Gaules et de la France*, X, 463.

**Fulbert, bishop, to the glorious duke of the
Aquitanians William.**

Invited to write something concerning the form
of fealty, I have briefly noted for you the following things from the authority of books. He who
swears fealty to his lord must always remember
these six things: harmless, safe, honorable, useful, easy, possible. Harmless, that is, he must not
harm his lord in his body. Safe, he must not harm
him in his secrets or in the fortifications by which
he is able to be safe. Honorable, so that he must
not harm him in his justice or in other affairs
which are seen to pertain to his honor. Useful,
that he might not be harmful to him in his possessions. Easy or possible, so that he not make
difficult any good which his lord could easily do
nor make anything impossible that is difficult. It
is just that the vassal avoid these evils, but he
does not merit his holding for so doing, for it is
not enough that he abstain from evil unless he
does what is good.

Therefore it remains that he should give his
lord counsel and aid in these same six above
mentioned things if he wishes to be seen worthy
of his benefice and to be safe in the fealty he has
sworn. The lord should act toward his vassal re-
ciprocally in all these things. If he does not do so,
he deserves to be considered of bad faith, just as
the vassal, if he were caught in collusion or in
doing or in consenting to them, would be perfidious or perjured.

I would have written to you at greater length if
I had not been occupied with many other things,
both the restoration of our city and of our church
which have recently been totally consumed by a
horrendous fire. Although for a time we could
not be turned away from this loss, through the
hope in the consolation of God and of you we
once more breathe.

HUGH OF LUSIGNAN

Agreement Between Lord And Vassal

AROUND 1020/25 HUGH OF LUSIGNAN, A POWERFUL AND AMBITIOUS chatelain in Poitou, wrote or dictated his account of his relations with William V of Aquitaine over the previous decades. Hugh contended that he had been unjustly deprived of lands and castles that had belonged to his ancestors. His description of his treatment at the hands of his lord provides unique glimpses into the realities of feudal relationships in the eleventh century.

Source: Ed. Jane Martindale, *English Historical Review* 84 (1969) pp. 528-548. Tr. George Beech.

William Count of the Aquitanians had an agreement with Hugh the Chiliarch to the effect that when Viscount Roso dies he [William] would give him his honor in commendation. Roho the bishop saw and heard this and he kissed the arm of the Count. Then Viscount Savary seized from Hugh land which he [Hugh] held from Count William and when the Viscount died the Count promised Hugh that he would make no agreement or accord with Ralph the dead man's brother until the land had been restored. This he said in the presence of all, but afterwards he secretly gave him [Ralph] the land. Hugh had an agreement with Viscount Ralph that he would marry his daughter [Ralph's] in return for that estate or for a larger one, or for other things. When the Count heard of this he was greatly angered and went humbly to Hugh and said to him, "Don't marry Ralph's daughter, I will give you whatever you want from me and you will be my friend before everyone else except my son." And Hugh did what the Count ordered him to do and out of love and fidelity he secretly rejected the woman. At the same time it happened that Joscelin of Parthenay castle died, and the Count said that he would turn over his honor and wife [Joscelin's] to Hugh, but that if he [Hugh] refused to accept them, he would no longer have confidence in him. In this affair Hugh did not encourage the Count at all in his own behalf or in anyone else's, nor did he discourage him. Thinking it over, he said to the Count, "I will do everything you order me to do." Making an agreement with Count

Fulk, the Count promised to give him [i.e. Fulk] something from his own benefices in place of that one. Fulk then promised that he would give to Hugh those things which belonged to him. As a part of this agreement the Count called for Viscount Ralph and said to him, "Hugh will not keep the agreement which he has with you because I forbid him to. But Fulk and I have an agreement that we will give him [i.e. Hugh] the honor and wife of Joscelin and we do this to punish you because you don't keep faith with me." And when Ralph heard this he was deeply sorry and said to the Count, "For the sake of God do not do that," and the Count said, "Make a pledge to me that you will not give him your daughter nor keep your agreement with him and I likewise will see that he does not possess the honor or the wife of Joscelin." And they did thus so that Hugh got neither the one nor the other. Ralph left to go to Count William who was in Montreuil castle, sending a message to Hugh that they should talk with one another. This was done and Ralph said to Hugh, "I tell you these things in advance in the faith that you will not reveal me; give me a pledge that you will aid me against Count William and I will keep your agreement with him and I will aid you against all men." But out of love for Count William Hugh refused to do this and Hugh and Ralph parted angrily. Then Ralph started war with Count William and out of love for the Count, Hugh went to war with Ralph and suffered greatly.

When Ralph died Hugh asked the Count to

restore to him the land which Ralph had seized from him. The Count said to Hugh, "I will not make an agreement with Viscount Josfred, the nephew of Ralph, nor with the men of Thouars castle, until I return your land." But the Count by no means did this but left and made an agreement with Viscount Josfred and with the men of Thouars castle and did not make an agreement with Hugh; and Hugh did not get his land but on account of the evil deed which Hugh did for the Count, Josfred started a war with Hugh and burned Mouzeuil castle and seized Hugh's knights and cut off their hands and did enough else. The Count in no way aided Hugh nor did he make an honest agreement between them, but Hugh in addition to this lost his land and on account of his assistance to the Count he lost still another which he was holding peacefully. And when Hugh saw that he was not going to get his land he seized 43 of the best knights of Thouars and he could have had justice and peace and his land back. And if he had been willing to accept a ransom he could have had 40,000 *solidi*. When the Count heard of this he ought to have been happy but he was angry and sent for Hugh saying to him, "Give me the men." And Hugh answered him, "Why do you ask these things of me my lord? It is only your fidelity [i.e. your lack of it] which causes me to lose things." The Count then said, "I don't ask you for them in order to do you wrong but because you are mine [i.e. my vassal] to do my will [i.e. to act according to my wishes] and so that everyone may know as a result of our agreement according to which I will get the men, that I will make an agreement with you that you will get your lands back and be repaid for the evil done you or else I will return the men to you. Believe and trust me and if anything should turn out badly for you, you will know because it was I who betrayed you." Then Hugh trusted in him and in God and handed over the men to the Count under such an agreement. Later on Hugh lost his land and got neither justice nor the men back.

The Count of the Poitevins and Bishop Gilbert had an agreement among themselves with Hugh's Uncle Joscelin. It concerned Vivonne castle to the effect that after the death of Bishop Gilbert the castle should go to Joscelin. While still

alive the Bishop had the men of that castle commend themselves to [i.e. become vassals of] Joscelin and turned over the tower to him; after the death of both men the Count made an agreement between Bishop Isembert and Hugh to the effect that half of the castle should be Hugh's, half from the demesne and two parts from the fiefs of the vassals. Therefore the Count had Hugh commend himself to Bishop Isembert. Then he took the best estate from them.

A Tribune named Aimery seized the castle called Civray from his lord Bernard and this castle was rightfully Hugh's as it had been his father's. Because of his anger at Aimery Count William urged Hugh to become the vassal of Bernard for that part of the castle which had belonged to his father so that both [i.e. Bernard and Hugh] could do war with Aimery. But Hugh did not want to be the vassal of Bernard. The Count let this request wait for a year and then growing angrier he urged Hugh all the more to become the vassal of Bernard. When a year had passed the Count came with great wrath to Hugh and said to him, "Why don't you make an agreement with Bernard? You owe so much to me that if I should tell you to make a peasant into a lord you should do it. Do what I tell you and if it should turn out badly for you, come and see me about it." Hugh believed him and became the man [i.e. vassal] of Bernard for the fourth part of the said castle. As his pledge to Hugh Bernard gave the Count four hostages. The Count said to Hugh, "Commend those hostages to me under such conditions that if Bernard should not keep those agreements made to you on faith, I will turn them over to you to custody and by my faith will be your helper." The Count promised this very strongly to Hugh [how strongly he himself well knows]. And Hugh trusted in his lord and took up a just war on account of the above castle and suffered great losses in men and other things. And the Count started to build a castle for him called Couhe but did not finish it but he spoke with Aimery and gave up the castle to him [i.e. Aimery] and in no way aided Hugh.

Later the Count became upset with Aimery on account of the castle called Chize which Aimery had seized and Hugh and the Count went to war together against him. He [i.e. the Count] besieged the castle of Malavallis in return for the evil deed which Aimery had done to him and captured it, and Hugh aided him as best he could. Before Hugh left the Count the latter promised him, just as a lord ought to promise satisfaction to his vassal, that he would make no agreement with Aimery nor have anything to do with him without Hugh, and that Malavallis would not be built without his [i.e. Hugh's] advice. But the Count did make an agreement with Aimery and permitted him to build Malavallis without the advice of Hugh. As long as Aimery lived Hugh got nothing back with respect to the aforesaid matters.

After the death of Aimery a great war began between the son of Aimery [also named Aimery] and Hugh. At the same time Hugh came to the Count and said to him, "Things are going badly for me now, my Lord, in that I have no part of the fief which you caused me to acquire." The Count answered him, "I am going to make a pact with them [i.e. Aimery's son and his men] which, if they keep it well, should be fine: if not, I will build the castle which I started." And the castle was constructed on the advice of Bernard who hitherto had assisted Hugh in the war. Then the men of Civray, when they saw how Hugh was oppressing them, were no longer able to hold out and made an agreement with Bernard giving him the castle and admitting him into it without consulting Hugh. Now both Bernard and Aimery were at war against Hugh and he was alone against them. Coming to the Count Hugh said to him, "My Lord, I am doing very badly because the lord of whom I became a vassal at your advice has just taken away my fief. I beg and urge you through the faith which a lord ought to render to his vassal that you see to it that I get either a favorable pact or my fief as you pledged to me, or that you turn over to me the hostages which I commended to you, and that in addition you aid me as you pledged to me." The Count, however, neither aided him nor made an agreement with him nor gave over his hostages, but gave them back to Bernard with no strings attached.

After this a war started between Bernard, Aimery, and Hugh. And when Hugh saw that the Count aided him in no way he went to seek the advice of Gerald the Bishop of Limoges and they both left to move against Bernard in La Marche

where they built a castle. But the Count who ought to have aided Hugh seized the castle from him and burned it. And he [i.e. the Count] and his son ordered all their men that no one should help Hugh unless he wished to die. Then Bernard in consultation with his men decided that they should do evil to Hugh on the advice of the Count and they [i.e. Bernard and his men] appointed a deadline fifteen days away. During those fifteen days the Count arranged a truce between Bernard and Hugh. Three days before the end of the truce the Count took Hugh along with his host to Apremont castle and a meeting was held in his castle. From there the Count went to Blaye where he was to have a meeting with Count Sancho and he told Hugh that he should come along. And Hugh responded, "My Lord, why do you ask me to go with you? You yourself know how short is the truce which I have with Bernard and he is threatening to do me ill." The Count said to him "Don't fear that they will do anything to you as long as you are with me," and he [i.e. the Count] took him along with him for force and against his wishes. And while they were staying at the meeting place Hugh's men heard that Bernard was attacking him. They sent a message to Hugh that he should come. Then Hugh said to the Count, "Bernard is attacking me." And the Count said, "Do not fear that they should have dared to attack you. Besides you would have needed that they attack in order that I might put them [i.e. Bernard and his men] to confusion and give you assistance." And in the very same hour the Count sent directions to Hugh through his own men that he should go on ahead and then he [the Count] followed him. When Hugh reached Lusignan Bernard was at Confolens castle and had captured the *burg* and the *barrium* [i.e. the cleared area and houses around the *burg*] and had burned everything except the spoils and the men taken prisoners, and had done enough other evil deeds. A messenger ran up to Hugh and said to him, "Bernard has your wife besieged in the old castle which is left over from the fire." Coming to the Count Hugh said to him, "My Lord, now help me because my wife is besieged." But the Count gave him no aid nor advice at all, and Bernard and his men turned back and did much harm to Hugh and his men, more than he could bear, fifty thousand *solidi* worth. And Hugh suffered this damage during the truce which the Count offered him at Blaye.

Not long after this Hugh went to Gencay castle and burned it and seized the men and women and took everything with him; and proceeding to the Count he said to him, "My Lord, give me permission to build the castle which I burned." And the Count said to him, "How can you build a castle when you are Fulk's vassal? He will demand it from you and you won't be able to keep it unless you turn it over to him." Hugh said, "My Lord, when I became the vassal of Fulk I told him that his men were seizing things which belonged to me and that if I was able to regain possession of them I would do it, but that I want to do this in such a way as to remain his vassal. And Fulk said to me, 'If you get angry at them, don't get angry at me.'" And when the Count heard that Fulk and Hugh had such an agreement he was pleased and said to Hugh, "Build the castle under such an agreement that if I am able to buy your share and mine from Count Fulk, one part [i.e. of the castle] will be mine and the other yours." And Hugh built the castle. Then Fulk asked the Count for it and the Count responded, "Ask Hugh for it." Then Fulk did this and Hugh responded, "When I became your vassal, I told you that if I was able to seize the castles from my enemies I would do it and that I would hold it [sic] from you, and I want to do this because this castle which you are demanding belonged to my relatives and I have a better right to it than those who were holding it." And Fulk said to him, "How can you, who are my vassal, hold something which I did not give you, against my will?" Then Hugh sought again the advice of the Count. The Count told him, "If he is willing to give you pledges that your enemies will not have the castle then you can't keep it; if not, keep it, because he will not be able to accuse you [i.e. of breaking feudal custom]." Hugh then asked Fulk to give him hostages, but he gave none saying, "I am going to see the Count and I will give him the hostages, and he can give you some of his own," and then the conference turned into an angry one. Fulk demanded Hugh's castle of the Count. "I will never give it up without pledges," said Hugh. Then the Count said to him, "I will give you a pledge; tell me which ones you want." Hugh said, "Get the ones you want from Count Fulk and give me what I'm asking for. Give me the man who has custody of the tower of Melle so that if Aimery should get the castle without my advice and evil should happen to me, that man will turn the tower over to me." The Count said to him, "I will not do this because it is not in my power to do it." Then Hugh said, "If you don't want to do this with Melle, make the same agreement with regard to Chize." But the Count was willing to do neither the one nor the other; and Hugh and his men saw that the Count was dealing badly with them, and they parted in anger. Then Hugh sent all kinds of necessities into the castle and intended to hold it against all comers if they would not give him pledges. Then the Count came outside his *civitatem* [presumably Poitiers] and asked Hugh to come to him and through Count William of Angouleme ordered him to submit himself to the mercy of the Count because he [i.e. the Count] could not change the situation which called for him to aid Fulk and he was fearful of losing [the friendship of] either Fulk or Hugh. Then Hugh committed himself to the friendship and trust of the Count his Lord and did this out of love for him [the Count] because he [i.e. the Count] was certain that Fulk had not been badly led. And the Count said, "Let Hugh do this for me and I will give him my faith just as a Lord ought to do to his vassal, and if evil should happen to him he will know that it was I who betrayed him and he will never trust in me again." And Hugh responded, "My Lord has spoken to me in such a way about many things and as a result has led me away [i.e. from my original opposition to him]." And not a single one of Hugh's men would advise him to trust the Count. But the Count reminded Hugh of all the good things which he had done for him and pressed him with his love and requests and appeals; then Hugh said to the Count, "I will trust every thing to you, but watch out lest you do me evil, for if you do, I will not be faithful to you nor will I serve you, nor will I render fidelity to you; but on account of the fact that I will be separated from you and you are not able to give me pledges, I want you to give me my fief as a hostage that [in case of your violation] I will never serve you and [I want you to] release me from that oath which I made to you." And the Court answered, "Gladly." And Hugh against the wishes of his men had turned the castle over to the Count under such an agreement that Aimery would not get possession of it without his [i.e. Hugh's] advice and that evil should not happen to him. When these reservations had been heard, Hugh accepted [and the Count gave] his fief as a pledge under such an agreement that if the Count should mislead him with regard to the agreement about Gencay, he would never again render service to him [as a vassal]. And the Count released him from the oaths so that he would never observe them and without any malevolence [on the part of the Count]. And the Count handed over Gencay without consulting Hugh and was given money and some domaine land. And it went very badly for Hugh with men killed, houses burned, booty taken, lands seized, and many other things which in truth cannot be enumerated. When this had ended the Count gave Hugh a respite and promised that he would give him a benefice either of something which was his by right or of something which would be pleasing to him. But when this period passed the Count did nothing for Hugh but sent an order to him, "Don't wait because I am not going to do anything for you. If all the world were mine I would not give you as much as a finger could hold with regard to this matter." When Hugh heard this he went to the court of the Count and informed him of his rights but it profited him not a bit. This saddened Hugh and in the presence of all who were there he renounced his allegiance to the Count except what he owed for the city [i.e. Poitiers] and his own person.

Before either Hugh or his men did any evil the men of the Count seized a benefice from Hugh's men in the name of war. When Hugh saw this he went to Chize castle which had been his uncle's but which Peter was holding unjustly, and whence much harm was being done to Hugh. He seized the tower and threw out Peter's men. And Hugh did this because he thought he had a right to it since it had belonged to his father or others of his relatives and he was losing that right. And when the Count heard of this he was greatly saddened and sent an order to Hugh that the latter should turn over to him the tower which he had taken away from Peter. Hugh sent back to the Count that he [the Count] should turn over to him [Hugh] his father's honor and the other things which he had seized in it, and in addition the entire honor which had belonged to Joscelin and which the Count had given him. The Count thought this over and then they arranged for a conference. The Count said to Hugh, "I will not give you those honors which you ask of me, but I will give you that honor which was your uncle's—the castle, the tower, and the entire honor—under such an agreement that you no longer demand of me that honor which was your father's, or others of your relatives, nor anything which you claim as your right." When he heard this Hugh greatly mistrusted the Count in that the latter with evil intent had taken much away from him in the past, and he said to the Count, "I don't dare to do this because I'm afraid that you'll threaten me with evil as you have done with regard to many other things." The Count said to Hugh, "I will make such pledges to you that you will no longer distrust me." Hugh asked him, "What kind of pledges?" The Count said, "I will produce a serf who will undergo an ordeal for you so that you will not doubt that the agreement which we make among ourselves will be kept nor that harm will ever again be done to you with regard to those affairs of the past, but the agreement will be kept firmly without any evil intent." When Hugh heard the Count speak in this manner he said, "You are my Lord, I will not accept a pledge from you, but I will simply rely on the mercy of God and of yourself." The Count said to Hugh, "Give up all those claims over which you have quarreled with me in the past and swear fidelity to me and my son and I will give you your uncle's honor or something else of equal value in exchange for it." Then Hugh said, "My Lord, I beg you through God and this blessed crucifix which is made in the figure of Christ that you do not make me do this if you and your son were intending to threaten me with trickery." And the Count said, "On my honor my son and I will do this without trickery." Hugh then said, "And when I shall have sworn fidelity to you, you will demand Chize castle of me, and if I should not turn it over to you, you will say that it is not right that I deny you the castle which I hold from you, and if I should turn it over to you, you and your son will seize it [i.e. and keep it] because you will have given nothing in pledge except the mercy of God and yourself." The Count said, "We will not do that, but if we should demand it of you, don't turn it over to us." Under the terms of such an agreement, or *finis* as it was also called, that the Count and his son should render fidelity to Hugh with no evil intentions, they received Hugh as their vassal in faith and trust. And they had Hugh abandon everything which he claimed from the past. And he swore fidelity to them and they gave him the honor of his uncle Joscelin just as the latter held it one year before he died.

Here end the agreements between the Count and Hugh.

GALBERT OF BRUGES

The Murder of Charles the Good

GALBERT, A NOTARY OF BRUGES, RECORDED AS AN EYE-WITNESS THE
events prior and subsequent to the murder of Count Charles the Good of
Flanders in 1127. This account shows the judicial measures by which the
count had attempted to consolidate his county at the expense of the lesser
nobility and chatelains who had gained power following the dissolution of
the Carolingian state. His murder and the subsequent disintegration of his
centralizing efforts indicate the strength of centrifugal forces in twelfth century society.

Source: James Bruce Ross, *The Murder of Charles the Good Count of Flanders* (New York:
Harper and Row, 1967).

---

[1] Charles becomes count of Flanders in 1119; his concern for peace and justice, 1119-24

Charles, son of Canute, king of Denmark, and
born of a mother who was descended from the
blood of the counts of the land of Flanders,[1]
because of this relationship grew up from boyhood to manly strength of body and mind in
our fatherland. After he was armed with the
honors of knighthood[2] he fought with distinction against his enemies and gained a fine reputation and glory for his name among the rulers
of the earth. Our barons had for many years
shown a preference for him as prince if by
chance such a possibility should occur.[3] Therefore when Count Baldwin, that extraordinary
brave youth, was dying, he, together with the
barons,[4] handed the realm over to his cousin
Charles and commended it to him under oath.
The pious count, acting with the prudence of
his predecessor, now took such measures to
strengthen the peace, to reaffirm the laws and
rights of the realm, that little by little public
order was restored in all parts, and by the
fourth year of his reign, thanks to his efforts,
everything was flourishing, everything was
happy, and joyful in the security of peace and
justice. When he saw that such a great boon of
peace made everyone happy, he gave orders
that throughout the limits of the realm all who
frequented markets or dwelt in towns should

live together in quiet and security without
resort to arms; otherwise they would be punished by the very arms they bore. To enforce
this, bows and arrows and subsequently all
arms were laid aside not only in those places
already protected by the count's peace but in
other places as well.

Thanks to this boon of peace, men governed
themselves in accordance with laws and justice,
devising by skill and study every kind of argument for use in the courts, so that when anyone
was attacked he could defend himself by the
strength and eloquence of rhetoric, or when he
was attacking, he might ensnare his enemy, who
would be deceived by the wealth of his oratory.
Rhetoric was now used both by the educated
and by those who were naturally talented, for
there were many illiterate people, endowed by
nature herself with the gift of eloquence and
rational methods of inference and argument,
whom those who were trained and skilled in the
rhetorical art were not able to resist or refute.
But, on the other hand, because these by their
deceits brought action in the courts against the
faithful and the lambs of God, who were less
wary, God, who sees all from on high, did not
fail to chastise the deceivers so that He might
reach by scourges those whom He had endowed
with the gift of eloquence for their salvation
because they had used this gift for their own
perdition.

[2] God desolates Flanders by famine, 1124-25

Therefore God inflicted the scourge of famine and afterwards of death on all who lived in our realm, but first He deigned by the terror of omens to recall to penitence those whom He had foreseen as prone to evil. In the year 1124 from the Incarnation of our Lord, in the month of August, there was visible to all the inhabitants of the lands an eclipse[5] on the body of the sun at about the ninth hour of the day,[6] and an unnatural failure of light so that the eastern part of the sun, darkened little by little, poured forth strange clouds on the other parts, not darkening the whole sun at the same time, however, but only partially. Nevertheless, the same cloud wandered over the whole circle of the sun, moving across from east to west, but only within the circle of the solar essence. Consequently, those who observed the condition of the peace and the wrongs in the courts, threatened everyone with the peril of famine and death. But when men were not corrected in this way, neither lords nor serfs, there came the hunger of sudden famine,[7] and subsequently the scourges of death attacked them. As it is said in the Psalms: "He called for a famine upon the land, and broke the whole staff of bread."

During this time no one was able to sustain himself by eating and drinking in his usual way, but, contrary to habit, a person ate as much bread in one meal as he had been accustomed to consume in several days before this time of famine. So he was glutted by this unusual quantity, and since all the natural passages of the organs were distended by the excess of food and drink, he fell ill. Men were wasting away from repletion and indigestion and yet they suffered from hunger until they drew the last breath. Many swelled up, and food and drink were loathsome to them although they had plenty of both. In this time of famine, in the middle of Lent,[8] the men of our land living near Ghent and the Leie and Scheldt rivers ate meat because bread was completely lacking. Some who tried to make their way to the cities and towns where they could buy bread[9] perished of hunger along the road, choking to death before they were halfway. Near the manors and farms[10] of the rich and the strongholds and

castles, the poor, bent low in their misery as they came for alms, fell dead in the act of begging. Strange to say, no one in our land retained his natural color but all bore a pallor like that of death. Both the well and the ill languished because those who were sound in body became ill on seeing the misery of the dying.

[3] Count Charles takes steps to relieve the poor

But the impious were not corrected in this way, for it is said that at this very time they had plotted the death of the most pious count Charles.[11] The count tried in every way possible to take care of the poor, distributing alms in the towns and throughout his domain, both in person and by his officials. At the same time he was feeding one hundred paupers in Bruges every day; and he gave a sizable loaf of bread to each one of them from before Lent until the harvests of the same year.[12] And likewise in his other towns he had made the same provision.[13] In the same year the lord count had decreed that whoever sowed two measures of land in the sowing time should sow another measure in peas and beans,[14] because these legumes yield more quickly and seasonably and therefore could nourish the poor more quickly if the misery of famine and want should not end in that year. He had also ordered this to be done throughout the whole county, in this way making provision for the poor in the future as well as he could.[15] He reprimanded those men of Ghent who had allowed poor people whom they could have fed to die of hunger on their doorsteps.

He also prohibited the brewing of beer because the poor could be fed more easily and better if the townspeople and country-people refrained from making beer in this time of famine. For he ordered bread to be made out of oats so that the poor could at least maintain life on bread and water. He ordered a fourth of a measure of wine to be sold for six pennies and not more dearly so that the merchants would stop hoarding and buying up wine and would exchange their wares, in view of the urgency of the famine, for other foodstuffs which they could acquire more quickly and which could be used more easily to nourish the poor. From his own table he took daily enough food to sustain one hundred and thirteen paupers. In addition he provided daily for one of the poor a set of new garments, including a shirt, tunic, cloak, breeches, hose, and shoes, from the beginning of that Lent and of his devout fasting (during which, betrayed, he fell asleep in the Lord) until the day when he died in Christ. And after he had seen to these arrangements and completed such a merciful distribution to the poor, he was in the habit of going to church where, kneeling in prayer, he would sing psalms to the Lord, and according to his custom would distribute pennies to the poor while prostrate before God.[16]

[4] Count Charles is offered and refuses the imperial crown, 1125

While the marquis Charles was reigning in his county of Flanders in the splendor of peace and fame, Henry, the Roman emperor, died, and the realm of that empire was made desolate and left without an heir to the throne. Therefore the leading men among the clergy and the people of the realm of the Romans and the Germans made a great effort to find someone for the office of emperor who was noble both in ancestry and character. After weighing the merits of rulers of various lands and kingdoms, those wise and powerful men of the realm decided, after due consideration, that they would formally send suitable delegates, namely, the chancellor of the archbishop of Cologne and with him Count Godfrey, to the count of Flanders, Charles the Pious, on behalf of the whole clergy and people of the kingdom and empire of the Germans, to beg and entreat him by virtue of his power and piety to assume the honors of empire and the regal dignities with their appurtenances, if only for the sake of charity. For all the best men among both clergy and people were hoping, ardently and rightly, that he would be elected so that if, God willing, he deigned to come to them, they could elevate him unanimously by the imperial coronation and establish him as king by the law of the preceding Catholic emperors. When Count Charles had heard the embassy and their urgent request, he took counsel with the nobles and peers of his land[17] as to what he should do. But those who

had rightly cherished and loved him, and who venerated him as a father, began to grieve and to lament his departure, predicting that it would prove the ruin of the fatherland if he should desert it. Those evil traitors, however, who were threatening his life, advised him to assume the German kingship and its dignities, pointing out to him how much glory and fame would be his as king of the Romans. Those wretches were trying by this guile and trickery to get rid of him; later when they had been unable to remove him while he was alive, they betrayed him while he was contending with them on behalf of the law of God and men.

And so Count Charles remained in his county because of the insistence of those who loved him, seeking and establishing for all, so far as possible, the peace and well-being of the fatherland; he was a Catholic, good and devout worshiper of God and a prudent ruler of men. When he wanted to perform good deeds of knighthood, he had no enemies around his land, either in the marches or on the frontiers and borders, either because his neighbours feared him or because, united to him in the bond of peace and love, they preferred to exchange offerings and gifts with him. So he undertook chivalric exploits for the honor of his land and the training of his knights in the lands of the counts or princes of Normandy or France, sometimes even beyond the kingdom of France; and there with two hundred knights on horseback he engaged in tourneys, in this way enhancing his own fame and the power and glory of his county. Whatever sin he committed by his worldliness he redeemed with God many times by almsgiving.

[5] Count Charles is offered but refuses the crown of the kingdom of Jerusalem, 1123

During his lifetime it happened that the king of Jerusalem was taken captive by the Saracens, and the city of Jerusalem sat desolate without her king. As we have learned, the Crusaders who were pursuing the course of Christian knighthood there hated that captive king because he was grasping and penurious, and had not governed the people of God well. Therefore they took counsel and by general consent sent a letter to Count Charles asking him to come to Jerusalem and receive the kingdom of Judaea, and in that place and in the holy city take possession of the crown of the Catholic realm and the royal dignity. But he was unwilling, after consulting his vassals, to desert the fatherland of Flanders, which in his lifetime he was to govern well, and would have ruled even better if those evil traitors, full of the demon, had not slain their lord and father, who was imbued with the spirit of piety and wisdom and courage. Alas, what sorrow, that they should rob the Church of God of such a great man whom the church and the people of the Eastern Empire, and the holy city of Jerusalem and its Christian population, had preferred and chosen, and even demanded to have as a king!

[6] In praise of Count Charles

Strength of mind and memory and even reason, the greater virtue of the mind, fail me in praising the good Count Charles; in comparison with him all you earthly princes are less worthy and less powerful, lacking experience and judgment, and disorderly in habits. For Count Charles held such a place among the devout sons of the Church that in his merits he excelled the leaders and many philosophers of the Christian faith; and although he had once been a sinner and guilty, at the end of his good life, from the fruit of penance, all things worked together for his good and for the eternal salvation of his soul. As it is said,

And none be counted happy till his death,
Till his last funeral rites are paid.

And, according to the Apostle, "We know that to them who love God all things work together for good, even to them that are called according to his purpose." For in a holy place and in holy prayer, and in holy devoutness of heart, and in the holy time of Lent, and in the holy act of almsgiving, and before the sacred altar and the sacred relics of Saint Donatian, archbishop of Rheims, and Saint Basil the Great, and Saint Maximus, the one who raised three dead, those foul dogs, full of the demon, those serfs, murdered their lord! Certainly there is no one so senseless, so stupid

and obtuse, as not to sentence those traitors to the vilest and most unheard-of punishments, those serfs who by unheard-of treachery did away with their lord, the very one whom they should most have protected.

It is certainly a marvelous and memorable fact that among the many emperors, kings, dukes, and counts whom we have seen, we have never yet seen or heard of any one whom it so well became to be lord and father, and advocate[18] of the churches of God. That he knew how to be lord, father, advocate, to be pious, gentle, compassionate, an honor to God and an ornament to the Church, cannot be doubted, for after the death of such a great man, everyone bore witness to his merits. Friends and enemies, foreigners and neighbors, nobles and common people, and the inhabitants of every land whatsoever, were convinced that he would be held worthy of great merit by God and men, because he died like a Christian ruler, seeking the justice of God and the welfare of those over whom he ruled. But the men whom he trusted tripped him up and betrayed him, as it is said in the Psalm: "Why, my own intimate friend, who shared my bread, has lifted his heel to trip me up."

[7] The discovery of the servile origin of the Erembald clan, 1126

Now after the clemency of God had withdrawn the scourges[19] and completely removed the troubles of the time, He began in His mercy to bestow plenty on the land, and He ordered the granaries to be filled with the produce of the fields and the earth to abound in wine and other foodstuffs, and by divine order the whole land flourished again in the loveliness of the seasons. The pious count, wishing to reestablish proper order in his realm, sought to find out who belonged to him, who were servile and who were free men in the realm. When cases were being heard in the courts,[20] the count was often present, and he learned from the judgments concerning secular liberty and the status of serfs that in important cases and general pleas free men scorned to answer charges made by servile ones. Those whom the count had been able to identify as belonging to him, he now set about trying to claim for himself. A certain provost, that Bertulf of Bruges, and his brother the castellan of Bruges, with their nephews Borsiard, Robert, Albert, and other leading members of that clan, were striving by every device of craft and guile to find a way by which they could slip out of servitude and cease belonging to the count; for they belonged to him, being of servile status. Finally, after due consideration, the provost gave his marriageable nieces, whom he had reared in his home, in wedlock to free knights, resorting to this policy of intermarriage as a means by which he and his kin might gain a certain measure of secular liberty.

But it happened that a knight who had married a niece of the provost challenged to single combat in the presence of the count another knight, who was free according to the descent of his family; and the latter replied vigorously with an indignant refusal, asserting that by birth he was not of servile status but rather of free rank, according to his family lineage, and for this reason he would not contend as an equal in single combat with his challenger. For, according to the law of the count, a free man who had taken to wife a female serf was no longer free after he had held her for a year, but had come to be of the same status as his wife. And so that knight mourned who had lost his liberty on account of his wife, through whom he had believed he could become freer[21] when he married her; and the provost and his kin mourned, and for that reason kept on trying in every way possible to free themselves from servitude to the count. Therefore when the count had learned from the judgment of the courts and the report of the elders of the realm that they—the Erembald clan—belonged to him beyond doubt, he set about trying to claim them as his serfs. Nevertheless, because the provost and his kin had not heretofore been molested or accused of servile status by the predecessors of the count, this would have been consigned to oblivion, having been laid to rest, as it were, and disregarded for so long, if it had not been brought to the attention of the courts by the challenge to combat.

[8] Bertulf and his nephew become desperate, 1127

But the provost, who with the whole line of his nephews was more powerful than anyone in the realm except the count and more eminent in reputation and in religion,[22] asserted that he himself was free, as were both his predecessors and successors in the clan, and he insisted that this was so with a certain irrationality and arrogance. And so he endeavored by laying plans and using influence to extract himself and his family from the possession and ownership of the count, and he often attacked the count in these terms:

"That Charles of Denmark[23] would never have succeeded to the countship if I had not been willing. But now, although he became count by my efforts, he does not remember how much I did for him but instead seeks to cast me and all my line back into serfdom, trying to find out from the elders whether we are his serfs.

"But let him try as much as he wants, we shall be free and we are free, and there is no man on earth who can make us into serfs!" He talked so boastfully in vain, however, for the count, on his guard, had found out that they were slandering him and had heard of their deceit and also of their treachery. And when the provost and his kin realized that they could not succeed in defending themselves but were, on the contrary, about to be deprived of their usurped liberty, he preferred to perish together with the whole line of his nephews rather than be handed over in servitude to the count. At last, in the guile of abominable deliberation, they began secretly to plot the death of the most pious count, and finally to fix on a place and an opportunity for killing him.

[9] Private war breaks out between Borsiard and Thancmar, 1127

When strife and conflict broke out between his nephews and those of Thancmar, whose side the count justly favored, the provost was delighted because it gave him an opportunity to betray the count, for he had called to the aid of his nephews all the knights of our region, using money, influence, and persuasion. They besieged Thancmar on all sides in the place where he had entrenched himself, and finally with a considerable force strongly attacked those within.[24] Breaking the bolts of the gates, they cut down the orchards and hedges of their enemies. Though the provost did not take part and acted as if he had done nothing, he actually did everything by direction and deception. He pretended in public that he was full of good will and told his enemies that he grieved to see his nephews engaged in so much strife and killing, although he himself had incited them to all these crimes. In that conflict many on both sides fell on that day wounded or dead. When the provost had learned that this fight was going on, he himself went to the carpenters who were working in the cloister of the brothers and ordered that their tools, that is, their axes, should be taken to that place for use in cutting down the tower and orchards and houses of his enemies.[25] Then he sent around to various houses in the town to collect axes which were quickly taken to that place. And when in the night his nephews had returned with five hundred knights and squires[26] and innumerable footsoldiers, he took them into the cloister and refectory of the brothers where he entertained them all with various kinds of food and drink and was very happy and boastful about the outcome.

And while he was harassing his enemies in this way, spending a great deal in support of those who were helping his nephews, first the squires and then the knights began to plunder the peasants, even seizing and devouring the flocks and cattle of the country people. The nephews of the provost were forcibly seizing the belongings of the peasants and appropriating them for their own use. But none of the counts from the beginning of the realm had allowed such pillaging to go on in the realm, because great slaughter and conflict came to pass in this way.

[10] The count takes measures against the nephews of Bertulf, February 27-28, 1127, and returns to Bruges

When the country people heard that the count had come to Ypres, about two hundred of them went to him secretly and at night, and kneeling at his feet begged him for his customary paternal help. They entreated him to order their goods to be returned to them, that is, their flocks and herds, clothes and silver, and all the other furniture of their houses which the nephews of the provost had seized together with those who had

fought with them continuously in that attack and siege. After listening solemnly to the complaints of those appealing to him, the count summoned his counselors, and even many who were related to the provost, asking them by what punishment and with what degree of severity justice should deal with this crime. They advised him to burn down Borsiard's house without delay because he had plundered the peasants of the count; and therefore strongly urged him to destroy that house because as long as it stood, so long would Borsiard indulge in fighting and pillaging and even killing, and would continue to lay waste the region. And so the count, acting on this advice, went and burned the house and destroyed the place to its foundations. Then that Borsiard and the provost and their accomplices were beside themselves with anxiety both because in this act the count had clearly lent aid and comfort to their enemies and because the count was daily disquieting them about their servile status and trying in every way to establish his rights over them.

After burning the house the count went on to Bruges. When he had settled down in his house, his close advisers came to him and warned him, saying that the nephews of the provost would betray him because now they could claim as pretext the burning of the house, although even if the count had not done this they were going to betray him anyway. After the count had eaten, mediators came and appealed to him to behalf of the provost and his nephews, begging the count to turn his wrath from them and to receive them mercifully back into his friendship. But the count replied that he would act justly and mercifully toward them if they would henceforth give up their fighting and pillaging; and he assured them, moreover, that he would certainly compensate Borsiard with a house that was even better. He swore, however, that as long as he was count, Borsiard should never again have any property in that place where the house had been burned up, because as long as he lived there near Thancmar he would never do anything but fight and feud with his enemies, and pillage and slaughter the people.

The mediators, some of whom were aware of the treachery, did not bother the count very much about the reconciliation, and since the servants were going about offering wine they asked the count to have better wine brought in. When they had drunk this, they kept on asking to be served again still more abundantly, as drinkers usually do, so that when they had finally received the very last grant from the count they could go off as if to bed. And by the order of the count everyone present was abundantly served with wine until, after receiving the final grant, they departed.[27]

[11] The Erembalds seal the plot against the count, during the night of March 1, 1127

Then Isaac and Borsiard, William of Wervik, Ingran, and their accomplices, after receiving the assent of the provost, made haste to carry out what they were about to do, by the necessity of divine ordination, through free will. For immediately those who had been mediators and intercessors between the count and the kinsmen of the provost went to the provost's house and made known the count's response, that is, that they had not been able to secure any mercy either for the nephews or their supporters, and that the count would treat them only as the opinion of the leading men of the land had determined in strict justice.[28]

Then the provost and his nephews withdrew into the inner room and summoned those whom they wanted. While the provost guarded the door, they gave their right hands to each other as a pledge that they would betray the count, and they summoned the young Robert to join in the crime, urging him to pledge by his hand that he would share with them what they were about to do and what they had pledged by their hands. But the noble young man, forewarned by the virtue of his soul and perceiving the gravity of what they were urging upon him, resisted them, not wishing to be drawn unwittingly into their compact until he could find out what it was they had bound themselves to do; and while they were pressing him, he turned away and hurried toward the door. But Isaac and William and the others called out to the provost guarding the door not to let Robert leave until by the pressure of his authority Robert should do what they had demanded. The young man, quickly influenced by the flattery and threats of the provost, came

back and gave his hand on their terms, not knowing what he was supposed to do with them, and, as soon as he was pledged to the traitors he inquired what he had done. They said:

"We have now sworn to betray that Count Charles who is working for our ruin in every way and is hastening to claim us as his serfs, and you must carry out this treachery with us, both in word and in deed."

Then the young man, struck with terror and dissolved in tears, cried out:

"God forbid that we should betray one who is our lord and the count of the fatherland. Believe me, if you do not give this up, I shall go and openly reveal your treachery to the count and to everyone, and, God willing, I shall never lend aid and counsel to this pact!"

But they forcibly detained him as he tried to flee from them, saying:

"Listen, friend, we were only pretending to you that we were in earnest about that treachery so that we could try out whether you want to stay by us in a certain serious matter; for there is something we have concealed from you up to this point, in which you are bound to us by faith and compact, which we shall tell you about in good time."

And so turning it off as a joke, they concealed their treachery.

Now each one of them left the room and went off to his own place. When Isaac had finally reached home, he pretended to go to bed, for he was awaiting the silence of the night, but soon he remounted his horse and returned to the castle.[29] After stopping at Borsiard's lodgings and summoning him and the others whom he wanted, they went secretly to another lodging, that of the knight, Walter. As soon as they had entered, they put out the fire that was burning in the house so that those who had been awakened in the house should not find out from the light of the fire who they were and what sort of business they were carrying on at that time of night, contrary to custom. Then, safe in the darkness, they took counsel about the act of treason to be done as soon as dawn came, choosing for this crime the boldest and rashest members of Borsiard's household, and they promised them rich rewards. To the knights who would kill the count they offered four marks and to the servingmen who would do the same, two marks, and they bound themselves by this most iniquitous compact. Then Isaac returned to his home about daybreak, after he had put heart into them by his counsel and made them ready for such a great crime.

[12] Borsiard and his accomplices slay the count on March 2, 1127; the news spreads

Therefore when day had dawned, so dark and foggy that you could not distinguish anything a spear's length away, Borsiard secretly sent several serfs out into the courtyard of the count[30] to watch for his entrance into the church. The count had arisen very early and had made offerings to the poor in his own house, as he was accustomed to do, and so was on his way to church. But as his chaplains reported, the night before, when he had settled down in bed to go to sleep, he was troubled by a kind of anxious wakefulness; perplexed and disturbed in mind, he was so disquieted by the many things on his mind that he seemed quite exhausted, even to himself, now lying on one side, now sitting up again on the bed. And when he had set out on his way toward the church of Saint Donatian, the serfs who had been watching for his exit ran back and told the traitors that the count had gone up into the gallery[31] of the church with a few companions. Then that raging Borsiard and his knights and servants, all with drawn swords beneath their cloaks, followed the count into the same gallery, dividing into two groups so that not one of those whom they wished to kill could escape from the gallery by either way, and behold! they saw the count prostrate before the altar, on a low stool, where he was chanting psalms to God and at the same time devoutly offering prayers and giving out pennies to the poor.

Now it should be known what a noble man and distinguished ruler those impious and inhuman serfs betrayed! His ancestors were among the best and most powerful rulers who from the beginning of the Holy Church had flourished in France, or Flanders, or Denmark, or under the Roman Empire. From their stock the pious count was born in our time and grew up from boyhood to perfect manhood, never departing from the noble habits of his royal ancestors or their natural integrity of life. And before he became count, after performing many notable and distinguished deeds, he took the road of holy pilgrimage to Jerusalem. After crossing the depths of the sea and suffering many perils and wounds for the love of Christ, he at last fulfilled his vow and with great joy reached Jerusalem. Here he also fought strenuously against the enemies of the Christian faith. And so, after reverently adoring the sepulcher of the Lord, he returned home. In the hardship and want of this pilgrimage the pious servant of the Lord learned, as he often related when he was count, in what extreme poverty the poor labour, and with what pride the rich are exalted, and finally with what misery the whole world is affected. And so he made it his habit to stoop to the needy, and be strong in adversity, not puffed up in prosperity; and as the Psalmist teaches, "The king's strength loves judgment," he ruled the country according to the judgment of the barons and responsible men.

When the life of such a glorious prince had undergone martyrdom, the people of all lands mourned him greatly, shocked by the infamy of his betrayal. Marvelous to tell, although the count was killed in the castle of Bruges on the morning of one day, that is, the fourth day of the week, the news of this impious death shocked the citizens of London, which is in England, on the second day afterwards about the first hour; and towards evening of the same day it disturbed the people of Laon who live far away from us in France.[32] We learned this through our students who at that time were studying in Laon, as we also learned it from our merchants who were busy carrying on their business on that very day in London. For no one could have spanned these intervals of time or space so quickly either by horse or by ship!

[13] Bertulf's past: his ambition, pride and simony

It was ordained by God that bold and arrogant descendants of Bertulf's ancestors should be left behind to carry out the crime of treachery. The others, prevented by death, were influential men in the fatherland in their lifetime, persons of eminence and of great wealth, but the provost passed his life among the clergy, extremely severe and not a little proud. For it was his habit when someone whom he knew perfectly well came into his presence, to dissemble, in his pride, and to ask disdainfully of those sitting near him, who that could be, and then only, if it pleased him, would he greet the newcomer. When he had sold a canonical prebend to someone he would invest him with it not by canonical election but rather by force, for not one of his canons dared to oppose him either openly or secretly. In the house of the brothers in the church of Saint Donatian the canons had formerly been deeply religious men and perfectly educated, that is, at the beginning of the provostship of this most arrogant prelate. Restraining his pride, they had held him in check by advice and by Catholic doctrine so that he could not undertake anything unseemly in the church. But after they went to sleep in the Lord, the provost, left to himself, set in motion anything that pleased him and toward which the force of his pride impelled him. And so when he became head of his family, he tried to advance beyond everyone in the fatherland his nephews who were well brought up and finally girded with the sword of knighthood. Trying to make their reputation known everywhere, he armed his kinsmen for strife and discord; and he found enemies for them to fight in order to make it known to everyone that he and his nephews were so powerful and strong that no one in the realm could resist them or prevail against them. Finally, accused in the presence of the count himself of servile status, and affronted by the efforts of the count himself to prove that he and all his lineage were servile, he tried, as we have said, to resist servitude by every course and device and to preserve his usurped liberty with all his might. And when, steadfast in his determination, he could not succeed otherwise, he himself, with his kinsmen, carried through the treachery, which he had long refused to consider, with frightful consequences involving both his own kinsmen and the peers of the realm.

[14] Omens and predictions of the crime; the character of Galbert's work

But the most pious Lord thought fit to recall His own by the terror of omens, for in our vicinity bloody water appeared in the ditches, as a sign of future bloodshed. They could have been called back from their crime by this if their hardened hearts had not already entered into a conspiracy for betraying the count. They often asked themselves, if they killed the count, who would avenge him? But they did not know what they were saying, for "who," an infinite word, meant an infinite number of persons, who cannot be reckoned in a definite figure; the fact is that the king of France with a numerous army and also the barons of our land with an infinite multitude came to avenge the death of the most pious count! Not even yet has the unhappy consequence of this utterance reached an end, for as time goes on they do not cease to avenge the death of the count upon all the suspect and the guilty and those who have fled in all directions and gone into exile. And so we, the inhabitants of the land of Flanders, who mourn the death of such a great count and prince, ever mindful of his life, beg, admonish, and beseech you, after hearing the true and reliable account of his life and death (that is, whoever shall have heard it), to pray earnestly for the eternal glory of the life of the soul and his everlasting blessedness with the saints. In this account of his passion, the reader will find the subject divided by days and the events of those days, up to the vengeance, related at the end of this little work, which God alone wrought against those barons of the land whom He has exterminated from this world by the punishment of death, those by whose aid and counsel the treachery was begun and carried through to the end.

[15] The murder of Count Charles, Tuesday, March 2, 1127

In the year one thousand one hundred and twenty-seven, on the sixth day before the Nones of March,[33] on the second day, that is, after the beginning of the same month, when two days of the second week of Lent had elapsed, and the fourth day was subsequently to dawn,[34] on the fifth Concurrent,[35] and the sixth Epact,[36] about dawn, the count at Bruges was kneeling in prayer in order to hear the early Mass in the church of Saint Donatian, the former archbishop of Rheims. Following his pious custom he was giving out alms to the poor, with his eyes fixed on reading the psalms, and his right hand outstretched to bestow alms; for his chaplain who attended to this duty had placed near the count many pennies which he was distributing to the poor while in the position of prayer.

The office of the first hour was completed and also the response of the third hour,[37] when "Our Father" is said, and when the count, according to custom, was praying, reading aloud obligingly; then at last, after so many plans and oaths and pacts among themselves, those wretched traitors, already murderers at heart, slew the count, who was struck down with swords and run through again and again, while he was praying devoutly and giving alms, humbly kneeling before the Divine Majesty. And so God gave the palm of the martyrs to the count, the course of whose good life was washed clean in the rivulets of his blood and brought to an end in good works. In the final moment of life and at the onset of death, he had most nobly lifted his countenance and his royal hands to heaven, as well as he could amid so many blows and thrusts of the swordsmen; and so he surrendered his spirit to the Lord of all and offered himself as a morning sacrifice to God. But the bloody body of such a great man and prince lay there alone, without the veneration of his people and the due reverence of his servants. Whosoever has heard the circumstances of his death has mourned in tears his pitiable death and has commended to God such a great and lamented prince, brought to an end by the fate of the martyrs.

[16] The murders continue; the flight of the count's friends and the panic of the merchants, March 2, 1127

They also killed the castellan of Bourbourg. First wounding him mortally, they afterward dragged him ignobly by his feet from the gallery into which he had gone up with the count, to the doors of the church and dismembered him outside with their swords. This castellan, however, after making confession of his sins to the priests of that very church, received the body and blood of Christ according to the Christian custom. For immediately after killing the count, the swordsmen, leaving the corpse of the count and the castellan at the point of death in the gallery, went out to attack those of their enemies who happened to be present at the court of the count, so that they could slay them at will as they moved about in the castle. They pursued into the count's house a certain knight named Henry whom Borsiard suspected of the death of his brother Robert. He threw himself at the feet of the castellan, Hacket, who had just gone into the house with his men to take possession of it and who now took Henry and the brother of Walter of Loker under his protection and saved them from their attackers.

At the same moment, there fell into the hands of the traitors two sons of the castellan of Bourbourg who meanwhile was confessing his sins to the priests in the gallery of the church; these sons of his were praised by everyone for their knighthood and also for their character. Walter and Gilbert they were called, brothers in blood, peers in knighthood, handsome in appearance, worthy to be loved by all who knew them. As soon as they had heard of the murder of the count and their father they tried to flee, but the wretched traitors, going after them on horseback, pursued them to the Sands at the exit of the town. A wicked knight named Eric, one of those who had betrayed the count, pulled one of the brothers off the horse on which he was fleeing and then together with the pursuers slew him. The other brother, who was rushing in flight to the threshold of his lodgings, they came upon face to face and pierced him through with their swords. As he fell, one of our citizens named Lambert Benkin cut him down as if he were a piece of wood. And so they sent those slaughtered brothers to the holy beatitude of the celestial life.

They also pursued for a mile Richard of Woumen, the mighty master of that stronghold whose daughter had married a nephew of Thancmar, against whom the provost and his nephews formerly stirred up strife and conflict. He with his vassals had gone up to the court of the count, like many of the barons who on the same day were getting ready to go to court.

The traitors, frustrated in their pursuit, returned to the castle where the clergy and people of our place had poured in and were wandering around, stunned by what had happened. Those who were known to have been friends of the count as long as he lived, were now, without doubt, in a state of fear, and, lying low for the time, they were avoiding being seen by the traitors; while those in the count's court who depended on his friendship quickly took flight and got away while the people were in a state of confusion. Gervaise, a chamberlain of the count, whom the hand of God armed first to avenge the death of his lord, fled on horseback toward those Flemings who were his kinsmen. A certain John, a servant of the count who looked after his room, and whom the count had loved most among his serving men, fled at dawn on horseback, riding by side paths until noon, and at noon reached Ypres where he broke the news of the death of the count and his men. At this time merchants from all the kingdoms around Flanders had come together at Ypres,[38] on the feast of Saint Peter's Chair, where the market and all the fairs were going on; they were in the habit of carrying on their business safely under the peace and protection of the most pious count. At the same time merchants from the kingdom of the Lombards had come to the same fair;[39] the count had bought from them for twenty-one marks a silver vessel which was marvelously made so that the liquid which it held disappeared as one looked at it.[40] When the news reached all these people from various places who had come together at the fair, they packed up their goods and fled by day and by night, bearing with them word of the disgrace of our land and spreading it everywhere.

Notes

1   The marriage of Adele by her father, Robert the Frisian, count of Flanders (1071-93), to Canute IV of Denmark was intended to strengthen a Flemish-Danish alliance against William the Con-

queror which crumbled in 1086 on Canute's assassination; following this event Adele fled to Flanders with her young son, Charles. Neither the exact date of the marriage nor of Charles's birth has been established, but he must have been born between *ca.* 1080 and 1086. He was still a "very small boy" (*parvulus*) on his arrival in Flanders, according to Walter of Therouanne's *Vita Karoli*, c. 2, MGH, SS XII, 540 (hereafter cited as Walter, giving only the chapter number).

2   That is, after he had undergone the ceremony of induction into the knightly order, when the candidate was girded with the sword and "dubbed" by his knightly sponsor.

3   If, that is, his cousin Count Baldwin VII (1111-19) should die without heirs, as it so happened. Baldwin, born in 1093, was injured on the Norman border while serving in the host of his feudal lord, Louis VI of France, in September, 1118, and died on June 19, 1119.

4   This was the normal procedure of succession in Flanders at the time, designation by the reigning count and confirmation by the barons.

5   Scientists have demonstrated that this solar eclipse was visible in Europe, at noon on the meridian of Paris on August 11, 1124. It is puzzling that Galbert describes the obscuration as moving from east to west; actually in a solar eclipse the moon travels across the sun from west to east.

6   Since the day was divided into two periods, each of twelve hours, beginning respectively at sunset and sunrise, the hours were variable.

7   This great famine is mentioned in many contemporary records. It is best explained in terms of a long, extremely cold and snowy winter in 1123-24, a late, cold, and rainy summer, followed by another bitter winter in 1124-25 and again in 1125-26.

8   That is, about March 4, 1125.

9   It is clear that grain was stored and could therefore be purchased not in the country but in the towns. The granaries of the counts, where the produce of the domain and payments in kind were assembled, were generally located in the "castles" (*castra*) of the counts, close to which mercantile settlements such as Bruges and Ghent had sprung up. A charter of Charles in 1123 refers to "my granary" at Veurne.

10 By *villas et curtes* Galbert probably refers to larger and smaller units of agrarian exploitation. The older great domain or villa was now breaking up into smaller units, manors or farms of various sizes and kinds. In the area around Bruges and

Ghent the domanial disintegration began early, probably in the tenth century.

11   Evidence that this chapter was written after the murder of Charles, March 2, 1127. It also reveals the current belief that a plot against the count had sprung up earlier than his legal action (in 1126) against the Erembald clan, the villains of Galbert's story. The complex motivation of the crime is discussed more fully below.

12   Galbert's calculation of the yearly calendar from Christmas rather than from Easter is in accord with the general practice of the time in Flanders, where the "Paschal style" did not appear until late in the twelfth century and then only concurrently with the still predominant "Christmas style."

13   Walter, c. 11, also speaks of Charles's order that a daily stipend be given to the needy on every one of his many farms, and of his personal distribution of food, money, and clothing wherever he was, in town, stronghold or manor (*urbe, oppido, vel villa*). One day at Ypres he gave out 7,800 loaves of bread.

14   Galbert obviously means measures of land sown with bread grains, probably wheat. A "measure" probably refers to the Flemish *ghemet*; the *ghemet* of Bruges contained 4,426.38 square meters, a little more than the English statute acre (4,047 square meters). Peas and beans were essential foods, used in a variety of ways. In hard times flour ground from them was mixed with the usual bread cereals.

15   This seems to imply that the original order affected only those parts of the count's domain which he exploited directly as a landlord.

16   The evidence of the use of money supports the theory that coins, especially in the form of silver pennies, were an indispensable instrument of daily life, even among the poor, at this time.

17   Galbert doubtless refers to a convoking of the count's *curia* or feudal court, a body of variable size, composed primarily of the great officials of his household, his more important direct vassals who came to fulfill one of their essential feudal functions, that of giving "counsel" to their lord, and other vassals who happened to be present.

18   "Advocate" may be used here in the general sense of "protector" (as it seems to be in Galbert's Introduction and in c. 6) but it also possesses a specific meaning since the counts of Flanders were the "superior-advocates" of almost all the abbeys in their realm. This function of military protection and limited judicial authority, which they exercised at the expense of the abbots and their officials, as well as of the lesser lay advocates, gave them a substantial control over these great and rich religious establishments.

19   "The scourges" doubtless refer to the famine of chapters 2 and 3. What follows seems to be a direct continuation of those chapters and therefore it is likely that chapters 4, 5, and 6 were a later interpolation.

20   Galbert is probably referring to the count's local tribunals or judicial assemblies exercising common law jurisdiction within most of the great territorial units of the domain, the castellanies, and hence called in French *tribuneaux de châtellenie*. They were presided over by the count's key local official and vassal, the castellan, and were composed of a variable number of *scabini (échevins)* or "judges," named by the count, free men of standing in the area, probably often knights of the petty nobility; they are often referred to as *échevinages*. These tribunals possessed a broad competence, both civil and penal, over free men, but none in cases of a strictly feudal nature or over the persons of vassals of the count.

21   "Freer" here probably means more "noble."

22   Walter, c. 14, stresses above all the wealth of Bertulf as a source of his power and pride. "Religion" here probably refers to Bertulf's ecclesiastical position rather than to his piety.

23   Derogatory, stressing the fact that Charles in his eyes was a foreigner, and perhaps implying some weakness in Charles's right to the succession. Bertulf's claim to have supported Charles when his succession was challenged by Clemence, the mother of Baldwin VII, is not sustained by any other evidence in the sources.

24   According to Walter, c. 17, the count had forced the unwilling adversaries to accept a truce (*treuga*) and thus halted their feud; the Erembalds now violate this peace and thus catch Thancmar off guard.

25   Adding Walter's account, c. 17, a clearer picture of Thancmar's country stronghold emerges. An enclosure, probably of wood, which his enemies break into through gates, contains orchards and hedges, forming an outer or lower courtyard, where everything is cut down or demolished in the first assault. Thancmar is driven into his upper or inner defense, a tower, probably wooden, since axes were to be used against it. Just where the "houses" were located is not clear.

26   Galbert, who is an accurate observer in so many respects, and who as a notary might be expected to be careful in the use of numbers, here follows a common medieval habit of inaccuracy in deal-

ing with large numbers. It would have been difficult to feed more than five hundred men in the quarters of the canons!

27 Galbert gives here a revealing picture of the count's "day," his conference with the intimates while eating, his audience to others later, his hospitality to all in the evening. The importance of wine in the social life of the time is clear; mass drinking was probably the chief indoor diversion of the fighting class. Some formalities in the drinking ceremony seem to be observed.

28 Galbert is referring to the judgment of the count's court at Ypres.

29 That is, the fortified enclosure of the "castle" which contained numerous buildings besides the count's house proper.

30 That is, the courtyard of the count's house within the castle.

31 The *solarium* was probably an open colonnaded gallery encircling the hexagonal core or "choir" of the church as in the tomb-chapel of Charlemagne at Aachen. From the narrative which follows, it seems to have been accessible only from the stairs in the two smaller towers which flanked the great "tower" or west-work. To the east it opened out into a chapel, directly over the apse or sanctuary, and to the west probably into another chapel over the "porch."

32 Galbert uses *Francia* here in the more restricted sense of the royal domain or Isle de France; the county of Flanders was, of course, a fief of the French crown and therefore part of "France" in the larger sense. If a courier with urgent news could double the average rate of 30 to 40 kilometers a day by land, it is not impossible that the word could reach Laon, about 200 kilometers

away as the crow flies, on the second day.

33 The Nones fell on the seventh day of the month in March, as in May, July, and October, not on the ninth as in the other months.

34 The days of the week were counted from Sunday as the first day, and so Tuesday, the day of the murder, was the "third" day.

35 The Concurrents were a series of numbers used in determining the date of Easter, using March 24 and Friday as key days.

36 The Epacts are a feature of the Lunar Year, the calculation of which was essential in the determination of Easter. "The age of the Moon on January 1 is called the Epacts (*adiectiones lunae*); if the number is 1 in a given year, it is 12 in the next and 23 in the third. The year was reckoned for this purpose as beginning on September 1 preceding the current year."

37 That is, Prime and Tierce, the canonical hours or offices which the clergy were chanting before the celebration of the Mass.

38 One of several Flemish fairs, international, long-term, as distinguished from local, weekly markets, which seem to date from the late eleventh century. Their appearance was probably due to the initiative of the counts, and was one of several measures undertaken to create a powerful economic bond across Flanders, from the Scheldt to the sea, and thus unify their lands.

39 The commercial expansion of the north Italian merchants (coming probably from the smaller cities such as Asti and Piacenza rather than Genoa) was even more precocious than that of England but Galbert's reference is the first sure evidence of their presence at the Flemish fairs.

40 Probably a false bottom!

THE FIRST CRUSADE

THE FOLLOWING FOUR TEXTS REFLECT THE IMPRESSIONS OF THE FIRST Crusade (1096-1099) from the Christian, Jewish, Muslim, and Byzantine perspectives.

1. Fulcher Of Chartres

FULCHER OF CHARTRES WAS THE CHAPLAIN OF BALDWIN I, LORD OF Edessa and first king of Jerusalem. Fulcher lived in Jerusalem from 1100 until at least 1127. Part of his account is based on his own experience, and part is drawn from other eyewitness chronicles.

Source: Frances Rita Ryan, SSJ, *A History of the Expedition to Jerusalem 1095-1127* (Knoxville, TN: University of Tennessee Press, 1969).

Here Beginneth the First Book Concerning the Deeds of the Franks, Pilgrims to Jerusalem

I The Council Held at Clermont.

1. In the year 1095 after the Incarnation of Our Lord, while Henry the so-called emperor was reigning in Germany[1] and King Philip in France,[2] evils of all kinds multiplied throughout Europe because of vacillating faith. Pope Urban II[3] then ruled in the city of Rome. He was a man admirable in life and habits who strove prudently and vigorously to raise the status of Holy Church ever higher and higher.

2. Moreover he saw the faith of Christendom excessively trampled upon by all, by the clergy as well as by the laity, and peace totally disregarded, for the princes of the lands were incessantly at war quarreling with someone or other. He saw that people stole worldly goods from one another, that many captives were taken unjustly and were most barbarously cast into foul prisons and ransomed for excessive prices, or tormented there by three evils, namely hunger, thirst and cold, and secretly put to death, that holy places were violated, monasteries and villas consumed by fire, nothing mortal spared, and things human and divine held in derision.

3. When he heard that the interior part of Romania had been occupied by the Turks and the Christians subdued by a ferociously destructive invasion, Urban, greatly moved by compassionate piety and by the prompting of God's love, crossed the mountains and descended into Gaul and caused a council to be assembled in Auvergne at Clermont, as the city is called. This council, appropriately announced by messengers in all directions, consisted of 310 members, bishops as well as abbots carrying the crozier.

4. On the appointed day Urban gathered them around himself and in an eloquent address carefully made known the purpose of the meeting. In the sorrowing voice of a suffering church he told of its great tribulation. He delivered an elaborate sermon concerning the many raging tempests of this world in which the faith had been degraded as was said above.

5. Then as a suppliant he exhorted all to resume the powers of their faith and arouse in themselves a fierce determination to overcome the machinations of the devil, and to try fully to restore Holy Church, cruelly weakened by the wicked, to its honorable status as of old.

II The Decree of Urban in the Same Council.

1. "Dearest brethren," he said, "I, Urban, supreme pontiff and by the permission of God

prelate of the whole world, have come in this time of urgent necessity to you, the servants of God in these regions, as a messenger of divine admonition. I hope that those who are stewards of the ministry of God shall be found to be good and faithful, and free from hypocrisy [I Cor. 4:1-2].

2. "For if anyone is devious and dishonest, and far removed from the moderation of reason and justice, and obstructs the law of God, then I shall endeavor with divine help to correct him. For the Lord has made you stewards over His household so that when the time comes you may provide it with food of modest savour. You will be blessed indeed if the Lord of the stewardship shall find you faithful [Matth. 24:45-46].

3. "You are called shepherds; see that you do not do the work of hirelings. Be true shepherds always holding your crooks in your hands; and sleeping not, guard on every side of the flock entrusted to you [Joan. 10:12-13].

4. "For if through carelessness or neglect a wolf carries off a sheep you will certainly not only lose the reward prepared for you by our Lord, but after first having been beaten by the rods of the lictor you will be summarily hurled into the abode of the damned.

5. "In the words of the Gospel, 'You are the salt of the earth' [Matth. 5:13]. But if you fail how will the salting be accomplished? Oh how many men must be seasoned! [Matth. 5:13; Marc. 9:50; Luc. 14:34]. It is needful for you to salt with the corrective salt of your wisdom the ignorant who gape overmuch after the lusts of the world. Otherwise they will be putrefied by their transgression and be found unseasoned when the Lord speaks to them.

6. "For if He shall find in them worms, that is sins, because of your slothful performance of duty He will forthwith order them, despised, cast into the abyss of filth [Marc. 9:44-48]. And because you will not be able to restore such loss to Him He will straightway banish you, damned in His judgment, from the presence of His love.

7. "But one that salteth ought to be prudent, farseeing, modest, learned, peacemaking, truth-seeking, pious, just, equitable, and pure. For how can the unlearned make others learned, the immodest others modest, and the impure others

pure? If one hates peace how can one bring about peace? Or if one has soiled hands how can he cleanse those who are soiled of other pollution? For it is read, 'If a blind man leads a blind man, both will fall into a pit' [Matth. 15:14; Luc. 6:39].

8. "Accordingly first correct yourself so that then without reproach you can correct those under your care. If you truly wish to be the friends of God then gladly do what you know is pleasing to Him.

9. "Especially see to it that the affairs of the church are maintained according to its law so that simoniacal heresy in no way takes root among you. Take care that sellers and buyers, scourged by the lash of the Lord [Matth. 21:12; Marc. 11:15; Luc. 19:45; Joan. 2:15], be miserably driven out through the narrow gates to utter destruction [Matth. 7:13; Luc. 13:24].

10. "Keep the church in all its ranks entirely free from secular power, cause a tithe of all the fruits of the earth to be given faithfully to God, and let them not be sold or retained.

11. "Whoever shall have seized a bishop, let him be accursed. Whoever shall have seized monks or priests or nuns, and their servants, or pilgrims and traders, and despoiled them, let him be accursed. Let thieves and burners of houses, and their accomplices, be banished from the church and excommunicated.

12. "'Thereafter we must consider especially,' said Gregory, 'how severely punished will be he who steals from another, if he is infernally damned for not being generous with his own possessions.' For so it happened to the rich man in the familiar Gospel story [Luc. 16:19-31]. He was not punished for stealing from another, but because having received wealth he used it badly.

13. "By these evils it has been said, dearest brethren, that you have seen the world disturbed for a long time and particularly in some parts of your own provinces as we have been told. Perhaps due to your own weakness in administering justice scarcely anyone dares to travel on the road with hope of safety for fear of seizure by robbers by day or thieves by night, by force or wicked craft, indoors or out.

14. "Wherefore the truce commonly so-called, which was long ago established by the holy fathers, should be renewed. I earnestly admonish

each of you to strictly enforce it in your own diocese. But if anyone, smitten by greed or pride, willingly infringes this truce, let him be anathema by virtue of the authority of God and by sanction of the decrees of this council."

III Urban's Exhortation Concerning a Pilgrimage to Jerusalem.[4]

1. When these and many other matters were satisfactorily settled, all those present, clergy and people alike, spontaneously gave thanks to God for the words of the Lord Pope Urban and promised him faithfully that his decrees would be well kept. But the pope added at once that another tribulation not less but greater than that already mentioned, even of the worst nature, was besetting Christianity from another part of the world.

2. He said, "Since, oh sons of God, you have promised Him to keep peace among yourselves and to faithfully sustain the rights of Holy Church more sincerely than before, there still remains for you, newly aroused by Godly correction, an urgent task which belongs to both you and God, in which you can show the strength of your good will. For you must hasten to carry aid to your brethren dwelling in the East, who need your help for which they have often entreated.

3. "For the Turks, a Persian people, have attacked them, as many of you already know, and have advanced as far into Roman territory as that part of the Mediterranean which is called the Arm of St. George. They have seized more and more of the lands of the Christians, have already defeated them in seven times as many battles, killed or captured many people, have destroyed churches, and have devastated the kingdom of God. If you allow them to continue much longer they will conquer God's faithful people much more extensively.

4. "Wherefore with earnest prayer I, not I, but God exhorts you as heralds of Christ to repeatedly urge men of all ranks whatsoever, knights as well as foot-soldiers, rich and poor, to hasten to exterminate this vile race from our lands and to aid the Christian inhabitants in time.

5. "I address those present; I proclaim it to those absent; moreover Christ commands it. For all those going thither there will be remission of sins if they come to the end of this fettered life while either marching by land or crossing by sea, or in fighting the pagans. This I grant to all who go, through the power vested in me by God.

6. "Oh what a disgrace if a race so despicable, degenerate, and enslaved by demons should thus overcome a people endowed with faith in Almighty God and resplendent in the name of Christ! Oh what reproaches will be charged against you by the Lord Himself if you have not helped those who are counted like yourselves of the Christian faith!

7. "Let those," he said, "who are accustomed to wantonly wage private war against the faithful march upon the infidels in a war which should be begun now and be finished in victory. Let those who have long been robbers now be soldiers of Christ. Let those who once fought against brothers and relatives now rightfully fight against barbarians. Let those who have been hirelings for a few pieces of silver [Matth. 27:3] now attain an eternal reward. Let those who have been exhausting themselves to the detriment of body and soul now labour for a double glory. Yea on the one hand will be the sad and the poor, on the other the joyous and the wealthy; here the enemies of the Lord, there His friends.

8. "Let nothing delay those who are going to go. Let them settle their affairs, collect money, and when winter has ended and spring has come, zealously undertake the journey under the guidance of the Lord."

IV Concerning the Bishop of Le Puy and Subsequent Events.

1. After these words were spoken and the audience inspired to enthusiasm, many of them, thinking that nothing could be more worthy, at once promised to go and to urge earnestly those who were not present to do likewise. Among them was a certain Bishop of Le Puy, Adhemar by name, who afterwards acting as vicar apostolic prudently and wisely governed the entire army of God and vigorously inspired it to carry out the undertaking.

2. So when these matters which we have mentioned were decided in the council and firmly

agreed upon by all, the blessing of absolution was given and all departed. After they had returned to their homes they told those who were not informed of what had been done. When the edict of the council had been proclaimed everywhere through the provinces, they agreed under oath to maintain the peace which is called the Truce [of God].

3. Indeed finally many people of varied calling, when they discovered that there would be remission of sins, vowed to go with purified soul whither they had been ordered to go.

4. Oh how fitting, and how pleasing it was to us all to see those crosses made of silk, cloth-of-gold, or other beautiful material which these pilgrims whether knights, or other laymen, or clerics sewed on the shoulders of their cloaks. They did this by command of Pope Urban once they had taken the oath to go. It was proper that the soldiers of God who were preparing to fight for His honor should be identified and protected by this emblem of victory. And since they thus decorated themselves with this emblem of their faith, in the end they acquired from the symbol the reality itself. They clad themselves with the outward sign in order that they might obtain the inner reality.

5. It is evident that because a good intention brings about the accomplishment of a good work, a good work brings about the salvation of the soul. If it is well to have good intentions it is still better after meditation to carry them out. Therefore it is best to lay up a store of good works so that through worthy deeds one acquires nourishment for the soul. Therefore let each one intend [to do] good so that he will finish by doing better and at length by deserving attain the best, which will not diminish in eternity.

6. In such a manner Urban, a wise man and reverenced

Meditated a labour whereby the world flowered.

For he restored peace and re-established the rights of the church in their former condition. He also made a vigorous effort to drive out the pagans from the lands of the Christians. And since he endeavored in every way to glorify everything which was of God, nearly everyone freely submitted in obedience to his paternal authority.

V Concerning the Dissension Between Pope Urban and Guibert.

1. But the Devil, who always seeks man's destruction and goes about like a lion, seeking whom he may devour [I Petr. 5:8], stirred up, to the confusion of the people, a certain rival to Pope Urban, Guibert by name.[5] This man, incited by pride and supported for a while by the impudence of the aforesaid emperor of the Bavarians,[6] began to usurp the apostolic office while Urban's predecessor Gregory, that is Hildebrand, rightfully held the see and excluded Gregory himself from the limits of St. Peter's Basilica.

2. And because Guibert acted thus perversely, the better people did not care to recognize him. Since Urban after the death of Hildebrand was legally elected and consecrated by the cardinal bishops,[7] the greater and more pious part of the people were in favor of obedience to him.

3. Guibert, however, urged on by the support of the said emperor and by the passion of most of the Roman citizens, kept Urban a stranger to the Monastery of the Blessed Peter as long as possible. But Urban during the time that he was excluded from his church traveled about the country reconciling to God the people who had gone somewhat astray.

4. Guibert even as he was puffed up by his primacy in the church showed himself to be a pope indulgent to sinners. He exercised the papal office, albeit unjustly, amongst his adherents and ridiculed the acts of Urban as invalid.

5. But Urban, in the year in which the Franks first passed through Rome on their way to Jerusalem,[8] obtained the whole apostolic power with the aid of a certain most noble matron, Mathilda by name, who was then very powerful in her native region about Rome.

6. Guibert was then in Germany. Thus there were two popes over Rome, but whom to obey many did not know, nor from whom to seek counsel or who should heal the sick. Some favored one, some the other.

7. But it was clear to the intelligence of men that Urban was the better; for he is rightly considered better who controls his passions just as if they were his enemies.

8. Guibert as the archbishop of the city of

Ravenna was very rich. He was resplendent in pomp and wealth. It was remarkable that such riches did not satisfy him. Ought he to be considered by all an exemplar of right living who, a lover of ostentation, boldly presumes to usurp the sceptre of God's authority? Certainly this office is not to be seized by force but accepted with fear and humility.

9. Nor is it a wonder that the whole world was disquieted and disturbed. For if the Church of Rome, the source of correction for all of Christianity, is troubled by any disorder, then immediately the members subject to it derive the malady through the chief nerves and are weakened by suffering along with it.

10. Yes, truly this church, which is indeed our mother, at whose bosom we were reared, by whose example we profited, and by whose counsel we were strengthened, was rudely smitten by that proud Guibert. And when the head is thus struck the members are hurt immediately.

If the head is afflicted the other members suffer.

11. Moreover when the head was sick in this way the members were enfeebled with pain because in all parts of Europe peace, virtue, and faith were brutally trampled upon by stronger men and lesser, inside the church and out. It was necessary to put an end to all these evils and, in accordance with the plan initiated by Pope Urban, to turn against the pagans the fighting which up to now customarily went on among the Christians.

12. Now therefore I must turn my pen to history in order to tell clearly the uninformed about the journey of those going to Jerusalem, what happened to them, and how the undertaking and the labour gradually came to a successful conclusion with the help of God. I, Fulcher of Chartres, who went with the other pilgrims, afterwards diligently and carefully collected all this in my memory for the sake of posterity, just as I saw it with my own eyes.[9]

VI The Time of Departure of the Christians Together with the Names of the Leaders of the Pilgrims.

1. In the year of 1096 of the Lord's Incarnation and in the month of March following the council, which, as has been said, Pope Urban held during November in Auvergne, some who were more speedy in their preparation than others began to set out on the holy journey. Others followed in April or May, in June or in July, or even in August or September or October as they were able to secure the means to defray expenses.

2. In that year peace and a very great abundance of grain and wine existed in all countries by the grace of God, so that there was no lack of bread on the trip for those who had chosen to follow Him with their crosses in accordance with His commands.

3. Since it is fitting to remember the names of the leaders of the pilgrims at that time I mention Hugh the Great, the brother of King Philip of France, the first of the heroes to cross the sea. Hugh landed with his men near Durazzo, a city in Bulgaria,[10] but rashly advancing with a small force was captured there by the citizens and conducted to the emperor at Constantinople. Here he stayed for some time, being not entirely free.

4. After him Bohemond of Apulia, a son of Robert Guiscard, of the nation of the Normans, passed with his army over the same route.

5. Next Godfrey, Duke of Lorraine, traveled through Hungary with a large force.

6. Raymond, Count of the Provençals, with Goths and Gascons, and also Adhemar, Bishop of Le Puy, crossed through Dalmatia.

7. A certain Peter the Hermit, having gathered to himself a crowd of people on foot but only a few knights, was the first to pass through Hungary. Afterwards Walter the Penniless, who was certainly a very good soldier, was the commander of these people. Later he was killed with many of his companions between Nicomedia and Nicaea by the Turks.

8. In the month of October, Robert, Count of the Normans, a son of William, King of the English, began the journey, having collected a great army of Normans, English, and Bretons. With him went Stephen, the noble Count of Blois, his brother-in-law, and Robert, Count of the Flemings, with many other nobles.

9. Therefore since such a multitude came from all Western countries, little by little and day by day the army grew while on the march from a

numberless host into a group of armies. You could see a countless number from many lands and of many languages. However, they were not gathered into a single army until we reached the city of Nicaea.

XV The Arrival of the Franks at Antioch and the Vicissitudes of the Siege.

1. In the month of October the Franks came to Antioch in Syria, a city founded by Seleucus, son of Antiochus. Seleucus made it his capital. It was previously called Reblata. Moreover it lay on the other side of the river which they called the Fernus or Orontes.[11] Our tents were ordered pitched before the city between it and the first milestone. Here afterwards battles were very frequently fought which were most destructive to both sides. When the Turks rushed out from the city they killed many of our men, but when the tables were turned they grieved to find themselves beaten.

2. Antioch is certainly a very large city, well fortified and strongly situated. It could never be taken by enemies from without provided the inhabitants were supplied with food and were determined to defend it. There is in Antioch a much-renowned church dedicated to the honor of Peter the Apostle where he, raised to the episcopate, sat as bishop after he had received from the Lord Jesus the primacy of the church and the keys to the Kingdom of Heaven.

3. There is another church too, circular in form, built in honor of the Blessed Mary, together with others fittingly constructed. These had for a long time been under the control of the Turks, but God, foreseeing all, kept them intact for us so that one day He would be honored in them by ourselves.

4. The sea is, I think, about thirteen miles from Antioch. Because the Fernus River flows into the sea at that point, ships filled with goods from distant lands are brought up its channel as far as Antioch. Thus supplied with goods by sea and land, the city abounds with wealth of all kinds.

5. Our princes when they saw how hard it would be to take the city swore mutually to cooperate in a siege until, God willing, they took it by force or stratagem.

6. They found a number of boats in the aforesaid river. These they took and fashioned into a pontoon bridge over which they crossed to carry out their plans. Previously they had been unable to ford the river.

7. But the Turks, when they had looked about anxiously and saw that they were beset by such a multitude of Christians, feared that they could not possibly escape them. After they had consulted together, Aoxianus, the prince and Amir of Antioch, sent his son Sanxado to the Sultan, that is the Emperor of Persia, urging that he should aid them with all haste. The reason was that they had no hope of other help except from Mohammed their advocate. Sanxado in great haste carried out the mission assigned to him.

8. Those who remained within the city guarded it, waiting for the assistance for which they had asked while they frequently concocted many kinds of dangerous schemes against the Franks. Nevertheless the latter foiled the stratagems of the enemy as well as they could.

9. On a certain day it happened that seven hundred Turks were killed by the Franks, and thus those who had prepared snares for the Franks were by snares overcome.[12] For the power of God was manifest there. All of our men returned safely except one who was wounded by them.

10. Oh how many Christians in the city, Greeks, Syrians, and Armenians, did the Turks kill in rage and how many heads did they hurl over the walls with *petrariae* and *fundibula*[13] in view of the Franks! This grieved our men very much. The Turks hated these Christians, for they feared that somehow the latter might assist the Franks against a Turkish attack.

11. After the Franks besieged the city for some time and had scoured the country roundabout in search of food for themselves and were unable to find even bread to buy, they suffered great hunger. For this reason all were very much discouraged, and many secretly planned to withdraw from the siege and to flee by land or by sea.

12. But they had no money on which to live. They were even obliged to seek their sustenance far away and in great fear by separating themselves forty or fifty miles from the siege, and there in the mountains they were often killed by the Turks in ambush.

13. We felt that misfortunes had befallen the Franks because of their sins and that for this reason they were not able to take the city for so long a time. Luxury and avarice and pride and plunder had indeed vitiated them.

14. Then the Franks, having again consulted together, expelled the women from the army, the married as well as the unmarried, lest perhaps defiled by the sordidness of riotous living they should displease the Lord. These women then sought shelter for themselves in neighboring towns.

15. The rich as well as the poor were wretched because of starvation as well as of the slaughter, which daily occurred. Had not God, like a good pastor, held His sheep together, without doubt they would all have fled thence at once in spite of the fact that they had sworn to take the city. Many though, because of the scarcity of food, sought for many days in neighboring villages what was necessary for life; and they did not afterward return to the army but abandoned the siege entirely.

16. At that time we saw a remarkable reddish glow in the sky and besides felt a great quake in the earth, which rendered us all fearful. In addition many saw a certain sign in the shape of a cross, whitish in color, moving in a straight path toward the East.[14]

XVI The Miserable Poverty of the Christians and the Flight of the Count of Blois.

1. In the year of our Lord 1098, after the area around Antioch had been stripped completely bare by the large number of our people, both the old and the young were increasingly distressed by excessive hunger.

2. Then the starving people devoured the stalks of beans still growing in the fields, many kinds of herbs unseasoned with salt, and even thistles which because of the lack of firewood were not well cooked and therefore irritated the tongues of those eating them. They also ate horses, asses, camels, dogs, and even rats. The poorer people ate even the hides of animals and the seeds of grain found in manure.

3. The people for the love of God endured cold, heat, and torrents of rain. Their tents became old

and torn and rotten from the continuous rains. For this reason many people had no cover but the sky.

4. Just as gold is thrice tried in the fire and seven times purified [Psalm. 12:7], so I believe the elect were tried by the Lord and by such suffering were cleansed of their sins. For although the sword of the Assassin did not fail to do its deadly work, many of the people suffered long agony and gladly ran the full course of martyrdom. Perhaps they took consolation from the example of Holy Job who purging his soul by torments of the body always remembered God [Job 2:12]. When they struggled against the pagans they labored for God.

5. Although God, who creates all, orders all that He has created and sustains what he has ordered, governs with vigor and is able to destroy or repair whatever He wishes, I feel that at the cost of suffering to the Christians He wills that the pagans shall be destroyed, they who have so many times foully trod underfoot all which belongs to God although with His permission and as the people deserved. In truth He has permitted the Christians to be slain for the augmentation of their salvation, the Turks, however, for the damnation of their souls. But those of the Turks predestined to salvation it pleased God to have baptized by our priests. "For those whom He predestined, them He called and also glorified" [Rom. 8:30].

6. What then? Some of our men as you have heard about withdrew from a siege which was so difficult, some from want, some from cowardice, some from fear of death, first the poor, then the rich.

7. Then Stephen, Count of Blois, left the siege and went home to France by sea. We all grieved on this account because he was a very noble man and was mighty in arms. On the day following his departure the city of Antioch was surrendered to the Franks. If he had persevered he would have greatly rejoiced with the rest, for what he did was a disgrace to him. For a good beginning does not profit one if one does not end well. In things regarding God I shall be brief lest I might go astray, for in these matters I must be careful not to wander from the truth.

8. From this month of October, as was said, the

siege of the city continued throughout the following winter and spring until the month of June. The Turks and Franks alternately staged many attacks and counterattacks. They conquered and were conquered. We, however, won more often than they. Once it happened that many Turks in fleeing fell into the Fernus River and miserably drowned.[15] On this side of the river and on the other side both people fought many times.

9. Our princes constructed forts in front of the city. By frequent sallies from them our men sturdily held back the Turks. As a result they often denied pasturage to the animals of the enemy. Nothing was brought in from the Armenians of the outlying areas; yet they often acted to our detriment.

XVII The Surrender of the City of Antioch.

1. When, however, God, appeased no doubt by their prayers, was pleased to end the labour of His people who had daily poured forth beseeching supplications to Him, in His love He granted that through the treachery of these same Turks the city should be secretly delivered up and restored to the Christians. Hear therefore of a treachery, and yet not a treachery.

2. Our Lord appeared to a certain Turk predestined by His grace and said to him, "Arise, you who sleep! I command you to return the city to the Christians." Although wondering about it the man kept the vision a secret.

3. Again the Lord appeared to him. "Return the city to the Christians," He said, "for I who command this am Christ indeed." Wondering therefore what he should do the man went to his master, the prince of Antioch, and made known the vision to him. The latter replied, "Do you wish, stupid man, to obey a ghost?" The man returned, and remained silent.

4. Again the Lord appeared unto him, saying, "Why have you not done what I have commanded? It is not for you to hesitate, for I who command this am the Lord of all." The Turk no longer doubting discreetly made a plot with our men by which they should obtain the city.

5. When this agreement was made, the Turk gave his son as a hostage to the Lord Bohemond to whom this plan had first been proposed and whom he had first influenced. On the appointed night the Turk admitted over the wall twenty of our men by means of rope ladders. At once, without delay, the gate was opened. The Franks, who were ready, entered the city. Forty more of our soldiers who had already entered by means of the ropes slew sixty Turks whom they found guarding the towers. Then all the Franks shouted together in a loud voice, "God wills it! God wills it!" For this was our signal cry when we were about to accomplish any good enterprise.

6. Hearing this the Turks were all extremely terrified. The Franks immediately began to attack the city, the dawn then growing lighter. When the Turks first noticed Bohemond's red banner, now waving aloft, the great tumult already raging round about, the trumpets of the Franks sounding from the top of the wall, and the Franks running about through the streets with drawn swords and savagely killing people, they were bewildered and began to flee here and there. As many Turks as could fled to the citadel situated on a lofty cliff.

7. Our common people indiscriminately seized whatever they found in the streets and houses, but the knights, who were experienced in the business of warfare, continued to seek out and kill the Turks.

8. The Amir of Antioch, Aoxianus by name, was beheaded while fleeing by an Armenian peasant, who at once brought the severed head to the Franks.

XVIII The Discovery of the Lance.

1. It happened moreover that after the city was taken a certain man found a lance in a hole in the ground under the Church of the blessed Apostle Peter. When it was discovered the man asserted that it was the very lance with which Longinus had, according to the Scriptures, pierced Christ in the right side [Joan. 19:34]. He said that this had been revealed to him by St. Andrew the Apostle.

2. And when it had been discovered and the man himself told the Bishop of Le Puy and Count Raymond, the Bishop thought the story false, but the Count hoped that it was true.

3. All the people when they heard this exulted

and glorified God. For almost a hundred days[16] the lance was held in great veneration and was carried gloriously by Count Raymond, who guarded it. Then it happened that many of the priests and laity hesitated, thinking that this was not the Lord's lance but another one dishonestly found by that doltish man.

4.   Wherefore after three days of fasting and prayers had been decided upon and finished by all, they lighted a heap of wood in the middle of the field in front of the town of Archas in the eighth month after the capture of Antioch; the bishops made the judicial benediction over the same fire; and the finder of the lance quickly ran clear through the midst of the burning pile to prove his honesty, as he had requested. When the man passed through the flames and emerged, they saw that he was guilty, for his skin was burned and they knew that within he was mortally hurt. This was demonstrated by the outcome, for on the twelfth day he died, seared by the guilt of his conscience.

5.   And since everyone had venerated the lance for the honor and love of God, when the ordeal was over those who formerly believed in it were now incredulous and very sad. Nevertheless Count Raymond preserved it for a long time afterward.

XXVI The Site of Jerusalem.

1.   The city of Jerusalem is located in a mountainous region which is devoid of trees, streams, and springs excepting only the Pool of Siloam, which is a bowshot from the city. Sometimes it has enough water, and sometimes a deficiency due to a slight drainage. This little spring is in the valley at the foot of Mount Zion in the course of the Brook Kedron which, in winter time, is accustomed to flow through the center of the Valley of Jehoshaphat.

2.   The many cisterns inside the city, reserved for winter rains, have a sufficiency of water. More, at which men and beasts are refreshed, are also found outside the city.

3.   It is generally conceded that the city is laid out in such proper proportion that it seems neither too small nor too large. Its width from wall to wall is that of four bowshots. To the west is the Tower of David with the city wall on each flank; to the south is Mount Zion a little closer than a bowshot; and to the east, the Mount of Olives a thousand paces outside the city.

4.   The aforesaid Tower of David is of solid masonry half-way up, of large squared blocks sealed with molten lead. Fifteen or twenty men, if well supplied with food, could defend it from all assaults of an enemy.

5.   In the same city is the Temple of the Lord, round in shape, built where Solomon in ancient times erected the earlier magnificent Temple. Although it can in no way be compared in appearance to the former building, still this one is of marvelous workmanship and most splendid appearance.

6.   The Church of the Lord's Sepulcher is likewise circular in form. It was never closed in at the top but always admits the light through a permanent aperture ingeniously fashioned under the direction of a skillful architect.

7.   I cannot, I dare not, I know not how to enumerate the many objects which it now contains or contained in the past lest in some way I deceive those reading or hearing about the matter. In the middle of the Temple, when we first entered it and for fifteen years thereafter, was a certain native rock. It was said that the Ark of the Lord's Covenant along with the urn and tables of Moses was sealed inside of it, that Josiah, King of Judah, ordered it to be placed there saying, "You shall never carry it from this place" [II Paralip. 35:3]. For he foresaw the future Captivity.

8.   But this contradicts what we read in the descriptions of Jeremiah, in the second book of the Maccabees, that he himself hid it in Arabia, saying that it would not be found until many peoples should be gathered together. Jeremiah was a contemporary of King Josiah; however, the king died before Jeremiah [II Mach. 2:4-9].

9.   They said that the angel of the Lord had stood upon the aforesaid rock [II Paralip. 3:1; II Sam. 24:18-25] and destroyed the people because of the enumeration of the people foolishly made by David and displeasing to the Lord [II Sam. 24:1-2, 15-17; I Paralip. 21:15]. Moreover this rock because it disfigured the Temple of the Lord was afterwards covered over and paved with marble. Now an altar is placed above it, and there the

clergy have fitted up a choir. All the Saracens held the Temple of the Lord in great veneration. Here rather than elsewhere they preferred to say the prayers of their faith although such prayers were wasted because offered to an idol set up in the name of Mohammed. They allowed no Christian to enter the Temple.

10. Another temple, called the Temple of Solomon, is large and wonderful, but it is not the one that Solomon built. This one, because of our poverty, could not be maintained in the condition in which we found it. Wherefore it is already in large part destroyed.

11. There were gutters in the streets of the city through which in time of rain all filth was washed away.

12. The Emperor Aeilus Hadrian[17] decorated this city magnificently and fittingly adorned the streets and squares with pavements. In his honor Jerusalem was called Aelia. For these and many other reasons Jerusalem is a most renowned and glorious city.

XXVII The Siege of the City of Jerusalem.

1. When the Franks beheld the city and realized that it would be difficult to take, our leaders ordered wooden ladders to be made. By carrying these to the wall and erecting them, and climbing with fierce energy to the top of the wall, they hoped with the help of God to enter the city.

2. These ladders were made, and on the seventh day after the arrival our leaders gave the command for the attack. At the sound of the trumpets at daybreak our men attacked the city on all sides with remarkable energy. But when they had continued the attack up to the sixth hour of the day and were not able to enter by means of the ladders which they had prepared because the ladders were too few, they reluctantly gave up the assault.

3. Then after consultation our leaders ordered the engineers to make machines of war. They hoped when these were moved up to the walls to attain the desired result with the help of God. Therefore this was done.

4. Meanwhile, however, our men did not suffer from lack of bread or meat. Yet because the area was dry, unwatered, and without streams our men as well as their beasts suffered for lack of water to drink. Wherefore, because necessity demanded it, they brought water daily to the siege from four or five miles away, laboriously carrying it in the skins of animals.

5. When the machines were ready, namely battering rams and *scrofae*, our men again prepared to attack the city. Among those contrivances they put together a tower made of short pieces of timber because there was no large stuff in that area. When the command was given they transported the tower, in sections, by night to a corner of the city. In the morning they quickly erected it, all assembled, not far from the wall, together with *petrariae* and other auxiliary weapons which they had prepared. After they had set it up and well protected it on the outside with hides, they pushed it little by little nearer the wall.

6. Then some soldiers, few it is true but brave, climbed upon the tower at a signal from the trumpet. The Saracens nevertheless set up a defense against them. With *fundibula* they hurled small burning brands soaked in oil and grease against the tower and the soldiers in it. Therefore many on both sides met sudden death in this fighting.

7. From the side where they were located, namely Mount Zion, Count Raymond and his men launched a heavy attack with their machines. From the other side where Duke Godfrey, Count Robert of Normandy, and Robert of Flanders were stationed there was still greater assault upon the wall. These were the events of that day.

8. The next day at the sound of the trumpets they undertook the same task with still more vigor. As a result they made a breach in the wall by battering it in one place with rams. The Saracens had suspended two timbers in front of the battlements and tied them there with ropes as a protection against the stones hurled at them by their assailants. But what they did for their advantage later turned to their detriment, by Divine Providence. For when the Franks had moved the aforesaid tower up to the wall they used falchions to cut the ropes by means of which the two beams were suspended. With these timbers they contrived a bridge and skillfully extended it from the tower to the top of the wall.

9. Already one stone tower on the wall, at which those working our machines had thrown flaming brands, was afire. This fire, gradually fed by the wooden material in the tower, caused so much smoke and flame that none of the city guards could remain there any longer.

10. Soon therefore the Franks gloriously entered the city at noon on the day known as Dies Veneris, the day in which Christ redeemed the whole world on the Cross. Amid the sound of trumpets and with everything in an uproar they attacked boldly, shouting "God help us!" At once they raised a banner on the top of the wall. The pagans were completely terrified, for they all exchanged their former boldness for headlong flight through the narrow streets of the city. The more swiftly they fled the more swiftly they were pursued.

11. Count Raymond and his men, who were strongly pressing the offensive in another part of the city, did not notice this until they saw the Saracens jumping off from the top of the wall. When they noticed it they ran with the greatest exultation as fast as they could into the city and joined their companions in pursuing and slaying their wicked enemies without cessation.

12. Some of the latter, Arabs as well as Ethiopians, fled into the Tower of David, and others shut themselves up in the Temples of the Lord and of Solomon. In the courts of these buildings a fierce attack was pressed upon the Saracens. There was no place where they could escape our swordsmen.

13. Many of the Saracens who had climbed to the top of the Temple of Solomon in their flight were shot to death with arrows and fell headlong from the roof. Nearly ten thousand were beheaded in this Temple. If you had been there your feet would have been stained to the ankles in the blood of the slain. What shall I say? None of them were left alive. Neither women nor children were spared.

XXVIII The Spoils Taken by the Christians.

1. How astonishing it would have seemed to you to see our squires and footmen, after they had discovered the trickery of the Saracens, split open the bellies of those they had just slain in order to extract from the intestines the bezants which the Saracens had gulped down their loathsome throats while alive! For the same reason a few days later our men made a great heap of corpses and burned them to ashes in order to find more easily the above-mentioned gold.

2. And also Tancred rushed into the Temple of the Lord and seized much gold and silver and many precious stones. But he restored these things, putting them or their equivalent back into the holy place. This was in spite of the fact that no divine services were conducted there at that time. The Saracens had practiced their rule of idolatry there with superstitious rite and moreover had not allowed any Christian to enter.

3. With drawn swords our men ran through the city
   Not sparing anyone, even those begging for mercy.
   The crowd fell just as rotten apples fall
   From shaken branches and acorns from swaying oaks.

2. *The account of Solomon Bar Simson*

SOLOMON BAR SIMSON WAS A MEMBER OF THE JEWISH COMMUNITY OF Mainz who wrote his *Chronicle* after 1140. Subsequent additions were made to the *Chronicle*, including lists of martyrs of Speyer, Worms, and Mainz and details of the self-immolations of Jewish communities.

Source: Shlomo Eidelberg, *The Jews and the Crusaders: Hebrew Chronicles of the First and Second Crusades* (Madison: the University of Wisconsin Press, 1977).

I will now recount the event of this persecution in other martyred communities as well—the extent to which they clung to the Lord, God of their fathers, bearing witness to His Oneness to their last breath.

In the year four thousand eight hundred and fifty-six, the year one thousand twenty-eight of our exile, in the eleventh year of the cycle Ranu, the year in which we anticipated salvation and solace, in accordance with the prophecy of Jeremiah: "Sing with gladness for Jacob, and shout at the head of the nations," etc.—this year turned instead to sorrow and groaning, weeping and outcry. Inflicted upon the Jewish People were the many evils related in all the admonitions; those enumerated in Scripture as well as those unwritten were visited upon us.

At this time arrogant people, a people of strange speech, a nation bitter and impetuous, Frenchmen and Germans, set out for the Holy City, which had been desecrated by barbaric nations, there to seek their house of idolatry and banish the Ishmaelites and other denizens of the land and conquer the land for themselves. They decorated themselves prominently with their signs, placing a profane symbol—a horizontal line over a vertical one—on the vestments of every man and woman whose heart yearned to go on the stray path to the grave of their Messiah. Their ranks swelled until the number of men, women, and children exceeded a locust horde covering the earth; of them it was said: "The locusts have no king [yet they go forth all of them by bands]." Now it came to pass that as they passed through the towns where Jews dwelled, they said to one another: "Look now, we are going a long way to seek out the profane shrine and to avenge ourselves on the Ishmaelites, when here, in our very midst, are the Jews—they whose forefathers murdered and crucified him for no reason. Let us first avenge ourselves on them and exterminate them from among the nations so that the name of Israel will no longer be remembered, or let them adopt our faith and acknowledge the offspring of promiscuity."[1]

When the Jewish communities became aware of their intentions, they resorted to the custom of our ancestors, repentance, prayer, and charity. The hands of the Holy Nation turned faint at this time, their hearts melted, and their strength flagged. They hid in their innermost rooms to escape the swirling sword. They subjected themselves to great endurance, abstaining from food and drink for three consecutive days and nights, and then fasting many days from sunrise to sunset, until their skin was shriveled and dry as wood upon their bones. And they cried out loudly and bitterly to God.

But their Father did not answer them; He obstructed their prayers, concealing Himself in a cloud through which their prayers could not pass, and He abhorred their tent, and He removed them out of His sight—all of this having been decreed by Him to take place "in the day when I visit"; and this was the generation that had been chosen by Him to be His portion, for they had the strength and the fortitude to stand in His Sanctuary, and fulfill His word, and sanctify His Great Name in His world. It is of such as these that King David said: "Bless the Lord, ye angels of His, ye almighty in strength, that fulfil His word," etc.

That year, Passover fell on Thursday, and the New Moon of the following month, Iyar, fell on

Friday and the Sabbath. On the eighth day of Iyar, on the Sabbath, the foe attacked the community of Speyer and murdered eleven holy souls who sanctified their Creator on the holy Sabbath and refused to defile themselves by adopting the faith of their foe. There was a distinguished, pious woman there who slaughtered herself in sanctification of God's Name. She was the first among all the communities of those who were slaughtered. The remainder were saved by the local bishop[2] without defilement [i.e., baptism], as described above.

On the twenty-third of Iyar they attacked the community of Worms. The community was then divided into two groups; some remained in their homes and others fled to the local bishop seeking refuge.[3] Those who remained in their homes were set upon by the steppe-wolves who pillaged men, women, and infants, children and old people. They pulled down the stairways and destroyed the houses, looting and plundering; and they took the Torah Scroll, trampled it in the mud, and tore and burned it. The enemy devoured the children of Israel with open maw.

Seven days later, on the New Moon of Sivan— the very day on which the Children of Israel arrived at Mount Sinai to receive the Torah— those Jews who were still in the court of the bishop were subject to great anguish. The enemy dealt them the same cruelty as the first group and put them to the sword. The Jews, inspired by the valor of their brethren, similarly chose to be slain in order to sanctify the Name before the eyes of all, and exposed their throats for their heads to be severed for the glory of the Creator. There were also those who took their own lives, thus fulfilling the verse: "The mother was dashed in pieces with her children." Fathers fell upon their sons, being slaughtered upon one another, and they slew one another—each man his kin, his wife and children; bridegrooms slew their betrothed, and merciful women their only children. They all accepted the divine decree wholeheartedly and, as they yielded up their souls to the Creator, cried out: "Hear, O Israel, the Lord is our God, the Lord is One." The enemy stripped them naked, dragged them along, and then cast them off, sparing only a small number whom they forcibly baptized in their profane waters. The number of

those slain during the two days was approximately eight hundred—and they were all buried naked. It is of these that the Prophet Jeremiah lamented: "They that were brought up in scarlet embrace dunghills." I have already cited their names above.[4] May God remember them for good.

When the saints, the pious ones of the Most High, the holy community of Mainz, whose merit served as shield and protection for all the communities and whose fame had spread throughout the many provinces, heard that some of the community of Speyer had been slain and that the community of Worms had been attacked a second time,[5] and that the sword would soon reach them, their hands became faint and their hearts melted and became as water. They cried out to the Lord with all their hearts, saying: "O Lord, God of Israel, will You completely annihilate the remnant of Israel? Where are all your wonders which our forefathers related to us, saying, 'Did You not bring us up from Egypt and from Babylonia and rescue us on numerous occasions?' How, then, have You now forsaken and abandoned us, O Lord, giving us over into the hands of evil Edom so that they may destroy us? Do not remove Yourself from us, for adversity is almost upon us and there is no one to aid us."

The leaders of the Jews gathered together and discussed various ways of saving themselves. They said, "Let us elect elders so that we may know how to act, for we are consumed by this great evil." The elders decided to ransom the community by generously giving of their money and bribing the various princes and deputies and bishops and governors. Then, the community leaders who were respected by the local bishop[6] approached him and his officers and servants to negotiate this matter. They asked: "What shall we do about the news we have received regarding the slaughter of our brethren in Speyer and Worms?" They [the Gentiles] replied: "Heed our advice and bring all your money into our treasury. You, your wives, and your children, and all your belongings shall come into the courtyard of the bishop until the hordes have passed by. Thus will you be saved from the errant ones."

Actually, they gave this advice so as to herd us together and hold us like fish that are caught in an evil net, and then to turn us over to the enemy, while taking our money. This is what actually happened in the end, and "the outcome is proof of the intentions." The bishop assembled his ministers and courtiers—mighty ministers, the noblest in the land—for the purpose of helping us; for at first it had been his desire to save us with all his might, since we had given him and his ministers and servants a large bribe in return for their promise to help us. Ultimately, however, all the bribes and entreaties were of no avail to protect us on the day of wrath and misfortune.

It was at this time that Duke Godfrey [of Bouillon], may his bones be ground to dust, arose in the hardness of his spirit, driven by a spirit of wantonness to go with those journeying to the profane shrine, vowing to go on this journey only after avenging the blood of the crucified one by shedding Jewish blood and completely eradicating any trace of those bearing the name "Jew," thus assuaging his own burning wrath. To be sure, there arose someone to repair the breach—a God-fearing man who had been bound to the most holy of altars—called Rabbi Kalonymos, the *Parnass* of the community of Mainz.[7] He dispatched a messenger to King Henry in the kingdom of Pula, where the king had been dwelling during the past nine years, and related all that had happened.

The king was enraged and dispatched letters to all the ministers, bishops and governors of all the provinces of his realm, as well as to Duke Godfrey, containing words of greeting and commanding them to do no bodily harm to the Jews and to provide them with help and refuge. The evil duke then swore that he had never intended to do them harm. The Jews of Cologne nevertheless bribed him with five hundred *zekukim* of silver, as did the Jews of Mainz. The duke assured them of his support and promised them peace.

However, God the maker of peace, turned aside and averted His eyes from His people, and consigned them to the sword. No prophet, seer, or man of wise heart was able to comprehend how the sin of the people infinite in number was deemed so great as to cause the destruction of so many lives in the various Jewish communities. The martyrs endured the extreme penalty normally inflicted only upon one guilty of murder.

Yet, it must be stated with certainty that God is a righteous judge, and we are to blame.

Then the evil waters prevailed.[8] The enemy unjustly accused them of evil acts they did not do, declaring: "You are the children of those who killed our object of veneration, hanging him on a tree; and he himself had said: 'There will yet come a day when my children will come and avenge my blood.' We are his children and it is therefore obligatory for us to avenge him since you are the ones who rebel and disbelieve in him. Your God has never been at peace with you. Although He intended to deal kindly with you, you have conducted yourselves improperly before Him. God has forgotten you and is no longer desirous of you since you are a stubborn nation. Instead, He has departed from you and has taken us for His portion, casting His radiance upon us."

When we heard these words, our hearts trembled and moved out of their places. We were dumb with silence, abiding in darkness, like those long dead, waiting for the Lord to look forth and behold from heaven.

And Satan—the Pope of evil Rome—also came and proclaimed to all the nations[9] believing in that stock of adultery—these are the stock of Seir—that they should assemble and ascend to Jerusalem so as to conquer the city, and journey to the tomb of the superstition whom they call their god. Satan came and mingled with the nations, and they gathered as one man to fulfill the command, coming in great numbers like the grains of sand upon the seashore, the noise of them clamorous as a whirlwind and a storm. When the drops of the bucket had assembled, they took evil counsel against the people of the Lord and said: "Why should we concern ourselves with going to war against the Ishmaelites dwelling about Jerusalem, when in our midst is a people who disrespect our god—indeed, their ancestors are those who crucified him. Why should we let them live and tolerate their dwelling among us? Let us commence by using our swords against them and proceed upon our stray path."

The heart of the people of our God grew faint and their spirit flagged, for many sore injuries had been inflicted upon them and they had been smitten repeatedly. They now came supplicating to God and fasting, and their hearts melted within them. But the Lord did as He declared, for we had sinned before Him, and He forsook the sanctuary of Shiloh—the Temple-in-Miniature— which He had placed among His people who dwelt in the midst of alien nations. His wrath was kindled and He drew the sword against them, until they remained but as the flagstaff upon the mountaintop and as the ensign on the hill, and He gave over His nation into captivity and trampled them underfoot. See, O Lord, and consider to whom Thou hast done thus: to Israel, a nation despised and pillaged, Your chosen portion! Why have You uplifted the shield of its enemies, and why have they gained in strength? Let all hear, for I cry out in anguish; the ears of all that hear me shall be seared: How has the staff of might been broken, the rod of glory—the sainted community comparable to fine gold, the community of Mainz! It was caused by the Lord to test those that fear Him, to have them endure the yoke of His pure fear.

One day a Gentile woman came, bringing a goose which she had raised since it was newborn. The goose would accompany her wherever she went. The Gentile woman now called out to all passersby: "Look, the goose understands my intention to go straying and desires to accompany me."

At that time, the errant ones gathered against us, and the burghers and peasants said to us: "Where is He in Whom you place your trust? How will you be saved? Now you shall see that these are the wonders which the crucified one works for them [the Crusaders] to signal that they should exact vengeance from their enemies." And they all came with swords to destroy us. But some of the leading burghers stood up to them, and prevented them from harming us.

At this point, the errant ones all united and battled the burghers, and the Gentiles fought with each other, until a Crusader was slain. Seeing this the Crusaders cried out: "The Jews have caused this," and nearly all of them reassembled, reviling and deriding them with the intention of falling upon them.

When the holy people saw this, their hearts melted. Upon hearing their words, the Jews, old and young alike, said: "Would that our death might be by the hands of the Lord, so that we should not perish at the hands of the enemies of the Lord! For He is a Merciful King, the sole sovereign of the universe."

They abandoned their houses; neither did they go to the synagogue save on the Sabbath preceding the month of Sivan—the final Sabbath before the evil decree befell us—when a small number of them entered the synagogue to pray. Rabbi Judah, son of Rabbi Isaac, also came there to pray with that *minyan*.[10] They wept exceedingly, to the point of exhaustion, for they saw that it was a decree of the King of Kings, not to be nullified.

A venerable student, Baruch, son of Isaac, was there, and he said to us: "Know in truth and honesty this decree has been issued against us, and we cannot be saved; for this past night I and my son-in-law Judah heard the souls praying in the synagogue in a loud voice, like weeping. When we heard the sound, we thought at first that perhaps some of the community had come from the court of the bishop to pray in the synagogue at midnight. In our anguish and bitterness of heart we ran to the door of the synagogue to see who was praying. The door was closed. We heard the sound and the loud wailing, but we did not understand a word of what was being said. We returned dismayed to our house—for it was close to the synagogue. Upon hearing this, we cried out: 'Ah Lord God! Wilt Thou make a full end of the remnant of Israel?'" Then they went and reported the occurrence to their brethren who were concealed in the court of the count and in the bishop's chambers, and all knew that this decree was of God. Thereupon, they, too, wept exceedingly, declaring themselves ready to accept God's judgment, saying: "Righteous art Thou, O Lord, and upright are Thy judgments."

On the New Moon of Sivan, Count Emicho,[11] the oppressor of all the Jews—may his bones be ground to dust between iron millstones—arrived outside the city with a mighty horde of errant ones and peasants. They encamped in tents, since the gates of the city were closed, for he, too, had said: "I desire to follow the stray course." He was made leader of the hordes and concocted a tale that an apostle of the crucified one had come to him and made a sign on his flesh to inform him that when he arrived at Magna Graecia, he [Jesus] himself would appear and place the kingly crown upon his head, and Emicho would vanquish his foes. This man was chief of our oppressors. He showed no mercy to the aged, or youths, or maidens, babes or sucklings—not even the sick. And he made the people of the Lord like dust to be trodden underfoot, killing their young men by the sword and disemboweling their pregnant women. They encamped outside the city for two days.

At this time, when the evildoer arrived at Mainz on his way to Jerusalem, the elders of the Jewish community approached their bishop, Ruthard,[12] and bribed him with three hundred *zekukim* of silver. Ruthard had intended to journey to the villages that were subject to the authority of the bishops, but the Jewish community came and bribed and entreated him, until they persuaded him to remain in Mainz, and he took the entire community into his inner chamber, with the words: "I have agreed to aid you." The count, too, declared: "I also wish to remain here in order to help you, but you will have to provide all our needs until those who bear the symbol have passed"; and the community agreed to these terms.

The two of them—the bishop and the count—thereupon acceded to the request of the Jews and said: "We shall die with you or remain alive with you." The community then said: "Since these two who are close to us have granted our request, let us now send out money to the evildoer Emicho, and give him letters of safe conduct so that the communities along the route will honor him. Perhaps the Lord will intercede in His abundant grace and cause him to refrain from his present intentions. It is for this very purpose that we have generously expended our money, giving the bishop, his officers, his servants, and the burghers about four hundred *zekukim* of silver." We dispatched seven pounds of gold to the evil Emicho—so as to aid ourselves, but it was of no avail whatever, and up to the present time we have had no respite from our affliction. We were not even comparable to Sodom and Gomorrah; for in their case they were offered reprieve if they could produce at least ten righteous people, whereas in our case not twenty, not even ten, were sought.

On the third day of Sivan,[13] a day of sanctification and abstinence for Israel in preparation for receiving the Torah, the very day on which our Master Moses, may he rest in peace, said: "Be ready against the third day"—on that very day the community of Mainz, saints of the Most High, withdrew from each other in sanctity and purity, and sanctified themselves to ascend to God all together. Those who had been "pleasant in their lives ... in their death they were not divided," for all of them were gathered in the courtyard of the bishop. God's wrath was kindled against His people, and He fulfilled the intention of the errant ones, who succeeded in their purpose; and all our wealth did not avail us, nor did our fasting, self-affliction, lamenting, or charity, and no one was found to stand in the breach—neither teacher nor prince—and even the holy Torah did not shelter its scholars. "And the daughter of Zion was shorn of all her splendor"—this refers to Mainz. Silenced were the voices of the leaders of the flock, "those who wage war," they that sway the many to righteousness; and silenced was the city of praise, the metropolis of joy, which had generously distributed great sums of money to the poor. An iron stylus writing upon a folio would not suffice to record her numerous good deeds extending back to ancient times—the city in which there were to be found simultaneously Torah and greatness and riches and glory and wisdom and modesty and good deeds, where "prohibition was added upon prohibition" so as to assure scrupulous adherence to the teaching of the Talmud: now this wisdom was completely destroyed, as happened to the dwellers of Jerusalem at the time of its destruction.

At midday the evil Emicho, oppressor of the Jews, came to the gate with his entire horde. The townspeople opened the gate to him, and the enemies of the Lord said to one another: "See, they have opened the gate for us; now let us avenge the blood of the crucified one."

When the people of the Holy Covenant, the saints, the fearers of the Most High, saw the great multitude, a vast horde of them, as the sand upon the seashore, they clung to their Creator. They donned their armor and their weapons of war, adults and children alike, with Rabbi Kalonymos, the son of Rabbi Meshullam, the *Parnass*, at their head. But, as a result of their sufferings and fasts, they did not have the strength to withstand the onslaught of the foe. The troops and legions surged in like a streaming river until finally Mainz was completely overrun from end to end. Emicho had it rumored that the enemy was to be driven from the city, and the Lord's panic was great within the city.

The Jews armed themselves in the inner court of the bishop, and they all advanced toward the gate to fight against the errant ones and the burghers. The two sides fought against each other around the gate, but as a result of their transgressions the enemy overpowered them and captured the gate. The hand of the Lord rested heavily on His people, and all the Gentiles assembled against the Jews in the courtyard to exterminate them. Our people's strength flagged when they saw that the hand of evil Edom was prevailing against them. The bishop's people, who had promised to help them, being as broken reedstaffs, were the first to flee, so as to cause them to fall into the hands of the enemy. The bishop himself fled from his church, for they wanted to kill him, too, because he had spoken in favor of the Jews. The enemy entered the courtyard on the third day of the week—a day of darkness and gloom, a day of clouds and thick darkness; let darkness and the shadow of death claim it for their own. Let God not inquire after it from above, nor let the light shine upon it. Alas for the day on which we saw the torment of our soul! O stars—why did you not withhold your light? Has not Israel been compared to the stars and the twelve constellations, according to the number of Jacob's sons? Why, then, did you not withhold your light from shining for the enemy who sought to eradicate the name of Israel?

When the people of the Sacred Covenant saw that the Heavenly decree had been issued and that the enemy had defeated them and were entering the courtyard, they all cried out together—old and young, maidens and children, menservants and maids—to their Father in Heaven. They wept for themselves and for their lives and proclaimed the justness of the Heavenly judgment, and they said to one another: "Let us be of good courage and bear the yoke of the Holy Creed, for now the enemy can only slay us by the sword, and death by the sword is the lightest of the four deaths. We shall then merit eternal life, and our souls will abide in the Garden of Eden in the presence of the great luminous speculum forever."

All of them declared willingly and wholeheartedly, "After all things, there is no questioning the ways of the Holy One, blessed be He and blessed be His Name, Who has given us His Torah and has commanded us to allow ourselves to be killed and slain in witness to the Oneness of His Holy Name. Happy are we if we fulfill His will, and happy is he who is slain or slaughtered and who dies attesting the Oneness of His Name. Such a one is destined for the World-to-Come, where he will sit in the realm of the saints—Rabbi Akiba and his companions, pillars of the universe, who were killed in witness to His Name. Moreover—for such a one a world of darkness is exchanged for a world of light, a world of sorrow for one of joy, a transitory world for an eternal world."

Then in a great voice they all cried out as one: "We need tarry no longer, for the enemy is already upon us. Let us hasten and offer ourselves as a sacrifice before God. Anyone possessing a knife should examine it to see that it is not defective, and let him then proceed to slaughter us in sanctification of the Unique and Eternal One, then slaying himself—either cutting his throat or thrusting the knife into his stomach."

Upon entering the courtyard, the enemy encountered some of perfect piety, including Rabbi Isaac, son of Rabbi Moses, uprooter of mountains. He extended his neck and was the first to be decapitated. The others wrapped themselves in their fringed prayer shawls and sat in the courtyard waiting to expedite the will of their Creator, not wishing to flee within the chambers just to be saved for temporal life, for lovingly they accepted Heaven's judgment. The foe hurled stones and arrows at them, but they did not scurry to flee; the enemy smote all whom they found there with their swords, causing slaughter and destruction.

Those Jews in the chambers, seeing what the enemy had inflicted upon the saints, all cried out: "There is none like our God unto whom it would be better to offer our lives." The women girded their loins with strength and slew their own sons and daughters, and then themselves. Many men also mustered their strength and slaughtered their wives and children and infants. The most gentle and tender of women slaughtered the child of her delight. They all arose, man and woman alike, and slew one another. The young maidens, the brides, and the bridegrooms looked out through the windows and cried out in a great voice: "Look and behold, O Lord, what we are doing to sanctify Thy Great Name, in order not to exchange You for a crucified scion who was despised, abominated, and held in contempt in his own generation, a bastard son conceived by a menstruating and wanton mother."

Thus the precious children of Zion, the people of Mainz, were tested with ten trials as was our Father Abraham, and as Hananiah, Mishael, and Azariah were. They, too, bound their children in sacrifice, as Abraham did his son Isaac, and willingly accepted upon themselves the yoke of fear of Heaven, of the King of Kings, the Blessed Holy One. Refusing to gainsay their faith and replace the fear of our King with an abominable stock, bastard son of a menstruating and wanton mother, they extended their necks for slaughter and offered up their pure souls to their Father in Heaven. The saintly and pious women acted in a similar manner, extending their necks to each other in willing sacrifice in witness to the Oneness of God's name—and each man likewise to his son and brother, brother to sister, mother to son and daughter, neighbor to neighbor and friend, bridegroom to bride, fiancé to his betrothed; each first sacrificed the other and then in turn yielded to be sacrificed, until the streams of blood touched and mingled, and the blood of husbands joined with that of their wives, the blood of fathers with that of their sons, the blood of brothers with that of their sisters, the blood of teachers with that of their pupils, the blood of bridegrooms with that of their brides, the blood of community deacons with that of their scribes, the blood of babes and sucklings with that of their mothers—all killed and slaughtered in witness to the Oneness of the Venerated and Awesome Name.

Let the ears hearing this and its like be seared, for who has heard or seen the likes of it? Inquire and seek: was there ever such a mass sacrificial offering since the time of Adam? Did it ever occur that there were a thousand and one offerings on one single day—all of them comparable to the sacrifice of Isaac, the son of Abraham? The earth trembled over just one offering that occurred on the myrrh mountain—it is said: "Behold, the valiant ones cry without," and the heavens are darkened. What have they [the martyrs] done? Why did the heavens not darken and the stars not withhold their radiance, why did not the sun and the moon turn dark? On a single day—the third of Sivan, the third day of the week—one thousand and one hundred[14] holy souls were killed and slaughtered, babes and sucklings who had not sinned or transgressed, the souls of innocent poor people. Wilt Thou restrain Thyself for these things, O Lord? It was for You that innumerable souls were killed! May You avenge the spilt blood of your servants, in our days and before our very eyes—Amen—and speedily!

The day the diadem of Israel fell, the students of the Torah fell, and the outstanding scholars passed away. The glory of the Torah fell, as it is written: "He hath cast down from heaven unto the earth the splendor of Israel." Gone were the sin-fearers, gone were the men of virtuous deed; ended were the radiance of wisdom and purity and abstinence; [ended was] the glory of the priesthood and of the men of perfect faith— repairers of the breach, nullifiers of evil decrees, and placaters of the wrath of their Creator; diminished were the ranks of those who give charity in secret. Gone was truth; gone were the explicators of the Word and the Law; fallen were the people of eminence and the sage—all on this day, on which so many sorrows befell us and we could turn neither to the right nor to the left from the fury of the oppressor. For since the day on which the Second Temple was destroyed, their like had not arisen, nor shall there be their like again—for they sanctified and bore witness to the Oneness of God's Name with all their heart and with all their soul and with all their might. Happy are they and happy is their lot, for all of them are destined for life eternal in the World-to-Come—and may my place be amongst them!

3. The account of Ibn Al-Athir

IBN AL-ATHIR (1160-1233) WAS A MESOPOTAMIAN INTELLECTUAL who wrote a history of the Muslim world. His account of the First Crusade is drawn from earlier sources and is colored by his own experience of later wars against the Latins, especially those of Saladin (1138-1193).

Source: Francesco Gabrieli (Italian translation), translated by E.J. Costello *Arab Historians of the Crusades* (Berkeley: University of California Press, 1969).

The Franks Seize Antioch (X, 185-8)

The power of the Franks first became apparent when in the year 478/1085-86 they invaded the territories of Islam and took Toledo and other parts of Andalusia, as was mentioned earlier. Then in 484/1091 they attacked and conquered the island of Sicily and turned their attention to the African coast. Certain of their conquests there were won back again but they had other successes, as you will see.

In 490/1097 the Franks attacked Syria. This is how it all began: Baldwin, their King, a kinsman of Roger the Frank who had conquered Sicily, assembled a great army and sent word to Roger saying: 'I have assembled a great army and now I am on my way to you, to use your bases for my conquest of the African coast. Thus you and I shall become neighbors.'

Roger called together his companions and consulted them about these proposals. 'This will be a fine thing both for them and for us!' they declared, 'for by this means these lands will be converted to the Faith!' At this Roger raised one leg and farted loudly, and swore that it was of more use than their advice. 'Why?' 'Because if this army comes here it will need quantities of provisions and fleets of ships to transport it to Africa, as well as reinforcements from my own troops. Then, if the Franks succeed in conquering this territory they will take it over and will need provisioning from Sicily. This will cost me my annual profit from the harvest. If they fail they will return here and be an embarrassment to me here in my own domain. As well as all this Tamïm will say that I have broken faith with him and violated our treaty, and friendly relations and communications between us will be disrupted. As far as we are concerned, Africa is always there. When we are strong enough we will take it.'

He summoned Baldwin's messenger and said to him: 'If you have decided to make war on the Muslims your best course will be to free Jerusalem from their rule and thereby win great honor. I am bound by certain promises and treaties of allegiance with the rulers of Africa.' So the Franks made ready and set out to attack Syria.

Another story is that the Fatimids of Egypt were afraid when they saw the Seljuqids extending their empire through Syria as far as Gaza, until they reached the Egyptian border and Atsiz invaded Egypt itself. They therefore sent to invite the Franks to invade Syria and so protect Egypt from the Muslims.[1] But God knows best.

When the Franks decided to attack Syria they marched east to Constantinople, so that they could cross the straits and advance into Muslim territory by the easier, land route. When they reached Constantinople, the Emperor of the East refused them permission to pass through his domains. He said: 'Unless you first promise me Antioch, I shall not allow you to cross into the Muslim empire.' His real intention was to incite them to attack the Muslims, for he was convinced that the Turks, whose invincible control over Asia Minor he had observed, would exterminate every one of them. They accepted his conditions and in 490/1097 they crossed the Bosphorus at Constantinople. Iconium and the rest of the area into which they now advanced belonged to Qilij Arslan ibn Sulaiman ibn Qutlumïsh, who marred their way with his troops. They broke through in rajab 490/July 1097, crossed Cilicia, and finally reached Antioch, which they besieged.

When Yaghi Siyan, the ruler of Antioch, heard of their approach, he was not sure how the Christian people of the city would react, so he made the Muslims go outside the city on their own to dig trenches, and the next day sent the Christians out alone to continue the task. When they were ready to return home at the end of the day he refused to allow them. 'Antioch is yours,' he said, 'but you will have to leave it to me until I see what happens between us and the Franks.' 'Who will protect our children and our wives?' they said. 'I shall look after them for you.' So they resigned themselves to their fate, and lived in the Frankish camp for nine months, while the city was under siege.

Yaghi Siyan showed unparalleled courage and wisdom, strength and judgment. If all the Franks who died had survived they would have overrun all the lands of Islam. He protected the families of the Christians in Antioch and would not allow a hair of their heads to be touched.

After the siege had been going on for a long time the Franks made a deal with one of the men who were responsible for the towers. He was a cuirass-maker called Ruzbih whom they bribed with a fortune in money and lands. He worked in the tower that stood over the river-bed, where the river flowed out of the city into the valley. The Franks sealed their pact with the cuirass-maker, God damn him! and made their way to the water-gate. They opened it and entered the city. Another gang of them climbed the tower with ropes. At dawn, when more than 500 of them were in the city and the defenders were worn out after the night watch, they sounded their trumpets. Yaghi Siyan woke up and asked what the noise meant. He was told that trumpets had sounded from the citadel and that it must have been taken. In fact the sound came not from the citadel but from the tower. Panic seized Yaghi Siyan and he opened the city gates and fled in terror, with an escort of thirty pages. His army commander arrived, but when he discovered on enquiry that Yaghi Siyan had fled, he made his escape by another gate. This was of great help to the Franks, for if he had stood firm for an hour, they would have been wiped out. They entered the city by the gates and

sacked it, slaughtering all the Muslims they found there. This happened in jumada I (491/April/May 1098). As for Yaghi Siyan, when the sun rose he recovered his self control and realized that his flight had taken him several *farsakh*[2] from the city. He asked his companions where he was, and on hearing that he was four *farsakh* from Antioch he repented of having rushed to safety instead of staying to fight to the death. He began to groan and weep for his desertion of his household and children. Overcome by the violence of his grief he fell fainting from his horse. His companions tried to lift him back into the saddle, but they could not get him to sit up, and so left him for dead while they escaped. He was at his last gasp when an Armenian shepherd came past, killed him, cut off his head and took it to the Franks at Antioch.

The Franks had written to the rulers of Aleppo and Damascus to say that they had no interest in any cities but those that had once belonged to Byzantium. This was a piece of deceit calculated to dissuade these rulers from going to the help of Antioch.

The Muslim Attack on the Franks, and its Results (X, 188-90)

When Qawam ad-Daula Kerbuqa heard that the Franks had taken Antioch he mustered his army and advanced into Syria, where he camped at Marj Dabiq. All the Turkish and Arab forces in Syria rallied to him except for the army from Aleppo. Among his supporters were Duqaq ibn Tutush, the Ata-beg Tughtikin, Janah ad-Daula of Hims, Arslan Tash of Sanjar, Sulaiman ibn Artuq and other less important amirs. When the Franks heard of this they were alarmed and afraid, for their troops were weak and short of food. The Muslims advanced and came face to face with the Franks in front of Antioch. Kerbuqa, thinking that the present crisis would force the Muslims to remain loyal to him, alienated them by his pride and ill-treatment of them. They plotted in secret anger to betray him and desert him in the heat of battle.

After taking Antioch the Franks camped there for twelve days without food. The wealthy ate their horses and the poor ate carrion and leaves from the trees. Their leaders, faced with this situation, wrote to Kerbuqa to ask for safe-conduct through his territory but he refused, saying 'You will have to fight your way out.' Among the Frankish leaders were Baldwin, Saint-Gilles, Godfrey of Bouillon, the future Count of Edessa, and their leader Bohemond of Antioch. There was also a holy man who had great influence over them, a man of low cunning, who proclaimed that the Messiah had a lance buried in the Qusyan, a great building in Antioch: 'And if you find it you will be victorious and if you fail you will surely die.' Before saying this he had buried a lance in a certain spot and concealed all trace of it. He exhorted them to fast and repent for three days, and on the fourth day he led them all to the spot with their soldiers and workmen, who dug everywhere and found the lance as he had told them. Whereupon he cried 'Rejoice! For victory is secure.' So on the fifth day they left the city in groups of five or six. The Muslims said to Kerbuqa: 'You should go up to the city and kill them one by one as they come out; it is easy to pick them off now that they have split up.' He replied: 'No, wait until they have all come out and then we will kill them.' He would not allow them to attack the enemy and when some Muslims killed a group of Franks, he went himself to forbid such behaviour and prevent its recurrence. When all the Franks had come out and not one was left in Antioch, they began to attack strongly, and the Muslims turned and fled. This was Kerbuqa's fault, first because he had treated the Muslims with such contempt and scorn, and second because he had prevented their killing the Franks. The Muslims were completely routed without striking a single blow or firing a single arrow. The last to flee were Suqman ibn Artuq and Janah ad-Daula, who had been sent to set an ambush. Kerbuqa escaped with them. When the Franks saw this they were afraid that a trap was being set for them, for there had not even been any fighting to flee from, so they dared not follow them. The only Muslims to stand firm were a detachment of warriors from the Holy Land, who fought to acquire merit in God's eyes and to seek martyrdom. The Franks killed them by the thousand and stripped their camp of food

and possessions, equipment, horses and arms, with which they re-equipped themselves.

The Franks Take Ma'arrat an-Nu'man (X, 190)

After dealing this blow to the Muslims the Franks marched on Ma'arrat an-Nu'man and besieged it. The inhabitants valiantly defended their city. When the Franks realized the fierce determination and devotion of the defenders they built a wooden tower as high as the city wall and fought from the top of it, but failed to do the Muslims any serious harm. One night a few Muslims were seized with panic and in their demoralized state thought that if they barricaded themselves into one of the town's largest buildings they would be in a better position to defend themselves, so they climbed down from the wall and abandoned the position they were defending. Others saw them and followed their example, leaving another stretch of wall undefended, and gradually, as one group followed another, the whole wall was left unprotected and the Franks scaled it with ladders. Their appearance in the city terrified the Muslims, who shut themselves up in their houses. For three days the slaughter never stopped; the Franks killed more than 100,000 men and took innumerable prisoners. After taking the town the Franks spent six weeks shut up there, then sent an expedition to 'Arqa, which they besieged for four months. Although they breached the wall in many places they failed to storm it. Munqidh, the ruler of Shaizar, made a treaty with them about 'Arqa and they left it to pass on to Hims. Here too the ruler Janah ad-Daula made a treaty with them, and they advanced to Acre by way of an-Nawaqir. However they did not succeed in taking Acre.

The Franks Conquer Jerusalem (X, 193-95)

Taj ad-Daula Tutush was the Lord of Jerusalem but had given it as a feoff to the amir Suqman ibn Artuq the Turcoman. When the Franks defeated the Turks at Antioch the massacre demoralized them, and the Egyptians, who saw that the Turkish armies were being weakened by desertion, besieged Jerusalem under the command of al-Afdal ibn Badr al-Jamali. Inside the city were

Artuq's sons, Suqman and Ilghazi, their cousin Sunij and their nephew Yaquti. The Egyptians brought more than forty siege engines to attack Jerusalem and broke down the walls at several points. The inhabitants put up a defence, and the siege and fighting went on for more than six weeks. In the end the Egyptians forced the city to capitulate, in sha'ban 489/August 1096.[3] Suqman, Ilghazi and their friends were well treated by al-Afdal, who gave them large gifts of money and let them go free. They made for Damascus and then crossed the Euphrates. Suqman settled in Edessa and Ilghazi went on into Iraq. The Egyptian governor of Jerusalem was a certain Iftikhar ad-Daula, who was still there at the time of which we are speaking.

After their vain attempt to take Acre by siege, the Franks moved on to Jerusalem and besieged it for more than six weeks. They built two towers, one of which, near Sion, the Muslims burnt down, killing everyone inside it. It had scarcely ceased to burn before a messenger arrived to ask for help and to bring the news that the other side of the city had fallen. In fact Jerusalem was taken from the north on the morning of Friday 22 sha'ban 492/15 July 1099. The population was put to the sword by the Franks, who pillaged the area for a week. A band of Muslims barricaded themselves into the Oratory of David and fought on for several days. They were granted their lives in return for surrendering. The Franks honored their word, and the group left by night for Ascalon. In the Masjid al-Aqsa the Franks slaughtered more than 70,000 people, among them a large number of Imams and Muslim scholars, devout and ascetic men who had left their homelands to live lives of pious seclusion in the Holy Place. The Franks stripped the Dome of the Rock[4] of more than forty silver candelabra, each of them weighing 3,600 drams, and a great silver lamp weighing forty-four Syrian pounds, as well as a hundred and fifty smaller silver candelabra and more than twenty gold ones, and a great deal more booty. Refugees from Syria reached Baghdad in ramadan, among them the qadi Abu sa'd al-H rawi. They told the Caliph's ministers a story that wrung their hearts and brought tears to their eyes. On Friday they went to the Cathedral Mosque and begged for help, weeping so that their hearers wept with them as they described the sufferings of the Muslims in that Holy City: the men killed, the women and children taken prisoner, the homes pillaged. Because of the terrible hardships they had suffered, they were allowed to break the fast.

*   *   *

It was the discord between the Muslim princes, as we shall describe, that enabled the Franks to overrun the country. Abu l-Muzaffar al-Abiwardi composed several poems on this subject, in one of which he says:

We have mingled blood with flowing tears, and there is no room left in us for pity (?)
To shed tears is a man's worst weapon when the swords stir up the embers of war.
Sons of Islam, behind you are battles in which heads rolled at your feet.
Dare you slumber in the blessed shade of safety, where life is as soft as an orchard flower?
How can the eye sleep between the lids at a time of disasters that would waken any sleeper?
While your Syrian brothers can only sleep on the backs of their chargers, or in vultures' bellies!
Must the foreigners feed on our ignominy, while you trail behind you the train of a pleasant life, like men whose world is at peace?
When blood has been spilt, when sweet girls must for shame hide their lovely faces in their hands!
When the white swords' points are red with blood, and the iron of the brown lances is stained with gore!
At the sound of sword hammering on lance young children's hair turns white.
This is war, and the man who shuns the whirlpool to save his life shall grind his teeth in penitence.
This is war, and the infidel's sword is naked in his hand, ready to be sheathed again in men's necks and skulls.
This is war, and he who lies in the tomb at Medina seems to raise his voice and cry: 'O sons of Hashim![5]

I see my people slow to raise the lance against the enemy: I see the Faith resting on feeble pillars.

For fear of death the Muslims are evading the fire of battle, refusing to believe that death will surely strike them.'

Must the Arab champions then suffer with resignation, while the gallant Persians shut their eyes to their dishonour?

The Capture of Bohemond of Antioch (X, 203-4)

In dhu l-qa'da of this year (493/September 1100) Kumushtikin ibn ad-Danishm nd Tailu, Prince of Malatia, Siwas and other territories, met Bohemond the Frank, one of the Frankish leaders, near Malatia. The former governor of Malatia had a treaty of friendship with Bohemond and asked for his help. Bohemond came with 5,000 men, but was defeated in battle by Ibn ad-Danishm nd and taken prisoner. Then seven Frankish Counts came from across the sea to seek Bohemond's release. They came to a fortress called Ankuriyya, took it and killed the Muslims they found there, before passing it on to another fort, which they besieged. Isma'il ibn ad-Danishm nd, who was defending the fort, mustered his great army, set an ambush for the Franks and then challenged them to battle. Battle was joined, the ambush sprung and of the 300,000 Franks only 3,000 escaped, during the night, and even they were wounded and exhausted. Ibn ad-Danishm nd attacked Malatia, took it and imprisoned the governor. The Frankish army from Antioch came out to challenge him, but he fought and defeated them. All this happened in the space of a few months.

4. Anna Comnena

Anna Comnena (1083-ca.1148), was the daughter of the Byzantine Emperor Alexius. She composed *The Alexiad*, a history of her father's reign, toward the end of her life. Although it is a glorification of his reign and is occasionally inaccurate in detail, it is generally a reliable and vivid description of her time.

Source: F.R.A. Sewter, *The Alexiad of Anna Comnena* (Harmondsworth: Penguin, 1969).

[Alexius] had no time to [rest] before he heard a rumour that countless Frankish armies were approaching. He dreaded their arrival, knowing as he did their uncontrollable passion, their erratic character and their irresolution, not to mention the other peculiar traits of the Kelt, with their inevitable consequences; their greed for money, for example, which always led them, it seemed, to break their own agreements without scruple for any clear reason. He had consistently heard this said of them and it was abundantly justified. So far from despairing, however, he made every effort to prepare for war if need arose. What actually happened was more far-reaching and terrible than rumour suggested, for the whole of the west and all the barbarians who lived between the Adriatic and the Straits of Gibraltar migrated in a body to Asia, marching across Europe country by country with all their households. The reason for this mass-movement is to be found more or less in the following events. A certain Kelt, called Peter, with the surname Koukoupetros,[1] left to worship at the Holy Sepulchre and after suffering much ill-treatment at the hands of the Turks and Saracens who were plundering the whole of Asia, he returned home with difficulty. Unable to admit defeat, he wanted to make a second attempt by the same route, but realizing the folly of trying to do this alone (worse things might happen to him) he worked out a clever scheme. He decided to preach in all the Latin countries. A divine voice, he said, commanded him to proclaim to all the counts in France that all should depart from their homes, set out to worship at the

Holy Shrine and with all their soul and might strive to liberate Jerusalem from the Agarenes.[2] Surprisingly, he was successful. It was as if he had inspired every heart with some divine oracle. Kelts assembled from all parts, one after another, with arms and horses and all the other equipment for war. Full of enthusiasm and ardour they thronged every highway, and with these warriors came a host of civilians, outnumbering the sand of the sea shore or the stars of heaven, carrying palms and bearing crosses on their shoulders. There were women and children, too, who had left their own countries. Like tributaries joining a river from all directions they streamed towards us in full force, mostly through Dacia. The arrival of this mighty host was preceded by locusts, which abstained from the wheat but made frightful inroads on the vines. The prophets of those days interpreted this as a sign that the Keltic army would refrain from interfering in the affairs of Christians but bring dreadful affliction on the barbarian Ishmaelites, who were the slaves of drunkenness and wine and Dionysos. The Ishmaelites are indeed dominated by Dionysos and Eros; they indulge readily in every kind of sexual licence, and if they are circumcised in the flesh they are certainly not so in their passions. In fact, the Ishmaelites are nothing more than slaves—trebly slaves—of the vices of Aphrodite.[3] Hence they reverence and worship Astarte and Ashtaroth, and in their land the figure of the moon and the golden image of Chobar[4] are considered of major importance. Corn, because it is not heady and at the same time is most nourishing, has been accepted as the symbol of Christianity. In the light of this the diviners interpreted the references to vines and wheat. So much for the prophecies. The incidents of the barbarians' advance followed in the order I have given and there was something strange about it, which intelligent people at least would notice. The multitudes did not arrive at the same moment, nor even by the same route—how could they cross the Adriatic *en masse* after setting out from different countries in such great numbers?—but they made the voyage in separate groups, some first, some in a second party and others after them in order, until all had arrived, and then they began their march across Epirus. Each army, as I have

said, was preceded by a plague of locusts, so that everyone, having observed the phenomenon several times, came to recognize locusts as the forerunners of Frankish battalions. They had already begun to cross the Straits of Lombardy in small groups when the emperor summoned certain leaders of the Roman forces and sent them to the area round Dyrrachium and Avlona, with instructions to receive the voyagers kindly and export from all countries abundant supplies for them along their route; then to watch them carefully and follow, so that if they saw them making raids or running off to plunder the neighboring districts, they could check them by light skirmishes. These officers were accompanied by interpreters who understood the Latin language; their duty was to quell any incipient trouble between natives and pilgrims. I would like here to give a clearer and more detailed account of the matter.

The report of Peter's preaching spread everywhere, and the first to sell his land and set out on the road to Jerusalem was Godfrey.[5] He was a very rich man, extremely proud of his noble birth, his own courage and the glory of his family. (Every Kelt desired to surpass his fellows.) The upheaval that ensued as men *and* women took to the road was unprecedented within living memory. The simpler folk were in very truth led on by a desire to worship at Our Lord's tomb and visit the holy places, but the more villainous characters (in particular Bohemond and his like) had an ulterior purpose, for they hoped on their journey to seize the capital itself, looking upon its capture as a natural consequence of the expedition. Bohemond disturbed the morale of many nobler men because he still cherished his old grudge against the emperor. Peter, after his preaching campaign, was the first to cross the Lombardy Straits, with 80,000 infantry and 100,000 horsemen. He reached the capital via Hungary.[6] The Kelts, as one might guess, are in any case an exceptionally hotheaded race and passionate, but let them once find an inducement and they become irresistible.

The emperor knew what Peter had suffered before from the Turks and advised him to wait for the other counts to arrive, but he refused, confident in the number of his followers. He crossed the Sea of Marmora and pitched camp near a small place called Helenopolis. Later some Normans, 10,000 in all, joined him but detached themselves from the rest of the army and ravaged the outskirts of Nicaea, acting with horrible cruelty to the whole population; they cut in pieces some of the babies, impaled others on wooden spits and roasted them over a fire; old people were subjected to every kind of torture. The inhabitants of the city, when they learnt what was happening, threw open their gates and charged out against them. A fierce battle ensued, in which the Normans fought with such spirit that the Nicaeans had to retire inside their citadel. The enemy therefore returned to Helenopolis with all the booty. There an argument started between them and the rest (who had not gone on the raid)—the usual quarrel in such cases—for the latter were green with envy. That led to brawling, whereupon the daredevil Normans broke away for a second time and took Xerigordos by assault. The sultan's reaction was to send Elkhanes with a strong force to deal with them. He arrived at Xerigordos and captured it; of the Normans some were put to the sword and others taken prisoner. At the same time Elkhanes made plans to deal with the remainder, still with Koukoupetros. He laid ambushes in suitable places, hoping that the enemy on their way to Nicaea would fall into the trap unawares and be killed. Knowing the Keltic love of money he also enlisted the services of two determined men who were to go to Peter's camp and there announce that the Normans, having seized Nicaea, were sharing out all the spoils of the city. This story had an amazing effect on Peter's men; they were thrown into confusion at the words 'share' and 'money'; without a moment's hesitation they set out on the Nicaea road in complete disorder, practically heedless of military discipline and the proper arrangement which should mark men going off to war. As I have said before, the Latin race at all times is unusually greedy for wealth, but when it plans to invade a country, neither reason nor force can restrain it. They set out helter-skelter, regardless of their individual companies. Near the Drakon they fell into the Turkish ambuscade and were miserably slaughtered. So great a multitude of Kelts and Normans died by the Ishmaelite sword that when they gathered the remains of the fallen,

lying on every side, they heaped up, I will not say a mighty ridge or hill or peak, but a mountain of considerable height and depth and width, so high was the mass of bones. Some men of the same race as the slaughtered barbarians later, when they were building a wall like those of a city, used the bones of the dead as pebbles to fill up the cracks. In a way the city became their tomb. To this very day it stands with its encircling wall built of mixed stones and bones. When the killing was over, only Peter with a handful of men returned to Helenopolis. The Turks, wishing to capture him, again laid an ambush, but the emperor, who had heard of this and indeed of the terrible massacre, thought it would be an awful thing if Peter also became a prisoner. Constantine Euphorbenus Catacalon (already mentioned often in this history) was accordingly sent with powerful contingents in warships across the straits to help him. At his approach the Turks took to their heels. Without delay Catacalon picked up Peter and his companions (there were only a few) and brought them in safety to Alexius, who reminded Peter of his foolishness in the beginning and added that these great misfortunes had come upon him through not listening to his advice. With the usual Latin arrogance Peter disclaimed responsibility and blamed his men for them, because (said he) they had been disobedient and followed their own whims. He called them brigands and robbers, considered unworthy therefore by the Savior to worship at His Holy Sepulchre. Some Latins, after the pattern of Bohemond and his cronies, because they had long coveted the Roman Empire and wished to acquire it for themselves, found in the preaching of Peter an excuse and caused this great upheaval by deceiving more innocent people. They sold their lands on the pretence that they were leaving to fight the Turks and liberate the Holy Sepulchre.

A certain Hugh,[7] brother of the King of France, with all the pride of a Nauatos in his noble birth and wealth and power, as he was about to leave his native country (ostensibly for a pilgrimage to the Holy Sepulchre) sent an absurd message to the emperor proposing that he (Hugh) should be given a magnificent reception: 'Know, Emperor, that I am the King of Kings, the greatest of all beneath the heavens. It is my will that you should meet me on my arrival and receive me with the pomp and ceremony due to my noble birth.' When this letter reached Alexius, John the son of Isaac the sebastocrator happened to be Duke of Dyrrachium, and Nicolas Mavrocatacalon, commander of the fleet, had anchored his ships at intervals round the harbor there. From this base he made frequent voyages of reconnaissance to prevent pirate ships sailing by unnoticed. To these two men the emperor now sent urgent instructions: the Duke was to keep watch by land and sea for Hugh's arrival and inform Alexius at once when he came; he was also to receive him with great pomp; the admiral was exhorted to keep a constant vigil—there must be no relaxation or negligence whatever. Hugh reached the coast of Lombardy safely and forthwith despatched envoys to the Duke of Dyrrachium. There were twenty-four of them in all, armed with breastplates and greaves of gold and accompanied by Count William the Carpenter[8] and Elias (who had deserted from the emperor at Thessalonica). They addressed the duke as follows: 'Be it known to you, Duke, that our Lord Hugh is almost here. He brings with him from Rome the golden standard of St. Peter.[9] Understand, moreover, that he is supreme commander of the Frankish army. See to it then that he is accorded a reception worthy of his rank and yourself prepare to meet him.' While the envoys were delivering this message, Hugh came down via Rome to Lombardy, as I have said, and set sail for Illyricum from Bari, but on the crossing he was caught by a tremendous storm. Most of his ships, with their rowers and marines, were lost. Only one ship, his own, was thrown up on the coast somewhere between Dyrrachium and a place called Pales, and that was half-wrecked. Two coastguards on the lookout for his arrival found him, saved by a miracle. They called to him, 'The duke is anxiously waiting for your coming. He is very eager to see you.' At once he asked for a horse and one of them dismounted and gave him his own gladly. When the duke saw him, saved in this way, and when he had greeted him, he asked about the voyage and heard of the storm which had wrecked his ships. He encouraged Hugh with fine promises and entertained

him at a magnificent banquet. After the feasting Hugh was allowed to rest, but he was not granted complete freedom. John the duke had immediately informed the emperor of the Frank's adventures and was now awaiting further instructions. Soon after receiving the news Alexius sent Boutoumites to Epidamnos (which we have on numerous occasions called Dyrrachium) to escort Hugh, not by the direct route but on a detour through Philippopolis to the capital. He was afraid of the armed Keltic hordes coming on behind him. Hugh was welcomed with honor by the emperor, who soon persuaded him by generous largess and every proof of friendship to become his liege-man and take the customary oath of the Latins.

This affair was merely the prelude. Barely fifteen days later Bohemond made the crossing to the coast of Kabalion. Hard on his heels came the Count Richard of the Principate. He too when he reached the Lombardy coast wanted to cross over to Illyricum. A three-masted pirate vessel of large tonnage was hired for 6,000 gold staters. She carried 200 rowers and towed three ship's boats. Richard did not make for Avlona, as the other Latin armies had done, but after weighing anchor changed direction a little and with a favorable wind sailed straight for Chimara (he was fearful of the Roman fleet). However, in escaping the smoke he fell into the fire: he avoided the ships lying in wait at different points in the Lombardy straits but crossed the path of the commander-in-chief of the whole Roman fleet, Nicolas Mavrocatacalon himself. The latter had heard of this pirate vessel some time before and had detached biremes, triremes and some fast cruisers from the main force; with these he moved from his base at Ason to Kabalion and there took up station. The so-called 'second count' was sent with his own galley (*Excussaton* to the ordinary seamen) to light a torch when he saw the rowers loose the stern-cables of the enemy ship and throw them into the sea. Without delay the order was carried out and Nicolas, seeing the signal, hoisted sail on some of his ships, while others were rowed with oars—they looked like millipedes—against Richard, who was now at sea. They caught him before he had sailed three stades from the land, eager to reach the opposite shore by Epidamnos.

He had 1,500 soldiers on board, plus eighty horses belonging to the nobles. The helmsman, sighting Nicolas, reported to the Frank: 'The Syrian fleet is on us. We're in danger of being killed by dagger and sword.' The count at once ordered his men to arm and put up a good fight. It was midwinter—the day sacred to the memory of Nicolas, greatest of pontiffs—but there was a dead calm and the full moon shone more brightly than in the spring. As the winds had fallen completely the pirate ship could no longer make progress under sail; it lay becalmed on the sea. At this point in the history I should like to pay tribute to the exploits of Marianus. He immediately asked the Duke of the Fleet, his father, for some of the lighter vessels and then steered straight for Richard's ship. He fell upon the prow and tried to board her. The marines soon rushed there when they saw that he was fully armed for battle, but Marianus, speaking in their language, told the Latins there was no need for alarm; he urged them not to fight against fellow-Christians. Nevertheless one of them fired a cross-bow and hit his helmet. The arrow drove clean through the top of it without touching a hair on his head—Providence thwarted it. Another arrow was quickly fired at the count, striking him on the arm; it pierced his shield, bored through his breastplate of scale-armour and grazed his side. A certain Latin priest who happened to be standing in the stern with twelve other fighting-men saw what had occurred and shot several times with his bow at Marianus. Even then Marianus refused to give up; he fought bravely himself and encouraged his men to follow his example, so that three times the priest's comrades had to be relieved because of wounds or fatigue. The priest, too, although he had been hit again and again and was covered with streams of blood from his wounds, still was undaunted. After a bitter contest which went on from evening till the next mid-day the Latins yielded much against their will to Marianus, when they had asked for and obtained an amnesty from him. The warrior-priest, however, even when the armistice was being arranged, did not cease from fighting. After emptying his quiver of arrows, he picked up a sling-stone and hurled it at Marianus, who protected his head with a shield, but that was broken into four and his helmet was shattered. The blow stunned him; he lost consciousness at once and for some time lay speechless, just as the famous Hector lay almost at his last gasp when struck by Ajax's stone. With difficulty he recovered his senses, pulled himself together and firing arrows against his enemy wounded him three times. The polemarch[10] (he was more that than a priest) was far from having had his fill of battle, although he had exhausted the stones and arrows and was at a loss what to do and how to defend himself against his adversary. He grew impatient, on fire with rage, gathering himself for the spring like a wild animal. He was ready to use whatever came to hand and when he found a sack full of barley-cakes, he threw them like stones, taking them from the sack. It was as if he were officiating at some ceremony or service, turning war into the solemnization of sacred rites. He picked up one cake, hurled it with all his might at Marianus' face and hit him on the cheek. So much for the story of the priest, the ship and its marines. As for Count Richard, he put himself in the hands of Marianus, together with his ship and her crew, and thereafter gladly followed him. When they reached land and were disembarking, the priest kept on making inquiries about Marianus; he did not know his name, but described him by the color of his garments. When at last he found him, he threw his arms round him and with an embrace boasted, 'If you had met me on dry land, many of you would have died at my hands.' He drew out a large silver cup, worth 130 staten, and as he gave it to Marianus and uttered these words, he died.

It was at this time that Count Godfrey made the crossing with some other counts and an army of 10,000 horsemen and 70,000 infantry. When he reached the capital he quartered his men in the vicinity of the Propontis, from the bridge nearer the Kosmidion[11] as far as the Church of St. Phocas. But when the emperor urged him to go over to the far side of the Propontis he put off the decision from day to day; the crossing was deferred with a series of excuses. In fact, of course, he was waiting for Bohemond and the rest of the counts to arrive. Peter had in the beginning undertaken his great journey to worship at the Holy Sepulchre, but the others (and in particular Bohemond) cherished their old grudge against Alexius and sought a good opportunity to avenge the glorious victory which the emperor had won at Larissa. They were all of one mind and in order to fulfil their dream of taking Constantinople they adopted a common policy. I have often referred to that already: to all appearances they were on pilgrimage to Jerusalem; in reality they planned to dethrone Alexius and seize the capital. Unfortunately for them, he was aware of their perfidy, from long experience. He gave written orders to move the auxiliary forces with their officers from Athyra to Philea *en masse* (Philea is a place on the coast of the Black Sea). They were to lie in wait for envoys from Godfrey on their way to Bohemond and the other counts coming behind him, or *vice versa*; all communications were thus to be intercepted. Meanwhile the following incident took place. Some of the counts who accompanied Godfrey were invited by the emperor to meet him. He intended to give them advice: they should urge Godfrey to take the oath of allegiance. The Latins, however, wasted time with their usual verbosity and love of long speeches, so that a false rumour reached the Franks that their counts had been arrested by Alexius. Immediately they marched in serried ranks on Byzantium, starting with the palaces near the Silver Lake; they demolished them completely. An assault was also made on the city walls, not with helepoleis (because they had none), but trusting in their great numbers they had the effrontery to try to set fire to the gate below the palace, near the sanctuary of St. Nicolas. The vulgar mob of Byzantines, who were utterly craven, with no experience of war, were not the only ones to weep and wail and beat their breasts in impotent fear when they saw the Latin ranks; even more alarmed were the emperor's loyal adherents. Recalling the Thursday on which the city was captured,[12] they were afraid that on that day[13] (because of what had occurred then) vengeance might be taken on them. All the trained soldiers hurried to the palace in disorder, but the emperor remained calm: there was no attempt to arm, no buckling on of scaled cuirass, no shield, no spear in hand, no girdling on of his sword. He sat firmly on the imperial throne, gazing cheerfully on them, encouraging and inspiring the hearts of

all with confidence, while he took counsel with his kinsmen and generals about future action. In the first place he insisted that no one whatever should leave the ramparts to attack the Latins, for two reasons: because of the sacred character of the day (it was the Thursday of Holy Week, the supreme week of the year, in which the Savior suffered an ignominious death on behalf of the whole world); and secondly because he wished to avoid bloodshed between Christians. On several occasions he sent envoys to the Latins advising them to desist from such an undertaking. 'Have reverence,' he said, 'for God on this day was sacrificed for us all, refusing neither the Cross, nor the Nails, nor the Spear—proper instruments of punishment for evil-doers—to save us. If you must fight, we too shall be ready, but after the day of the Savior's resurrection.' They, far from listening to his words, rather reinforced their ranks, and so thick were the showers of their arrows that even one of the emperor's retinue standing near the throne, was struck in the chest. Most of the others ranged on either side of the emperor, when they saw this, began to withdraw, but he remained seated and unruffled, comforting them and rebuking them in a gentle way—to the wonder of all. However, as he saw the Latins brazenly approaching the walls and rejecting sound advice, he took active steps for the first time. His son-in-law Nicephorus (my Caesar) was summoned. He was ordered to pick out the best fighters, expert archers, and post them on the ramparts; they were to fire volleys of arrows at the Latins, but without taking aim and mostly off-target, so as to terrify the enemy by the weight of the attack, but at all costs to avoid killing them. As I have remarked, he was fearful of desecrating that day and he wished to prevent fratricide. Other picked men, most of them carrying bows, but some wielding long spears, he ordered to throw open the gates of St. Romanus and make a show of force with a violent charge against the enemy; they were to be drawn up in such a way that each lancer had two peltasts to protect him on either side. In this formation they would advance at a walking pace, but send on ahead a few skilled archers to shoot at the Kelts from a distance and alter direction, right or left, from time to time; when they saw that the space between the two armies had been reduced to a narrow gap, then the officers were to signal the archers accompanying them to fire thick volleys of arrows at the horses, not at the riders, and gallop at full speed against the enemy. The idea was partly to break the full force of the Keltic attack by wounding their mounts (they would not find it easy to ride in this condition) and partly (this was more important) to avoid the killing of Christians. The emperor's instructions were gladly followed. The gates were flung open; now the horses were given their head, now reined in. Many Kelts were slain, but few of the Romans on that day were wounded. We will leave them and return to the Caesar, my lord. Having taken his practised bowmen, he set them on the towers and fired at the barbarians. Every man had a bow that was accurate and far-shooting. They were all young, as skilled as Homer's Teucer in archery. The Caesar's bow was truly worthy of Apollo. Unlike the famous Greeks of Homer he did not 'pull the bow-string until it touched his breast and draw back the arrow so that the iron tip was near the bow'; he was making no demonstration of the hunter's skill, like them. But like a second Hercules he shot deadly arrows from deathless bows and hit the target at will. At other times, when he took part in a shooting contest or in a battle, he never missed his aim: at whatever part of a man's body he shot, he invariably and immediately inflicted a wound there. With such strength did he bend his bow and so swiftly did he let loose his arrows that even Teucer and the two Ajaxes were not his equal in archery. Yet, despite his skill, on this occasion he respected the holiness of the day and kept in mind the emperor's instructions, so that when he saw the Franks recklessly and foolishly coming near the walls, protected by shield and helmet, he bent his bow and put the arrow to the bow-string, but purposely shot wide, shooting sometimes beyond the target, sometimes falling short. Although, for the day's sake, he refrained from shooting straight at the Latins, yet whenever one of them in his foolhardiness and arrogance not only fired at the defenders on the ramparts, but seemingly poured forth a volley of insults in his own language as well, the Caesar did bend his bow. 'Nor

did the dart fly in vain from his hand', but pierced the long shield and cleft its way through the corselet of mail, so that arm and side were pinned together. 'Straightway he fell speechless to the ground', as the poet says, and a cry went up to heaven as the Romans cheered their Caesar and the Latins bewailed their fallen warrior. The battle broke out afresh, their cavalry and our men on the walls both fighting with courage; it was a grim, dour struggle on both sides. However, when the emperor threw in his guards, the Latin ranks turned in flight. On the next day Hugh advised Godfrey to yield to the emperor's wish, unless he wanted to learn a second time how experienced a general Alexius was. He should take an oath, he said, to bear his true allegiance. But Godfrey rebuked him sternly. 'You left your own country as a king,' he said, 'with all that wealth and a strong army; now from the heights you've brought yourself to the level of a slave. And then, as if you had won some great success, you come here and tell me to do the same.' 'We ought to have stayed in our own countries and kept our hands off other peoples',' replied Hugh. 'But since we've come thus far and need the emperor's protection, no good will come of it unless we obey his orders.' Hugh was sent away with nothing achieved. Because of this and reliable information that the counts coming after Godfrey were already near, the emperor sent some of his best officers with their troops to advise him once more, even to compel him to cross the straits. No sooner were they in sight when the Latins, without a moment's hesitation, not even waiting to ask them what they wanted, launched an attack and began to fight them. In this fierce engagement many on both sides fell and all the emperor's men who had attacked with such recklessness were wounded. As the Romans showed greater spirit the Latins gave way. Thus Godfrey not long after submitted; he came to the emperor and swore on oath as he was directed that whatever cities, countries or forts he might in future subdue, which had in the first place belonged to the Roman Empire, he would hand over to the officer appointed by the emperor for this very purpose. Having taken the oath he received generous largess, was invited to share Alexius' hearth and table, and was entertained at a magnificent banquet, after which he crossed over to Pelekanum and there pitched camp. The emperor then gave orders that plentiful supplies should be made available for his men.

In the wake of Godfrey came Count Raoul, with 15,000 cavalry and foot-soldiers. He encamped with his attendant counts by the Propontis near the Patriarch's Monastery; the rest he quartered as far as Sosthenion along the shore. Following Godfrey's example he procrastinated, waiting for the arrival of those coming after him, and the emperor who dreaded it (guessing what was likely to happen) used every means, physical and psychological, to hurry them into crossing the straits. For instance, Opus was summoned— a man of noble character, unsurpassed in his knowledge of things military—and when he presented himself before the emperor he was despatched overland with other brave men to Raoul. His instructions were to force the Frank to leave for the Asian side. When it was clear that Raoul had no intention of going, but in fact adopted an insolent and quite arrogant attitude to the emperor, Opus armed himself and set his men in battle order, maybe to scare the barbarian. He thought this might persuade him to set sail. But the Keltic reaction was immediate: with his available men he accepted the challenge, 'like a lion who rejoices when he has found a large prey'. There and then he started a violent battle. At this moment Pegasios arrived by sea to transport them to the other side and when he saw the fight on land and the Kelts throwing themselves headlong at the Roman ranks, he disembarked and himself joined in the conflict, attacking the enemy from the rear. In this fight many men were killed, but a far greater number were wounded. The survivors, under the circumstances, asked to be taken over the straits; reflecting that if they joined Godfrey and told him of their misfortunes he might be stirred to action against the Romans, the emperor prudently granted their request; he gladly put them on ships and had them transported to the Savior's tomb, especially since they themselves wanted this. Friendly messages, offering great expectations, were also sent to the counts whom they were awaiting. Consequently, when they arrived, they willingly carried out his

instructions. So much for Count Raoul. After him came another great contingent, a numberless heterogeneous host gathered together from almost all the Keltic lands with their leaders (kings and dukes and counts and even bishops). The emperor sent envoys to greet them as a mark of friendship and forwarded politic letters. It was typical of Alexius: he had an uncanny prevision and knew how to seize a point of vantage before his rivals. Officers appointed for this particular task were ordered to provide victuals on the journey—the pilgrims must have no excuse for complaint for any reasons whatever. Meanwhile they were eagerly pressing on to the capital. One might have compared them for number to the stars of heaven or the grains of sand poured out over the shore; as they hurried towards Constantinople they were indeed 'numerous as the leaves and flowers of spring' (to quote Homer). For all my desire to name their leaders, I prefer not to do so. The words fail me, partly through my inability to make the barbaric sounds—they are so unpronounceable—and partly because I recoil before their great numbers. In any case, why should I try to list the names of so enormous a multitude, when even their contemporaries became indifferent at the sight of them? When they did finally arrive in the capital, on the emperor's orders they established their troops near the monastery of Saint Cosmas and Saint Damian, reaching as far as the Hieron. It was not nine heralds, after the old Greek custom, who 'restrained them with cries', but a considerable number of soldiers who accompanied them and persuaded them to obey the emperor's commands. With the idea of enforcing the same oath that Godfrey had taken, Alexius invited them to visit him separately. He talked with them in private about his wishes and used the more reasonable among them as intermediaries to coerce the reluctant. When they rejected advice—they were anxiously waiting for Bohemond to come—and found ingenious methods of evasion by making new demands, he refuted their objections with no difficulty at all and harried them in a hundred ways until they were driven to take the oath. Godfrey himself was invited to cross over from Pelekanum to watch the ceremony. When all, including Godfrey, were assembled and after the

oath had been sworn by every count, one nobleman dared to seat himself on the emperor's
throne. Alexius endured this without a word,
knowing of old the haughty temper of the Latins,
but Count Baldwin went up to the man, took him
by the hand and made him rise. He gave him a
severe reprimand: 'You ought never to have done
such a thing, especially after promising to be the
emperor's liege-man. Roman emperors don't let
their subjects sit with them. That's the custom
here and sworn liege-men of His Majesty should
observe the customs of the country.' The man
said nothing to Baldwin, but with a bitter glance
at Alexius muttered some words to himself in his
own language: 'What a peasant! He sits alone
while generals like these stand beside him!' Alexius saw his lips moving and calling one of the
interpreters who understood the language asked
what he had said. Being told the words he made
no comment to the man at the time, but kept the
remark to himself. However, when they were all
taking their leave of him, he sent for the arrogant,
impudent fellow and asked who he was, where
he came from and what his lineage was. 'I am a
pure Frank,' he replied, 'and of noble birth. One
thing I know: at a cross-roads in the country
where I was born is an ancient shrine; to this any
one who wishes to engage in single combat goes,
prepared to fight; there he prays to God for help
and there he stays awaiting the man who will
dare to answer his challenge. At that cross-roads
I myself have spent time, waiting and longing for
the man who would fight—but there was never
one who dared.' Hearing this the emperor said,
'If you didn't get your fight then, when you
looked for it, now you have a fine opportunity for
many. But I strongly recommend you not to take
up position in the rear of the army, nor in the van;
stand in the centre with the *hemilochitae*.[14] I know
the enemy methods. I've had long experience of
the Turk.' The advice was not given to him alone,
but as they left he warned all the others of the
manifold dangers they were likely to meet on the
journey. He advised them not to pursue the
enemy too far, if God gave them the victory, lest
falling into traps set by the Turkish leaders they
should be massacred.

So much for Godfrey, Raoul and those who
came with them. Bohemond arrived at Apros

with the other counts. Knowing that he himself
was not of noble descent, with no great military
following because of his lack of resources, he
wished to win the emperor's goodwill, but at the
same time to conceal his own hostile intentions
against him. With only ten Kelts he hurried to
reach the capital before the rest. Alexius understood his schemes—he had long experience of
Bohemond's deceitful, treacherous nature—and
desired to talk with him before his companions
arrived; he wanted to hear what Bohemond had
to say and while he still had no chance of corrupting the rest (they were not far away now) he
hoped to persuade him to cross over to Asia.
When Bohemond came into his presence, Alexius
at once gave him a smile and inquired about his
journey. Where had he left the counts? Bohemond
replied frankly and to the best of his knowledge
to all these questions, while the emperor politely
reminded him of his daring deeds at Larissa and
Dyrrachium; he also recalled Bohemond's former
hostility. 'I was indeed an enemy and foe then,'
said Bohemond, 'but now I come of my own free
will as Your Majesty's friend.' Alexius talked at
length with him, in a somewhat discreet way trying to discover the man's real feelings, and when
he concluded that Bohemond would be prepared
to take the oath of allegiance, he said to him, 'You
are tired now from your journey. Go away and
rest. Tomorrow we can discuss matters of common interest.' Bohemond went off to the Cos-
midion, where an apartment had been made
ready for him and a rich table was laid full of del-
icacies and food of all kinds. Later the cooks
brought in meat and flesh of animals and birds,
uncooked. 'The food, as you see, has been prepared by us in our customary way,' they said,
'but if that does not suit you here is raw meat
which can be cooked in whatever way you like.'
In doing and saying this they were carrying out
the emperor's instructions. Alexius was a shrewd
judge of a man's character, cleverly reading the
innermost thoughts of his heart, and knowing the
spiteful, malevolent nature of Bohemond, he
rightly guessed what would happen. It was in
order that Bohemond might have no suspicions
that he caused the uncooked meat to be set before
him at the same time, and it was an excellent
move. The cunning Frank not only refused to

taste any of the food, but would not even touch it with his finger-tips; he rejected it outright, but divided it all up among the attendants, without a hint of his own secret misgivings. It looked as if he was doing them a favor, but that was mere pretence: in reality, if one considers the matter rightly, he was mixing them a cup of death. There was no attempt to hide his treachery, for it was his habit to treat servants with utter indifference. However, he told his own cooks to prepare the raw meat in the usual Frankish way.

On the next day he asked the attendants how they felt. 'Very well,' they replied and added that they had suffered not the slightest harm from it. At these words he revealed his hidden fear: 'For my own part,' he said, 'when I remembered the wars I have fought with him, not to mention the famous battle, I was afraid he might arrange to kill me by putting a dose of poison in the food.' Such were the actions of Bohemond. I must say I have never seen an evil man who in all his deeds and words did not depart far from the path of right; whenever a man leaves the middle course, to whatever extreme he inclines he takes his stand far from virtue. Bohemond was summoned then and required, like the others, to take the customary Latin oath. Knowing what his position was he acquiesced gladly enough, for he had neither illustrious ancestors nor great wealth (hence his forces were not strong—only a moderate number of Keltic followers). In any case Bohemond was by nature a liar. After the ceremony was over, Alexius set aside a room in the palace precincts and had the floor covered with all kinds of wealth: clothes, gold and silver coins, objects of lesser value filled the place so completely that it was impossible for anyone to walk in it. He ordered the man deputed to show Bohemond these riches to open the doors suddenly. Bohemond was amazed at the sight. 'If I had had such wealth,' he said, 'I would long ago have become master of many lands.' 'All this,' said the man, 'is yours today—a present from the emperor.' Bohemond was overjoyed. After accepting the gift and thanking him for it, he went off to rest at his lodging-place. Yet when the things were brought to him, although he had expressed such admiration before, he changed. 'I never thought I should be so insulted by the emperor,' he said. 'Take them

away. Give them back to the sender.' Alexius, familiar with the Latins' characteristic moodiness, quoted a popular saying: 'His mischief shall return upon his own head.' Bohemond heard about this, and when he saw the servants carefully assembling the presents to carry them away, he changed his mind once more; instead of sending them off in anger he smiled on them, like a sea-polyp which transforms itself in a minute. The truth is that Bohemond was an habitual rogue, quick to react to fleeting circumstance; he far surpassed all the Latins who passed through Constantinople at that time in rascality and courage, but he was equally inferior in wealth and resources. He was the supreme mischief-maker. As for inconstancy, that followed automatically— a trait common to all Latins. It was no surprise then that he should be overjoyed to receive the money he had formerly refused. When he left his native land, he was a soured man, for he had no estates at all. Apparently he left to worship at the Holy Sepulchre, but in reality to win power for himself—or rather, if possible, to seize the Roman Empire itself, as his father had suggested. He was prepared to go to any length, as they say, but a great deal of money was required. The emperor, aware of the man's disagreeable, ill-natured disposition, cleverly sought to remove everything that contributed to Bohemond's secret plans. When therefore Bohemond demanded the office of Domestic of the East, he was not granted his request; he could not 'out-Cretan the Cretan', for Alexius was afraid that once possessed of authority he might use it to subjugate all the other counts and thereafter convert them easily to any policy he chose.

At the same time, because he did not wish Bohemond to suspect in any way that his plans were already detected, he flattered him with fine hopes. 'The time for that is not yet ripe, but with your energy and loyalty it will not be long before you have even that honor.' After a conversation with the Franks and after showing his friendship for them with all kinds of presents and honors, on the next day he took his seat on the imperial throne. Bohemond and the others were sent for and warned about the things likely to happen on their journey. He gave them profitable advice. They were instructed in the methods normally used by the Turks in battle; told how they should draw up a battle-line, how to lay ambushes; advised not to pursue far when the enemy ran away in flight. In this way, by means of money and good advice, he did much to soften their ferocious nature. Then he proposed that they should cross the straits. For one of them, Raymond the Count of Saint-Gilles,[15] Alexius had a deep affection, for several reasons: the count's superior intellect, his untarnished reputation, the purity of his life. He knew moreover how greatly Raymond valued the truth: whatever the circumstances, he honored truth above all else. In fact, Saint-Gilles outshone all Latins in every quality, as the sun is brighter than the stars. It was for this that Alexius detained him for some time. Thus, when all the others had taken their leave of him and made the journey across the straits of the Propontis to Damalion,[16] and when he was now relieved of their troublesome presence, he sent for him on many occasions. He explained in more detail the adventures that the Latins must expect to meet with on their march; he also laid bare his own suspicions of their plans. In the course of many such conversations on this subject he unreservedly opened the doors of his soul, as it were, to the count; he warned him always to be on his guard against Bohemond's perfidy, so that if attempts were made to break the treaty he might frustrate them and in every way thwart Bohemond's schemes. Saint-Gilles pointed out that Bohemond inherited perjury and guile from his ancestors—it was a kind of heirloom. 'It will be a miracle if he keeps his sworn word,' he said. 'As far as I am concerned, however, I will always try to the best of my ability to observe your commands.' With that he took his leave of the emperor and went off to join the whole Keltic army. Alexius would have liked to share in the expedition against the barbarians, too, but he feared the enormous numbers of the Kelts. He did think it wise, though, to move to Pelekanum. Making his permanent headquarters near Nicaea, he could obtain information about their progress and at the same time about Turkish activities outside the city, as well as about the condition of the inhabitants inside. It would be shameful, he believed, if in the meantime he did not himself win some military success. When a favorable opportunity

arose, he planned to capture Nicaea himself; that would be preferable to receiving it from the Kelts (according to the agreement already made with them). Nevertheless he kept the idea to himself. Whatever dispositions he made, and the reasons for them, were known to himself alone, although he did entrust this task to Boutoumites (his sole confidant). Boutoumites was instructed to suborn the barbarians in Nicaea by all kinds of guarantees and the promise of a complete amnesty, but also by holding over them the prospect of this or that retribution—even massacre—if the Kelts took the city. He had long been assured of Boutoumites' loyalty and he knew that in such matters he would take energetic measure. The history of the foregoing events has been set out in chronological order from the beginning.

Notes   *Fulcher of Chartres*

1   Henry IV (1054-1106), German king and antagonist of the Cluny reform papacy, had been crowned Emperor of the Romans by antipope Clement III in 1084. Fulcher's sympathies with the reform party are apparent here and below.

2   Philip I (1060-1108), already in trouble with the church for his bigamous relations with Bertrada of Montfort, was re-excommunicated at Clermont in November, 1095.

3   Urban II (1088-1100) was the friend and disciple of Gregory VII (1073-85), the great champion of the Cluny reform movement.

4   This heading does not fit chap. iii because the chapter does not mention Jerusalem, the Holy Sepulcher, or the Holy Land. The chapter is broad in scope and includes the rescue of the Byzantines as a large part of the purpose of the crusade. As this and some other chapter headings do not fit the chapters they entitle, it is probable that the divisions in the text were made and titled by a later scribe, not by Fulcher.

5   Guibert had been the Archbishop of Ravenna. In the famous investiture controversy between the Emperor Henry IV and Pope Gregory VII [Hildebrand], Guibert sided with Henry and as a result was chosen (anti-) pope in 1080, taking the name of Clement III. He died in 1100.

6   Fulcher sarcastically refers to Henry IV not as Emperor of the Romans but of the Bavarians. Henry had become Duke of Bavaria in 1055 and drew much of his strength from that area.

7   Gregory died in 1085, and his successor, Victor

III, reigned briefly from 1086 to 1087. Then the former Cluny monk, the Frenchman Odo de Lagny, Cardinal Bishop of Ostia, was elected pope in 1088, taking the name of Urban II.

8 Fulcher, in referring to the year (1096) when the Franks first passed through Rome, must have been writing after they had passed through again, that is, after the members of the Crusade of 1101 went through. By "Franks" Fulcher meant "crusaders" because most crusaders at that time (though by no means all) were Frenchmen.

9 Fulcher here identifies himself by name and as a member of the First Crusade. The phrase "successful conclusion" indicates that he wrote it at some time after, and not before, the conclusion of that crusade in 1099.

10 The reference to Durazzo, Albania, as a part of Bulgaria dates back to the great Bulgarian monarchy of Czar Samuel (d. 1014), destroyed by the Byzantine Emperor Basil by 1018.

11 The Franks arrived at Antioch on October 20-21, 1097.

12 This refers to a demonstration against a neighboring Turkish fortress called Hârim (Harene, Aregh) in mid-November, 1097. Fulcher's figure, seven hundred, is hearsay.

13 *Fundibula*, like *petrariae*, were machines for hurling stones. The two types seem to have been much the same.

14 The auroral display and earthquake were on December 30, 1097, according to Raymond of Aguilers. The "sign in the sky" may have been something imagined in the auroral display.

15 This may refer to skirmishes of November 18, 1097, or March 6, 1098.

16 *i.e.*, until late in September, 1098.

17 The Roman Emperor Hadrian (117-38).

Notes *Solomon Bar Simson*

1 Our narrator's derogatory references to the Holy Family were influenced by an earlier work known as *Ma'aseh Yeshu*, and also as *Toldot Yeshu*.

2 Bishop John of Speyer (1090-1104).

3 The name of the bishop of Worms of this period was Adalbert or Allenbrand.

4 This is an allusion to the register of martyrs which preceded Bar Simson's account.

5 It seems that Emicho ignored the order of Emperor Henry and attacked Speyer on 3 May 1096. The same troops assaulted the Jews in Worms on 18 May. A second attack on the Worms community by a local mob occurred on 25 May.

6 Archbishop Ruthard of Mainz (1089-1109).

7 The official leader of the community—an office generally reserved for men of unquestionable character and piety.

8 The "evil waters" refer to baptism.

9 This is a reference to the speech of Pope Urban II at Clermont on 27 November 1095.

10 A reference to the quorum of ten adult male Jews required for congregational prayer.

11 Emicho, count of Leiningen, commanded a band of Crusaders.

12 Archbishop Ruthard of Mainz.

13 Corresponding to 27 May 1096.

14 Rabbi Eliezer bar Nathan reports that 1,300 were killed in Mainz.

Notes *Ibn Al-Athir*

1 The Fatimids were also Muslims, but they were heretics and so opposed to the rest of *sunni* Islam.

2 One *farsakh* (parasang) is about four miles.

3 The date given here is wrong; the Egyptians took Jerusalem in August 1098.

4 The rock from which, the Muslims believe, Muhammad ascended into heaven. Over it was built the so-called 'Mosque of 'Umar', the chief Islamic monument in Jerusalem. It was from this Mosque that the conquerors took their booty. Near by, but separate from it, is the 'Farthest Mosque' (al-Masjid al-Aqsa), where according to Ibn al-Athir the armies of the Cross showed even greater barbarity. The two sanctuaries are often confused in both Arabic and European sources.

5 The Prophet, who from the tomb raises his voice to rebuke his descendants (the sons of Hashim), that is, the unworthy Caliphs whose opposition to the Crusades is only half-hearted.

Notes *Anna Comnena*

1 He was known to his contemporaries as Peter the Little but we know him as Peter the Hermit.

2 Another name (like Ishaelites) for the Turks, i.e. descendants of Hagar.

3 Anna is unfair to the Mohammedans, but other authors accuse them of excessive wine-bibbing. She seems to be unaware that Aphrodite, Astarte and Ashtaroth are identical goddesses of love.

4 Chobar (or Chabar), meaning 'The Great', was the name given by the Saracens to the goddess of love.

5 Godfrey of Bouillon, Duke of Lower Lorraine.

6 The Crusaders arrived at Constantinople on 1

August 1096. They crossed the Bosphorus on 6 August. The attack on Nicaea, which was the headquarters of the Seljuq sultan (Kilij Arslan), took place in September.

7   Hugh of Vermandois, younger son of Henry I of France and Anne of Kiev. Despite his extraordinary bombast he had made little mark in French politics.

8   William of Melun. Apparently surnamed 'the Carpenter' because of his strength.

9   Given by the pope to soldiers leaving to fight the infidels.

10   The *polemarch* is an army rank—a commander-in-chief of soldiers.

11   The Monastery of St. Kosmas.

12   A reference to the revolt of the Comneni.

13   2 April 1097 (also a Thursday).

14   Junior officers in the army.

15   Anna calls him Isangeles. He was Count of Toulouse and Marquis of Provence, hoped to lead the Crusaders in the field and was a rival of Bohemond.

16   In April 1097.

THE FOURTH LATERAN COUNCIL

THE COUNCIL CALLED BY INNOCENT III IN 1215 WAS THE GREATEST ecclesiastical assembly of the century. It was attended by over four hundred bishops, eight hundred priests, and representatives of all the princes of Europe. The canons of the council, given below, attempted to address the essential doctrinal issues of Christianity as well as the problem of clerical and lay disciplines.

Source: Harry Rothwell, (ed.) *English Historical Documents 1189-1327* (London: Eyre and Spottiswoods, 1975).

Canons of the Fourth Lateran Council, 1215

1. We firmly believe and simply confess, that there is one only true God, eternal, without measure, omnipotent, unchangeable, incomprehensible and ineffable, the Father, the Son, and the Holy Spirit: three persons indeed, but one simple essence, substance, or nature altogether; the Father of none, the Son of the Father alone, and the Holy Spirit proceeding; consubstantial, and co-equal, co-omnipotent, and co-eternal; one principle of all things; the creator of all things visible and invisible, spiritual and corporal, who by His omnipotent virtue at once from the beginning of time established out of nothing both forms of creation, spiritual and corporal, that is the angelic and the mundane, and afterwards the human creature, composed as it were of spirit and body in common. For the devil and other demons were created by God naturally good, but they became evil by their own doing. Man, however, sinned by the suggestion of the devil.

This Holy Trinity, undivided as regards common essence, and distinct in respect of proper qualities of person, in accordance with the perfectly ordered plan for the ages, gave the teaching of salvation to the human race first by means of Moses and the holy prophets and others His servants. Finally the only-begotten son of God, Jesus Christ, incarnate of the whole Trinity in common, being conceived of Mary ever Virgin by the cooperation of the Holy Spirit, made very man, compounded of a reasonable soul and human flesh, one person in two natures, shewed the way of life in all its clearness. He, while as regards His divinity He is immortal and incapable of suffering, nevertheless, as regards His humanity, was made capable of suffering and mortal. He also, having suffered for the salvation of the human race upon the wood of the cross and died, descended to hell, rose again from the dead, and ascended into heaven; but descended in spirit and rose again in flesh, and ascended in both alike to come at the end of the world to judge the quick and the dead, and to render to every man according to his works, both to the reprobate and to the elect, who all shall rise again with their own bodies which they now wear, that they may receive according to their works, whether they be good or bad, these perpetual punishment with the devil, and those everlasting glory with Christ.

There is moreover one universal church of the faithful, outside which no man at all is saved, in which the same Jesus Christ is both the priest and the sacrifice, whose body and blood are truly contained in the sacrament of the altar under the species of bread and wine, the bread being transubstantiated into the body and the wine into the blood by the divine power, in order that, to accomplish the mystery of unity, we ourselves may receive of His that which He received of ours. This sacrament no one can perform but a priest, who has been duly ordained, according to the keys of the church, which Jesus Christ Himself granted to the apostles and their successors.

But the sacrament of baptism, which is consecrated in water by invoking the indivisible Trinity, that is the Father, and the Son, and the Holy Spirit, is profitable to the salvation of children and adults alike when duly conferred in proper church fashion by anyone, whosoever he be. And if anyone, after receiving baptism, has fallen into sin, he can always be redeemed by true penitence. Not only virgins and the continent, but married people too, find favor with God by right faith and good works and deserve to attain eternal blessedness.

2. We condemn therefore and reject the little book or treatise which the abbot Joachim has put out against Mr. Peter Lombard on the unity or essence of the Trinity, calling him a heretic and madman because he said in his *Sentences*, "There is a supreme reality which is Father, Son and Holy Ghost and it does not beget, neither is it begotten, nor does it proceed," from which he asserts that Peter Lombard makes God not so much a Trinity as a quaternity, that is to say three persons and the common essence, a sort of fourth, declaring plainly that there is no reality which is Father, Son and Holy Ghost, neither is it essence, substance or nature, although he concedes that Father, Son and Holy Ghost are one essence, one substance, and one nature. He professes, however, that such a unity is not true and proper, but, as it were, a collective and analogous unity in the way many men are called one people and many believers one church, according to "The multitude of them that believed were of one heart and one soul", and "He that is joined unto the Lord is one spirit" with him; also "He that planteth and he that watereth are one", and all of us "are one body in Christ": again, in the book of Kings, "My people and thy people are one." But to establish this opinion he adduces above all what Christ says in the gospel about believers: "I wish, Father, that they may be one in us, even as we are one, that they may be made perfect in one." For (so he says) Christians are not one, i.e. a single reality common to all: they are one in this way, i.e., one church because of the unity of the catholic faith and finally one kingdom because of the indissoluble union of charity. Thus one reads in the canonical Epistle of John, "For there are three that bear record in heaven, the Father, the Word, and the Holy Ghost, and these three are one," and immediately the author adds, "And there are three that bear witness in earth, the spir-

it, the water, and the blood, and these three are one", according to certain manuscripts.

But we, with the approbation of the holy and universal council, believe and confess with Peter [Lombard] that there is one single supreme reality, incomprehensible indeed and ineffable, who truly is Father, Son and Holy Ghost, the three persons together and each of them separately, and therefore in God there is a Trinity only, not a quaternity, because each of the three persons is that reality, that is to say essence, substance or divine nature, which alone is the principle of all things, apart from which another cannot be found, and that reality does not beget, neither is it begotten, nor does it proceed, but it is the Father who begets, the Son who is begotten, and the Holy Ghost which proceeds, so there are distinctions of person and unity of nature. Although therefore one person is the Father, another is the Son, another the Holy Ghost, there is not another, but that which is the Father is the Son and the Holy Ghost, altogether the same, so, according to the orthodox and catholic faith, they are believed to be consubstantial. For the Father by begetting everlastingly the Son gave him his substance, as he himself testifies, "What the Father gave me is greater than all," and it cannot be said that he gave part of his substance to him and kept part for himself, as the substance of the Father is indivisible inasmuch as it is utterly simple; but neither can it be said that the Father transferred his substance to the Son in begetting him, as if he so gave it to the Son that he did not keep it himself, otherwise he would have ceased to be substance. It is clear therefore that in being born the Son received the substance of the Father without any diminution of it, and so the Father and the Son have the same substance and thus the Father and the Son and the Holy Ghost proceeding from both are the same reality. When therefore Truth prays to the Father for those believing in him, saying, "I wish that they may be one in us, as we also are one," this word "one" is taken to mean in the case of believers the union of charity in grace, in the case of divine persons the unity of identity in nature, as Truth says elsewhere, "Be ye perfect even as your heavenly Father is perfect," as if it were to say more plainly, "Be ye perfect" with the perfection of grace "as your heavenly Father is perfect" with the perfection of nature—each, that is, after his fashion, for between the Creator and a creature there can be remarked no similarity so great that a greater dissimilarity cannot be seen between them.

If therefore anyone ventures to defend or approve the opinion or teaching of the said Joachim on this matter, he is to be refuted by all as a heretic. By this however we do not wish to do anything at all to the detriment of the monastery of Fiore, of which Joachim was the founder, because there the foundation is according to rule and the observance is in a healthy state; particularly as this same Joachim ordered all his writings to be sent to us for approval or correction at the judgment of the apostolic see and composed a letter, signed by his own hand, in which he firmly confesses that he holds the faith held by the Roman church, the mother and teacher, by the divine plan, of all believers. We reject and condemn also the utterly perverse opinion of the impious Aymer whose mind the father of lies has blinded to such an extent that his teaching must be reckoned not so much heretical as insane.

3. We excommunicate and anathematise every heresy setting itself up against this holy, orthodox, catholic faith which we have expounded above, and condemn all heretics by whatever names they go under: they have various faces indeed, but tails tied one to another, for they have vanity in common. Those condemned as heretics shall be handed over to the secular authorities present or to their bailiffs for punishment by the penalty deserved, clerks first being degraded from their orders. The goods of these condemned are, if they are laymen, to be confiscated, if clerks, assigned to the churches from which they drew their stipend. Those found no more than suspect of heresy shall, unless they prove their innocence by a suitable purgation having regard to the reasons for suspicion and the character of the person, be struck by the sword of anathema, and until adequate satisfaction has been made they shall be avoided by everybody, so that if they continue under excommunication for a year they shall be condemned as heretics forthwith. Secular authorities, whatever functions they discharge, shall be instructed, exhorted and, if necessary, compelled by ecclesiastical censure, as they wish to be reputed Christian and treated as such, to take for the defence of the faith public oath that they will concern themselves and do their utmost in good faith to expel from lands under their jurisdiction all heretics pointed out by the church: accordingly from now on whenever anyone is raised to a position of authority spiritual or temporal he shall be bound to confirm this chapter on oath. If however a temporal lord, required and instructed by the church, neglects to purge his land of this heretical filth he shall be bound by the metropolitan and the other bishops of the same province with the bond of excommunication, and if he disdains to render satisfaction within the year it shall be reported to the supreme pontiff in order that he may forthwith declare his vassals absolved from their fealty to him, and make the land available for occupation by catholics, who when they have evicted the heretics are to have possession of it without opposition and keep it in the purity of the faith— saving the right of the principal lord, provided that in this matter he opposes no obstacle and puts no impediment in the way. The same rule is to be no less observed for those who do not have principal lords. Catholics who having taken the cross undertake to expel heretics shall enjoy the indulgence and be protected by the holy privilege allowed to those going to the help of the Holy Land. We decree that adherents of, besides receivers, defenders and helpers of heretics are liable to excommunication and firmly ordain that if any such, after being marked with excommunication refuses to render satisfaction within the year he shall forthwith be *ipso facto* branded with infamy, not to be admitted to public office or advisory functions or the electing of anyone to such, and his testimony shall not be acceptable; he shall also be *intestabilis*, i.e. he shall not have the right to make a will and he may not enter upon the succession to an inheritance; no one moreover shall be forced to answer to him about any matter whatever, but he shall answer to others. If he chances to be a judge, his sentence shall have no force, nor shall any causes be brought to his court; if he is an advocate his pleading shall not be listened to at all; if a notary, documents

drawn up by him shall have no weight whatever, but be condemned with their condemned author; other cases we order to be treated similarly. If however he is a clerk he shall be deprived of every office and benefice, so that the heavier punishment may be employed against him whose fault is the greater. If any refuse to avoid heretics after they have been pointed out by the church they shall be struck by the sentence of excommunication until proper satisfaction has been made. Clerks shall not, of course, administer the church's sacraments to such pestilent folk or presume to give them Christian burial or accept their alms or offerings; otherwise they shall be deprived of their office and never be restored to it without a special indult of the apostolic see. Similarly with regulars of whatever sort, and on them this too shall be inflicted—that their privileges are not to be respected in the diocese in which they have presumed to commit such excesses. Because some "under a form of godliness denying (as the Apostle says) the power thereof" claim for themselves the authority to preach when the same Apostle says, "How shall they preach except they be sent?", all who are prohibited or not yet sent but presume to usurp publicly or privately the office of preaching without having received the authority of the apostolic see or the catholic bishop of the place shall be bound by the bond of excommunication, and unless they repent very promptly shall be punished by another appropriate penalty. We add moreover that every archbishop or bishop shall personally or through his archdeacon or other suitable and upright persons visit twice or at least once a year any parish of his in which there are said to be heretics and there compel three or more men of good reputation, or even if it seems expedient the whole neighborhood, to swear that if anyone knows of heretics there or of any who hold secret conventicles or any whose life and habits differ from the normal way of living of Christians he will make it his business to point them out to the bishop. He, the bishop, shall summon the accused to his presence and if they do not clear themselves[1] of the accusation, or if after clearance they relapse into their former errors of faith, they shall be punished in accordance with canon law. If any of them, however, refuse with

damnable obstinacy to be bound by oath and will not swear, they shall be from that very fact reckoned as heretics. We will, command and strictly order, on the strength of their obedience, bishops to see carefully to the effective execution of these things all over their dioceses, if they wish to escape canonical punishment; for if any bishop is negligent or slack over clearing the ferment of heresy from his diocese when it shows itself by unmistakable signs he shall be deposed from his office as bishop and in his place another suitable person substituted who has the will and the power to overthrow heresy.

4. Although we should like to cherish and honor the Greeks, who in our time are returning to the obedience of the apostolic see, by maintaining as much as we can under the Lord their customs and rites, we neither want to nor should defer to them in things which breed danger to souls and detract from the decorum of the church. For after the Greek church withdrew with certain associates and supporters from the obedience of the apostolic see the Greeks began to loathe the Latins so much that, among other wicked things they did out of contempt for them, they would not, when Latin priests had celebrated on their altars, themselves sacrifice on them before they had washed them, as if by this they had been defiled. Also, those baptized by Latins these Greeks had the temerity to rebaptize and there are some still, we are told, who do not fear to do it. Wishing therefore to do away with such a scandal in the church of God, we on the advice of the holy council strictly command them not to venture to do such things in future and to conform like obedient sons to the holy Roman church, their mother, so that there may be "one fold and one shepherd". If anyone does venture to do such a thing he shall be struck with the sword of excommunication and deprived of every ecclesiastical office and benefice.

5. Renewing the ancient privileges of the patriarchal see, we decree with the approbation of the holy universal council that, after the Roman church, which by the divine plan, has as mother and ruler of all Christians the primacy of ordinary power over all other churches, the churches

of Constantinople shall have the first place, that of Alexandria the second, that of Antioch the third, that of Jerusalem the fourth, each of them keeping its own authority—so that after their pontiffs have received the pallium, which is the distinguishing mark of the plenitude of the pontifical office, from the Roman pontiff and taken the oath of fealty and obedience to him, they may lawfully confer the pallium on their own suffragans and receive from them for themselves the canonical profession and for the Roman church the promise of obedience. They shall have the standard of the divine cross carried before them everywhere save in Rome or wherever the pope (or his legate) is present wearing the insignia of apostolic dignity. In all provinces under their jurisdiction appeal, when necessary, shall be made to them, except for appeals lodged with the apostolic see, to which all must humbly defer.

6.   As is known to have been ordained of old by the holy fathers, metropolitans should not fail to hold provincial councils every year with their suffragans to consider diligently and in the fear of God the correction of excesses and the reform of morals, especially in the clergy, reciting the canonical rules (particularly those laid down by the present general council) to secure their observance, inflicting on transgressors the punishment due. In order that this may be the more effectively achieved, they are to set up in each diocese suitable persons, discreet that is and honest, who throughout the year shall carefully find out simply and summarily without any jurisdiction what things deserve correction or reform and faithfully report those things to the metropolitan and suffragans and others at the ensuing council, that they after careful deliberation may proceed against these things and others suitably and decently. What they decree, they shall cause to be observed, making it known in diocesan synods, which shall be held annually in each diocese. Whoever neglects to act upon this salutary statute is to be suspended from his benefices and his office until he is released by the decision of his superior.

7.   By an irrevocable decree we ordain that persons in authority over churches shall prudently and diligently give their minds to correcting the excesses and reforming the morals of those, especially the clergy, subject to them, lest the blood of these be required at their hands. So that they can perform the task of correcting and reforming freely, we decree that no custom or appeal can impede the execution of their [sentences], unless they have exceeded the rules to be observed in such things. Let, however, the excesses of canons of a cathedral church which by custom have been corrected by the chapter be corrected by it, in churches which have had such a custom until now, at the instance and on the orders of the bishop within a sufficient time-limit, which the bishop shall fix. If this is not done, then the bishop, mindful of God and putting a stop to all opposition, shall not delay to correct them by ecclesiastical censure as the care of souls requires, and not omit to correct their other excesses too as the charge of souls requires, due order nevertheless being observed in all things. For the rest, if canons stop celebrating divine service without manifest and reasonable cause, particularly in contempt of the bishop, the bishop may celebrate in the cathedral church notwithstanding if he wishes, and on complaint from him the metropolitan as our delegate for this may, when he has established the truth of the matter, chastise them with ecclesiastical censure in such fashion that for fear of the punishment they shall not venture such action in future. Let those in authority over churches carefully see to it therefore that they do not turn this salutary decree into a way of getting money or other exaction, but operate it zealously and faithfully if they wish to avoid canonical punishment, since the apostolic see will, with divine authority, watch over these things most particularly.

8.   "By what right and in what way a prelate ought to proceed to enquire into and punish the excesses of subordinates is clearly shown from the testimony assembled in the New and Old Testament, from which the subsequent canon law sanctions derive," as we said distinctly some time ago and now with the approbation of the holy council confirm. For one reads in the gospel that the bailiff who was "denounced to his lord for having wasted his goods" heard from him,

"What is this I hear of thee? Give an account of thy bailiwick for now thou canst no more be bailiff." And in Genesis God says, "I will go down now, and see whether they have done altogether according to the cry of it which is come to me." From which authorities it is clearly proved that not only when a subordinate but even a prelate commits some excess and through complaint and rumour it reaches the ears of his superior, not from the ill-disposed and slanderous but from prudent and honest people, not just once but often (which complaint implies and rumour is manifest proof of), he, the superior, ought in the presence of senior people of the church to enquire into the truth and if the case demands it canonical distress shall smite the fault of the offender—not as if he were accuser and judge but with rumour informing and complaint denouncing, as one carrying out the duty of his office. While this is to be done in the case of subordinates, it must still more carefully be done in the case of prelates, who are set "as a mark for the arrow". And because they cannot please everybody since they are bound *ex officio* not only to reprove but also to blame, nay even at times to suspend, sometimes to bind, they frequently incur the hatred of many people and are liable to ambushes. For this reason the holy fathers wisely decreed that accusation of prelates is not to be allowed easily, for fear that if the columns are shaken the building may fall, unless there is careful provision for shutting the door against not only false but also malicious accusation. They wished so to provide for prelates not to be accused unjustly that they would take care all the same not to offend out of arrogance and they found a suitable preventative for either evil, viz, that a criminal accusation, which entails the *diminutio capitis*, i.e. degradation, shall in no wise be allowed unless it is preceded by the *inscriptio legitima*.[2] But when anyone is so notorious for his excesses that complaint now cannot be ignored any longer without scandal or without danger allowed to continue, action is to be taken without the slightest hesitation to enquire into and punish his excesses, not out of hate but out of charity; with the condition that if it is a matter of grave excess, though not one involving his degradation, he shall be deprived of all office, in accor-

dance with the gospel sentence that the bailiff is to be removed from his bailiwick who cannot give a proper account of it. He ought therefore to be present about whom enquiry is to be made, unless out of contumacy he absents himself, and the points to be enquired into should be set out before him so that he can be in a position to defend himself, and not only the depositions of the witnesses but also their names, in order that he may know what has been said and who said it, are to be revealed to him, also legitimate exceptions and replications are to be allowed, lest through the suppression of names the audacious may prefer false charges or through the barring of exceptions, bear false witness. A prelate ought to be all the more zealous to correct the excesses of his subordinates, the more to blame he would be for leaving their offences unpunished. Against them, notorious cases aside, although three procedures are possible, viz, by accusation, denunciation and inquest, let careful precautions nevertheless be taken in all cases lest for the sake of a slight gain grave loss may be incurred: just as the *legitima inscriptio* ought to precede the accusation, so a kindly warning ought to come before denunciation and entry of complaint before inquest, always with the rule applied that the method of pronouncing sentence shall be according to the mode of trial. This order, however, need not in our view be observed in all respects as regards regulars, who can at need be more easily and freely removed from their offices.

9.   Since in many parts peoples of different languages with various rites and usages within the common faith are mixed together in the same city and diocese, we strictly command the bishops of cities or dioceses of this sort to appoint suitable men to celebrate divine service for them in the various rites and languages, administer the ecclesiastical sacraments to them and instruct them by word and by example alike. We utterly forbid one and the same city or diocese to have more than one bishop, like a body with more than one head as if it were a monster, yet if for the reasons aforesaid necessity requires it, the bishop of the place may after careful deliberation set up a catholic bishop appropriate for those nations as vicar for himself in the aforesaid matters, who will in all

respects be under and obedient to him—as to which, if anyone behaves otherwise he shall know he is smitten by the sword of excommunication, and if he does not then recover his senses he is to be deposed from all ecclesiastical office, the help of the secular arm being invoked if necessary to curb such presumption.

10. Among the other things pertaining to the saving of Christian souls the bread of the gospel is recognized as the most necessary of all, for as the body is nourished by material food so is the soul by spiritual, because "Man does not live by bread alone, but by every word that proceedeth out of the mouth of God." Hence, since it often happens that bishops because of their manifold occupations or bodily ailments or enemy attacks or other reasons—not to mention lack of learning, in them a most grievous fault, not to be tolerated in future—are unable themselves to do all the preaching of the gospel to the people that is needed, especially in large and scattered dioceses, we by a general constitution decree that bishops are to choose men effective in action and speech, suitable for executing the office of sacred preaching to advantage, to visit zealously the peoples committed to them in their place when they themselves cannot and edify them by word and example, and they are to furnish these men, when they need them, with what is appropriate and necessary lest for lack of the things necessary they be forced to abandon an undertaking. We order, in consequence, suitable men to be appointed as well in cathedral as in other conventual churches for the bishops to have as coadjutors and cooperators not only in preaching but also in hearing confessions and enjoining penances and everything else pertaining to the saving of souls. If any one neglects to carry this out, he shall be subject to rigorous punishment.

11. As because of their poverty some have neither the opportunity to study nor chance of advancement, the Lateran council[3] provided by pious decree that "in each cathedral church some competent benefice should be given to a master, whose duty it should be to instruct for nothing the clerks of that church and other poor scholars, thus at once relieving the need of the teacher and opening up the path of knowledge to those who are learning". Since, however, this decree is very little observed in many churches, we confirm it, adding that not only in every cathedral church but also in others, whose resources are adequate, a suitable master, elected by the chapter or the greater and sounder part of the chapter, shall be established by the prelate. He is to instruct for nothing the clerks of those churches and of others in grammar and in other branches of study as far as possible. The metropolitan church shall maintain nonetheless a theologian to teach holy writ to priests and others and above all instruct them in those things which are recognized as having to do with the cure of souls. To each of the masters there is to be assigned by the chapter the income of a single prebend, and just as much by the metropolitan for the theologian, without his being made on that account a canon, though he shall get the revenues of one as long as he remains prepared to teach. If the metropolitan church finds the two a burden, let it provide for the theologian in the way stated, but for the grammarian get adequate provision made in another church of the city or diocese.

12. In each kingdom or province let there be held every three years, saving the right of diocesan bishops, a general chapter of abbots and of priors without an abbot of their own who have not been accustomed to hold one. They should all attend, if there is no canonical impediment, at one of the monasteries which is suitable for the purpose, with this limitation—that none of them shall bring with him more than six mounts and eight persons. Let them call in as a favor at the start of this innovation two neighboring Cistercian abbots to furnish appropriate counsel and assistance, as they have long been accustomed to holding such chapters and are very knowledgeable. They, with no opposition, shall coopt two they think would be a help from their own order, and these four shall preside over the general chapter, in such a way that from this no one of them assumes leadership; so, if need be, they can, after careful deliberation, be changed. This kind of chapter shall last several consecutive days, as is Cistercian practice, and in it there is to be care-

ful consideration of the reform of the order and the observance of the rule, and what is decided with the approval of those four is to be inviolably observed by all, without any excuse, opposition or appeal. It shall be settled as well where the chapter is to be held next time. Those attending are to lead a common life and divide between them, proportionately, the common expenses. If they cannot all be put up in the same house, let them stay many together at least in several houses. In the same chapter too let there be appointed discreet religious who will make it their business to visit, in the way prescribed for them and on our behalf, every abbey of monks and of nuns of the kingdom or province to correct and reform what in their view needs correction and reform. If they consider that the superior of the place should be removed outright from the running of it, they shall denounce him to his bishop, that he may remove him, and if he does not do it, the visitors shall refer the matter to the consideration of the papal see. This same thing we will and command canons regular to observe according to their order. If any difficulty arises out of this innovation which cannot be resolved by the said visitors, let it be referred without fuss to the judgment of the papal see, the rest of what after careful discussion they have agreed upon being observed without being called in question again. On the other hand, diocesan bishops shall make it their business so to reform the monasteries under their jurisdiction that when the said visitors come they find more in them worthy of commendation than of correction; and shall be most careful lest the said monasteries are oppressed by them with undue burdens, for, just as we wish the rights of superiors to be upheld, we do not wish to support wrongs done to inferiors. Furthermore, we strictly command both diocesan bishops and those who preside at chapters to restrain by ecclesiastical censure, with no appeal from it, advocates, patrons, vidames, rectors and consuls, magnates and knights, or any others, from presuming to commit offences against monasteries in respect of their persons or their things, and should they have committed such an offence they shall without fail force them to give satisfaction, so that monasteries may serve Almighty God freely and quietly.

13.   For fear too great a diversity of religious orders should lead to grave confusion in the church of God, we firmly forbid anyone in future to invent a new religious order: whoever wishes to become a religious must adopt one of the approved orders. Similarly, anyone wishing to found a new religious house must accept the rule and constitutions of one of the approved religious orders. We forbid also anyone to presume to have a place as a monk in more than one monastery.

14.   That the morals and conduct of clerks may be improved, let all strive to live continently and chastely, especially those established in holy orders; let them seek to avoid completely the sin of lust—particularly that on account of which the anger of God comes down from heaven upon the sins of disobedience—in order that they may be able to minister in the sight of Almighty God with a pure heart and clean body. Lest too easy a pardon afford an incentive to sin, we decree that they who are caught giving way to the sin of incontinence shall in proportion to the degree of their sin be punished according to the rules of canon law, which we wish to be most effectively and rigorously observed in order that those whom the fear of God does not hold back from evil temporal punishment at least may restrain from sin. If anyone, therefore, suspended because of this, presumes to celebrate the divine service he shall not only be deprived of ecclesiastical benefices but also for this twofold transgression be forever deposed from office. Prelates who venture to support such in their wickednesses, especially for money or other temporal advantage, shall be subject to like punishment. Those who, in the manner of their country, have not renounced the marriage bond shall if they fall into sin be punished more severely, since they can avail themselves of lawful matrimony.

15.   All clerks shall carefully abstain from gluttony and drunkenness, by which means they may temper the wine to themselves and themselves to the wine; and let no one be urged to drink, as drunkenness both causes the loss of one's senses and rouses the temptation to lust. Accordingly we decree that that abuse is to be

utterly abolished whereby in certain parts drinkers bind each other to drink measure for measure and he in their judgment is most praised who has made most people drunk and drained the deepest cups. If anyone shows himself to blame in these things, unless he makes suitable satisfaction when warned by his superior he is to be suspended from his benefice or office. Hunting and bird-catching we forbid for all clerks, hence let them not presume to have either hunting dogs or falcons.

16. Clerks are not to practice secular callings or business, especially if they are dishonorable, not to watch mimes, entertainers and actors and not to frequent taverns at all, unless compelled of necessity to do so on a journey. They are not to play at dice or the little dice[4] or be present at such games. They are to have a suitable crown and tonsure and apply themselves to the divine services and other good pursuits. They are to wear outer garments that are closed, not noticeable by being too short or too long; they are not to indulge in red or green cloths, long sleeves or shoes with embroidery or with curved toes, bridles, pectorals and spurs that are gilded or have other unnecessary ornamentation. Priests and those in minor dignities are not to wear cloaks with sleeves at divine service inside the church, and not even elsewhere, unless a justifiable fear requires a change of dress. They are not to wear buckles or belts ornamented with gold or silver, or even rings except those whose dignity it befits to have them. All bishops are to wear outer garments of linen in public and in church unless they are monks, when they should wear the monastic habit: they are not to wear their cloaks loose in public, but fastened on either side behind the neck or at the chest.

17. We grieve to relate that not only certain lesser clerks but also some prelates spend nearly half the night in unnecessary feasting and forbidden conversation, not to mention other things, and leaving for sleep what is left of the night, they are barely roused at the dawn chorus of the birds and doze away the whole morning. There are also others who celebrate mass barely four times a year or, what is worse, do not bother to attend it,

and if they are present while it is being celebrated, they flee the silence of the choir and pay attention to the conversation of the laity outside and, while they are listening to things being said that they are not required to, their ears are not intent on the service. These things and the like we utterly forbid therefore on pain of suspension and strictly command them on the strength of their obedience to celebrate the divine service, day and night alike, as far as God allows them, with zeal and devotion.

18. No clerk may decree or pronounce a sentence of death; nor may he carry out a punishment which involves blood or be there when it is carried out. If anyone presumes to inflict injury on churches or ecclesiastical persons by transgressing this decree he shall be restrained by ecclesiastical censure. Nor shall any clerk write or dictate letters requiring a punishment which involves blood: in the courts of princes let this responsibility be given to laymen, not clerks. Also let no clerk be put in command of mercenaries, crossbowmen or suchlike men of blood; and no subdeacon, deacon, or priest is to practise the art of surgery, which involves burning and cutting; and none is to bestow any blessing or consecration on a purgation by ordeal of boiling water or of cold water or of the red-hot iron, saving nevertheless previously promulgated prohibitions concerning single combats or duels.

19. We do not wish it to be left uncorrected that certain clerks store their own furniture, and that of others, in churches, so that they look more like lay houses than houses of God, regardless of the fact that God would not suffer a vessel to be carried through the temple. There are others too who not only let churches fall into neglect, but also leave the sacred vessels and the liturgical vestments and the altar-cloths too and the very communion-cloths so dirty that at times they horrify some people. Now because the zeal of God's house has eaten us up, we firmly prohibit such furniture to be allowed into churches unless on account of enemy attacks or sudden fire or other emergencies they have to be taken in; yet so that when the emergency is over things are taken back to where they were. We command too that orato-

ries, vessels, communion-cloths and the aforementioned vestments be kept clean and fresh. For
it seems too absurd to neglect an uncleanness in
sacred things which would be disgraceful even in
profane.

20. We order the chrism and the eucharist in all
churches to be kept locked away in a safe place so
that no audacious hand can reach them to do
anything horrible or impious. If he who is
responsible for keeping them is careless and
leaves them about he shall be suspended from
office for three months, and if through his carelessness anything unspeakable happens to them
he shall be subject to greater punishment.

21. Every Christian of either sex after reaching
the years of discretion shall confess all his sins at
least once a year privately to his own priest and
try as hard as he can to perform the penance
imposed on him; and receive with reverence the
sacrament of the eucharist at least at Easter,
unless for some reasonable cause, on the advice
of his own priest, he thinks he should temporarily refrain from taking it. Otherwise he shall be
barred from entering a church in his lifetime and
at death shall not have Christian burial. This
salutary decree shall be published frequently in
churches, so that no one can find the veil of an
excuse in the blindness of ignorance. Should,
however, anyone for good reasons wish to confess his sins to another priest, let him first ask for
and get the permission of his own priest, otherwise the other will not be able to absolve him or
bind him. As for the priest, he should be discerning and prudent so that like a practised doctor he
can pour wine and oil on the wounds of the
injured, diligently enquiring into the circumstances both of the sinner and of the sin, from
which to choose intelligently what sort of advice
he ought to give him and what sort of remedy to
apply, various means availing to heal the sick. Let
him take the utmost care not to betray the sinner
in some measure by word or sign or any other
way whatever, but if he needs sage advice, let
him seek it cautiously without mentioning the
person: he who presumes to reveal a sin dis-
closed in the confessional we decree is to be not
only deposed from his priestly office but also

shut up to do penance for life in a monastery of
strict observance.

22. As physical illness is sometimes the result of
sin—the Lord said to a sick man whom he had
cured, "Go and sin no more, lest worse befall
you,"—we by the present decree ordain and
strictly command doctors, when it happens
before anything else to call in doctors of souls, so
that after his spiritual health has been seen to, the
sick man may respond better to the bodily medicine—for when the cause ceases, the effect ceases.
This among other things has occasioned this
decree: that some on a sickbed, when advised by
doctors to arrange for the good of their souls, fall
into a state of despair, whereby they incur more
easily the danger of death. If any doctor shall
transgress this our decree, after it has been published by the local prelates, he shall be barred
from entering a church more, until he has performed the appropriate penance for this sort of
transgression. Furthermore, as the soul is much
more precious than the body, we forbid on pain
of eternal anathema any doctor to prescribe anything for a sick man for his bodily health which
might endanger his soul.

23. Lest for lack of a shepherd a rapacious wolf
attack the Lord's flock and a bereaved church suffer grave injury to its goods and wishing in this
matter to counteract the danger to souls and provide protection for churches, we decree that a
cathedral or monastic church may not be without
a prelate for more than three months, and if, there
being no lawful impediment, an election is not
made within that time, those who should have
elected shall be for that occasion deprived of the
power to elect and it shall devolve upon him who
is recognized as the immediate superior. He on
whom the power has devolved shall, ever mindful of the Lord, not delay more than three months
in supplying, with the counsel of his chapter and
of other discreet men, the bereaved church
canonically with a suitable person from that
church or another church if one is not to be found
in that, if he wishes to escape canonical penalty.

24. Owing to the various forms of election
which some try to invent, both many impedi-

ments are produced and great dangers threaten bereaved churches. Because of this we decree that when an election is to be made, with all present who ought, want to and conveniently can be there, there shall be chosen three worthy of trust from the college who shall carefully find out in confidence one by one everybody's vote, and having written them down, shall quickly make known the result of this voting,[5] and no appeal shall be allowed to obstruct it, so that after scrutiny he shall be elected on whom the whole or the greater or sounder part of the chapter agrees. Or else the power of electing shall be committed to some suitable men, who acting for everybody shall provide the bereaved church with a pastor. Otherwise no election made shall be valid, unless perchance it was made by all unanimously as if by divine inspiration and without flaw. Those who attempt to elect contrary to the aforesaid forms shall be deprived of the power of electing on that occasion. What we absolutely forbid is that anyone should appoint a proxy in the business of election unless he is away from the place where he ought to receive the summons and, detained by a lawful impediment, cannot come— as to which, if need be, he shall take an oath—and that if he wishes he may commission someone from the electoral college in his stead. We condemn also clandestine elections and decree that as soon as an election has taken place it be solemnly published.

25. Whoever consents to election of himself by misuse of secular power contrary to canonical freedom shall both be deprived of the advantage of having been elected and be rendered ineligible; nor can he without a dispensation be elected to any dignity. Those who presume to take part in this sort of election, which we declare *ipso jure*, invalidated, shall be suspended completely from their offices and benefices for three years and during that time deprived of the power to elect.

26. There is nothing more harmful to the church of God than the elevation of unworthy prelates to the government of souls. Wishing therefore to apply the necessary medicine for this malady, we ordain by an irrevocable decree that when anyone is raised to the government of souls he who

has the right to confirm him shall diligently examine both the election procedure and the character of the person elected, so that if everything is in order he may give him his confirmation, because if it were incautiously given in advance and everything was not in order, not only would the one unworthily promoted have to be rejected but also the one who promoted unworthily would have to be punished. The latter, we decree, is to suffer this punishment: if it is clearly a matter of negligence on his part, especially if he has confirmed the election of a man of insufficient learning or disgraceful life or uncanonical age, not only shall he be deprived of the power of confirming the first one to follow that man, but also (lest by any chance he escapes punishment) be debarred from receiving the fruits of his own benefice until he can justly obtain a pardon; if convicted of having intentionally transgressed in the matter, let him suffer a heavier penalty. Bishops too shall endeavor to promote to holy orders and ecclesiastical dignities such as are able to discharge worthily the office committed to them, if they themselves wish to escape canonical penalty. For the rest, those who are immediately under the Roman pontiff shall, to get confirmation of their office, appear personally before him if it can be conveniently done or send suitable persons, by means of whom careful inquiry into election procedure and into those who are elected can be made, so that in the end, on the strength of his informed judgment, they may attain the full authority of their office, when nothing in the canon law stands in their way—provided meanwhile that those who are in very distant posts, that is outside Italy, may by dispensation, if they were elected peaceably, where it meets the church's needs or is to its advantage administer in things spiritual and temporal, but shall alienate nothing whatever belonging to the church. They may be given the customary consecration or benediction.

27. As the governing of souls is the art of arts, we strictly command bishops carefully to prepare those who are to be promoted to the priesthood and instruct them, either personally or through other suitable men, in the divine services and the sacraments of the church, in order that they may

know how to celebrate them properly: since if they presume in future to ordain the ignorant and unskilled (which could indeed be easily detected) we decree that both those who ordain and those who are ordained are to be subject to punishment. For it is better, particularly in the ordaining of priests, to have a few good than many bad ministers, because if the blind leads the blind both will fall into the ditch.

28. Certain people persistently demand leave to resign and having got it omit to do so. But in demanding such resignation they would seem to have in mind either the good of the churches over which they preside or their own well-being, neither of which things do we wish to be impeded by the advice of those seeking their own or even by any fickleness of purpose: we therefore decree that they are to be compelled to resign.

29. With great foresight it was prohibited in the Lateran council[6] for anyone to receive divers ecclesiastical dignities and several parish churches contrary to the ordinances of canon law on pain both of the receiver losing what he has thus received and of the one bestowing being deprived of the power to bestow. But as, owing to the presumption and greed of some, the said statute has borne no fruit, or very little, we, wishing to counter with a surer and stronger remedy, ordain by the present decree that whoever receives a benefice with cure of souls attached, if he already has such a benefice shall automatically be deprived of that and if perchance he tries to keep it let him be deprived of the other one also. Also he who has the giving of the first benefice shall freely bestow it, after the receiving of the second, on a person on whom he considers it can be worthily be bestowed, but if he delays more than three months over bestowing it not only shall the bestowal of it devolve upon another in accordance with the statute of the Lateran council but also he shall be forced to assign for the use of the church of the benefice in question as much from his own income as is established was obtained from it while it was vacant. The very same we decree is to be done with regard to minor dignities, adding that no one shall presume to have several dignities or minor dignities

in one and the same church even if they do not have cure of souls. As to men of birth and lettered persons, who should be honored by greater benefices, they when reason demands it can be dispensed by the apostolic see.

30. It is very serious and improper that certain heads of churches, when they could promote serious men to ecclesiastical benefices, fear not to adopt unworthy people recommended neither by upright living nor by learning, following the inclination of their heart, not the judgment of their reason. How much churches lose by this every man of right mind knows. Wishing therefore to cure this malady, we order them to pass over the unworthy and choose suitable people, who have both the desire and the ability to serve God and churches well, and let careful enquiry be made about this each year in provincial council, so that he who is found guilty after a first and a second correction shall be suspended by that council from conferring benefices, and a prudent and honest person appointed in that same council to take the place of the one suspended in conferring benefices; and the very same is to be done with regard to chapters who offend in these things. An offence by a metropolitan shall however be left by the council to be reported to the judgment of a superior. So that this salutary provision shall have its full effect, a sentence of suspension of this kind shall definitely not be lifted without the authority of the Roman pontiff or of the appropriate patriarch—that in this too the four patriarchal sees may be specially honored.

31. To abolish a very bad corruption indeed which has been on the increase in many churches, we firmly prohibit sons of canons, particularly as they are bastards, being made canons in secular churches where their fathers are established; and if in spite of this it is attempted, we decree it not valid. And they who, as has been said, venture to make canons of such shall be suspended from their benefices.

32. A vicious custom that ought to be uprooted has established itself in some parts, namely that patrons of parish churches, and certain other persons, claim the incomes from them wholly for

themselves, leaving the priests deputed to serve them so small a portion that they cannot fittingly live on it. We have learnt for certain that in some regions parish priests get for their support only a quarter of a quarter, that is a sixteenth, of the tithes. Whence it is said that in these regions scarcely any parish priest can be found who has even a modicum of education. As the ox ought not to be muzzled when it treadeth out the corn, and he who serves the altar ought to live from the altar, we decree therefore, any custom of a bishop or patron or anyone else notwithstanding, that a sufficient portion shall be assigned to the priests. He who has a parish church shall serve it not by a vicar but personally in the due form which the care of that church requires, unless perchance the parish church is annexed to a prebend or a dignity. In which case we allow that he who has such a prebend or dignity should, as he must serve in a greater church, make it his business to have in the parish church a suitable, canonically instituted perpetual[7] vicar, who, as has been said, shall have a fitting portion from the revenues of that church: otherwise, he shall know that by the authority of this decree he is deprived of that church and it is to be given freely to someone else who is willing and able to do as we have said. What we utterly forbid is that anyone should presume deceitfully to confer from the revenues of a church which has to maintain its own priest a pension on another as it were as a benefice.

33.   Procurations due, by reason of visitation, to bishops, archdeacons, or anyone else, also to legates or nuncios of the apostolic see, should by no means, without manifest and necessary cause, be exacted, save when they actually incur the expense of visitation, and then they shall observe the moderation in transport and retinue decreed in the Lateran council.[8] We add this modification as regards legates and nuncios of the apostolic see, that when they must necessarily stay in some place, so that this place may not be excessively burdened because of them they may receive moderate procurations from other churches or persons who have not yet been burdened with their procurations, on condition that the number of procurations shall not exceed the number of days they stayed in that place, and when any per-

son has not sufficient means on his own, two or more may be combined into one. Rather, those performing the office of visitation shall not seek their own but the things which are Jesus Christ's, by devoting themselves to preaching, exhortation, correction, and reformation, that they may bring back the fruit which does not perish. He who presumes to contravene this shall both restore what he has received and pay the same amount as compensation to the church he has thus burdened.

34.   Many prelates, to meet the cost of a procuration or some service to a legate or some other person, extort more from their subordinates than they pay out, and trying to gain from their loss, seek booty rather than aid from those under them. This we forbid to be done in future. And if perchance anyone ventures to do it let him both restore what has been thus extorted and be forced to distribute an equivalent amount to the poor. A superior with whom a complaint has been lodged about this shall, if he is negligent in executing this decree, suffer canonical punishment.

35.   In order that due honor be paid to judges and thought taken for litigants in the matter of trouble and expense, we decree that when anybody sues an adversary before the competent judge, he shall not before judgment has been given appeal to a superior judge without reasonable cause, but proceed with his suit before that one and it shall not be open to him to obstruct by saying that he has sent a messenger to a superior judge or even procured letters from him before they were remitted to the judge delegate. When, however, in his view he has reasonable cause for appealing, and has stated before that same judge the grounds of the appeal and these are such that if they were proved they would be reckoned legitimate, the superior judge shall take cognisance of the appeal. If he finds it not reasonable he shall send the appellant back to the inferior judge and sentence him to bear the costs of the other party; otherwise he shall proceed with the case, saving the constitutions about referring major cases to the apostolic see.

36.   As when the cause ceases the effect ceases,

we decree that if a judge ordinary or a judge delegate has pronounced a comminatory or interlocutory sentence on anything, an order for the execution of which would prejudice one of the parties and on good advice refrains from putting it into effect, he shall proceed freely with the hearing of the case, notwithstanding any appeal made against such comminatory or interlocutory sentence (provided his action is not open to question on any other legal ground), in order that the action may not be held up for frivolous reasons.

37. Some abusing the grace of the holy see try to sue out writs from it to distant judges so that the one sued, tired of the trouble and expense of the action, shall have to give in to or come to terms with the bringer of the action. But since a way should not be opened by a court of justice for wrongs which observance of the law forbids, we decree that nobody can be dragged outside his diocese, unless it was procured with the assent of both parties and it expressly mentions this constitution. There are others, too, who, turning to a new kind of trade, to revive complaints that are dormant or to introduce new questions invent causes, for which they sue out writs from the apostolic see without authority from their superiors and offer them for sale, either to the party sued that he may not be vexed by an outlay of trouble and expense because of them, or to the bringer of the action that he through them may tire out the adversary with undue vexations. But since lawsuits should be shortened rather than prolonged, we by this general edict decree that if anybody on any question presumes in future to sue out papal writs without special mandate from his superior, both the writs shall be invalid and he himself punished as a maker of false documents, unless he happens to be one of those from whom a mandate rightly ought not to be required.

38. Against a false assertion of an unjust judge an innocent litigator is never at any time able to prove the truth by a denial, as the act of denying is not in the nature of things at all a direct proof. So, lest the false should prejudice the truth or iniquity prevail over equity, we decree that in both ordinary and extraordinary judicial proceedings the judge shall always employ either a public official,[9] if he can get one, or two suitable men to draw up faithfully all judicial acts (that is to say, citations, adjournments, objections and exceptions, petitions and answers, interrogations, confessions, depositions of witnesses, productions of documents, interlocutions, appeals, renunciations, final decisions and the rest of the things that call for proper drafting) specifying places, times and persons; and everything thus written is to be given to the parties on condition that the originals are kept by the writers, so that if dispute arises over the handling of the case by the judge the truth can be established from them. With the application of this measure such deference will be paid to upright and experienced judges that justice will not be impaired for the innocent by imprudent and wicked judges. A judge who neglects to observe this decree shall, if any difficulty results from his neglect, be punished by a superior judge with the punishment he deserves, nor shall there be a presumption in favor of his procedure save to the extent that it accords with the legal documents.

39. It often happens that a man unjustly deprived of something loses in effect the right to it, because of the difficulty of proof when the one who deprived him of it has transferred it to a third party, there being no remedy at law for the deprived by means of an action for restitution against the possessor, the advantage of possession having changed hands. Wherefore, notwithstanding the strict civil law, we decree that if anyone in future knowingly receives such a thing (taking over as it were, too, the fault of the depredator because there is not much difference, particularly as regards peril to the soul, between unjustly withholding and seizing the property of another), as a help against this sort of possessor the deprived is to have the benefit of restitution.

40. It sometimes happens that a plaintiff who, on account of the contumacy of the opposing party, has the possession of a thing adjudged to him to look after, is not able to get it into his possession within a year because of force or fraud over it, or having got it loses it, and thus, since in the opinion of many he does not qualify as the

true possessor at the end of the year, the defendant profits by his wickedness. Therefore so that a contumacious party shall not be in a better position than one who obeys a citation, we decree in the name of canonical equity that in the case aforesaid the plaintiff shall when a year has elapsed be accepted as the true possessor. Furthermore, we prohibit generally submission of spiritual matters to the arbitration of a layman, because it is not fitting for a layman to arbitrate in such things.

41. As "Whatsoever is not of faith is sin", we define by synodal decree that no prescription, canonical or civil, is valid without good faith, since generally any statute or custom is to be discounted which cannot be observed without committing mortal sin. So that it behooves one who claims a prescriptive right to have had no knowledge at any stage that the thing was someone else's.

42. Just as it is our will that laymen should not usurp the rights of clerks, so it ought to be our will that clerks should not lay claim to the rights of laymen. For which reason we forbid every clerk in future on the pretext of ecclesiastical freedom to extend his jurisdiction to the detriment of secular justice: let him be content with the written laws and the customs up to now approved, in order that by a right distribution "the things that are Caesar's" may be rendered unto Caesar and "the things that are God's" rendered unto God.

43. Some laymen try to encroach too far upon divine right when they force churchmen who hold nothing temporal from them to take oaths of fealty to them. Because, according to the apostle, a servant "to his own master standeth or falleth", we prohibit by the authority of holy council such clerks to be compelled to take an oath of this sort to secular persons.

44. Laymen, however devout, have no power to dispose of church property: their lot is to obey, not to be in command. We deplore it, then, when in some of them charity grows so cold that the freedom of the church, which not only the holy fathers but secular rulers too have buttressed by many privileges, they do not fear to attack by their decrees, or rather their devices; by not only alienating fiefs and other ecclesiastical possessions and usurping jurisdictions but also illegally appropriating mortuaries as well as other things connected with spiritual property. It being our wish to ensure the immunity of churches from these things and to provide against such great injuries, we pronounce, with the approval of holy council, such decrees and the claiming of fiefs or other ecclesiastical goods appropriated under a decree of a lay power without the lawful assent of the ecclesiastical authorities, not valid, as it could be termed not a decree but a deprivation or molestation. Those who expropriate the church are to be curbed by its censures.

45. In certain provinces, patrons or vidames and advocates of churches display so much arrogance that they not only create difficulties and snares when vacant churches have to be provided with suitable pastors but also presume to dispose of church possessions and other church goods as they like, and, dreadful to relate, fear does not deter them from murdering prelates. Since therefore what has been devised as a protection ought not to be turned into a roundabout way of oppression, we expressly forbid patrons or advocates or vidames in future to appropriate the aforesaid things to a greater extent than they are entitled to by law; and if contrary to this they do presume, they are to be curbed with the utmost severity of the canon law. Equally, with the approbation of the sacred council we decree that if patrons or advocates or feudatories or vidames or others with benefices venture with unspeakable daring either in person or through others to kill or maim the rector of any church or other clerk of that church they shall surrender completely, patrons the right of patronage, feudatories the fief, vidames the dignity of vidame, the beneficed their benefice. And lest the punishment be less well remembered than the offence, not only shall nothing from the aforesaid things pass to their heirs, but also their posterity to the fourth generation shall by no means be admitted into a college of clerks or attain a position of any authority in houses of regulars, save when out of compassion they are given dispensation.

46. With regard to consuls and rulers of cities and others who endeavor to oppress churches and churchmen by tallages or levies or other exactions, the Lateran council,[10] wishing to preserve ecclesiastical immunity, strictly forbade such presumption on pain of anathema, ordering offenders and their abettors to be subject to excommunication until they give suitable satisfaction. If, however, when for instance the bishop and his clergy together foresee a necessity or advantage so great that without any coercion, for the common good or the common need when the resources of laymen do not suffice, they consider churches should give subsidies, the aforesaid laymen shall humbly and devoutly receive them and give thanks. But as some are imprudent, let the Roman pontiff, whose business it is to see to the common good, be consulted beforehand. We decree further that, since as things now stand the malice of certain people towards the church of God has not abated, decrees and sentences promulgated by those excommunicated on this score or at their command shall be deemed null and void and never at any time to be valid. Besides, as fraud and guile ought not to protect anyone, let no one be duped by foolish error into resisting anathema during his time of authority as if after it he would not be compelled to give due satisfaction; for we decree that both he who has refused to give satisfaction and his successor (if he has not satisfied within a month) are to remain bound by ecclesiastical censure until suitable satisfaction is given, since he who succeeds to an office succeeds to its responsibilities.

47. With the approbation of the holy council we forbid anybody to venture to promulgate sentence of excommunication on anyone save after sufficient warning in the presence of suitable persons, who can if necessary testify to this warning. If anybody does contravene this, even if the sentence of excommunication is just, he shall know that entry to a church is forbidden him for a month and he shall nonetheless be punished with another penalty if that seems expedient. Let him also be careful not to proceed to the excommunication of anyone without manifest and reasonable cause. If perchance he does so proceed and, on being humbly requested, does not take the trouble to revoke the process without imposing punishment, the injured party may put in a complaint of unjust excommunication to a superior judge. This superior, if he can do it without danger from the delay, shall send him back to the one who excommunicated him with orders for him to be absolved by some suitably appointed date, otherwise he, the superior, will, either personally or through another as shall be expedient, on receiving sufficient security give him absolution. Whenever a case of unjust excommunication is made out against an excommunicator, he shall be condemned to pay the excommunicated compensation for damages, and be nonetheless punished in another way at the will of the superior judge if the nature of the offence calls for it—for it is not a light offence to inflict so great a punishment on someone innocent—unless it can be shown that he acted in error, particularly if he is of praiseworthy reputation. If, however, against the sentence of excommunication nothing reasonable is proved by the complainant, it is he who for the trouble caused by an unjustified complaint shall be condemned to be punished by having to pay compensation or in another way at the discretion of the superior judge, unless in his case it can be shown that there is the excuse of error, and moreover he shall be compelled upon security to give satisfaction for that for which he was justly excommunicated or be subjected once more to the initial sentence until fully adequate satisfaction without remission has been given. Should, however, the judge of first instance acknowledge his error and be prepared to revoke the sentence but he for whose benefit it was passed appeals, for fear it may be revoked without satisfaction being exacted, appeal shall not be admitted in this regard unless the error is such that there can properly be doubt about it; in this case the judge, giving sufficient security that he will stand trial before the judge appealed to or one delegated by him, shall absolve the excommunicate and thus not be subject at all to the prescribed punishment—every precaution being taken that he does not wish with the wicked purpose of harming somebody pretend to have erred, if he wishes to escape strict canonical punishment.

48. As there is a special provision forbidding

anybody to venture to promulgate sentence of excommunication on anyone save after sufficient warning[11] and as we wish to provide against the possibility of the one warned being able, by means of a fraudulent objection or appeal, to avoid examination by the giver of the warning, we decree that if he alleges he considers the judge suspect he shall, before this same judge, bring an action of just suspicion, and he himself in agreement with his adversary (or, if he happens not to have an adversary, with the judge) shall choose the arbiters or if it happens that they cannot reach agreement they shall choose without evil intent he one and the other another to take cognisance of the action of suspicion. If they, the arbiters, cannot reach an agreed decision they shall call in a third, so that what two of them decree shall have binding force. They are to know also that this they are bound, in accordance with the command strictly enjoined by us in virtue of obedience under the testimony of the divine judgment, faithfully to give effect to. If the action of suspicion is not legally established before them within a sufficient time the judge shall exercise his jurisdiction. If on the other hand it is legally established, with the assent of the objector the judge objected to shall commit the matter to a suitable person or transmit it to a superior judge that he may conduct it as it should be conducted. Furthermore, if a person warned is resorting to appeal and his transgression is manifest from the evidence or by his confession or in some other lawful way—as the remedy of appeal has not been established to defend iniquity but to protect innocence—such an appeal is not to be allowed. If his transgression is in any doubt, the appellant, in order that he may not by the subterfuge of a frivolous appeal, impede the action of the judge, shall set out before him the verifiable grounds of the appeal, such that if they were verified would have to be considered legitimate. Then if he has an adversary, by a date to be fixed by the same judge according to the distance between places, the circumstances, and the nature of the business, he shall proceed with the appeal, and if he does not trouble to proceed with it, forthwith the judge himself shall proceed, notwithstanding the appeal. If no adversary appears, the judge shall proceed *ex officio* and once the grounds of the appeal have been verified before the superior judge, the superior shall exercise his office as judge. But if the appellant fails to get the grounds of his appeal verified he shall be sent back to him from whom it has been established he appealed maliciously. We do not however wish the above two constitutions to apply to regulars, who have their own special observances.

49. Under the threat of divine judgment we absolutely forbid anyone out of cupidity to dare to bind someone with the bond of excommunication or to absolve anyone so bound, especially in those regions where by custom when an excommunicate is absolved he is punished by a money penalty; and we decree that when it is established that a sentence of excommunication was unjust he who imposed it shall be compelled by ecclesiastical censure to restore the money thus extorted, and, unless he demonstrably acted in error, he shall pay his victim as much again and if perchance he cannot pay he shall be punished in another way.

50. It should not be judged reprehensible if men's decrees are varied at some time or other in accordance with changing circumstances, especially when urgent necessity or evident advantages requires it, since God himself, of the things he decreed in the Old Testament, has changed some in the New. Since therefore the prohibitions about contracting marriage in the second or third degree of affinity and about uniting the offspring of a second marriage to the kindred of the first husband frequently lead to difficulty and sometimes endanger souls, we, inasmuch as when the prohibition ceases the effect ceases, revoke with the approval of the holy council decrees published on this subject and by the present constitution decree that contracting parties connected in these ways may in future be freely united. Also the prohibition of marriage shall not in future exceed the fourth degree of the consanguinity and affinity, since in grades beyond that such prohibition cannot now be generally complied with without grave harm. The number four agrees well with bodily marriage—of which the apostle says, "The husband hath not power of his own body, but the wife, neither has the wife

power of her own body, but the husband"—
because there are four humors in the body, which
is composed of the four elements. As the prohibition of marriage is now restricted to the fourth
degree it is our will that it should be unqualified,
notwithstanding decrees published before on this
subject whether by others or by us, so that if any
presume to be united contrary to this prohibition
they shall not be protected by length of time,
since lapse of time does not diminish a sin but
increases it, and the graver offences are, the
longer they keep the unfortunate soul in
bondage.

51.   As the prohibition of marriage in the three
remotest degrees is repealed, we wish it to be
strictly observed in the others. Hence, following
in the steps of our predecessors, we absolutely
prohibit clandestine marriages, forbidding also
any priest to presume to be present at such. For
which reason we extend the particular custom of
certain countries to countries generally, decreeing
that when marriages are to be contracted they
shall be published in the churches by the priests,
a suitable period being fixed beforehand within
which whoever wants and is able to may adduce
a lawful impediment. Those priests shall nevertheless find out whether any impediment exists.
When it seems probable that there is an impediment to contracting a union, the contract shall be
expressly forbidden, until it is clear from documents produced what ought to be done about it.
If any presume to enter into such clandestine
marriages or forbidden marriages in a prohibited
degree even in ignorance, the issue begotten of
such union shall be reckoned truly illegitimate
with no help to be had from the ignorance of the
parents, since they by contracting such unions
could be regarded as not devoid of knowledge or
at least as affecting ignorance. Likewise the offspring shall be reckoned illegitimate if both parents, knowing of a lawful impediment, presume
to contract marriage in the presence of the
church, contrary to every prohibition. Certainly a
parish priest who does not trouble to forbid such
unions or any regular also, whatever his order,
who ventures to be present at them, shall be suspended from office for three years, and more
severely punished if the nature of the office

demands it. And for those too who presume to be
united in such fashion, even in a permitted
degree, an adequate penance shall be enjoined. If
however any one, to impede a legitimate union,
alleges out of wickedness an impediment, he
shall not escape ecclesiastical punishment.

52.   Although, contrary to normal practice, it
was at one time of a certain necessity decided
that in reckoning degrees of consanguinity and
affinity hearsay evidence should be valid seeing
that owing to the short life of man witnesses cannot testify from personal knowledge in a reckoning as far as the seventh degree, nevertheless,
because from numerous instances and definite
proofs we have learnt that many dangers for lawful unions have arisen from this, we decree that
in this matter witnesses from hearsay are not to
be admitted in future (since the prohibition does
not now go beyond the fourth degree) unless
there exist persons of weight who are trustwor-
thy and who testified before the cause was begun
to things they learnt from their elders: not merely from one of them, since he alone if he were
alive would not suffice, but from at least two, and
they not of bad repute and suspect, but trustwor-
thy and quite unexceptionable, since it would
seem rather absurd to admit those whose actions
would be rejected; nor if one got from a number
what he testifies to, or if a number with bad rep-
utations got what they testify to from men with
good, should he be admitted as if he were more
than one, or they as if they were suitable witnesses, since, according to normal legal practice, the
assertion of a single witness is not sufficient even
if he were resplendent with authority, and legal
actions are forbidden to those of bad repute. Such
witnesses shall declare on oath that in bearing
witness in the cause they do not act from hate or
fear or love or for advantage; shall indicate persons by their exact names or by gesture or by sufficient description; shall distinguish by clear
reckoning every degree of relationship on either
side; and, finally, shall include in their oath the
statement that what they depose in evidence they
got from their forefathers and they believe it to be
correct. Still, they shall not be sufficient unless
they declare on oath that to their knowledge the
persons belonging to at least one of the aforesaid

degrees regard each other as blood-relations. For it is preferable to allow some unions that are contrary to the laws of man than to contravene the law of God by parting those lawfully joined.

53. In some regions there are mingled certain peoples who in accordance with their rites by custom do not pay tithes, although they are counted as Christians. To these people some landed lords assign their lands to be cultivated in order, by cheating churches of the tithes, to get greater revenues from them. Wishing therefore to provide for the immunity of churches from these things, we ordain that, when lords make over their lands for cultivation to such persons in such a way, they shall pay the tithes to the churches without objection and in full, themselves, and if necessary be compelled to do so by ecclesiastical censure. Those tithes are of necessity payable inasmuch as they are due by divine law and accepted local custom.

54. It is not in man's power for the seed to answer to the hopes of the sower, since in the words of the apostle, "Neither is he that planteth anything, neither he that watereth, but God that giveth the increase," he who from the dead seed bringeth forth much fruit, and some from excess of greed endeavor to cheat over the tithes, deducting from the crops and first-fruits the rents and dues, which meanwhile are got by untithed. But since as a sign of universal dominion, and by a certain special title as it were, the Lord has reserved tithes to himself, we, wishing to prevent both injury to churches and danger to souls, decree that in virtue of this general dominion payment of tithes is to precede payment of dues and rents, or at least those who receive untithed rents and dues shall, seeing that a thing carries with it its burden, be forced by ecclesiastical censure to tithe them for the churches to whom by right they are due.

55. Lately abbots of the Cistercian order assembled in general chapter wisely decreed at our instance that brothers of that order shall not in future buy property from which tithes are due to churches, unless it might be for founding new monasteries. And if such property is conferred on

them by the pious devotion of the faithful or bought for founding new monasteries, they shall assign them for cultivation to others by whom the tithes shall be paid to churches, lest because of their privileges churches be permanently deprived. We accordingly decree that on lands assigned to others and on future acquisitions, even if they cultivate them with their own hands or at their own expense, they shall pay tithes to the churches to which because of the lands they were previously paid, unless they think fit to compound with those churches. Considering this sort of statute as acceptable and right, we will that it be extended to other regulars who enjoy like privileges and we command prelates of churches to be readier and prompter in affording them full justice with regard to those who wrong them and to be at pains to maintain their privileges more carefully and completely.

56. Many regulars, we understand, and sometimes secular clerks, in letting houses or granting fiefs add, to the prejudice of parish churches, a covenant that the tenants and vassals should pay them the tithes and choose burial in their ground. Since it springs from avarice, we utterly disapprove of such a pact and decree that whatever is received because of such a pact shall be surrendered to the parish church.

57. In order that charters which the Roman church has granted to certain religious may remain intact, we have come to the conclusion that certain things in them should be clarified, lest through being not well understood they lead to abuse, on which account they could justly be revoked, for he deserves to lose his charter who abuses power granted to him.

The apostolic see has rightly given an indult to certain regulars that Christian burial shall not be denied to those who have become members of their fraternity if perchance the churches they belong to are under interdict and they happen to die, unless they are excommunicate or interdicted by name, and they may carry away members of their fraternity whom heads of churches will not permit to be buried in their churches to their own churches for burial, unless they were excommunicate or interdicted by name. But by members of their fraternity we understand this: either those who while still in this world have offered themselves to their order and changed their secular habit, or those who in their lifetime have given them their property, keeping for as long as they live the usufruct of it. They are only to be buried in the churches of these regulars or in churches not under interdict belonging to others which they have elected to be buried in, for if it were understood of anybody acquiring membership of their fraternity by paying them twopence or threepence a year ecclesiastical discipline would be at the same time loosened and cheapened, though even they may get a certain remission allowed them by the apostolic see.

Another indult has been given to such regulars: that if any of their brothers sent by them to receive dues or fraternity—money come to any city, castle or place which happens to be under an interdict, churches shall be opened once a year at their "joyous advent" for divine services to be celebrated there, the excommunicate being excluded. This we wish to be understood thus— that in the same city or castle or place one church only shall be opened to the brothers of that order as has been said once a year. Because although it is said in the plural "churches shall be opened at their joyous advent", this on a rational explanation refers not to churches of one place but churches of the said places as a whole: for if in this way they visited all the churches of one place the sentence of interdict would incur too much contempt.

They who venture to usurp anything for themselves contrary to the above-written explanations shall undergo severe punishment.

58. The indult which has been given to some religious we extend to bishops in respect of their episcopal office, granting that when a country is under a general interdict they can sometimes— the excommunicate and persons interdicted being excluded—behind closed doors, in a lowered voice, and without the ringing of bells celebrate divine service, unless this has been expressly forbidden them. We grant this, however, to those who have not in any way occasioned the interdict, lest they introduce any guile or fraud and turn the gain into a wicked loss.

59. What to certain religious is forbidden by the apostolic see we will and command to be extended to all: that no religious may without the leave of his abbot and the majority of his chapter be surety for anyone or accept a loan from another for a sum bigger than that decided on by the common opinion. Otherwise the community shall not be held at all responsible for these things, unless perchance the matter has manifestly redounded to the advantage of the house. And he who presumes to contravene this statute shall be subject to the severest discipline.

60. From complaints we get from bishops in various parts of the world, we have become aware of grave and great excesses committed by certain abbots, who not content with the frontiers of their own authority reach out to those of the episcopal dignity, taking cognisance of matrimonial causes, enjoining public penances, granting even letters of indulgence and like presumptions, from which it sometimes happens that for many episcopal authority is cheapened. Wishing therefore to provide in these things for both the dignity of bishops and the well-being of abbots, we by the present decree strictly forbid any of the abbots to presume to reach for such things, if he wishes to avoid danger for himself, unless perchance any of them by special concession or other legitimate cause is able to defend himself in respect of such things.

61. For any regulars to presume to receive churches or tithes from lay hands without the consent of the bishops or to admit to any divine services those under excommunication or those interdicted by name is known to have been prohibited under the Lateran Council. We now prohibit it more strongly and will see that the offenders are punished by penalties which are adequate. We confirm, nevertheless, that in churches which do not fully belong to them they shall, in accordance with the statutes of that council, present priests who are to be instituted to the bishops for examination by them about the care of the people: to themselves they are to avoid evidence of sufficient sense in things temporal. They shall not dare to remove them once they are instituted without first consulting the bishops; indeed we

add that they shall try to present those who are either noted for their way of life or recommended on verifiable grounds by the bishops.

62. Because some put up saints' relics for sale and display them indiscriminately the Christian religion is very often disparaged. So, in order that it may not be disparaged in future, we ordain by the present decree that ancient relics from now on are not to be shown outside the reliquary or put up for sale. As for newly-discovered relics, let no one venture to venerate them publicly without their having first been approved by the authority of the Roman pontiff. Neither should prelates in future allow those who come to their churches in order to venerate to be deceived by vain fictions or false documents, as has commonly happened in many places for the getting of alms. We forbid, too, questors of alms, some of whom deceive one another, advancing in their preaching a number of errors, to be recognized unless they show genuine letters from the pope or the diocesan bishop. Even then they shall be allowed to put forward to the people nothing beyond what is contained in those letters. We have indeed thought it well to give a copy of the form of letter which the apostolic see generally grants to such persons, in order that diocesan bishops may model their own letters on it. It is thus:

Since, as the apostle says, "we shall all stand before the judgment seat of Christ" to receive as we have "done in the body, whether it be good or bad", it behooves us to prepare for the day of the last judgment by works of mercy and for the sake of eternity to sow on earth what, God giving us it back multiplied, we should collect in heaven— keeping a firm hope and confidence, since "He that soweth sparingly shall reap also sparingly, and he that soweth in blessings, of blessings shall also reap" for life eternal. To support the brethren and the indigent who flock into such and such hospital its own resources do not suffice. We therefore admonish and exhort you all in the Lord and for the remission of your sins enjoin you from the goods God has conferred upon you to bestow pious alms and to give them grateful charitable assistance so that through your help their need may be cared for and you, by these and other good things which, God inspiring you,

you have done, can attain eternal happiness.

Let those who are sent in quest of alms be modest and discreet, they are not to put up in taverns or other unsuitable places or incur unnecessary expense, being careful above all not to bear the garb of false religion. Moreover, because of indiscriminate and excessive indulgences, which certain heads of churches are not afraid to grant, the keys of the church are brought into contempt and at the same time penitential satisfaction loses force; we accordingly decree that when a church is dedicated the indulgence shall be not for more than a year, whether it is dedicated by one bishop or by more than one, and then for the anniversary of the dedication the remission granted shall not exceed forty days of the penance imposed. We order the letters of indulgence which are granted for various reasons at different times to fix this number of days also, since the Roman pontiff himself, who possesses the plenitude of power, generally observes this moderation in such things.

63. As we have learnt for certain, shameful and wicked exactions and extortions are levied in many places and by many persons, sellers of doves in the temple as it were, for the consecration of bishops, the blessing of abbots and the ordaining of clerks, and it is fixed how much is to be paid for this or that and how much for another or yet another, and, verging on the utterly damnable, there are some who strive to defend such base and crooked conduct on the grounds of old-established custom. Wishing to abolish so great an abuse, we thoroughly reject a custom such as this, which should rather be termed a corruption, and firmly decree that no one shall presume to exact anything under any pretext whatever for conferring things or for things conferred; otherwise both he who receives and he who gives so absolutely condemned a payment as this shall be condemned with Gehazi and Simon.

64. The stain of simony has discolored many nuns to such an extent that they admit scarcely any as sisters without payment—wishing to cover this vice with the pretext of poverty. We absolutely forbid this to happen in future and ordain that whoever commits such wickedness in

future, both she who admits and she who is admitted, whether she is just a nun or in authority, shall be expelled from her convent without hope of reinstatement and thrust into a house of stricter observance to do perpetual penance. As to those who have thought fit to provide that they be removed from the convents they entered wrongly and placed in other houses of the same order. But if perchance there are too many of them to be conveniently placed elsewhere they are, by dispensation, so as not to roam about and perhaps imperil their souls in the world, to be admitted afresh to the same convent, with a change of superior and of the inferior offices of the houses. This, we decree, is to be observed with regard to monks and other regulars also. Yet, that they may not be able to excuse themselves on grounds of simplicity or ignorance, we command diocesan bishops to have this published all over their dioceses each year.

65. We have heard that certain bishops on the death of rectors of churches put these churches under an interdict and do not allow anyone to be instituted to them until they themselves have had a certain sum of money paid to them. Further, when a knight or a clerk enters a house of religion or chooses burial with religious, although he may have left nothing to the house, they cunningly make difficulties until their hand touches something in the way of a present. Therefore, since one should abstain not only from evil but also, according to the apostle, "from all appearance of evil", we absolutely forbid exactions of this sort: and any transgressor shall restore double what was exacted, this to be faithfully used for the benefit of places prejudiced by the exactions.

66. It comes frequently to the ears of the pope that certain clerks exact and extort payments for funeral rites for the dead, the blessing of those being married, and the like, and if it happens that their greed is not satisfied they deceitfully set up false impediments. In retaliation some laymen, from a ferment of heretical wickedness, try to break with what is for holy church a laudable custom introduced by the pious devotion of the faithful, on the pretext of canonical scruples. For which reason we alike forbid the wicked exac-

tions to be made in these matters and order the pious customs to be kept, ordaining that the sacraments of the church are to be given freely, but also that those who maliciously try to alter a laudable custom are, when the truth is known, to be restrained by the bishop of the place.

67. The more Christianity is restrained from exacting interest that much more strongly does the dishonesty of the Jews in these matters grow, so that in a short time they exhaust the means of Christians. Wanting therefore in this business to see that Christians are not savagely opposed by Jews, we ordain by conciliar decree that if in future on any pretext whatever Jews extort oppressive and excessive interest from Christians they shall be allowed no contact with Christians until they have made suitable amends for the excessive burden. Christians too, if need be, shall be compelled by ecclesiastical censure without appeal to abstain from dealings with them. We enjoin upon rulers not to be hostile to Christians on this account, but, rather, zealous in restraining Jews from such great oppression. And by the same penalty Jews shall, we decree, be compelled to compensate churches for tithes and offerings due to them which they used to receive from Christians for houses and other possessions before these went by whatever title to the Jews, so that churches may be preserved from loss.

68. In some provinces a difference of dress distinguishes Jews or Saracens from Christians, but in certain others such confusion has developed that they are indistinguishable. Whence it sometimes happens that by mistake Christians unite with Jewish or Saracen women and Jews or Saracens with Christian. Therefore, in order that so reprehensible and outrageous a mixing cannot for the future spread under cover of the excuse of an error of this kind, we decree that such people of either sex in every Christian province and at all times shall be distinguished from other people by the character of their dress in public, seeing that in addition one finds that this was enjoined upon them by Moses himself. On the days of Lamentation and on Passion Sunday they shall not appear in public at all, because some of them on such days, so we have heard, do not blush to parade in

their most elegant clothes and are not afraid to ridicule the Christians, who exhibit a memorial of the most holy Passion and display signs of grief. What we most strictly forbid is for them to venture to burst out at all in derision of the Redeemer. And as we ought not to ignore the insulting of Him who atoned for our sins, we order secular rulers to inflict condign punishment upon those who so venture, to restrain them from daring at all to blaspheme Him who was crucified for us.

69. It would be too absurd for a blasphemer of Christ to be in a position of authority over Christians and what the council of Toledo providently laid down on this we, because of the boldness of transgressors, here renew, forbidding Jews to be appointed to public office, since with such authority they are very hostile to Christians. Whoever commits such office to them shall by the provincial council—which we order to be held annually—be first admonished then curbed by an appropriate sanction. The officer so appointed shall be denied communion with Christians in business and in other things as long as whatever he has got from Christians by reason of his office thus acquired is not converted in accordance with the stipulations of the diocesan bishop to the use of poor Christians, and the office he disrespectfully assumed he shall surrender out of shame. We extend this same thing to pagans.

70. Some, we have learnt, who have come voluntarily to the water of holy baptism do not wholly cast off the old man to put on completely the new, when, keeping parts of their old rite, they upset by such mixing the decorum of the Christian religion. But since it is written Woe unto the man who goes into a land two ways and A garment ought not to be put on woven of linen and wool together, we decree that such persons shall be completely stopped by heads of churches from observing their old rite, in order that those who freely offered themselves to the Christian religion may by a salutary coercion be kept from its observance, for it is a lesser evil not to know the way of the Lord than to go back on it after knowing it.

71. It being our ardent aspiration to liberate the Holy Land from infidel hands, we decree, on the advice of men of experience who are fully aware of the circumstances of time and place and with the approbation of the holy council, that crusaders are to make ready so that all who have arranged to go by sea shall assemble in the kingdom of Sicily on the calends of June after next,[12] some as necessary and fitting at Brindisi, the others at Messina and places neighboring it on either side, where we too have arranged to be in person at that time, God willing, in order that by our counsel and aid the Christian army may be in good order for setting out with divine and apostolic benediction. By the same date also they should take care to be ready who have decided to go by land. These shall forewarn us meanwhile, in order that we may grant them a suitable legate *a latere* for counsel and aid. Priests and other clerks, subordinates and prelates as well, who may be in the Christian army shall devote themselves to prayer and exhortation, teaching the troops by word and example alike to have always before their eyes the fear and love of God and to say or do nothing which might offend the divine majesty. And if ever they fall into sin they shall through true penitence soon rise again, humble of mind and body and observing moderation in way of life and of dress, avoiding all discord and rivalry, having put completely aside all bitterness and envy, so that thus armed with spiritual and material weapons they shall fight the enemies of the faith more safely, relying not on their own power but on that of God. To these clerks we grant that they may receive the fruits of their benefices in full for three years as if they were resident in the churches and, if necessary, have power to put them in pawn for that length of time. To prevent this holy purpose being hindered or delayed, we strictly enjoin on all heads of churches each in his own jurisdiction diligently to warn and induce those who have given up the cross to resume it, and them and others who have taken the cross and those who will take it to fulfil their vows to God, and if necessary compel them to do so without further demur by sentences of excommunication against their persons and of interdict on their lands—those only being excepted who find themselves faced with an

obstacle of such a sort that their vow may, in accordance with regulations laid down by the apostolic see, rightly be commuted or postponed.

Furthermore, to prevent anything connected with this matter of Jesus Christ being left undone, we will and command that patriarchs, archbishops, bishops, abbots and others who have cure of souls shall make it their business to preach the cross to those in their charge, earnestly entreating in the name of the Father, the Son and the Holy Ghost, one only true and eternal God, kings, dukes, princes, margraves, counts, barons and other magnates, also the communities of cities, vills and towns, that those who do not go in person to help of the Holy Land should contribute, according to their means, the appropriate number of fighting men with their necessary expenses for three years, for the remission of their sins as is explained in encyclicals and for greater assurance will also be explained below. We wish not only those who furnish their own ships but also those who are zealous enough to build ships for this purpose to participate in this remission. To those who refuse, if there chance to be any so ungrateful to the Lord our God, we firmly declare in the name of the apostle they are to know they will be answerable to us before the awful judge at the latter day of strict judgment for this and let them ask themselves beforehand with what conscience, with what composure they can confess before the only-begotten Son of God Jesus Christ, to whom "the Father gave all things into his hands", if in this matter which is as it were peculiarly his they refuse to serve Him who was crucified for sinners, by whose beneficence they are sustained, nay more, by whose blood they are redeemed. Lest, however, we appear to put on men's shoulders heavy and unbearable burdens which we are unwilling to move a finger for, like those who say "by all means" but do not do, behold we from what we have been able to save over and above necessary and moderate expenses do grant and give to this work thirty thousand pounds, besides the ship which we are providing for the crusaders of Rome and neighboring districts, and will nonetheless appropriate to this same purpose three thousand marks of silver which we have left over from the alms of certain faithful, the rest having been faithfully dis-

tributed for the needs and benefit of the said Land by the hands of Albert, patriarch of Jerusalem, of blessed memory, and the masters of the Temple and the Hospital. But desiring to have other heads of churches and all clerks participate and share in both the merit and the reward, we, with the general approbation of the council, have decreed that all clerks, subordinate as well as prelates, shall give a twentieth part of their ecclesiastical revenues for three years in aid of the Holy Land by means of those appointed for the purpose by apostolic provision, the only exceptions being that certain religious are rightly to be exempted from this taxation, likewise those who have taken or will take the cross and are to go in person.

As for us and our brethren the cardinals of the holy Roman church, we shall pay a full tenth. And let them all know that they are obliged to observe this faithfully on pain of excommunication: so that those who knowingly commit fraud in this matter shall incur sentence of excommunication. Because those who continue in the service of the ruler of heaven ought certainly in justice to enjoy special privilege and as the date of departure is somewhat more than a year ahead, crusaders shall be exempt from levies, tallages and other burdens, and we take their persons and goods under the protection of St Peter and ourselves once the cross has been taken, ordaining that they are to be safeguarded by the archbishops, bishops and all prelates of the church, deputies to be specially appointed *ad hoc* for their protection so that until there is certain knowledge of their death or of their return their goods may remain intact and undisturbed. If anyone contravenes this he shall be curbed by ecclesiastical censure. If any of those setting out are bound by oath to pay interest, we command their creditors to be compelled by the same punishment to release them from the oath they have taken and to desist from exacting interest. But if any of the creditors does force them to pay interest we order him to be compelled by similar punishment to restore it. Jews we order to be compelled by the secular power to remit interest and until they do so all intercourse shall be refused them by Christians on pain of excommunication. For the benefit of those who are unable at present to pay off their debts to Jews, secular rulers shall so provide for them that from the start of their journey until there is certain knowledge of their death or return they shall not be subject to the inconvenience of interest, the Jews being compelled, after deduction of necessary expenses, to reckon the revenue they have received meanwhile from property held as security towards reduction of the debt: such a benefit does not seem to do much harm in that it defers payment in a way which does not devour the debt. Heads of churches who are negligent in doing justice to crusaders and their families are to know that they will be severely punished.

Furthermore, because corsairs and pirates greatly hinder help to the Holy Land by capturing and plundering those going to or returning from it, we bind with the chain of excommunication those who help and support them. We forbid under threat of anathema anyone to be knowingly party to any contract of sale or purchase with them. We enjoin rulers of cities and their territories to restrain and constrain them from this iniquity: otherwise, because to be unwilling to overthrow wrongdoers is none other than to encourage them and he is not without a touch of secret complicity who does not oppose a manifest crime, it is our wish and command that ecclesiastical discipline be used against their persons and lands by heads of churches. Furthermore, we excommunicate and anathematise those false and impious Christians who affronting Christ himself and Christian people carry arms and iron and timber for galleys to the Saracens. Those too who sell them galleys or ships and those who pilot Saracen pirate ships or give them any advice or help with machines or anything else to the detriment of the Holy Land we decree are to be punished by being deprived of their possessions and are to be the slaves of those who capture them; and we order such a sentence to be renewed on Sundays and feast-days in every maritime city and the bosom of the church not to be opened for them unless they send in aid of the Holy Land the whole of what they have received of such damnable wealth and the same amount of their own so that they get a punishment proportionate to their offence. But if, perchance, they cannot pay, those guilty of such things shall be punished

otherwise in order that through their punishment the audacity to attempt like things may be crushed in others. In addition we prohibit and on pain of anathema forbid all Christians for four years to send or take their ships across to the lands of Saracens in eastern parts, in order that by this a greater supply of shipping may be got ready for those wanting to cross to the help of the Holy Land and the said Saracens deprived of the not inconsiderable help they have been used to getting from it. Although tournaments have been forbidden on pain of a certain penalty in various councils in a general way, we, because the business of a crusade is greatly impeded by them at the present time, strictly forbid them to be held for three years. Because it is of the utmost necessity for the accomplishment of this business that rulers of Christian peoples should keep peace with each other, we ordain on the advice of the holy universal council that a general peace shall be kept throughout Christendom for at least four years, so that heads of churches may bring those at variance to conclude a peace or observe firmly and inviolably a truce. Those who refuse to agree shall be most strictly compelled to do so by excommunication of their persons and an interdict on their lands, unless their wrongdoing is so great that they ought not to have the enjoyment of such peace; but if perchance they make light of the church's censure they can, not without cause, dread the invocation by ecclesiastical authority of the secular arm against them as disturbers of the business of Him who was crucified. We therefore trusting in the mercy of Almighty God and the authority of the blessed apostles Peter and Paul, by that power of binding and unbinding which God has given us, though unworthy, grant to all who in person and at their own expense go on this journey full pardon of their sins about which they are profusely contrite in heart and have spoken in confession and at the retribution of the just we promise the further benefit of eternal salvation. To those who do not go there in person but send entirely at their own expense according to their means and status men suitably equipped, and similarly to those who although at others' expense, go in person, we grant full pardon of their sins. We will and grant that all those shall participate too in this remission in proportion to the nature of their help and the intensity of their piety who contribute suitably from their goods to the support of the Holy Land or give useful advice and assistance. Likewise, the universal synod gives its full support and blessing to all starting out on this common enterprise that it may contribute worthily to their salvation.

Notes

1   By compurgation or ordeal
2   The accuser is named and he will be liable to a penalty if his accusation is not sustained.

3   Third Lateran Council, 1179
4   *taxillos* (another form of dice)
5   *publicent in communi* (i.e. totals, not the individual votes)
6   Third Lateran Council, 1179
7   i.e. with security of tenure, not removable
8   Third Lateran Council, 1179
9   *publica persona* (i.e. a notary)
10 Third Lateran Council, 1179
11 The reference is to the preceding canon, No. 47.
12 i.e. on 1 June 1217

MENDICANTS

The Rule of Saint Francis of Assisi

FRANCIS OF ASSISI (1182-1226) WAS THE MOST IMPORTANT RELIGIOUS figure of the thirteenth century. Francis's dedication to a life of poverty and simplicity caught the imagination of Europeans and resulted in the rapid increase of his followers. In 1210 Pope Innocent III approved a simple rule for Francis and his followers which was simply a collection of Gospel precepts emphasizing poverty and preaching. By the 1220s, when the Franciscans numbered in the thousands, a more formal rule was needed. The following, written by Francis in 1223 and approved by the papacy, became the official rule of the Franciscans.

Source: E. F. Henderson (ed.), *Select Historical Documents* (London: George Bell, 1894).

1. This is the rule and way of living of the minorite brothers: namely to observe the holy Gospel of our Lord Jesus Christ, living in obedience, without personal possessions, and in chastity. Brother Francis promises obedience and reverence to our lord pope Honorius, and to his successors who canonically enter upon their office, and to the Roman Church. And the other brothers shall be bound to obey brother Francis and his successors.

2. If any persons shall wish to adopt this form of living, and shall come to our brothers, they shall send them to their provincial ministers; to whom alone, and to no others, permission is given to receive brothers. But the ministers shall diligently examine them in the matter of the catholic faith and the ecclesiastical sacraments. And if they believe all these, and are willing to faithfully confess them and observe them steadfastly to the end; and if they have no wives, or if they have them and the wives have already entered a monastery, or if they shall have given them permission to do so—they themselves having already taken a vow of continence by the authority of the bishop of the diocese, and their wives being of such age that no suspicion can arise in connection with them:—the ministers shall say unto them the word of the holy Gospel, to the effect that they shall go and sell all that they have and strive to give it to the poor. But if

they shall not be able to do this, their good will is enough. And the brothers and their ministers shall be on their guard and not concern themselves for their temporal goods; so that they may freely do with those goods exactly as God inspires them. But if advice is required, the ministers shall have permission to send them to some God-fearing men by whose counsel they shall dispense their goods to the poor. Afterwards there shall be granted to them the garments of probation; namely two gowns without cowls and a belt, and hose and a cape down to the belt; unless to these same ministers something else may at some time seem to be preferable in the sight of God. But, when the year of probation is over, they shall be received into obedience; promising always to observe that manner of living, and this Rule. And, according to the mandate of the lord pope, they shall never be allowed to break these bonds. For according to the holy Gospel, no one putting his hand to the plough and looking back is fit for the kingdom of God. And those who have now promised obedience shall have one gown with a cowl, and another, if they wish it, without a cowl. And those who are compelled by necessity, may wear shoes. And all the brothers shall wear humble garments, and may repair them with sack cloth and other remnants, with the benediction of God. And I warn and exhort them lest they despise or judge men whom they shall see clad in soft garments and in colors, using delicate food and drink; but each one shall the rather judge and despise himself.

3. The clerical brothers shall perform the divine service according to the order of the holy Roman Church; excepting the psalter, of which they may have extracts. But the lay brothers shall say twenty four Paternosters at matins, five at the service of praise, seven each at the first, third, sixth, and ninth hour, twelve at vespers, seven at the completorium; and they shall fast from the feast of All Saints to the Nativity of the Lord; but as to the holy season of Lent, which begins from the Epiphany of the Lord and continues forty days, which the Lord consecrated with his holy fast— those who fast during it shall be blessed of the Lord, and those who do not wish to fast shall not be bound to do so; but otherwise they shall fast until the Resurrection of the Lord. But at other times the brothers shall not be bound to fast save on the sixth day (Friday); but in time of manifest necessity the brothers shall not be bound to fast with their bodies. But I advise, warn and exhort my brothers in the Lord Jesus Christ, that, when they go into the world, they shall not quarrel, nor contend with words, nor judge others. But they shall be gentle, peaceable and modest, merciful and humble, honestly speaking with all, as is becoming. And they ought not to ride unless they are compelled by manifest necessity or by infirmity. Into whatever house they enter they shall first say: peace be to this house. And according to the holy Gospel it is lawful for them to eat of all the dishes which are placed before them.

4. I firmly command all the brothers by no means to receive coin or money, of themselves or through an intervening person. But for the needs of the sick and for clothing the other brothers, the ministers alone and the guardians shall provide through spiritual friends, as it may seem to them that necessity demands, according to time, place and cold temperature. This one thing being always regarded, that, as has been said, they receive neither coin nor money.

5. Those brothers to whom God has given the ability to labor, shall labor faithfully and devoutly; in such way that idleness, the enemy of the soul, being excluded, they may not extinguish the spirit of holy prayer and devotion; to which other temporal things should be subservient. As a reward, moreover, for their labor, they may receive for themselves and their brothers the necessaries of life, but not coin or money; and this humbly, as becomes the servants of God and the followers of most holy poverty.

6. The brothers shall appropriate nothing to themselves, neither a house, nor a place, nor anything; but as pilgrims and strangers in this world, in poverty and humility serving God, they shall confidently go seeking for alms. Nor need they be ashamed, for the Lord made Himself poor for us in this world. This is the height of most lofty poverty, which has constituted you my most beloved brothers heirs and kings of the kingdom of Heaven, has made you poor in possessions, has exalted you in virtues. This be your portion, which leads on to the land of the living. Adhering to it absolutely, most beloved brothers, you will wish to have for ever in Heaven nothing else than the name of our Lord Jesus Christ. And wherever the brothers are and shall meet, they shall show themselves as of one household; and the one shall safely manifest to the other his necessity. For if a mother loves and nourishes her son in the flesh, how much more zealously should one love and nourish one's spiritual brother? And if any of them fall into sickness, the other brothers ought to serve him, as they would wish themselves to be served.

7. But if any of the brothers at the instigation of the enemy shall mortally sin: for those sins concerning which it has been ordained among the brothers that recourse must be had to the provincial ministers, the aforesaid brothers must be bound to have recourse to them, as quickly as they can, without delay. But those ministers, if they are priests, shall with mercy enjoin penance upon them. But if they are not priests, they shall cause it to be enjoined upon them through others, priests of the order; according as it seems to them to be most expedient in the sight of God. And they ought to be on their guard lest they grow angry and be disturbed on account of the sin of any one; for wrath and indignation impede love in themselves and in others.

8. All the brothers shall be bound always to have one of the brothers of that order as general minister and servant of the whole fraternity, and shall be firmly bound to obey him. When he dies, the election of a successor shall be made by the provincial ministers and guardians, in the chapter held at Pentecost; in which the provincial ministers are bound always to come together in whatever place shall be designated by the general minister. And this, once in three years; or at another greater or lesser interval, according as shall be ordained by the aforesaid minister. And if, at any time, it shall be apparent to the whole body of the provincial ministers and guardians that the aforesaid minister does not suffice for the service and common utility of the brothers: the aforesaid brothers to whom the right of election has been given shall be bound, in the name of God, to elect another as their guardian. But after the chapter held at Pentecost the ministers and the guardians can, if they wish it and it seems expedient for them, in that same year call together, once, their brothers, in their districts, to a chapter.

9. The brothers may not preach in the bishopric of any bishop if they have been forbidden to by him. And no one of the brothers shall dare to preach at all to the people, unless he have been examined and approved by the general minister of this fraternity, and the office of preacher have been conceded in him. I also exhort these same brothers that, in the preaching which they do, these expressions shall be chaste and chosen, to the utility and edification of the people; announcing to them vices and virtues, punishment and glory, with briefness of discourse; for the words were brief which the Lord spoke upon earth.

10. The brothers who are the ministers and servants of the other brothers shall visit and admonish their brothers and humbly and lovingly correct them; not teaching them anything which is against their soul and against our Rule. But the brothers who are subjected to them shall remember that, before God, they have discarded their own wills. Wherefore I firmly command them that they obey their ministers in all things which they have promised God to observe, and which are not contrary to their souls and to our Rule. And wherever there are brothers who know and recognize that they can not spiritually observe the Rule, they may and should have recourse to their ministers. But the ministers shall receive them lovingly and kindly, and shall exercise such familiarity towards them, that they may speak and act towards them as masters to their servants; for so it ought to be, that the ministers should be the servants of all the brothers. I warn and exhort, moreover, in Christ Jesus the Lord, that the brothers be on their guard against all pride, vainglory, envy, avarice, care and anxiety for this world, detraction and murmuring. And they shall not take trouble to teach those ignorant of letters, but shall pay heed to this that they desire to have the spirit of God and its holy workings; that they pray always to God with a pure heart; that they have humility, patience, in persecution and infirmity; and that they love those who persecute, revile and attack us. For the Lord saith: "Love your enemies, and pray for those that persecute you and speak evil against you; Blessed are they that suffer persecution for righteousness' sake, for of such is the kingdom of Heaven; He that is steadfast unto the end shall be saved."

11. I firmly command all the brothers not to have suspicious intercourse or to take counsel with women. And, with the exception of those whom special permission has been given by the Apostolic Chair, let them not enter nunneries. Neither may they become fellow god-parents with men or women, lest from this cause a scandal may arise among the brothers or concerning brothers.

12. Whoever of the brothers by divine inspiration may wish to go among the Saracens and other infidels, shall seek permission to do so from their provincial ministers. But to none shall the ministers give permission to go, save to those whom they shall see to be fit for the mission.

Furthermore, through their obedience I enjoin on the ministers that they demand from the lord pope one of the cardinals of the holy Roman Church, who shall be the governor, corrector and protector of that fraternity, so that, always being subjected and lying at the feet of that same holy Church, steadfast in the catholic faith, we may observe poverty and humility, and the holy Gospel of our Lord Jesus Christ; as we have firmly promised.

CLARE OF ASSISI

Testament

CLARE (1194-1253) HAD ALREADY ACQUIRED A REPUTATION FOR piety when, upon hearing Francis preach in 1212, she determined to imitate his life. Despite concerted opposition from her family, she and a few companions established a life somewhat similar to that of Francis at San Damiano. Although she and Francis had initially hoped that she might provide leadership to women wishing to lead a life similar to his, ecclesiastical opposition made this impossible. The rule imposed on the Poor Clares by Innocent III was essentially that of the Benedictines. Under his successor Honorius III, the Poor Clares were required to lead a strictly cloistered life.

Her *Testament* emphasizes the fundamental principles of her religious orientation: poverty, humility, and penance in the tradition of Francis to the extent permitted women by the thirteenth century Church.

Source: Ignatius Brady, *The Legend and Writings of Saint Clare of Assisi* (New York: St. Bonaventure, 1953).

In the Name of the Lord, Amen.

1. Among the many graces which we have received and continue daily to receive from the liberality of the Father of mercies (II. 1:3), and for which we must give deepest thanks to our glorious God, our vocation holds first place. Indeed, because it is the more perfect and the greater among these graces, so much the more does it claim our gratitude. Therefore the Apostle says: "Know your vocation" (cf 1 Cor. 1:26).

2. The Son of God became for us the Way (John 14:16) and that Way our Blessed Father Francis, His true lover and imitator, has shown and taught us by word and example.

3. Therefore, beloved Sisters, we must consider the immense benefits which God has conferred upon us, but especially those which He has deigned to work in us through His beloved servant, our Father the Blessed Francis, not only after our conversion but even while we yet dwelt among the vanities of the world.

4. For when the Saint as yet had neither Friars nor companions and, shortly after his conversion, was repairing the Church of San Damiano and there, filled completely with divine consolation, was led to abandon the world wholly and forever, in great joy and in the illumination of the Holy Spirit he prophesied concerning us what the Lord later fulfilled. For at that time he mounted the wall of the church and cried with a loud voice in the French tongue to certain poor folk of the neighborhood: "Come and help me in building the Monastery of San Damiano; for here will dwell Ladies whose good name and holy life will glorify our Heavenly Father throughout His holy Church."

5. In this therefore we can behold the great kindness of God toward us, who of the abundance of His mercy and love deigned to speak thus through His Saint of our vocation and election. And it was not of us alone that our most blessed Father prophesied these things, but of all others likewise who were about to enter the holy calling to which God has called us.

6. With what solicitude, therefore, and fervour of mind and body must we not observe the commandments of God and of our Father, that with the help of God we may return to Him with

increase the talent He has given us! For the Lord has placed us as an example and mirror not only for other men, but also for our Sisters whom God has called to our way of life, that they in turn should be a mirror and an example to those living in the world.

Since therefore the Lord has called us to such heights of holiness that in us our other Sisters may behold themselves who are to be an example to mankind, we are truly bound to bless the Lord and praise Him and to be strengthened in Him more and more to do good. Wherefore if we live according to the pattern given us, we shall leave others a noble example and after life's short labour gain the prize of eternal happiness.

7. After the most high celestial Father had deigned to enlighten my heart by His mercy and grace to do penance after the example and teaching of our most Blessed Father Francis shortly after his own conversion, I voluntarily promised him obedience with the few Sisters whom the Lord had given me soon after my conversion, according to the light of His grace which the Lord had given us by the holy life and teaching of His servant.

8. But when the Blessed Father saw that though we were weak and frail of body, we shirked neither privation nor poverty, hardship, tribulation, ignominy, nor the contempt of the world, but rather, as he and his Friars often saw for themselves, that after the example of the Saints and his Friars we accounted all these as great delight, he rejoiced in the Lord. And moved to love for us, he bound himself always to have, in his own person or through his Order, the same diligent care and special solicitude for us as for his own Friars.

9. And thus by the will of God and of our most blessed Father Francis we came to dwell at the church of San Damiano. There in a short time the Lord by His mercy and grace increased our number that what He had prophesied through His Saint might come to pass. Before this we had dwelled in another place, but for a little while only.

10. Afterwards he wrote for us a form of life,

especially that we should persevere always in holy poverty. Nor was he content while living to exhort us by many words and examples to the love and observance of most holy poverty, but also gave us many writings that after his death we would in no wise turn aside from it, even as the Son of God while He lived in this world wished never to desert this same holy poverty. And our most blessed Father Francis, following the footsteps of Christ, never while he lived departed in example or in teaching from His holy poverty, which he had chosen for himself and for his Friars.

11. And I, Clare, the unworthy handmaid of Christ and of the Poor Sisters of the Monastery of San Damiano, and the little plant of the holy Father, considered with my Sisters our most high calling and the command of so great a Father, and the frailty of the other Sisters, which we feared in ourselves after the death of our holy Father Francis, who was our pillar of strength, and after God our one consolation and our support. Therefore we have bound ourselves again and again to our Lady most holy Poverty, that after my death the Sisters present and to come may never in any way abandon her.

12. And as I have ever been zealous and careful to observe and have the others observe the holy poverty which we have promised the Lord and our Holy Father Francis, so the other Abbesses who shall follow me in my office are bound always to observe holy poverty unto the end and to cause it to be observed by their sisters.

Indeed, for greater surety I took care to have our profession of holy Poverty, which we promised our Father, strengthened by the privileges granted us by the Lord Pope Innocent, in whose Pontificate we had our beginning, and by his successors, that at no time or in any fashion we might ever depart from it.

13. Wherefore on bended knees and prostrate in body and soul I recommended all my Sisters present and to come to our holy Mother, the Roman Church, to the Supreme Pontiff, and especially to the Lord Cardinal who has been appointed for the religion of the Friars Minor and for us. And

for love of that Lord who was poor in the crib, who lived a poor life, and who hung naked on the gibbet of the Cross, may the Lord Cardinal always cause his little flock to observe the holy poverty which we have promised God and our most blessed Father Francis, and may he always strengthen and preserve them in this poverty. For this is the little flock which the Lord and Father had begotten in His holy Church by the word and example of the blessed Father Francis, who followed the poverty and humility of His beloved Son and of the glorious Virgin, His Mother.

14. The Lord gave us our most blessed Father Francis as Founder, Planter and Helper in the service of Christ and in those things which we have promised God and him our Father; and in his lifetime he was ever solicitous in word and in work to cherish and foster us, his little plants. Wherefore I also recommend and entrust my Sisters, present and to come, to the successor of our blessed Father Francis and to the whole Order, that they may always help us to advance to better things in the service of God and above all to observe most holy poverty in a more perfect way.

15. If it should ever happen that the aforesaid Sisters leave this place and go elsewhere, they are bound nevertheless, wherever they may be after my death, to observe the aforesaid manner of poverty which we have promised God and our most blessed Father Francis.

16. In such an event, let that Sister who fills my office and the other Sisters be ever careful and prudent not to acquire or receive more land around such a place than strict necessity demands for a garden wherein to grow vegetables. But if at any time it should be expedient for the proper solitude of the monastery to have more land beyond the limits of the garden, they may not permit more to be acquired than strict necessity demands. And this land shall not be cultivated nor sown but is to remain always untouched and uncultivated.

17. I admonish and exhort in the Lord Jesus Christ all my Sisters present and to come that they strive always to follow the way of holy simplicity, humility and poverty and to live worthily and holily, as we have been taught by our blessed Father Francis from the beginning of our conversion to Christ. Thereby, though not by our own merits but only through the mercy and bounteous grace of the Father of mercies, they may always diffuse the fragrance of their good name to our other Sisters near and afar off.

18. Love one another with the charity of Christ, and let the love which you have in your hearts be shown outwardly by your deeds that, inspired by this example, the Sisters may always grow in the love of God and in mutual charity.

19. And I beseech that Sister who shall be entrusted with the care of the Sisters to govern others more by her virtues and holy life than by her office, so that, encouraged by her example, they may obey her not only out of duty but rather out of love. Let her be prudent and watchful toward her Sisters as a good Mother toward her daughters; and from the alms which the Lord shall give her let her take care to provide for them according to the needs of each one. Let her also be so kind and approachable that they may reveal their necessities without fear and have recourse to her at any hour with all confidence as may seem good to them for themselves or for their Sisters.

20. But the Sisters who are under her should remember that they have renounced their own wills for God's sake. Therefore I will that they obey their Mother as they have of their own free will promised the Lord; and thus the Mother, seeing their charity and humility and the unity that exists among them, will carry more lightly the burdens of her office, and what is painful and bitter will, by their holy living, be turned to sweetness for her.

21. And because straight is the way and the path one walks, and narrow the gate by which one enters into life, so few there are that walk thereon and enter through it (Cf. Matt. 7, 13:14); and if there are some that walk that way for a time, how few indeed are those who persevere thereon. Happy those to whom it is given to walk

that way and to persevere to the end! (Cf. Matt. 10:22).

22. Let us take care, therefore, if we have entered the way of the Lord, lest by our own fault or negligence or ignorance at any time and in any way we turn aside therefrom and so do injury to so great a Lord and His Virgin Mother, and to our blessed Father Francis and to the Church Triumphant and the Church Militant. For it is written: "Cursed are they who turn aside from Thy commandments!" (Ps. 118:21).

23. For this reason I bend my knees to the Father of our Lord Jesus Christ (Eph. 3:14), that through the prayers and merits of the glorious and holy Virgin Mary, His Mother, and of our most blessed Father Francis and all the Saints, the Lord Himself who has given us a good beginning will give also the increase (cf. 1 Cor. 3, 7), and likewise constant perseverance to the end. Amen.

24. This writing, that it may be better observed, I leave to you, my most beloved and dearest Sisters present and to come, as a sign of the blessing of the Lord and of our most blessed Father Francis, and of my blessing, who am your Mother and Handmaid.

CANONIZATION PROCESS OF ST. DOMINIC

DOMINIGO DE GUZMAN (1170-1221) BEGAN HIS RELIGIOUS CAREER AS
a regular canon of the cathedral of Osma in 1206 but within ten years was
preaching against the Albigensian heretics of southern France. Like Francis,
he attracted numerous followers who formed a mendicant preaching order,
the Order of Preachers known as the Dominicans. The following texts were
part of the testimony presented in the course of his canonization process,
which resulted in his canonization as a saint in 1234.

Source: Simon Tugwell, O.P., *Early Dominicans: Selected Writings* (New York: Paulist
Press, 1987).

Testimony of Brother Ventura (August 6)

(2) Brother Ventura of Verona, prior of the convent of the Order of Preachers in Bologna, said on
oath that it was thirteen years and more since he
entered the Order of Preachers on the advice and
encouragement of the blessed father Dominic, the
founder of the Order of Preachers and its first
Master, and made profession in his hand and
received the habit from him. At that time the
blessed father Dominic had, after the Pope, full
authority over the whole Order of Friars Preachers, to shape and organize and correct it. "In the
same year," he said, "the first General Chapter of
the Order was held at Bologna, and I was present
at it."

He also said that he was with the blessed father
Dominic and enjoyed great intimacy with him in
his comings and goings throughout the province
of Lombardy, being associated with him in his
travelling and when he was staying somewhere,
and in eating, drinking, sleeping and praying.

(3) He also said that on a journey or wherever he
was, he wanted to be always preaching or talking
or arguing about God, either in person or
through his companions. He was also persistent
in prayer, and said Mass every day if he could
find a church, though he never did so without
weeping. When he arrived at a hostel, if there
was a church there he would go there first. When
he was staying somewhere other than one of the
convents, when he heard others saying Matins he
would get up at once and recite Matins devoutly

with his companions. After Compline, when he
was on a journey, wherever he was, he observed
silence with his companions and with everybody
else, and did not want it to be broken until the
hour of Terce the next day. When he was travelling, he would lie down at night on some straw,
fully clothed, barely even taking his shoes off.

(4) He also said that when he was travelling he
observed to the full the Order's fasts, from the
feast of Holy Cross until Easter, that is, and every
Friday in summer. He was content to eat whatever food was set before him, except that he would
not eat any meat whatsoever. It made him very
happy if the provision of food was coarse and
poor, as the witness testifies he had often
observed. As soon as he arrived at any convent of
the Order, he called the brethren together and
preached to them, bringing them all no little consolation.

(5) He also said that when he was stopping in
any convent, he conformed to the common usage
of the others in what he ate and in everything
else, and he wanted them all to do likewise.

He never saw him doing or saying anything
different from this.

He never saw him speaking ill of anyone, or
ever saw him utter an idle word.

He said that the blessed Dominic was wise, sensible, patient, kind and very compassionate; he
thinks he never saw any mortal man so endowed
with virtues, although he has seen many religious
people in different parts of the world.

He also said that he heard his general confession at the time of his death in Bologna, and he reckoned from this that he had never sinned mortally, and that he had kept his virginity all his life, because the blessed father accused himself to him in confession of once revealing to some people that he was a virgin, though he did so to be useful to them.

(6) When he came to any place where there were any religious houses, he visited them all, preaching and encouraging them to regular observance. There was no one so troubled that he would not go away comforted if he came and listened to his words. He did this particularly in parts of Lombardy like Milan and the Cistercian monastery of Colomba. He also said that he preached nearly every day unless he was prevented, or gave the brethren a conference, during which he would weep a lot and make others weep too. He was strict in punishing the faults of the brethren, and was a great enthusiast for the Rule, but at the same time his words were so pleasant that the brethren endured the penances imposed by their loving father with the utmost patience and eagerness. He was constant in his attendance at the Divine Office, and used to spend the night in prayer, weeping a lot. When the witness was asked how he knew this, he said that he often found him in church praying and weeping, and sometimes overcome by sleep. Sometimes when he was tired because of his vigils, he would go to sleep at table.

(7) He also said that when the blessed Dominic had been visiting the lord Ugolino, Cardinal of Ostia and papal legate, in Venice, he returned to Bologna in very hot weather, late at night, and then spent a long time talking with the witness and with brother Rudolph about the affairs of the Order, and these fathers urged him to go and rest, but he refused and went into the church and prayed, and then said Matins with the brethren at the proper time. It was from his staying up that night that he got the pain in his head and the sickness which resulted in his going to the Lord. When he was ill, he refused to lie in a bed, but lay on some sacking instead. He had the novices called to him and gave them advice about their salvation. He appeared to be, and indeed he really was, cheerful and happy in his sickness.

(8) When his illness got worse, the blessed father had himself carried to Santa Maria del Monte, which was said to be a healthier place. There he sent for the prior, who came with twenty brethren from the community; he gave them a long talk. When he had received the holy oil there, the prior of Santa Maria said, "I shall bury him in this church, and I will not allow him to be taken away." When the blessed Dominic realized this, he said to those of his brethren who were standing by, "Quick, take me away from here. God forbid that I should be buried anywhere except under the feet of my brethren." So he was taken back to the church of St. Nicholas, and the brethren were actually afraid he was going to die on the way.

An hour later, he called the witness and said to him, "Make yourselves ready." When he, the prior, and the other brethren had got ready in the proper way for the commendation of his soul and had gathered around him, the holy father said to the prior and the brethren, "Wait a little longer." While this was going on, the prior said to him, "Father, you know that you are leaving us desolate and sad. Remember to pray for us to the Lord." And brother Dominic lifted his hands to heaven and said, "Holy Father, you know that I have gladly persevered in your will, and I have watched over and kept those whom you gave me. Now I commend them back to you. Watch over them and keep them." He said that the brethren had told him that when they asked about themselves, he replied, "I shall be more useful to you and more fruitful after my death than I was in my life." After this, saint Dominic said to the prior and the brethren, "Begin." And during the office of the commendation of his soul, the blessed father was saying the words with the brethren, because his lips were moving. While the brethren were saying, "Come to help him, you saints of God, and receive his soul," he breathed his last.

His funeral was attended by lord Ugolino, Cardinal of Ostia, who is now the Pope, and by the lord patriarch of Aquileia and by many venerable bishops and abbots. The Mass was sung at the funeral by the lord Ugolino.

(9) That year everybody noticed an extraordinary fragrance in the whole church, especially near the tomb, and the witness in particular says that he noticed it himself. There were also a lot of miracles worked that year and in the following years for people who came to the tomb of the blessed Dominic, bringing wax images and all kinds of things. When several people tried to present silk cloths to cover the tomb of the blessed Dominic, the brethren would not allow them to, for fear they would be accused of greed.

(10) When the body of the blessed Dominic was due to be moved, for several days the *podestà* of Bologna and many noble citizens guarded it to prevent it from being stolen. When the tomb was opened, in the presence of the *podestà* and many citizens of Bologna and other noble men, including religious, bishops and laymen, the brethren found a wooden coffin, shut with iron nails; and such a fragrance came out that they were all amazed, saying that they had never smelled anything like it. So the body was moved by the archbishop and other prelates to the new tomb, and the extraordinary fragrance remained the whole time. Master Jordan held the holy body in his hands and gave it to the three hundred or so brethren who had come to the General Chapter to kiss. When the witness was asked how he knew all this, he said that he was present at all of it.

(11) He also said that the blessed Dominic had such charity that he wanted to extend it to everybody, even the damned, and he used sometimes to weep for them.

Testimony of Brother William of Monferrato (August 7)

(12) The second sworn witness was brother William of Monferrato, of the Order of Preachers, whose disposition was as follows.

"Going to Rome once," he said, "when I was still in the world, I went to stay in the house of the bishop of Ostia, who is now the Pope, to spend Lent there, and there I consorted with brother Dominic who used to come and see the cardinal frequently, and I recognized him as a holy man and I liked his way of life. I began to love him and I often spoke with him about the salvation of others, and, though I have lived with many people, I never met anyone more holy.

"I went to Paris to study theology for two years, and there I received the habit of the Preachers from the blessed Dominic, although we had previously agreed to go and convert unbelievers.

"I accompanied him when he was going to Rome and elsewhere. Whether he was ill or well, I always found him remarkably strict in his observance. He gave dispensations to the other brethren, but not to himself. Even when he was ill, he kept the Order's fasts. When he had an attack of dysentery on his way to Rome, he would not break the Order's fasts or eat meat or take anything extra with his food except some herbs or a bit of turnip." When the witness was asked how he knew this, he replied that he was with him and saw it all, especially at Viterbo where he had been very ill.

(13) "When he was badly treated in any place where he was staying, in the way of food and drink and bedding and such things, I never saw him complaining, but only his extraordinary patience. When he settled down to rest, he prayed for a long time and wept so much that he used to wake his companions up. He spent more time in prayer than asleep. He slept in his tunic and cappa, with his stockings and belt on. He always slept without a mattress, and more often on a plank than on bedding.

"He always observed silence at the times laid down in the Order, and he avoided idle words and spoke always with God or about God." Asked how he knew this, the witness said that, as one of the blessed Dominic's principal companions, he lived with him by day and by night, whether he was travelling or staying somewhere, and he saw and heard all this.

(14) "I must also say, and I believe it to be true, because of his holy way of life, that the blessed father always preserved his virginity; another reason why I believe it is that I have heard it from

many reliable people, especially the Bishop of Osma, with whom he had been for a long time, and from some of the bishop's canons, with whom he had also lived; I do not remember their names."

(15) He also says that he was present at the translation of the blessed Dominic, when his body was moved from its previous burial place into the church, to the place where it is now. The brethren, including the Provincial, did not want any seculars to be present, because they were afraid it would stink, since water had already seeped into that tomb; but they could not prevent the *podestà* at Bologna and twenty four noble citizens from being there, and some of them guarded the tomb for several days before it was opened. When the stone was taken away, a wooden coffin was revealed, in which the body of the saint was lying, and then a pleasant, sweet smell came out and none of them could decide what it smelled like.

(16) After this translation, many people of various states of life said that they had received graces of healing. "But I do not remember their names, because I was a diffinitor at the Chapter and was too caught up in other things to pay attention to them."

Testimony of Brother Amizo of Milan (August 8)

(17) The third sworn witness was brother Amizo of Milan, the prior of Padua, whose deposition was as follows.

Master Dominic, he said, was a humble man, gentle, patient, kind, quiet, peaceful, modest and very balanced in everything he did and said. He was a loyal comforter of other people, particularly his own brethren. He was an outstanding enthusiast for regular observance, a great lover of poverty, both in the food and in the clothing of the brethren of his Order, and also in their buildings and churches and in the style and ornamentation of their church vestments. During his lifetime he was very keen on this and took great pains to see that the brethren did not use purple or silk vestments in their churches on themselves

or on the altars, and that they did not have vessels of gold or silver, except chalices.

(18) He also said that he was persistent in prayer, by day and by night. He followed the Order's observance fully in choir and in the refectory and elsewhere. He was very fervent in prayer and in preaching, and, because he was zealous for souls, he encouraged his brethren most insistently to be the same. He loved other religious and spoke most highly of them.

(19) He preserved his virginity up to the time of his death, as nearly everybody said. He also said that he was present when the *podestà* of Bologna, with the Master of the Order of Preachers and many others, had the new tomb and the coffin of the blessed Dominic's body opened, and how they all smelled a wonderful fragrance, such as they had never smelled before.

Testimony of Brother Buonviso (August 9)

(20) The fourth sworn witness was brother Buonviso of the Order of Preachers. He was with the blessed Dominic, as he says, at Bologna, in the cloister of St. Nicholas, and at Rome and at Milan, and he looked after him when he was ill. So he said that when the brethren left the church in the evening to go and rest, the blessed Dominic used to remain secretly in the church to pray, and the witness used to watch him and sometimes heard him praying with shouts and groans. He had no place of his own to lie down; if drowsiness ever overcame him, he would go to sleep on a board or a bench or on the bier they used for the dead. He used to lie down at night exactly as he was, as he had been walking about during the day.

(21) When the blessed Dominic went to Rome with the witness, whenever he left a city or village he always took his shoes off and carried them under his arm, though his companion was quite willing to carry them for him, and when he approached a town or village he would put them on again. When they came to a particular path which was full of stones, the blessed father said to his companion, "Here, poor wretch that I am, I

was once forced to put my shoes on when I was coming along this path." When his companion asked him why, he said, "Because the rain had made these stones so sharp that I could not bear it." Also on one occasion when it rained very heavily while they were travelling and St. Dominic was caught in it, he quite happily began to sing a hymn; the witness saw this and heard it, because he was travelling with him. When he came to the rivers that were swollen because of the heavy rain, he beat them down with the sign of the cross and went over, encouraging his nervous companions to cross too.

During the celebration of Mass and during the psalmody, tears used to flow in great abundance from his eyes.

(22) When they were in a hostel, he never asked for provision to be made to suit his own taste, but always that of the others. And when he was badly treated, he showed all the signs of being particularly pleased. When the blessed Dominic was ill at Milan with a fever, the witness says that when the fever came on, he became quite lifted up to God and afterwards he had someone read to him.

"When I, brother Buonviso, was procurator at Bologna, once when there was no bread for the brethren at lunch time, St. Dominic sat down at table with them and lifted up his hands in prayer, looking towards heaven, and then two extremely handsome young men came into the refectory with two baskets, with the purest white bread in one, and some figs in the other, and they distributed the bread and the figs to each one of the brethren. I write this and I know this because I was there when it happened and saw it."

He also said that the blessed father was very humble, loving, kind, compassionate, patient, sober, zealous for poverty and for the salvation of souls, and a lover of all religious and religious orders. In himself he kept the Rule strictly. He never returned curse for curse, but blessed those who cursed.

(23) When the *podestà* of Bologna and a great number of the citizens of Bologna together with the Master of the Order and the Provincial of Lombardy opened the new tomb and the coffin

where the bones of the blessed Dominic were, a wonderful fragrance came out, such that they all said that nobody had ever smelled anything like it. "I smelled it myself and was present when this happened."

(24) The witness said that when he was a novice and had no skill in preaching, because he had not yet studied scripture, the holy father told him to go to Piacenza to preach. He excused himself, but he spoke so charmingly that he induced him to go, saying that the Lord would be with him and would put words in his mouth. God did in fact give him such grace in his preaching that many people were converted and three entered the Order.

Testimony of John of Spain (August 10)

(25) The fifth sworn witness was brother John of Spain of the Order of Preachers, who was received into the Order by the blessed Dominic in Toulouse, at the church of St. Romain, at the time of the council of Innocent III. He lived with brother Dominic on his journeys and in various places, by day and night.

He also said that he prayed more persistently than all the other brethren. He used to take the discipline with a triple chain, particularly at night, either giving it to himself or getting someone else to give it to him, and there are many brethren who can attest this, who beat him at his request. He punished people who broke the Rule severely yet mercifully. He was very upset whenever he punished anyone for any fault.

(26) He was zealous for souls and used to send his brethren out to preach, bidding them look to the salvation of others. He had such confidence in God's goodness that he even sent unlearned men out to preach, saying to them, "Do not be afraid; the Lord will be with you and will put power in your mouths." And it turned out as he said.

When the blessed Dominic was at Toulouse, in the church already referred to, he sent the witness to Paris with five other clerical brethren and one lay brother, to study and preach there and to establish a convent. This was contrary to the wishes of Count Simon de Montfort and the archbishop of Narbonne and the bishop of Toulouse and several other prelates, but he told the prelates, the Count and the brethren, "Do not contradict me. I know quite well what I am doing." He told the witness and the others not to have any fear, because everything would work out well. He also sent some others to Spain with similar instructions.

While the witness and his companions were studying in Paris and applying themselves to the salvation of souls, they were given the church of St. Jacques, situated in the gate of Orléans, by Master John, the dean of St. Quentin, who was at that time a Regent Master in theology in Paris, and by the masters and students of the whole University of Paris. There they established a convent. Many brethren were received into the Order, and they were given a great many properties and revenues and some estates, particularly in the regions of Toulouse and Albi. The witness said that in the days when the Order of Preachers owned estates and many properties in these places and used to carry money with them when they travelled and ride on horseback and wear surplices, brother Dominic worked hard to get the brethren of the Order to abandon and make light of all such temporal things and to devote themselves to poverty and to give up riding on horseback and take nothing with them when they travelled. So their properties in the kingdom of France were given to some nuns belonging to the Cistercian Order, and other properties were given to other people.

To allow the brethren to devote themselves more energetically to study and preaching, brother Dominic wanted them to have uneducated laybrothers, who would be in charge of the educated brethren in the administration and provision of all worldly goods; but the clerical brethren refused to have laybrothers in charge of them, in case what happened to the brethren of Grandmont at the hands of their laybrothers should happen to them too.

(27) St. Dominic was loved by everybody, rich and poor, Jew and pagan (there were many of these in Spain), in fact by everybody except for the heretics and the enemies of the church whom he pursued and refuted in debate and in preaching.

He lay down at night just as he was during the day, except that he took his shoes off. When he was travelling from one land to another, he took his shoes off, and when he arrived anywhere he put them on again, and he did this in all the towns and villages he came to. He refused to have anyone help him carry his shoes. He used to get great delight from anything untoward that happened to him on the way. For example, if he tripped over a stone his face would light up as he said, "This is doing penance!"

He had a great love of poverty, and he encouraged the brethren to love it too. He exulted in cheap clothes, though he liked them to be clean.

(28) He was most sparing in what he ate and drank. He hardly ever took anything extra, if he was offered it, and he observed the Rule strictly himself, though he gave dispensations to others.

When he was walking about in a city or town, he barely lifted his eyes from the ground.

He did not have any place of his own to lie down in, as the other brethren did. (Asked how he knew this, he said that if he had a place of his own, he would have discovered it, because he had been most persistent in trying to find out.)

He was elected bishop two or three times, but always refused, preferring to live in poverty with his brethren to having any bishopric. The sees he refused were those of Béziers and Comminges.

(29) He rarely spoke except about God or with God in prayer, and he encouraged the brethren to do likewise. He was happy when he was with other people, but in prayer he sobbed and wept.

He remained a virgin all his life, and this was what everybody said.

He often said that it was his desire to be whipped and cut up for the name of Christ, and finally to die.

In letters and in his spoken words he encouraged the brethren to apply themselves to the study of the New and Old Testaments more than to any other reading. He always carried round with him the gospel of Matthew and the letters of Paul, and he read them so often that he knew them by heart.

The canons with whom he had lived before the

Order was founded related that when the blessed Dominic was still in the world, as a student at Palencia, he sold his books and furniture to feed the poor during a time of famine. At his example many other people began to do the same thing.

Testimony of Brother Rudolph of Faenza (August 11)

(30) The sixth sworn witness was brother Rudolph of Faenza of the Order of Preachers, who was the priest in charge of the church of St. Nicholas of the Vines in Bologna, and who gave this church to the brethren, with the permission of the bishop of Bologna, at the request of the lord Ugolino, bishop of Ostia, who was papal legate at the time and is now the Pope.

The witness says that he was with the blessed Dominic in Bologna, in church, at the office, in the dormitory, in the refectory, by day and by night, because he, the witness, was procurator for the brethren and had entered the Order many years before and had made profession before the blessed Dominic came to Bologna, and so he knew him well.

(31) "The blessed father Dominic," the witness says, "nearly always spent the night in church, praying and weeping there, as I saw by the light of the lamp which is in the church, and sometimes I saw him standing on the tip of his toes with his hands stretched up. Because of the intimacy I had with him I sometimes went and prayed beside him, and I saw in him a fervour in prayer such as I have never seen the like of.

"The blessed father wore an iron chain next to the skin. When I stripped him after his death, I took this chain as a great treasure, but eventually I gave it to Master Jordan at his urgent request.

"At night he used to lie down dressed just as he was for walking about during the day. He would lie down on some planks or on the ground or sometimes on a trellis, and he did not take anything off except his shoes. Because of his long vigils in church, he sometimes used to go to sleep at table. He was regularly there with the brethren in choir and in the refectory, and he took the same food as the others.

"When I was procurator for the brethren in

Bologna," the witness says, "I once prepared an extra dish for the brethren, and he came to me after lunch and said, 'Why are you killing the brethren by giving them extra dishes?'. When we were short of bread or other food, I often went to him to tell him what we needed. He used to say, 'Go to church and pray'. He would do the same, and I found that God provided whatever we were short of. Even a little supply of bread put out at his command for a whole lot of brethren was abundantly sufficient for them all. He kept the Rule completely in every respect, with regard to food and fasting and everything else, and he took care to see that it was observed by the others.

(32) "Finally, I never saw a man whose service of God pleased me more than did that of the blessed Dominic. He longed for the salvation of all men, including Christians and Saracens, and especially the Cumans, to whom he wanted to go.

"He was happy, kind, patient, cheerful, compassionate, and a comforter of the brethren. If he saw any of the brethren offending in any point, he walked past as if he had not seen it, but later, looking perfectly calm, he would address him with soothing words and say to him, 'Brother, you have done wrong; do penance.' In this kind way he led them all to do penance and to make amends; and though his words were humble when he spoke to offenders, he still punished their offenses severely.

"He had a supreme love of poverty and encouraged the others to practice poverty too. For instance, Signor Oderico Gallicani once gave the brethren in Bologna a certain piece of property worth five hundred Bolognese pounds; when the blessed Dominic arrived, he tore up the title deeds and returned the property, saying, 'Preachers ought to live by alms.' If ever they had enough in the house to support the brethren for the day, he would not let them beg on that day, and if anyone gave them any alms, he ordered them to return it. He wanted them to have small houses and cheap clothes and even cheap vestments in church. He did not want the brethren to concern themselves with temporal affairs, except those who had been made responsible for them. When he saw that anyone was suitable to be a preacher, he did not want him to be given any other job.

"Whether he was travelling or at home, he always wanted to talk about God or the salvation of souls. I never heard an idle or harmful word from his mouth, or anything derogatory.

(33) "He was very fervent in his preaching and often used to weep while preaching, which made the people weep too.

"At the first General Chapter in Bologna, in the presence of the brethren, he said that he deserved to be deposed and that they ought to depose him. But the fathers refused to do this, so he appointed diffinitors who were to have the authority to do this for the duration of the Chapter. 'I am slack,' he said, 'and useless, so put me out of office.'

"When he was sick at Bologna, the time he died, the brethren stood round him, in tears. Then the blessed Dominic exhorted them to keep the observances of their religious life, and told them not to be afraid, because he would be more useful to them after his death. 'I was holding his head with a towel,' the witness says, 'wiping away the sweat from his face. One of the brethren came to the blessed Dominic and said, "Father, where do you want your body to be buried?" He said, "Under the feet of my brethren."' While the brethren were saying the commendation of his soul, the blessed father said the words with them. But when they got to 'Come to help him, you saints of God, come to meet him, you angels of the Lord, and receive his soul and present it before the Most High,' he breathed his last. All this took place in one of the cells at St. Nicholas. I never saw him sleeping in a bed with a feather mattress, or even on sacking except when he died, because he was on sacking then. When he breathed his last, he lifted his hands toward heaven."

(34) He also said that he prepared his tomb and the wooden coffin, since he was procurator. His body was shut in with iron nails and he guarded it carefully until it was put in the tomb. Nor did anyone put any perfumes there, because the witness was present the whole time. He also said that he was one of those who opened the tomb in

which the blessed father had been buried first, when his body was moved to the place where it is now. It was he who broke the wall of the tomb with iron hammers; the wall was very strong and was sealed with strong, hard cement. He also raised the stone which was on top, with an iron bar, because the tomb was protected by large stones and sealed with cement. He had had all this done most carefully at the outset, to make sure that people did not steal the body. And when the witness raised the stone that was on top with the iron bar, and the tomb was opened, a great fragrance came out, an overwhelming fragrance, very pleasant and sweet; he did not recognize it. All those who smelled it agreed that there had never been any fragrance like it. It still remains in the bones of the blessed Dominic.

Testimony of Brother Stephen of Spain (August 9)

(35) The seventh sworn witness was brother Stephen of the Order of Preachers, the Provincial of Lombardy. He said that "it is fifteen years since I first knew Master Dominic, the founder of the Order of Preachers and its first Master; before I knew him personally I heard from reliable people that while he was still a student he sold his books and fed the poor during a time of famine. He said, 'I refuse to study dead skins while men are dying of hunger.' At his example, other men of great authority did the same sort of thing."

Round about this time, he began to preach in the district of Toulouse against the heretics there, with the bishop of Osma, and he started the Order of Preachers.

(36) He also said that when he, the witness, was a student at Bologna, the blessed Dominic came to Bologna and preached there. "After I had confessed my sins to him, one evening when I was at dinner with some friends in the house where we were staying, the blessed Dominic sent two of the brethren to me to say, 'Brother Dominic says you are to come to him.' I told them to go away and said I would come when I had finished my dinner, but they said, 'He says you are to come now.' So I left everything and went to him. I found him

with many of the brethren at the church of St. Nicholas." He said to the brethren who were standing by, "Quick, show him how to do a *venia*." When he had done a *venia*, he put himself in his hands. Then the blessed Dominic received him into the Order, saying, "I am giving you arms with which you will be able to fight the devil all the days of your life." The witness was surprised at the time and afterwards, wondering what had prompted Dominic to summon him and clothe him in the habit of the Friars Preachers, because he had not discussed his conversion with him beforehand. He thought that it must have been because of some divine revelation and inspiration that he did it.

(37) He also said that the blessed Dominic was a great comforter of the brethren and of other people who were in distress. "For instance," the witness says, "When I was a novice, I suffered a great many trials, but I endured them all at the encouragement of the holy man. The same thing happened to many of the novices, as they told me."

The witness was with the blessed Dominic at Bologna for a whole year, in the cloister of St. Nicholas, and became very intimate with him there, and he never heard him speak a single malicious or idle word. When he preached, his words were so moving that they made both him and his hearers weep with compunction. Whether he was at home or on a journey, he always spoke about God or other profitable subjects, and he urged the others to do the same.

After Compline, when the common prayer was finished, he made the brethren go to the dormitory, while he remained in the church to pray. And while he prayed, he used to reach such a pitch of groaning and lamenting that the brethren who were nearby were woken up by it. He often used to spend the whole night in church, up to the time of Matins. At Matins he would go round both sides of choir, urging and encouraging the brethren to sing loudly and with devotion. The holy man was so devoted to his vigils of prayer "that I never saw him leave the church and go to any place of his own to sleep, only to the bier."

(38) When he was celebrating Mass, particularly during the words of the Canon, he used to weep and show all the signs of a most intensely fervent love. He was enthusiastic for regular life and was a great observer of the Rule of the Order. He had a supreme love of poverty, and encouraged the brethren to imitate him in this, so he would not accept any properties he was offered nor did he want the brethren to accept them. He had cheap clothes made out of coarse, though clean material, and he wore a very cheap, short scapular, and would never hide it with his cappa, even in the presence of important people. When brother Rudolph raised the cells by an arm's length, because the brethren used to have poor, mean, low cells, and this was in the absence of the blessed Dominic, when the holy father came back, he said, "Do you so quickly want to abandon poverty and build great palaces?" So he ordered them to abandon the work, and it duly remained unfinished as long as he was alive. He put it in his Rule that the brethren were to use cheap clothes and buildings and that they were not to take money with them when they travelled, but were to live off alms. He was most sparing in food and drink, to such an extent that when the brethren had two dishes, he contented himself with one. While the brethren went on eating after he had finished, he used to go to sleep, because of the long vigils he kept in church.

(39) It was generally said that he preserved his virginity until the end of his life. "I heard his confession several times and could never discover that he had committed a mortal sin." He was patient and happy in all trials. When he was in need, or the brethren lacked anything, in food or in clothing, he showed every sign of happiness.

Since brother John of Vicenza announced to the people in a sermon a revelation he had received about the blessed Dominic, and since he, the witness, began to think about moving his body, great graces in increasing abundance have been seen plainly both in the brethren and in the people who listened to the life and miracles of the blessed Dominic. In the cities of Lombardy a huge number of heretics has been burned, and more than a hundred thousand people who did not know whether they ought to belong to the Roman church or to the heretics have been sincerely converted to the Catholic faith of the Roman church by the preaching of the Friars Preachers. Their sincerity is shown by the fact that these converts, who had previously been defending the heretics, are now pursuing them and detest them, and in almost all the cities of Lombardy and the Marches the statutes which were opposed to the church have been handed over to the Friars Preachers to correct and emend and bring into line with Catholic truth. They have eradicated feuds and established peace between many cities, they have subdued usury and arranged for repayments, ever since the life and miracles of the blessed Dominic began to be famous.

(40) The witness also said that he was present when the body of the blessed Dominic was moved from the tomb under the ground to the marble tomb, and he says that they broke the limestone and the very hard cement with picks and other iron instruments, and then opened the tomb, on which there was a thick, strong stone; inside they found a wooden coffin, from which a marvellous fragrance was coming. The Master of the Order took the bones and put them in a new coffin, in the presence of many of the brethren and the archbishop of Ravenna and many other bishops and prelates and the *podestà* of Bologna with many noble citizens, and they put the new coffin in a stone monument, where it is now. The fragrance lasted for many days afterwards in the hands of those who had touched the relics.

Testimony of Brother Paul of Venice (August 16)

(41) The eighth sworn witness was brother Paul of Venice of the Order of Preachers, who received the habit at Bologna fourteen years ago and made profession in the hands of Master Reginald. After his profession, when the blessed Dominic came to Bologna, the witness was very intimate with him and walked with him round the Marches of Treviso and was with him in eating and drinking, when he was staying anywhere and when he was travelling, in the Divine Office, by day and by night, for about two years. "In all this time, I

never heard from him an idle word or a derogatory or flattering word or any damaging word." On the contrary, when he was travelling, he saw him either praying or preaching or giving his time to prayer or meditation. When he was travelling, he would tell his companions to go on ahead, saying, "Let us think about our Savior." Wherever he was, he always spoke either about God or to God, and he encouraged the brethren to do the same, and put it in his Rule. He was never seen to be angry or upset or worried by the toil of travelling, but was patient and happy in all adversities.

(42) He had a supreme love of poverty for himself and for his Order. When some of the people of Bologna wanted to give the brethren certain properties, he refused them, saying that he wanted his brethren to live off alms. And he put it in the Constitutions that properties should not be accepted in the Order.

When he left any town he used to take his shoes off and walk barefoot. He wore the cheapest of habits. "I sometimes saw the blessed Dominic seeking alms from door to door and receiving bread like any pauper. For example, at Dugliolo one day when he was begging for alms, someone offered him a whole loaf of bread, and the father knelt down and took it with great humility and devotion.

"When he was travelling, I never saw him lie in a bed, though he did sometimes lie on some bedding. Once when I visited the church of Porto Legnago with him, the father had a place prepared for his companions to lie down, but he went into the church and spent the night there until Matins, and then he said Matins with the clergy. When he was travelling, he kept the Order's fasts, though he made his companions eat because of the labour of the journey. In the convent of St. Nicholas in Bologna I looked for a long time to see if he had any place of his own to lie down in, and I found that he had not; he slept either on the ground or on a wicker trellis or on a wooden board, and very often he spent the night in church. When he prayed he wept a great deal, because sometimes when I went to fetch him from prayer I saw his face wet with tears. Every day, even when he was travelling, he wanted to sing Mass, if he could find a convenient church for it.

(43) "He longed jealously for the salvation of believers and unbelievers alike. He sometimes said to me, 'When we have established our Order, we shall go to the Cumans and preach the faith of Christ to them and win them for the Lord.'

He wanted the Rule to be observed strictly by himself and by the others. He reprimanded offenders justly and so affectionately that no one was ever upset by his correction and punishment. He conformed to the community in his food and in the Office. When he spent the night in church, he was still always there with the rest to celebrate Matins. He used to encourage the brethren in choir, now on one side, now on the other, to sing well and excellently and to recite the psalms with devotion.

"He was patient, kind, compassionate, sober, loving, humble and chaste, and he was always a virgin. I never knew anyone to compare with him in holiness of life.

"When he was travelling, he preached to the people who joined his party and urged them on to follow the good.

(44) "I was present at Bologna when his body was moved, when such a delightful fragrance came from it that everyone prostrated themselves on the ground and gave thanks to God. The whole church was filled with the fragrance.

(45) "When I was coming to Bologna from Venice to give evidence about the life of the blessed Dominic, my usual kidney pains attacked me so severely that I thought I would not be able to give evidence at the time appointed. I went to the tomb of the blessed Dominic and when I had prayed about this, I was completely freed from the pain."

Testimony of Brother Frugerio of Pennabilli (August 17)

(46) The ninth sworn witness was brother Frugerio of Pennabilli of the Order of Preachers, who had been in the Order for fourteen years and had made profession in the hands of Master Reginald and received the habit from him in the church of Mascarella, which was the first place in Bologna where the Order of Preachers was established. After his profession, with permission from Master Reginald, the witness went to visit his family, and when he returned to Bologna he found the blessed Dominic at the church of St. Nicholas, where the brethren had moved. He lived with him there for more than four months. He was also with him in the convent of Florence and in the convent in Rome, and also travelling to Rome and through various other towns, being with him in the Office, in eating and talking, hearing his confession, in prayer and in discussing God with him, by day and by night.

The blessed Dominic was very devoted in his prayer, both when he was travelling and when he was in a convent, so much so that he, the witness, could not see that he ever slept in a bed, although one was sometimes prepared for him. But sometimes when he was tired, as a result of keeping vigil too long at night, he would go to sleep on the ground or on a piece of wood. When he was celebrating Mass he wept a good deal.

(47) When he was talking to the brethren he used to weep and he made them weep too.

"I never heard an idle or harmful word from him, whether of flattery or of detraction." He always spoke about God or with God, and he used to preach to anyone he met on the way when he was travelling, and he urged the brethren to do the same. This was why he wanted to put this in his Rule. He was zealous for souls, not only those of Christians, but also Saracens and other unbelievers. As evidence of this, he proposed to go to the pagans and die there for the faith, once he had organized his brethren.

He treated himself roughly and observed the Order's fasts very strictly when he was travelling, and would not eat before the set time, even though he made his companions eat. He used a single tunic in winter and in summer. He exhorted the brethren to practise the poverty which he himself loved so much. He used a cheap tunic. He was quick to rebuke and correct any of the brethren who were wearing clothes that were at fault. This was why he directed that they should not accept properties, but should live off alms, and he put this in the Rule. He wanted the brethren to have cheap houses and cheap reading desks, so that they would display poverty in everything.

(48) He himself observed the Rule strictly and wanted it to be observed by the others. He convicted and corrected offenders with gentleness and kindness in such a way that no one was upset, even though the penances were sometimes very severe.

"He was never defiled by any mortal sin, as far as I could tell from his confession, which I heard. He was kind and patient in all trials, rejoicing in adversities, loving, compassionate, a comforter of the brethren and of others. He was adorned with all the virtues to such a degree that I never saw anyone like him."

(49) *I, Aldrovando, son of the late Tebaldo, notary by imperial authority, received these witnesses, on the instructions of Master Tancred, archdeacon of Bologna, Dom Thomas, prior of Santa Maria di Reno, and brother Palmiero of Campagnola, the judges appointed by the lord Pope, and I put them in official form and wrote them out in the year of our Lord 1233 in the sixth indiction, in the earlier part of August.*

THOMAS OF CANTIMPRÉ

Defense of the Mendicants

THOMAS OF CANTIMPRÉ (1210-1263/80) WAS BORN IN THE AREA OF
Brussels. He became an Austin canon in Cantimpré before joining the
Dominican order in Louvain. He studied in Cologne and Paris and was the
author of lives of contemporary saints, an account of the mendicant orders,
and a compilation of natural history. The following text is a description and
defense of his fellow mendicants against other forms of religious life.

Translation: Simon Tugwell, O.P., *Early Dominicans: Selected Writings* (New York:
Paulist Press, 1974).

I had often heard of the ways in which the friars
had to do without things, sometimes in considerable hardship, but I wanted to try it for myself,
and will tell you simply what happened to me
with the friars in my own native land. I arrived
on foot in some town which I did not know, so
tired from the journey that I thought my heart
would soon fail from my excessive weakness.
The friars went to the priest's house, but could
not even get a crust of the very black bread which
the servants of his household were using. From
there they went far and wide through the town
and got nothing, except a piece of bran bread
from a poor little lady who lived on the edge of
the town—a large gift indeed, in fact a huge
benefaction! So we sat down in the open air and
ate the bread. And though the husks in the bread
pricked our mouths as we ate, I never in my life
enjoyed such a delicious meal. This made me
reflect, not without a certain depression of spirit,
on what those blessed men had been enduring all
over the place, often in much worse situations
than this, while I could not sustain such discomfort for even a single day. So I shall keep quiet
about this kind of thing, which is constantly happening to them.

But there is just one thing which I do want to
mention here. It is possible to distinguish three
different kinds of way of life followed by our
clergy. The secular clergy work at their studies,
the canons, whether secular or regular, devote
themselves to the celebration of the Divine Office,
and the monks and other religious apply all their

energy to the careful practice of their regular
observances. But the friars, both the Preachers
and the Minors, in accordance with the requirements of their Orders, seem to follow all three
ways of life at one and the same time. They study
with the clerics, they devote themselves to the
Divine Office with the canons, and, in common
with the monks and other religious, they practise
community life with its accusations and beatings
and fasting, and, in part, they also practise
silence, and almost every day they all take the
discipline after Compline; in addition to that,
they have certain observances of their own, so
that, for instance, the Preachers wear a rough
rope next to the skin round their loins, and wear
woollen clothes which get prickly with all their
sweat as they travel round on foot. And apart
from all that, they have chosen to live without
owning any properties at all. What a labour it is
for the Friars Minor to beg their bread every day!
And what a labour it is for all the Preachers who
go out generally to beg after August, to collect
enough bread for the rest of the year, so that their
study will not be hindered or prevented!

You most faithful and long-suffering men, do
not be ashamed to beg your bread; Christ the
Lord begged for a drink of water from a Samari-
tan woman. Do not be afraid to be called and to
be beggars; Christ himself, who is the Truth,
declared that the poor are blessed. This is attested to by both the New and Old Testaments.

Christ is my witness in saying all of this. I am
not seeking any special glory for these two

Orders. They have their judge and it is he who seeks glory for them. I am simply constrained to reply to their critics, who consider these new religious Orders to be superstitious and silly, and reckon their travelling ground to be frivolous; to use their own word, they call the friars "gyrovagues." Well, my brethren, you need not be ashamed to be called or to be gyrovagues. You are in the company of Paul, the teacher of the nations, who completed the preaching of the gospel all the way from Spain to Illyria. While they sit home in their monasteries—and let us hope that it is with Mary—you go touring round with Paul, doing the job you have been given to do. And I am hopeful that if you suffer oppression in the world, you will still have peace in Christ, perhaps even as much peace or more than they have who sit grumbling in their place of quiet, stirring up quarrels among themselves or with their superiors. And if they are free from quarrels, as they will perhaps claim, let them sit there if they want to, with all their warm clothes on, enjoying their peace, but then they should allow the friars, whom they call gyrovagues, to travel round the world in their meagre tunics and in rags, rescuing from the jaws of the demons souls that were redeemed by the life-giving death of Christ, while they, in their peaceful and carefree existence, turn a blind eye while such souls go down to Hell. If they were real religious and real lovers of Christ, these people who malign and criticize and ridicule the friars like this, what a welcome they would give them, how glad they would be to rejoice with the friars, who apply themselves to rescuing and saving the souls Christ thought it worthwhile to ransom with his own precious Blood, valuing them so much that he made nothing of doing whatever he could for the sake of their salvation.

While we are on the subject, let me record a vision seen by a Cistercian monk who was so holy that it would appear wicked and impious not to believe him. Caught up in spirit, he saw the patroness of the Cistercian Order, the loving Mother of Jesus Christ. The blessed Virgin said to him, "I commend to your charity my brethren and my sons, so that you will love them truly and pray for them all the more earnestly." He agreed to this happily, confident that she meant the brethren of his own Order. But she said, "I have other brethren too whom I take to myself, to be cherished and protected by my patronage." With these words, she drew back her cloak and revealed the brethren of the Order of Preachers gathered safely there, and she said to him, "These are men whose life's work it is to make sure that my beloved Son's blood was not shed in vain."

Brother Walter of Trier, of the Order of Preachers, told me a similar story. There was a lady in Saxony, a recluse with a high reputation for sanctity. When she heard of the Order of Preachers, in its early days, she was very excited by its name and passionately wanted to see some of the friars. Eventually, when the opportunity offered, she did see two young friars. She was amazed and said to the Lord, "What is this, Lord? Has the preaching of your word been usurped by such unskilled babies as these?" Soon after she had said this, the Mother of Christ appeared to her and drew back her cloak and showed her the brethren of the Order, saying, "Do not despise any such as these, because I am the one who guides and protects them, and I direct their feet into the way of peace."

Now, reader, see how truly the Mother of Truth said this. Particularly in the beginning of the Order, but also in our own day, we have seen young men with no experience, delicately brought up, only recently converted from the world, touring round the world in pairs, not overthrown even though they are among wicked people, innocent among the harmful, simple as doves among the cunningly malicious, but at the same time prudent as serpents in their care of themselves. Who would not be amazed at boys like this, now even more than before, not being burned though they are in the thick of the blazing furnace, while religious who belong to other Orders which are very strictly kept away from the turmoil of the world can hardly win through without tremendous difficulty, as we have, alas, seen and heard all too often? The friars are tormented by work, distracted by all kinds of different business, and yet they survive unbroken; but these others have nothing else to attend to except their own mental and bodily health, and yet they still wobble. To what are we to ascribe this? To their own strength? Surely not. Rather to the Mother of Christ. If there are some who fall, because they are flesh as well as spirit, it is because they have idly tried to support themselves on a broken reed of Egypt instead of on Mary, the pillar of heaven.

So let our evil-mouthed and impious detractors beware of going against the patronage of the Mother of Christ by persecuting her children; if they do, they are liable to incur her anger, because she supports and defends her children. A certain Pope in our days, whose name we pass over in silence, out of respect for the Holy See, issued letters against the privileges which had been granted by himself and the four previous Popes to these two Orders, one of which is called by the Creator from all eternity "Beauty," through the prophet Zechariah, and that is the Order of Preachers, the other of which is called "Rope," by which we may obviously understand the Minors. We have it from people who were in the Roman court at the time, and there can be no doubt about it, that on the same day that he wrote these letters he was struck down by paralysis and lost his ability to talk; nor did he ever again regain his health or leave his bed. What is more, he was seen after his death by a certain holy man living outside the walls of Rome, being handed over to the two saints of God, Francis and Dominic, to be judged.

ON THE ETERNALITY OF THE WORLD

THE INTRODUCTION OF ARISTOTELIAN PHILOSOPHY IN THE COURSE OF the twelfth and thirteenth century revolutionized European thought at the same time that universities were radically restructuring the context within which learning took place. The issue of the eternality of the world is a prime example of the problems presented the intellectuals of the thirteenth century. Scripture is unequivocal: the universe is created. Aristotle is equally unambiguous: the world is eternal. The three Paris professors whose works follow represented the three reactions to this apparent contradiction between faith and reason. The Franciscan Bonaventure (ca. 1217-1274) was certain that he could demonstrate by philosophical argumentation that the world was created. Siger of Brabant, (ca. 1240-ca. 1284), a professor in the arts faculty, taught what he considered to be an authentic Aristotelian response. The Dominican Thomas Aquinas (1225-1274) attempted to defend reason from the conservatives who wished to condemn Aristotelian philosophy and from the radicals who wished to show that it contradicted Scripture.

Translation: C. Vollert, SJ, L.H. Kendzierski, and R.M. Byrne, *On the Eternality of the World* (Milwaukee: Marquette University Press, 1964).

St. Bonaventure

(In *II Sent*. d.1, a.1, q.2)

The question is: Has the world been produced in time or from eternity. That it has not been produced in time is shown:

1. By the arguments based on motion, the first of which is demonstrative in the following way: *Before every motion and change, there is the motion of the first moveable thing (primum mobile)*; but everything which begins to be begins by way of motion or change; therefore that motion (viz., of the first moveable thing) is before all that which begins to be. But that motion could not have preceded itself or its movable thing (*mobile*); therefore it could not possibly have a beginning. The first proposition is a basic one and its proof is as follows: It is a basic principle in philosophy that "in every kind the complete is prior to the incomplete of that kind"; but movement toward place is the more perfect among all the kinds of motion inasmuch as it is the motion of a complete being, and circular motion is both the swifter and the more perfect among all the kinds of local motion;

but the motion of the heaven is of this kind, therefore most perfect, therefore the first. Therefore it is evident that, etc.

2. This is likewise shown by an absurdity consequent upon the alternative. *Everything which comes to be comes to be through motion or change*; consequently, if motion comes to be it comes to be through motion or change, and with regard to this latter motion the question is similarly raised. Therefore, either there is to be an infinite regress or a positing of some motion lacking a beginning; if the motion, then also the moveable thing and, consequently, also the world.

3. Similarly, a demonstrative argument based on time is as follows: *Everything which begins to be either begins to be in an instant or in time*. If, therefore, the world begins to be, it does so either in an instant or in time. But before every time there is time, and time is before every instant. Consequently there is time before all those things which have begun to be. But it could not have been before the world and motion; therefore the world has not had a beginning. The first proposition is *per se* known. The second, namely that

before every time there is time, is evident from the fact that if it is flowing, it was of necessity flowing beforehand. Similarly, it is evident that there is time before every instant since time is a circular measure suited to the motion and the movable thing; but every point in a circle is a beginning even as it is an end; therefore every instant of time is a beginning of the future even as it is a terminus of the past. Accordingly, before every "now" there has been a past. It is evident, therefore, etc.

4. Again, this is shown by the absurdity consequent upon the alternative. If time is produced, it is produced either in time or in an instant; therefore in time. But in every time there is a prior and a posterior, both a past and a future. Consequently, if time has been produced in time, there has been time before every time, and this is impossible. Therefore, etc.

These are Aristotle's arguments based on the character of the world itself.

5. Besides these, there are other arguments based on the character of the producing cause. In general, there can be reduced to two, the first of which is demonstrative and the second based on the absurdity consequent upon the alternative. The first is as follows: *Given an adequate and actual cause, the effect is given*; but God from eternity has been the adequate and actual cause of this world; therefore, etc. The major premise is *per se* known. The minor, namely that God is the adequate cause, is evident. Since He needs nothing extrinsic for the creating of the world, but only the power, wisdom and goodness which have been most perfect in God from eternity, evidently He has, from eternity, been the adequate cause. That He has also been the actual cause is evident as follows: God is pure act and is His own act of willing, as Aristotle says; and our philosophers (*Sancti*) say that He is His own acting. It follows, therefore, etc.

6. Also, by the absurdity of the alternative. *Everything which begins to act or produce, when it was not producing beforehand, passes from rest into act.* If, therefore, God begins to produce the world, He passes from rest into act; but all such

things are subject to rest and change or mutability. Therefore God is subject to rest and mutability. This, however, contradicts His absolute goodness and absolute simplicity, and, consequently, is impossible. It is to blaspheme God; and to say that the world has had a beginning amounts to the same thing.

These are the arguments which the commentators and more recent men (*moderniores*) have added over and beyond the arguments of Aristotle; or, at least, they are reducible to these.

But there are arguments to the contrary, based on *per se* known propositions of reason and philosophy.

1. The first of these is: It is impossible to add to the infinite. This is *per se* evident because everything which receives an addition becomes more; "but nothing is more than infinite". If the world lacks a beginning, however, it has had an infinite duration, and consequently there can be no addition to its duration. But this is certainly false because every day a revolution is added to a revolution; therefore, etc. If you were to say that it is infinite in past time and yet is actually finite with respect to the present, which now is, and, accordingly, that it is in this respect, in which it is finite, that the "more" is to be found, it is pointed out to you that, to the contrary, it is in the past that the "more" is to be found. This is an infallible truth: If the world is eternal, then the revolutions of the sun in its orbit are infinite in number. Again, there have necessarily been twelve revolutions of the moon for every one of the sun. Therefore the moon has revolved more times than the sun, and the sun an infinite number of times. Accordingly, that which exceeds the infinite as infinite is discovered. But this is impossible; therefore, etc.

2. The second proposition is: *It is impossible for the infinite in number to be ordered*. For every order flows from a principle toward a mean. Therefore, if there is no first, there is no order; but if the duration of the world or the revolutions of the heaven are infinite, they do not have a first; therefore they do not have an order, and one is not before another. But since this is false, it follows that they have a first. If you say that it is necessary to posit a limit (*statum*) to an ordered series

only in the case of things ordered in a causal relation, because among causes there is necessarily a limit, I ask why not in other cases. Moreover, you do not escape in this way. For there has never been a revolution of the heaven without there being a generation of animal from animal. But an animal is certainly related causally to the animal from which it is generated. If, therefore, according to Aristotle and reason it is necessary to posit a limit among those things ordered in a causal relation, then in the generation of animals it is necessary to posit a first animal. And the world has not existed without animals; therefore, etc.

3.   The third proposition is: *It is impossible to traverse what is infinite.* But if the world had no beginning, there has been an infinite number of revolutions; therefore it was impossible for it to have traversed them; therefore impossible for it to have come down to the present. If you say that they (i.e., numerically infinite revolutions) have not been traversed because there has been no first one, or that they well could be traversed in an infinite time, you do not escape in this way. For I shall ask you if any revolution has infinitely preceded today's revolution or none. If none, then all are finitely distant from this present one. Consequently, they are all together finite in number and so have a beginning. If some one is infinitely distant, then I ask whether the revolution immediately following it is infinitely distant. If not, then neither is the former (infinitely) distant since there is a finite distance between the two of them. But if it (i.e. the one immediately following) is infinitely distant, then I ask in a similar way about the third, the fourth, and so on to infinity. Therefore, one is no more distant than another from this present one, one is not before another, and so they are all simultaneous.

4.   The fourth proposition is: *It is impossible for the infinite to be grasped by a finite power.* But if the world had no beginning, then the infinite is grasped by a finite power; therefore, etc. The proof of the major is *per se* evident. The minor is shown as follows. I suppose that God alone is with a power actually infinite and that all other things have limitation. Also I suppose that there has never been a motion of the heaven without

there being a created spiritual substance who would either cause or, at least, know it. Further, I also suppose that a spiritual substance forgets nothing. If, therefore, there has been no revolution of the heaven which he would not know and which would have been forgotten. Therefore, he is actually knowing all of them and they have been infinite in number. Accordingly, a spiritual substance with finite power is grasping simultaneously an infinite number of things. If you assert that this is not unsuitable because all the revolutions, being of the same species and in every way alike, are known by a single likeness, there is the objection that not only would he have known the rotations, but also their effects as well, and these various and diverse effects are infinite in number. It is clear, therefore, etc.

5.   The fifth proposition is: *It is impossible that there be simultaneously an infinite number of things.* But if the world is eternal and without a beginning, then there has been an infinite number of men, since it would not be without there being men—for all things are in a certain way for the sake of man and a man lasts only for a limited length of time. But there have been as many rational souls as there have been men, and so an infinite number of souls. But, since they are incorruptible forms, there are as many souls as there have been; therefore an infinite number of souls exist. If this leads you to say that there has been a transmigration of souls or that there is but the one soul for all men, the first is an error in philosophy, because, as Aristotle holds, "appropriate act is in its own matter." Therefore, the soul, having been the perfection of one, cannot be the perfection of another, even according to Aristotle. The second position is even more erroneous, since much less is it true that there is but the one soul for all.

6.   The last argument to this effect is: *It is impossible for that which has being after non-being to have eternal being,* because this implies a contradiction. But the world has being after non-being. Therefore it is impossible that it be eternal. That it has being after non-being is proven as follows: everything whose having of being is totally from another is produced by the latter out of nothing;

but the world has its being totally from God; therefore the world is out of nothing. But not out of nothing as a matter (*materialiter*); therefore out of nothing as an origin (*originaliter*). It is evident that everything which is totally produced by something differing in essence has being out of nothing. For what is totally produced is produced in its matter and form. But matter does not have that out of which it would be produced because it is not out of God (*ex Deo*). Clearly, then, it is out of nothing. The minor, viz., that the world is totally produced by God, is evident from the discussion of another question.

Conclusion

Whether positing that all things have been produced out of nothing would imply saying that the world is eternal or has been produced eternally.

I answer: It has to be said that to maintain that the world is eternal or eternally produced by claiming that all things have been produced out of nothing is entirely against truth and reason, as the last of the above arguments proves; and it is so against reason that I do not believe that any philosopher, however slight his understanding, has maintained this. For such a position involves an evident contradiction. But, with the eternity of matter presupposed, to maintain an eternal world seems reasonable and understandable, and this by way of two analogies which can be drawn. For the procession of earthly things from God is after the fashion of an imprint (*vestigium*). Accordingly, if a foot and the dust in which its print were formed were eternal, nothing would prevent our understanding that the footprint is co-eternal with the foot and, nevertheless, it still would be an imprint from the foot. If matter, or the potential principle, were in this fashion coeternal with the maker, what would keep that imprint from being eternal? Rather, on the contrary, it would seem quite fitting that it should be.

Again, another reasonable analogy offers itself. For, from God the creature proceeds as a shadow, the Son as brightness. But as soon as there is light, there is immediately brightness, and immediately shadow if there should be an opaque object in its way. If, therefore, matter, as opaque, is coeter-

nal with the maker, just as it is reasonable to posit the Son, the brightness of the Father, to be coeternal, so it seems reasonable that creatures or the world, shadow in relation to the Highest Light, is eternal. Moreover, this view is more reasonable than its contrary, viz., that matter has been eternally incomplete, without form or the divine influence, as certain philosophers have maintained. In fact, it is more reasonable to such an extent that even that outstanding philosopher, Aristotle, has fallen into this error, according to the charges of our philosophers (*Sancti*), the exposition of the commentators, and the apparent meaning of his text.

On the other hand, modern scholars say that the Philosopher has never thought this nor did he intend to prove that the world had no beginning *in any way at all*, but rather that it did not begin *by way of a natural motion*.

Which of these interpretations is the truer one I do not know. This one thing I do know, that if he held that the world has not begun *according to nature*, he maintained what is true, and his arguments based on motion and time are conclusive. But if he thought that it has *in no way begun*, he has clearly erred, as has been shown above by many arguments. Moreover, in order to avoid self-contradiction, he had to maintain either that the world has not been made, or that it has not been made out of nothing. In order to avoid an actual infinity, however, he had to hold for either the corruption of the rational soul, or its unicity, or its transmigration; thus, in any case, he had to destroy its beatitude. So it is that this error has both a bad beginning and the worst of endings.

1. To the first objection, regarding motion, viz., that there is a first among all motions and changes because there is a most perfect one, it must be granted as true with respect to *natural* motions and changes and there is nothing against it. But with respect to the *supernatural* change, through which that *mobile* (i.e., the heaven) has proceeded into being, it is not true. For this latter change precedes every created thing, and so precedes the *primum mobile* and, of course, its motion.

2. To the objection, every motion passes into being through motion, it must be answered that

motion does not pass into being *through itself* nor *in itself*, but *with another* and *in another*. And since God has, in the same instant, made the *mobile* and, as mover, acted upon the *mobile*, then He has cocreated the motion with the *mobile*. If, however, you were to seek further with regard to that creating, it must be said that there a limit is reached as in the very first of things. Further on, this will be made better known.[1]

3. To the third objection, regarding the "now" of time, it must be said that just as there is a twofold indicating of a point in a circle, either when the circle is being made or after it has been made, and just as when it is being made there is a placing and indicating of a first point but when it already is there is no locating of a first, so also with regard to time there is a twofold acceptance of the "now." In the very production of time, there has been a first "now" before which there has been no other and which was the beginning of time in which all things are said to have been produced. But with respect to time after it has been made, it is true that it is the terminus of the past and it is in the fashion of a circle. But things have not been produced in this way in a time already complete. Thus it is clear that the Philosopher's arguments do not at all establish this conclusion. With regard to the statement that before every time is time, this is true in terms of dividing time from within, but not in the sense of preceding as outside time.

4. To the objection concerning time, as to when has it begun, it must be said that it began in its own beginning (*principium*). But the source (*principium*) of time is the instant or "now"; and so it began in an instant. Also, the argument: Time has not been in an instant and so has not begun in an instant does not stand because things which are successive are not in their own beginning. This same thing can be said in another way since there are two ways of speaking about time, either according to its essence or according to its being (*esse*). If one speaks of it according to its essence, then the "now" is the whole essence of time, and that has begun to be with the mobile thing, not in another "now" but in its own self since it has been established in the very beginning and thus

it has not had another measure. If one speaks of it according to its being, then it has begun with the motion of change, viz., it has not begun by way of creation, but rather through the change of the changeable, and especially of the *primum mobile*.

5. To the objection based on the adequacy and actuality of the cause, it must be said that the adequate cause of any effect is to two kinds, either as operative through its *nature* or as operative through *will* or *reason*. If operative through *nature*, then, as soon as it is, it produces its effect. On the other hand, if operative through *will*, even though it be adequate, it is not necessarily operative as soon as it is, since a cause of this sort is operative by way of wisdom and discernment and so takes suitability into account. Therefore, inasmuch as eternity did not befit the nature of the creature itself, it was not fitting that God should grant this most excellent of states to any thing. Accordingly, the divine will, which operates by way of wisdom, has produced the world not from eternity but in time, since, as He has produced, so has He disposed and so has He willed. For He has willed from eternity to produce then when He has produced, just as I will now to hear Mass tomorrow. It is thus evident that the adequacy of the cause is not pertinent to this question.

Similarly with regard to actuality, it must be said that a cause can be in act in two ways, either in itself, as I were to say: The sun shines, or in its effect (*in effectu*), as if I were to say: The sun illumines. In the first way God has always been in act, since He is pure act unadulterated by the merely possible. In the other way He is not always in act, for He has not always been producing.

6. To the sixth objection: If from being non-producing He has become producing, He has changed from rest to act, it must be said that there is a type of agent in which action and production add something over and beyond the agent and producer. Such an agent is changed in some way when from non-acting it becomes acting, and in this case rest precedes operation and by operation completion is achieved. But there is another agent which is its own action, and nothing at all

is added to such an agent when it produces nor does anything come to be in it which it was not beforehand. An agent of this sort neither receives completion in operating nor is it idle in non-operating, nor, when from non-producing it comes to be producing, it is changed from rest to act. But such is God, even according to the philosophers, who have asserted God to be the most simple of beings. It is evident, therefore, that their argument is a foolish one. For if He had produced things from eternity in order to avoid idleness, then He would not be, *without things*, the perfect good, nor consequently would He *with things*, since that which is most perfect is perfect by its own self. Moreover, if because of His immutability it were necessary that things be from eternity, then He could produce nothing new now. And what kind of God would He be who is now essentially incapable of anything? All these consequences imply nonsense rather than philosophy or an argumentation.

If you were to ask how this is to be understood, viz., that God acts by His own self and yet does not begin to act, the answer would have to be that, even though this cannot be fully understood because of the conjoined imagination, nevertheless it can be established by argumentation necessitating assent; and anyone who withdraws from sense experience in order to consider the intelligibles will, to some extent perceive it. For if anyone were to ask whether an angel could make a pottery cup or throw a stone in spite of no hands, the answer would be that he could because he is capable, by his own power alone and without an organ, of what the soul is capable of with the body and its members. If, therefore, an angel, because of its simplicity and perfection, exceeds man to such an extent that he can do, without an organ as a means, that for which man necessarily requires an organ, can even do through one [power] what man is capable of only through many, how much more can God, Who is at the very limit of the whole of simplicity and perfection, produce all things without any means by the command of His own will which is nothing other than Himself, and thereby remain immutable in producing! In this way a man can be led to an understanding of this truth. But that man will grasp it more perfectly who can consider these

two aspects of his Maker, namely that He is most perfect and most simple. Because He is most perfect, all the perfections there are to be attributed to Him; because most simple, these introduce no diversity into Him, and accordingly no change or mutability. So it is, "remaining at rest He causes all things to be moved."

Collationes in Hexaemeron IV, 13

The sixth division is into cause and caused; and here there are many errors. For some say that the world has been from eternity. Wise men agree that something could not come to be from nothing and in this way be from eternity, since it is necessarily the case that, just as when a thing passes into nothing it ceases to be, so also when it comes to be from nothing it begins to be. But some seem to have posited an unoriginated matter; from this it follows that God does not make anything. For He does not make matter, since it is unoriginated. Nor does He make form since either it comes to be from something or from nothing; not from matter since the being (*essentia*) of form cannot come from the being (*essentia*) of matter; and not from nothing since, as they suppose, God can make nothing from nothing. But let perish the notion that the power of God has matter as its supporting foundation.

Collationes in Hexaemeron V, 29

And it is in this way that the Philosopher proceeds to prove the world eternal on the basis that circular local motion, because it is perfect, precedes every motion and change. But I answer: It must be said that the perfect is before the diminished when speaking of the simply perfect, but not when speaking of the perfect in a genus, as is the case with local motion.

Collationes in Hexaemeron VI, 2-5

2. Just as it has been said of the angels, *God separated the light from the darkness*, so also it may be said of the philosophers. But what was the first step that some have taken toward darkness? It was this: although all of them have seen that the first cause is the beginning of all things as well as

their end, still they have differed from one another about an intermediary. For some have denied that the exemplars of things are in that first cause. The leader of this group seems to have been Aristotle who at the beginning and at the end of his *Metaphysics*, and in many other places, condemns Plato's Ideas. Accordingly, he says that God knows only Himself, does not need knowledge of any other thing, and moves as desired and loved. On this ground these men assert that He has no knowledge of the particular. As a consequence, Aristotle especially attacks the Ideas in his *Ethics* where he says that the highest good cannot be an *Idea*. His arguments do not hold, and the commentator [on the *Ethics*, Eustratius] has destroyed them.

3.   From this error follows a further error, namely, that God does not have foreknowledge or providence since He does not have within Himself the intelligibilities (*rationes*) of things through which He might know them. Also they say that the only truth about the contingent is not truth. And from this it follows that all things come to be either by chance or by the necessity of fate. Because it is impossible to come to be by chance, the Arabs introduce the necessity of fate, namely, that the sphere-moving substances are the necessary causes of all things. From this it follows that the truth that there is an earthly disposition of earthly things according to penalties and glory is obscured. For if those substances unerringly move, nothing is affirmed regarding hell, nor that there is a devil. Nor, as it seems, has Aristotle ever asserted that there is a devil, and that there is a beatitude after this life. This threefold error, then, consists in hiding away within darkness, exemplareity, divine providence and the disposition of earthly things.

4.   There follows upon these a threefold blindness or mental dullness. First, about the eternity of the world, as Aristotle seems to hold according to all the Greek doctors, such as Gregory of Nyssa, Gregory Nazianzenus, Damascene, Basil, as well as according to all the Arabic commentators, who say that Aristotle taught this and they seem to speak his words. You will never find him saying that the world had a source or a beginning; rather he argued against Plato who alone

seems to have held that time had a beginning. And this is in direct conflict with the light of truth.

From this follows another blindness, about the unicity of the intellect. For if an eternal world is posited, some one of these consequences follows necessarily; either there is an infinite number of souls since men would have been infinite in number, or the soul is perishable, or there is a transition from body to body, or the intellect is one in all men, the error attributed to Aristotle by the Commentator.

From these two it follows that after this life there is neither happiness nor punishment.

5.   These men, therefore, have fallen into errors, nor have they been "separated from the darkness"; and such errors as these are the very worst. Nor has the abysmal pit been as yet locked up. This is the darkness of Egypt; for although great light might be discerned in them in knowledges prior to this, still it is entirely extinguished through the aforementioned errors. And some men, seeing that Aristotle was so outstanding in other matters and in them spoke the truth, cannot believe that he has not said what is true in these matters.

Collationes in Hexaemeron VII, 1-2

1.   *God saw the light, that it was good, and He divided the light from darkness*, etc. This text has been discussed in order to explain vision by the understanding naturally bestowed upon us. He causes us to see this, *that it was good*, both in the order of scientific consideration and also in that of sapiential contemplation. In the order of scientific consideration, inasmuch as He illumines as light, namely, as the truth of things, as the truth of speech, and as the truth of conduct. In the order of sapiential contemplation, inasmuch as He illumines through the influx into the soul of a ray from the eternal light, in order that the soul may see that light in its own self as in a mirror, in the separate Intelligence as in a transmitting medium as it were (*medio quodam delativo*), in the eternal light as in a subject-source (*in subjecto fontano*). Also it has been said that He divided the light from darkness, because certain ones have

attacked the Ideas, and as a result a threefold understanding of truth has been hidden in darkness, namely, the truth about the angelic fall, which follows if the angel would not have his perfection except through motion. From this there follows a threefold blindness, namely, about the eternity of the world, about the unicity of the intellect, and about punishment and glory.

2. The first one Aristotle seems to posit, as well as the last one since he does not place happiness in an afterlife; with regard to the middle one, the Commentator says he thought this. On the eternity of the world, he could be excused because he understood this as a philosopher, speaking as a naturalist, saying that it could not begin to be through nature. That Intelligences would have their perfection through motion, this he could have said inasmuch as they are not useless, because there is nothing useless in the very ground work of nature. Likewise that he placed happiness in this life may be because, although he thought it eternal, about that he did not interject his own view (*se*), perhaps because it was not part of his treatment of the question. About the unicity of the intellect it could be said that he understood the intellect to be one by reason of the inflowing light, not by reason of itself, since it is many according to subject.

Breviloquium II, 1-3

1. These matters regarding the Trinity having been, in a summary fashion, grasped, some remarks now have to be made about that creature that is the world. What must be held in this matter is, briefly, as follows: The whole of the earthly contrivance has been produced in being in time (*ex tempore*) and from nothing (*de nihilo*) by one, sole, and highest first Principle whose power, though itself immeasurable, has disposed *all things in a certain weight, number, and measure.*

2. From these points, understood in a general way, about the production of things, truth is gained and error rejected. By "in time" is excluded the error of those positing an eternal world. By "from nothing" is excluded the error of those positing an eternal material principle. By "by one

Principle" is excluded the error of the Manichees positing a plurality of principles. By "sole and highest" is excluded the error of those positing that God has produced lower creatures through the ministry of the Intelligences. By adding "in a certain weight, number, and measure" it is pointed out that the creature is an effect of the creating Trinity under a threefold causality: *efficient*, by which in the creature there is unity, mode and measure; *exemplar*, by which there is in creature truth, species, and number; *final*, by which there is in the creature goodness, order and weight. And, indeed, these are found in every creature, as a vestige of the Creator, whether they are corporeal or spiritual or composed of both.

3. The basis for understanding the aforesaid is as follows: For there to be perfect order and repose among things, all things must be reduced to one principle which indeed is first so that it may give repose to others and most perfect so that it may give completion to all others. The first principle through which there is repose can be one and only one. This first principle, if it produces the world, since it could not produce it out of its own self, must produce it out of nothing. And because production out of nothing posits being (*esse*) after non-being (*non-esse*) on the part of the produced and immeasurability in producing power on the part of the producing principle, and since this belongs to God alone, it is necessary that the world as a creature be produced in time by that immeasurable power acting *per se* and immediately.

Siger of Brabant

Question on the Eternity of the World

The first question is whether the human species and in general the species of all individuals began to exist only by way of the propagation of generable and corruptible things when it had no previous existence whatsoever; and it seems that this is so.

That species of which any individual began to exist when it had no previous existence at all is new and began to have existence since it universally and entirely had no previous existence. The human species is such, and in general the species of all individuals generable and corruptible, because every individual of this type of species began to exist when it had no previous existence. And, therefore, any species of such things is also new and began, since in all cases it had not previously existed. The major is stated thus: because the species does not have being nor is caused except in singulars and in causing singulars. If, therefore, any individual of some species has been created when it had not existed before, the species of those beings will be such a kind.

Secondly, this same conclusion is also able to be reached in a different manner thus: universals, just as they do not have existence in singulars, so neither are they caused. Every being is caused by God. Therefore, if man has been caused by God, since he is some being of the world, it is necessary that he come to exist in a certain determined individual; just as the heaven and whatever else has been caused by God. Because, if man does not have an individual eternity, as has the sensible heaven according to philosophers, then the human species will have been caused by God so that it began to exist when it had not existed before.

To prove this one must consider, in the first place, how the human species was caused, and in general any other universals of generable and corruptible things; and in this way an answer should be made to the question and the aforementioned argument.

Secondly, since the foregoing argument admits that universals exist in singulars, one must seek or consider how this may be true.

Thirdly, because some species began to exist when it had surely not existed before, and because it follows that potentiality precedes act in duration, it should be seen which of these preceded the other in duration. For, this presents a difficulty within itself.

I

Concerning the first, therefore, we should know that the human species has not been caused, according to philosophers, except through generation. Now, because in general the being of all things is in matter which is in potency to form, they are made by a generation which is either essential or accidental. From this, however, that the human species has been made by God through generation, it follows that it does not proceed directly from Him. The human species, however, and in general the species of all things which are in matter, since it is made through generation, is not generated essentially but accidentally. It is not generated essentially, because if any one were to study those things which are made universally, then every thing which is made is made from this determined and individual matter. For, although arguments and knowledge are concerned with universals, yet operations are regarding singulars. Now, however, determined matter does not pertain to the meaning of species, and therefore is not generated essentially; and this is held by Aristotle in VII *Metaphysicae*. The same reason why form is not generated is also the reason why the composite which is species is not generated. And I call the species a composite, just as Callias in his own nature is this soul in this body, so also animal is soul in body. The common nature of form and species that they are not generated essentially is because individuated matter pertains to the consideration or reasoning of neither of the things from which generation essentially comes, through the transmutation of the thing from non-being to being, or from privation to form. The human species, however, although not generated essentially has nevertheless been generated accidentally, because it thus happens if man, just as he has been abstracted in thought from individual matter and from the individual, so he might be abstracted in existence. Then, just as he is not generated essentially, it might be thought that he is also not generated accidentally; but, because man in his being is this man, Socrates or Plato, then Socrates is also a man, as Aristotle says in VII *Metaphysicae*, that generating a brass sphere generates a sphere because a brass sphere is a sphere. And since just as Socrates is a man, so is Plato, and so with the others. Hence it is that man is generated through the generation of any individual, and not only of one determined individual.

Now, from the explanation it is clear in what way the human species is considered by philosophers eternal and caused. For, it is not to be thought of as eternal and caused as if it existed abstracted from individuals. Nor is it eternally caused in the sense that it exists in an eternally caused individual, as the species of heaven or an intelligence; but rather because in the individuals of the human species one is generated before the other eternally, and the species has to be and to be caused through an individual's existing and being caused. Hence it is that the human species always exists and that it did not begin to be after previous non-existence. For, to say that it began to be after it had not existed before is to say that there began to be a certain individual before whom no other individual of that species had existed. And since the human species had not been caused otherwise than generated through the generation of individual before individual, the human species or that which is called by the name of man begins to exist because universally everything generated begins to exist—begins, nevertheless, to exist when it existed and had previously existed. For, man begins to be through the generation of Socrates who is generated; he exists, nevertheless, through the existence of Plato of the previous generation. Those things are not contradictory about the universal; just as there is nothing repugnant for a man to run and not to run. Indeed, man runs in the person of Socrates, and man does not run in the person of Plato. From the fact, nevertheless, that Socrates runs, it is not true to say that man universally and entirely does not run. So also, in the fact that Socrates is generated man begins to be, is not to say that man begins to be in such a way that he had not in any wise previously existed.

From the previous discourse the solution to the aforementioned argument is clear.

And first, it must be said that this argument as just stated, namely, that species is new and began to exist when it had not previously existed, must be denied. Any individual of this kind began to be when it did not previously exist because even though it be true that no individual man began to be after not existing, yet no individual of this kind begins to be unless another one had previously existed. Species does not have existence so much through the existence of one of its individuals as another, and so the human species does

not begin to be when it had not existed before. For, to admit that the species is such is to say that not only a certain individual of it began to be when he had not been before, but any individual of it began to be when neither he nor another individual of that species had existed before.

And the given reason is similar to the reasoning by which Aristotle speculates in IV *Physicorum*, whether past time is finite. All past time whether near or remote is a certain *then*, and the certain *then* has a measured distance to the present *now*; therefore all past time is finite. And each of the aforementioned propositions is clear from the meaning of that *then* which Aristotle speaks of in IV *Physicorum*. The solution of this reasoning, according to Aristotle, is that although every second is finite, nevertheless since in time there is a *then* before the *then* to infinity, therefore not all past time is finite. For, what is composed of things finite in quantity yet infinite in number has to be infinite. So also, although there is no individual man but that he has begun to exist when he had not existed before, yet there is an individual before the individual to infinity; it is thus that man does not begin to be when he had in no wise existed before, and neither does time. And the case is similar—just as past time has to be through a certain *then*, so also species have to be through the existence of any one of its individuals.

Finally, as regards the form of the reasoning as proposed in the second way, it must be said that the universal does not have existence nor is caused except in singulars; since it is also said that all being has been caused by God, it must be conceded that man also exists as a being of the world and caused by God. But, since it is brought in the discussion and inferred that man has come into existence in some determined individual, it must be said that this conclusion is in no wise to be drawn from the premises; indeed, that reasoning is a hindrance to itself. For, it is accepted in the first place, that man does not have existence except in singulars nor is caused except in singulars; and it is clear that according to this reasoning he has existence and is created through one or through another. For this reason, therefore, it must be concluded that it is reasonable that man has come into existence in some determined individual. Indeed, the human species comes and came into being accidentally by the generation of individual before individual to infinity. This is not to say, however, that it (the human species) comes into existence only in some determined individual and when it had not existed before. Whence we should wonder about those arguing thus since they want to argue that the human species had begun through its being made; and yet that it was not made essentially but rather by the making of the individual, as they confess. To show their intention they ought to show that individual has not been generated before individual to infinity. This, however, they do not show but they propose one false theory, that the human species is not able to have been made eternal by God unless it had been created in some determined and eternal individual, just as the species of heaven was made eternal; and when they find no eternal being among the individuals of man, they think that they have demonstrated that the whole species began to exist when it had not been at all before.

II

The second question is whether universals are in particulars, and it is clear that they are not since Aristotle says in II *De Anima*, that universals in themselves exist in the mind. And Themistius in a similar book, says that concepts are similar things which are universals, which the mind collects and stores within itself. And the same Themistius, in *super principium De Anima*, says that genus is a certain concept gathered from the slight similitude of the singulars; the concepts however are in the conceiving mind, and universals, since they are concepts, are also in the mind.

But on the other hand, universals are universal things for otherwise they might not be said of particulars; and for this reason universals are not within the mind.

Moreover, the thing itself, which is the subject for universality, the man or the stone, is not in the mind. Also, the intention of universality must consist in its being called and denominated universal; and hence man and stone since they are called universals, the intention of universality is in these. Either both, the thing and the intention,

or neither is in the mind. Because, if man and stone in respect to the fact that they are, are not in the mind, it seems that neither are they there in respect to the fact that they are universals.

The solution. The universal, because it is a universal, is not a substance, as Aristotle states in VII *Metaphysicae*. And so this is clear. The universal, in that it is a universal, is different from any singular. If, therefore, the universal, in that it is universal, would be a substance, then it would be differing in substance from any of the singulars, and each (singular) would be a substance in act, both singular and universal; the act however, would be distinguished. Therefore universals would be distinct substances and separated from particulars; on this account with Aristotle it amounts to the same thing to say that universals are substances as to say that they are separated from particulars. And if the universal, in that it is universal, is not a substance, then it is evident that there are two things in the universal, namely, the thing which is denominated universal, the man or stone, which is not in the mind, and the intention itself of universality, and this is in the mind; so that the universal in that it is universal does not exist except in the mind, as is evident in this way. For, nothing is called a universal because it exists of its own nature commonly and abstractly from particulars, or by the work of the intellect in the nature of things; because if in its own nature, in its very being, it were to exist abstractly from particulars, it would not be spoken of them since it would be separated from them and we would not need an active intellect. Moreover, the active intellect does not give things any abstraction in existence from individual matter or from particulars, but gives to them an abstraction according to intellection by producing an abstract intellection of those things. If, therefore, the man or stone are universals, it is not except that these things are known universally and abstractly from individual matter. These things do not exist thus in the nature of things because if understood, those things, the man and the stone, do not have existence except in the mind. Since the abstract comprehension of these things is not in things, then those things, because they are universals, are in the mind. And this can also be seen in like cases.

A certain thing is said to be known because there is a knowledge of it and it happens that it is understood. The thing itself, however, with respect to what it is, although it be outside the mind, yet in respect to its being understood, that is, insofar as there is understanding of it, exists only in the mind. Because, if universals are universals, and they are understood as such, namely, abstract and common to particulars, then the universals as universals do not exist except in the mind. And this is what Averroes says in *super IIIum De Anima*, that universals as universals are entirely intelligibles; not as beings but as intelligibles. The intelligible, however, as intelligible, that is, insofar as there is an understanding of it, is entirely in the soul. Thus also Themistius says that universals are concepts.

But it must be observed that the abstract and common understanding of any nature, although it be something common, as a common understanding of particulars, yet is not common according to its being predicated of particulars in that it has to be abstracted from particulars; but that which is abstractly and commonly understood and of consequence is so signified, is spoken concerning particulars. For this reason: because that very nature which is spoken of and comprehended as a general thing is in things and is therefore spoken concerning particulars. Although those things are known and understood abstractly and commonly, they do not exist as such; therefore things of this kind are not predicated of particulars according to the ideas of genus and species.

And one must also consider that it is not necessary that the universal exist in actuality before it may be known because the universal in actuality is intelligible in actuality. Now, it is one and the same actuality whether of the intelligible in actuality or of the intellect in actuality; just as it is one motion whether of the active or of the passive, although they be different. But the intelligible in potency certainly precedes the understanding of it; however, such a thing is not universal also except in potency, and so it is not necessary that the universal have to be universal except in potency before it is understood.

Nevertheless, some have held the contrary in this discussion because the very activity of understanding precedes in the natural order the object causing that act. Now, however, the universal, in that it is universal, moves the intellect and is the object which causes the act of understanding; on this account it seems to them that the universal is not universal in that it is so understood, indeed, because the universal in the natural order is universal before it is so understood and is the cause of that understanding of it.

But the solution of this is that nature by which is caused the act of the intelligible and of the intellect, which is the intellect in act, is the active intellect and also the phantasm which naturally precede that act. In what manner, however, these two concur to cause the act of understanding must be sought in *super IIIum De Anima*. But this must be said that the universal is not a universal before the concept and the act of understanding, as at least that act is of the active intellect. For, the understanding of the thing which is in the possible intellect, since it is possible as regards the subject, belongs to the active intellect as efficient. Thus the universal does not have formally that which is universal from the nature which causes the act of understanding. Indeed, as has been mentioned before, it is the concept and the actuality from which the universal receives its universality. Therefore universals, in that they are universals, are entirely in the mind. On this account they are not generated by nature inasmuch as they are universals, neither essentially nor accidentally. For, the nature which is stated and understood universally is in particular things and is generated accidentally.

To the first objection it must be said that the fact that universals are universal things can be understood in two ways; either because they exist universally or because they are understood universally. Universals, however, are not universal things in the first manner as if they existed universally in the nature of things, for then they would not be concepts of the mind. But universals are universal things in a second manner, that is, they are understood universally and abstractly; in this way universals, insofar as they are universals and since they are concepts, cannot be spoken of as particulars as such. For, the idea of genus or species is not said of them, but the very nature which is thus understood as that which is itself included, is not in the mind, and is said of particulars.

In regard to another point, it must be said that things are rightly named after something which does not exist in reality. For, a thing understood is named from the understanding of it which is not in it but in the mind; and so also the universal is named from the universal and abstract under-standing of it which is not in it but in the mind.

III

Consequently we must investigate the third question. Although act precedes potency in thought, for potentiality is defined through act, as we say the builder is able to build, potency nevertheless is prior to act in substance and in perfection in a thing which proceeds from poten-cy to act because the things which are later in generation are, in substance and perfection, prior, since generation proceeds from the imperfect to the perfect and from potentiality to act. Act is also before potentiality in substance and perfection in the respect that potentiality and act are looked at in different ways; because eternal things are prior to corruptible things in substance and perfection. But nothing eternal, in respect that it is such a thing, is in potentiality. In corruptible things, however, there is an admixture of potency.

The question is whether act precedes potential-ity in time, or potentiality the act.

And it seems that the act does not precede potentiality in time because in eternal beings one is not before the other in time. But when the act of a certain species and the potentiality to that act are looked upon according to the species, they are both eternal. For, man is always in act and is always able to be man. Therefore the act thought of in relation to the species does not precede potentiality in time.

Moreover, in this matter in which one is to come from the other in a cycle to infinity, there is none which is first in time. But the seed is from the man and the man from the seed to infinity. Therefore, in those things the one does not pre-cede the other in time. Just as in the case of the seed from which a man is generated there is another generating man previously existing, so also previous to that generating man, since he

himself was generated, there must have been a seed from which he was generated.

What is first in the order of generation is first in the order of time. But potentiality is prior to act in the order of generation since generation proceeds from potentiality to act, and therefore it is prior in the order of time.

Moreover, there is no reason why act should precede potentiality in time except that by a power a being is made in act through some agent of its own kind existing in act. But, although from this it follows that the act of the agent precedes in time the act and perfection of the generated thing by that agent, nevertheless, it does not seem to happen that the act of the one generating pre-cedes in time that which is in potentiality to the act of generation. Nor from this also does act sim-ply precede potentiality in time, although some act precedes some potentiality to that act. For, just as being in potentiality comes into actuality through something of its own species in act, so also the thing existing in act in that species is gen-erated from something existing in potentiality to the act of that species. For, just as that which is in potentiality, namely a man, is brought into act by a man in act, so also the man generating is gener-ated from the previous seed and from a man in potency; and so in that reasoning the hen has pre-ceded the egg in time and the egg the hen, as peo-ple argue.

On the other side is Aristotle in IX *Metaphysi-cae*. For, he holds that although what proceeds from potentiality to act is the same in number, yet potentiality precedes the act in time, neverthe-less, the same being in relation to species and existing in act precedes potentiality.

Moreover, everything existing in potentiality is brought into actuality through something exist-ing in act and at length is brought into the order of moving things by a mover existing completely in act who did not previously have in his power to be anything except in act. Therefore, according to this, act is seen simply to precede potency in time.

To prove this we must first consider that some-thing numerically the same which has existence at some time in potentiality and some time in act is able to be prior in time than it is. But because this potency is preceded by act in another, since every being in potentiality comes into actuality by that which is in some way of its species, therefore it is not proper to say simply that potentiality precedes act in time.

Secondly, one must consider that if the whole universe of caused beings were at some time not being, as certain poets, theologians, and natural philosophers claimed, Aristotle says in XII *Metaphysicae*, then potentiality would precede act simply. And also if some entire species of being, as the human species, would begin to exist when it had never existed before, just as some think they have demonstrated, the potentiality for the actuality of that species would simply precede the act. But each of these is impossible, as is evident from the first consideration.

For, if the whole universe of beings at some time had been in potentiality, so that none of the beings would be totally in act—always an agent in act and the mover—then the beings and the world would not now be except in potentiality, and matter of itself would come into act, which is impossible. Thus Aristotle says in XII *Metaphysicae*, and so does his Commentator, that for things to be at rest in an infinite time and afterward to be in motion is the same as for matter to be self-moving.

From the second question it is evident that this is impossible. For, since the prime mover and agent is always in act, and something in potency is not prior to something in act, it follows that it always moves and acts and makes anything or does anything without an intermediate movement. From this, however, that it is always moving and so acting, it follows that no species of being proceeds to actuality, but that it has proceeded before, so that the same species which were, return in a cycle; and so also opinions and laws and religions and all other things so that the lower circle around from the circling of the higher, although because of the antiquity there is no memory of the cycle of these. We say these things as the opinion of the Philosopher, although not asserting them as true. One, nevertheless, should notice that a certain species of being is able to go into act when it did not exist except in potentiality, although at another time it also was in act, as is evident. For, it happens in the heavens that a certain spectacle and constellation appear in the heavens previously not existing, the effect of which is properly another species of being here below, which is then caused and which yet previously existed.

Thirdly, it must be considered that when it is taken that the potency to an act and the act educing that potency are of the same kind in the generator and thing generated, it is not said in so taking them that act precedes potentiality simply nor potentiality act, unless the act is taken according to the species and the proper potentiality is taken according to the individual. For, a man in act, and a certain man in act, inasmuch as he is generating, precedes in time that which is being in potency, namely, man generated. But because in this order, just as being in potency proceeds into act through something existing in act, and so act precedes any given potentiality, so also everything existing in act in this species goes from potentiality to act, and so potentiality in this species precedes any given act. Therefore neither simply precedes the other in time, but one comes before the other to infinity, as was stated.

In the fourth question we must consider that in a certain order of moving and acting beings it is necessary that thing which proceeds from potentiality to act come to some act that educes that potentiality to actuality, and this act does not have to go from potentiality to act. Therefore, since every being in potentiality goes to actuality through some being of its own species in act, not all being, however, in actuality and generating proceeds from potentiality to act. Hence it is that in any given being in potentiality to some act, the act of the species in a certain way, although not entirely for the same reason, precedes that potentiality from which it proceeds to act, precede. And therefore, the act is simply said to precede potentiality in time, as has been explained, namely, because the first mover leading into act all being in potentiality does not precede in time the being in potentiality, since the being in potentiality is regarded in the rank of prime matter. For, just as God always exists, according to Aristotle, so also does the potential man, since he is regarded as prime matter. Moreover, the prime mover does not precede in time the being in potentiality, since he is regarded as in prime matter. Moreover, the prime mover does not precede in time the being in potentiality, since it is looked upon as in matter properly considered in relation to species, as man is in the seed. For, it is never true, according to Aristotle, to say that God existed, unless potential man existed or had existed, as in the seed. But in a third manner from what has been said, act simply precedes potentiality in time because in any being in potentiality, as given in proper matter, the act of that potentiality having to educe the potency to act, precedes in time. It is not thus with any given being in act that the potentiality to that act precedes it in time, as is evident in prime movers educing to actuality all beings in potentiality. In the aforementioned we utilize, as also does Aristotle, prime movers as species of things which are educed from potentiality to actuality, the act would not simply precede the potentiality in time, as Aristotle has said in IX *Metaphysicae*, saying that act precedes potentiality in time, adding the reason, because one act is always taken as before another up to the one which is always the prime mover.

From this the solution of the reasoning of those opposed is clear.

To the first problem, therefore, it must be said that being in potentiality is not eternal unless when it is regarded as in prime matter. For, when taken as its proper matter, according to which anything is said to exist properly in potentiality, as is said in IX *Metaphysicae*, it is new, unless it were taken according to species. For, just as nothing generated is corruptible in infinite time, so also nothing generable is not generated in infinite time since the generable has been taken as in proper matter and in a position near to generation, as the Commentator says in *super Ium Caeli et Mundi*.

To the second problem it must be said, as has been mentioned, that in the order of things generating existing in act which also proceed from potentiality to act, there is no being in act before the being in potentiality, but one there is always before the other to infinity. Because every being in potentiality is the essential order of moving and acting beings at length comes to some being existing in act which does not go from potentiality to act; hence it is that on account of that order the act is said simply to precede that potency.

To the third problem it must be said that it is

well established that in a being which is the same in number proceeding from potency to act, potency precedes act; but that, nevertheless, before the being in potency there is another of the same species in act, educing it from potency to act.

To the last problem we must say that it is truly spoken that act precedes potentiality, because all being in potentiality goes into actuality through something existing in act. Nor do those two things which are contradictory hinder one another. In the first place, this is not so because the being in act educing that which is in potentiality into act precedes in time not only the act in the being generated, but also the potentiality proper to the actuality of the being generated because of the fact that not only is the act of the generated being from the one generating, but also the being in potentiality to the act of the generated being is also from the one generating, as the seed from the man. And universally, proper matters are from the prime mover educing each thing from potentiality to act. In the second place, what is opposed does not hinder, as is evident from what has been said above. Although in the order of moving beings, on the basis of which the argument is made, it is necessary to admit that before being in act, there is a being in potency from which it proceeds into act, so also before being in potency there is a being in act which educes itself from potentiality to act; nevertheless, in another order of moving things it is necessary to hold that there is a being in act which educes into act what is in potency, since the being in potency from which it is made does not precede it, as is evident.

St. Thomas Aquinas

On the Eternity of the World

1. If we suppose, in accord with Catholic faith, that the world has not existed from eternity but had a beginning of its duration, the question arises whether it could have existed forever. In seeking the true solution of this problem, we should start by distinguishing points of agreement with our opponents from points of disagreement.

If the question is phrased in such a way as to

inquire whether something besides God could have existed forever, that is, whether a thing could exist even though it was not made by God, we are confronted with an abominable error against faith. More than that, the error is repudiated by philosophers, who avow and demonstrate that nothing at all can exist unless it was caused by Him who supremely and in a uniquely true sense has existence.

However, if we inquire whether something has always existed, understanding that it was caused by God with regard to all the reality found in it, we have to examine whether such a position can be maintained. If we should decide that this is impossible, the reason will be either that God could not make a thing that has always existed, or that the thing could not thus be made, even though God were able to make it. As to the first alternative, all parties are agreed that God could make something that has always existed, because of the fact that His power is infinite.

2. Accordingly our task is to examine whether something that is made could have existed forever. If we reply that this is impossible, our answer is unintelligible except in two senses or because there are two reasons for its truth: either because of the absence of passive potentiality, or because of incompatibility in the concepts involved.

The first sense may be explained as follows. Before an angel has been made, an angel cannot be made, because no passive potentiality is at hand prior to the angel's existence, since the angel is not made out of pre-existing matter. Yet God could have made the angel, and could also have caused the angel to be made, because in fact He has made angels and they have been made. Understanding the question in this way, we must simply concede, in accordance with faith, that a thing caused by God cannot have existed forever, because such a position would imply that a passive potentiality has always existed, which is heretical. However, this does not require the conclusion that God cannot bring it about that some being should exist forever.

Taken in the second sense, the argument runs that a thing cannot be so made because the concepts are incompatible, in the same way as affirmation and denial cannot be simultaneously true;

yet certain people assert that even this is within God's power. Others contend that not even God could make such a thing, because it is nothing. However, it is clear that He cannot bring this about, because the power by which it is supposed to be effected would be self-destructive. Nevertheless, if it is alleged that God is able to do such things, the position is not heretical, although I think it is false, just as the proposition that a past event did take place involves a contradiction. Hence Augustine, in his book against Faustus, writes as follows: "Whoever says, 'If God is omnipotent, let Him bring it about that what has been made was not made,' does not perceive that what he really says is this: 'If God is omnipotent, let Him bring it about that what is true is false for the very reason that it is true.'" Still, some great masters have piously asserted that God can cause a past event not to have taken place in the past; and this was not esteemed heretical.

3. We must investigate, therefore, whether these two concepts are logically incompatible, namely, that a thing has been created by God and yet has existed forever. Whatever may be the truth of the matter, no heresy is involved in the contention that God is able to bring it about that something created by Him should always have existed. Nevertheless I believe that, if the concepts were to be found incompatible, this position would be false. However, if there is no contradiction in the concepts, not only is it not false, but it is even possible; to maintain anything else would be erroneous. Since God's omnipotence surpasses all understanding and power, anyone who asserts that something which is intelligible among creatures cannot be made by God, openly disparages God's omnipotence. Nor can anyone appeal to the case of sin; sins, as such, are nothing.

The whole question comes to this, whether the ideas, to be created by God according to a thing's entire substance, and yet to lack a beginning of duration, are mutually repugnant or not. That no contradiction is involved, is shown as follows: A contradiction could arise only because of one of the two ideas or because of both of them together; and in the latter alternative, either because an efficient cause must precede its effect in duration, or because non-existence must precede existence in duration; in fact, this is the reason for saying that what is created by God is made from nothing.

4. Consequently, we must first show that the efficient cause, namely God, need not precede His effect in duration, if that is what He Himself should wish.

In the first place, no cause producing its effect simultaneously need precede its effect in duration. Now God is a cause producing His effect, not by way of motion, but instantaneously. Therefore He need not precede His effect in duration. The major premise is clear from induction, based on all instantaneous changes, such as illumination, and the like. It can also be demonstrated by reasoning. In any instant in which a thing is asserted to exist, the beginning of its action can likewise be asserted, as is evident in all things capable of generation; the very instant in which fire begins to exist, it emits heat. But in instantaneous action, the beginning and the end of the action are simultaneous, or rather are identical, as in all indivisible things. Therefore, at any moment in which there is an agent producing its effect instantaneously, the terminus of its action can be realized. But the terminus of the action is simultaneous with the effect produced. Consequently no intellectual absurdity is implied if we suppose that a cause which produces its effect instantaneously does not precede its effect in duration. There would be such an absurdity in the case of causes that produce their effects by way of motion, because the beginning of motion must precede its end. Since people are accustomed to think of productions that are brought about by way of motion, they do not readily understand that an efficient cause does not have to precede its effect in duration. And that is why many, with their limited experience, attend to only a few aspects, and so are overhasty in airing their views.

This reasoning is not set aside by the observation that God is a cause acting through His will, because the will, too, does not have to precede its effect in duration. The same is true of the person who acts through his will, unless he acts after deliberation. Heaven forbid that we should attribute such a procedure to God!

5. Moreover, the cause which produces the entire substance of a thing is no less able to produce that entire substance than a cause producing a form is in the production of a form; in fact, it is much more powerful, because it does not produce its effect by educing it from the potentiality of matter, as is the case with the agent that produces a form. But some agent that produces only a form can bring it about that the form produced by it exists at the moment the agent itself exists, as is exemplified by the shining sun. With far greater reason, God, who produces the entire substance of a thing, can cause His own effect to exist whenever He Himself exists.

Besides, if at any instant there is a cause with which the effect proceeding from it cannot co-exist at that same instant, the only reason is that some element required for complete causality is missing; for a complete cause and the effect caused exist together. But nothing complete has ever been wanting in God. Therefore an effect caused by Him can exist always, as long as He exists, and so He need not precede it in duration.

Furthermore, the will of a person who exercises his will suffers no loss in power. But all those who undertake to answer the arguments by which Aristotle proves that things have always had existence from God for the reason that the same cause always produces the same effect, say that this consequence would follow if He were not an agent acting by His will. Therefore, although God is acknowledged to be an agent acting by His will, it nevertheless follows that He can bring it about that what is caused by Him should never have been without existence.

And so it is clear that no logical contradiction is involved in the assertion that an agent does not precede its effect in duration. As regards anything that does not imply logical contradiction, however, God cannot bring it into being.

6. We now proceed to inquire whether logical contradiction is latent in the position that a created thing was never without existence. The reason for doubting is that, since such a thing is said to have been made from nothing, non-existence must seemingly precede its existence in the order of duration. The absence of any contradiction is shown by Anselm in the eighth chapter of his

Monologium, where he explains how a creature may be said to have been made from nothing. "The third interpretation," he states, "according to which something is said to have been made from nothing, is reasonable if we understand that the thing was, indeed, made, but that there is nothing from which it was made. In a like sense we may say that, when a man is saddened without cause, his sadness arises from nothing. In this sense, therefore, no absurdity will follow if the conclusion drawn above is kept in mind, namely, that with the exception of the supreme essence all things that exist were made by it out of nothing, that is, not out of something." According to this explanation, then, it is clear that no order is established between what was made and nothing, as though what is made would first have to be nothing, and would afterward be something.

7.   To proceed further, let us suppose that the order alluded to above, namely, relationship to nothingness, remains asserted, so that the sense is this: the creature is made from nothing [*ex nihilo*] that is, it is made after nothing. The term "after" unquestionably connotes order. But order is of various kinds; there is an order of duration and an order of nature. If, therefore, the proper and the particular do not follow from the common and the universal, it will not be necessary, just because the creature is said to exist subsequent to nothingness, that it should first have been nothing, in the order of duration, and should later be something. It is enough that in the order of nature it is nothing before it is a being; for that which befits a thing in itself is naturally found in it before that which it merely has from another. But a creature does not have existence except from another; regarded as left simply to itself, it is nothing; prior to its existence, therefore, nothingness is its natural lot. Nor, just because nothingness does not precede being in duration, does a thing have to be nothing and being at the same time. For our position is not that, if the creature has always existed, it was nothing at some time. We maintain that its nature is such that it would be nothing if it were left to itself; just as, if we say that the air was always illuminated by the sun, we must hold that the air

has been made luminous by the sun. And because everything that comes from what is not contingent, that is, from that which does not happen to exist along with that which is said to become, we must assert that the air was made luminous from being not luminous or from being dark; not in the sense that it was ever non-luminous or dark, but in the sense that it would be such if it were left to itself alone. And this is brought out more clearly in the case of stars and planets that are always being illuminated by the sun.

8.   Thus it is evident that the statement that something was made by God and nevertheless was never without existence, does not involve any logical contradiction. If there were some contradiction, it is surprising that Augustine did not perceive it, as this would have been a most effective way of disproving the eternity of the world; and indeed he brings forward many arguments against the eternity of the world in the eleventh and twelfth books of *De civitate Dei*; yet he completely ignores this line of argumentation. In fact, he seems to suggest that no logical contradiction is discernible here. Thus in Book X, chap. 31 of *De civitate Dei*, he says of the Platonists: "They found a way of accounting for this by explaining that it was not a beginning of time but a principle of subordination. They point out that if a foot had always, from eternity, been planted in the dust, there would always be a footprint underneath, and no one would doubt that the footprint had been made by someone stepping there; and yet the foot would not be prior to the print, although the print was made by the foot. In the same way, they continue, the world and the gods created in it have always existed, since He who made them has always existed, and nevertheless they were made." Augustine never charges that this is unintelligible, but proceeds against his adversaries in another way. He also says in Book XI, chap. 4: "They who admit that the world was made by God, yet do not wish it to have a beginning in time but only a beginning of its creation, so that it was always made in some sense that is scarcely intelligible, do indeed say something." How and why this is scarcely intelligible, was touched on in the first argument.

9. Another surprising thing is that the best philosophers of nature failed to discern this contradiction. In the fifth chapter of the same book, Augustine, writing against those who were mentioned in the preceding reference, remarks: "Our present discussion is with those who agree with us that God is incorporeal and is the Creator of all natures, with the exception of His own." And, regarding the latter, he adds, further on: "They surpassed all other philosophers in prestige and authority." The same situation emerges if we carefully consider the position of those who held that the world has always existed; for in spite of this they teach that it was made by God, and perceived no logical inconsistency in this doctrine. Therefore they who do descry such inconsistency with their hawk-like vision are the only rational beings, and wisdom was born with them!

10. Yet, since certain authorities seem to be on their side, we have to show that the foundation furnished by these authorities is fragile. Damascene, for instance, in the eighth chapter of the first book, observes: "What is brought to existence from non-existence is not of such a nature as to be co-eternal with Him who is without beginning and exists forever." Similarly Hugh of St. Victor says, in the beginning of his book, *De Sacramentis*: "The ineffable power of omnipotence could not have anything co-eternal with it, so as to have aid in creating."

The minds of these authorities and of others like them is clarified by what Boethius says in the last book of the *Consolation*: "Certain people, when they learn about Plato's view that this world did not have a beginning in time and is to have no end, wrongly conclude that the created world is thus made co-eternal with its Creator. But it is one thing to be carried through an endless life, which is what Plato attributed to the world, and quite another to embrace the whole presence of endless life all at once, which is manifestly proper to the divine mind."

11. Hence it is clear that the difficulty feared by some does not follow, that is, that the creature would be on a par with God in duration. Rather we must say that nothing can be co-eternal with God, because nothing can be immutable save God alone. The statement of Augustine in *De civitate Dei*, XII, chap. 15, is to the point: "Since the flight of time involves change, it cannot be co-eternal with changeless eternity. Accordingly, even though the immortality of the angels does not run on in time, and is not past as though it were no longer present, or future as though it had not yet arrived, yet their movements, by which successive times are traversed, do change over from the future into the past. And therefore they cannot be co-eternal with the Creator, in whom we cannot say that any movement has occurred that no longer endures, or that any will occur that has not yet taken place." He speaks in like vein in the eighth book of his commentary on Genesis: "Because the nature of the Trinity is absolutely changeless, it is eternal in such a way that nothing can be co-eternal with it." And he utters similar words in the eleventh book of the *Confessions*.

12. They also bring in arguments which philosophers have touched on, and then undertake to solve them. One among them is fairly difficult; it concerns the infinite number of souls: if the world has existed forever, the number of souls must now be infinite. But this argument is not to the purpose, because God could have made the world without men and souls; or He could have made men at the time He did make them, even though He had made the rest of the world from eternity. Thus the souls surviving their bodies would not be infinite. Besides, no demonstration has as yet been forthcoming that God cannot produce a multitude that is actually infinite.

There are other arguments which I forbear to answer at the present time. A reply has been made to them in other works. Besides, some of them are so feeble that their very frailty seems to lend probability to the opposite side.

Summa Contra Gentiles

Chapter 31
That Creatures Need Not Have Existed Always

We have still to show that created things need not have existed from eternity.

If the entire created universe or any single creature necessarily exists, this necessity must arise either from the creature itself or from some other being. The necessity cannot be derived from the creature itself. For we showed above that every being must proceed from the first Being. But anything that does not enjoy self-existence cannot possibly derive necessary existence from itself, because what exists necessarily cannot lack existence; and thus that which of itself has necessary existence, also has of itself the impossibility of not being. Consequently, it cannot be a non-being; hence it is a being.

If, however, the necessity in question is derived from some other being, it must come from a cause that is extrinsic, because everything that is received within a creature owes its existence to another. Now an extrinsic cause is either efficient or final. The effect of an efficient cause exists necessarily when the agent acts necessarily, for the effect depends on the efficient cause in consequence of the agent's action. Hence, if the agent is not constrained by any necessity to the action of producing the effect, the effect does not have to follow with absolute necessity. But God is not compelled by any necessity to the action of producing creatures, as was shown above. Therefore, as far as the necessity that depends on an efficient cause is concerned, no creature has to exist with absolute necessity.

The same is true of the necessity that depends on a final cause. For things that are means to an end do not acquire necessity from the end unless the end cannot be attained without them, as life cannot be preserved without food, or cannot be so well attained, as in the case of a journey without a horse. But the end of the divine will, by which things were brought into existence, cannot be anything else than God's goodness, as was shown in Book I, and the divine goodness does not depend on creatures either for its existence, since it necessarily exists itself, or for its well-being, since it is absolutely perfect in itself. All this has been proved above. Therefore no creature's existence is absolutely necessary; consequently we do not have to hold that some creature has always existed.

Again, nothing that proceeds from the will is absolutely necessary, unless the will happens to be impelled by necessity to will something. But God brings creatures into existence, not by any necessity of His nature, but by His will, as we have proved; nor does He necessarily will creatures to be, as was shown in Book I. Hence it is not absolutely necessary for any creature to be, and therefore it is not necessary that creatures should always have existed.

Furthermore, we showed above that God does not act with an action that is outside Himself; that is, no action of His issues forth from Him to terminate in a creature, in the way that heat issues from fire and terminates in wood. God's willing is His acting, and things are as God wishes them to be. But God is under no necessity to will that a creature should have existed always, since He does not have to will that a creature should exist at all, as was shown in Book I. Therefore it is not necessary for any creature to have existed always.

Besides, a thing does not proceed necessarily from a voluntary agent except by reason of some obligation. But, as was shown above, God is under no obligation to produce creatures, if the universal production of creatures is considered absolutely. Therefore God does not produce a creature out of necessity. Consequently, although God is eternal, it is not necessary for Him to have produced any creature from eternity.

Moreover, as we proved above that absolute necessity in created things results, not from a relationship to the first principle that is necessarily self-existent, but from a relationship to other causes that are not necessarily self-existent. But the necessity that stems from a relationship to something that is not necessarily self-existent, does not require a thing to have existed always. Thus, if something runs, it must be in motion; but it need not have been always in motion, because the act of running itself is not absolutely necessary. Consequently, there is no cogent reason why creatures should have existed always.

Chapter 32
Arguments of Those Who Seek to Prove the Eternity of the World from God's Standpoint

However, since many have held that the world has existed always and of necessity, and have endeavored to demonstrate their position, we must present their arguments, with a view to showing that they do not necessarily lead to the conclusion that the world is eternal. We shall set forth, first, arguments derived from God's standpoint; secondly, those that are derived from the point of view of creatures; thirdly, those that are derived from the manner in which things were made, according to the contention that they began to exist anew.

To prove the eternity of the world from God's standpoint, the following arguments are alleged.

1. Every agent that is not always in action, is moved either directly or indirectly; directly, as when a fire, which was not always burning, begins to burn, either because it is freshly kindled or is just now being carried over and placed next to some fuel; indirectly, in the way that an agent begins to move an animal by some new motion that affects it, either from within, as when an animal, awaking after the digestive process is finished, begins to roam around, or from without, as when some fresh incentives entice the animal to undertake some new action. But God is not moved either directly or indirectly, as was proved in Book I. Therefore God always acts in the same way, and it is by His action that created things are brought into being. Accordingly, creatures have always existed.

2. Again, an effect proceeds from its efficient cause by the action of that cause. But God's action is eternal; otherwise He would become an actual agent after being a potential agent, and He would have to be actualized by some prior agent; which is impossible. Therefore the things created by God have existed from eternity.

3. Furthermore, given a sufficient cause, its effect must necessarily follow. For if, given the cause, the effect does not follow with necessity, it would be possible, given the cause, that the effect could exist and yet not exist; but what is possible needs something to reduce it to act. Hence some cause will have to be found to make the effect actual; and so the first cause was not sufficient. God, however, is the sufficient cause of the production of creatures; otherwise, He would not be

a cause in reality, but would rather be a cause in potentiality, since He would become a cause by the addition of something; and that is clearly impossible. Accordingly, since God has existed from eternity, it seems that the creature, too, must have existed from eternity.

4. Likewise, a voluntary agent does not delay in carrying out his purpose of making something unless he is awaiting some future event that has not yet taken place. And this sort of thing sometimes occurs within the agent himself, as when full power for acting or the removal of some obstacle impeding such power is awaited. Sometimes, too, it is outside the agent, as when someone in whose presence the action is to be performed is expected, or at least when a suitable time that has not yet arrived is awaited. For if the will is fully equipped, its power is straightway carried into execution, unless it labors under some defect; thus the movement of a limb immediately follows the will's command, if no defect is found in the motive power that is to carry out the movement. Hence it is clear that, when one wishes to do something and it is not done at once, the failure must be ascribed either to a defect in power, the removal of which is looked for, or to the fact that the will is not fully equipped to perform the action. And I assert that the will is fully equipped when one wills absolutely to do something, not absolutely, but on some condition that is not yet verified, or unless a present obstacle is removed. Evidently, however, that which God now wills to exist, He has eternally willed to exist, for no new movement of the will can occur in Him. Nor could any defect or impediment obstruct His power; and nothing else could be awaited as an incentive for the universal production of creatures, since apart from God nothing is uncreated, as was proved above. Therefore the conclusion that God has brought creatures into existence from eternity seems imperative.

5. Besides, an intellectual agent does not choose one thing in preference to another unless the one is more excellent than the other. But where there is no difference, there cannot be any superiority in excellence. Hence, where no difference is discernible, no choice will be made of one thing

rather than of another. This is the reason why no action will proceed from an agent equally indifferent to either of two alternatives, just as no action proceeds from matter; for potentiality of this sort is like the potentiality of matter. But there can be no difference between non-being and non-being. Hence one non-being is not preferable to another.

Now beyond the entire universe of creatures there is nothing except the eternity of God. But no difference in periods of time can be designated in nothingness; hence we cannot say that a thing ought to be made at one moment rather than at another. Likewise, such a difference in moments cannot be designated in eternity, the whole of which is uniform and simple, as was shown in Book I. The consequence is, therefore, that God's will is equally disposed to the production of creatures throughout all eternity. Accordingly, it is His will either that creatures should never be produced within His eternity, or that they should always have been produced. Obviously, however, it is not His will that creatures should never have been produced throughout His eternity, since creatures evidently came into being at the behest of His will. The conclusion, therefore, that the created world has always existed, is apparently necessary.

6. Again, things that are directed to an end derive their necessity from that end; this is especially true of things that are done voluntarily. Hence, as long as the end remains the same, things directed to the end preserve the same dispositions or are produced in the same way, unless a new relation arises between them and the end. But the end of creatures issuing forth from the divine will is the divine goodness, which alone can be the end of the divine will. Since, therefore, the divine goodness remains the same throughout all eternity, both in itself and in reference to the divine will, creatures are apparently brought into being by the divine will in the same manner throughout all eternity. For if they are assumed to be quite without existence prior to some definite time at which they are supposed to have begun their existence, they cannot be said to have acquired any new relation to their end.

7. Moreover, since the divine goodness is supremely perfect, all things are said to have come forth from God by reason of His goodness, not in the sense that any advantage might accrue to Him from creatures, but in the sense that goodness has the tendency to communicate itself so far as possible; goodness is manifested by such self-communication. Since all things share in the goodness of God so far as they have being, the more permanent they are, the more they share in God's goodness; that is why the perpetual existence of a species is said to be divine. But the divine goodness is infinite. Accordingly it has the tendency to communicate itself in an infinite way, and not merely at a particular time. Therefore the divine goodness seems to be a reason requiring the eternal existence of some creatures.

Such, then, are the arguments drawn from the side of God; they seemingly lead to the conclusion that creatures have existed forever.

Chapter 33
Arguments of Those Who Seek to Prove the Eternity of the World from a Consideration of Creatures

There are also other arguments, derived from the viewpoint of creatures, that seem to indicate the same conclusion.[2]

1. Things that have no potentiality to non-existence cannot be without existence. But among creatures there are some that have no potentiality to non-existence. For only creatures that possess matter subject to contrariety can have potentiality to non-existence, since potentiality to existence and non-existence is potentiality to privation and form, whose subject is matter; and privation is always connected with the contrary form, since matter cannot exist without any form at all. But there are certain creatures that have no matter subject to contrariety, either because they are entirely devoid of matter, such as intellectual substances, as will be shown later on, or because they have no contrary, such as heavenly bodies, as is proved by their movement, which has no contrary. Hence it is impossible for certain creatures not to exist. Of necessity, therefore, they must exist always.

2. Likewise, every thing endures in being in proportion to its power of being, except by accident, as in those things that are destroyed by violence. But some creatures are endowed with power to exist, not for a limited time, but forever. Such are heavenly bodies and intellectual substances; they are incorruptible because they have no contrary. Consequently everlasting existence is their due; on the other hand, that which begins to exist, does not always exist. In the case of incorruptible things, therefore, a beginning of existence is out of the question.

3. Furthermore, whenever anything begins to be moved for the first time, either the mover or the thing moved or both must behave otherwise now, when there is movement, than previously, when there was no movement. For, according as a mover actually moves, it has a certain reference or relation to the thing that is moved. However, a new relation does not arise without some change in both or at least one of the extremes. But a thing that is in a different state now than formerly, is moved. Therefore, prior to newly initiated movement, another movement, either in the moveable thing or in the mover, has to precede. Accordingly, every movement must either be eternal or must have some other movement preceding it. Hence there was always movement, and consequently there were always moveable things. And so creatures have always existed, since God Himself is absolutely immovable, as was proved in Book I.

4. Besides, every agent that generates its like intends to preserve perpetual existence in the species, since existence cannot be perpetually preserved in the individual. But natural desire cannot be futile. Therefore the species of things capable of generation must be perpetual.

5. Further, if time is everlasting, motion, too, must be everlasting, since time is the measure of motion. Consequently movable things also must be everlasting, since movement is the act of the moveable. But time must be everlasting, for time is inconceivable without a *now*, just as a line is inconceivable without a point. But *now* is always the end of the past and the beginning of the future; this is the very definition of *now*. And so

any given *now* has time preceding and following it. And thus no *now* has time preceding and following it. And thus no *now* can be either first or last. Consequently moveable things, which are created substances, must exist from eternity.

6. Again, we must either affirm or deny. Therefore, if the affirmation of a thing is implied in its negation, that thing must always exist. Such a thing is time. For if we say that time did not always exist, we assert that it did not exist before it existed; similarly, if time is not to exist always in the future, its non-existence must come after its existence. But there can be no before or after in duration unless there is time, since time is the measure of before and after. And thus time would have to exist before it began, and continue into the future after it ceased. Accordingly time must be eternal. Now time is an accident, and an accident cannot exist without a subject. Its subject, however, is not God, who is above time; for He is absolutely immutable, as was proved in Book I. Consequently some created substance is eternal.

7. Moreover, many propositions are of such a kind that he who denies them must affirm them. For instance, whoever denies that there is truth, supposes that truth exists, for he supposes that the negative proposition he utters is true. The case is similar with him who denies the principle that contradictories are not simultaneous, for by denying this he asserts that the denial he voices is true and that the opposite affirmation is false, and thus that both are not verified about the same thing. Therefore, if a thing whose denial entails its affirmation must exist always, as we have just proved, the aforesaid propositions and all propositions derived from them are eternal. But these propositions are not God. Therefore something besides God must be eternal.

These arguments, then, and others like them can be adduced on the part of creatures to prove that creatures have always existed.

Chapter 34
Arguments to Prove the Eternity of the World from the Viewpoint of the Creative Action

Other reasons can be alleged on the part of the

creative action itself to prove the same conclusion.[3]

1.   What is commonly asserted by all, cannot be wholly false. For a false opinion betrays a certain weakness of intellect, just as a false judgment about a proper object of sense results from a weakness in the sense. But defects are accidental, because they are outside the intention of nature. What is accidental, however, cannot exist always and in all beings; thus the judgment which every taste registers about flavors cannot be false. Accordingly a judgment that is pronounced by all men about a truth cannot be erroneous. Now it is the common opinion of all philosophers that nothing is made from nothing. Consequently it must be true. Therefore, if anything is made, it must be made from something. And if the latter thing is also made, it, too, must be made from something else. But this process cannot go on indefinitely, for then no generation would ever be completed, since an infinite number of stages cannot be traversed. Hence we must come to some first thing that was not made. But every being that has not existed forever must have been made. Therefore that being from which all other things were originally made must be eternal. But this being is not God, because He cannot be the matter of anything, as was proved in Book I. Consequently something outside of God must be eternal, namely, prime matter.

2.   Moreover, if a thing is not in the same state now as before, it must have undergone some change, for this is precisely what we mean by mutation: that a thing is not in the same state now as before. But everything that begins to exist anew, is not in the same state now as before; and the reason is, that some motion or change has taken place. All motion or change occurs in some subject, for motion is the act of a moveable thing. Since motion precedes that which is brought about by it, seeing that motion terminates in such a thing, some moveable subject must exist prior to anything that is made. And as an infinite regression along this line is impossible, we must come to some first subject that never began but always existed.

3.   Besides, everything that begins to exist anew, had a possible existence before it actually existed; otherwise it was impossible for it to exist and necessary for it not to exist. Thus it would forever have been a non-being and would never have begun to be. But that which has the possibility of existing is a subject that is potentially a being. Therefore, before anything begins to exist anew, a subject that is potentially a being must pre-exist. And since we cannot go back in this way indefinitely, we must suppose some primary subject that did not begin to exist anew.

4.   Again, no permanent substance exists while it is being made. For it is made that it may exist; hence if it were already existing, it would not still have to be made. But while it is being made, there must be some subject that is worked upon; for, since the process of making is an accident, it requires a subject. Accordingly everything that is made has some pre-existing subject. And since this cannot go on indefinitely, the conclusion follows that the first subject was not made, but is eternal. From this the further conclusion follows that something besides God is eternal, for He Himself cannot be the subject of making or of movement.

These, then, are the arguments to which some thinkers give their adherence, as though they were demonstrations vindicating their contention that created things must have existed forever. In this they contradict the Catholic faith, which insists that nothing outside God has existed forever, and that all things, except the one eternal God, have had a beginning of their existence.

Chapter 35
Solution of the Arguments Alleged Above, and First of Those Derived from the Standpoint of God

We have now to show that the foregoing arguments do not necessarily conclude. We shall consider, first, those that are alleged on the part of the agent.

Even if the effects produced by God begin to exist anew, He Himself need not be moved either directly or indirectly, as the *first* objection argued.

Newness of effect can, indeed, indicate a change in the agent to the extent that it demonstrates newness of action; a new action cannot be performed by an agent unless the latter is moved in some way, at least from inactivity to action. Yet newness of a divine effect does not demonstrate newness of action in God, since His action is His essence, as was brought out above. And therefore newness of effect cannot demonstrate such change when God is the agent.

Nevertheless it does not follow that, if the action of the First Agent is eternal, His effect must be eternal, as the *second* argument inferred. We showed above that God acts voluntarily in producing things. However, He does not act in such a manner that some other, intermediate action is elicited by Him, in the way that in us the action of our motive power intervenes between the act of the will and the effect, as we have shown previously; God's act of understanding and willing is necessarily identical with His act of making. An effect issues from the intellect and the command of the will. Just as any other condition of the thing made is determined by the intellect, so a time is set for it; art not only determines that a thing should be of a definite quality, but assigns a time for it. For example, a physician prescribes that a medicine should be given at this or that time; if his act of will were in itself powerful enough to produce the effect, the effect would follow in due time from the previous decision, without any new action on his part. Hence there is nothing to prevent us from saying that God's action existed from eternity, although its effect was not produced from eternity but occurred at the time eternally appointed for it.

This consideration also makes it clear that, even though God is the sufficient cause producing the existence of things, we do not have to conclude that His effect is eternal just because He Himself exists eternally, as the *third* argument contended. Given a sufficient cause, its effect does, indeed, follow. This is not true, however, of an effect that is foreign to the cause, such as would result from an insufficiency in the cause, as if, for example, a hot body failed to emit heat. The proper effect of the will is the production of that which the will decides; if something else than what the will decrees were to result, the

effect would not be proper to the cause but would be alien to it. But, to repeat what we have said, just as the will determines that a thing should be of a definite nature, so it wills that the thing should exist at a particular time. In order that the will may be a sufficient cause, therefore, the effect need not exist when the will itself exists, but only at the time which the will appoints for it. The case is different with things proceeding from a cause that acts naturally, because the action of nature is determined by the nature itself; given the existence of the cause, the effect must follow. The will, however, acts in a way that is governed, not by its existence, but by its intention. And therefore, just as the effect of a natural agent is determined by the agent's existence, if the latter is a sufficient cause, so the effect of a voluntary agent is produced in accord with the agent's purpose.

All this makes it manifest that the effect of the divine will is not unduly retarded, as the *fourth* argument suggested, even though it did not always exist, notwithstanding the fact that it was willed. Not only the existence of the effect, but the time of its existence, is subject to the divine will. Therefore the thing willed, that is, the existence of a creature at a definite time, is not retarded, because the creature began to exist at the moment appointed by God from eternity.

We cannot admit any diversity of parts in some sort of duration prior to the beginning of all creation, as was supposed in the *fifth* argument. For nothingness has neither measure nor duration. And God's duration, which is eternity, has no parts, but is absolutely simple, without before and after, since God is immovable, as was explained in Book I. Hence there is no question of comparing the beginning of all creation with diverse parts designated in some pre-existing measure, with which the beginning of creatures might be in agreement or disagreement, so that an agent would have to have a reason for bringing creatures into existence at this particular instant of that duration rather than at some preceding or subsequent instant. Such a reason would indeed be required if some duration divisible into parts existed outside the universe of created beings, as is the case with particular agents that produce their effect in time, yet do not produce time itself. But God brought creatures and time into being together. Hence the question to consider is not, why He produced them now rather than earlier, but only why He did not endow them with eternal existence. Comparison with place will clarify this point. Particular bodies are produced in a definite place, as well as at a definite time. And because time and place, by which they are enveloped, are extrinsic to them, there must be a reason why they are produced in this place and at this time rather than another. But there is no reason for inquiring why the whole of heaven was located here and not there, for beyond it there is no place, and the entire place for all things was produced along with it. In their quest of such a reason, some fell into the error of attributing infinity to bodies. Similarly, outside the totality of creation there is no time, since time was produced simultaneously with the universe; hence we need not go into the reason why it exists now and not earlier, and so we will not be let to concede the infinity of time. We have only to ask why it did not exist always, or why it came into being after non-being, or why it had a beginning at all.

To pursue this inquiry the *sixth* argument was proposed; it is based on a consideration of the end, which alone can induce necessity in things that are done voluntarily. The end of the divine will cannot be anything else than God's goodness. However, God does not act in order to bring this end into being, in the way that a craftsman acts in constructing his handiwork; for God's goodness is eternal and unchangeable, so that nothing can be added to it. Nor can God be said to act for His own self-improvement. Again, He does not act to acquire this end for Himself, as a king engages in warfare to gain possession of a city, for God is His own goodness. It remains, consequently, that He acts for an end in the sense that He produces an effect which is to share in the end. In this production of things for the sake of an end, the uniform relation of an end to agent is not to be regarded as an argument in favor of the eternity of His work; we should rather focus our attention on the relation of the end to the effect that is produced for the end. Thus we perceive that the effect is produced in such a way as to be more fittingly directed to the end. Hence the fact

that the end is uniformly related to the agent does not justify us in concluding that the effect is eternal.

Lastly, it is not necessary that the divine effect should have existed always, for the reason that it would thus be more suitably directed to the end, as the *seventh* argument seemed to imply. Indeed, it is more suitably directed to the end for the very reason that it did not exist always. For every agent that produces an effect designed to participate in the agent's own form aims at reproducing its own likeness in the effect. Fittingly, therefore, God willed to produce creatures for participation in His goodness; by resembling the divine goodness they would represent it. Such a representation cannot reach the level of equality, in the way that a univocal effect represents its cause, so that effects produced by infinite goodness would have to be eternal; no, God is represented by creatures as the transcendent is represented by that which is surpassed. But the transcendence of the divine goodness over creation is best brought out by the fact that creatures have not always existed. This fact clearly shows that all things outside of God have Him as the author of their being, and that His power is under no necessity to produce such effects, as nature is with regard to natural effects; and consequently that He is a voluntary and intelligent agent. Some thinkers have entertained view opposed to these truths, because they assume the eternity of creatures.

Accordingly there is nothing on the part of the agent that compels us to hold the eternity of creation.

Chapter 36
Solution of the Arguments Alleged on the Part of the Things Produced

Likewise there is nothing on the part of creatures that necessarily induces us to assert their eternity.

The necessity of existing which is found in creatures and is the basis of the *first* argument for this position, is a necessity of order, as was shown previously. But the necessity of order does not force the thing that is subject to such necessity to have existed forever, as was pointed out above. Although the substance of heaven necessarily exists, since it lacks potentiality to non-existence, this necessity is consequent on its substance. Therefore, once heaven's substance has been brought into being, this necessity entails the impossibility of not existing; but if the production of its substance is taken into consideration, such necessity does not obviate heaven's non-existence.

Similarly, the power of existing always, from which the *second* argument was drawn, presupposes the production of the substance. Therefore, since the production of the substance is in question, such power cannot be a conclusive argument for the eternity of that substance.

The objection next adduced does not compel us to acknowledge the eternity of motion. It is plain from the preceding chapter that without any change in Himself, God the agent can accomplish something new, something that is not eternal. But if something can be done by Him anew, it is clear that something can also be put in motion by Him anew, for newness of motion follows on the decision of the eternal will that motion is not to be eternal.

Likewise, the tendency of natural agents to perpetuate their species, which was the source of the *fourth* argument, presupposes that natural agents have already been produced. Hence this argument is out of place except with regard to natural things that have already been brought into being; it is irrelevant when there is question of the production of these things. Whether a process of generation that will go on forever has to be admitted, will be examined later.

Also the *fifth* argument, based on time, presupposes rather than proves the eternity of motion. According to Aristotle's teaching, the *before* and *after* and continuity of time are dependent on the *before* and *after* and continuity of motion; hence the same instant is clearly the beginning of the future and the end of the past, because some assignable point in motion is the beginning and end of the various segments of motion. Not every instant, therefore, will have to be of this kind, unless every assignable point in time is taken to be midway between before and after in motion— which is to suppose that motion is eternal. But if we suppose that motion is not eternal, we can say that the first instant of time is the beginning of the future without being the end of any past. Nor

is the contention that some *now* is a beginning and not an end incompatible with the succession of time, on the ground that a line, in which a point is placed as a beginning and not an end, is stationary and not transitory; for even in a particular movement, which of course is not stationary but transitory, some point can be designated as only the beginning without being the end of movement. Otherwise all motion would be perpetual, which is impossible.

In the hypothesis that time began, the assertion that it did not exist before it existed does not compel us to admit that the very supposition of its non-existence implies its existence, as the *sixth* argument inferred. For the *before* we speak of as preceding time does not imply any flight of time in reality, but only in our imagination. When we say that time exists after not existing, we mean that no time was flowing prior to this designated *now*. In the same way, when we say that there is nothing above heaven, we do not mean that there is some place beyond heaven which may be said to be *above* in relation to it, but that there is no place higher than heaven. In both cases the imagination can add a certain dimension to the existing thing. However, just as such addition is no reason for attributing the infinite quantity to a body, as is indicated in Book III of the *Physics*, so neither is it a reason for admitting that time is eternal.

The truth of the propositions which even the one who denies the propositions must concede, as maintained in the seventh *argument*, involves the necessity of the order which exists between predicate and subject. Such necessity does not require a thing to exist forever, except, indeed, the divine intellect, in which all truth is rooted, as was shown in Book I.

Clearly, therefore, the arguments derived from creatures do not compel us to assert the eternity of the world.

Chapter 37
Solution of the Arguments Drawn from the Creative Action

Our remaining task is to show that none of the arguments derived from the viewpoint of the production of things imposes the same conclusion.

The position common to philosophers who contend that nothing is made from nothing, which is the starting point of the *first* argument, is true with regard to the kind of making they had in mind. Since all our knowledge begins with sense perception, which has to do with individual things, human speculation mounted from particular to universal considerations. Hence they who investigated the origin of things considered only particular instances of production, and inquired how this fire or this stone came into being. And so they who came first, limiting their consideration of the production of things to an excessively superficial examination, maintained that a thing is made merely according to certain accidental modifications, such as rarity, density, and the like, and asserted in consequence that "to be made" was nothing but "to be altered"; that is, they thought that everything was made from something actually existing. But their successors, who entered more deeply into the process by which things are made, advanced to a consideration of the production of things in terms of their substance; they taught that a thing need not be made from actually existing being, except in accidentals, and that in its essentials it is made from potential being. Yet this sort of production, which is that of a being made from some other being, is the making of a particular being, one that is made inasmuch as it is this being, such as a man or a fire, but not universally, inasmuch as it simply is; for there existed previously a being that was transformed into this being. Penetrating, then, still more deeply into the origin of things, they considered at last the procession of all created being from a single first cause, as is clear from the arguments listed above to prove this truth. In this procession of all being from God, it is impossible for anything to be made from something else previously existing; otherwise it would not be the making of created being in its entirety.

This kind of making eluded the early naturalists, who shared the common opinion that nothing is made from nothing. Or, if any of them did arrive at the notion, they did not think that the term "making" properly expressed it, since the word "making" implies motion or change, whereas in this origin of all being from one first

being, the transformation of one being into another is inconceivable, as we have shown. For this reason, the investigation of this kind of origin of things is the concern, not of the philosopher of nature, but of the metaphysician, who studies universal being, including such things as are dissociated from motion. By virtue of a certain similarity, however, we transfer the term "making" even to such origin, and so we say that those beings are made whose essence or nature takes its origin from other beings.

Consequently it is evident that the *second* argument, which is based on the nature of motion, does not lead to a necessary conclusion. Creation cannot be called change except metaphorically, so far as a created thing is regarded as having existence after non-existence. In this sense one thing is said to issue from another even when no change from one thing into another takes place, for the sole reason that one of them succeeds the other, as day comes forth from night. Nor can the nature of motion that is here alleged be of any avail, for what does not exist at all is not in any particular state; hence we cannot conclude that, once a thing begins to exist, it is in a different state now from what it was before.

Therefore it is also plain that no passive potentiality has to precede the existence of all created being, as the *third* argument attempted to prove. Such a necessity does, indeed, obtain in things that originally come into being by way of motion, seeing that motion is the act of a being existing in potentiality. Before a created thing existed, its existence was possible, because of the power of the agent that initially endowed it with existence, or by reason of the compatibility of the terms, in which no contradiction is found. Possibility in this latter sense involves no reference to potentiality, as the Philosopher asserts in Book V of his *Metaphysics*. For the predicate, "to be," is not incompatible with the subject, "world" or "man," as "commensurate" [predicated of the side of a square] is incompatible with "diagonal." And thus it follows that the existence of the world or of a man is not impossible, and consequently that before they existed their existence was possible, even in the absence of potentiality. But things that come into being by way of motion must previously be possible by reason of some passive potentiality; such are things the Philosopher has in mind when he employs this argument in Book VII of the *Metaphysics*.

This also explains why the *fourth* argument fails to prove its point. For in things that are made by way of motion, *to be made* and *to be* are not simultaneous, since their production involves succession. But in things that are not made by way of motion, their making does not precede their existence.

Therefore it is quite evident that nothing prevents us from maintaining that the world has not always existed. And this is what the Catholic faith teaches: "In the beginning God created heaven and earth" (Genesis 1:1); and in Proverbs 8:22 it is said of God: "Before He made anything from the beginning," etc.

Chapter 38
Arguments by Which Some Endeavor to Prove that the World is not Eternal

We come now to a group of arguments brought forward by certain thinkers to prove that the world has not always existed; they are drawn from the following considerations.

1.   That God is the cause of all things, has been demonstrated. But a cause must precede in duration the things that are produced by its action.

2.   Again, since all being has been created by God, it cannot be said to have been made from some being, and so we conclude that it was made from nothing. Consequently its existence must be subsequent to non-existence.

3.   Another reason is that an infinite series would by now have been crossed. For the past has been traversed, and if the world has always existed, an infinite number of days or of solar revolutions have gone by.

4.   A further consequence is that an addition is made to the infinite, for new additions are daily being made to the days or solar revolutions which have passed.

5.   Still another consequence is that we are pro-ceeding to infinity in efficient causes, in the hypothesis that generation has always taken place. This has to be admitted if the world has existed forever, for the father is the cause to his son, and another man is the cause of the father, and so on, back into the endless past.

6.   Furthermore, it will follow that an infinite multitude exists, namely, the immortal souls of an infinite number of men dead and gone.

Since these arguments do not conclude with strict necessity, although they are not entirely devoid of probability, it is enough to touch on them briefly, so that the Catholic faith may not seem to rest on inept reasonings rather than on the unshakable basis of God's teaching. And so we deem it suitable to show how such arguments are met by those who have maintained the eternity of the world.

The *first* contention, that an agent necessarily precedes the effect wrought by its action, is true of causes which produce something by way of motion, because the effect is not achieved until the motion has come to a stop, whereas the agent must exist even when the motion begins. But in causes that act instantaneously the same conclusion need not follow. Thus, as soon as the sun reaches the point of the east, it at once lights up our hemisphere.

Also the *second* argument is invalid. For if the proposition, "Something is made from something," is not granted, the contradictory to be asserted is, "Something is not made from something," and not, "Something is made from nothing," except in the latter sense. We cannot conclude from this that a thing comes into existence subsequent to non-existence.

Again, the *third* argument lacks cogency. For, even though the infinite does not exist all at once if it is actual, it can exist successively; understood in this sense, any infinite is finite. Therefore, since each of the preceding revolutions was finite, it could make a full turn. But if they are all viewed as existing simultaneously, on the supposition that the world had always existed, a first revolution cannot be assigned. And so there could be no transition to the present, for transition always requires two extremes.

The *fourth* argument, too, is weak. There is

nothing to prevent an addition to the infinite on the side on which it is finite. On the supposition that time is eternal, it must be infinite on the part of what went before, but finite on the part of what came after, for the present marks the end of the past.

The *fifth* objection is likewise devoid of cogency. According to philosophers, infinite procession is impossible when there is a question of efficient causes that act together at the same time, because the effect would have to depend on an infinite number of co-existing actions. But, according to those who propose the theory of an endless series of generations, infinite procession is not impossible in the case of causes that do not act simultaneously. Here the infinity is accidental to the causes; whether the father of Socrates is another man's son or not, affects him only accidentally. But when a stick moves a stone, its movement by the hand that holds it is not accidental; the stick moves only to the extent that it is moved.

Notes

1 St. Bonaventure, *In II Sent.* d.1, p. 1, a. 3, q. 2, ad 5m. St. Bonaventure's point seems to be that to ask whether there is a creating of creating is to ask a meaningless question.
2 These arguments are answered in chap. 36.
3 These arguments are refuted in chap. 37.

JACQUES FOURNIER

Inquisition Records

IN 1320 THE BISHOP OF PAMIERS, JACQUES FOURNIER (CA. 1280-1342), later Pope Benedict XII, interrogated the inhabitants of the village of Montaillou on the supposition of Cathar heresy in the village. This extraordinarily detailed record allows one to see not only the procedures of the Inquisition and the nature of fourteenth century heterodox belief, but the private lives of ordinary villagers.

The following testimony is that of a member of the minor nobility, Béatrice de Planissoles.

Source: Jean Duvernoy, *Le registre d'inquisition de Jacques Fournier* (Paris: Mouton, 1978).

Witnesses against Béatrice, widow of Othon of Lagleize of Dalou

In the year of our lord 1320, the 19th of June. It came to the knowledge of the reverend father in Christ our lord Jacques, by the grace of God bishop of Pamiers, that Béatrice, widow of Othon, of Lagleize, of Dalou, who lives at Varilhes, had made comments that smelled of Manichean heresy or touched it, and especially against the sacrament of the altar, he wished, with the assistance of Gaillard of Pomiès, substitute for my lord the inquisitor of Carcassonne, to inform himself on the events which preceded, and he received the following witnesses:

Guillaume Roussel of Dalou, sworn witness and ordered to say the truth said:

Ten years ago, it seems to me, but I do not remember exactly the period or the day, I was at the home of Béatrice, in her house near the church of Dalou, and two of her daughters were near Béatrice, one of whom had about six or seven years and the other four or five and some other people. I do not recall the names of these latter.

They started to talk about priests and the sacrament of the altar which is the business of priests. Béatrice said, I think, that she was astounded:"If God was in the sacrament of the altar how did he allow himself to be eaten by the priests (or by a priest)?" Hearing that, I left the house in confusion.

—Why did you hide this for so long?—Because I was not interrogated before and also because I did not think that I was doing wrong in not denouncing it myself.

—Did Béatrice say this as a joke?—It did not seem to me that she was joking, the more I paid attention to what came from her facial expression and her words.

—Did Béatrice go to church willingly?—No, not until she was reprimanded by Barthélemy, a priest vicar of this church. Afterwards, she went to church.

—Who were the people who were very intimate with this Béatrice, who might have known her secrets?—Grazide, widow of Bernard Pujol, of Dalou, Bernarde, wife of Garisot, who lives at Varilhes, Mabille, wife of Raimond Gouzey of Herm, Sibille, maid servant of Michel Dupont of Foix, Esperte, wife of Arnaud of Varilhes.

The same day and year as above, Guillaume of Montaut, rector of the church of Dalou, sworn witness and interrogated on what had preceded said:

Twelve years ago, it seems to me, although I do not exactly recall the period or the day, I was at the church of Dalou, and there I found Mabille Vaquier, of Dalou, now deceased. She told me that she had reprimanded this Béatrice who was the wife of her uncle because she did not go to church and also because she had heard her say evil things which had upset her. What she had said was, "You believe that what the priests hold at the altar is the body of Christ? Surely, if it was the body of Christ, even if it was as large as this mountain, the priests would already have eaten it all themselves!" And for this reason, Jean had himself had insulting words with Béatrice.

And he said nothing else although he was diligently interrogated.

Confession of Béatrice, widow of Othon de Lagleize of Dalou

In the year of the Lord 1320, the Wednesday after the feast of Saint James the Apostle (23 July 1320), the reverend father in Christ my lord Jacques, by the grace of God bishop of Pamiers, addressed a letter of citation against Béatrice, widow of Othon de Lagleize, living in Varilhes, the contents of which follows:

Brother Jacques, by the divine commiseration bishop of Pamiers, to his well-loved in Christ curate of Varilhes or his vicar, greetings in the Lord.

We order you to require immediately Béatrice, widow of Othon de Lagleize and Jeanne, wife of Guillaume de Reumaze the younger, to appear next Saturday before us in our seat of Pamiers in person, to answer certain facts touching the Catholic faith, about which we desire to know the truth and the reasons for it.

Given in the above mentioned seat, the Wednesday before the feast of Saint James the Apostle, the year of the Lord 1320. Return the letter sealed with your seal in evidence of having accomplished this order.

The designated Saturday the above mentioned Béatrice cited by the curate of Varilhes, as is evident from the seal of the above mentioned priest on the back of the above mentioned letter of summons, appeared before my lord the bishop of the above mentioned see, and my lord the bishop informed her that she was strongly suspected of heresy according to his sources, and that she had to speak the pure and simple truth on all of the points about herself as well as about others living and dead.

The above-mentioned Béatrice said nothing to the above order, neither about herself nor about others, and she did not wish to do so. My lord bishop, wishing to direct her to say the truth and not to hide it and not wishing to see her fall into perjury, asked her without demanding an oath, if she had ever affirmed that if the sacrament of the altar was the true body of Christ, he would not allow himself to be eaten by priests, and that if it was as large as Mount Margail, which is near Dalou, it would long ago have been eaten by the priests alone. She answered no.

He asked her if she had seen, received in her home, or had gone to see Pierre, Jacques, and Guillaume Authié or other heretics. She answered no, except that she had once seen Pierre Authié exercising his profession of notary and in this capacity he had prepared the act of sale of a property belonging to her husband. She had approved this sale by oath, and Pierre Authié had prepared the instrument of sale and of its ratification. He was not yet considered a heretic at this time, and she had not seen him since.

On the question of my lord bishop, she said that she had once received the late Gaillarde Cuq in her home for a night, but she did not hear from her spells, or see magic, or receive evil teachings from her.

My lord bishop, hearing that Béatrice did not wish to say or avow these things and without oath wishing to act with benevolence toward her and to listen more, assigned the following Tuesday for her to appear before the above mentioned see, ordering her to be present that day in person and to be ready to answer these facts and all others concerning the faith under oath. Béatrice accepted this day willingly, promising by her own oath to appear before my lord the bishop as ordered and to answer these facts under oath and to do and accomplish all that would be necessary in this matter. She was thus graciously postponed until the Tuesday by my lord bishop.

On that Tuesday the above mentioned Béatrice did not appear, although she was waited for all the day, and for this reason the lord bishop formally noted her absence and declared her defiant.

After this the above mentioned Béatrice, fleeing, was sought by the men of my lord bishop carrying his letters to all bailiffs, officers and judges and was found by them while she was hiding in Mas-Saintes-Puelles, in the diocese of Saint Papoul. She was taken prisoner by the men of my lord bishop and the sergeants of the court of Mas-Saintes-Puelles, to my lord bishop and presented to him the 1st of August of the above year. The below listed objects were found on her person. These were all shown in the presence of my lord bishop and she recognized that they were all hers and that she had fled with them.

My lord bishop ordered that she be held strongly suspect concerning the Catholic faith, both because of the preceding information and by her flight and the objects found on her. Wishing to hear about her, he received from her an oath to say the pure, simple and entire truth both about herself and about others living and dead as witness, in matters concerning the Catholic faith. When she had sworn this oath, he asked her:

—Are you guilty of heresy? Have you had relations and intimacy with Pierre, Guillaume, Jacques Authié, the heretics, and with other heretics, by adoring them, seeing them, giving or sending them anything, or favoring them in any other manner?—No, on my oath, except that which I said about Pierre Authié, when I ratified the act of sale which my dead husband the knight Béof de Roquefort made.

When I contracted marriage with this Bérenger, at the wedding ceremony, I saw Guillaume Authié dancing. This was about twenty-four years ago.

—Do you know of other persons living or dead who had this sort of relations or intimacy or who committed anything of this sort?—No. But, when I was a little girl and I was at Celles, about six years before marrying my first husband, the people were hurrying one day to see the body of Christ at the church of this place. I heard a mason (I don't know his name but I think he was Oudin) ask where these people were going. They answered that they were going to see the body of Christ. He said, "They need not hurry so for that because if the body of Christ was as large as the Pech de Boulque, it would long ago have been eaten like a pasta!"

And I sometimes repeat these words that I heard this man say, without believing them, and I told them at Dalou. I do not recall if it was when the people were going to see the body of the Lord at Dalou or on other occasions. It seems to me that it was about fourteen years ago that I repeated these words.

—To whom, on presence of whom?—I do not recall.

(August 7, 1320, in the chamber before the bishop and Gaillard de Pomiès)

Twenty-six years ago during the month of August (I do not recall the day), I was the wife of the late knight Bérenger de Roquefort, castelain of Montaillou. The late Raimond Roussel, of Rades, was the intendant and the stewart of our household which we held at the castle of Montaillou. He often asked me to leave with him and to go to Lombardy with the good Christians who are there, telling me that the Lord had said that man must quit his father, mother, wife, husband, son and daughter and follow him, and that he would give him the kingdom of heaven. When I asked him, "How could I quit my husband and my sons?" he replied that the Lord had ordered it and that it was better to leave a husband and sons whose eyes rot than to abandon him who lives for eternity and who gives the kingdom of heaven.

When I asked him "How is it possible that God created so many men and women if many of them are not saved?" he answered that only the good Christians will be saved and no others, neither religious nor priests, nor anyone except these good Christians. Because, he said, just as it is impossible for a camel to pass through the eye of a needle, it is impossible for those who are rich to be saved. This is why the kings and princes, prelates and religious, and all those who have wealth, cannot be saved, but only the good Christians. They remained in Lombardy, because they did not dare live here where the wolves and the dogs would persecute them. The wolves and the dogs were the bishops and the Dominicans, who persecute the good Christians and chase them from this country.

He said that he had listened to some of these good Christians. They were such that once one had heard them speak one could not do without them and if I heard them one time, I would be one of theirs for ever.

When I asked how we could flee together and go to the good Christians, because, when my husband found out, he would follow us and kill us, Raimond answered that when my husband would take a long trip and be far from our country, we could leave and go to the good Christians. I asked him how we would live when we were there. He answered that they would take care of us and give us enough with which to live. "But," I told him, "I am pregnant. What could I do with the child that I am carrying when I leave with you for the good Christians?" "If you give birth to it in their presence, it will be an angel. With the help of God they will make a king and a holy thing of him because he will be born without sin, not having frequented the people of this world, and they would be able to educate him perfectly in their sect, since he would know no other."

He also told me that all spirits sinned at the beginning with the sin of pride, believing that they could know more and be worth more than God, and for that they fell to earth. These spirits later take on bodies, and the world will not end before all of them have been incarnated into the bodies of men and women. Thus it is that the soul of a new born child is as old as that of an old man.

They also said that the souls of men and women who were not good Christians, after leaving their bodies, enter the bodies of other men and women a total of nine times. If in these nine bodies they do not find the body of a good Christian, the soul is damned. If on the contrary, they find the body of a good Christian, the soul is saved.

I asked him how the spirit of a dead man or woman could enter the mouth of a pregnant woman and from there into the mouth of the fruit that she carries in her womb. He answered that the spirit could enter the fruit of the woman's womb by any part of her body. When I asked him why children do not speak from birth, since they have the old souls of other persons, he answered that God does not wish it. He also told me that the spirits of God which sinned lived wherever they could.

Thus he urged me to leave with him so that we could go together to the good Christians, mentioning various noble women who had gone there.

Alesta and Serena, women of Châteauverdun, painted themselves with colors which made them appear foreign so that they could not be recognized and went to Toulouse. When they arrived at an inn, the hostess wanted to know if they were heretics and gave them live chickens, telling them to prepare them because she had things to do in town, and left the house.

When she had returned she found the chickens still alive and asked them why they had not prepared them. They responded that if the hostess would kill them, they would prepare them but that they would not kill them. The hostess heard that and went to tell the inquisitors that two heretics were in her establishment. They were arrested and burned. When it was time to go to the stake, they asked for water to wash their faces, saying that they would not go to God painted thusly.

I told Raimond that they would have done better to abandon their heresy than to allow themselves to be burned, and he told me that the good Christians did not feel fire because fire with which they are burned cannot hurt them.

Raimond also told me that one of these two women, when she was leaving her house at Châteauverdun, had a child in a crib that she wanted to see before leaving. She kissed it, the child smiled, and as she was beginning to move away from the place where it lay, she returned toward it. The child began to laugh and this process began again so that she could not leave. Finally she ordered its nurse to take it, which she did. Thus she was able to leave.

And Raimond told me this to encourage me to do the same!

He told me that Stephanie, the wife of the late Guillaume Arnaud, one of the ladies of Châteauverdun, had abandoned everything and had gone to the good Christians. Prades Tavernier, who since has been accepted as a heretic and is called André, left with her. He told me all of this to convince me to leave, but I answered that if two or three women of my rank left with us, I would then have an excuse that I would not have if, still young, I left with him, because people would immediately say that we had left our country to satisfy our lust.

After having so often shared his heretical discourses with me in various times and places and invited me to leave with him, finally one evening after we had dined together, he secretly entered the bedroom where I slept and put himself under my bed.

I put the house in order and went to bed and when all was quiet and asleep and I was asleep myself, Raimond came out from under my bed and slipped into it in his night shirt and started to act as though he wished to lie with me carnally. "What is going on?" I said. He told me to be quiet. I answered, "What do you mean, be quiet, you peasant?" And I started to shout and to call my maid servants who slept beside me in this bedroom telling them that there was a man with me in my bed.

When he heard this he left the bed and the bedroom. The next day he said that he had acted badly in hiding near me. I answered, "I see now that your invitations to go to the good Christians were intended only to possess me and know me carnally. If I had not been afraid that my husband would believe that I did something dishonorable with you, I would immediately put you in the dungeon."

We did not speak further of heretical questions and shortly after Raimond left our house and returned home to Prades.

—Did you believe and do you still believe what he told you about the good Christians, about the sin of the spirits of heaven, about the reincarnation of souls?—No.

—Did you ever reveal the statements which you heard from this Raimond?—No, except to a Franciscan friar of the convent of Limoux in sacramental confession.

—Did anyone else hear the heretical statements which this Raimond made to you?—I do not recall that there was anyone else present.

Alazaïs Gonelle from Gébetz in the diocese of Alet often came to talk with me and she told me on behalf of Raimond that it would be good for us to leave for Lombardy and the good Christians to save our souls because no one could be saved except in their sect. If I wanted to go with Raimond she herself, Alazaïs, would go with us and she knew that if anyone left for Lombardy and the good Christians, Algée de Martre, from Camurac in the diocese of Alet, would leave with them.

This Alazaïs had been the concubine of Guillaume Clergue, the brother of the rector of Montaillou, and this Algée is the sister of the mother of this rector. But I did not see this Algée.

—What did you understand by these good Christians concerning whom Raimond and Alazaïs spoke constantly?—By good Christians I understood the heretics.

About 25 years ago, when I was living in Montaillou, one day during the month of July, Alazaïs, the wife of Bernard Ribas of Montaillou, knocked at the door. I sent to see what she wanted. She said that she wanted some vinegar. I ordered some to be given her. She said that she did not want it, but that she wanted to speak with me. I replied that I could not, and she departed. The same day she returned and knocked at the door. I sent to find out what she wanted and she said that her daughter was in agony and she asked me to come down to her house because her daughter very much wanted to see me. I answered that I could not come down to her house because it had not been long enough since I had given birth. This Alazaïs returned again to me the same day asking and begging that I go see her daughter, which I could not do.

The same day I had made a candle which is called a "recolor" to go to the church of Sainte-Marie-de-Carnesses. I summoned a woman who lived at the home of the rector of Montaillou (this woman was from Limbrassac) and we both went to the church. Descending to Montaillou, we met this Alazaïs who was leading two geese; she told me to come to her home to see her daughter Guillemette (the wife of Pierre Clergue of Montaillou). I told her that I could not go and she told me that her brother Prades Tavernier was there and wished to speak with me because Stéphanie, the wife of Guillaume Arnaud de Châteauverdun, had given him a message which he wished to transmit to me.

But since it was notorious that the Prades Tavernier had left the country with this Stéphanie to go to the heretics, I said to Alazaïs to leave me alone because I did not wish to speak with Prades. She then left me and I did not see this Prades Tavernier, and I did not speak with him since his departure from the region with this Stéphanie.

About 21 years ago, a year after the death of my husband, I wanted to go to the church of Montaillou to confess during Lent. When I was there, I went to Pierre Clergue, the rector, who was hearing confessions behind the altar of Saint Mary. As soon as I had knelt before him, he embraced me, saying that there was no woman in the world that he loved as much as me. In my surprise, I left without having confessed.

Later, around Easter, he visited me several times, and he asked me to give myself to him. I said one day that he so bothered me in my home that I would rather give myself to four men than to a single priest because I had heard it said that a woman who gave herself to a priest could not see the face of God. To which he answered that I was an ignorant fool because the sin is the same for a woman to know her husband or another man, and the same whether the man were husband or priest. It was even a greater sin with a husband he said, because the wife did not think that she had sinned with her husband but realized it with other men. The sin was therefore greater in the first case.

I asked him how he, who was a priest, could speak like that, since the church said that marriage had been instituted by God, and that it was the first sacrament instituted by God between Adam and Eve, as a result of which it was not a sin when spouses know each other. He answered, "If it was God who instituted marriage between Adam and Eve and if he created them, why didn't he protect them from sin?" I understood then that he was saying that God did not create Adam and Eve and that he had not instituted marriage between them. He added that the Church taught many things which were contrary to truths. Ecclesiastics said these things because without them it would inspire neither respect nor fear. Because, except for the Gospels and the Lord's Prayer, all of the other texts of Scripture were only "affitilhas," a word in the vernacular which designates what one adds on one's own to what one has heard.

I answered that in this case ecclesiastics were throwing the people into error.

(August 8, 1320, in the Chamber of the bishop before the bishop and Gaillard de Pomiès)

Speaking of marriage, he told me that many of the rules concerning it do not come from divine will who did not forbid people to marry their sisters or other persons related by blood, since at the beginning brothers knew their sister. But when several brothers had one or two pretty sisters, each wanted to have her or them. The result was many murders among them and this is why the Church had forbidden brothers to know their sisters or blood relatives carnally. But for God the sin is the same whether it is an outside woman, a sister, or another relative, because the sin is as great with one woman as with another, except that it is a greater sin between a husband and wife, because they do not confess it and they unite themselves without shame.

He added that the marriage was complete and consummated as soon as a person had promised his faith to the other. What is done at the church between spouses, such as the nuptial benediction, was only a secular ceremony which had no value and had been instituted by the Church only for secular splendor.

He further told me that a man and a woman could freely commit any sort of sin as long as they lived in this world and act entirely according to their pleasure. It was sufficient that at their death they be received into the sect or the faith of the good Christians to be saved and absolved of all the sins committed during this life. Because, he said, Christ said to his apostles to leave father, mother, spouse, and children, and all that they possessed, to follow him, in order to have the kingdom of heaven. Peter answered Christ, "If we, who have left everything and followed you, will have the kingdom of heaven, what will be the share of those who are ill and cannot follow you?" The Lord answered Peter that his "friends" would come and impose their hands on the heads of the ill. The ill would be healed and healed, they would follow him and have the kingdom of heaven.

The rector said that these "friends of God" were the good Christians, whom others call heretics. The imposition of the hands that they give to the dying saves them and absolves them of all their sins.

To prove that it was better for the world if brothers married sisters, he told me, "You see that we are four brothers. I am a priest and do not want a wife. If my brothers Guillaume and Bernard had married Esclarmonde and Guillemette, our sisters, our house would not have been ruined by the need of giving them a dowry. It would have remained whole. With a wife who would have been brought into the house for Raimond, our brother, we would have had enough spouses and our house would have been richer. It would therefore have been better if the brother married the sister or the sister the brother, because when she leaves her paternal house with great wealth in order to marry an outsider, the house is ruined."

And with these opinions and many others he influenced me to the point that in the octave of Saints Peter and Paul I gave myself to him one night in my home. This was often repeated and he kept me like this for one and one half years, coming two or three times each week to spend the night in my house near the chateau of Montaillou.

I myself came two nights to his house so that he could unite himself with me. He even knew me carnally Christmas night and still this priest said the mass the next morning although there were other priests present.

And when, on this night of the Nativity, he wanted to have relations with me, I said to him, "How could you want to commit so great a sin on so holy a night?" He answered that the sin was the same to have intercourse with a woman on any other night or on Christmas night. Since this time and many others he said mass the morning after having known me the night before without having confessed since there was no other priest and since I often asked him how he could celebrate the mass after having committed such a sin the night before, he answered that the only valid confession is one which one makes to God, who knows the sin before it is committed, and who alone can absolve it. But the confession that one makes to a priest who is ignorant of the sin until it is revealed to him and who does not have the power to absolve sin has no value and is only made for the ostentation and the splendor of this world. Because only God can absolve sins, man cannot.

He added that I should not confess to another priest the sin which I committed with him but only to God, who knew it and who could absolve me, because a man could not do it. In order to incite me to believe that not even the sovereign pontiff nor the other bishops nor the priests who depend on them do not have this power, he alleged that saint Peter was not a Pope during his life but after his death and that his bones were thrown into a pit where they remained many years. When they were discovered, they were washed and placed in the chair on which the Roman pontiffs sit. But, since the bones of Saint Peter did not have the power to absolve when they were enthroned and apostolized, nor did Peter thus become "apostolic" nor did the Roman pontiffs who are made popes on this chair have the power to pardon. Only the good Christians who suffer persecution and death are able to do so, like saints Laurence, Stephen, and Barthélemy, but not the bishops and the priests subject to the Roman church, who are heretics and persecutors of the good Christians. God took this power from them and retained it for himself, and transmitted it only to the good Christians who he knew and announced in advance that they would suffer persecution.

I then asked him since confession to priests had no value, since they could not absolve, and since the penances that they imposed were without value, why he himself heard confessions, absolved, and imposed penances. This priest said that it was necessary for him and for other priests to do this, even though they meant nothing, because otherwise he would lose his income and no one would give them anything if they did not do what the Church ordered.

But only the good Christians and those who were received by them after having adored them could absolve all other people from their sins. And it was not necessary that those who wished to be absolved by them of their sins confess to them. It was sufficient to give themselves to God and to the good Christians, and they would absolve them simply by the imposition of hands.

He told me all this and what will follow in my home, sometimes near a window that looked out on the road, while I was delousing his head, sometimes near the fire, sometimes when I was in bed. We avoided being overheard by others as much as possible when we broached this subject. I do not recall if Sibille my maid servant, the daughter of Arnaud Teisseyre of Montaillou, who became the concubine of Raimond Clergue, heard anything.

The priest told me that God only made the spirits and that which did not decay or corrode, because the works of God endure for ever. But all of the body which one sees and which one feels, that is to say the heaven and the earth and all that is in them, except only the spirits, were the work of the devil, who rules the world, who made them. It is because it is he who made them that all things are in the process of corruption, because he cannot make anything that is stable or solid.

He told me at this time that God, in the beginning, made a man who spoke and walked. Seeing it, the devil made the body of another man which could neither walk nor speak. God said to him, "Why did you make a sort of person that can neither walk nor speak?" The devil answered that he could not, and said to God to make his person walk and speak. God said that he would willingly do so, if what he put in this man would be for him, God. The devil agreed. God breathed into the mouth of the man that the devil had made and this man began to walk and to talk. Since then the soul of man belongs to God and the body to the devil.

He also told me that God had made all the spirits of heaven. These spirits sinned in their pride, wishing to equal God, and because of this sin they fell from heaven through the air and onto the earth. They live in and penetrate the bodies that they encounter, indifferently, when able, whether bodies of animals or animals of humans. And these spirits in the bodies of animals are as capable of reason and understanding as are those in human bodies, except that they cannot speak in the bodies of animals. And the fact that the spirits which are in the bodies of animals are endowed with reason and with understanding results, he said, in the fact that they flee from that which is dangerous for them and search what is good for them. This is why it is a sin to kill any animal or a person, because each has reason and understanding. He also said that it is necessary that all these spirits enter a human body to be able to do penance for this sin of pride, and this must be done before the end of the world. It is only in the bodies of humans, according to him, that these spirits can do penance for this sin. They cannot do it in the bodies of beasts.

He also told me that these spirits who sinned thusly, if they can enter the body of a good Christian, rejoice greatly, and, as soon as they leave his body, they return to heaven from which they fell. If they do not enter the body of a good Christian but into the body of another man or another woman, when they leave they enter, if they can, into the body of another man or woman up to nine times, if they do not enter the body of a good Christian man or woman. If they do enter, as soon as they exit, they return to heaven from whence they had fallen.

But if in these nine bodies which they enter successively, there is no good Christian, when they leave the last body they are entirely lost and cannot do any further penance. He told me that all of this is true in general, but the spirits which consented to the betrayal of Christ, as was the case of Judas and some of the other Jews, as soon as they left their bodies, were immediately lost and could not do penance, and they did not enter the bodies of people to do penance. But those who were present at the betrayal of Christ without having consented to it, enter into nine other bodies like the others.

This priest also told me that only the spirits who enter the bodies of good Christians will be saved and no others, whether they be Christian, Jew or Saracen. According to him all of the good Christians, those who worship them believing in them and having been received into their sect, have been saved. And he said that for this reason his mother Mengarde was saved because she had done much good for the good Christians and Roqua and Raimond Roché his son who were immured for heresy for a time received all of their subsistence from her house. Her mother was kind to these two people because they had been heretics and believers.

This priest also told me that these spirits which were in heaven and which had sinned in revolting against God divided. Some of them plotted and rebelled against God, and these were first to leave heaven. Their sin was so serious that later God did not wish to accept penance and they were sent to hell and are demons. But there were other spirits that did not plot the revolt against God and did not rebel openly but who wished to follow those who had planned this revolt. Those fell onto the earth and in the air and are incorporated into the bodies of men and animals, do penance, and are saved or damned as has been previously said.

He also said that the good Christians do not believe that God causes the seeds of things that multiply, flower, and ripen on the earth. Because if it were so, since God could also make things grow on bare rock as well as on fertile soil, the seeds thrown on stone would grow as well as those on earth. But this takes place, he said, because soil is rich, and God does not intervene.

He also told me that the good Christians do not believe that Christ took flesh from the holy Virgin nor did he descend to take flesh from her because, before she was born Christ had existed from all eternity. But he simply "adombrad" himself in Mary without taking anything from her. Explaining this word "adombration" this priest told me that, just as the wine that is in a cask is within its shadow without taking anything from it, but is only contained in it, in the same way Christ lived in the virgin Mary without taking anything from her, but was simply in her as is the contents in a container.

He also told me that Christ, although he dined with his disciples, never ate or drank, although he appeared to do so.

He told me that from the time that Christ was crucified on the cross, no one should venerate or adore it since an outrage against Christ had been committed on it.

He also told me that there was no church of God except there where there is a good Christian because he is the Church of God, but elsewhere there is no church of God and the other men are not the church of God.

He also told me that when the good Christians are burned for their faith they are the martyrs of Christ. He also told me that when these good Christians have received anyone into their sect, that person must no longer eat or drink except cold water, and he said that when the people thus die of weakness they become the saints of God.

He also told me that the fires in which they are burned do not make the good Christians suffer, because God assists them so that they will not suffer from this fire and that they will not have great pain.

The above-mentioned Raimond Roussel told me that a man was seriously ill and a priest came to him and asked him if he wanted to see and receive the body of the Lord. The man replied that he wanted to see the body of Christ more than anything else in the world. This priest went to get the body of the Lord and bring it to the sick man. He took it from the pix and held it in his hands showing it to the sick man and questioned him on the articles of faith especially asking if he believed that it was the body of Christ. The indignant patient said to the priest, "You miserable whore of a peasant, if what you are holding were the body of Christ, and if it was as large as a great mountain, you and the other priests would long ago have eaten it all!" And he refused to receive the body of Christ.

Pierre Clergue, the rector, told me that this world which the devil had made is decaying and will totally destroy itself, and before this happens, God will assemble his friends and draw them to himself so that they do not see so great a catastrophe as that of the destruction of the world.

When I went down from the region of Alion to contract a marriage with my second husband, Othon de Lagleize of Dalou, this rector told me that he was very displeased that I was going down into that low country because no one would dare speak further with me about the good Christians or come see me to save my soul. I was going to live with wolves and dogs, of whom, he said, none would be saved. He called all the Catholics who are not good Christians wolves and dogs.

He nevertheless said that if one day my heart told me to be received into the sect of good Christians, I should let him know early because he would do all that he could so that the good Christians would receive me into their sect and save my soul. I answered him that I did not want to be received into that sect but that I wanted to be saved in the faith in which I was, quoting my sister Gentille, who had first said this.

These heretical conversations continued between us for around two years and this priest taught me all of this.

—Did you believe and do you still believe these heresies that this rector of the church of Montaillou, Pierre Clergue, told you and in which he instructed you?—The last year, when I left the region of Alion from Easter until the following August, I completely and fully believed these errors to the point that I would not have hesitated to undergo any suffering to

defend them. I believed that they were truth taught by the priest whom, because he was a priest, I believed what he said. But when I was at Crampagna with my second husband and I heard the preaching of the Dominicans and Franciscans and I visited with faithful Christians, I abandoned these errors and heresies and I confessed at the penitential court of a Franciscan of the convent of Limoux in the Church of Notre Dame de Marseille where I had gone to see my sister Gentille, who lived at Limoux and who was the wife of the late Paga de Post. I made this confession fifteen years ago and I remained around five years without confessing heretical opinions that I had heard and believed although I confessed my other sins during these five years.

At the time when I believed these heresies, I did not see (nor did I see before or after) any heretics that I knew to be heretics, although I believed that they were good men because they suffered martyrdom for God and this priest had taught me that it was only in their sect that one could be saved.

I greatly regret having ever heard these heretical opinions and even more for having believed these heresies, and I am ready to accept the penance that my lord the bishop may wish to impose on me for them.

(August 9, 1320, in the chamber of the bishopric, before the bishop and Gaillard de Pomeèsès)

Nineteen years ago at the Assumption of Mary (15 August 1301) I left Prades in the region of Alion where I lived in a house near the church and went to Crampagna to marry Othon de Lagleize. Before leaving Prades, Bernard Belot of Montaillou, who died on the wall of Carcassonne, came to see me and told me that the rector of Montaillou, Pierre Clergue, was very unhappy with me because I was going into the low country where I could not have good Christians to save my soul. Because these good Christians did not trust the people of the low country and that they did not dare to speak with them about their sect or their life. This is why this priest feared that I would lose my soul if I went down to the low country where there were no good Christians. This

Bernard also told me that the good Christians, if they dared, would ask me to see them, because, he said, no one could be confirmed in their faith if he had not seen them and heard them speak. I answered that I did not wish to see them and that I did not have the heart to wish to do so. He told me to send them something as a sign of recognition in the same way that when a person received a benefit from another, he has the obligation to pray to God for that person. These good Christians, he told me, only pray for those from whom they receive something. I asked him, "What should I send them?" He answered that it was sufficient that I send them something if I wished that they pray to God for you. I gave him five Paris sous, the current coin, to take to the good Christians and I said, "I do not know who will have this money, but may it be for the love of God."

At the time that I lived in Montaillou and Prades, the rumour was circulating among the believers that the heretics were visiting the houses of the brothers Raimond and Bernard Belot, who lived together, those of Alazaïs den Riba, sister of the heretic Prades Tavernier, and of Guillaume Benet, brother of Arnaud Benet of Ax, who were all from Montaillou. It was said that they served as guides for these heretics and that they knew their routes.

The same year that I sent this money to the heretics by the intermediary of Bernard Belot, I was at Crampagna with Guillaume Othon my second husband around the feast of St. Michael in September. Bernard Belot came to see me at Crampagna in the house or the estate called Carol, where I was then living, and told me that the rector of Montaillou sent greetings and also sent me by his intermediary an act of marriage concerning my marriage with my first husband in which was found the assignment of my dowry. I had deposited this act with the rector. Since I was not concerned about this act because I had already settled with the heirs of my first husband, I thought that Bernard was bringing me a message from the rector, and I spoke with him in secret. He said that the rector greeted me and asked me to remember the discussions we had about the sect and the stature and way of life of the good men. I

answered that I did not wish to remember and that on the contrary it very much displeased me to have ever heard or to have spoken of them. I told him that it was better to hear the opinions of the Dominicans and Franciscans than to speak of the sect and the way of life of the heretics, and this Bernard told me that my heart had changed quickly and that the discussions that he and the rector had held with me were lost. He had thought right away, he said, that when I descended into the low country they had lost their good words. I answered that in the future he was not to send me such messages because if my husband knew something bad would happen. "In the future, do not return, because if you visit this house my husband will believe right away something evil about me, either dishonest conduct or some other evil."

Thus he left me, unhappy with my answer, and said that he did not believe that their good words could have been so quickly lost.

Twenty-two years ago, I was gravely ill at Varilhes in the house of my late husband Othon. This priest came one day to the synod at Pamiers and he entered my home to visit me. When he was with me he sat at the head of my bed where I lay and asked me how I was, gently stroking my hand and arm. I answered that I was seriously ill. He then said to my late daughter Béatrice who was there to leave the room because he wanted to speak to me in private. When she had left, he asked me how my heart was. I answered him that it was very weak and that I was afraid of the discussions that we had together (I meant by that the heretical opinions described above that the priest had told me). I was so afraid of them that I did not dare to confess these sins to any priest for fear that he would judge me of suspicious faith. He told me not to fear that because God knew my sin and alone could absolve the sins I had and that I need not confess to any priest. He also told me that I would soon be cured and that when he went down to Pamiers he would see me and that we would discuss these matters. This said, he left me and since then I have not seen him. He nevertheless sent me an engraved cup and some sugar.

About twenty-one years ago, I was at Montaillou after the death of my first husband. One day, around Christmas, I was in the home of Alazaïs Maury of Montaillou. We were warming ourselves by the fire and since we were there Gauzia, the wife of Bernard Clergue, arrived and in front of me asked this Alazaïs if Guillemette, the widow of Pierre Faure of Montaillou, was dead. Alazaïs answered yes and that she had been buried. Gauzia then said, "Did you do it well?" Alazaïs answered, "Yes, by my faith, well." Gauzia then said, "And you did it very, very well? You did not omit anything?" Alazaïs answered that it had been done "well" and that there had been no obstacle to doing it. Gauzia then said, "Thank God!" Having said this, she sat down by the fire. I did not understand why this discussion had taken place between these two women nor what they meant to say, but a few days later I met Alazaïs, I don't remember where, and I asked her what these words between her and Gauzia meant. She answered that they meant nothing. I said that on the contrary one did not say such things for nothing. Then she told me that she did not dare reveal to me what they meant because she feared that I would denounce her. I promised on my faith to keep her secret. She then told me that the good Christians had come to the house of the ill woman, Guillemette, and she had been received into their sect to become a good Christian. After that, they had ordered her not to eat or to drink except for cold water, and she did so, neither eating not drinking anything but cold water. She stayed in this state for around fifteen days until her death.

From this time on Alazaïs began to visit me and she spoke to me about the good Christians, saying that they were holy and good people and that one should have more confidence in them than in the clergy because they bore many persecutions for Christ and that the clerics do not bear persecution but that they have the pleasures of this world.

She said that a person should not quit the sect of the good Christians for any danger or misfortune. She also said that one can only be saved in their sect and in their faith. Regardless of what sins one has committed in the present life, if one has been received by them at the end, those sins are remitted and one is saved.

She also said that these good Christians hide and do not dare show themselves because the Church persecutes and destroys them and that it is a great work of charity to do them good. She said that she and her husband Raimond Maury often did them good deeds taking on their poverty and depriving themselves of food to give it to them and often sending them flour and other things that they had, always of the best quality. I said, "These good Christians accept flour?" She answered yes, and I then gave her a quarter of a barrel of flour to give to the good persons on my behalf. I do not know if she gave them the flour or not.

Because of the opinions that I heard concerning these heretics from Raimond Roussel and the priest, I believed that what Alazaïs had told me was true concerning these good Christians. This is why I sent them flour through her. Afterwards I did not further speak with this Alazaïs about the heretics.

Around the same time Alazaïs, wife of Pens Azéma of Montaillou had a son named Raimond Azéma, who was said by some to frequent the heretics. One evening at nightfall I was at her home. Raimond arrived carrying a basket in which he seemed to have something and he quickly left. I asked Alazaïs where her son was going at such an hour. She answered me that he was going somewhere. I asked her to be more precise, and she answered that I was "chilarda" (that means I had big eyelids) and that she would not reveal where her son was going. I said, "And why not?" She said that I would not keep the secret. I assured her of the contrary and also asked her what her son was carrying in the basket. She said that actually her son was carrying food in the basket and that when I had insisted and asked her many times to whom he was carrying this food, she finally told me that he was taking it to the good persons whom the others called heretics, and yet these were good and holy people who underwent many persecutions for Christ. One must not abandon their faith out of any human fear because all that one sees in the world was made by the devil who rules the world and all will be destroyed like spider webs except for spirits which were made by God. She also told me that people cannot be saved except in their faith and belief, and that it is sufficient to have been received into their sect to be saved regardless of the sins that one has committed during one's life, and that it is a great thing that one can save one's soul by believing in these people and in dying in one's home. I only answered that her son would be in great trouble if he was stopped carrying this basket to the good Christians. Since then I did not speak with her about this subject. The above-mentioned Raimond drowned in the Douctuyre near the church of Notre-Dame de Vals.

About twenty years ago, when I was living in Prades, one day, I do not remember exactly, I was going to Cassou to visit my sister Ava, wife of Verèze, who was in labour. The following Sunday I went to the church of Unac which is the parish church of Cassou. When I was there Raimonde, widow of Guillaume-Bernard of Luzenac, who had also come, embraced and kissed me (because she was a member of my family), and told me near the entry of the church, "And you, my cousin who is in this good region, you have not yet seen these good people? If I lived there, I would see them willingly." I asked her whom she called "good people." She answered that she meant the good Christians. I told her that I had not seen any and that I did not have the heart to see them. She told me that once I had seen them and listened to them, I would no longer want to hear anyone else, and that after having listened one time, I would always be in a good state, wherever I went. We said nothing more on this subject and we entered the church and heard mass.

(August 12, before the bishop and Gaillard de Pomiès)

During the life time of my husband, Raimond Clergue, alias Pathau, natural son of Guillaume Clergue (he himself brother of Pons Clergue who was the father of Pierre Clergue the curate of Montaillou) took me by force in the castle. A year later, at the death of my hus-

band Bérenger de Roquefort, he kept me publicly. This did not prevent this curate, Pierre Clergue, to solicit me, even though he knew that his cousin Raimond had possessed me.

"How can you ask this," I said to him. "You know very well that your cousin Raimond had me. He will reveal everything!" The rector answered me that this was neither necessary nor a problem. "I know well what has happened, but I can be of more use to you and give you more presents than this bastard!" He told me that they could both support me, he the curate and Raimond. I answered that I would not permit this at any cost because there would be bad feelings between them because of me and that both would revile me because of the other.

And after the priest possessed me, I had no further relations with this Raimond, although he tried from time to time. Since then Raimond and the priest shared a secret hatred because of that, but I did not know it.

When I was at Dalou, after having contracted marriage with my second husband, Othon de Lagleize, a marriage which took place at the Assumption of Mary, this priest came to Dalou to the following grape harvests and pretended to be from Limoux. Entering my house he told me that my sister Gentille, who lived in Limoux, sent greetings, and I allowed him to enter. We both went into the cellar and he knew me carnally, while Sibille, the daughter of the late Armaud Teisseyre, stayed at the door of the cellar.

The previous evening she had brought me a silk blouse of Barcelona workmanship which had one red and another yellow lace as a gift from this rector and she told me that he would come the following day so that no one would come and that if someone else did arrive he would not think that anything had happened between the rector and me because this servant was standing in the middle of the open cellar door in which the priest and I were coupling. Having committed this sin, I took him out of the house. When we were at the outside door, I told him that I had given five sous to Bernard Belot. "Did he tell you?" He answered that he had told him and that I had done a good thing to give him those five sous. I was thinking of the five sous that I had given this Bernard to take to the heretics on my behalf and I believe that this is what the priest understood.

When he came to see me at Varilhes, when I was ill, as has been said and when he told me to remember the discussions that we had at Montaillou about the good Christians, and that I should not confess, he also told me that he was holding the inquisition over the heads of the people of Montaillou. "How can that be! You now persecute the good Christians and their believers, you who usually wish them well?" He answered that he continued to wish them well, but that he wanted to revenge himself against many people of the place who hated him in whatever he could and that later he would arrange things with God.

Twelve years ago I was at Dalou. One day, a priest brought the body of the Lord to the bridge of Dalou where Pierre du Pont was who wished to receive communion. I went to this house and saw and heard the priest question the ill man on the articles of faith and also ask him if he believed that it was the true body of Christ by which we are saved. The sick person said that he believed and devotedly asked for the body of Christ with joined hands. I returned home with Grazide Pujol of Dalou. On the way I said that he had received the body of the Lord better than that man described above who said that if the body of the Lord was that which the priests say is the body of the Lord and if it were as large as a mountain, it would already have been eaten only by the priests. Grazida told me to be silent because if one heard me say such things, they would be taken badly. I answered that I did not say them evilly but that I was repeating the words that this bad man had said.

—Did you ever believe that the true body of the Lord was not in the sacrament of the altar?—No.

—Did you say to anyone else these words or their equivalent?—I do not remember, but if I do recall, I will admit it.

—Have you told others the heretical opinions that Raimond Roussel, this priest, and other above mentioned people told you?—

No.—Have you heard these heretical opinions from others than those named above by you?—No.

—Did anyone ever tell you that the devil was the principle and the maker of corporeal creatures in the sense that they were not made or produced by God or by anyone but that he made them by himself and of himself principally, in the same way that God is a principle not made or produced by an other spirit?—I have not heard this. These people did not tell me either that God made the devil or the contrary.

—Did you ever hear from these people that there was a good God and a bad God?—No. They called God he who made the spirits, and the maker of the world they called the devil and the director of the world. I never heard them call him "Hylè (matter)."

—Have you heard these or others say that the good God made two worlds and the bad God ten other worlds, and that the bad God with his ten worlds and those who were in his worlds had fought the good God and his worlds, and that things which are in the worlds of God and that he had been in part the victor over the good God and had conquered a part of him?—No.

—Have you heard these or others say that the spirits were of the substance of God or part of God?—No, except for what I have already said.

(August 13, in the episcopal chamber, before the bishop)

—Have you heard these or others say that there are two souls in people, one of which inclines people to do evil (and that it is the one of the devil) and the other to do good (and that it is part of God)?—No.

—Have you heard them say that all of the spirits created by God were of the same nature and condition?—This priest told me that all the spirits were created by God in heaven of the same condition but that some adhered to God and remained in heaven with him and that others revolted against God (and those were put in hell and are demons) and others, although they did not rebel against God, still followed the rebels, and these fell on the earth and in the air. These are the spirits which enter the bodies of dumb beasts and of men and women, as has been said.

—Did you hear them say that the devil, moved by pride or envy against God, made this world and all that is in it except for the spirits, in order to seem the equal of God?—No, but only that the devil made all visible things. I did not hear why he made them.

—Did you hear them say that the scriptures of the Old Testament are not of the good God?—Only that the priest told me that all of the Scriptures except for the Gospels and the Lord's Prayer, were "affitilhas" and lies.

—Did you hear them say that the Son descended in Mary and "adombrad" himself in her?—I heard the priest say that it was not the Father who descended but that he sent the Holy Spirit, who "adombrad" himself in Mary.

—Did they call Mary the mother of God if according to this priest the Holy Spirit did not take flesh in her?—Yes.

—Did you hear them or others say that Christ was dead?—This priest said that he had been crucified but I do not recall hearing from him that he was dead.

—When he spoke to you of Jesus Christ, did you at times hear him called true man?—This priest called him true God but I do not recall having heard him call him true man.

—Did he say that Jesus Christ rose from the dead?—He said that Christ rose, but I do not recall if he said that he rose from the dead.

—Did you hear him say that Christ will judge the good and the bad at the last judgment?—Yes.

—That all the resurrected with their bodies will come to the last judgment of Christ?—He said "We will all come to the judgment of Christ, at which there will be many called but few chosen, and this few chosen was only the good Christians, and those who will be received by them at their deaths. No matter how much one believed in the good Christians during one's life, if one was not received into their sect at death, one is not saved."

He said also that no one, regardless of his order, state, or condition, except for the good Christians, and those whom they receive at

their deaths, will be saved. And although he said that all would come to the judgment of Christ, I never heard him or the others who believe in the heretics say that persons will be raised or will come to the judgment of Christ with their own bodies.

—Did this priest or the other believers deny baptism by water, confession, the sacrament of the altar, holy orders, extreme unction?—I never heard them speak of other sacraments or deny them, except those of penance and marriage.

(She said nothing more about the Manichean sect)

August 22, in the episcopal chamber, before the bishop and Brother Gaillard de Pomiès)

Mengarde, the widow of Pons Clergue, once told me after the death of my first husband, in her house, while we were speaking of Roqua and of his son Raimond Roché, who had been immured for heresy, that it was good that they had been done a good turn. I answered that it was good because she was a good woman. Mengarde told me, "If you well know, it is good to do good to this Roqua." Later paying attention to these words, I thought that this Mengarde had told me that with attention because she was in agreement with this Roqua about the heresy.

While I was living at Prades, after the death of my first husband, I was living in a small house between those of Jean Clergue, rector of Prades, and the inn of Pierre Guilhem of that place. Since this house touched that of the curate, everything which took place there could be heard by those in the other house. Pierre Clergue, curate of Montaillou, who had come to see me, told me that he would send Jean, his student, whose family name I do not know, to get me the next night to sleep with him. I accepted.

Therefore I was home when the first hour sounded, waiting for this student. He arrived and I followed him through a very dark night and we arrived at the church of St. Pierre de Prades, where we entered. We found Pierre Clergue who had prepared a bed in the church. I said, "O, how can we do such a thing in the church of Saint Pierre?" He answered, "What a great wrong it will do to St. Peter!" This said we went to bed together in the church and this night he knew me carnally in this church. Afterward, before dawn, he showed me out of the church himself and took me to the door of the house where I was living.

I had said to him at the beginning of our relations, "What will I do if I become pregnant by you? I will be dishonored and lost." He answered that he had a good herb which, if a man wears it when he is with a woman, he can not engender nor can a woman conceive. I said to him, "What is this herb? Is it not the one that the cheese makers put on their pots of milk into which they have put rennet and which prevents the milk from curdling as long as it is on the pot?" He told me not to bother trying to know what kind of herb it was but that it was a herb that had this power and that he had some.

Since that time when he wanted to take me, he wore something rolled up and tied in a piece of linen the thickness and length of an ounce or of the first digit of my little finger, with a long thread which he passed around my neck. And this thing which he said was this herb hung down between my breasts to the base of my stomach. He always placed it thus when he wanted to know me and it remained on my neck until he rose. And if sometimes during the same night this priest wanted to know me two or more times, he asked me, before we coupled, where this herb was. I would take it by finding it by the thread which I had at my neck and place it in his hand. He took it and placed it before the base of my stomach with the thread passing between my breasts. This is how he coupled with me and no other way. I asked him one day to leave this herb with me. He refused because he said that then I could give myself to another man without becoming pregnant. He would not give it to me so that I would refrain from so doing out of fear of the consequences. He did this in particular thinking of his cousin Raimond Clergue, alias Pathau, who had first kept me before this priest, his fraternal cousin, had me, because they were jealous of each other.

He again told me that he did not want me to have a child from him while my father, Philippe de Planissoles was alive, because the latter would have been too ashamed, but that after his death he wanted me to have his child.

After this, the same year, on the 25th of the month of August, the above named Béatrice swore juridically before the bishop of Pamiers before my lord bishop, assisted by Brother Gaillard of Pomiès, substitute of my lord the inquisitor of Carcassonne, in presence of the religious person Brother Guillaume Séguier, prior of the convent of Preachers (Dominicans) of Pamiers, the discrete person master Bernard Gaubert, jurist, and me, the undersigned notary. Because she was very ill and in bed and her death was expected, my lord bishop told her that if she had hidden anything concerning heresy in the confession that she had made above about herself or others, or if she had accused a person against truth and justice, she should admit it and reveal it, or she should exonerate the persons she had unjustly accused. And my lord the bishop commanded this at the peril of her soul. She responded, exonerating the rector and accusing the above named Raimond Roussel concerning the following articles:

Although in her confession she had said that the above mentioned rector had told her that God had only made the spirits and that the devil made all bodies that one sees and feels, such as the earth, the sky, and all found there, except for the spirits, and as a result spirits remain forever but corporeal things disintegrate and corrode, now, called to a better memory, she says that it was not the rector who told her this, but the above named Raimond Roussel, and that he said this near the gate of the castle of Montaillou.

What she said that the rector had said, that Christ did not come down from heaven and did not take flesh of Mary but that the Holy Spirit "adombrated" itself in her, in explaining the word adombration in the above manner, it had not been the rector who said this but Raimond Roussel in the same place as in the previous article.

She said under her own oath and in peril of her soul, that all the rest, together and in parts, that she reported on the facts of heresy against herself, this rector, and other persons, both living and dead, and which is contained in the above confessions, were true.

The above was read to her so that she could understand them and the heretical articles that she had admitted in her previous confessions against herself, the rector, and Raimond Roussel were read to her in the vernacular language. She confirmed them entirely and fully and said that they were true, except what she had retracted in her previous confession (not the articles, but who had told them to her).

Asked if she had instructed any other person on these articles or on some of them, if it was not as she had stated, she answered no.

—Why did you flee when you were called by my lord bishop and you appeared on the accusation of heresy? Did someone advise you to flee or to absent yourself?—I fled out of the fear that I had of my lord the bishop because of the heresy that I had committed and above all because my lord, when I appeared before him the first time, called me by the name of my father Philippe who had been accused of this crime.

I realized some time before my lord the bishop called me that he was going to do so, and I sent to Barthelémy Amilhac, a priest who had conducted himself evilly with me for a certain time, to discuss it with him and to take council with him to know what I should do if I was accused of heresy by my lord the bishop. He came to Varlhes where I was living, but without entering the town, and we spoke. I told him that I had understood that my lord had interrogated witnesses against me concerning heresy and that I was afraid that I would be accused of this crime.—Did it seem more appropriate to him to flee than to appear on this accusation?—He asked me, "Do you consider yourself guilty?" I answered no, and that he could be sure that if I have committed anything of this sort I would have told him, whom I had loved so much.

This priest told me that then it was better to appear since I did not feel guilty because my lord the bishop, he told me, would not do me an injustice. Having said this he left.

Afterward I appeared, summoned by my lord, I was terrified, and returning to Varilhes, I dreamed of fleeing and I gathered all the things that I wanted to take with me. I said to no one that I wanted to flee. On the contrary, to my daughter Condors, I said that I was returning to my lord the bishop on the day that he had ordered me. I promised her this, embraced her, and then fled toward Belpech in the diocese of Mirepoix. As soon as I arrived there I sent word to Barthélémy, this priest, at Mézerville where he was staying. He came immediately to find me at Belpech.

Arriving and seeing my trousseau of clothes that I had carried with me he said, "Why have you come here? What do you intend to do, carrying so many clothes with you?" I took him aside and told him that I had been summoned by my lord the bishop and that I had appeared, and that he had told me that I had said that the body of the Lord was not in the sacrament of the altar, and that if he had been as large as a mountain, it would have already been eaten by the priests alone. He had also said that I had seen Pierre, Guillaume and Jacques Authié the heretics, that I had listened to them and that I had performed magic on their advice. Even though I did not feel guilty, as I said to this priest, because I had not seen the heretics Pierre and Guillaume Authié since they had become heretics, I wanted nevertheless to flee and to go to the home of my daughter Gentille at Limoux to hide.

He answered that I had done very wrong to flee, that it was necessary to return and to appear before my lord bishop. I said that I would not do so even if he gave me the whole bishopric of Pamiers. The priest said, "If that is how it is and I can not retain you, take this money," and he gave me eight *Tournois* of money. We ate together. He again told me that he would not abandon me unless I wanted him to do so before I was at Limoux, but that after the feast of the Invention of Saint Stephen (August 8), the feast when he had to go to Mézerville, because it was the feast of the altar of the church of that place, he would accompany me to Limoux. In the meantime he pawned or sold a book or otherwise obtained money so

that we could make the trip to Limoux together. From there, he told me that we would go to
Mas-Saintes-Puelles, which is on the outskirts,
and where no one would look for me. After
this feast, we would leave together. I was
delighted to hear it, and we, this priest, I, and a
sergeant of Belpech whose name I do not
know, went to Mas-Saintes-Puelles, where I
was arrested by the people of my lord the bishop and taken by them to him.

Likewise it was established that certain very
suspect things that had been collected by her
for witchcraft were found among her things
and that she recognized them as hers, and that
she had possessed them. These were: two
umbilical cords of infants found in her purse;
cloth stained by blood which seemed to be
menstrual blood in a leather sack with a
[roquette] seed and slightly burned incense
grains; a mirror and a small knife wrapped in a
piece of linen; the seed of a plant wrapped in
muslin; a piece of dried bread which is called
"tinhol"; a number of written formulas, and
pieces of linen. Since it was established that for
these reasons there was a great suspicion that
this Béatrice was a witch and used spells, my
lord the bishop asked her why she possessed
these items. She answered:

I had the cords of the male children of my
daughters and I kept them because a Jewish
woman, since baptized, had told me that if I
carried them with me and I had a legal suit, I
would not lose. This is why I took these from
my grandchildren and kept them. I never had
the occasion to verify their efficacy.

These clothes stained with blood are from
the menstrual blood of my daughter Philippa
and because this baptized Jew had told me that
if I kept some of her first blood and that I gave
it to her husband or to another man to drink he
would never be interested in another woman.
This is why, when a long time ago my daughter Philippa was young and had her first
menses, I looked at her face and seeing that she
was congested, I asked her what was wrong.
She answered that she was bleeding from her
vulva. I then remembered the words of this
baptized Jew. I cut a piece of the slip of my
daughter Philippa which was stained with this

blood and since it seemed to me that there was
not enough, I gave my daughter another piece
of linen "blouset" so that, when she had her
period, she could stain and impregnate this
cloth. She did this and then I dried the cloth
with the intention, when her husband married
her, of giving it to him to drink, by extracting it
from this cloth that I had stained. Philippa
married this year and I had the intention of
giving it to her fiance to drink. But I thought
that it would be better to wait until the marriage was consummated and that it should be
Philippa herself who would give it to her husband to drink. And since, when I was arrested,
the marriage had not yet been consummated
between Philippa and her husband, and that
they had not yet celebrated the wedding, I did
not give it to him to drink.

I did not put these clothes with the incense
grains in order to cast a spell. It was by chance.
My daughter had a headache this year and
someone told me that incense mixed with
other things cures this illness. This is why
some of the grains remained in my possession
in this bag. I did not have any intention to do
anything with them.

Neither the mirror, the wrapped knife, nor
the pieces of linen cloth, were intended for
magic or a spell.

As for the seed wrapped in muslin, it is a
seed of a plant called the bugle. It was given to
me by a pilgrim who said that it was efficacious against epilepsy. Since my grandson, the
son of my daughter, Condors, suffers from it
this year, I wanted to use it. But my daughter
said that she had taken him to the church of
Saint-Paul and that he had been cured of this
illness, and that she did not want me to do anything to her son for his illness. Thus I did not
use it.

—Have you made other spells, have you
taught them, have you learned them from anyone?—No. At times however I believed that
Barthelémy, this priest, had cast some sort of
spell because I loved him too much and I too
much wanted to be with him, even though,
when I met him, I had already entered
menopause. I often asked him but he always
denied it.

In light of the fact that she had plainly confessed to in matters of heresy and witchcraft both about herself and others living or dead, that she had greatly repented having committed this and that she wanted to return to union with the Church and the Catholic faith; that she had asked absolution and was also ready to do the penance that my lord the bishop judged good to impose on her for the above listed acts; for these reasons my lord bishop, having received from her the abjuration of heresy and the promise under oath according to the formula of the Church, gave her absolution of the sentences which she had incurred for the crimes of heresy and witchcraft, if she had fully confessed and repented of what had preceded. If not it was not the intention of my lord bishop, as he told her, to absolve these sentences. The above named Béatrice promised nevertheless, if she should later remember anything concerning heresy, to report it both concerning herself and concerning others living or dead.

The formula of this abjuration and of this engagement under oath is the following:

I, Béatrice, appearing juridically before you, reverend father in Christ my lord Jacques, by the grace of God bishop of Pamiers, I entirely abjure all heresy raised against our lord Jesus Christ and the Holy Catholic Church, and all beliefs of heretics, of whatever sects condemned by the Roman Church, and especially the sect to which I had adhered and all complicity, participation, defense, and frequenting of these heretics, under the penalty of that which is due by law to one who has relapsed into heresy abjured by law.

Likewise, I abjure and promise to pursue according to my ability the heretics of any sect condemned by the Roman Church and especially the sect to which I adhered and the believers, frauds, dissimulators, and defenders of these heretics as well as those whom I know or believe to be in flight by reason of heresy and to have any of them arrested and handed over to my lord bishop or the inquisitors of heretical deviation to the extent of my power every time and in every place that I learn of the existence of one or more of them.

Likewise, I swear and promise to hold, guard and defend the Catholic faith that the Holy Roman Church preaches and observes.

Likewise, I promise to obey and to defer to the orders of the church, of my lord the bishop and of the inquisitors and to come on the day and days specified before them or their replacements every time and in every place that I receive the order or the demand from them by messenger or by letter or in other manners. I promise never to flee or to knowingly absent myself in a spirit of rebellion and to receive and to accomplish as far as I am able the penalties of the penance that they will have judged it good to impose on me. And to this end I obligate my person and my property.

After which the above year, the 5th of March, the above named Béatrice appeared juridically before my lord bishop and the religious person Brother Jean de Beaude of the Order of Preachers, (Dominicans) Inquisitor of heretical deviation in the kingdom of France commissioned by the apostolic See in the episcopal chamber. In fidelity to the oath that she had sworn, she confessed that the extract of her deposition was correct and she concluded in the present case, asking for sentencing on the facts and requesting that one act toward her with mercy. And my lord bishop concurred with her.

And my lords the bishop and the inquisitor assigned to the above named Béatrice a day to hear the definitive sentence on the preceding, that is, the following Sunday, March 8, before the third hour, in the house of the Preachers (Dominicans) of Pamiers.

Done in the year and day above, in the presence of the religious persons Brothers Gaillard of Pomiès, prior of the convent of the Brothers Preachers of Pamiers, Arnaud of Carla, of the same convent, Brother Pierre, companion of my lord the inquisitor, David and Bernard of Centelles, monks of Fontfroide of the Order of Citeaux, and of my lord Germain de Castelnau, archdeacon of the church of Pamiers, witnesses for these summoned, and us Guillaume Peyre-Barthe, notary of my lord the archbishop and Barthelémy Adalbert, notary of the Inquisition, who have been present at what preceded and have received and written it.

And the Sunday assigned to the above named Béatrice, she appeared in the cemetery of Saint-Jean-Martyr of Pamiers and was given the sentence by my lords the bishop and the inquisitor which reads as follows, "Know all ye, etc." See this sentence in the Book of sentences of the Inquisition.[1]

And I, Rainaud Jabbaud, cleric of Toulouse, sworn in the matter of the inquisition, on the order of my lord the bishop, have faithfully corrected this confession against the original.

Notes

1 She was sentenced to death on the walls of Carcassonne but the sentence was commuted to wearing a double cross (indicating a heretic) on her clothing for the remainder of her life.

MARSILIUS OF PADUA

Discourses

Marsilius of Padua (ca. 1275-1342), rector of the University of Paris, dedicated his 1324 attack on ecclesiastical claims to political power to the Emperor Louis of Bavaria. His political ideology, which based political power on the consent of the people, entirely denied papal and episcopal claims to secular political authority. He was an equally ardent defender of the position of the Spiritual Franciscans, who insisted on the primacy of radical poverty in keeping with the tradition of Francis.

Source: Alan Gewirth, *Marsilius of Padua, The Defender of Peace* (New York: Columbia University Press, 1951).

CHAPTER III: ON THE CANONIC STATEMENTS AND OTHER ARGUMENTS WHICH SEEM TO PROVE THAT COERCIVE RULERSHIP BELONGS TO BISHOPS OR PRIESTS AS SUCH, EVEN WITHOUT THE GRANT OF THE HUMAN LEGISLATOR, AND THAT THE SUPREME OF ALL SUCH RULERSHIPS BELONGS TO THE ROMAN BISHOP OR POPE

Having thus distinguished the meanings of these terms with which the largest part of our inquiry will deal, we now enter more securely upon our principal task. First of all, we shall adduce the authorities of the holy Scripture which might lead someone to think that the Roman bishop called pope is the supreme judge, in the third sense of "judge" or "judgment," over all the bishops or priests and other ecclesiastic ministers in the world, and also over all rulers, communities, groups, and individuals of this world, of whatever condition they may be.

2. Let us first quote the passage of Scripture in the sixteenth chapter of Matthew, where Christ says to St. Peter: "And I will give to thee the keys of the kingdom of heaven: and whatsoever thou shalt bind on earth, it shall be bound also in heaven: and whatsoever thou shalt loose on earth, it shall be loosed also in heaven." For through this passage, certain Roman bishops have assumed for themselves the authority of the supreme jurisdiction mentioned above. For by the "keys" given to St. Peter by Christ, they wish to understand plenitude of power over the whole regime of men; just as Christ had this plenitude of power over all kings and rulers, so did he grant it to St. Peter and his successors in the Roman episcopal seat, as Christ's general vicars in this world.

3. A second passage of Scripture in support of the same position is taken from the words of Christ in the eleventh chapter of Matthew, when he said: "All things are delivered to me by my father"; and again in the twenty-eighth chapter when he said: "All power is given to me in heaven and in earth." Since, therefore, St. Peter and his successors in the episcopal seat at Rome were and are Christ's vicars, as they say, it seems that all power or plenitude of power has been given to them, and consequently jurisdictional authority over everyone.

4. A third passage to the same effect is taken from the eighth chapter of Matthew and the fifth chapter of Mark, where it is written: "And the devils besought him," that is, Christ, "saying, If thou cast us out hence, send us into the herd of swine. And he said to them, Go. But they going out went into the swine: and, behold, the whole herd ran violently down a steep place into the sea, and they perished in the waters." From these words it appears that Christ disposed of temporal things as if they were all his own; for otherwise he would have sinned in destroying the herd of swine. But it is wrong to say that Christ,

whose flesh did not see corruption, sinned. Since, therefore, St. Peter and his successors the Roman bishops are and were the special vicars of Christ, as some say, they can dispose of all temporal things as judges in the third sense of the word, and they, like Christ, have plenitude of power and dominion over them all.

5.   Again, the same is shown by what is written in the twenty-first chapter of Matthew, the eleventh of Mark, and the nineteenth of Luke: "Then Jesus sent two disciples, saying to them, Go ye into the village that is over against you, and immediately you shall find an ass tied, and a colt with her"; or, "a colt tied, upon which no man yet hath sat," as in Mark and Luke. "Loose them and bring them to me." From these words the same conclusion can be reached, and by the same mode of deduction, as from the passage quoted immediately above.

6.   Moreover, the same point is proved from the twenty-second chapter of Luke, where these words are found: "Behold, here are two swords," said the apostles, replying to Christ. "And he," that is, Christ, "said to them: It is enough." By these words, according to some men's interpretation, it must be understood that there are in the present world two governments, one ecclesiastic or spiritual, the other temporal or secular. Since, therefore, Christ said to the apostles: "It is enough," namely, for you to have these two swords, he seems to have meant that both swords should belong to the authority of the apostles, and particularly to St. Peter as the leading apostle. For if Christ had not wanted the temporal sword to belong to them, he should have said: It is too much.

7.   Again, it seems that the same must be believed from the twenty-first chapter of John, where Christ spoke to St. Peter as follows: "Feed my sheep, feed my lambs, feed my sheep," repeating the same phrase three times, just as we have quoted. From these words some draw the following interpretation: that St. Peter and his successors the Roman bishops ought absolutely to be in charge over all of Christ's faithful sheep,

that is, the Christians, and especially over the priests and deacons.

8.   Moreover, this clearly seems to be the view of St. Paul in the first epistle to the Corinthians, Chapter 6, where he writes: "Know ye not that we shall judge angels? how much more secular things?" Therefore, judgments in the third sense over secular things seem to pertain to priests or bishops, and especially to the first of them, the Roman bishop. Again, the Apostle seems to have thought the same in the first epistle to the Corinthians, Chapter 9, when he said: "Have not we power to eat," etc. And the same in the second epistle to the Thessalonians, Chapter 3. In these passages he seems explicitly to hold that God gave him power over the temporalities of the faithful, and consequently jurisdiction over them.

9.   The same is again shown from the first epistle to Timothy, Chapter 5, where the Apostle wrote to Timothy: "Against a priest receive not an accusation, but under two or three witnesses." From this, then, it seems that the bishop has jurisdiction at least over priests, deacons, and other ministers of the temple, inasmuch as it pertains to him to hear accusations against them.

We shall omit to quote proofs in support of the proposed conclusion and its opposite from the Old Scripture or Testament, for a reason which we shall indicate in Chapter IX of this discourse.

And so, from the aforesaid authorities of the holy Scripture, and other similar ones, and from such interpretations of them, someone might be led to think that the highest of all rulerships belongs to the Roman bishop.

10.   Following upon these, it is fitting to adduce some quasi-political arguments which might perhaps lead men to fancy and believe the aforesaid conclusion. The first of these arguments is as follows. As the human body is to the soul, so is the ruler of bodies to the ruler of souls. But the body is subject to the soul with respect to rule. Therefore too the ruler of bodies, the secular judge, must be subject to the rule of the judge or ruler of souls, and especially of the first of them all, the Roman pontiff.

11.   Again, another argument from almost the same root: As corporeals are to spirituals, so is the ruler of corporeals to the ruler of spirituals. But it is certain that corporeals are by nature inferior and subject to spirituals. Therefore the ruler of corporeals, the secular judge, must be subject to the ruler of spirituals, the ecclesiastic judge.

12.   Moreover, as end is to end, and law to law, and legislator to legislator, so is the judge or ruler in accordance with the one of these to the judge or ruler in accordance with the other. But the end toward which the ecclesiastic judge, the priest or bishop, directs, the law by which he directs, and the maker of that law, are all superior to and more perfect than the end, the law, and the maker to which and by which the secular judge directs. Therefore the ecclesiastic judge, bishop or priest, and especially the first of them all, is superior to every secular judge. For the end toward which the ecclesiastic judge directs is eternal life; the law by which he directs is divine; and its immediate maker is God, in whom neither error nor malice can lodge. But the end toward which the secular judge aims to direct is sufficiency of this worldly life; the law by which he directs is human; and the immediate maker of this law is man or men, who are subject to error and malice. Therefore, the latter are inferior to and less worthy than the former. Therefore, too, the secular judge, even the supreme one, is inferior to and less worthy than the ecclesiastic judge, the supreme priest.

13.   Moreover, a person or thing is absolutely more honorable than another when the action of that first person or thing is absolutely more honorable than the action of the second. But the action of the priest or bishop, the consecration of the blessed body of Christ, is the most honorable of all the actions which can be performed by man in the present life. Therefore, any priest is more worthy than any non-priest. Since, therefore, the more worthy should not be subject to the less worthy, but rather above it, it seems that the secular judge should not be above the priest in jurisdiction, but rather subordinate to him, and especially to the first of them all, the Roman pontiff.

14.   The same is again shown with more specific reference to the Roman ruler, called emperor. For any person who has the authority to establish this ruler's government and to transfer it at pleasure from nation to nation is superior to this ruler in judgment, in the third sense of "judgment." But the Roman pontiff proclaims that he is such a person, inasmuch as he transferred the Roman empire from the Greeks to the Germans, as was set forth in the seventh of his decretals, *On Oaths*; and the same is stated even more explicitly by the modern so-called bishop of the Romans, in an edict of his addressed to Ludwig, duke of Bavaria, elected king of the Romans.

15.   Another argument to the same effect is that a great difficulty seems to arise if we assume that Christ's vicar, the Roman bishop, and the other bishops who are successors of the apostles, are subject to the sentence of any secular ruler. For since the secular ruler may sin against divine and human law, whereupon he must be corrected, as was said in Chapter XVIII of Discourse I, and since he, being supreme over all laymen, does not have a superior or an equal, inasmuch as a plurality of governments was rejected in Chapter XVII of Discourse I, it will seem that coercive jurisdiction over him belongs to the Roman bishop, and not conversely.

By the above, therefore, it might seem possible to prove that bishops or priests have coercive jurisdiction, and that to the supreme Roman pontiff belongs the supreme rulership of all in this world. We seem adequately to have set forth both the authorities of the holy Scripture and certain quasi-political and human arguments in support of this position.

CHAPTER IV: ON THE CANONIC SCRIPTURES, THE COMMANDS, COUNSELS, AND EXAMPLES OF CHRIST AND OF THE SAINTS AND APPROVED DOCTORS WHO EXPOUNDED THE EVANGELIC LAW, WHEREBY IT IS CLEARLY DEMONSTRATED THAT THE ROMAN OR ANY OTHER BISHOP OR PRIEST, OR CLERGYMAN, CAN BY VIRTUE OF THE WORDS OF SCRIPTURE CLAIM OR ASCRIBE TO HIMSELF NO COERCIVE RULERSHIP OR CONTENTIOUS JURISDICTION, LET ALONE THE SUPREME JURISDICTION OVER ANY CLERGYMAN OR LAYMAN; AND THAT, BY CHRIST'S COUNSEL AND

EXAMPLE, THEY OUGHT TO REFUSE SUCH RULERSHIP, ESPECIALLY IN COMMUNITIES OF THE FAITHFUL, IF IT IS OFFERED TO THEM OR BESTOWED ON THEM BY SOMEONE HAVING THE AUTHORITY TO DO SO; AND AGAIN, THAT ALL BISHOPS, AND GENERALLY ALL PERSONS NOW CALLED CLERGYMEN, MUST BE SUBJECT TO THE COERCIVE JUDGMENT OR RULERSHIP OF HIM WHO GOVERNS BY THE AUTHORITY OF THE HUMAN LEGISLATOR, ESPECIALLY WHERE THIS LEGISLATOR IS CHRISTIAN

We now wish from the opposite side to adduce the truths of the holy Scripture in both its literal and its mystical sense, in accordance with the interpretations of the saints and the expositions of other approved doctors of the Christian faith, which explicitly command or counsel that neither the Roman bishop called pope, nor any other bishop or priest, or deacon, has or ought to have any rulership or coercive judgment or jurisdiction over any priest or non-priest, ruler, community, group, or individual of whatever condition; understanding by "coercive judgment" that which we said in Chapter II of this discourse to be the third sense of "judge" or "judgment."

2. The more clearly to carry out this aim, we must not overlook that in this inquiry it is not asked what power and authority is or was had in this world by Christ, who was true God and true man, nor what or how much of this power he was able to bestow on St. Peter and the other apostles and their successors, the bishops or priests; for Christian believers have no doubts on these points. But we wish to and ought to inquire what power and authority, to be exercised in this world, Christ wanted to bestow and in fact (de facto) did bestow on them, and from what he excluded and prohibited them by counsel or command. For we are bound to believe that they had from Christ only such power and authority as we can prove to have been given to them through the words of Scripture, no other. For it is certain to all the Christian believers that Christ, who was true God and true man, was able to bestow, not only on the apostles but also on any other men, coercive authority or jurisdiction over all rulers or governments and over all the other individuals in this world; and even more perhaps, as for example the

power to create things, to destroy or repair heaven and earth and the things therein, and even to be in complete command of angels; but these powers Christ neither bestowed nor determined to bestow on them. Hence Augustine, in the tenth sermon *On the Words of the Lord in Matthew*, wrote the following: " 'Learn of me' not how to make a world, not how to create all visible and invisible things, nor how to do miracles in the world and revive the dead; but: 'because I am meek and humble of heart.' "

3. Therefore for the present purpose it suffices to show, and I shall first show, that Christ himself came into the world not to dominate men, nor to judge them by judgment in the third sense, nor to wield temporal rule, but rather to be subject as regards the status of the present life; and moreover, that he wanted to and did exclude himself, his apostles and disciples, and their successors, the bishops or priests, from all such coercive authority or worldly rule, both by his example and by his words of counsel or command. I shall also show that the leading apostles, as Christ's true imitators, did this same thing and taught their successors to do likewise; and moreover, that both Christ and the apostles wanted to be and were continuously subject in property and in person to the coercive jurisdiction of secular rulers, and that they taught and commanded all others, to whom they preached or wrote the law of truth, to do likewise, under pain of eternal damnation. Then I shall write a chapter on the power or authority of the keys which Christ gave to the apostles and their successors in office, bishops and priests, so that it may be clear what is the nature, quality, and extent of such power, both of the Roman bishop and of the others. For ignorance on this point has hitherto been and still is the source of many questions and damnable controversies among the Christian faithful, as was mentioned in the first chapter of this discourse.

4. And so in pursuit of these aims we wish to show that Christ, in his purposes or intentions, words, and deeds, wished to exclude and did exclude himself and the apostles from every office of rulership, contentious jurisdiction, government, or coercive judgment in this world. This

is first shown clearly beyond any doubt by the passage in the eighteenth chapter of the gospel of John. For when Christ was brought before Pontius Pilate, vicar of the Roman ruler in Judaea, and accused of having called himself king of the Jews, Pontius asked him whether he had said this, or whether he did call himself a king, and Christ's reply included these words, among others: "My kingdom is not of this world," that is, I have not come to reign by temporal rule or dominion, in the way in which worldly kings reign. And proof of this was given by Christ himself through an evident sign when he said: "If my kingdom were of this world, my servants would certainly fight, that I should not be delivered to the Jews," as if to argue as follows: If I had come into this world to reign by worldly or coercive rule, I would have ministers for this rule, namely, men to fight and to coerce transgressors, as the other kings have; but I do not have such ministers, as you can clearly see. Hence the interlinear gloss: "It is clear that no one defends him." And this is what Christ reiterates: "But now my kingdom is not from hence," that is, the kingdom about which I have come to teach.

8.   Moreover, the same is shown very evidently by Christ's words and example in the following passage of the twelfth chapter of Luke: "And one of the multitude said to him, Master, speak to my brother, that he divide the inheritance with me. But he," that is Christ, "said to him, Man, who hath appointed me judge or divider over you?" As if to say: I did not come to exercise this office, nor was I sent for this, that is, to settle civil disputes through judgment; but this, however, is undoubtedly the most proper function of secular rulers or judges. Now this passage from the gospel contains and demonstrates our proposition much more clearly than do the glosses of the saints, because the latter assume that the literal meaning, such as we have said, is manifest, and have devoted themselves more to the allegorical or mystical meaning. Nevertheless, we shall now quote from the glosses for a stronger confirmation of our proposition, and so that we may not be accused of expounding Scripture rashly. These words of Christ, then, are expounded by St. Ambrose as follows: "Well does he who descend-

ed for the sake of the divine avoid the earthly, and does not deign to be judge over disputes and appraiser of wealth, being the judge of the living and the dead and the appraiser of their merits." And a little below he adds: "Hence not undeservedly is this brother rebuffed, who wanted the dispenser of the heavenly to concern himself with the corruptible." See, then, what Ambrose thinks about Christ's office in this world; for he says that "well does he avoid the earthly," that is, the judgment of contentious acts, "who descended for the sake of the divine," that is, to teach and minister the spiritual; in this he designated Christ's office and that of his successors, namely, to dispense the heavenly or spiritual; that spiritual of which Ambrose spoke in his gloss on the first epistle to the Corinthians, Chapter 9, which we quoted in Chapter II of this discourse under the third meaning of this word "spiritual."

9.   It now remains to show that not only did Christ himself refuse rulership or coercive judgment in this world, whereby he furnished an example for his apostles and disciples and their successors to do likewise, but also he taught by words and showed by example that all men, both priests and non-priests, should be subject in property and in person to the coercive judgment of the rulers of this world. By his word and example, then, Christ showed this first with respect to property, by what is written in the twenty-second chapter of Matthew. For when the Jews asked him: "Tell us therefore, what dost thou think? Is it lawful to give tribute to Caesar, or not?" Christ, after looking at the coin and its inscription, replied: "Render therefore to Caesar the things that are Caesar's, and to God the things that are God's." Whereon the interlinear gloss says, "that is, tribute and money." And on the words: "Whose image and inscription is this?" Ambrose wrote as follows: "Just as Caesar demanded the imprinting of his image, so too does God demand that the soul be stamped with the light of his countenance." Note, therefore, what it was that Christ came into the world to demand. Furthermore, Chrysostom writes as follows: "When you hear: 'Render to Caesar the things that are Caesar's,' know that he means only those things which are not harmful to piety, for if they were,

the tribute would be not to Caesar but to the devil." So, then, we ought to be subject to Caesar in all things, so long only as they are not contrary to piety, that is, to divine worship or commandment. Therefore, Christ wanted us to be subject in property to the secular ruler. This too was plainly the doctrine of St. Ambrose, based upon this doctrine of Christ, for in his epistle against Valentinian, entitled *To the People*, he wrote: "We pay to Caesar the things that are Caesar's, and to God the things that are God's. That the tribute is Caesar's is not denied."

10. The same is again shown from the seventeenth chapter of Matthew, where it is written as follows: "They that received the didrachmas came to Peter, and said, Doth not your master pay the didrachmas?" and then, a little below, is written what Christ said to Peter: "But that we may not scandalize them, go to the sea and cast in a hook, and that fish which shalt first come up, take: and when thou hast opened its mouth, thou shalt find a piece of money: take that, and give it to them for me and thee." Nor did the Lord say only, " Give it to them," but he said, "Give it to them for me and thee." And Jerome on this passage says: "Our Lord was in flesh and in spirit the son of a king, whether we consider him to have been generated from the seed of David or the word of the Almighty Father. Therefore, being the son of kings, he did not owe tribute." And below he adds: "Therefore, although he was exempt, yet he had to fulfill all the demands of justice, because he had assumed the humility of the flesh." Moreover, Origen on the words of Christ: "That we may not scandalize them," spoke more to the point and in greater conformity to the meaning of the evangelist, as follows: "It is to be understood," that is, from Christ's words, "that while men sometimes appear who through injustice seize our earthly goods, the kings of this earth send men to exact from us what is theirs. And by his example the Lord prohibits the doing of any offense, even to such men, either so that they may no longer sin, or so that they may be saved. For the son of God, who did no servile work, gave the tribute money, having the guise of a servant which he assumed for the sake of man."

How, then, is it possible, on the strength of the words of the evangelic Scripture, that the bishops and priests be exempt from this tribute, and from the jurisdiction of rulers generally, unless by the rulers' own gratuitous grant, when Christ and Peter, setting an example for others, paid such tribute? And although Christ, being of royal stock in flesh, was perhaps not obliged to do this, yet Peter, not being of royal stock, had no such reason to be exempt, just as he wanted none. But if Christ had thought it improper for his successors in the priestly office to pay tribute and for their temporal goods to be subject to the secular rulers, then without setting a bad example, that is, without subjecting the priesthood to the jurisdiction of secular rulers, he could have ordained otherwise and have made some arrangement about those tax collectors, such as removing from them the intention of asking for such tribute, or in some other appropriate way. But he did not think it proper to do so, rather he wanted to pay; and from among the apostles, as the one who was to pay with him the tribute, he chose Peter, despite the fact that Peter was to be the foremost teacher and pastor of the church, as will be said in Chapter XVI of this discourse, in order that by such an example none of the others would refuse to do likewise.

11. The passage of Scripture which we quoted above from the seventeenth chapter of Matthew is interpreted in the way we have said by St. Ambrose in the epistle entitled *On Handing Over the Basilica*, where he writes as follows: "He," that is, the emperor, "demands tribute, it is not denied. The fields of the church pay tribute." And a little further on he says, more to the point: "We pay to Caesar the things that are Caesar's, and to God the things that are God's. The tribute is Caesar's, it is not denied." Expressing more fully this which we have called the meaning of the above-quoted passage of Scripture, St. Bernard in an epistle to the archbishop of Sens wrote as follows: "This is what is done by these men," namely, those who suggested that subjects rebel against their superiors. "But Christ ordered and acted otherwise. 'Render,' he said, 'to Caesar the things that are Caesar's, and to God the things that are God's.' What he spoke by word of mouth, he

soon took care to carry out in deed. The institutor of Caesar did not hesitate to pay the tax to Caesar. For he thus gave you the example that you should do likewise. How, then, could he deny the reverence due to the priests of God, when he took care to show it even for the secular powers?"

And we must note what Bernard said, that Christ, in taking care to pay the tax to the secular powers, showed "due," and therefore not coerced, "reverence." For everyone owes such tax and tribute to the rulers, as we shall show in the following chapter from the words of the Apostle in the thirteenth chapter of the epistle to the Romans, and the glosses thereon of the saints and doctors; although perhaps not every tax is owed everywhere by everyone, such as the entry tax[1] which was not owed by the inhabitants, although the custodians or collectors sometimes wrongly demanded and exacted it from simple inhabitants or natives, such as were the apostles. And therefore, in agreement with Origen, who I believed grasped the meaning of the evangelist on this point better than did Jerome, I say that it seemed customary and was perhaps commonly established in states, especially in Judaea, that entry taxes were not to be paid by inhabitants or natives, but only by aliens. And hence Christ said to Peter: "Of whom do the kings of the earth receive tribute?" etc., by "tribute" meaning that entry tax which the tax collectors were demanding. For Christ did not deny that the children of the earth, that is, natives, owe "tribute," taking the word as a common name for every tax; on the contrary, he later said of it, excepting no one: "Render to Caesar the things that are Caesar's"; and this was also expressed by the Apostle in agreement with Christ, when he said, in the thirteenth chapter of the epistle to the Romans: "For this cause also you pay tribute," that is, to rulers, "for they are the ministers of God." By "children," therefore, Christ meant the children of kingdoms, that is, persons born or raised therein, and not the children of kings by blood; otherwise his words would not seem to have been pertinent, for very often he spoke in the plural both for himself and for Peter, who was certainly not the child of such kings as those discussed by Jerome. Moreover, if Christ was of David's stock in flesh, so too were very many other Jews,

although not perhaps Peter. Again, the tribute was not then being exacted by David or by anyone of his blood; why, therefore, should Christ have said, "The kings of the land ... then the children are free,"[2] saying nothing about the heavenly king? But it is certain that neither Christ nor Peter was a child of Caesar, either in flesh or in spirit. Moreover, why should Christ have asked the above question? For everyone certainly knows that the children of kings by blood do not pay tribute to their parents. Jerome's exposition, therefore, does not seem to have been as much in agreement with Scripture as was Origen's. But the above words of Scripture show that Christ wanted to pay even undue tribute in certain places and at certain times, and to teach the Apostle and his successors to do likewise, rather than to fight over such things. For this was the justice of counsel and not of command which Christ, in the humility of the flesh which he had assumed, wanted to fulfill and to teach others to fulfill. And the Apostle, like Christ, also taught that this should be done. Hence, in the first epistle to the Corinthians, Chapter 6: "Why do ye not rather take wrong? why do ye not rather suffer yourselves to be defrauded?" than to quarrel with one another, as he had said before.

12.   Moreover, not only with respect to property did Christ show that he was subject to the coercive jurisdiction of the secular ruler, but also with respect to his own person, than which no greater jurisdiction could be had by the ruler over him or over anyone else, for which reason it is called "capital jurisdiction" (merum imperium) by the Roman legislator.[3] That Christ was thus subject can be clearly shown from the twenty-seventh chapter of Matthew; for there it is written that Christ allowed himself to be seized and brought before Pilate, who was the vicar of the Roman emperor, and he suffered himself to be judged and given the extreme penalty by Pilate as judge with coercive power; nor did Christ protest against him as not being a judge, although he perhaps indicated that he was suffering an unjust punishment. But it is certain that he could have undergone such judgment and punishment at the hands of priests, had he so desired, and had he deemed it improper for his successors to be sub-

ject to the secular rulers and to be judged by them.

But since this view is borne out at great length in the nineteenth chapter of John, I shall here adduce what is written there. When Christ had been brought before Pilate, vicar of Caesar, to be judged, and was accused of having called himself king of the Jews and son of God, he was asked by Pilate: "Whence art thou?" But having no reply from Jesus, Pilate spoke to him the following words, which are quite pertinent to our subject; here is the passage: "Pilate therefore saith to him, Speakest thou not to me? Knowest thou not that I have power to crucify thee, and I have power to release thee? Jesus answered: Thou shouldst not have any power against me, unless it were given thee from above." See, then, Jesus did not deny that Pilate had the power to judge him and to execute his judgment against him; nor did he say: This does not pertain to you of right (de jure) but you do this only in fact (de facto). But Christ added that Pilate had this power "from above." How from above? Augustine answers: "Let us therefore learn what he," that is, Christ, "said, and what he taught the Apostle," that is, Paul, in the epistle to the Romans, Chapter 13. What, then, did Christ say? What did he teach the Apostle? "That there is no power," that is, authority of jurisdiction, "except from God," whatever be the case with respect to the act of him who badly uses the power. "And that he who from malice hands over an innocent man to the power to be killed, sins more than does the power itself if it kills the man from fear of another's greater power. But God had certainly given to him," that is, Pilate, "power in such manner that he was under the power of Caesar."

The coercive judicial power of Pilate over the person of Christ, therefore, was from God, as Christ openly avowed, and Augustine plainly showed, and Bernard clearly said in his epistle to the archbishop of Sens: "For," as he wrote, "Christ avows that the Roman ruler's power over him is ordained of heaven," speaking of Pilate's power and with reference to this passage of Scripture. If, then, the coercive judiciary power of Pilate over Christ was from God, how much more so over Christ's temporal or carnal goods, if he had possessed or owned any? And if over

Christ's person and temporal goods, how much more over the persons and temporal goods of all the apostles, and of their successors, all the bishops or priests?

Not only was this shown by Christ's words, but it was confirmed by the consummation of the deed. For the capital sentence was pronounced upon Christ by the same Pilate, sitting in the judgment seat, and by his authority that sentence was executed. Hence in the same chapter of John this passage is found: "Now when Pilate had heard these words, he brought Jesus forth, and sat down in the judgment seat"; and a little below is added: "Then therefore he delivered him," that is, Jesus, "to them to be crucified." Such was the Apostle's view regarding Christ, when he said in the third chapter of the epistle to the Galatians: "But when the fullness of the time was come, God sent his son, made of a woman, made under the law," and therefore also under the judge whose function it was to judge and command in accordance with the law, but who was not, however, a bishop or a priest.

13.   Not only did Christ wish to exclude himself from secular rulership or coercive judicial power, but he also excluded it from his apostles, both among themselves and with respect to others. Hence in the twentieth chapter of Matthew and the twenty-second chapter of Luke this passage is found: "And there was also a strife among them," that is, the apostles, "which of them should seem to be the greater. And he," Christ, "said to them, The kings of the Gentiles lord it over them, and they that have power over them are called beneficent." (But in Matthew this clause is written as follows: "And they that are the greater exercise power upon them.") "But you not so: but he that is the greater among you, let him become as the younger; and he that is the leader, as he that serveth." "But whosoever will be the greater among you shall be your servant: even as the Son of man is not come to be ministered unto, but to minister," that is, to be a servant in the temporal realm, not to lord it or rule, for in spiritual ministry he was first, and not a servant among the apostles. Whereon Origen comments: "'You know that the princes of the Gentiles lord it over them,' that is, they are not content merely to rule

their subjects, but try to exercise violent lordship over them," that is, by coercive force if necessary. "But those of you who are mine will not be so; for just as all carnal things are based upon necessity, but spiritual things upon the will, so too should the rulership of those who are spiritual rulers," prelates, "be based upon love and not upon fear." And Chrysostom writes, among other remarks, these pertinent words:

> The rulers of the world exist in order to lord it over their subjects, to cast them into slavery and to despoil them [namely, if they deserve it] and to use them even unto death for their [that is, the rulers'] own advantage and glory. But the rulers [that is, prelates] of the church are appointed in order to serve their subjects and to minister to them whatever they have received from Christ, so that they neglect their own advantage and seek to benefit their subjects, and do not refuse to die for their salvation. To desire the leadership of the church is neither just nor useful. For what wise man is there who wants to subject himself of his own accord to such servitude and peril, as to be responsible for the whole church? Only he perhaps who does not fear the judgment of God and abuses his ecclesiastic leadership for secular purposes, so as to change it into secular leadership.

Why, then, do priests have to interfere with coercive secular judgments? for their duty is not to exercise temporal lordship, but rather to serve, by the example and command of Christ. Hence Jerome: "Finally he," that is, Christ, "sets forth his own example, so that if they," the apostles, "do not respect his words they may at least be ashamed of their deeds,"[4] that is, wielding temporal lordship. Hence Origen on the words: "And to give his life a redemption for many," wrote as follows:

> The rulers of the church should therefore imitate Christ, who was approachable, and spoke to women, and placed his hands upon the children, and washed the feet of his disciples, so that they might do the same for their brethren. But we are such [he is speaking of the prelates of his day] that we seem to exceed even the worldly rulers in pride, either misunderstanding or despising the commandment of Christ, and we demand fierce, powerful armies, just as do kings.

But since to do these things is to despise or be ignorant of Christ's commandment, the prelates must first be warned about it, which is what we shall do in this treatise, by showing what authority belongs to them; then, if they disregard this, they must be compelled and forced by the secular rulers to correct their ways, lest they corrupt the morals of others. These, then, are the comments made on the passage in Matthew. On Luke, Basil writes: "It is fitting that those who preside should offer bodily service, following the example of the Lord who washed the feet of his disciples."

Christ, then, said: "The kings of the Gentiles lord it over them. But you," that is, the apostles, "not so." So Christ, king of kings and lord of lords, did not give them the power to exercise the secular judgments of rulers, nor coercive power over anyone, but he clearly prohibited this to them, when he said: "But you not so." And the same must consequently be held with respect to all the successors of the apostles, the bishops or priests. This too is what St. Bernard clearly wrote to Eugene, *On Consideration*, Book II, Chapter IV, discussing the above words of Christ: "The kings of the Gentiles lord it over them," etc. For Bernard wrote, among other things:

> What the apostle [Peter] has, this did he give, namely, the guardianship, as I have said, of the churches. But not lordship? Hear him. "Neither as lording it over the clergy," he says, "but being made a pattern of the flock." And lest you think he spoke only from humility, but not with truth, the voice of the Lord is in the gospel: "The kings of the Gentiles lord it over them, and they that have power over them are called beneficent." And he adds: "But you not so." It is quite plain, then, that lordship is forbidden to the apostles. Go, then, if you dare, and usurp either the apostolate if you are a lord or lordship if you are an apostle. You are plainly forbidden to have both. If you wish to

have both at once, you shall lose both. In any case, do not think you are excepted from the number of those about whom God complains in these words: "They have reigned, but not by me: they have been princes, and I knew not."

And so from the evangelic truths which we have adduced, and the interpretations of them made by the saints and other approved teachers, it should be clearly apparent to all that both in word and in deed Christ excluded and wished to exclude himself from all worldly rulership or governance, judgment, or coercive power, and that he wished to be subject to the secular rulers and powers in coercive jurisdiction.

CHAPTER XIII: ON THE STATUS OF SUPREME POVERTY, WHICH IS USUALLY CALLED EVANGELICAL PERFECTION; AND THAT THIS STATUS WAS HELD BY CHRIST AND HIS APOSTLES

Having thus distinguished the senses and meanings of the terms given above, we shall now infer some conclusions. The first of these is that no one can lawfully handle, individually or in common with others, some temporal thing, whether his own or someone else's, or something pertaining thereto, like the use or the usufruct, without right or without having a right to the thing or to something pertaining thereto—taking "right" in its first and second senses. For every deed which is not commanded or permitted to be done by right is not lawful, as everyone can clearly see from the definition of "lawful"; nor must we linger to prove this, since it is almost self-evident to all men.

2. The second conclusion which we can infer from what we have said is that one can handle a thing, or something pertaining thereto, lawfully according to one law, such as the divine, and unlawfully according to another, such as the human; and likewise conversely; and again, one can do the same thing lawfully or unlawfully according to each law. This is not difficult to see, since the commands, prohibitions, and permissions in these laws sometimes differ and disagree with one another and sometimes agree. Consequently, when one acts in accordance with the command or permission of one kind of law, one acts lawfully according to it; but if this act is prohibited by the other kind of law, one does it unlawfully according to that other law; if it is permitted by both kinds of law, one acts lawfully according to both. But if it is prohibited by both, one does it unlawfully according to both laws. Whether anything which is permitted to be done or omitted by divine law, is commanded or prohibited by human law, and conversely, still remains to be considered; for it does not pertain to our present inquiry. It is, however, certain that many things are permitted by human law, like fornication, drunkenness, and other sins, which are prohibited by divine law.

3. And now I wish to show that even apart from having any ownership, in the first three senses, of any temporal thing or of anything pertaining thereto, a person may lawfully handle it in private (in the third sense of "private") or even possess it in common with someone else (understanding the third sense of "possession"), and also lawfully destroy it. This is so, I maintain, regardless of whether that thing, or something pertaining thereto, be consumable in some one use or not; whether it be private to him (in the third sense of "private") or be common to him with another person or persons; whether it be his own, that is, rightfully acquired by him, or belong to someone else who, having rightfully (in the first sense) acquired it, consents to his handling it.

I demonstrate this proposition as follows. That temporal thing (or something pertaining thereto) which a person handles or holds apart from having ownership of it (in the first three senses of ownership), in accordance with divine law or human law or both, he can handle and destroy lawfully, apart from having ownership of it (in the above senses) whether in private or in common with others. But, regardless of whether a thing (or something pertaining thereto) be his own or belong to someone else who consents to his handling it, a person can, in accordance with these laws, handle the thing, as has been said, apart from having the aforementioned ownership of it. Therefore he can lawfully handle the thing without having ownership of it.

The first proposition of this deduction is self-evident from the definition of "lawful." The second I prove by an argument taken from induction, first with regard to a thing which belongs to a person privately or in common with someone else, or which he has rightfully acquired through his own act or someone else's, as by gift or legacy, by hunting, or fishing, or by some other lawful labor or deed of his. For suppose that a person has thus acquired a thing. It is then certain that he can use and handle it in accordance with the laws, as is plain from induction. Also it is clear that anyone who has the capacity can lawfully renounce a right introduced on his behalf, since, according to human and divine law, a benefit is not bestowed on an unwilling person. Therefore, a person who can by his own or by another's deed acquire ownership of a thing, or of its use, will be able to renounce such ownership. Since, therefore, the same person, if he wants to, acquires both the power lawfully to use a thing and the power to claim it and to prohibit another person from it, he can lawfully renounce the power of laying claim to the thing (or something pertaining thereto) or of prohibiting another therefrom (which power is none other than ownership taken in its first three legal senses), without renouncing the power of using the thing (or something pertaining thereto). This latter power falls under the right taken in its second sense, and is by some men called "simple use of a thing" (*simplex facti usus*) without the right of using (*jus utendi*), by "right of using" meaning "ownership" in any of its three senses given above.

4.   Moreover, a thing which belongs to no one (*in nullius bonis est*) a person can lawfully use in accordance with the laws; but when someone has renounced the power to lay claim to a thing and to prohibit another person therefrom, that thing can then belong to no one; therefore a person can lawfully use it. Since, therefore, a person who renounces the aforesaid power does not have the aforesaid ownership of the thing, it is apparent that one can lawfully handle and use a thing apart from having any of the aforesaid legal ownership.

5.   Again, those things are separate from each other, of which one can for any time be given up by lawful vow, and the other not. But the aforesaid ownership of a thing, or the power to lay claim to and prohibit from a temporal thing or something pertaining thereto, can be given up for any time by lawful vow; while the lawful having or simple use of a thing cannot by lawful vow be given up for any time. Therefore these two cases are properly separate from each other. The first proposition of this deduction is self-evident from the definition of "lawful"; for the same thing cannot at once be lawful and unlawful according to the same law. The second proposition I shall prove with respect to each part. And first, that to give up for any time the aforesaid ownership by vow is lawful: for that vow is lawful which can be derived from the counsel of Christ. But such giving up is what Christ counseled, when in Matthew, Chapter 20, he said: "And every one that hath forsaken house or lands ... for my name's sake, shall receive an hundredfold, and shall inherit everlasting life." The same counsel is to be found in Matthew, Chapter 5, and Luke, Chapter 6, when Christ said: "And him that taketh away thy cloak, forbid not to take thy coat also." "And if any man will sue thee at the law, and take away thy coat, let him have thy cloak also." Whereon Augustine: "If he gives this command with regard to necessary things," that is, he counsels that one should not sue at law, "how much more so with regard to superfluities?" And in accordance with this teaching of Christ, the Apostle said in I Corinthians, Chapter 6: "Now therefore there is utterly a fault among you, because you go to law one with another. Why do ye not rather take wrong? Why do ye not rather suffer yourselves to be defrauded?" (supply: rather than sue someone at law, even justly, in order to lay claim to a temporal thing?). Whereon the gloss according to Augustine, after quoting the above passages of the gospel, adds: "This," that is, to sue at law justly, "the Apostle tolerates in the weak, since such judgments have to be made among brethren in the church with brethren sitting as judges." And then, because of some doubts regarding Augustine's meaning, the gloss adds:

Correctly to understand the above words of Augustine, where he says that "it is a sin to go to law with a brother," it must here be stated what is fitting for the perfect in such matters and what is not, and what is allowed to the weak and what is not. The perfect, then, are allowed to demand what is theirs simply, that is, without suit, litigation or judgment; but it is not fitting for them to have recourse to a lawsuit before a judge. The weak, however, are allowed to demand what is theirs both by starting a lawsuit before a judge and by having judgments against a brother.

Therefore, a lawful vow can be taken with respect to the giving up of ownership. But if it is not lawful for the perfect to sue before a coercive judge, then they do not have the power lawfully to lay claim to a thing, which power is the ownership discussed above; for they have renounced such power by a vow which they are allowed at no time to contravene, especially while it still stands.

And as for the other part of the second proposition, that the lawful having of a thing or of its use, or the simple use of a thing, cannot be given up for any time—this is clear enough: for nothing which is prohibited by divine law can lawfully fall under a vow. But such giving up is prohibited by divine law, because it is a species of homicide. For he who observed such a vow would knowingly kill himself from hunger or cold or thirst; which is explicitly prohibited by divine law, as in Matthew, Chapter 19, Mark, Chapter 10, and Luke, Chapter 18, where Christ, confirming some commands of the old law, says: "Thou shalt not kill," etc. Therefore, the simple use of a thing, or the lawful having of it, is separate from all the afore-mentioned kinds of ownership, or the power of laying claim to and prohibiting from the thing or something pertaining thereto.

6.   From this too it clearly follows of necessity that it is insane heresy to assert that a thing or its use cannot be had apart from the aforesaid ownership. For he who says this thinks nothing other than that Christ's counsel cannot be fulfilled; which is an open lie and, as we have said, must be shunned as vicious and heretical.

7.   Nor is any difficulty presented by the objection that, while one may lawfully vow to give up an *act* of litigation, yet one cannot thus vow to give up the *habit* or the active legal *power* to claim the thing and prohibit it from someone else before a coercive judge, which power we have called ownership. For this statement is false, since every habit or legal power, acquired or acquirable, the act of which can be given up by lawful vow, can itself be given up in the same way, as is apparent by induction in all objects of deliberation which fall under vows. For he who vows chastity or obedience gives up by his vow not only the acts, but also the lawful power to perform these acts which had previously belonged to him by right (taken in the first sense). Again, it is inconsonant with the truth to say that a person has lawful power to perform acts all of which are unlawful, since a power is not called lawful or unlawful, nor is the difference between these known, otherwise than through the lawfulness or unlawfulness of the acts which emerge or can emerge from that power. Since, therefore, all the acts which emerge from the lawful power which a person had before his vow, are unlawful after the vow has been taken, it is clear that the person taking the vow has retained no lawful power to perform these acts.

8.   Next I show that apart from having any ownership (in the senses given above), a person can have lawful use of something which belongs to another man, even to the extent of consuming the thing itself, if he exercises this use with the consent of the owner. For since the thing is assumed to be entirely in the ownership (or power to claim) of another person, it is certain that such ownership is not transferred to anyone else except by the deed and the express consent of its owner, and with no dissent on the part of the person to whom such ownership (or power to claim) of such a thing or of its use is to be transferred. Suppose, therefore, that the owner does not wish to transfer such ownership of a thing or of its use to some other person. Suppose, too, that this other person dissents from receiving such ownership, as for instance, because he has given up the ownership of all temporal things by an explicit

vow, as befits those who are perfect. Suppose, further, that an owner consents to have some perfect person use some thing of his, even to the extent of consuming the thing, and that the perfect person, who has given up ownership of every thing, wishes to use such thing with the owner's consent. I say, then, that the person who thus uses the thing, uses it lawfully, and that he nevertheless has no ownership whatsoever (in the senses given above) of the thing or of its use. That he has no ownership of the thing, or of its use, is apparent from the assumed conditions with regard both to the will of the owner and to the condition of the person who is to receive the use of the thing, who has completely given up such ownerships. That he uses the thing lawfully is apparent from the definition of "lawful," since everyone is permitted by law to use a thing belonging to someone else even to the extent of consuming it, if there intervenes the express consent of the owner of the thing.

9. Now if we take ownership or control in its last sense, as meaning the human will or freedom, with that natural motive power which is not acquired but innate in us, then I say that neither lawfully nor unlawfully can we freely handle a thing, or something pertaining thereto, without having such ownership or control, nor can we give up such ownership or control. And for the sake of brevity, I pass over this without proof, since it is almost self-evident, inasmuch as without these powers no one can continue to exist.

10. From these statements, then, it can be seen that not all lawful or rightful (in the first or second sense or both) power over a temporal thing or over its use is ownership, although conversely all lawful ownership (in the first three legal senses) of a thing or of its use or both, is lawful or rightful power. And hence, when one argues in this fashion: there is lawful or rightful power over a thing or its use, therefore there is lawful or rightful ownership of the thing or of its use—one makes an invalid inference. For a person can lawfully have and handle a thing, whether it is his in private or in common or whether it belongs to another—in which case the owner or the person

who has lawfully acquired it must give his consent—without acquiring any legal ownership of it.

11. Having set forth these premises, we now enter more fully upon our main task. We say first that the existence of poverty or of poor persons is almost self-evident, and is found in many passages of Scripture, from which it will suffice to quote one, in Mark, Chapter 12, where Christ says: "Verily I say unto you, that this poor widow hath cast more in than all of them."

12. Next I show similarly by Scripture that poverty is meritorious as a means toward eternal life, for the Truth has said, in Luke, Chapter 6: "Blessed be the poor: for yours is the kingdom of God," that is, you merit it, for in this life no one except christ is actually blessed, but rather merits it.

13. And from this it necessarily follows that poverty is a virtue, if one becomes habituated thereto by many acts of thus willing to lack temporal goods; or else poverty is an act which is productive of a virtue or elicited from a virtue; for everything which is meritorious is a virtue or an act of virtue. Again, every counsel of Christ pertains essentially to virtue; but poverty is such a counsel, as is sufficiently clear from Matthew, Chapters 5 and 19 and from many other passages of the evangelic Scripture.

14. From this it necessarily follows that the poverty to which we here refer as a virtue is that voluntary poverty which was defined in the third and fourth senses of poverty given above. For there is no virtue or deed of virtue without choice, and there is no choice without consent, as is sufficiently clear from the second and third books of the *Ethics*. This can be confirmed by Matthew, Chapter 5, where Christ said: "Blessed are the poor in spirit," by "spirit" meaning will or consent, although some of the saints interpret "spirit" to mean pride, which interpretation is not, however, very appropriate, inasmuch as there immediately follow in the same chapter these words: "Blessed are the meek."[5] But whatever be the interpretation of this passage, there is

no doubt, according to the views of the saints, that if poverty is deserving of the kingdom of the heavens, as Christ says, it must be not primarily the external lack of temporal goods, but an internal habit of the mind, whereby one freely wishes to be lacking in such goods for the sake of Christ. Whence on the words in Luke, Chapter 6: "Blessed are the poor," etc., Basil writes: "Not everyone who is oppressed by poverty is blessed. For there are many persons who are poor in means, but most avaricious in desire, and these are not saved by their poverty, but damned by their desire. For nothing which is involuntary can be blessed, since every virtue is marked by free will." Poverty, then, is a meritorious virtue, and consequently voluntary. But external lack is not in itself a virtue, inasmuch as it does not lead to salvation without the proper desire; for a person might be lacking in temporal goods under coercion and against his will, and yet he would be condemned because of his inordinate desire for these goods. This was also the view of the Apostle on this subject, when in II Corinthians, Chapter 8, he said: "For if there be first a willing mind, it is accepted according to that a man hath"— "accepted," that is, meritorious.

15. Moreover, if this choice to be lacking in temporal goods is to be meritorious, it must be made for the sake of Christ. Hence the Truth says in Matthew, Chapter 19: "And everyone that hath forsaken houses ... for my name's sake." Whereon Jerome: "He who has forsaken carnal things for the sake of the Savior, will receive spiritual things, whose worth is to that of carnal things as the number one hundred is to a small number." And further on: "Those who because of faith in Christ have shunned all secular desires, riches, and pleasures in order to preach the gospel, will be benefited a hundredfold and will possess eternal life."

16. Again, since that which is opposed to avarice is essentially meritorious, it is essentially a virtue; such is voluntary poverty for the sake of Christ; for avarice is a vice. This virtue of voluntary poverty bears an analogy to moral liberality, although it differs from it in its end and is of a more perfect species, at least so far as concerns the mean in the thing itself, as will be clear from what follows; and hence both of them cannot be placed in the same indivisible species.[6]

17. From these considerations, therefore, it can be seen that meritorious poverty is the virtue whereby a person wishes for the sake of Christ to be deprived of and to lack all the temporal goods, usually called riches, which are over and above what is necessary for his subsistence.

18. Whence too it manifestly follows that this virtue is not the habit or act of charity, as some seem to think. For poverty is not the habit or act which is essentially and primarily opposed to the actual or habitual hatred of God, because if it were, then more than one thing would be primarily opposed to one thing. For although the vice which is opposed to each theological virtue is incompatible with charity, yet from this it does not follow that charity is every theological virtue, since such vices are not opposed to charity primarily.

19. Nor is any difficulty presented by the argument that the virtue whereby we tend toward God through love, and the virtue whereby we recede from an inordinate desire for temporal things, are essentially the same virtue, just as the motion whereby a thing leaves some terminus and the motion whereby it tends in the opposite direction are essentially the same motion; and that since by charity we essentially tend toward God, therefore it is by this same virtue, and not by a different one, that we seem to depart from the love of temporal things.

20. The weakness of this argument can be seen primarily through our previous statement. For although by charity we essentially and primarily tend toward God through love, yet its opposite, from which we essentially and primarily depart, is hatred of God, not the unlawful love of temporal things. This is so even though this latter departure sometimes is a consequence of charity, because when one departs from the love of temporal goods, there follows virtuous poverty, which is essentially and primarily such a voluntary giving up of temporal things as is necessari-

ly followed by the departure from what is opposed to it essentially and primarily, namely, the unlawful love of temporal things. For if our opponent reasoned truly, the conclusion from true premises would be as follows: that charity is well-nigh every virtue, since charity is necessarily followed by most of the virtues, like faith and hope, whereby we essentially and primarily depart from heresy and despair, respectively.

21. Moreover, charity cannot fall under vow, because it is a command. But the afore-mentioned poverty, especially as taken in the fourth sense, falls under a vow. Therefore, charity is not essentially virtuous poverty, nor conversely, although poverty follows upon charity just as do most of the other theological virtues.

22. Moreover, I say that the highest mode or species of this virtue is the explicit vow of the wayfarer, whereby for the sake of Christ he renounces and wishes to be deprived of and to lack all acquired legal ownership, both in private and in common, or the power to claim and to prohibit another from temporal things (called "riches") before a coercive judge. And by this vow, also, the wayfarer wishes, for the sake of Christ, to be deprived of and to lack, both in private and in common, all power, holding, handling, or use of temporal things over and above what is necessary quantitatively and qualitatively for his present subsistence. Nor does he wish at one time to have such goods, however lawfully they may come to him, in an amount sufficient to supply several of the future needs or necessities either of himself alone or of himself together with a determinate other person or persons in common. Rather, he wishes to have at one time only what is necessary for a single need, as the immediately actual and present need of food and shelter; but with this sole exception, that the person who takes this vow should be in such place, time, and personal circumstance that he can acquire for himself, on each successive day, a quantity of temporal things sufficient to supply his aforesaid individual need, but only one at a time, not more. This mode or species of meritorious poverty is the status which is considered to be necessary for evangelical perfection, as will

clearly be seen from what follows. Agnate this mode of meritorious poverty, or this status of a person who does not have possessions in private (in the third sense) or even in common with another (in the sense of "common" which is opposed to the above sense of "private"), we shall henceforth, for the sake of brevity, call "supreme poverty," and the person who wishes to have this status we shall call, in keeping with the custom of theologians, "perfect."

23. That this mode of meritorious poverty is the supreme one can be shown from this, that through it all the other meritorious counsels of Christ are observed. For in the first place, men give up by a vow all the temporal things which it is possible for a wayfarer to give up; secondly, most of the impediments to divine charity are removed for those who take this vow; thirdly, they are put in condition to endure many secular passions, humiliations, and hardships, and are willingly deprived of many secular pleasures and vanities; and in a word, they are put in the best condition to observe all the commands and counsels of Christ. That he who takes such a vow completely gives up temporal things to the extent that it is possible and lawful for the wayfarer to do so, is evident. For he wishes to have at one time nothing except what is necessary to supply a single present or almost present need of food and clothing; less than this no faithful wayfarer is allowed to have, since if he wished to have less than was necessary for sustenance of his life, he would knowingly be a homicide, which by divine law at least no one is allowed to be. Therefore, he who wishes to have temporal things in such quantity that he is not allowed to have less, wishes to have the minimum of them; and he who gives up such a quantity of them that he is not allowed to give up more, gives up the maximum. But this is what the wayfarer does in accordance with the aforesaid mode of meritorious poverty, which we have called the supreme mode. But that this is in accord with the counsel of Christ is evident. For he gave a counsel concerning this vow in Luke, Chapter 14, when he said: "So likewise, whosoever he be of you that forsaketh not all that he hath, he cannot be my disciple."

24. That the person who takes this vow removes from his path most of the impediments to divine charity, is evident. For the love and will to save temporal things turns a man toward them, and consequently turns him so much the more away from love or affection for God. Whence the Truth in Matthew, Chapter 6: "Where your treasure is, there will your heart be also." To no avail is the excuse that the person who has these things does not turn his love toward them. For listen to Christ, who in Matthew, Chapter 13, and Mark, Chapter 4, says that "the deceitfulness of riches chokes the word." Whereon Jerome: "Riches are flatterers which do one thing and promise another." And hence, Christ counseled complete renunciation of temporal things for the person who wishes to be perfect, in Luke, Chapter 18: "Sell all that thou hast, and distribute unto the poor." Whereon Bede: "Whoever wishes to be perfect, then, must sell the things which he has: not partly, as Ananias and Sapphira did, but completely." And on the same passage, Theophylact adds these pertinent words: "He urges supreme poverty. For if there remains anything," that is, any temporal things, "he is its slave," namely, the person who saves such things for himself. For such things by their very nature move inordinately the emotions of their possessors. Expounding the same counsel of Christ in Matthew, Chapter 19, Raban adds a remark in support of the same position which is quite pertinent. He writes: "There is a difference between having money and loving money. But it is safer neither to have nor to love riches." For, as Jerome says on the same passage: "It is difficult to despise riches when one possesses them." For "they are stickier than lime," as Thomas says, discussing the same counsel of Christ in Luke, Chapter 18. Therefore, the person who gives up riches so far as it is possible and lawful for the wayfarer to do so, removes from his path the greatest impediments to charity.

25. Also he exposes himself to many secular passions, humiliations and hardships; he willingly deprives himself of many worldly pleasures and advantages. While this is self-evident from experience, let us quote the wise Solomon in Ecclesiastes, Chapter 10: for "all things," he says,

"obey money," that is, the person who has money. And on the other hand, as it is written in Proverbs, Chapter 15: "All the days of the poor are evil"; for the poor man "has many afflictions," as the gloss thereon says. Again in Proverbs, Chapter 19: "Wealth maketh many friends; but the poor man is separated from his neighbor." But that it is meritorious and advisable to bear sorrows in this world and to abstain from pleasures, is evident from Matthew, Chapters 5 and 19, and Luke, Chapter 6, where it is written with regard to the bearing of sorrows: "Blessed are the poor," "Blessed are they that mourn," "Blessed are they which are persecuted," "Blessed are ye that hunger," together with the other statements there added; and with regard to abstinence from pleasures: "Everyone that hath forsaken houses and brethren," with the other things there listed, "shall receive an hundredfold, and shall inherit everlasting life." This same position is expounded by the glosses of the saints thereon, which I have omitted to quote for the sake of brevity and because this matter is sufficiently well known. This too was the view of the Apostle, in Romans, Chapter 8: "For I reckon," he writes, "that the sufferings of this present time are not worthy to be compared with the glory which shall be revealed in us." And therefore the adversities of this world are meritorious for those who willingly bear them. The same view was taken in II Corinthians, Chapter I, when the Apostle said "that as ye are partakers of the sufferings, so shall ye be also of the consolation." Whereon Ambrose: "For your hardships will be repaid with equal," that is, proportional, "glory." But groups of persons who have ownership of temporal things in common do not entirely put themselves in condition thus to bear secular sufferings and hardships: indeed, they do so in lesser degree than do many poor secular married couples who sometimes have private possessions, and who nevertheless are more often in need of things required for sufficiency of life than are they who only possess such things in common.

26. Furthermore, that through this mode of meritorious poverty, which we have called the supreme mode, all the commands and counsels

of Christ can be observed to the highest degree, will be apparent to anyone who reads the gospel, especially the chapters we have indicated. For how can a person who has chosen to endure such poverty be avaricious or proud, incontinent or intemperate, ambitious, pitiless, unjust, timid, slothful, or jealous; why should he be mendacious or intolerant, for what reason malevolent toward others? On the contrary, he who has put himself in this condition seems to have an open door to all the virtues, and also to the serene fulfillment of all the commands and counsels. This is so plain to anyone who considers it that I omit the proof, for the sake of brevity.

27. Thus, therefore, the supreme mode or species of meritorious poverty is that which we have described above; for through it, all the commands and meritorious counsels of Christ can be more fully and more securely observed. And from this description it is apparent, first, that the perfect person ought, by an explicit vow, to renounce temporal things so far as their ownership is concerned, both because this is the counsel of Christ, as we have shown above from Luke, Chapter 14, and because the perfect person by thus manifesting his poverty renders himself more contemptible in the sight of others and makes a fuller abandonment of secular honors. Whence in Luke, Chapter 9: "If any man will come after me, let him deny himself." From this, moreover, it follows that no one can observe supreme poverty before attaining the complete use of reason. And from this description it also follows that the perfect person ought neither to have nor to acquire or save anything for himself, that is, for the purpose of supplying his future needs, but should look out only for the immediate present, except in the case which we have mentioned in the description above. Whence in Matthew, Chapter 7: "Take therefore no thought for the morrow: for the morrow shall take thought for the things of itself." Whereon the gloss: " 'for the morrow,' that is, for the future; but he grants that thought must be taken with regard to the present. It is not proper to take thought for the future, since the divine ordinance provides for this; but gratefully accepting what the present offers, let us leave the care of the

uncertain future to God, who takes care of us." And the same counsel is given in Matthew, Chapter 7, when Christ said to his disciples: "Behold the fowls of the air: for they sow not, neither do they reap, nor gather into barns; yet your heavenly father feedeth them." And a little below he adds: "Therefore take no thought, saying, What shall we eat, or what shall we drink, or wherewith shall we be clothed? For after all these things do the Gentiles seek."

28. Now when we said that the perfect person is not allowed to provide for himself for the morrow, we did not mean that if anything remained from his lawful daily acquisitions, he ought to throw it away and in no manner save it, but that he ought to save it only with the firm intention of properly distributing it to any poor person or persons he met who were more needy than he. Whence in Luke, Chapter 3: "He that hath two coats, let him impart to him that hath none: and he that hath meat, let him do likewise"; understanding by "two coats" and "meat" that which remains over and above one's own present needs.

We said that the surplus must be given to *any* poor person; for a community of men who save or have goods for certain definite persons only, such as the community of monks, canons, and the like, is not a perfect community; for the perfect community, like that of Christ and his apostles, extends to all the faithful, as is clear from the Acts, Chapter 4. And if it chanced to extend to infidels also, it would perhaps be still more meritorious, according to Luke, Chapter 6: "Do good to them which hate you."

But the perfect person lawfully can and should keep surplus goods, so long as he has the firm intention of dealing with them as we have said. Whence in John, Chapter 6: "Gather up the fragments that remain, that nothing be lost. Therefore they gathered them together, and filled twelve baskets with the fragments of the twelve barley loaves." This view was also expressed by the gloss on the words in Matthew, Chapter 18: "Take that piece of money"; for the gloss says: "So great was the poverty of the Lord that he did not have wherewith to give tribute. Judas had the common goods in the bags, but he said that it was wrong to convert to one's own uses the goods of the poor." Which shows that what had been stored up belonged to the poor, that is, it was saved with that intention.

29. And from this it is clear that they are wrong who say that perfection is attained by vowing to accept nothing for distribution to the poor who are weak or otherwise incapable of acquiring for themselves the necessities of life. For, as is clear from II Corinthians, Chapters 8 and 9, the Apostle acquired goods with this purpose, and there is no doubt that he did so lawfully and meritoriously. And this is also apparent from the gloss on the words in John, Chapter 21: "Feed my sheep," etc. But since the matter is quite evident, I omit to quote these passages, for the sake of brevity.

30. From our above description of supreme poverty it also necessarily follows that the perfect person neither can nor ought to save or keep in his power any real estate, like house or field, unless he has the firm intention of giving it away as soon as he can, or exchanging it for money or for something else which can immediately and conveniently be distributed to the poor. For since house or field could not as such be conveniently distributed to the poor without incurring the difficulty of giving too much to some and too little to others, we must follow the counsel of Christ, and do what he advised when he said, in Matthew, Chapter 19, Luke, Chapter 8, and Mark, Chapter 10: "Go and sell." Nor did Christ say: Give to the poor everything that you have; nor did he say: Throw away everything that you have; but rather he said: "Go and sell," for by selling the distribution of wealth can be more conveniently made. Such too was the counsel of the apostles, and those to whom they gave this counsel followed it out, wishing to distribute their goods to the poor conveniently. Whence in Acts, Chapter 4: "For as many as were possessors of lands or houses sold them, and brought the prices of the things that were sold. And distribution was made unto every man according as he had need."

31. From the above it is also apparent that no perfect person can acquire the ownership (in the first, second, and third senses) of any temporal thing, as we have proved above from Matthew, Chapter 5, and Luke, Chapter 6. And we have confirmed this through the Apostle in I Corinthians, Chapter 6; and we made it sufficiently clear by the words of Augustine and the gloss on that scriptural passage. Since the matter is evident, I have omitted to quote these passages for the sake of brevity.

32. Nor should we pay attention to the argument that perfect men may lawfully save real estate in order to distribute the annual income thereof to the poor. For it is more meritorious because of love of Christ and pity for one's neighbor to distribute at once to the poor both the real estate and the income thereof, rather than the latter alone; and besides, it is more meritorious to give away the real estate alone rather than its income alone. For in this way help can be given to many poor and needy persons at once, who might perhaps through want become ill or die before the income became available, or commit an act of violence, theft, or some other evil. Again, a person who kept the real estate might die before the time when the income was distributed, and thus he would never have the merit therefrom that he could have had.

Entirely the same view must be held with respect to any kind of chattels, which similarly, when thus kept, naturally affect to an inordinate degree the desire of the person who holds them. But if the virtue here considered is believed to be charity, as some seem to think, then undoubtedly this mode of charity, that is, with supreme poverty, is more perfect than having private or common ownership of a temporal thing, as is plain from the preceding reasonings.

33. But now advancing to the principal proposition, we wish to show that Christ while he was a wayfarer observed the supreme species or mode of meritorious poverty.[7] For that which is first in each sphere is greatest; but Christ under the New Law was the first of the wayfarers who merited eternal life; therefore he was the greatest of all in perfection; therefore observed this status with respect to temporal things, for without this it is impossible, according to the common law, to attain the greatest degree of meritoriousness.

Again, if he had not observed this mode of poverty, then some other wayfarer could have been or might in the future be more perfect in merit than Christ according to the common law, which it is impious to believe. For Christ asserted that this status was required for perfection in merit, when he said: "If you wish to be perfect, sell all whatsoever that thou hast and distribute unto the poor"; nor did he add: the things that thou hast in private or in common, but he meant this to be taken universally, so that he stressed its universal meaning by saying: "all whatsoever." For he who has the ownership or keeping of temporal things in common with another person or persons, in a way other than the one described by us, has not given up all the temporal things which it is possible to give up, nor is he exposed to so many secular sufferings or deprived of so many advantages as is he who renounces temporal things both as private property and in common, nor is he thus free from solicitude for these things, nor does he observe all the counsels of Christ equally as much as does he who completely gives us temporal things.

34.   And now I wish to show that while Christ observed supreme poverty, he did have some possessions both as private property and in common. That he had private property (in the third sense) is shown by the passage in Mark, Chapter 2: "For there were many, and they followed him. And the scribes and sinners saw him eat with publicans and sinners." Now it is certain that he lawfully had as private or individual property that which he put to his mouth and ate. Moreover, his clothes were his private or individual property, as is sufficiently clear from Matthew, Chapter 27, Mark, Chapter 15, Luke, Chapter 23, and John, Chapter 19. Whence in Matthew, in the chapter mentioned: "They took the robe off from him, and put his own raiment on him." Thus too in John, in the chapter just mentioned: "Then the soldiers, when they had crucified Jesus, took his garments." Thus too in Mark and Luke, whose passages are omitted for the sake of brevity. Christ, therefore, even while observing supreme poverty, lawfully or rightfully had temporal things as his private property, and wanted them and it was fitting that he want them; otherwise he would have sinned mortally, for being a true man he was subject to hunger, as is apparent from Matthew, Chapter 21, and Mark, Chapter 18, and hence he needed food, which he had to take when he was able to do so, for otherwise he would have gravely sinned, by knowingly starving himself to death.

35.   Christ also lawfully had some things in common while observing supreme poverty. Whence in John, Chapter 12: "This Judas said, not that he cared for the poor; but because he was a thief, and had the bags," that is, the common belongings of Christ and the apostles and the other poor persons. That these were held in common is apparent from the fact that Christ ordered some of them to be distributed to the hungry crowds of the poor, as is sufficiently clear from Matthew, Chapter 14. The "bags" were the repositories wherein was kept the alms money which had been given to them. This is again shown by the fourteenth chapter of the same book: "For some of them thought that Judas had the bag." Also it is shown by the gloss on the passage in Matthew, Chapter 18: "Take that piece of money," etc., whereon the gloss says: "Judas had the common goods in the bags." Thus too the apostles, while observing supreme poverty, had belongings in common among themselves and with other poor persons, after the resurrection of Christ. Whence in Acts, Chapter 4: "But they had all things in common." And similarly they had some things as private property, namely, their own food and clothing, which they applied for their private use, just as did Christ.

36.   Next I wish to give a necessary proof of what constitutes the principal thesis of this chapter and the ones immediately preceding and following, namely, that Christ the wayfarer, giving a preeminent manifestation of the height of perfection, had no acquired ownership (in the first, second, or third sense), in private or in common, of any temporal thing or of its use. For if he had assumed for himself such ownership, he would not have observed all the counsels, and especially that form of poverty which is the highest one possible for the wayfarer. But Christ observed all these counsels in the most perfect manner of any

wayfarer. Therefore, Christ did not have or want to have such ownership of temporal things, which the Scripture in many passages calls "possession," as in Luke, Chapter 14: "Whosoever he be of you that forsaketh not all that he possesseth"; so too in Matthew, Chapter 10: "Possess neither gold, nor silver, nor brass in your purses," that is, do not keep these unless perhaps for a lawful occasion, namely, for the purpose and needs mentioned above, such as for the sake of the powerless poor, as Paul did, or from urgent necessity of time, place, and personal condition; which cases will be made clearer in the following chapter. Although even in the afore-mentioned cases the person who has taken a vow of supreme poverty is not allowed to have ownership, for such ownership necessarily excludes the fulfillment of Christ's counsel regarding supreme poverty. Christ, therefore, did not have the aforesaid ownership of temporal things, nor can it be had by any imitator of him, that is, by anyone who wishes to observe supreme poverty.

37. In consequence of these considerations, I say that it cannot be proved from the holy Scripture that Christ, however condescending he may have been to the weak, had the aforesaid ownership or possession of temporal goods in private or in common, although some of the saints are believed to have held this view. For by parity of reasoning one might conclude that Christ did everything which was permitted lest he should seem to have condemned the status of persons who did such things. If this argument were sound, Christ would have accepted and exercised secular rulership or contentious jurisdiction over litigation, whereas the opposite of this was irrefutably shown in Chapter IV of this discourse; so too, he would have married, would have engaged in lawsuits before a coercive judge, and would have done everything else that was permitted; but that Christ did these things no one can prove by Scripture, but rather the opposite. For it was not necessary or fitting for him to do such things in order that he should not seem to have condemned the status of those persons who did them, and who are called "weak." For it does not follow that

because Christ was not married, therefore he seemed to be condemning the status of those who were married; and similarly in the other cases. For he himself sufficiently expressed the difference between the things which it is necessary to do or omit for salvation—the commands or prohibitions—and the things which are not necessary for salvation, which the saints call "supererogatory." For when someone asked Christ what things were necessary for eternal salvation, Christ replied: "If thou wilt enter into life, keep the commandments." And again when the person asked him what things were supererogatory, Christ did not reply: If thou wilt enter into life, but he said to him: "If thou wilt be perfect." In these words in Matthew, Chapter 19, Luke, Chapter 18, and Mark, Chapter 10, Christ explicitly showed that for eternal life the observance of the commandments was sufficient, for he made no reply, to the person asking about this, other than to say: "Keep the commandments, if thou wilt enter into life." And hence it was not necessary or fitting for Christ to do all the things that were permitted, in order that he should not seem to have condemned the status of persons who did such things, for he had already made it clear that men can be saved by observing only the commandments or commands, taking "command" in its more general sense as both affirmative and negative; but it was more fitting for Christ to observe the counsels, as for example to maintain supreme poverty and not to marry, in order to afford to all others an example of such observance; which, as we read in Scripture, he actually carried out both in word and in deed. For speaking of his poverty in Matthew, Chapter 8, and Luke, Chapter 9, he said: "The foxes have holes, and the birds of the air have nests; but the Son of man hath not where to lay his head." Whereon the gloss: "I am so poor that I do not have a shelter of my own." For "so great was the poverty of the Lord that he did not have wherefrom to give tribute," as the gloss says on the words in Matthew, Chapter 18: "Take that piece of money, and give to them for me and you." But we never read that Christ had a castle or fields or treasure chests in order that he might not seem to be condemning the status of those who did have such things.

38.   But if Christ had done things that were permitted, he could none the less have equally obeyed all the counsels, for he, who was the legislator, was able to do such things in order that he should not seem to be condemning the status of those who did them. Hence he would not have wanted in an unqualified sense to do such things, as do the weak who want them for their own advantage; but he would have wanted to do such things for a different purpose, wanting them and at the same time, in a certain way, not wanting them, since he wanted them not for himself but for the aforesaid reason. But all other perfect men can in no way properly want such ownership, if they are to observe the counsels to the full. For they cannot want such ownership in order that they may not seem to be condemning the status of others, as it does not pertain to them to approve or condemn anyone's status, because they neither were nor are nor will be legislators. If therefore they wanted such ownership, they would want it as weak persons, not as perfect ones. So, then, it would have been lawful for Christ to do these things that were permitted, if he had wanted to, while at the same time observing all the counsels to the full; but it can be lawful for no one else to do so, for the reason already stated.

39.   But if it be asked who can be so perfect as to wish to have, at one time, only such an amount of temporal goods as is merely sufficient for one's own present or immediate need, I reply that Christ and other men did so desire, although such men are few, because "strait is the gate, and narrow is the way ... and few there be that find it," as it is written in Matthew, Chapter 7. And do you tell me, I beg: How many voluntary martyrs are there in these times, how many heroic men, how many Catos, Scipios, and Fabricii?

Notes

1   This is the *pedagium*, a tax paid to the ruler of a territory by those who came into the territory from outside.

2   Matthew 17:24-25. The complete text, required to make sense of the fragment quoted by Marsilius, is as follows: "The kings of the earth, of whom do they receive tribute or custom? Of their own children, or of strangers? And he said: Of strangers. Jesus said to him: Then the children are free."

3   For this untranslatable phrase see *Corp. jur. civ., Digest* II. i. 3: "Capital jurisdiction is to have the power of the sword to punish criminal men, which jurisdiction is also called power" (*Merum est imperium habere gladii potestatem ad animadvertendum facinorosos homines, quod etiam potestas appelatur*).

4   Marsilius' misinterpretation of Jerome's meaning necessitates a mistranslation of this passage. What Jerome says is that the apostles "may at least be shamed to deeds" (*erubescant ad opera*), i.e., deeds such as Christ wanted them to perform, not the "wielding temporal lordship" with which Marsilius taxes them.

5   Matthew 5:3,4. The saints referred to are Chrysostom and Augustine; in Thomas Aquinas *Catena aurea* (XI, 55).

6   For the indivisible species, see Aristotle *Posterior Analytics* II. 13. 96b 15 ff.; *Metaphysics* V. 10. 1018b 4. For the mean "in the thing itself," see Aristotle *Nicomachean Ethics* II. 6. 1106a 25 ff., where it is pointed out that the "mean" in which the moral virtues consist is a mean "relatively to us" rather than a mean in terms of the thing or object with which the virtue is concerned. For liberality as a moral virtue, see *ibid.* IV. 1. 1119b 21 ff.

7   Marsilius here argues against the bull of John XXII, *Cum inter nonnullos*, of Nov. 12, 1323 (*Corp. jur can., Extravag. Joh. XXII* Tit. 14. cap. 4), which condemned the doctrine that Christ had absolute poverty. Marsilius' position on this and other issues is in turn condemned in John's bull, *Quia quorundam mentes*, of Nov. 10, 1324 (*ibid.* Tit. 14. cap. 5).

THE BOOK OF MARGERY KEMPE

MARGERY KEMPE (1373-1439) WAS THE DAUGHTER OF A PROSPEROUS merchant of Lynn. At 20 she was married to John Kempe. Her writings, the first autobiography in English, reflect the tensions of her dual life: wife and mother on the one hand and pilgrim and mystic on the other.

Source: W. Butler-Bowdon, *The Book of Margery Kempe* (New York: the Devin-Adair Company, 1944)

The First Book

CHAPTER 1

Her marriage and illness after childbirth. She recovers.

When this creature was twenty years of age, or some deal more, she was married to a worshipful burgess (of Lynne) and was with child within a short time, as nature would. And after she had conceived, she was belaboured with great accesses till the child was born and then, what with the labour she had in childing, and the sickness going before, she despaired of her life, weening she might not live. And then she sent for her ghostly father, for she had a thing on her conscience which she had never shewn before that time in all her life. For she was ever hindered by her enemy, the devil, evermore saying to her that whilst she was in good health she needed no confession, but to do penance by herself alone and all should be forgiven, for God is merciful enough. And therefore this creature oftentimes did great penance in fasting on bread and water, and other deeds of alms with devout prayers, save she would not shew that in confession.

And when she was at any time sick or diseased, the devil said in her mind that she should be damned because she was not shriven of that default. Wherefore after her child was born, she, not trusting to live, sent for her ghostly father, as is said before, in full will to be shriven of all her lifetime, as near as she could. And when she came to the point for to say that thing which she had so long concealed, her confessor was a little too hasty and began sharply to reprove her, before she had fully said her intent, and so she would no more say for aught he might do. Anon,

for the dread she had of damnation on the one side, and his sharp reproving of her on the other side, this creature went out of her mind and was wondrously vexed and laboured with spirits for half a year, eight weeks and odd days.

And in this time she saw, as she thought, devils opening their mouths all inflamed with burning waves of fire, as if they would have swallowed her in, sometimes ramping at her, sometimes threatening her, pulling her and hauling her, night and day during the aforesaid time. Also the devils cried upon her with great threatenings, and bade her that she should forsake Christendom, her faith, and deny her God, His Mother and all the Saints in Heaven, her good works and all good virtues, her father, her mother and all her friends. And so she did. She slandered her husband, her friends and her own self. She said many a wicked word, and many a cruel word; she knew no virtue nor goodness; she desired all wickedness; like as the spirits tempted her to say and do, so she said and did. She would have destroyed herself many a time at their stirrings and have been damned with them in Hell, and in witness thereof, she bit her own hand so violently, that the mark was seen all her life after.

And also she rived the skin on her body against her heart with her nails spitefully, for she had no other instruments, and worse she would have done, but that she was bound and kept with strength day and night so that she might not have her will. And when she had long been laboured in these and many other temptations, so that men weened she should never have escaped or lived, then on a time as she lay alone and her keepers were from her, Our Merciful Lord Jesus Christ, ever to be trusted, worshipped be His Name, never forsaking His servant in time of need, appeared to His creature who had forsaken Him, in the likeness of a man, most seemly, most beauteous and most amiable that ever might be seen with man's eye, clad in a mantle of purple silk, sitting upon her bedside, looking upon her with so blessed a face that she was strengthened in all her spirit, and said to her these words:—

'Daughter, why hast thou forsaken Me, and I forsook never thee?'

And anon, as He said these words, she saw verily how the air opened as bright as any lightning. And He rose up into the air, not right hastily and quickly, but fair and easily, so that she might well behold Him in the air till it was closed again.

And anon this creature became calmed in her wits and reason, as well as ever she was before, and prayed her husband as soon as he came to her, that she might have the keys of the buttery to take her meat and drink as she had done before. Her maidens and her keepers counselled him that he should deliver her no keys, as they said she would but give away such goods as there were, for she knew not what she said, as they weened.

Nevertheless, her husband ever having tenderness and compassion for her, commanded that they should deliver to her the keys; and she took her meat and drink as her bodily strength would serve her, and knew her friends and her household and all others that came to see how Our Lord Jesus Christ had wrought His grace in her, so blessed may He be, Who ever is near in tribulation. When men think He is far from them, He is full near by His grace. Afterwards, this creature did all other occupations as fell to her to do, wisely and soberly enough, save she knew not verily the call of Our Lord.

CHAPTER 2

Her worldly pride. Her attempt at brewing and milling, and failure at both. She amends her ways.

When this creature had thus graciously come again to her mind, she thought that she was bound to God and that she would be His servant. Nevertheless, she would not leave her pride or her pompous array, which she had used before-

time, either for her husband, or for any other man's counsel. Yet she knew full well that men said of her full much villainy, for she wore gold pipes on her head, and her hoods, with the tippets, were slashed. Her cloaks also were slashed and laid with divers colours between the slashes, so that they should be the more staring to men's sight, and herself the more worshipped.

And when her husband spoke to her to leave her pride, she answered shrewdly and shortly, and said that she was come of worthy kindred— he should never have wedded her—for her father was sometime Mayor of the town of N...[1] and afterwards he was alderman of the High Guild of the Trinity in N... And therefore she would keep the worship of her kindred whatever any man said.

She had full great envy of her neighbours, that they should be as well arrayed as she. All her desire was to be worshipped by the people. She would not take heed of any chastisement, nor be content with the goods that God had sent her, as her husband was, but ever desired more and more.

Then for pure covetousness, and to maintain her pride, she began to brew, and was one of the greatest brewers in the town of N... for three years or four, till she lost much money, for she had never been used thereto. For, though she had ever such good servants, cunning in brewing, yet it would never succeed with them. For when the ale was fair standing under barm as any man might see, suddenly the barm would fall down, so that all the ale was lost, one brewing after another, so that her servants were ashamed and would not dwell with her.

Then this creature thought how God had punished her aforetime—and she could not take heed—and now again, by the loss of her goods. Then she left and brewed no more.

Then she asked her husband's mercy because she would not follow his counsel aforetime, and she said that her pride and sin were the cause of all her punishing, and that she would amend and that she had trespassed with good will.

Yet she left not the world altogether, for she now bethought herself of a new housewifery. She had a horse-mill. She got herself two good horses and a man to grind men's corn, and thus she trusted to get her living. This enterprise lasted not long, for in a short time after, on Corpus Christi Eve, befell this marvel. This man, being in good health of body, and his two horses sturdy and gentle, had pulled well in the mill before-time, and now he took one of these horses and put him in the mill as he had done before, and this horse would draw no draught in the mill for anything the man might do. The man was sorry and essayed with all his wits how he should make this horse pull. Sometimes he led him by the head, sometimes he beat him, sometimes he cherished him and all availed not, for he would rather go backward than forward. Then this man set a sharp pair of spurs on his heels and rode on the horse's back to make him pull, and it was never the better. When the man saw it would work in no way, he set up this horse again in the stable, and gave him corn, and he ate well and freshly. And later he took the other horse and put him in the mill, and like his fellow did, so did he, for he would not draw for anything the man might do. Then the man forsook his service and would no longer remain with the aforesaid crea-ture. Anon, it was noised about the town of N... that neither man nor beast would serve the said creature.

Then some said she was accursed; some said God took open vengeance upon her; some said one thing and some said another. Some wise men, whose minds were more grounded in the love of Our Lord, said that it was the high mercy of Our Lord Jesus Christ that called her from the pride and vanity of the wretched world.

Then this creature, seeing all these adversities coming on every side, thought they were the scourges of Our Lord that would chastise her for her sin. Then she asked God's mercy, and forsook her pride, her covetousness, and the desire that she had for the worship of the world, and did great bodily penance, and began to enter the way of everlasting life as shall be told hereafter.

CHAPTER 3

Her vision of Paradise. She desires to live apart from her husband. Does penance and wears a haircloth.

On a night, as this creature lay in her bed with her husband, she heard a sound of melody so sweet and delectable, that she thought she had been in Paradise, and therewith she started out of her bed and said:—

'Alas, that ever I did sin! It is full merry in Heaven.'

This melody was so sweet that it surpassed all melody that ever might be heard in this world, without any comparison, and caused her, when she heard any mirth or melody afterwards, to have full plenteous and abundant tears of high devotion, with great sobbings and sighings after the bliss of Heaven, not dreading the shames and the spites of this wretched world. Ever after this inspiration, she had in her mind the mirth and the melody that was in Heaven, so much, that she could not well restrain herself from speaking thereof, for wherever she was in any company she would say oftentimes:—'It is full merry in Heaven.'

And they that knew her behaviour beforetime, and now heard her speaking so much of the bliss of Heaven, said to her:—

'Why speak ye so of the mirth that is in Heav-en? Ye know it not, and ye have not been there, any more than we.' And were wroth with her, for she would not hear nor speak of worldly things as they did, and as she did beforetime.

And after this time she had never desired to commune fleshly with her husband, for the debt of matrimony was so abominable to her that she would rather, she thought, have eaten or drunk the ooze and the muck in the gutter than consent to any fleshly communing, save only for obedi-ence.

So she said to her husband:—'I may not deny you my body, but the love of my heart and my affections are withdrawn from all earthly crea-tures, and set only in God.'

He would have his will and she obeyed, with great weeping and sorrowing that she might not live chaste. And oftentimes this creature coun-selled her husband to live chaste, and said that they often, she knew well, had displeased God by their inordinate love, and the great delectation they each had in using the other, and now it was good that they should, by the common will and consent of them both, punish and chastise them-selves wilfully by abstaining from the lust of their bodies. Her husband said it was good to do so, but he might not yet. He would when God willed. And so he used her as he had done before. He would not spare her. And ever she prayed to God that she might live chaste; and three or four years after, when it pleased Our Lord, he made a vow of chastity, as shall be written afterwards, by leave of Jesus.

And also, after this creature heard this heavenly melody, she did great bodily penance. She was shriven sometimes twice or thrice on a day, and specially of that sin she so long had (hid), concealed and covered, as is written in the beginning of the book.

She gave herself up to great fasting and great watching; she rose at two or three of the clock, and went to church, and was there at her prayers unto the time of noon and also all the afternoon. Then she was slandered and reproved by many people, because she kept so strict a life. She got a hair-cloth from a kiln, such as men dry malt on, and laid it in her kirtle as secretly and privily as she might, so that her husband should not espy it. Nor did he, and she lay by him every night in his bed and wore the hair-cloth every day, and bore children in the time.

Then she had three years of great labour with temptations which she bore as meekly as she could, thanking Our Lord for all His gifts, and was as merry when she was reproved, scorned and japed for Our Lord's love, and much more merry than she was beforetime in the worship of the world. For she knew right well she had sinned greatly against God and was worthy of more shame and sorrow than any man could cause her, and despite of the world was the right way Heavenwards, since Christ Himself had chosen that way. All His apostles, martyrs, confessors and virgins, and all that ever came to Heaven, passed by the way of tribulation, and she, desiring nothing so much as Heaven, then was glad in her conscience when she believed that she was entering the way that would lead her to the place she most desired.

And this creature had contrition and great compunction with plenteous tears and many boisterous sobbings for her sins and for her unkindness against her Maker. She repented from her childhood for unkindness, as Our Lord would put it in her mind, full many a time. Then,

beholding her own wickedness, she could but sorrow and weep and ever pray for mercy and forgiveness. Her weeping was so plenteous and continuing, that many people thought she could weep and leave off, as she liked. And therefore many men said she was a false hypocrite, and wept before the world for succour and worldly goods. Then full many forsook her that loved her before while she was in the world, and would not know her. And ever, she thanked God for all, desiring nothing but mercy and forgiveness of sin.

CHAPTER 4

Her temptation to adultery with a man, who, when she consents, rejects her.

The first two years when this creature was thus drawn to Our Lord, she had great quiet in spirit from any temptations. She could well endure to fast, and it did not trouble her. She hated the joys of the world. She felt no rebellion in her flesh. She was so strong, as she thought, that she dreaded no devil in Hell, as she did such great bodily penance. She thought that she loved God more than He did her. She was smitten with the deadly wound of vainglory, and felt it not, for she many times desired that the crucifix should loosen His hands from the Cross, and embrace her in token of love. Our Merciful Lord Jesus Christ, seeing this creature's presumption, sent her, as is written before, three years of great temptations, one of the hardest of which I purpose to write as an example to those who come after, so that they should not trust in themselves, or have joy in themselves, as she had. For, no dread, our ghostly enemy sleepeth not, but he full busily searcheth our complexions and dispositions and where he findeth us most frail, there, by Our Lord's sufferance, he layeth his snare, which no man may escape by his own power.

So he laid before this woman the snare of lechery, when she believed that all fleshly lust had wholly been quenched in her. And so for a long time she was tempted with the sin of lechery, for aught that she could do. Yet she was often shriven, she wore her hair-cloth, and did great bodily penance and wept many a bitter tear, and prayed full often to Our Lord that He should preserve her and keep her, so that she should not fall into temptation, for she thought she would rather be dead than consent thereto. All this time she had no lust to commune with her husband; but it was very painful and horrible unto her.

In the second year of her temptation, it so fell that a man whom she loved well, said unto her on St. Margaret's Eve before evensong that, for anything, he would lie by her and have his lust of his body, and she should not withstand him, for if he did not have his will that time, he said he would anyhow have it another time; she should not choose. And he did it to see what she would do, but she thought that he had meant it in full earnest at that time, and said but little thereto. So they parted then and both went to hear evensong, for her church was that of Saint Margaret. This woman was so laboured with the man's words that she could not hear her evensong, nor say her Paternoster, or think any other good thought, but was more troubled than ever she was before.

The devil put into her mind that God had forsaken her, or else she would not be so tempted. She believed the devil's persuasion, and began to consent because she could think no good thought. Therefore thought she that God had forsaken her, and when evensong was done, she went to the man aforesaid, so that he could have his lust, as she thought he had desired, but he made such simulation that she could not know his intent, and so they parted asunder for that night. This creature was so laboured and vexed all that night, that she never knew what she might do. She lay by her husband, and to commune with him was so abominable to her that she could not endure it, and yet it was lawful unto her, in lawful time, if she would. But ever she was laboured with the other man, to sin with him inasmuch as he had spoken to her. At last, through the importunity of such temptation, and lack of discretion, she was overcome and consented in her mind, and went to the man to know if he would then consent to her, and he said he never would, for all the gold in this world; he would rather be hewn as small as flesh for the pot.

She went away all shamed and confused in herself at seeing his stability and her own insta-bility. Then thought she of the grace that God had given her before; how she had two years of great quiet in her soul, repenting of her sin with many bitter tears of compunction, and a perfect will never again to turn to her sin, but rather to die. Now she saw how she had consented in her will to do sin, and then fell she half into despair. She thought she must have been in Hell for the sorrow she felt. She thought she was worthy of no mercy, for her consent was so wilfully done, nor ever worthy to do Him service, because she was so false to Him. Nevertheless she was shriven many times and often, and did whatever penance her confessor would enjoin her to do, and was governed by the rules of the Church. That grace, God gave his creature, blessed may he be, but He withdrew not her temptation, but rather increased it, as she thought.

Therefore she thought He had forsaken her, and dared not trust to His mercy, but was afflicted with horrible temptations to lechery and despair all the next year following. But Our Lord, of His mercy, as she said herself, gave her each day for the most part two hours of sorrow for her sins, with many bitter tears. Afterwards, she was laboured with temptation to despair as she was before, and was as far from feelings of grace, as they that never felt any, and that she could not bear, and so she gave way to despair. But for the time that she felt grace, her labours were so wonderful that she could evil fare with them, but ever mourned and sorrowed as though God had forsaken her.

CHAPTER 5

She speaks with Our Lord, Who orders her to abstain from flesh-meat, and to contemplate and meditate.

Then on the Friday before Christmas Day, as this creature was kneeling in a chapel of Saint John, within a Church of St. Margaret in N..., weeping wondrous sore, and asking mercy and forgiveness for her sins and trespasses, Our merciful Lord Christ Jesus, blessed may He be, ravished her spirit and said unto her:—

'Daughter, why weepest thou so sore? I am coming to thee, Jesus Christ Who died on the cross, suffering bitter pains and passions for thee. I, the same God, forgive thee thy sins to the uttermost point, and thou shalt never come to Hell or Purgatory, but when thou shalt pass out of this world, within a twinkling of an eye, thou shalt have the bliss of Heaven, for I am the same God that hath brought thy sins to thy mind and made thee be shriven thereof. And I grant thee contrition to thy life's end. Therefore I bid thee and command thee, boldly call Me "Jesus Christ, thy love", for I am thy love, and shall be thy love without end. And, daughter, thou hast a haircloth on thy back. I will that thou put it away, and I shall give thee a haircloth in thy heart that shall please Me much better than all the haircloths in the world. Also, my dearworthy daughter, thou must forsake that which thou lovest best in this world, and that is the eating of flesh. Instead of that flesh, thou shalt eat of My flesh and My blood, that is the Very Body of Christ in the Sacrament of the Altar. This is My will, daughter, that thou receive My Body every Sunday, and I shall flow so much grace into thee, that all the world shall marvel thereof. Thou shalt be eaten and gnawed by the people of the world as any rat gnaweth stockfish. Dread thee nought, daughter, for thou shalt have victory over all thine enemies. I shall give thee grace enough to answer every clerk in the love of God. I swear to thee by My Majesty that I will never forsake thee in weel or in woe. I shall help thee and keep thee, so that no devil in Hell shall part thee from Me, nor angel in Heaven, nor man on earth, for devils in Hell may not, and angels in Heaven will not, and man on earth shall not. And, daughter, I will thou leave thy bidding of many beads, and think such thoughts as I shall put into thy mind. I shall give thee leave to pray till six of the clock, saying what thou wilt. Then shalt thou be still and speak to Me in thought and I shall give to thee high meditation and very contemplation. I bid thee go to the anchorite at the Preaching Friars and shew him My secrets and My counsels which I shew to thee, and work after his counsel, for My Spirit shall speak in him to thee.'

Then this creature went forth to the anchorite as she was commanded, and shewed him the revelations, as they were revealed to her. Then the anchorite, with great reverence and weeping, thanking God, said:—

'Daughter, ye suck even on Christ's breast, and ye have an earnest-penny of Heaven. I charge you to receive such thoughts as God gives, as meekly and devoutly as ye can, and to come to me and tell me what they are, and I shall, with the leave of Our Lord Jesus Christ, tell you whether they are of the Holy Ghost or of your enemy the devil.'

CHAPTER 6

The birth of Our Lady. Her speech with Saint Elizabeth. The birth of Our Lord.

Another day, she gave herself up to meditation as she had been bidden and lay still, not knowing what she might best think of. Then she said to Our Lord Jesus Christ:

'Jesus, of what shall I think?'

Our Lord answered to her mind:—'Daughter, think of My Mother, for she is the cause of all the grace that thou hast.'

Then, anon, she saw Saint Anne, great with child, and she prayed Saint Anne that she might be her maiden, and her servant. And anon, Our Lady was born, and then she arranged to take the child to herself and keep it till it was twelve years of age, with good meat and drink, with fair white clothing and white kerchiefs.

Then she said to the blessed child:—'Lady, you shall be the Mother of God.'

The blessed child answered and said:—'I would I were worthy to be the handmaiden of her that should conceive the Son of God.'

The creature said:—'I pray you, Lady, if that grace befall, you renounce not my service.'

The blissful child passed away for a certain time, the creature being quite quiet in contemplation, and afterwards came again and said:—

'Daughter, now am I become the Mother of God.'

And then the creature fell down on her knees with great reverence and great weeping and said:—

'I am not worthy, Lady, to do you service.'

'Yes, daughter,' said she, 'follow thou me, thy service liketh me well.'

Then went she forth with Our Lady and with Joseph, bearing with her a pottle of wine and honey, and spices thereto. Then went they forth to Elizabeth, Saint John the Baptist's mother, and when they met together, each worshipped the other, and so they dwelt together, with great grace and gladness twelve weeks. And Saint John was born, and Our Lady took him up from the earth with all manner of reverence, and gave him to his mother, saying of him that he should be a holy man, and blessed him. Afterwards they took leave of each other with compassionate tears. Then the creature fell down on her knees to Saint Elizabeth, and begged her to pray for her to Our Lady that she might do her service and pleasure.

'Daughter,' said Elizabeth, 'me-seemeth thou dost right well thy duty.'

Then went the creature forth with Our Lady to Bethlehem and purchased her shelter every night with great reverence, and Our Lady was received with glad cheer. Also she begged for Our Lady fair white cloths and kerchiefs to swathe her Son in, when He was born; and when Jesus was born, she provided bedding for Our Lady to lie in with her Blessed Son. Later she begged meat for Our Lady and her Blessed Child, and she swathed Him with bitter tears of compassion, having mind of the sharp death He would suffer for love of sinful men, saying unto Him:—

'Lord, I shall fare fair with You. I will not bind You tight. I pray You be not displeased with me.'

CHAPTER 7

The adoration of the Magi. She accompanies Our Lady into Egypt.

And afterwards on the twelfth day, when three Kings came with their gifts, and worshipped Our Lord in His Mother's lap, this creature, Our Lady's handmaiden, beholding all the process in contemplation, wept wondrous sore.

And when she saw that they would take their leave to go home again into their country, she could not bear that they should go from the Presence of Our Lord, and for wonder that they should go, she cried wondrous sore. Soon after came an angel, and bade Our Lady and Joseph to go from the country of Bethlehem into Egypt. Then went this creature forth with Our Lady, day by day finding her harbourage with great reverence and many sweet thoughts and high meditations, and also high contemplation, sometimes continuing in weeping two hours and often

longer in mind of Our Lord's Passion without ceasing, sometimes for her own sin, sometimes for the sin of the people, sometimes for the souls in Purgatory, sometimes for them that were in poverty and dis-ease, for she desired to comfort them all.

Sometimes she wept full plenteously and full boisterously for desire of the bliss of Heaven, and because she was so long deferred therefrom. She greatly coveted to be delivered out of this wretched world. Our Lord Jesus Christ said to her mind that she should abide and languish in love, 'for I have ordained thee to kneel before the Trinity, to pray for all the world, for many hundred thousand souls shall be saved by thy prayers. So ask, daughter, what thou wilt, and I will grant thee thine asking.'

The creature said:—'Lord, I ask mercy and preservation from everlasting damnation for me and all the world. Chastise us here how Thou wilt and in Purgatory also, and of Thy great mercy, keep us from damnation.'

CHAPTER 8

She asks Our Lord to be her executor and to give Master N. half of the reward of her good deeds.

Another time, as this creature lay in her prayer, the Mother of Mercy, appearing to her, said:—

'Daughter, blessed may thou be, thy seat is made in Heaven, before my Son's knee, and whom thou wilt have with thee.'

Then asked her Blessed Son:—'Daughter, whom wilt thou have fellow with thee?'

'My dearworthy Lord, I ask for my ghostly father, Master N...'

'Why asketh thou more for him than thine own father or thine husband?'

'Because I may never requite him for his goodness to me, and the gracious labour he has taken over me in hearing my confession.'

'I grant thee thy desire for him; yet shall thy father be saved, and thy husband also, and all thy children.'

Then this creature said:—'Lord, after Thou has forgiven me my sin, I make Thee mine executor of all the good works that Thou workest in me. In praying, in thinking, in weeping, in going on pilgrimage, in fasting, or in speaking any good word, it is fully my will, that Thou give Master N... half of it to the increase of his merit, as if he did them himself. And the other half, Lord, spread on Thy friends and Thine enemies, and on my friends and mine enemies, for I will have but Thyself for my share.'

'Daughter, I shall be a true executor to thee and fulfil all thy will; and for the great charity that thou hast to comfort thy fellow Christians, thou shalt have double reward in Heaven.'

CHAPTER 9

Our Lord promises to slay her husband's lust. She is injured by falling stones and timber in church.

Another time, as she prayed to God that she might live chaste by leave of her husband, Christ said to her:—

'Thou must fast on Friday, both from meat and drink, and thou shalt have thy desire ere Whitsunday, for I shall suddenly slay (the fleshly lust) in thy husband.'

Then on the Wednesday in Easter week, after her husband would have had knowledge of her, as he was wont before, and when he came nigh to her, she said:—'Jesus Christ, help me,' and he had no power to touch her at that time in that way, nor ever after with any fleshly knowledge.

It befell on a Friday before Whitsun Eve, as this creature was in a church of Saint Margaret at N... hearing her mass, she heard a great noise, and a dreadful. She was sore amazed through fear of the voice of the people, who said God should take vengeance on her. She knelt on her knees, holding down her head, with her book in her hand, praying Our Lord Jesus Christ for grace and mercy.

Suddenly there fell down from the highest part of the church roof, from under the foot of the spar, on her head and back, a stone which weighed three pounds, and a short end of a beam weighing six pounds, so that she thought her back was broken asunder, and she feared she would be dead in a little while.

Soon afterwards, she cried, 'Jesus, mercy!' and anon, her pain was gone.

A good man, called John of Wyreham, seeing this wonder and supposing she had been greatly injured, came and pulled her by the sleeve and said:—

'Dame, how fare ye?'

The creature, whole and sound, then thanked him for his cheer and his charity, much marvelling and greatly a-wonder that she felt no pain, having had so much a little before. For twelve weeks afterwards, she felt no pain. Then the spirit of God said to her soul:—

'Hold this for a great miracle, and if the people will not believe this, I will work many more.'

A worshipful doctor of divinity, named Master Aleyn, a White Friar, hearing of this wonderful work, inquired of this creature all the details of the process. He, desiring the work of God to be magnified, got the same stone that fell on her back and weighed it, and then got the beam-end that fell on her head, which one of the keepers of the church had laid on the fire to burn. This worshipful doctor said it was a great miracle, and Our Lord was highly to be magnified for preserving this creature against the malice of her enemy, and told it to many people and many people magnified God much in this creature. Many also would not believe it, and thought it more a token of wrath and vengeance, rather than believe it was any token of mercy and kindness.

CHAPTER 10

She wishes to visit certain places for spiritual reasons and starts with her husband for York.

Soon after, this creature was urged in her soul to go and visit certain places for ghostly health, inasmuch as she was cured, but might not without the consent of her husband. She asked her husband to grant her leave, and he, full trusting it was the will of God, soon consenting, they went to such places as she was inclined.

Then Our Lord Jesus Christ said to her:—'My servants desire greatly to see thee.'

Then she was welcomed and made much of in divers places, wherefore she had great dread of vainglory, and was much afraid. Our Merciful Lord Jesus Christ, worshipped be His Name, said to her:—

'Dread not, daughter, I will take vainglory from thee, for they that worship thee, worship Me; they that despise thee, despise Me and I will chastise them therefor. I am in thee and thou in Me, and they that hear thee, hear the voice of

God. Daughter, there is no so sinful man living on earth, that, if he will forsake his sin and live after thy counsel, such grace as thou promisest him, I will confirm for thy love.'

Then her husband and she went forth to York and divers other places.

CHAPTER 11

On the way back from York, she and her husband argue as to their carnal relationship to each other.

It befell on a Friday on Midsummer Eve in right hot weather, as this creature was coming from York-ward carrying a bottle with beer in her hand, and her husband a cake in his bosom, that he asked his wife this question:—

'Margery, if there came a man with a sword, who would strike off my head, unless I should commune naturally with you as I have done before, tell me on your conscience—for ye say ye will not lie—whether ye would suffer my head to be smitten off, or whether ye would suffer me to meddle with you again, as I did at one time?'

'Alas, sir,' said she, 'why raise this matter, when we have been chaste these eight weeks?'

'For I will know the truth of your heart.'

And then she said with great sorrow:—'Forsooth, I would rather see you being slain, than that we should turn again to our uncleanness.'

And he replied:—'Ye are no good wife.'

She then asked her husband what was the cause that he had not meddled with her for eight weeks, since she lay with him every night in his bed. He said he was made so afraid when he would have touched her, that he dare do no more.

'Now, good sir, amend your ways, and ask God's mercy, for I told you nearly three years ago that ye[2] should be slain suddenly, and now is this the third year, and so I hope I shall have my desire. Good sir, I pray you grant me what I ask, and I will pray for you that ye shall be saved through the mercy of Our Lord Jesus Christ, and ye shall have more reward in Heaven than if ye wore a hair-cloth or a habergeon.[3] I pray you, suffer me to make a vow of chastity at what bishop's hand God wills.'

'Nay,' he said, 'that I will not grant you, for now may I use you without deadly sin, and then might I not do so.'

Then she said to him:—'If it be the will of the Holy Ghost to fulfil what I have said, I pray God that ye may consent thereto; and if it be not the will of the Holy Ghost, I pray God ye never consent to it.'

Then they went forth towards Bridlington in right hot weather, the creature having great sorrow and dread for her chastity. As they came by a cross, her husband sat down under the cross, calling his wife to him and saying these words unto her:—'Margery, grant me my desire, and I shall grant you your desire. My first desire is that we shall lie together in bed as we have done before; the second, that ye shall pay my debts, ere ye go to Jerusalem; and the third, that ye shall eat and drink with me on the Friday as ye were wont to do.'

'Nay, sir,' said she, 'to break the Friday, I will never grant you whilst I live.'

'Well,' said he, 'then I shall meddle with you again.'

She prayed him that he would give her leave to say her prayers, and he granted it kindly. Then she knelt down beside a cross in the field and prayed in this manner, with a great abundance of tears:—

'Lord God, Thou knowest all things. Thou knowest what sorrow I have had to be chaste in my body to Thee all these three years, and now might I have my will, and dare not for love of Thee. For if I should break that manner of fasting which Thou commandest me to keep on the Friday, without meat or drink, I should now have my desire. But, Blessed Lord, Thou knowest that I will not contravene Thy will, and much now is my sorrow unless I find comfort in Thee. Now, Blessed Jesus, make Thy will known to me unworthy, that I may follow it thereafter and fulfil it with all my might.'

Then Our Lord Jesus Christ with great sweetness, spoke to her, commanding her to go again to her husband, and pray him to grant her what she desired, 'And he shall have what he desireth. For, my dearworthy daughter, this was the cause that I bade thee fast, so that thou shouldst the sooner obtain and get thy desire, and now it is granted to thee. I will no longer that thou fast. Therefore I bid thee in the Name of Jesus, eat and drink as thy husband doth.'

Then this creature thanked Our Lord Jesus

Christ for His grace and goodness, and rose up and went to her husband, saying to him:—

'Sir, if it please you, ye shall grant me my desire, and ye shall have your desire. Grant me that ye will not come into my bed, and I grant you to requite your debts ere I go to Jerusalem. Make my body free to God so that ye never make challenge to me, by asking any debt of matrimony. After this day, whilst ye live, I will eat and drink on the Friday at your bidding.'

Then said her husband:—'As free may your body be to God, as it hath been to me.'

This creature thanked God, greatly rejoicing that she had her desire, praying her husband that they should say three Paternosters in worship of the Trinity for the great grace that He had granted them. And so they did, kneeling under a cross, and afterwards they ate and drank together in great gladness of spirit. This was on a Friday on Midsummer's Eve. Then went they forth Bridlingtonward and also to many other countries and spoke with God's servants, both anchorites and recluses, and many others of Our Lord's lovers, with many worthy clerks, doctors of divinity and bachelors also, in divers places. And this creature, to many of them, shewed her feelings and her contemplations, as she was commanded to do, to find out if any deceit were in her feelings.

CHAPTER 16

She and her husband go to Lambeth to visit the Archbishop of Canterbury, whom she reproves for the bad behaviour of his clergy and household.

Then went this creature forth to London with her husband unto Lambeth, where the Archbishop lay at that time; and as they came into the hall in the afternoon, there were many of the Archbishop's clerks and other reckless men, both squires and yeomen, who swore many great oaths and spoke many reckless words, and this creature boldly reprehended them, and said they would be damned unless they left off their swearing and other sins that they used.

And with that, there came forth another woman of the same town in a furred cloak, who forswore this creature, banned her, and spoke full cursedly to her in this manner:—

'I would thou wert in Smithfield, and I would bring a faggot to burn thee with. It is a pity thou art alive.'

This creature stood still and answered not, and her husband suffered it with great pain, and was full sorry to hear his wife so rebuked.

Then the Archbishop sent for this creature into his garden. When she came into his presence, she saluted him as best she could, praying him of his gracious lordship to grant her authority to choose her confessor and to be houselled[4] every Sunday, if God would dispose her thereto, under his letter and his seal through all his province. And he granted her full benignly all her desire without any silver or gold, nor would he let his clerks take anything for the writing or the sealing of the letter.

When this creature found this grace in his sight, she was well comforted and strengthened in her soul, and so she showed this worshipful lord her manner of life, and such grace as God wrought in her mind and in her soul, to find out what he would say thereto, and whether he found any default either in her contemplation or in her weeping.

And she told him also the cause of her weeping, and the manner of dalliance that Our Lord spoke to her soul; and he found no default in her, but praised her manner of living, and was right glad that Our Merciful Lord Christ Jesus showed such grace in our days, blessed may He be.

Then this creature boldly spoke to him for the correction of his household, saying with reverence:—

'My lord, Our Lord of all, Almighty God has not given you your benefice and great worldly wealth to keep His traitors and them that slay Him every day by great oaths swearing. Ye shall answer for them, unless ye correct them, or else put them out of your service.'

Full benignly and meekly he suffered her to speak her intent, and gave her a fair answer, she supposing it would then be better. And so their dalliance continued till stars appeared in the firmament. Then she took her leave, and her husband also.

Afterwards they came again to London, and many worthy men desired to hear her dalliances and communication, for her communication was so much in the love of God that her hearers were often stirred thereby to weep right sadly.

And so she had there right great cheer, and her husband because of her, as long as they remained in the city.

Afterwards they came again to Lynne, and then went this creature to the anchorite at the Preaching Friars in Lynne and told him what cheer she had, and how she had sped whilst she was in the country. And he was right glad of her coming home, and held it was a great miracle, her coming and going to and fro.

And he said to her:—'I have heard much evil language of you since ye went out, and I have been sore counselled to leave you and no more to associate with you, and there are promised me great friendships, on condition that I leave you. And I answered for you thus:—

'"If ye were in the same plight as ye were when we parted asunder, I durst well say that ye were a good woman, a lover of God, and highly inspired by the Holy Ghost. And I will not forsake her for any lady in this realm, if speaking with the lady means leaving her. Rather would I leave the lady and speak with her, if I might not do both, than do the contrary".'

CHAPTER 17

She visits Norwich and has an interview with the Vicar, who believes in her, and later on helps her when under examination.

On a day, long before this time, while this creature was bearing children and she was newly delivered of a child, Our Lord Jesus Christ said to her that she should bear no more children, and therefore He bade her to go to Norwich.

And she said:—'Ah! dear Lord, how shall I go? I am both faint and feeble.'

'Dread thee not. I shall make thee strong enough. I bid thee go to the Vicar of Saint Stephen's and say that I greet him well, and that he is a highly chosen soul of Mine, and tell him he pleaseth Me much with his preaching and shew him thy secrets, and My counsels such as I shew thee.'

Then she took her way Norwich-ward, and came into his church on a Thursday a little before noon. And the Vicar went up and down with another priest, who was his ghostly father, who lived when this book was made. And this creature was clad in black clothing at that time.

She saluted the Vicar, praying him that she might speak with him an hour or else two hours at afternoon, when he had eaten, in the love of God.

He, lifting up his hands and blessing her, said:—'Benedicite. How could a woman occupy an hour or two hours in the love of Our Lord? I shall never eat meat till I learn what ye can say of Our Lord God in the time of an hour.'

Then he sat himself down in the church. She, sitting a little aside, showed him all the words that God had revealed to her in her soul. Afterwards she shewed him all her manner of life from her childhood, as nigh as it would come to her mind; how unkind she had been against Our Lord Jesus Christ, how proud and vain she had been in her behaviour, how obstinate against the laws of God, and how envious against her fellow Christians. Later, when it pleased Our Lord Christ Jesus, how she was chastised with many tribulations and horrible temptations and afterwards how she was fed and comforted with holy meditations and specially in the memory of Our Lord's Passion.

And, while she conversed on the Passion of Our Lord Jesus Christ, she heard so hideous a melody that she could not bear it. Then this creature fell down, as if she had lost her bodily strength, and lay still a great while, desiring to put it away, and she might not. Then she knew well, by her faith, that there was great joy in Heaven where the least point of bliss, without any comparison, passeth all the joy that ever might be thought or felt in this life.

She was greatly strengthened in her faith and more bold to tell the Vicar her feelings, which she had by revelation both of the quick and the dead, and of his own self.

She told him how sometimes the Father of Heaven spoke to her soul as plainly and as verily as one friend speaks to another by bodily speech. Sometimes in the Second Person in Trinity, sometimes all Three Persons in Trinity, and one substance in Godhead spoke to her soul, and informed her in her faith and in His love, how she should love Him, worship Him and dread

Him, so excellently that she never heard of any book, either Hylton's book or Bride's[5] book, or Stimulus Amoris, or Incendium Amoris, or any other that she ever heard read, that spoke so highly of the love of God. But she felt that, as highly working in her soul, as if she could have shewn what she felt.

Sometimes Our Lady spoke to her mind; sometimes St. Peter, sometimes St. Paul, sometimes St. Katherine, or whatever Saint in Heaven she had devotion to, appeared in her soul and taught her how she should love Our Lord, and how she should please Him. Her dalliance was so sweet, so holy and so devout, that this creature might not oftentimes bear it, but fell down and wrestled with her body, and made wondrous faces and gestures with boisterous sobbings, and great plenty of tears, sometimes saying 'Jesus, Mercy', and sometimes, 'I die'.

And therefore many people slandered her, not believing that it was the work of God, but that some evil spirit vexed her in her body or else that she had some bodily sickness.

Notwithstanding the rumours and the grutching of the people against her, this holy man, the Vicar of Saint Stephen's Church of Norwich, whom God hath exalted, and through marvellous works shewn and proved for holy, ever held with her and supported her against her enemies, unto his power, after the time that she, by the bidding of God, had shewn him her manner of governance and living, for he trustfully believed that she was well learned in the law of God, and endued with the grace of the Holy Ghost, to Whom it belongeth to inspire where He will. And though His voice be heard, it is not known in the world from whence it cometh or whither it goeth.

This holy Vicar, after this time, was confessor to this creature always when she came to Norwich, and houselled her with his own hands.

And when she was at one time admonished to appear before certain officers of the Bishop, to answer to certain articles which would be put against her by the stirring of envious people, the good Vicar, preferring the love of God before any shame of the world, went with her to hear her examination, and delivered her from the malice of her enemies. And then it was revealed to this creature that the good Vicar would live seven years after, and then should pass hence with great grace, and he did as she foretold.

CHAPTER 18

At Norwich she visits a White Friar, William Sowth-feld, and an anchoress, Dame Jelyan.

This creature was charged and commanded in her soul that she should go to a White Friar, in the same city of Norwich, called William Sowthfeld, a good man and a holy liver, to shew him the grace that God wrought in her, as she had done to the good Vicar before. She did as she was commanded and came to the friar on a forenoon, and was with him in a chapel a long time, and shewed him her meditations, and what God had wrought in her soul, to find out if she were deceived by any illusion or not.

This good man, the White Friar, ever whilst she told him her feelings, holding up his hands, said:—'Jesu Mercy and gramercy.'

'Sister,' he said, 'dread not for your manner of living, for it is the Holy Ghost working plenteously His grace in your soul. Thank Him highly for His goodness, for we all be bound to thank Him for you, Who now in our days will inspire His grace in you, to the help and comfort of us all, who are supported by your prayers and by such others as ye be. And we are preserved from many mischiefs and diseases which we should suffer, and worthily, for our trespass. Never were such good creatures amongst us. Blessed be Almighty God for His goodness. And therefore, sister, I counsel you that ye dispose yourself to receive the gifts of God as lowly and meekly as ye can, and put no obstacle or objection against the goodness of the Holy Ghost, for He may give His gifts where He will, and of unworthy He maketh worthy, of sinful He maketh rightful. His mercy is ever ready unto us, unless the fault be in ourselves, for He dwelleth not in a body subject to sin. He flieth all false feigning and falsehood: He asketh of us a lowly, a meek and a contrite heart, with a good will. Our Lord sayeth Himself:— "My Spirit shall rest upon a meek man, a contrite man, and one dreading My words."

'Sister, I trust to Our Lord that ye have these conditions either in your will or your affection, or else in both, and I believe not that Our Lord suffereth them to be deceived endlessly, that set all their trust in Him, and seek and desire nothing but Him only, as I hope ye do. And therefore believe fully that Our Lord loveth you and worketh His grace in you. I pray God to increase it and continue it to His everlasting worship, for His mercy.'

The aforesaid creature was much comforted both in body and in soul by this good man's words, and greatly strengthened in her faith.

Then she was bidden by Our Lord to go to an anchoress in the same city, named Dame Jelyan, and so she did, and showed her the grace that God put into her soul, of compunction, contrition, sweetness and devotion, compassion with holy meditation and high contemplation, and full many holy speeches and dalliance that Our Lord spake to her soul; and many wonderful revelations, which she shewed to the anchoress to find out if there were any deceit in them, for the anchoress was expert in such things, and good counsel could give.

The anchoress, hearing the marvellous goodness of Our Lord, highly thanked God with all her heart for His visitation, counselling this creature to be obedient to the will of Our Lord God and to fulfil with all her might whatever He put into her soul, if it were not against the worship of God, and profit of her fellow Christians, for if it were, then it were not the moving of a good spirit, but rather of an evil spirit. 'The Holy Ghost moveth ne'er a thing against charity, for if He did, He would be contrary to His own self for He is all charity. Also He moveth a soul to all chasteness, for chaste livers are called the Temple of the Holy Ghost, and the Holy Ghost maketh a soul stable and steadfast in the right faith, and the right belief.

'And a double man in soul is ever unstable and unsteadfast in all his ways. He that is ever doubting is like the flood of the sea which is moved and born about with the wind, and that man is not likely to receive the gifts of God.

'Any creature that hath these tokens may steadfastly believe that the Holy Ghost dwelleth in his soul. And much more when God visiteth a creature with tears of contrition, devotion, and compassion, he may and ought to believe that the Holy Ghost is in his soul. Saint Paul saith that the Holy Ghost asketh for us with mourning and weeping unspeakable, that is to say, He maketh us to ask and pray with mourning and weeping so plenteously that the tears may not be numbered. No evil spirit may give these tokens, for Saint Jerome saith that tears torment more the devil than do the pains of Hell. God and the devil are ever at odds and they shall never dwell together in one place, and the devil hath no power in a man's soul.

'Holy Writ saith that the soul of a rightful man is the seat of God, and so I trust, sister, that ye be. I pray God grant you perseverance. Set all your trust in God and fear not the language of the world, for the more despite, shame and reproof that ye have in the world, the more is your merit in the sight of God. Patience is necessary to you, for in that shall ye keep your soul.'

Much was the holy dalliance that the anchoress and this creature had by communing in the love of Our Lord Jesus Christ the many days that they were together.

This creature shewed her manner of living to many a worthy clerk, to worshipful doctors of divinity, both religious men and others of secular habit, and they said that God wrought great grace with her, and bade her she should not be afraid—there was no deceit in her manner of living. They counselled her to be persevering, for their greatest dread was that she should turn and not keep her perfection. She had so many enemies and so much slander, that they thought she might not bear it without great grace and a mighty faith.

Others who had no knowledge of her manner of governance, save only by outward sight or else by jangling of other persons perverting the judgment of truth, spoke full evil of her and caused her much enmity and much distress, more than she would otherwise have had, had their evil language never been spoken. Nevertheless the anchorite of the Preaching Friars in Lynne, who was the principal ghostly father of this creature, as is written before, took it on charge of his soul that her feelings were good and sure, and that there was no deceit in them, and he by the spirit of prophecy, told her that, when she should go Jerusalem-ward, she would have much tribulation with her maiden, and how Our Lord would try her sharply and prove her full straitly.

Then said she to him:—'Ah! Good sir, what shall I do when I am far from home, and in strange countries, and my maiden is against me? Then is my bodily comfort gone, and ghostly comfort from any confessor such as ye be, I wot not where to get.'

'Daughter, dread ye nothing, for Our Lord Himself shall comfort you His own self, Whose comfort surpasseth all other, and when all your friends have forsaken you, Our Lord will make a broken-backed man lead you forth whither ye will go.'

And so it befell as the anchorite had prophesied in every point, and as, I trust, shall be written more fully afterwards.

Then this creature, in a manner complaining, said to the anchorite:—

'Good sir, what shall I do? He that is my confessor in your absence is right sharp with me; he will not believe my feelings; he setteth naught by them; he holdeth them but trifles and japes, and that is great pain to me, for I love him well and would fain follow his counsel.'

The anchorite answering her, said:—'It is no wonder, daughter, if he cannot believe in your feelings so soon. He knoweth well that ye have been a sinful woman, and therefore he weeneth that God would not be homely with you in so short a time. After your conversion, I would not for all this world be so sharp to you as he is. God, for your merit, hath ordained him to be your scourge, and he fareth with you as a smith with a file maketh the iron bright and clean to the sight, which before appeared rusty, dirty, and evil-colored. The more sharp he is to you the more clearly shineth your soul in the sight of God, and God hath ordained me to be your nurse and your comfort. Be ye lowly and meek and thank God for both one and the other.'

On a time, before this creature went to her prayers to find out what answer she should give to the widow, she was commanded in her spirit to bid the widow leave her confessor that was, at that time if she would please God, and go the anchorite at the Preaching Friars in Lynne and show him her life.

When this creature gave this message, the widow would not believe her words, nor her ghostly father either, unless God should give her the same grace that He gave this creature, and she charged this creature that she should no more come to her place.

And because this creature told her that she had to feel love and affection for her ghostly father, therefore the widow said it had been good for this creature that her love and her affection were set as hers was.

Then Our Lord bade this creature write a letter and send it her. A master of divinity wrote a letter at her request and sent it to the widow with these clauses that follow:

One clause was that the widow should never have the grace that this creature had. Another was that, though this creature never came into her house, it would please God right well.

Our Lord soon after said to this creature: 'It were better for her than all this world, if her love were set as thine is, and I bid thee go to her ghostly father and tell him that, as he will not believe thy words, they shall be parted asunder sooner than he thinketh, and they that be not of her counsel shall know it ere he does, whether he will or not. Lo! Daughter, here mayest thou see how hard it is to part a man from his own will.'

And all this procedure was fulfilled in truth, as the creature had said, before twelve years after. Then this creature suffered much tribulation and great grief, because she said these words, as Our Lord bade her. And ever she increased in the love of God and was more bold than she was before.

CHAPTER 19

The lady whose husband is in Purgatory.

Before this creature went to Jerusalem, Our Lord sent her to a worshipful lady, so that she should speak with her in counsel and do His errand to her. The lady would not speak with her unless her ghostly father were present, and she said she was well pleased. And then, when the lady's ghostly father had come, they went into a chapel, all three together, and then this creature said with great reverence and many tears:—

'Madam, Our Lord Jesus Christ bade me tell you that your husband is in Purgatory, and that ye shall be saved, but that it shall be long ere ye come to Heaven.'

And then the lady was displeased, and said her

husband was a good man—she believed not that he was in Purgatory. Her ghostly father held with this creature, and said it might right well be as she said, and confirmed her words with many holy tales.

And then this lady sent her daughter, with many others of her household with her, to the anchorite who was principal confessor to this creature, so that he should forsake her or else he would lose her friendship. The anchorite said to the messengers that he would not forsake this creature for any man on earth, because to such creatures as would inquire of him her manner of governance and what he thought of her, he said she was God's own servant, and also he said that she was the tabernacle of God.

And the anchorite said unto her own person to strengthen her in her faith:—

'Though God take from you all tears and dalliance, believe nevertheless that God loveth you and that ye shall be right sure of Heaven for what ye have had beforetime, for tears with love are the greatest gift which God may give on earth, and all men that love God ought to thank Him for you.'

Also, there was a widow who prayed this creature to pray for her husband, and find out if he had any need of help. And as this creature prayed for him, she was answered that his soul would be thirty years in Purgatory, unless he had better friends on earth. Thus she told the widow and said:—

'If ye will give alms, three pounds or four, in Masses and alms-giving to poor folk, ye shall highly please God and give the soul great ease.'

The widow took little heed of her words and let it pass.

Then this creature went to the anchorite and told him how she had felt, and he said the feeling was of God, and the deed in itself was good, even though the soul had no need there-of, and counselled that it should be fulfilled. Then this creature told this matter to her ghostly father, so that he should speak to the widow, and so for a long time this creature heard no more of this matter.

Afterwards Our Lord Jesus Christ said to this creature:—'That thing I bade should be done for the soul, it is not done. Ask now thy ghostly father.'

And so she did, and he said it was not done.

She said again:—'My Lord Jesus Christ told me so right now.'

CHAPTER 20

The Host flutters at the Consecration.

On a day as this creature was hearing her Mass, a young man and a good priest was holding up the Sacrament in his hands, over his head, and the Sacrament shook and flickered to and fro, as a dove flickereth with her wings. And when he held up the Chalice with the Precious Sacrament, the Chalice moved to and fro, as if it would have fallen out of his hands. When the Consecration was done, this creature had great marvel of the stirring and moving of the Blessed Sacrament, desiring to see more Consecrations, and watching if it would do so again.

Then said Our Lord Jesus Christ to the creature:—'Thou shalt no more see It in this manner; therefore thank God that thou hast seen. My daughter, Bride, saw Me never in this wise.'

Then said this creature, in her thought:—

'Lord, what betokeneth this?'

'It betokeneth vengeance.'

'Ah! Good Lord, what vengeance?'

Then said Our Lord again to her:—'There shall be an earthquake; tell it to whom thou wilt, in the name of Jesus. For I tell thee forsooth, right as I spoke to Saint Bride, right so I speak to thee, daughter, and I tell thee truly that it is true, every word that is written in Bride's book, and by thee it shall be known for very truth. And thou shalt fare well, daughter, in spite of all thine enemies; the more envy they have of thee for My grace, the better shall I love thee. I were not rightful God unless [I loved] thee, for I know thee better than thou dost thyself, [whatsoever men][6] say of thee. Thou sayest I have great patience in the sin of the people, and thou sayest truth, but if thou saw the sin of the people as I do, then wouldst thou have much more marvel in My patience and much more sorrow in the sin of the people than thou hast.'

Then the creature said:—'Alas! dearworthy Lord, what shall I do for the people?'

Our Lord answered:—'It is enough to thee to do as thou dost.'

Then she prayed:—'Merciful Lord Christ Jesus, in Thee is all mercy and grace and goodness.

Have mercy, pity and compassion on them. Show Thy mercy and Thy goodness to them, help them, send them true contrition, and never let them die in their sin.'

Our Merciful Lord said:—'I may no more, daughter, of My rightfulness do for them than I do. I send them preaching and teaching, pestilence and battles, hunger and famine, loss of their goods with great sickness and many other tribulations, and they will not believe My words, nor will they know My visitation. And therefore I shall say to them thus:—

'"I made My servants pray for you and ye despised their works and their living."'

CHAPTER 21

Our Lord speaks on the merits of maidenhood, marriage and widowhood.

At the time that this creature had revelations, Our Lord said to her:—'Daughter, thou art with child.'

She said to Him:—'Ah! Lord, what shall I do for the keeping of my child?'

Our Lord said:—'Dread thee not. I shall arrange for a keeper.'

'Lord, I am not worthy to hear Thee speak, and thus to commune with my husband. Nevertheless, it is to me great pain and great dis-ease.'

'Therefore it is no sin to thee, daughter, for it is rather to thee reward and merit, and thou shalt have never the less grace, for I will that thou bring Me forth more fruit.'

Then said the creature:—'Lord Jesus, this manner of living belongeth to Thy holy maidens.'

'Yea, daughter, trow thou right well that I love wives also, and specially those wives who would live chaste if they might have their will, and do their business to please Me as thou dost; for, though the state of maidenhood be more perfect and more holy than the state of widowhood, and the state of widowhood more perfect than the state of wedlock, yet, daughter, I love thee as well as any maiden in the world. No man may hinder Me in loving whom I will, and as much as I will, for love, daughter, quencheth all sin. And therefore ask of Me the gifts of love. There is no gift so holy as is the gift of love, nor anything to be desired so much as love, for love may purchase

what it can desire. And therefore, daughter, thou mayest no better please God than continually to think on His love.'

Then this creature asked Our Lord how she should best love Him, and Our Lord said:—

'Have mind of thy wickedness and think of My goodness.'

She said again:—'I am the most unworthy creature that ever Thou shewedest grace unto on earth.'

'Ah! daughter,' said Our Lord, 'fear thee nothing. I take no heed what a man hath been, but I take heed what he will be. Daughter, thou hast despised thyself; therefore thou shalt never be despised of God. Have mind, daughter, what Mary Magdalene was, Mary of Egypt, Saint Paul, and many other saints that are now in Heaven, for of unworthy, I make worthy, and of sinful, I make rightful. And so have I made thee worthy. To Me, once loved, and ever more loved by Me. There is no saint in Heaven that thou wilt speak with, but he shall come to thee. Whom God loveth, they love. When thou pleasest God, thou pleasest His Mother, and all the saints in Heaven. Daughter, I take witness of My Mother, of all the angels in Heaven, and of all the saints in Heaven, that I love thee with all My heart, and I may not forget thy love.'

Our Lord said then to His Blissful Mother:— 'Blessed Mother, tell ye My daughter of the greatness of the love I have unto her.'

Then this creature lay still, all in weeping and sobbing as if her heart would have burst for the sweetness of speech that Our Lord spoke unto her soul.

Immediately afterwards, the Queen of Mercy, God's Mother, dallied to the soul of this creature, saying:—

'My dearworthy daughter, I bring thee sure tidings, as witness my sweet Son Jesus, with all the angels and all the saints in Heaven who love thee full highly. Daughter, I am thy Mother, thy Lady and thy Mistress, to teach thee in all wise how thou shalt please God best.'

She taught this creature and informed her so wonderfully, that she was abashed to say it or tell it to any—the matters were so high and so holy— save only to the anchorite who was her principal confessor, for he had most knowledge of such things. And he charged this creature, by virtue of obedience, to tell him whatever she felt, and so she did.

CHAPTER 22

Our Lord praises her and promises her eternal life.

As this creature lay in contemplation for weeping, in her spirit she said to Our Lord Jesus Christ:—

'Ah! Lord, maidens dance now merrily in Heaven. Shall not I do so? For, because I am no maiden, lack of maidenhood is to me now great sorrow; me-thinketh I would I had been slain when I was taken from the font-stone, so that I should never have displeased Thee, and then shouldst Thou, blessed Lord, have had my maidenhood without end. Ah! dear God, I have not loved thee all the days of my life and that sore rueth me; I have run away from Thee, and Thou hast run after me; I would fall into despair, and Thou wouldst not suffer me.'

'Ah! Daughter, how often have I told thee that thy sins are forgiven thee, and that we are united (in love) together without end. Thou art to Me a singular love, daughter, and therefore I promise thee thou shalt have a singular grace in Heaven, daughter, and I promise thee that I shall come to thine end at thy dying with My Blessed Mother, and My holy angels and twelve apostles, Saint Katherine, Saint Margaret, Saint Mary Magdalene and many other saints that are in Heaven, who give great worship to Me for the grace that I give to thee, thy God, thy Lord Jesus. Thou needest dread no grievous pains in thy dying, for thou shalt have thy desire, that is to have more mind of My Passion than of thine own pain. Thou shalt not dread the devil of Hell, for he hath no power in thee. He dreadeth thee more than thou dost him. He is wroth with thee because thou tormentest him more with thy weeping than doth all the fire in Hell; thou winnest many souls from him with thy weeping. And I have promised thee that thou shouldst have no other Purgatory than the slander and speech of the world, for I have chastised thee Myself as I would, by many great dreads and torments that thou hast had with evil spirits, both asleep and awake for many years. And therefore I shall preserve thee at thine end

through My mercy, so that they shall have no power over thee either in body or in soul. It is a great grace and miracle that thou hast thy bodily wits, for the vexation that thou hast had with them aforetime.

'I have also, daughter, chastised thee with the dread of My Godhead, and many times have I terrified thee with great tempests of winds, so that thou thoughtst vengeance would have fallen on thee for sin. I have proved thee by many tribulations, many great griefs, and many grievous sicknesses, insomuch that thou hast been anointed for death, and all, through my Grace, hast thou escaped. Therefore dread thee naught, daughter, for with Mine own hands which were nailed to the Cross, I will take thy soul from thy body with great mirth and melody, with sweet smells and good odours, and offer it to My Father in Heaven, where thou shalt see Him face to face, living with Him without end.

'Daughter, thou shalt be right welcome to My Father, and My Mother, and to all My saints in Heaven, for thou hast given them drink full many times with the tears of thine eyes. All My holy saints shall rejoice at thy coming home. Thou shall be full filled with all manner of love that thou covetest. Then shalt thou bless the time that thou wert wrought, and the Body that thee hath (dearly) bought. He shall have joy in thee and thou in Him without end.

'Daughter, I promise thee the same grace that I promised Saint Katherine, Saint Margaret, Saint Barbara, and Saint Paul, insomuch that what creature on earth unto the Day of Doom asketh thee any boon and believeth that God loveth thee, he shall have his boon or else a better thing. Therefore they that believe that God loveth thee, they shall be blessed without end. The souls in Purgatory shall rejoice in thy coming home, for they know well that God loveth thee specially. And men on earth shall rejoice in God for thee, for He shall work much grace for thee and make all the world to know that God loveth thee. Thou hast been despised for My love and therefore thou shalt be worshipped for My love.

'Daughter, when thou art in Heaven, thou shalt be able to ask what thou wilt, and I shall grant thee all thy desire. I have told thee beforetime that thou art a singular lover, and therefore thou shalt have a singular love in Heaven, a singular reward, and a singular worship. And, forasmuch as thou art a maiden in thy soul, I shall take thee by the one hand in Heaven, and My Mother by the other hand, and so shalt thou dance in Heaven with other holy maidens and virgins, for I may call thee dearly bought, and Mine own dearworthy darling. I shall say to thee, Mine own blessed spouse:—"Welcome to Me with all manner of joy and gladness, here to dwell with Me and never to depart from Me without end, but ever to dwell with Me in joy and bliss, which no eye may see, nor ear hear, nor tongue tell, nor heart think, that I have ordained for thee and all My servants who desire to love and please Me as thou dost."'

CHAPTER 23

The vicar who thought of leaving his benefice. Margery's revelations as to the fate of departed souls, and of sick people.

There came once a vicar to this creature, praying her to pray for him, and to find out whether he would more please God by leaving his cure and his benefice, or by keeping it still, for he thought he profited not among his parishioners. The creature being at her prayers, having mind of this matter, Christ said unto her spirit:—

'Bid the vicar keep still his cure and his benefice, and be diligent in preaching and teaching them in person, and sometimes to procure others to teach them My laws and My commandments, so that there be no default on his part, and if they do never the better, his merit shall be never the less.'

So she gave her message as she was commanded, and the vicar still kept his cure.

As this creature was in a church of Saint Margaret in the choir, where a corpse was present, and he that was husband of the same corpse, whilst she lived, was there in good health to offer her Mass-penny, as was the custom of the place, Our Lord said to the aforesaid creature:—

'Lo! Daughter, the soul of this corpse is in Purgatory, and he that was her husband is now in good health, and yet he shall be dead in a short time.'

And so it befell, as she felt by revelation.

Also, as this creature lay in the choir at her prayers, a priest came to her and prayed her to pray for a woman who lay at point of death. As this creature began to pray for her, Our Lord said to her:—

'Daughter, there is great need to pray for her, for she hath been a wicked woman, and she shall die.'

And she answered:—'Lord, as thou lovest me, save her soul from damnation.'

Then she wept with plenteous tears for that soul, and Our Lord granted her mercy for the soul, commanding her to pray for her.

This creature's ghostly father came to her, moving her to pray for a woman who lay at point of death, to man's sight, and anon Our Lord said she should live and fare well, and so she did.

A good man, who was a great friend of this creature and helpful to the poor people, was very sick for many weeks together. And much mourning was made for him, for men thought he would never have lived, his pain was so amazing in all his joints and all his body. Our Lord Jesus said to her spirit:—

'Daughter, be not afraid for this man, he shall live and fare right well.'

And so he lived many years after, in good health and prosperity.

Another good man, who was a reader, lay sick also, and when this creature prayed for him, it was answered to her mind that he should linger a while, and later would be dead of the same sickness, and so he was a short time after.

Also a worshipful woman, and as men believed, a holy woman, who was a special friend of this creature, was right sick, and many people thought she should have been dead. Then, this creature praying for her, Our Lord said:—

'She shalt not die these ten years, for ye shall, after this, make full merry together, and have full good communication as ye have had before.'

And so it was, in truth. This holy woman lived many years after.

Many more such revelations this creature had in feeling; to write them all would be hindrance, peradventure, of more profit.

These are written to show the homeliness and goodliness of Our Lord Jesus Christ, and for no commendation of this creature.

These feelings and many more than are written, both of living and of dying, of some to be saved, of some to be damned, were to this creature great pain and punishment. She would rather have suffered any bodily penance than these feelings, if she might have put them away, for the dread she had of illusions and deceits of her ghostly enemies. She had sometimes such great trouble with such feelings when they fell not true to her understanding, that her confessor feared that she would have fallen into despair therewith. And then, after her trouble and her great fears, it would be shewn unto her soul how the feelings should be understood.

CHAPTER 24

The priest who wrote the book proves Margery's revelations to be true. The man who tried to borrow money. The other who tried to sell a breviary.

The priest who wrote this book, to prove this creature's feelings many and divers times asked her questions, and information of things that were to come, unknown and uncertain at that time to any creature as to what would be the outcome, praying her, though she was loath and unwilling to do such things, to pray to God therefore, and ascertain, when Our Lord would visit her with devotion, what would be the outcome, and truly, without any feigning, tell him how she felt, or else he would not gladly write the book.

And so this creature, compelled somewhat for fear that he would not otherwise have followed her intent to write this book, did as he prayed her, and told him her feelings as to what would befall in such matters as he asked her, if her feelings were truth. And thus he proved them for very truth. And yet he would not always give credence to her words, and that hindered him in the manner that followeth.

It befell on a time, that there came a young man to this priest, which young man the priest had never seen before, complaining to the priest of poverty and distress into which he had fallen by misfortune, explaining the cause of the misfortune, saying also that he had taken holy orders to be a priest. For a little hastiness, defending himself, as he had no choice unless he was to be dead through the pursuit of his enemies, he smote a man, or perhaps two, where-through, as he said, they were dead or likely to die.

And so he had fallen into irregularities and might not execute his orders without dispensation of the Court of Rome, and for this reason he fled from his friends, and dared not go into his country for dread of being taken for their death.

The aforesaid priest, giving credence to the young man's words inasmuch as he was an amiable person, fair featured, well favoured in cheer and countenance, sober in his language and dalliance, priestly in his gesture and vesture, having compassion on his distress, purposing to get him friends unto his relief and comfort, went to a worshipful burgess in Lynne, a mayor's equal, and a merciful man, who lay in great sickness, and long had done so, complaining to him and his wife, a full good woman, of the misfortune of this young man, trusting to have fair alms as he oftentimes had for others that he asked for.

It happened that the creature, of whom this book is written, was present there and heard how the priest pleaded for the young man, and how the priest praised him. And she was sore moved in her spirit against that young man, and said they had many poor neighbors who, they knew well enough, had great need of being helped and relieved, and it should rather be alms to help them that they knew well for well disposed folk, and their own neighbors, than strangers that they knew not, for many speak and seem full fair outwardly to the sight of the people. God knoweth what they are in their souls!

The good man and his wife thought she spoke right well, and therefore they would grant him no alms.

At that time the priest was evil-pleased with this creature, and when he met her alone, he repeated how she had hindered him so that he could get no alms for the young man, who was a well-disposed man, as he thought, and much commended his behaviour.

The creature said:—'Sir, God knoweth what his behaviour is, for, as far as I know, I have never seen him and yet I have understanding what his behaviour should be; and therefore, Sir, if ye will act by my counsel, and after what I feel, let him choose and help himself as well as he can, and meddle ye not with him, for he will deceive you at the last.'

The young man resorted always to the priest, flattering him and saying that he had good friends in other places, who would help him if they knew where he was, and that in a short time; and also they would thank those persons who had supported him in his distress. The priest, trusting it would be as this young man told him, lent him silver, with good will, to help him. The young man prayed the priest to hold him excused if he saw him not for two days or three, for he would go a little way, and come again in a short time and bring him back his silver right well and truly. The priest, having confidence in his promise, was well content, granting him good love and leave unto the day on which he had promised to come again.

When he was gone, the aforesaid creature, understanding by feeling in her soul that Our Lord would show that he was an untrue man, and would come back no more, she, to prove whether her feeling was true or false, asked the priest where the young man was, that he had praised so much.

The priest said he had walked a little way and he trusted that he would come again. She said she supposed he would no more see him, and no more he did ever after. And then he repented that he had not done after her counsel.

A short time after this was past, there came another false rascal, an old man, to the same priest and proffered him a breviary, a good little book, for sale. The priest went to the aforesaid creature, praying her to pray for him, and find out whether God willed that he should buy the book or not, and while she prayed, he cheered the man as well as he could, and then came again to this creature and asked how she felt.

'Sir,' she said, 'buy no book from him, for he is not to be trusted, and that ye will well know if ye meddle with him.'

Then the priest prayed the man that he might see his book. The man said he had not got it on him. The priest asked how he came by it. He said he was executor to a priest who was of his kindred, and he charged him to sell it, and dispose of it for him.

'Father,' said the priest—because of rever-

ence—'why do ye offer me this book rather than other men or other priests, when there are so many more thriftier and richer priests in this church than I am, and I wot well ye had no knowledge of me before this time?'

'Forsooth, Sir,' he said, 'no more I had. Nevertheless I have good will toward your person, and also it was his will, who owned it before, that, if I knew any young priest that me-thought quiet and well-disposed, he should have this book before any other man, and for less price than any other man, that he might pray for him, and these causes make me come to you rather than to another.'

The priest asked him where he dwelt.

'Sir,' he said, 'but five miles from this place in Penteney Abbey.'

'There have I been,' said the priest, 'but I have not seen you.'

'No, Sir,' said he again, 'I have been there but a little while, and now have I there an allowance of food, thanks be to God.'

The priest prayed him that he might have a sight of the book and see if they might agree.

He said:—'Sir, I hope to be here again next week and to bring it with me, and, Sir, I promise you, ye shall have it before any other man, if ye like it.' The priest thanked him for his good will and so they parted asunder, but the man never came to the priest afterwards, and the priest knew well that the aforesaid creature's feeling was true.

CHAPTER 25

The dispute between the church and the chapels regarding the font.

Furthermore, here followeth a right notable matter of the creature's feeling, and it is written here for convenience inasmuch as it is, in feeling, like the matters that be written before, notwithstanding that it befell long after the matters which follow.

It happened in a worshipful town where there was one parish church and two chapels annexed, the chapels having and administering all the Sacraments, except only christening and purifications, through sufferance of the parson, who was a monk of Saint Benedict's Order, sent from the house of Norwich, keeping residence with three of his brethren in the worshipful town before written.

Through some of the parishioners desiring to make the chapels like the parish church by pursuance of a bull from the Court of Rome, there befell great dispute and great trouble between the prior, who was their parson and curate, and the aforesaid parishioners, who desired to have fonts and purifications in the chapels, as there were in the parish church. And especially in the one chapel which was the greater and fairer, they would have a font.

There was pursued a bull, under which a font was granted to the chapel, provided that it was no derogation to the parish church. The bull was put in plea and divers days were spent in form of law to prove whether the font, if it were put in, would be derogatory to the parish church or not. The parishioners who pursued were right strong, and had great help of lordship, and also, most of all, they were rich men, worshipful merchants, and had gold enough, that can speed in every need; and it is ruth that need should speed ere truth.

Nevertheless, the prior who was their parson, though he was poor, manfully withstood them with the help of some of his parishioners who were his friends, and love the worship of their parish church. So long was this matter in plea that it began to irk them on both sides, and it was never the nearer an end.

Then was the matter put to my Lord of Norwich—Alnewyk—to see if he might by treaty bring it to an end. He labored this matter diligently; and to set it at rest and peace, he proffered the aforesaid parishioners much of their desire with certain conditions, insomuch that they that held with the parson and with their parish church, were full sorry, dreading greatly that they that sued to have a font would obtain and get their intent and so make the chapel equal to the parish church.

Then the priest who afterwards wrote this book, went to the creature of whom this treatise maketh mention, as he had done before in time of plea, and asked her how she felt in her soul on this matter, whether they should have a font in the chapel or not.

'Sir,' said the creature, 'dread ye not, for I understand in my soul, though they should give [even][7] a bushel of nobles[8] they could not have it.'

'Ah! Mother,' said the priest, 'my lord of Norwich hath offered it to them on certain conditions, and they have a time for consideration to say nay or yea, whichever they will, and therefore I am afraid they will not refuse it, but be right glad to have it.'

This creature prayed to God that His will might be fulfilled, and, forasmuch as she had the revelation that they would not have it, she was the more bold to pray Our Lord to withstand their intent and slacken their boasting.

And so, as Our Lord willed, they obeyed not nor liked the conditions which were offered them, for they trusted fully to get their intent by lordship and process of law; and, as God willed, they were deceived of their intent, and because they would have all, they lost all.

And so, blessed may God be, the parish church stood fast in their worship and her degree, as she had done for two hundred years before and more, and the inspiration of Our Lord was by experience proved very true and sure in the aforesaid creature.

CHAPTER 26

She starts from Yarmouth on her way to the Holy Land. She has trouble with her companions owing to her weeping and piety. She reaches Constance.

When the time came that this creature should visit those holy places where Our Lord was quick and dead, as she had by revelation years before, she prayed the parish priest of the town where she was dwelling, to say for her in the pulpit, that, if any man or woman claimed any debt from her husband or herself, they should come and speak with her ere she went, and she, with the help of God would make a settlement with each of them, so that they should hold themselves content. And so she did.

Afterwards, she took her leave of her husband and of the holy anchorite, who had told her, before, the process of her going and the great disease that she would suffer by the way, and when all her fellowship forsook her, how a broken-backed man would lead her forth in safety, through the help of Our Lord.

And so it befell indeed, as shall be written afterward.

Then she took her leave of Master Robert, and prayed him for his blessing, and so, forth of other friends. Then she went forth to Norwich, and offered at the Trinity, and afterwards she went to Yarmouth and offered at an image of Our Lady, and there she took her ship.

And next day they came to a great town called Zierikzee, where Our Lord of His high goodness visited this creature with abundant tears of contrition for her own sins, and sometime for other men's sins also. And especially she had tears of compassion in mind of Our Lord's Passion. And she was houselled each Sunday where there was time and place convenient thereto, with great weeping and boisterous sobbing, so that many men marvelled and wondered at the great grace that God had wrought in His creature.

This creature had eaten no flesh and drunk no wine for four years ere she went out of England, and so now her ghostly father charged her, by virtue of obedience, that she should both eat flesh and drink wine. And so she did a little while; afterwards she prayed her confessor that he would hold her excused if she ate no flesh, and suffer her to do as she would for such time as pleased him.

And soon after, through the moving of some of her company, her confessor was displeased because she ate no flesh, and so were many of the company. And they were most displeased because she wept so much and spoke always of the love and goodness of Our Lord, as much at the table as in other places. And therefore shamefully they reproved her, and severely chid her, and said they would not put up with her as her husband did when she was at home and in England.

And she answered meekly to them:—'Our Lord, Almighty God, is as great a Lord here as in England, and as good cause have I to love Him here as there, blessed may He be.'

At these words, her fellowship was angrier than before, and their wrath and unkindness to this creature was a matter of great grief, for they were held right good men and she desired great-

ly their love, if she might have it to the pleasure of God.

And then she said to one of them specially:— 'Ye cause me much shame and great grievance.'

He answered her anon:—'I pray God that the devil's death may overcome thee soon and quickly,' and many more cruel words he said to her than she could repeat.

And soon after some of the company in whom she trusted best, and her own maiden also, said she could no longer go in their fellowship. And they said that they would take away her maiden from her, so that she should no strumpet be, in her company. And then one of them, who had her gold in keeping, left her a noble with great anger and vexation to go where she would and help herself as she might, for with them, they said, she should no longer abide; and they forsook her that night.

Then, on the next morning, there came to her one of their company, a man who loved her well, praying her that she would go to his fellows and meeken herself to them, and pray them that she might go still in their company till she came to Constance.

And so she did, and went forth with them till she came to Constance with great discomfort and great trouble, for they did her much shame and much reproof as they went, in divers places. They cut her gown so short that it came but little beneath her knee, and made her put on a white canvas, in the manner of a sacken apron, so that she should be held a fool and the people should not make much of her or hold her in repute. They made her sit at the table's end, below all the others, so that she ill durst speak a word.

And, notwithstanding all their malice, she was held in more worship than they were, wherever they went.

And the good man of the house where they were hostelled, though she sat lowest at the table's end, would always help her before them all as well as he could, and sent her from his own table such service as he had, and that annoyed her fellowship full evil.

As they went by the way Constance-ward, it was told them that they would be robbed and have great discomfort unless they had great grace.

Then this creature came to a church and went in to make her prayer, and she prayed with all her heart, with great weeping and many tears, for help and succour against their enemies.

Then Our Lord said to her mind:—'Dread thee naught, daughter, thy fellowship shall come to no harm whilst thou art in their company.'

And so, blessed may Our Lord be in all His works, they went forth in safety to Constance.

CHAPTER 27

At Constance, the Papal legate befriends her. She meets William Wever, of Devonshire. She goes to Bologna and Venice.

When this creature and her fellowship had come to Constance, she heard tell of an English friar, a master of divinity, and the Pope's legate, who was in that city. Then she went to that worshipful man and shewed him her life from the beginning to that hour, as nigh as she might in confession, because he was the Pope's legate and a worshipful clerk.

And afterwards she told him what discomfort she had with her fellowship. She told him also what grace God gave her of contrition and compunction, of sweetness and devotion and of many divers revelations that God had revealed to her, and the fear that she had of illusions and deceits of her ghostly enemies, of which she lived in great dread, desiring to put them away, and to feel none, if she might withstand them.

And when she had spoken, the worshipful clerk gave her words of great comfort, and said it was the work of the Holy Ghost, commanding and charging her to obey them and receive them when God should give them and to have no doubts, for the devil hath no power to work such grace in a soul. And also he said that he would support her against the evil will of her fellowship.

Afterwards, when it pleased her fellowship, they prayed this worthy doctor to dinner, and the doctor told the aforesaid creature, warning her to sit at the meat in his presence as she did in his absence, and to keep the same manner of behaviour as she kept when he was not there.

When the time had come for them to sit at meat, every man took his place as he liked; the worshipful legate and doctor sat first, and then the others, and, at the last, the said creature at the board's end, sitting and speaking no word, as she was wont to do, when the legate was not there.

Then the legate said to her:—

'Why are ye no merrier?'

And she sat still and answered not, as he himself had commanded her to do.

When they had eaten, the company made great complaint against this creature to the legate, and said that, utterly, she could no longer be in their company, unless he commanded her to eat flesh as they did and stop her weeping, and that she should not talk so much of holiness.

Then the worshipful doctor said:—'Nay, sirs, I will not make her eat flesh whilst she can abstain and be the better disposed to Our Lord. If one of you made a vow to go to Rome barefoot, I would not dispense him of his vow whilst he could fulfil it, nor will I bid her to eat flesh whilst our Lord giveth her strength to abstain. As for her weeping, it is not in my power to restrain it, for it is the gift of the Holy Ghost. As for her speaking, I will pray her to cease till she cometh where men will hear her with better will than ye do.'

The company was wroth, and in great anger. They gave her over to the legate and said utterly that they would no more associate with her. He full benignly and kindly received her as though she had been his mother, and received her gold, about twenty pounds, and yet one of them withheld wrongfully about sixteen pounds.

And they withheld also her maiden, and would not let her go with her mistress, notwithstanding that she had promised her mistress and assured her that she would not forsake her for any need.

And the legate made arrangements for this creature and made her his charge as if she had been his mother.

Then this creature went into a church and prayed Our Lord that He would provide her with a leader.

And anon Our Lord spoke to her and said:—

'Thou shalt have right good help and a good leader.'

Immediately afterwards there came to her an old man with a white beard. He was from Devonshire, and said:—

'Damsel, will ye pray me for God's love, and for Our Lady's, to go with you and be your guide, for your countrymen have forsaken you?'

She asked, what was his name?

He said:—'My name is William Wever.'

She prayed him, by the reverence of God and of Our Lady, that he would help her at her need, and she would well reward him for his labour, and so they agreed.

Then went she to the legate and told him how well Our Lord had ordained for her, and took her leave of him and of her company who so unkindly had rejected her, and also of her maiden who was bounden to have gone with her. She took her leave with full heavy face and rueful, having great grief in as much as she was in a strange country, and knew not the language, or the man who would lead her, either.

And so the man and she went forth in great dread and gloom. As they went together, the man said to her:—

'I am afraid thou wilt be taken from me, and I shall be beaten for thee, and lose my jacket.'

She said:—'William, dread you not. God will keep us right well.'

And this creature had every day mind of the Gospel which telleth of the woman that was taken in adultery, and brought before Our Lord.

And she prayed:—'Lord, as thou drove away her enemies, so drive away mine enemies, and keep well my chastity that I vowed to Thee, and let me never be defiled, for if I am, Lord, I make my vow, that I will never come back to England whilst I live.'

Then they went forth day by day and met with many jolly men. And they said no evil word to this creature, but gave her and her man meat and drink, and the good wives where they were housed, laid her in their own beds for God's love, in many places where they came.

And Our Lord visited her with great grace of ghostly comfort as she went by the way. And so God brought her forth till she came to Bologna. And after she had come there, there came thither also her other fellowship, which had forsaken her before. And when they heard say that she had come to Bologna ere they had, then had they great wonder, and one of their fellowship came to

her praying her to go to his fellowship and try if they would receive her again into their fellowship. And so she did.

'If ye will go in our fellowship, ye must make a new covenant, and that is this—ye shall not speak of the Gospel where we are, but shall sit still and make merry, as we do, both at meat and at supper.'

She consented and was received again into their fellowship. Then went they forth to Venice and dwelt there thirteen weeks; and this creature was houselled every Sunday in a great house of nuns, and had great cheer among them, where Our Lord Jesus Christ visited this creature with great devotion and plenteous tears, so that the good ladies of the place were much marvelled thereof.

Afterwards, it happened, as this creature sat at meat with her fellowship, that she repeated a text of the Gospel that she had learnt beforetime with other good words, and then her fellowship said she had broken covenant. And she said:—

'Yea, sirs, forsooth I may no longer keep your covenant, for I must needs speak of My Lord Jesus Christ, though all this world had forbidden it to me.'

Then she took to her chamber and ate alone for six weeks, unto the time that Our Lord made her so sick that she weened to have been dead, and then suddenly He made her whole again. And all the time her maiden let her alone and made the company's meat and washed their clothes, and, to her mistress, under whom she had taken service, she would no deal attend.

CHAPTER 28

She sails from Venice and reaches Jerusalem. Much trouble owing to her crying.

Also this company, which had put the aforesaid creature from their table, so that she should no longer eat amongst them, engaged a ship for themselves to sail in. They bought vessels for their wine, and obtained bedding for themselves, but nothing for her. Then she, seeing their unkindness, went to the same man where they had been, and bought herself bedding as they had done, and came where they were and shewed them what she had done, purposing to

sail with them in that ship which they had chartered.

Afterwards, as this creature was in contemplation, Our Lord warned her in her mind that
she should not sail in that ship, and He assigned
her to another ship, a galley, that she should sail
in. Then she told this to some of the company,
and they told it forth to their fellowship, and
then they durst not sail in the ship they had
chartered. So they sold away their vessels which
they had got for their wines, and were right fain
to come to the galley where she was, and so,
though it was against her will, she went forth
with them in their company, for they durst not
otherwise do.

When it was time to make their beds, they
locked up her clothes, and a priest, who was in
their company, took away a sheet from the aforesaid creature, and said it was his. She took God to
witness that it was her sheet. Then the priest
swore a great oath, by the book in his hand, that
she was as false as she might be, and despised her
and strongly rebuked her.

And so she had ever much tribulation till she
came to Jerusalem. And ere she came there, she
said to them that she supposed they were grieved with her.

'I pray you, Sirs, be in charity with me, for I am
in charity with you, and forgive me that I have
grieved you by the way. And if any of you have
in anything trespassed against me, God forgive it
you, and I do.'

So they went forth into the Holy Land till they
could see Jerusalem. And when this creature saw
Jerusalem, riding on an ass, she thanked God
with all her heart, praying Him for His mercy
that, as He had brought her to see His earthly city
of Jerusalem, He would grant her grace to see the
blissful city of Jerusalem above, the city of Heav-
en. Our Lord Jesus Christ, answering her
thought, granted her to have her desire.

Then for the joy she had, and the sweetness she
felt in the dalliance with Our Lord, she was on
the point of falling off her ass, for she could not
bear the sweetness and grace that God wrought
in her soul. Then two pilgrims, Duchemen, went
to her, and kept her from falling; one of whom
was a priest, and he put spices in her mouth to
comfort her, thinking she had been sick. And so

they helped her on to Jerusalem, and when she
came there, she said:—

'Sirs, I pray you be not displeased though I
weep sore in this holy place where Our Lord
Jesus Christ was quick and dead.'

Then went they to the temple in Jerusalem and
they were let in on the same day at evensong
time, and abode there till the next day at evensong time. Then the friars lifted up a cross and
led the pilgrims about from one place to another
where Our Lord suffered His[9] ... and His Passion,
every man and woman bearing a wax candle in
one hand. And the friars always, as they went
about, told them what Our Lord suffered in every
place. The aforesaid creature wept and sobbed as
plenteously as though she had seen Our Lord
with her bodily eye, suffering His Passion at that
time. Before her in her soul she saw Him verily
by contemplation, and that caused her to have
compassion. And when they came up on to the
Mount of Calvary, she fell down because she
could not stand or kneel, and rolled and wrestled
with her body, spreading her arms abroad, and
cried with a loud voice as though her heart
would have burst asunder; for, in the city of her
soul, she saw verily and clearly how Our Lord
was crucified. Before her face, she heard and saw,
in her ghostly sight, the mourning of Our Lady,
of Saint John, and Mary Magdalene and of many
others that loved Our Lord.

And she had such great compassion and such
great pain, at seeing Our Lord's pain that she
could not keep herself from crying and roaring
though she should have died for it. And this was
the first cry[10] that ever she cried in any contemplation. And this manner of crying endured
many years after this time, for aught any man
might do, and therefore, suffered she much
despite and much reproof. The crying was so
loud and so wonderful that it made the people
astounded unless they had heard it before, or
unless they knew the cause of the crying. And she
had them so often that they made her right weak
in her bodily might, and especially if she heard of
Our Lord's Passion.

And sometimes, when she saw the crucifix, or
if she saw a man with a wound, or a beast,
whichever it were, or if a man beat a child before
her, or smote a horse or other beast with a whip,

if she saw it or heard it, she thought she saw Our Lord being beaten or wounded, just as she saw it in the man or the beast either in the field or the town, and by herself alone as well as amongst the people.

First when she had her cryings in Jerusalem, she had them often, and in Rome also. And when she came home to England, first at her coming home, it came but seldom, as it were once a month, then once a week, afterwards daily, and once she had fourteen in one day, and another day she had seven, and so on, as God would visit her, sometimes in church, sometimes in the street, sometimes in her chamber, sometimes in the fields, whenever God would send them, for she never knew the time nor the hour when they would come. And they never came without passing great sweetness of devotion and high contemplation. And as soon as she perceived that she would cry, she would keep it in as much as she might that the people should not hear it, to their annoyance. For some said that a wicked spirit vexed her; some said it was a sickness; some said she had drunk too much wine; some banned her; some wished she was in the harbour; some wished she was on the sea in a bottomless boat; and thus each man as he thought. Other ghostly men loved her and favoured her the more. Some great clerks said Our Lady cried never so, nor any saint in Heaven, but they knew full little what she felt, nor would they believe that she could not stop crying if she wished.

And therefore when she knew that she would cry, she kept it in as long as she might, and did all she could to withstand it or put it away, till she waxed as livid as any lead, and ever it would labour in her mind more and more till the time it broke out. And when the body might no longer endure the ghostly labour, but was overcome with the unspeakable love that wrought so fervently in her soul, then she fell down and cried wondrous loud, and the more she laboured to keep it in or put it away, so much the more would she cry, and the louder. Thus she did on the Mount of Calvary, as is written before.

Thus she had as very contemplation in the sight of her soul, as if Christ had hung before her bodily eye in His Manhood. And when through the dispensation of the high mercy of Our Sovereign Savior Christ Jesus, it was granted to this creature to behold so verily His precious tender body, all rent and torn with scourges, fuller of wounds than ever was a dove-house of holes, hanging on the Cross with the crown of thorns upon His head, His beautiful hands, His tender feet nailed to the hard tree, the rivers of blood flowing out plenteously from every member, the grisly and grievous wound in His precious side shedding blood and water for her love and her salvation, then she fell down and cried with a loud voice, wonderfully turning and wresting her body on every side, spreading her arms abroad as if she would have died, and could not keep herself from crying, and from these bodily movements for the fire of love that burnt so fervently in her soul with pure pity and compassion.

It is not to be marvelled at, if this creature cried and made wondrous faces and expressions, when we may see each day with the eye both men and women, some for the loss of worldly goods, some for affection of their kindred, or worldly friendships, through over much study and earthly affection, and most of all for inordinate love and fleshly affection, if their friends are parted from them, they will cry and roar and wring their hands as if they had no wits or senses, and yet know they well that they are displeasing God.

And, if a man counsel them to leave or cease their weeping and crying, they will say that they cannot; they loved their friend so much, and he was so gentle and so kind to them, that they may in no way forget him. How much more might they weep, cry, and roar, if their most beloved friends were with violence taken in their sight and with all manner of reproof, brought before the judge, wrongfully condemned to death, and especially so spiteful a death as Our Merciful Lord suffered for our sake. How would they suffer it? No doubt they would both cry and roar and avenge themselves if they might, or else men would say they were no friends.

Alas! Alas! for sorrow that the death of a creature, who hath often sinned and trespassed against their Maker, shall be so immeasurably mourned and sorrowed. And it is an offence to God, and a hindrance to the souls beside them.

And the compassionate death of Our Savior by

which we are all restored to life, is not kept in mind by us unworthy and unkind wretches, nor do we support Our Lord's own secretaries whom He hath endued with love, but rather detract and hinder them as much as we may.

CHAPTER 29

She visits the Holy Sepulchre, Mount Sion and Bethlehem.

When this creature with her fellowship came to the grave where Our Lord was buried, anon, as she entered that holy place, she fell down with her candle in her hand, as if she would have died for sorrow. And late she rose up again with great weeping and sobbing, as though she had seen Our Lord buried even before her.

Then she thought she saw Our Lady in her soul, how she mourned and how she wept for her Son's death, and then was Our Lady's sorrow her sorrow.

And so, wherever the friars led them in that holy place, she always wept and sobbed wonderfully, and especially when she came where Our Lord was nailed on the Cross. There cried she, and wept without measure, so that she could not restrain herself.

Also they came to a stone of marble that Our Lord was laid on when He was taken down from the Cross, and there she wept with great compassion, having mind of Our Lord's Passion.

Afterwards she was houselled on the Mount of Calvary, and then she wept, she sobbed, she cried so loud that it was a wonder to hear it. She was so full of holy thoughts and meditations and holy contemplations on the Passion of Our Lord Jesus Christ, and holy dalliance that Our Lord Jesus Christ spoke to her soul, that she could never express them after, so high and so holy were they. Much was the grace that Our Lord shewed to this creature whilst she was three weeks in Jerusalem.

Another day, early in the morning, they went again amongst great hills, and their guides told her where Our Lord bore the Cross on His back, and where His Mother met with Him, and how she swooned and fell down and He fell down also. And so they went forth all the forenoon till they came to Mount Sion. And ever this creature wept abundantly, all the way that she went, for compassion of Our Lord's Passion. On Mount Sion is a place where Our Lord washed His disciples' feet and, a little therefrom, He made His Maundy with His disciples.

And therefore this creature had great desire to be houselled in that holy place where Our Merciful Lord Christ Jesus first consecrated His precious Body in the form of bread, and gave it to His disciples. And so she was, with great devotion and plenteous tears and boisterous sobbings, for in this place is plenary remission, and so there is in four other places in the Temple. One is on the Mount of Calvary; another at the grave where Our Lord was buried; the third is at the marble stone that His precious Body was laid on, when It was taken from the Cross; the fourth is where the Holy Cross was buried; and in many other places in Jerusalem.

And when this creature came to the place where the apostles received the Holy Ghost, Our Lord gave her great devotion. Afterwards she went to the place where Our Lady was buried, and as she knelt on her knees the time of two masses, Our Lord Jesus Christ said to her:—

'Thou comest not hither, daughter, for any need except merit and reward, for thy sins were forgiven thee ere thou came here and therefore thou comest here for the increasing of thy reward and thy merit. And I am well pleased with thee, daughter, for thou standest under obedience to Holy Church, and because thou wilt obey thy confessor and follow his counsel who, through authority of Holy Church, hath absolved thee of thy sins and dispensed thee so that thou shouldst not go to Rome and Saint James unless thou wilt thine own self. Notwithstanding all this, I command thee in the Name of Jesus, daughter, that thou go visit these holy places and do as I bid thee, for I am above Holy Church, and I shall go with thee and keep thee right well.'

Then Our Lady spoke to her soul in this manner, saying:—

'Daughter, well art thou blessed, for my Son Jesus shall flow so much grace into thee that all the world shall wonder at thee. Be not ashamed, my dearworthy daughter, to receive the gifts that my Son shall give thee, for I tell thee in truth, they shall be great gifts that He shall give thee. And therefore, my dearworthy daughter, be not ashamed of Him that is thy God, thy Lord and thy love, any more than I was, when I saw Him hanging on the Cross—my sweet Son, Jesus—to cry and to weep for the pain of my sweet Son Jesus Christ. Mary Magdalene was not ashamed to cry and weep for my Son's love. Therefore, daughter, if thou will be partaker in our love, thou must be partaker in our sorrow.'

This sweet speech and dalliance had this creature at Our Lady's grave, and much more than she could ever repeat.

Afterwards she rode on an ass to Bethlehem, and when she came to the temple and the crib where Our Lord was born, she had great devotion, much speech and dalliance in her soul, and high ghostly comfort with much weeping and sobbing, so that her fellows would not let her eat in their company, and therefore she ate her meat by herself alone.

And then the Grey Friars, who had led her from place to place, received her to them and set her with them at the meat so that she should not eat alone. And one of the friars asked one of her fellowship if she were the woman of England whom, they had heard said, spoke with God. And when this came to her knowledge, she knew well that it was the truth that Our Lord said to her, ere she went out of England:—

'Daughter, I will make all the world to wonder at thee, and many a man and many a woman shall speak of Me for love of thee, and worship Me in thee.'

CHAPTER 30

She visits the Jordan, Mount Quarentyne, Bethania and Rafnys. Starts for Rome, and at Venice meets Richard, the broken-backed man, and goes on in his company.

Another time, this creature's fellowship would go to the Flood of Jordan and would not let her go with them. Then this creature prayed Our Lord that she might go with them, and He bade that she should go with them whether they would or not. Then she went forth by the grace of God, and asked no leave of them.

When she came to the Flood of Jordan, the weather was so hot that she thought her feet would have burnt for the heat that she felt.

Afterwards she went with her fellowship to Mount Quarantyne. There Our Lord fasted forty days, and there she prayed her fellowship to help her up on to the Mount. And they said, 'Nay', for they could not well help themselves. Then had she great sorrow, because she might not come on to the hill. And anon, happed a Saracen, a well-favoured man, to come by her, and she put a groat into his hand, making him a sign to bring her on to the Mount. And quickly the Saracen took her under his arm and led her up on to the high Mount, where Our Lord fasted forty days.

Then was she sore athirst, and had no comfort in her fellowship. Then God, of His great goodness, moved the Grey Friars with compassion, and they comforted her, when her countrymen would not know her.

And so she was ever more strengthened in the love of Our Lord and the more bold to suffer shame and reproof for His sake in every place where she came, for the grace that God wrought in her of weeping, sobbing, and crying, which grace she might not withstand when God would send it. And ever she proved her feelings true, and those promises that God had made her while she was in England and other places also. They befell her in effect just as she had felt before, and therefore she durst the better receive such speeches and dalliance, and the more boldly work thereafter.

Afterwards, when this creature came down from the Mount, as God willed, she went forth to the place where Saint John the Baptist was born. And later she went to Bethania, where Mary and Martha dwelt, and to the grave where Lazarus was buried and raised from death into life. And she prayed in the chapel where Our Blessed Lord appeared to His blissful Mother on Easter Day at morn, first of all others. And she stood in the same place where Mary Magdalene stood when Christ said to her:—

'Mary, why weepest thou?'

And so she was in many more places than be written, for she was three weeks in Jerusalem and the country thereabout, and she had ever great devotion as long as she was in that country.

The friars of the Temple made her great cheer and gave her many great relics, desiring that she should have dwelt still amongst them if she would, for the faith they had in her. Also the Saracens made much of her, and conveyed her, and led her about the country wherever she would go; and she found all people good to her and gentle, save only her own countrymen.

And as she came from Jerusalem unto Rafnys, then would she have turned again to Jerusalem for the great grace and ghostly comfort that she felt when she was there, and to purchase herself more pardon.

Then Our Lord commanded her to go to Rome and, so, forth home to England, and said to her:—

'Daughter, as oftentimes as thou sayest or thinkest "Worshipped be those Holy Places in Jerusalem that Christ suffered bitter pain and Passion in", thou shalt have the same pardon as if thou wert there with thy bodily presence, both to thyself and to all that thou wilt give it to.'

And as she went forth to Venice, many of her fellowship were right sick, and Our Lord said to her:—

'Dread thee not, daughter, no man shall die in the ship that thou art in.'

And she found her feelings right true. When Our Lord had brought them again to Venice in safety, her countrymen forsook her and went away from her, leaving her alone. And some of them said that they would not go with her for a hundred pound.

When they had gone away from her, then Our Lord Jesus Christ, Who ever helpeth at need, and never forsaketh His servants who truly trust in His mercy, said to this creature:—

'Dread thee not, daughter, for I will provide for thee right well, and bring thee in safety to Rome and home again into England without any villainy to thy body, if thou wilt be clad in white clothes, and wear them as I said to thee whilst thou wert in England.'

Then this creature, being in great grief and distress, answered Him in her mind: ...

'If Thou be the spirit of God that speaketh in my soul, and I may prove Thee for a true spirit with the counsel of the Church, I shall obey Thy will; and if Thou bringest me to Rome in safety, I shall wear white clothes, though all the world should wonder at me, for Thy love.'

'Go forth, daughter, in the Name of Jesus, for I am the spirit of God, which shall help thee in all thy need, go with thee, and support thee in every place, and therefore mistrust Me not. Thou foundest Me never deceivable, and I bid thee nothing do, but that which is worship to God, and profit to thy soul. If thou will do thereafter, then I shall flow on thee great plenty of grace.'

Then anon, as she looked on one side, she saw a poor man sitting, who had a great hump on his back. His clothes were all clouted and he seemed a man of fifty winters' age. Then she went to him and said:—

'Good man, what aileth your back?'

He said:—'Damsel, it was broken in a sickness.'

She asked, what was his name, and what countryman he was. He said his name was Richard, and he was of Ireland. Then thought she of her confessor's words, who was a holy anchorite, as is written before, who spoke to her whilst she was in England in this manner:—

'Daughter, when your fellowship hath forsaken you, God will provide a broken-backed man to lead you forth, wherever you will go.'

Then she, with a glad spirit, said to him:—

'Good Richard, lead me to Rome, and you shall be rewarded for your labor.'

'Nay, damsel,' said he, 'I wot well thy countrymen have forsaken thee, and therefore it were hard on me to lead thee. Thy countrymen have both bows and arrows with which they might defend both thee and themselves, and I have no weapons save a cloak full of clouts, and yet I dread me that mine enemies will rob me, and peradventure take thee away from me and defile thy body, and therefore I dare not lead thee, for I would not, for a hundred pounds, that thou hadst a villainy in my company.'

And she said again:—'Richard, dread you not; God shall keep us both right well and I shall give you two nobles for your labor.'

Then he consented and went forth with her. Soon after, there came two Grey Friars and a woman that came with them from Jerusalem, and she had with her an ass, which bore a chest and an image therein, made after Our Lord.

Then said Richard to the aforesaid creature:—

'Thou shalt go forth with these two men and the woman and I will meet thee morning and evening, for I must get on with my job and beg my living.'

So she did after his counsel and went forth with the two friars and the woman. And none of them could understand her language, and yet they provided for every day, meat, drink, and harborage as well as they did for themselves and rather better, so that she was ever bounden to pray for them.

Every evening and morning, Richard with the broken back came and comforted her as he had promised.

The woman who had the image in the chest, when they came into good cities, took the image out of her chest and set it in worshipful wives' laps; and they would put shirts thereon, and kiss it as if it had been God Himself.

When the creature saw the worship and reverence that they gave to the image, she was taken with sweet devotion and sweet meditations, so that she wept with great sobbing and loud crying; and she was moved so much the more, because while she was in England, she had high meditations on the birth and the childhood of Christ, and she thanked God forasmuch as she saw these creatures having as great faith in what she saw with her bodily eye, as she had had before with her ghostly eye.

When these good women saw this creature weeping, sobbing and crying so wonderfully and mightily that she was nearly overcome therewith, then they arranged a good soft bed and laid her thereon, and comforted her as much as they could for Our Lord's sake, blessed may He be.

CHAPTER 31

Her ring is stolen and recovered. She reaches Assisi, and meets Dame Margaret Florentyne, with whom she goes on to Rome.

The aforesaid creature had a ring, which Our Lord had commanded her to have made whilst she was at home in England, and she had engraved thereon, 'Jesus Christ est amor meus'. She had much thought how she should keep this ring from thieves and stealing, as she went about the countries, for she thought she would not have lost the ring for a thousand pounds and much more, because she had it made by the bidding of

God; and also, she wore it by His bidding, for she purposed beforetime, ere she had it by revelation, never to have worn a ring.

So it happed her to be harbored in a good man's house, and many neighbors came in to cheer her for her perfection and her holiness, and she gave them the measure of Christ's grave which they received full kindly, having great joy thereof, and thanked her highly therefor.

Afterwards this creature went to her chamber and let her ring hang by her purse-string, which she bore at her breast. In the morning on the next day, when she would have taken her ring, it was gone. She could not find it. Then had she great grief, and complained to the good wife of the house, saying in this wise:—

'Madam, my good wedding ring to Jesus Christ, as one might say, it is away.'

The good wife, understanding what she meant, prayed her to pray for her, and she changed her face and countenance strangely, as though she had been guilty. Then this creature took a candle in her hand and sought all about her bed where she had lain all night, and the good wife of the house took another candle in her hand and busied herself seeking also about the bed; and at last she found the ring under the bed on the boards. And with great joy she told the good wife that she had found her ring. Then the good wife, submitting herself, prayed this creature for forgiveness, as well as she could. 'Good Christian, pray for me.'

Afterwards this creature came to Assisi, and there she met with a Friar Minor, an Englishman; and a devout clerk, he was held to be. She told him of her manner of living, of her feelings, of her revelations, and of the grace that God wrought in her soul by holy inspirations and high contemplations, and how Our Lord dallied to her soul in a manner of speaking. Then the worshipful clerk said she was much beholden to God, for he said he had never heard of anyone living in this world, who was so homely with God by love and homely dalliance, as she was, thanked be God for His gifts, for it is His goodness, and no man's merit.

Upon a time, as this creature was in church at Assisi, there was shewn Our Lady's kerchief which she wore here on earth, with many lights and great reverence. Then this creature had great devotion. She wept, she sobbed, she cried with great plenty of tears and many holy thoughts. She was also there on Lammas Day, when there is great pardon with plenary remission, to purchase grace, mercy and forgiveness for herself, for all her friends, for all her enemies, and for all the souls in Purgatory.

And there was a lady who had come from Rome to purchase her pardon. Her name was Margaret Florentyne, and she had with her many Knights of Rhodes, many gentlewomen, and much good baggage.

Then Richard, the broken-backed man, went to her, praying her that this creature might go with her to Rome, and himself also, so as to be kept from the peril of thieves. And then that worshipful lady received them into her company and let them go with her to Rome, as God willed. When the aforesaid creature had come into Rome, they that were her fellows aforetime, who had put her out of their company were in Rome also, and having heard that such a woman had come thither, they had great wonder how she came there in safety.

Then she went and got her white clothes and was clad all in white, as she was commanded to do, years before, in her soul by revelation, and now it was fulfilled in effect.

Then was this creature received into the Hospital of Saint Thomas of Canterbury in Rome, and she was houselled every Sunday with great weeping, boisterous sobbing, and loud crying, and was highly beloved by the Master of the Hospital and all his brethren. And then, through the stirring of her ghostly enemy, there came a priest, that was held a holy man in the Hospital and also in other places of Rome, who was one of her fellows, and one of her own countrymen. And notwithstanding his holiness, he spoke so evil of this creature and slandered so her name in the Hospital that, through his evil language, she was put out of the Hospital, so that she might no longer be shriven or houselled therein.

Notes

1 Lynne, now King's Lynn, is evidently referred to. This anonymity is dropped later on.
2 i.e., 'your lust'. *See* Chapter 9, line 5.
3 A habergeon, or coat of mail, was worn as a penance, in addition to its primary purpose of bodily protection.
4 To go to Holy Communion.
5 Saint Bridget of Sweden.
6 Words missing owing to damage to the MS.
7 Word missing in MS.
8 The value of a noble was six shillings and eightpence.
9 Word missing in MS.
10 Outcry; scream.

POPE GREGORY VII AND KING HENRY IV

The Investiture Controversy

ALTHOUGH THE INVESTITURE CONTROVERSY WAS A PAN-EUROPEAN phenomenon, the critical eleventh-century phase most affected the development of the Empire. The contest between Gregory VII (1073-1085) and emperor Henry IV (1056-1106) was largely a propaganda war fought for the allegiance of the German episcopate and nobility. The series of letters of Gregory and Henry present the positions of each side and their attempts to best their opponents in public opinion.

Source: Theodor E. Mommsen and Karl F. Morrison, *Imperial Lives and Letters of the Eleventh Century* (New York: Columbia U. Press, 1962); Ephraim Emerton, *The Correspondence of Pope Gregory VII* (New York: Columbia University Press, 1932).

The Correspondence of Pope Gregory VII

Book III, 3 (July 20, 1075.)

Gregory ... to King Henry, greeting ...

Among other praiseworthy actions, my beloved son, to which you are reported to have risen in your efforts at self-improvement, there are two that have specially commended you to your holy mother, the Roman church: first, that you have valiantly withstood those guilty of Simony; and second, that you freely approve, and strenuously desire to enforce, the chastity of the clergy as servants of God. For these reasons you have given us cause to expect of you still higher and better things with God's help. Wherefore we earnestly pray that you may hold fast by these, and we beseech our Lord God that he may deign to increase your zeal more and more.

But now, as regards the church of Bamberg, which according to the ordinance of its founder [King Henry II] belongs to the Holy and Apostolic See as the shoulder to the head, that is, as a most intimate member, by a certain special bond of duty, we are greatly disturbed and we are forced by the obligation of our office to come to the rescue of its distress with all our powers. That simoniac so-called bishop Hermann, summoned to a Roman synod this present year, failed to appear. He came within a short distance of Rome,

but there halted and sent forward messengers with ample gifts, trying, with his well-known trickery, to impose upon our innocence and, if possible, to corrupt the integrity of our colleagues by a pecuniary bargain. But when this turned out contrary to his hopes, convinced of his own damnation he hastily retreated and, soothing the minds of the clergy who were with him by smooth and deceitful promises, declared that if he were able to regain his own country he would resign his bishopric and enter the monastic life.

How he kept these promises Your Highness, beloved son, well knows. With increasing audacity he plundered the clergy who were upholding the welfare and the honor of their church, and had not your royal power restrained him, as we are informed, he would have completely ruined them. After careful consideration of these outrages we removed him from his episcopal and priestly office. Further, as he dared to oppress the church of Bamberg, under the apostolic patronage of St. Peter, more cruelly and more harshly than before, we placed him in the bonds of anathema until he should lay down his usurped dignity and, nevertheless, present himself for trial before the Apostolic See.

Now, therefore, most excellent son, we ask Your Highness and urge you by our dutiful obligation to take counsel with men of piety and so to regulate the affairs of that church according to

God's order, that you may be worthy of divine protection through the intercession of St. Peter, in whose name and under whose patronage the church was founded.

What I have written regarding this case to our colleague Siegfried, bishop of Mainz, and the clergy and people of Bamberg, you may learn with certainty from the letters dispatched to them.[1]

To King Henry IV, Admonishing Him to Show More Deference to the Holy See and Its Decrees
Book III, 10, p. 263. Dec. 8, 1075 [or Jan. 8, 1076].

Gregory, bishop, servant of God's servants, to King Henry, greeting and the apostolic benediction—but with the understanding that he obeys the Apostolic See as becomes a Christian king.

Considering and weighing carefully to how strict a judge we must render an account of the stewardship committed to us by St. Peter, prince of the Apostles, we have hesitated to send you the apostolic benediction, since you are reported to be in voluntary communication with men who are under the censure of the Apostolic See and of a synod. If this is true, you yourself know that you cannot receive the favour of God nor the apostolic blessing unless you shall first put away those excommunicated persons and force them to do penance and shall yourself obtain absolution and forgiveness for your sin by due repentance and satisfaction. Wherefore we counsel Your Excellency , if you feel yourself guilty in this matter, to make your confession at once to some pious bishop who, with our sanction, may impose upon you a penance suited to the offense, may absolve you and with your consent in writing may be free to send us a true report of the manner of your penance.

We marvel exceedingly that you have sent us so many devoted letters and displayed such humility by the spoken words of your legates, calling yourself a son of our Holy Mother Church and subject to us in the faith, singular in affection, a leader in devotion, commending yourself with every expression of gentleness and reverence, and yet in action showing yourself most bitterly hostile to the canons and apostolic decrees in those duties especially required by loyalty to the Church. Not to mention other cases, the way you have observed your promises in the Milan affair, made through your mother and through bishops, our colleagues, whom we sent to you, and what your intentions were in making them is evident to all. And now, heaping wounds upon wounds, you have handed over the sees of Fermo and Spoleto—if indeed a church may be given over by any human power to persons entirely unknown to us, whereas it is not lawful to consecrate anyone except after probation and with due knowledge.

It would have been becoming to you, since you confess yourself to be a son of the Church, to give more respectful attention to the master of the Church, that is, to Peter, prince of the Apostles. To him, if you are of the Lord's flock, you have been committed for your pasture, since Christ said to him: "Peter, feed my sheep," and again: "To thee are given the keys of Heaven, and whatsoever thou shalt bind on earth shall be bound in Heaven and whatsoever thou shalt loose on earth shall be loosed in Heaven." Now, while we, unworthy sinner that we are, stand in his place of power, still whatever you send to us, whether in writing or by word of mouth, he himself receives, and while we read what is written or hear the voice of those who speak, he discerns with subtle insight from what spirit the message comes. Wherefore Your Highness should beware lest any defect of will toward the Apostolic See be found in your words or in your messages and should pay due reverence, not to us but to Almighty God, in all matters touching the welfare of the Christian faith and the status of the Church. And this we say although our Lord deigned to declare: "He who heareth you heareth me; and he who despiseth you despiseth me."

We know that one who does not refuse to obey God in those matters in which we have spoken according to the statutes of the holy fathers does not scorn to observe our admonitions even as if he had received them from the lips of the Apostle himself. For if our Lord, out of reverence for the chair of Moses, commanded the Apostles to observe the teaching of the scribes and pharisees who sat thereon, there can be no doubt that the apostolic and gospel teaching, whose seat and foundation is Christ, should be accepted and maintained by those who are chosen to the service of teaching.

At a synod held at Rome during the current year, and over which Divine Providence willed us to preside, several of your subjects being present, we saw that the order of the Christian religion had long been greatly disturbed and its chief and proper function, the redemption of souls, had fallen low and through the wiles of the Devil had been trodden under foot. Startled by this danger and by the manifest ruin of the Lord's flock we returned to the teaching of the holy fathers, declaring no novelties nor any inventions of our own, but holding that the primary and only rule of discipline and the well-trodden way of the saints should again be sought and followed, all wandering paths to be abandoned, for we know that there is no other way of salvation and eternal life for the flock of Christ and their shepherds except that shown by him who said: "I am the door and he who enters by me shall be saved and shall find pasture." This was taught by the Apostles and observed by the holy fathers and we have learned it from the Gospels and from every page of Holy Writ.

This edict [against lay investiture], which some who place the honor of men above that of God call an intolerable burden, we, using the right word, call rather a truth and a light necessary for salvation, and we have given judgment that it is to be heartily accepted and obeyed, not only by you and your subjects but by all princes and peoples who confess and worship Christ—though it is our especial wish and would be especially fitting for you, that you should excel others in devotion to Christ as you are their superior in fame, in station and in valour.

Nevertheless, in order that these demands may not seem to you too burdensome or unfair we have sent you word by your own liegemen not to be troubled by this reform of an evil practice but to send us prudent and pious legates from your own people. If these can show in any reasonable way how we can moderate the decision of the holy fathers [at the Council] saving the honor of the eternal king and without peril to our own soul, we will condescend to hear their counsel. It would in fact have been the fair thing for you,

even if you had not been so graciously admonished, to make reasonable inquiry of us in what respect we had offended you or assailed your honor, before you proceeded to violate the apostolic decrees. But how little you cared for our warnings or for doing right was shown by your later actions.

However, since the long-enduring patience of God summons you to improvement, we hope that with increase of understanding your heart and mind may be turned to obey the commands of God. We warn you with a father's love that you accept the rule of Christ, that you consider the peril of preferring your own honor to his, that you do not hamper by your actions the freedom of that Church which he deigned to bind to himself as a bride by a divine union, but, that she may increase as greatly as possible, you will begin to lend to Almighty God and to St. Peter, by whom also your own glory may merit increase, the aid of your valour by faithful devotion.

Now you ought to recognize your special obligation to them for the triumph over your enemies which they have granted you, and while they are making you happy and singularly prosperous, they ought to find your devotion increased by their favor to you. That the fear of God, in whose hand is all the might of kings and emperors, may impress this upon you more than any admonitions of mine, bear in mind what happened to Saul after he had won a victory by command of the prophet, how he boasted of his triumph, scorning the prophet's admonitions, and how he was rebuked by the Lord, and also what favor followed David the King as a reward for his humility in the midst of the tokens of his bravery.

Finally, as to what we have read in your letters and do not mention here we will give you no decided answer until your legates, Radbod, Adalbert and Odescalcus, to whom we entrust this, have returned to us and have more fully reported your decision upon the matters which we commissioned them to discuss with you.

The Roman Lenten Synod of 1076
Book III, 10(a), (Feb. 14-20, 1076).

In the year of the Incarnation 1075, our lord Pope Gregory held a synod at Rome in the church of

Our Savior which is called the Constantiniana. A great number of bishops and abbots and clergy and laymen of various orders were present.

At this synod, among the decrees promulgated was the excommunication of Siegfried, archbishop of Mainz, in the following form:

In accordance with the judgment of the Holy Spirit and by authority of the blessed Apostles Peter and Paul, we suspend from every episcopal function, and exclude from the communion of the body and blood of the Lord, Siegfried, archbishop of Mainz, who has attempted to cut off the bishops and abbots of Germany from the Holy Roman Church, their spiritual mother—unless perchance in the hour of death, and then only if he shall come to himself and truly repent. Those who voluntarily joined his schism and still persist in their evil deeds, we also suspend from all episcopal functions. Those, however, who consented against their will we allow time until the feast of St. Peter; but if within that term they shall not have given due satisfaction in person or by messengers in our presence, they shall thenceforth be deprived of their episcopal office.

Excommunication of the bishops of Lombardy

The bishops of Lombardy who, in contempt of canonical and apostolic authority, have joined in a sworn conspiracy against St. Peter, prince of the Apostles, we suspend from their episcopal functions and exclude them from the communion of Holy Church.

[Here follows a list of excommunications of prelates and laymen beyond the Alps, ending with the proclamation against King Henry IV.]

Excommunication of Henry IV

O blessed Peter, prince of the Apostles, mercifully incline thine ear, we [sic] pray, and hear me, thy servant, whom thou hast cherished from infancy and hast delivered until now from the hand of the wicked who have hated and still hate me for my loyalty to thee. Thou art my witness, as are also my Lady, the Mother of God, and the blessed Paul, thy brother among all the saints, that thy Holy Roman Church forced me against my will to be its ruler. I had no thought of ascending thy throne as a robber, nay, rather would I have chosen to end my life as a pilgrim than to seize upon

thy place for earthly glory and by devices of this world. Therefore, by thy favor, not by any works of mine, I believe that it is and has been thy will, that the Christian people especially committed to thee should render obedience to me, thy especially constituted representative. To me is given by thy grace the power of binding and loosing in Heaven and upon earth.

Wherefore, relying upon this commission, and for the honor and defense of thy Church, in the name of Almighty God, Father, Son and Holy Spirit, through thy power and authority, I deprive King Henry, son of the emperor Henry, who has rebelled against thy Church with unheard-of-audacity, of the government over the whole kingdom of Germany and Italy, and I release all Christian men from the allegiance which they have sworn or may swear to him, and I forbid anyone to serve him as king. For it is fitting that he who seeks to diminish the glory of thy Church should lose the glory which he seems to have.

And, since he has refused to obey as a Christian should or to return to the God whom he has abandoned by taking part with excommunicated persons, has spurned my warnings which I gave him for his soul's welfare, as thou knowest, and has separated himself from thy Church and tried to rend it asunder, I bind him in the bonds of anathema in thy stead and I bind him thus as commissioned by thee, that the nations may know and be convinced that thou art Peter and that upon thy rock the son of the living God has built his Church and the gates of hell shall not prevail against it.

A General Apology to All the Faithful in Germany
Epistolae collectae, Book IV, 14 1076.

Gregory ... to all bishops, dukes, counts and other loyal defenders of the faith in Germany, greeting ...

We hear that certain among you are in doubt regarding our excommunication of the king and are asking whether he was lawfully condemned; also whether our sentence was pronounced with due deliberation and under authority of a legal right of inquiry. We have therefore taken pains to make clear to the understanding of all by what motives, as our conscience bears witness, we were led to this act of excommunication. And we do this, not so much in order to make public by our own complaint the several cases which, alas! are only too well known, as to silence the accusations of those who feel that we took up the sword of the spirit rashly and were moved rather by our own impulses than by a holy fear and a zeal for justice.

While we were still in the office of deacon, sinister and dishonorable rumors came to us regarding the conduct of the king, and we sent him frequent admonitions both by letter and by legates, for the sake of the imperial station and personal character of his father and mother as well as from our hope and wishes for his improvement, warning him to desist from his evil ways and, mindful of his noble birth and station, so to order his life as would be fitting for a king and, God willing, for an emperor. And later, when we had reached the dignity of Supreme Pontiff—unworthy as we were—and he had grown in years and in vice, we, knowing that God would require his soul at our hands the more strictly now that authority and freedom were given to us above all others, besought him the more earnestly in every way, by argument, by persuasion and by threats, to amend his life. He replied with frequent letters of devotion, pleading his frail and fickle youth and the evil counsels of those in power at his court and promising from day to day that he would comply with our instructions—he promised in words, but in fact he trampled them under foot with ever-increasing misbehaviour.

In the meantime we summoned to repentance certain of his intimates by whose intrigues and advice he had profaned bishoprics and many monasteries, for money installing wolves instead of shepherds. We ordered them, while there was still time, to give back the church property, which they had received with sacrilegious hand through this accursed commerce, to its rightful owners and to give satisfaction to God for their sins by penitential service. But when we learned that they refused to do this after due time and continued in their accustomed evil ways, we cut them off from the communion and body of the whole Church as guilty of sacrilege and as servants and members of the Devil, and we warned the king to banish them from his household and from his counsels and to desist from all association with them as persons under excommunication.

But again, when the Saxon uprising against the king was gaining strength and he saw that the resources and defenses of the kingdom were failing him to a great extent, he wrote us a letter of supplication full of humility. In this letter he confessed his fault before Almighty God and St. Peter and ourself and besought us by our apostolic authority to correct his offenses in church affairs against the canon law and the decrees of holy fathers. He also promised to obey us in all respects and to give us his faithful aid and counsel. And afterward, being admitted to penance by our colleagues and legates, Humbert, bishop of Palestrina, and Gerald, bishop of Ostia, whom we had sent to him, he reaffirmed all these promises in their hands, taking his oath by the sacred scarfs which they wore around their necks.

Then some time later, after a battle with the Saxons, he performed his sacrifices of gratitude to God for his victory by promptly breaking his vows of amendment, fulfilling none of his promises, receiving the excommunicated persons into his intimate counsels and bringing ruin upon the churches as he had done before.

With the greatest grief, then, although we had lost almost all hope of his improvement after he had treated with scorn the gifts of the heavenly king, we decided to make a further attempt, desiring rather that he should listen to apostolic gentleness than that he should suffer from our severity. We therefore wrote warning him to remember his promises and consider to whom they had been made; not to imagine that he could deceive God, whose anger when he begins to give judgment is the more severe the longer his patience has endured; and not to dishonour God, who has honored him, or use his power in contempt of God and in despite of apostolic authority, knowing as he does that God resists the proud but shows favor to the humble.

Besides this, we sent to him three clergymen,

his own subjects, through whom we gave him private warnings to do penance for his crimes, horrible to describe, but known to many and published through many lands and for which the authority of law, human and divine, commands that he should not only be excommunicated until he should give due satisfaction, but should be deposed from his royal office without hope of restitution.

Finally we warned him that, unless he should exclude the excommunicated persons from his intimacy, we could pass no other sentence upon him but that, being cut off from the Church, he should join the fellowship of the condemned, with whom, rather than with Christ, he has chosen to take his part. And yet, if he were willing to listen to our warnings and reform his conduct, we called upon God—and we call upon him still—to bear witness how greatly we should rejoice in his honor and his welfare, and with what affection we should welcome him into the bosom of Holy Church as one who, being the chief of a nation and ruling over a widespread kingdom, is bound to be the defender of the Catholic peace and righteousness.

On the other hand, his actions prove how little he cares either for our written words or for the messages sent by our legates. He was angered that anyone should reprove or correct him, and could not be led back to any improvement, but, carried away by a still greater fury of self-confidence, he did not stop until he had caused almost all the bishops in Italy and as many as he could in Germany to suffer shipwreck of their faith and had compelled them to refuse the obedience and honor which they owed to St. Peter and the Apostolic See and which had been granted to these by Our Lord Jesus Christ.

When, therefore, we saw that we had reached the limit: namely, first, that he refused to give up his relations with those who had been excommunicated for sacrilege and the heresy of Simony; second, because he was not willing, I will not say to perform, but even to promise repentance for his crimes, for the penance which he had sworn to in the hands of our legates was a fraudulent one; finally, because he had dared to divide the body of Christ, that is, the unity of the Church—

for all these crimes, I say, we excommunicated him through the decision of a council. Since we could not bring him back to the way of salvation by gentle means, we tried, with God's help, to do so by severity, and if—which God forbid!—he should not be afraid even of the severest penalty, our soul should at least be free from the charge of negligence or timidity.

If, then, anyone thinks that this sentence was imposed illegally or without reason, if he is willing to apply common sense to the sacred law he will take our part, will listen patiently to what is taught, not by ourself but by divine authority, and is sanctioned by the unanimous opinion of the holy fathers, and he will agree with us. We do not believe that any true believer who knows the canon law can be caught by this error and can say in his heart, even though he dare not openly proclaim it, that this action was not well taken. Nevertheless, even if—which God forbid!—we had bound him with this chain without due cause or in irregular form, the judgment is not to be rejected on this ground, as the holy fathers declare, but absolution is to be sought in all humility.

Now do you, my beloved, who have not desired to forsake the righteousness of God on account of the wrath of the king or of any danger, take no thought of the folly of those who "shall be consumed for their cursing and lying," but stand fast like men and comfort yourselves in the Lord. Know that you are on the side of him who, as unconquered king and glorious victor, will judge the living and the dead, rendering to each one according to his works. Of his manifold rewards you may be assured if you remain faithful to the end and stand firm in his truth. For this we pray God without ceasing, that he may give you strength to be established by the Holy Spirit in his name. May he turn the heart of the king to repentance and cause him to understand that we and you love him far more truly than those who now favor and support his evil doing.

And if, under God's blessing, he shall return to his senses, no matter what he may be plotting against us, he shall find us always ready to receive him back into holy communion in accordance with your affectionate counsel.

To All in Authority in Germany, Urging Their Support in His Struggle with Henry IV
Book IV, 1, (July 25, 1076).

Gregory ... to all his brethren in Christ, bishops, abbots and priests, dukes, princes and knights, all dwellers in the Roman Empire who truly love the Christian faith and the honor of St. Peter, greeting ...

We render thanks to Almighty God, who for the exceeding love he bore to us did not spare his own son, but gave him for us all, to protect and govern his Church, beyond all our deserts, beyond the expectation even of good men. You know, beloved brethren, that in this time of peril when Antichrist is busy everywhere by means of his members, scarce one is to be found who truly loves God and his honor, or who prefers his commands rather than earthly profit and the favor of the princes of this world. But he who rejects not his own and daily changes sinners from his left side to his right has looked upon you with calm and favoring countenance and has set you up against his enemies to the healing of many nations, that it might please you rather to be steadfast in the perils of this present life than to set the favor of men above the glory and honor of the eternal king. So doing you will not pass over with deaf ears that saying of the prince of the Apostles, "Ye are a chosen generation, a royal priesthood," and also, "We ought to obey God rather than men."

You well know, my brethren, for how long a time our Holy Church has had to bear the unheard-of wickedness and manifold wrongdoing of the king—would that I could call him Christian or [truly] your king—and what misfortunes it has suffered at his hands under the lead of our ancient enemy. Already during our diaconate we sent him words of warning out of our affection for him and our devotion to his parents, and after we came to the priestly office—unworthy as we are—frequently and earnestly have we striven, with the help of pious men, to bring him to his senses. But how he has acted against all this, how he has rendered evil for good, and how he has raised his heel against St. Peter and striven to rend in twain the Church which God

entrusted to him you know, and it has been spread abroad throughout the world. But, since it belongs to our office to regard men and not their vices, to resist the wicked that they may repent, and to abhor evil but not men, we admonish you by authority of St. Peter, prince of the Apostles, and call upon you as our beloved brethren to endeavor in every way to snatch him from the hand of the Devil and rouse him to a true repentance, that we may be able with God's help to bring him back in brotherly love into the bosom of that Church which he has sought to divide. This, however, in such ways that he may not be able by some fraud to disturb the Christian faith and trample our Holy Church under his feet.

But if he will not listen to you and shall choose to follow the Devil rather than Christ and shall prefer the counsel of those who have long been under excommunication for simoniacal heresy to yours, then we shall find ways under divine inspiration to rescue the already declining Church Universal by serving God rather than man.

Now do you, my brethren and fellow priests, by authority of St. Peter, receive and bring back into the bosom of our Holy Mother Church as many as shall repent of those who have not been ashamed to set the king above Almighty God and to deny the law of Christ, if not in words, at least by their deeds—as the Apostle says, "They profess that they know God; but in works they deny him"—these receive, that you may be worthy to rejoice in Heaven with the angels of God. In all things keep before your eyes the honor of your holy father, the prince of the Apostles. But all those, bishops or laymen, who, led astray by fear or the favor of men, have not withdrawn from association with the king, but by favoring him have not feared to hand over the king's soul and their own to the Devil—have no dealings or friendship with these unless they shall repent and perform the proper acts of penance. For these are they who hate and slay their own souls and the king's as well, and are not ashamed to throw the kingdom, their fatherland and the Christian faith into confusion. For, as we are subject to the word of the prophet: "If thou speakest not to warn the wicked from his wicked way ... his soul will I require at thine hand," and again, "Cursed be he that shall hold back his sword from blood," that is, shall hold back the word of reproof from smiting those of evil life, so they, unless they obey, are subject to the wrath of the divine judgment and to the penalties of idolatry, as Samuel bears witness. And God is our witness that we are moved against evil princes and faithless priests by no question of worldly advantage, but by our sense of duty and by the power of the Apostolic See which continually weighs upon us. It were better for us, if need were, to pay the debt of mortality at the hands of tyrants rather than to consent in silence to the ruin of the Christian law through fear or for any advantage. We know what our fathers said: "He who does not oppose evil men out of regard for his station gives his consent; and he who removes not that which ought to be cut out is guilty of the offense."

May Almighty God, from whom all good things proceed, guard and strengthen your hearts through the merits of Our Lady, the Queen of Heaven, and the intercession of the blessed Apostles Peter and Paul, and may he always pour upon you the grace of his Holy Spirit that you may do what is pleasing to him. May you be worthy to rescue his Bride, our Mother, from the jaws of the wolf, and may you attain to his supreme glory, cleansed of all your sins.

To Bishop Hermann of Metz, in Defense of the Excommunication of Henry IV
Book IV, 2, (Aug. 25, 1076).

Gregory ... to Hermann, bishop of Metz, greeting ...

You have asked a great many questions of me, a very busy man, and have sent me an extremely urgent messenger. Wherefore I beg you to bear with me patiently if my reply is not sufficiently ample.

The bearer will report to you as to my health and as to the conduct of the Romans and the Normans in regard to me. As to the other matters about which you inquire—would that the blessed Peter himself, who is many times honored or wronged in me his servant, such as I am, might give the answers!

There is no need to ask me who are the excommunicated bishops, priests or laymen; since beyond a doubt they are those who are known to be in communication with the excommunicated king Henry—if, indeed, he may properly be called king. They do not hesitate to place the fear and favor of men before the commands of the eternal King nor to expose their king to the wrath of Almighty God by giving him their support.

He too feared not to incur the penalty of excommunication by dealing with followers who had been excommunicated for the heresy of Simony nor to draw others into excommunication through their dealings with him. How can we think of such things but in the words of the Psalmist: "The fool hath said in his heart there is no God," or again: "They are all gone astray in their wills."

Now to those who say: "A king may not be excommunicated," although we are not bound to reply to such a fatuous notion, yet, lest we seem to pass over their foolishness impatiently we will recall them to sound doctrine by directing their attention to the words and acts of the holy fathers. Let them read what instructions St. Peter gave to the Christian community in his ordination of St. Clement in regard to one who had not the approval of the pontiff. Let them learn why the Apostle said, "Being prompt to punish every disobedience"; and of whom he said, "Do not even take food with such people." Let them consider why Pope Zachary deposed a king of the Franks and released all his subjects from their oaths of allegiance. Let them read in the records [*registra*] of St. Gregory how in his grants to certain churches he not merely excommunicated kings and dukes who opposed him but declared them deprived of their royal dignity. And let them not forget that St. Ambrose not only excommunicated the emperor Theodosius but forbade him to stand in the room of the priests within the church.

But perhaps those people would imagine that when God commended his Church to Peter three times saying, "Feed my sheep," he made an exception of kings! Why do they not see, or rather confess with shame that, when God gave to Peter as leader the power of binding and loosing in heaven and on earth he excepted no one, withheld no one from his power? For if a man says that he cannot be bound by the ban of the Church, it is evident that he could not be loosed by its authority, and he who shamelessly denies this cuts himself off absolutely from Christ. If the Holy Apostolic See, through the princely power divinely bestowed upon it, has jurisdiction over spiritual things, why not also over temporal things? When kings and princes of this world set their own dignity and profit higher than God's righteousness and seek their own honor, neglecting the glory of God, you know whose members they are, to whom they give their allegiance. Just as those who place God above their own wills and obey his commands rather than those of men are members of Christ, so those of whom we spoke are members of Antichrist. If then spiritual men are to be judged, as is fitting, why should not men of the world be held to account still more strictly for their evil deeds?

Perchance they imagine that royal dignity is higher than that of bishops; but how great the difference between them is, they may learn from the difference in their origins. The former came from human lust of power; the latter was instituted by divine grace. The former constantly strives after empty glory; the latter aspires ever toward the heavenly life. Let them learn what Anastasius the pope said to Anastasius the emperor regarding these two dignities, and how St. Ambrose in his pastoral letter distinguished between them. He said: "If you compare the episcopal dignity with the splendor of kings and the crowns of princes, these are far more inferior to it than lead is to glistening gold." And knowing this, the emperor Constantine chose, not the highest, but the lowest seat among the bishops; for he knew that God resists the haughty, but confers his grace upon the humble.

Meantime, be it known to you, my brother, that, upon receipt of letters from certain of our clerical brethren and political leaders we have given apostolic authority to those bishops to absolve such persons excommunicated by us as have dared to cut themselves loose from the king. But as to the king himself, we have absolutely forbidden anyone to dare to absolve him until we shall have been made certain by competent witnesses of his sincere repentance and reparation; so that at the same time we may determine, if

divine grace shall have visited him, in what form we may grant him absolution, to God's glory and his own salvation. For it has not escaped our knowledge that there are some of you who, pretending to be authorized by us, but really led astray by fear or the favor of men, would presume to absolve him if I [sic] did not forbid them, thus widening the wound instead of healing it. And if others, bishops in very truth, should oppose them, they would say that these were actuated, not by a sense of justice, but by personal hostility.

Moreover ordination and consecration by those bishops who dare to communicate with an excommunicated king become in the sight of God an execration, according to St. Gregory. For since they in their pride refuse to obey the Apostolic See, they incur the charge of idolatry, according to Samuel. If he is said to be of God who is stirred by divine love to punish crime, certainly he is not of God who refuses to rebuke the lives of carnal men so far as in him lies. And if he is accursed who withholds his sword from blood—that is to say, the word of preaching from destroying the life of the flesh—how much more is he accursed who through fear or favor drives his brother's soul into everlasting perdition! Furthermore you cannot find in the teaching of any of the holy fathers that men accursed and excommunicated can convey to others that blessing and that divine grace which they do not fear to deny by their actions.

Meanwhile, we order you to ask our brother, the venerable archbishop of Trier, to forbid the bishop of Toul to interfere in the affairs of the abbess of Remiremont and, with your assistance, to annul whatever action he has taken against her.

But, concerning Matilda, daughter to us both and faithful servant of St. Peter, I will do as you wish. I am not yet quite clear as to her future status—*deo gubernante*. I wish you, however, clearly to understand that although I remember her late husband Godfrey as a frequent offender against God, I am not affected by his enmity toward me nor by any other personal feeling, but moved by my fraternal affection for you and by Matilda's prayers I pray God for his salvation.

May Almighty God, through the mediation of

Mary, Queen of Heaven, ever virgin, and the authority of the blessed Apostles Peter and Paul granted by him to them, absolve you and all our brethren who uphold the Christian faith and the dignity of the Apostolic See from all your sins, increase your faith, hope and charity and strengthen you in your defense of his law that you may be worthy to attain to everlasting life.

To All the Faithful in Germany, Counseling Them to Choose a New King in the Event that Henry IV Can Not Be Brought to Repentance
Book IV, 3, (Sept. 3, 1076).

Gregory ... to all the beloved brethren in Christ, fellow bishops, dukes, counts and all defenders of the Christian faith dwelling in the kingdom of Germany, greeting and absolution from all their sins through the apostolic benediction.

If you weigh carefully the decree in which Henry, king so-called, was excommunicated in a holy synod by judgment of the Holy Spirit, you will see beyond a doubt what action ought to be taken in his case. It will there be seen why he was bound in the bondage of anathema and deposed from his royal dignity, and that every people formerly subject to him is released from its oath of allegiance.

But because, as God knows, we are not moved against him by any pride or empty desire for the things of this world, but only by zeal for the Holy See and our common mother, the Church, we admonish you in the Lord Jesus and beg you as beloved brethren to receive him kindly if with his whole heart he shall turn to God, and to show toward him not merely justice which would prohibit him from ruling, but mercy which wipes out many crimes. Be mindful, I beg you, of the frailty of our common human nature and do not forget the pious and noble memory of his father and his mother, rulers the like of whom cannot be found in this our day.

Apply, however, the oil of kindness to his wounds in such a way that the scars may not grow foul by neglect of the wine of discipline and thus the honor of Holy Church and of the Roman Empire fall in widespread ruin through our indif-ference. Let those evil counselors be far removed from him, who, excommunicated for the heresy of Simony, have not scrupled to infect their master with their own disease and by diverse crimes have seduced him into splitting our Holy Church in twain and have brought upon him the wrath of God and of Saint Peter. Let other advisors be given him who care more for his advantage than their own and who place God above all earthly profit. Let him no longer imagine that Holy Church is his subject or his handmaid but rather let him recognize her as his superior and his mistress. Let him not be puffed up with the spirit of pride and defend practices invented to check the liberty of Holy Church, but let him observe the teaching of the holy fathers which divine power taught them for our salvation.

But if he shall have given you reliable information as to these and other demands which may properly be made upon him, we desire that you give us immediate notice by competent messengers so that, taking counsel together, we may with God's help decide upon the right course of action. Above all, we forbid, in the name of St. Peter, that any one of you should venture to absolve him from excommunication until the above-mentioned information shall have been given to us and you shall have received the consent of the Apostolic See and our renewed answer. We are distrustful of the conflicting counsels of different persons and have our suspicions of the fear and favor of men.

But now, if through the crimes of many [others]—which God forbid!—he shall not with whole heart turn to God, let another ruler of the kingdom be found by divine favor, such an one as shall bind himself by unquestionable obligations to carry out the measures we have indicated and any others that may be necessary for the safety of the Christian religion and of the whole empire. Further, in order that we may confirm your choice—if it shall be necessary to make a choice—and support the new order in our time, as we know was done by the holy fathers before us, inform us at the earliest possible moment as to the person, the character and the occupation of the candidate. Proceeding thus with pious and practical method you will deserve well of us in the present case and will merit the favour of the

Apostolic See by divine grace and the blessing of St. Peter, prince of the Apostles.

As to the oath which you have taken to our best beloved daughter, the empress Agnes, in case her son should die before her, you need have no scruples, because, if she should be led by over-fondness for her son to resist the course of justice or, on the other hand, should defend justice and consent to his deposition, you will know how to do the rest. This, however, would seem to be advisable: that when you have come to a firm decision among yourselves that he shall be removed, you should take counsel with her and with us as to the person to be entrusted with the government of the kingdom. Then either she will give her assent to the common judgment of us all, or the authority of the Apostolic See will release all bonds which stand in the way of justice.

With regard to the excommunicated persons, I remind you that I have already given to those of you who defend the Christian faith as bishops authority to absolve them, and I hereby confirm this—provided only that they truly repent and with humble hearts apply for penance.

To the German Princes, Giving an Account of Canossa
Book IV, 12, (End of Jan., 1077).

Whereas, for love of justice you have made common cause with us and taken the same risks in the warfare of Christian service, we have taken special care to send you this accurate account of the king's penitential humiliation, his absolution and the course of the whole affair from his entrance into Italy to the present time.

According to the arrangement made with the legates sent to us by you we came to Lombardy about twenty days before the date at which some of your leaders were to meet us at the pass and waited for their arrival to enable us to cross over into that region. But when the time had elapsed and we were told that on account of the troublous times—as indeed we well believe—no escort could be sent to us, having no other way of coming to you we were in no little anxiety as to what was our best course to take.

Meanwhile we received certain information that the king was on the way to us. Before he entered Italy he sent us word that he would make satisfaction to God and St. Peter and offered to amend his way of life and to continue obedient to us, provided only that he should obtain from us absolution and the apostolic blessing. For a long time we delayed our reply and held long consultations, reproaching him bitterly through messengers back and forth for his outrageous conduct, until finally, of his own accord and without any show of hostility or defiance, he came with a few followers to the fortress of Canossa where we were staying. There, on three successive days, standing before the castle gate, laying aside all royal insignia, barefooted and in coarse attire, he ceased not with many tears to beseech the apostolic help and comfort until all who were present or who had heard the story were so moved by pity and compassion that they pleaded his cause with prayers and tears. All marveled at our unwonted severity, and some even cried out that we were showing, not the seriousness of apostolic authority, but rather the cruelty of a savage tyrant.

At last, overcome by his persistent show of penitence and the urgency of all present, we released him from the bonds of anathema and received him into the grace of Holy Mother Church, accepting from him the guarantees described below, confirmed by the signatures of the abbot of Cluny, of our daughters, the Countess Matilda and the Countess Adelaide, and other princes, bishops and laymen who seemed to be of service to us.

And now that these matters have been arranged, we desire to come over into your country at the first opportunity, that with God's help we may more fully establish all matters pertaining to the peace of the Church and the good order of the land. For we wish you clearly to understand that, as you may see in the written guarantees, the whole negotiation is held in suspense, so that our coming and your unanimous consent are in the highest degree necessary. Strive, therefore, all of you, as you love justice, to hold in good faith the obligations into which you have entered. Remember that we have not bound ourselves to the king in any way except by frank statement—as our custom is—that he may expect our aid for his safety and his honor, whether through justice or through mercy, and without peril to his soul or to our own.

To Hermann of Metz, in Defense of the Papal Policy toward Henry IV
Book VIII, 21, (March 15, 1081).

Gregory ... to his beloved brother in Christ, Hermann, bishop of Metz, greeting ...

We know you to be ever ready to bear labor and peril in defense of the truth, and doubt not that this is a gift from God. It is a part of his unspeakable grace and his marvelous mercy that he never permits his chosen ones to wander far or to be completely cast down; but rather, after a time of persecution and wholesome probation, makes them stronger than they were before. On the other hand, just as among cowards one who is worse than the rest is broken down by fear, so among the brave one who acts more bravely than the rest is stirred thereby to new activity. We remind you of this by way of exhortation that you may stand more joyfully in the front ranks of the Christian host, the more confident you are that they are the nearest to God the conqueror.

You ask us to fortify you against the madness of those who babble with accursed tongues about the authority of the Holy Apostolic See not being able to excommunicate King Henry as one who despises the law of Christ, a destroyer of churches and of the empire, a promoter and partner of heresies, nor to release anyone from his oath of fidelity to him; but it has not seemed necessary to reply to this request, seeing that so many and such convincing proofs are to be found in Holy Scripture. Nor do we believe that those who abuse and contradict the truth to their utter damnation do this as much from ignorance as from wretched and desperate folly. And no wonder! It is ever the way of the wicked to protect their own iniquities by calling upon others like themselves; for they think it of no account to incur the penalty of falsehood.

To cite but a few out of the multitude of proofs: Who does not remember the words of our Lord and Savior Jesus Christ: "Thou art Peter and on this rock I will build my Church, and the gates of hell shall not prevail against it. And I will give

thee the keys of the kingdom of heaven and whatsoever thou shalt bind on earth shall be bound in heaven and whatsoever thou shalt loose on earth shall be loosed in heaven." Are kings excepted here? Or are they not of the sheep which the Son of God committed to St. Peter? Who, I ask, thinks himself excluded from this universal grant of the power of binding and loosing to St. Peter unless, perchance, that unhappy man who, being unwilling to bear the yoke of the Lord, subjects himself to the burden of the Devil and refuses to be numbered in the flock of Christ? His wretched liberty shall profit him nothing; for if he shakes off from his proud neck the power divinely granted to Peter, so much the heavier shall it be for him in the day of judgment.

This institution of the divine will, this foundation of the rule of the Church, this privilege granted and sealed especially by a heavenly decree to St. Peter, chief of the Apostles, has been accepted and maintained with great reverence by the holy fathers, and they have given to the Holy Roman Church, as well in general councils as in their other acts and writings, the name of "universal mother." They have not only accepted her expositions of doctrine and her instructions in [our] holy religion, but they have also recognized her judicial decisions. They have agreed as with one spirit and one voice that all major cases, all especially important affairs and the judgments of all churches ought to be referred to her as to their head and mother, that from her there shall be no appeal, that her judgments may not and cannot be reviewed or reversed by anyone.

Thus Pope Gelasius, writing to the emperor Anastasius, gave him these instructions as to the right theory of the principate of the Holy and Apostolic See, based upon divine authority:

Although it is fitting that all the faithful should submit themselves to all priests who perform their sacred functions properly, how much the more should they accept the judgment of that prelate who has been appointed by the supreme divine ruler to be superior to all priests and whom the loyalty of the whole later Church has recognized as such. Your Wisdom sees plainly that no human capacity [*concilium*] whatsoever can equal that of him whom the word of Christ raised above all others and whom the reverend

Church has always confessed and still devotedly holds as its Head.

So also Pope Julius, writing to the eastern bishops in regard to the powers of the same Holy and Apostolic See, says:

You ought, my brethren, to have spoken carefully and not ironically of the Holy Roman and Apostolic Church, seeing that our Lord Jesus Christ addressed her respectfully [*decenter*], saying, "Thou art Peter and upon this rock I will build my church, and the gates of hell shall not prevail against it; and I will give thee the keys of the kingdom of heaven." For it has the power, granted by a unique privilege, of opening and shutting the gates of the celestial kingdom to whom it will.

To whom, then, the power of opening and closing in Heaven is given, shall he not be able to judge the earth? God forbid! Do you remember what the most blessed Apostle Paul says: "Know ye not that we shall judge angels? How much more things that pertain to this life?"

So Pope Gregory declared that kings who dared to disobey the orders of the Apostolic See should forfeit their office. He wrote to a certain senator and abbot in these words:

If any king, priest, judge or secular person shall disregard this decree of ours and act contrary to it, he shall be deprived of his power and his office and shall learn that he stands condemned at the bar of God for the wrong that he has done. And unless he shall restore what he has wrongfully taken and shall have done fitting penance for his unlawful acts he shall be excluded from the sacred body and blood of our Lord and Savior Jesus Christ and at the last judgment shall receive condign punishment.

Now then, if the blessed Gregory, most gentle of doctors, decreed that kings who should disobey his orders about a hospital for strangers should be not only deposed but excommunicated and condemned in the last judgment, how can anyone blame us for deposing and excommunicating Henry, who not only disregards apostolic judgments, but so far as in him lies tramples upon his mother the Church, basely plunders the whole kingdom and destroys its churches—unless indeed it were one who is a man of his own kind?

As we know also through the teaching of St. Peter in his letter touching the ordination of Clement, where he says: "If any one were friend to those with whom he [Clement] is not on speaking terms, that man is among those who would like to destroy the Church of God and, while he seems to be with us in the body, he is against us in mind and heart, and he is a far worse enemy than those who are without and are openly hostile. For he, under the forms of friendship, acts as an enemy and scatters and lays waste the Church." Consider then, my best beloved, if he passes so severe a judgment upon him who associates himself with those whom the pope opposes on account of their actions, with what severity he condemns the man himself to whom the pope is thus opposed.

But now, to return to our point: Is not a sovereignty invented by men of this world who were ignorant of God subject to that which the providence of Almighty God established for his own glory and graciously bestowed upon the world? The Son of God we believe to be God and man, sitting at the right hand of the Father as High Priest, head of all priests and ever making intercession for us. He despised the kingdom of this world wherein the sons of this world puff themselves up and offered himself as a sacrifice upon the cross.

Who does not know that kings and princes derive their origin from men ignorant of God who raised themselves above their fellows by pride, plunder, treachery, murder—in short, by every kind of crime—at the instigation of the Devil, the prince of this world, men blind with greed and intolerable in their audacity? If, then, they strive to bend the priests of God to their will, to whom may they more properly be compared than to him who is chief over all the sons of pride? For he, tempting our High Priest, head of all priests, son of the Most High, offering him all the kingdoms of this world, said: "All these will I give thee if thou wilt fall down and worship me."

Does anyone doubt that the priests of Christ are to be considered as fathers and masters of kings and princes and of all believers? Would it not be regarded as pitiable madness if a son should try to rule his father or a pupil his master and to bind with unjust obligations the one through whom he expects to be bound or loosed, not only on earth but also in heaven? Evidently recognizing this the emperor Constantine the Great, lord over all kings and princes throughout almost the entire earth, as St. Gregory relates in his letter to the emperor Mauritius, at the holy synod of Nicaea took his place below all the bishops and did not venture to pass any judgment upon them but, even addressing them as gods, felt that they ought not to be subject to his judgment but that he ought to be bound by their decisions.

Pope Gelasius, urging upon the emperor Anastasius not to feel himself wronged by the truth that was called to his attention said: "There are two powers, O august Emperor, by which the world is governed, the sacred authority of the priesthood and the power of kings. Of these the priestly is by so much the greater as they will have to answer for kings themselves in the day of divine judgment"; and a little further: "Know that you are subject to their judgment, not that they are to be subjected to your will."

In reliance upon such declarations and such authorities, many prelates have excommunicated kings or emperors. If you ask for illustrations: Pope Innocent excommunicated the emperor Arcadius because he consented to the expulsion of St. John Chrysostom from his office. Another Roman pontiff deposed a king of the Franks, not so much on account of his evil deeds as because he was not equal to so great an office, and set in his place Pippin, father of the emperor Charles the Great, releasing all the Franks from the oath of fealty which they had sworn to him. And this is often done by Holy Church when it absolves fighting men from their oaths to bishops who have been deposed by apostolic authority. So St. Ambrose, a holy man but not bishop of the whole Church, excommunicated the emperor Theodosius the Great for a fault which did not seem to other prelates so very grave and excluded him from the Church. He also shows in his writings that the priestly office is as much superior to royal power as gold is more precious than lead. He says: "The honor and dignity of bishops admit of no comparison. If you liken them to the splendor of kings and the diadem of princes, these are as lead compared to the glitter of gold.

You see the necks of kings and princes bowed to the knees of priests, and by the kissing of hands they believe that they share the benefit of their prayers." And again: "Know that we have said all this in order to show that there is nothing in this world more excellent than a priest or more lofty than a bishop."

Your Fraternity should remember also that greater power is granted to an exorcist when he is made a spiritual emperor for the casting out of devils, than can be conferred upon any layman for the purpose of earthly dominion. All kings and princes of this earth who live not piously and in their deeds show not a becoming fear of God are ruled by demons and are sunk in miserable slavery. Such men desire to rule, not guided by the love of God, as priests are, for the glory of God and the profit of human souls, but to display their intolerable pride and to satisfy the lusts of their mind. Of these St. Augustine says in the first book of his Christian doctrine: "He who tries to rule over men—who are by nature equal to him—acts with intolerable pride." Now if exorcists have power over demons, as we have said, how much more over those who are subject to demons and are limbs of demons! And if exorcists are superior to these, how much more are priests superior to them!

Furthermore, every Christian king when he approaches his end asks the aid of a priest as a miserable suppliant that he may escape the prison of hell, may pass from darkness into light and may appear at the judgment seat of God freed from the bonds of sin. But who, layman or priest, in his last moments has ever asked the help of any earthly king for the safety of his soul? And what king or emperor has power through his office to snatch any Christian from the might of the Devil by the sacred rite of baptism, to confirm him among the sons of God and to fortify him by the holy chrism? Or—and this is the greatest thing in the Christian religion—who among them is able by his own word to create the body and blood of the Lord? or to whom among them is given the power to bind and loose in Heaven and upon earth? From this it is apparent how greatly superior in power is the priestly dignity.

Or who of them is able to ordain any clergyman in the Holy Church—much less to depose him for any fault? For bishops, while they may ordain other bishops, may in no wise depose them except by authority of the Apostolic See. How, then, can even the most slightly informed person doubt that priests are higher than kings? But if kings are to be judged by priests for their sins, by whom can they more properly be judged than by the Roman pontiff?

In short, all good Christians, whomsoever they may be, are more properly to be called kings than are evil princes; for the former, seeking the glory of God, rule themselves rigorously; but the latter, seeking their own rather than the things that are of God, being enemies to themselves, oppress others tyrannically. The former are the body of the true Christ; the latter, the body of the Devil. The former rule themselves that they may reign forever with the supreme ruler. The power of the latter brings it to pass that they perish in eternal damnation with the prince of darkness who is king over all the sons of pride.

It is no great wonder that evil priests take the part of a king whom they love and fear on account of honors received from him. By ordaining any person whomsoever, they are selling their God at a bargain price. For as the elect are inseparably united to their Head, so the wicked are firmly bound to him who is head of all evil— especially against the good. But against these it is of no use to argue, but rather to pray God with tears and groans that he may deliver them from the snares of Satan, in which they are caught and after trial may lead them at last into knowledge of the truth.

So much for kings and emperors who, swollen with the pride of this world, rule not for God but for themselves. But since it is our duty to exhort everyone according to his station, it is our care with God's help to furnish emperors, kings and other princes with the weapons of humility that thus they may be strong to keep down the floods and waves of pride. We know that earthly glory and the cares of this world are wont especially to cause rulers to be exalted, to forget humility and, seeking their own glory, strive to excel their fellows. It seems therefore especially useful for emperors and kings, while their hearts are lifted

up in the strife for glory, to learn how to humble themselves and to know fear rather than joy. Let them therefore consider carefully how danger- ous, even awesome is the office of emperor or king, how very few find salvation therein, and how those who are saved through God's mercy have become far less famous in the Church by divine judgment than many humble persons. From the beginning of the world to the present day we do not find in all authentic records [seven] emperors or kings whose lives were as distinguished for virtue and piety as were those of a countless multitude of men who despised the world—although we believe that many of them were saved by the mercy of God. Not to speak of Apostles and Martyrs, who among emperors and kings was famed for his miracles as were St. Mar- tin, St. Antony and St. Benedict? What emperor or king ever raised the dead, cleansed lepers or opened the eyes of the blind? True, Holy Church praises and honors the emperor Constantine, of pious memory, Theodosius and Honorius, Charles and Louis, as lovers of justice, champions of the Christian faith and protectors of churches, but she does not claim that they were illustrious for the splendor of their wonderful works. Or to how many names of kings or emperors has Holy Church ordered churches or altars to be dedicat- ed or masses to be celebrated?

Let kings and princes fear lest the higher they are raised above their fellows in this life, the deeper they may be plunged in everlasting fire. Wherefore it is written: "The mighty shall suffer mighty torments." They shall render unto God an account for all men subject to their rule. But if it is no small labor for the pious individual to guard his own soul, what a task is laid upon princes in the care of so many thousands of souls! And if Holy Church imposes a heavy penalty upon him who takes a single human life, what shall be done to those who send many thousands to death for the glory of this world? These, although they say with their lips, *mea culpa*, for the slaughter of many, yet in their hearts they rejoice at the increase of their glory and neither repent of what they have done nor regret that they have sent their brothers into the world below. So that, since they do not repent with all their hearts and will not restore what they have gained by human bloodshed, their penitence before God remains without the fruits of a true repentance.

Wherefore they ought greatly to fear, and they should frequently be reminded that, as we have said, since the beginning of the world and throughout the kingdoms of the earth very few kings of saintly life can be found out of an innumerable multitude, whereas in one single chair of successive bishops—the Roman—from the time of the blessed Apostle Peter nearly a hundred are counted among the holiest of men. How can this be, except because the kings and princes of the earth, seduced by empty glory, prefer their own interests to the things of the Spirit, whereas pious pontiffs, despising vainglory, set the things of God above the things of the flesh. The former readily punish offenses against themselves but are not troubled by offenses against God; the latter quickly forgive those who sin against them but do not easily pardon offenders against God. The former, far too much given to worldly affairs, think little of spiritual things; the latter, dwelling eagerly upon heavenly subjects, despise the things of this world.

All Christians, therefore, who desire to reign with Christ are to be warned not to reign through ambition for worldly power. They are to keep in mind the admonition of that most holy pope Gregory in his book on the pastoral office: "Of all these things what is to be followed, what held fast, except that the man strong in virtue shall come to his office under compulsion? Let him who is without virtue not come to it even though he be urged thereto." If, then, men who fear God come under compulsion with fear and trembling to the Apostolic See where those who are properly ordained become stronger through the merits of the blessed Apostle Peter, with what awe and hesitation should men ascend the throne of a king where even good and humble men like Saul and David become worse! What we have said above is thus stated in the decrees of the blessed pope Symmachus—though we have learned it by experience: "He, that is St. Peter, transmitted to his successors an unfailing endowment of merit together with an inheritance of innocence"; and again: "For who can doubt that he is holy who is

raised to the height of such an office, in which if he is lacking in virtue acquired by his own merits, that which is handed down from his predecessor is sufficient. For either he [Peter] raises men of distinction to bear this burden or he glorifies them after they are raised up."

Wherefore let those whom Holy Church, of its own will and with deliberate judgment, not for fleeting glory but for the welfare of multitudes, has called to royal or imperial rule—let them be obedient and ever mindful of the blessed Gregory's declaration in that same pastoral treatise: "When a man disdains to be the equal of his fellow men, he becomes like an apostate angel. Thus Saul, after his period of humility, swollen with pride, ran into excess of power. He was raised in humility, but rejected in his pride, as God bore witness, saying: 'Though thou wast little in thine own sight, wast thou not made the head of the tribes of Israel?'" and again: "I marvel how, when he was little to himself he was great before God, but when he seemed great to himself he was little before God." Let them watch and remember what God says in the Gospel: "I seek not my own glory," and, "He who would be first among you, let him be the servant of all." Let them ever place the honor of God above their own; let them embrace justice and maintain it by preserving to everyone his right; let them not enter into the counsels of the ungodly, but cling to those of religion with all their hearts. Let them not seek to make Holy Church their maidservant or their subject, but recognizing priests, the eyes of God, as their masters and fathers, strive to do them becoming honor.

If we are commanded to honor our fathers and mothers in the flesh, how much more our spiritual parents! If he that curseth his father or his mother shall be put to death, what does he deserve who curses his spiritual father or mother? Let not princes, led astray by carnal affection, set their own sons over that flock for whom Christ shed his blood if a better and more suitable man can be found. By thus loving their own son more than God they bring the greatest evils upon the Church. For it is evident that he who fails to provide to the best of his ability so great and necessary an advantage for our holy mother, the

Church, does not love God and his neighbor as befits a Christian man. If this one virtue of charity be wanting, then whatever of good the man may do will lack all saving grace.

But if they do these things in humility, keeping their love for God and their neighbor as they ought, they may count upon the mercy of him who said: "Learn of me, for I am meek and lowly of heart." If they humbly imitate him, they shall pass from their servile and transient reign into the kingdom of eternal liberty.

The Letters of Henry IV

Henry declares to the Roman clergy and people that Hildebrand is his enemy. He sends them a copy of his decree of deposition (Letter 11) and exhorts them to take a new pope after forcing Hildebrand to step down (1076).[1]

Henry, King by the grace of God, sends grace, greeting, and every good thing to the clergy and people of the entire holy Roman Church:

That fidelity is believed firm and unshaken which is always kept unchanged for one whether he is present or absent—fidelity altered neither by the extended absence of him to whom it is owed nor through the wearisome passage of a long time. We know that this is the sort of fidelity which you keep for us; we are thankful, and we ask that it continue unchanged. Specifically, we ask that just as you act now, so in the future you will steadfastly be friends of our friends and enemies of our enemies.

Noting particularly among the latter the monk Hildebrand, we urge you to enmity against him, since we have found him to be an assailant and an oppressor of the Church, as well as a waylayer of the Roman commonwealth, and of our kingdom, as may be known clearly from the following letter sent to him by us:

[In the original of Letter 10, the full text of Letter 11 is given here. Letter 10 continues:]

This is the text of our letter to the monk Hildebrand, which we have also written to you so that our will may be both yours and ours—nay rather, so that your love may bring satisfaction to God

and to us. Rise up against him, therefore, O most faithful, and let the man who is first in the faith be first in his condemnation. We do not say, however, that you should shed his blood, since after his deposition life would indeed be a greater penalty for him than death. We say rather that if he prove unwilling to descend, you should force him to do so and receive into the Apostolic See another, elected by us with the common counsel of all the bishops and of yourselves, one who will be willing and able to cure the wounds which that man has inflicted upon the Church.

Henry charges Hildebrand with having stolen his hereditary privileges in Rome, striven to alienate Italy, abused the bishops, and threatened his office and his life. He reports the sentence of deposition issued by the Diet of Worms, and as patrician of the Romans, he commands him to descend from the throne of St. Peter (1076).

Henry, King by the grace of God, to Hildebrand:

Although hitherto I hoped for those things from you which are expected of a father and obeyed you in all respects to the great indignation of our vassals,[2] I have obtained from you a requital suitable from one who was the most pernicious enemy of our life and kingly office. After you had first snatched away with arrogant boldness all the hereditary dignity owed me by that See, going still further you tried with the most evil arts to alienate the kingdom of Italy.[3] Not content with this, you have not feared to set your hand against the most reverend bishops, who are united to us like most cherished members and have harassed them with most arrogant affronts and the bitterest abuses against divine and human laws. While I let all these things go unnoticed through patience, you thought it not patience but cowardice and dared to rise up against the head itself, announcing, as you know, that (to use your own words) you would either die or deprive me of my life and kingly office.

Judging that this unheard of defiance had to be confuted not with words, but with action, I held a general assembly of all the foremost men of the kingdom, at their supplication. When they had made public through their true declaration (which you will hear from their own letter) those things which they had previously kept silent through fear and reverence, they took public action to the end that you could no longer continue in the Apostolic See. Since their sentence seemed just and righteous before God and men, I also give my assent, revoking from you every prerogative of the papacy which you have seemed to hold, and ordering you to descend from the throne of the city whose patriciate is due me through the bestowal of God and the sworn assent of the Romans.

Renunciation of Gregory VII by the German Bishops (Synod of Worms, 1076)

Siegfried, archbishop of Mainz, Udo of Trier, William of Utrecht, Herman of Metz, Henry of Liége, Ricbert of Verdun, Bido of Toul, Hozeman of Speier, Burchard of Halberstadt, Werner of Strassburg, Burchard of Basel, Otto of Constance, Adalbero of Würzburg, Rupert of Bamberg, Otto of Regensburg, Egilbert of Freising, Ulric of Eichstätt, Frederick of Münster, Eilbert of Minden, Hezilo of Hildesheim, Benno of Osnabrück, Eppo of Naumburg, Imadus of Paderborn, Tiedo of Brandenburg, Burchard of Lausanne, and Bruno of Verona, to Brother Hildebrand:

When you had first usurped the government of the Church, we knew well how, with your accustomed arrogance, you had presumed to enter so illicit and nefarious an undertaking against human and divine law. We thought, nevertheless, that the pernicious beginnings of your administration ought to be left unnoticed in prudent silence. We did this specifically in the hope that such criminal beginnings would be emended and wiped away somewhat by the probity and industry of your later rule. But now, just as the deplorable state of the universal Church cries out and laments, through the increasing wickedness of your actions and decrees, you are woefully and stubbornly in step with your evil beginnings.

Our Lord and Redeemer impressed the goodness of peace and love upon his Faithful as their distinctive character, a fact to which there are more testimonies than can be included in the brevity of a letter. But by way of contrast, you have inflicted wounds with proud cruelty and cruel pride, you are eager for profane innovations, you delight in a great name rather than in a good one, and with unheard-of self-exaltation, like a standard bearer of schism, you distend all the limbs of the Church which before your times led a quiet and tranquil life, according to the admonition of the Apostle. Finally, the flame of discord, which you stirred up through terrible factions in the Roman church, you spread with raging madness through all the churches of Italy, Germany, Gaul, and Spain. For you have taken from the bishops, so far as you could, all that power which is known to have been divinely conferred upon them through the grace of the Holy Spirit, which works mightily in ordinations. Through you all administration of ecclesiastical affairs has been assigned to popular madness. Since some now consider no one a bishop or priest save the man who begs that office of Your Arrogance with a most unworthy servility, you have shaken into pitiable disorder the whole strength of the apostolic institution and that most comely distribution of the limbs of Christ, which the Doctor of the Gentiles so often commends and teaches. And so through these boastful decrees of yours—and this cannot be said without tears—the name of Christ has all but perished. Who, however, is not struck dumb by the baseness of your arrogant usurpation of new power, power not due you, to the end that you may destroy the rights due the whole brotherhood? For you assert that if any sin of one of our parishioners comes to your notice, even if only by rumour, none of us has any further power to bind or to loose the party involved, for you alone may do it, or one whom you delegate especially for this purpose. Can anyone schooled in sacred learning fail to see how this assertion exceeds all madness?

We have judged that it would be worse than any other evil for us to allow the Church of God to be so gravely jeopardized—nay rather, almost destroyed—any longer through these and other presumptuous airs of yours. Therefore, it has pleased us to make known to you by the common counsel of all of us something which we have left unsaid until now: that is, the reason why you cannot now be, nor could you ever have been, the head of the Apostolic See.

In the time of the Emperor Henry [III] of good memory, you bound yourself with a solemn oath that for the lifetime of that Emperor and for that of his son, our lord the glorious King who now presides at the summit of affairs, you would neither obtain the papacy yourself nor suffer another to obtain it, insofar as you were able, without the consent and approbation either of the father in his lifetime or of the son in his. And there are many bishops today who were witnesses of this solemn oath, who saw it then with their own eyes and heard it with their own ears. Remember also that in order to remove jealous rivalry when ambition for the papacy tickled some of the cardinals, you obligated yourself with a solemn oath never to assume the papacy both on the plea and on the condition that they did the same thing themselves. We have seen in what a holy way you observed each of these solemn vows. Again, when a synod was celebrated in the time of Pope Nicholas [II], in which one hundred twenty-five bishops sat together, it was decided and decreed under anathema that no one would ever become pope except by the election of the cardinals and the approbation of the people, and by the consent and authority of the king. And of this council and decree, you yourself were author, advocate, and subscriber.

In addition to this, you have filled the entire Church, as it were, with the stench of the gravest of scandals, rising from your intimacy and cohabitation with another's wife who is more closely integrated into your household than is necessary. In this affair, our sense of decency is affected more than our legal case, although the general complaint is sounded everywhere that all judgments and all decrees are enacted by women in the Apostolic See, and ultimately that the whole orb of the Church is administered by this new senate of women. For no one can complain adequately of the wrongs and the abuse suffered by the bishops, whom you call most undeservedly sons of whores and other names of this sort.

Since your accession was tainted by such great perjuries, since the Church of God is imperiled by so great a tempest arising from abuse born of your innovations, and since you have degraded

your life and conduct by such multifarious infamy, we declare that in the future we shall observe no longer the obedience which we have not promised to you. And since none of us, as you have publicly declared, has hitherto been a bishop to you, you also will now be pope to none of us.

Henry charges Hildebrand with having thrown the whole Church into confusion and with having threatened his life and office. He declares that Hildebrand was not ordained of God, but is damned by the precept of St. Paul and by the judgment of all Henry's bishops; and he commands him to descend from the Apostolic See (1076).

Henry, King not by usurpation, but by the pious ordination of God, to Hildebrand, now not Pope, but false monk:

You have deserved such a salution as this because of the confusion you have wrought; for you left untouched no order of the Church which you could make a sharer of confusion instead of honor, of malediction instead of benediction.

For to discuss a few outstanding points among many: Not only have you dared to touch the rectors of the holy Church—the archbishops, the bishops and the priests, anointed of the Lord as they are—but you have trodden them under foot like slaves who know not what their lord may do. In crushing them you have gained for yourself acclaim from the mouth of the rabble. You have judged that all these know nothing, while you alone know everything. In any case, you have sedulously used this knowledge not for edification, but for destruction, so greatly that we may believe Saint Gregory, whose name you have arrogated to yourself, rightly made this prophesy of you when he said: "From the abundance of his subjects, the mind of the prelate is often exalted, and he thinks that he has more knowledge than anyone else, since he sees that he has more power than anyone else."

And we, indeed, bore with all these abuses, since we were eager to preserve the honor of the Apostolic See. But you construed our humility as fear, and so you were emboldened to rise up even against the royal power itself, granted to us by

God. You dared to threaten to take the kingship away from us—as though we had received the kingship from you, as though kingship and empire were in your hand and not in the hand of God.

Our Lord, Jesus Christ, has called us to kingship, but has not called you to the priesthood. For you have risen by these steps: namely, by cunning, which the monastic profession abhors, to money; by money to favor; by favor to the sword. By the sword you have come to the throne of peace, and from the throne of peace you have destroyed the peace. You have armed subjects against their prelates; you who have not been called by God have taught that our bishops who have been called by God are to be spurned; you have usurped for laymen the bishops' ministry over priests, with the result that these laymen depose and condemn the very men whom the laymen themselves received as teachers from the hand of God, through the imposition of the hands of bishops.

You have also touched me, one who, though unworthy, has been anointed to kingship among the anointed. This wrong you have done to me, although as the tradition of the holy Fathers has taught, I am to be judged by God alone and am not to be deposed for any crime unless—may it never happen—I should deviate from the Faith. For the prudence of the holy bishops entrusted the judgment and the deposition even of Julian the Apostate not to themselves, but to God alone. The true pope Saint Peter also exclaims, "Fear God, honor the king." You, however, since you do not fear God, dishonour me, ordained of Him.

Wherefore, when Saint Paul gave no quarter to an angel from heaven if the angel should preach heterodoxy, he did not except you who are now teaching heterodoxy throughout the earth. For he says, "If anyone, either I or an angel from heaven, preach any other gospel unto you than that which we have preached unto you, let him be accursed." Descend, therefore, condemned by this anathema and by the common judgment of all our bishops and of ourself. Relinquish the Apostolic See which you have arrogated. Let another mount the throne of Saint Peter, another who will not cloak violence with religion but who will teach the pure doctrine of Saint Peter.

I, Henry, King by the grace of God, together with all our bishops, say to you: Descend! Descend!

In this encyclical letter to his bishops, Henry admonishes them to help the beleaguered Church against Hildebrand, who has destroyed the peace between the kingship and the priesthood and has recently abused royal envoys. He invites them to participate in an assembly at Worms on Whitsun (1076).

Henry, King by the grace of God, sends to A., the grace, greeting, and love which he sends not to all men, but only to a few:

In the greatest affairs there is need for the greatest counsels of the greatest men, who externally should have power and within should not be lacking in good will, so that they may be both willing and able to deliberate well about that matter for which they wish well. For in the advancement of any enterprise, neither power without good will nor good will without power is useful. O most faithful subject, you possess, we think, each of these in equal proportion. To tell the truth, although as one of the great, you possess great power, your good will for our advantage and for that of our kingdom grows even greater than this great power—if we know you well and have properly noted your fidelity. From past actions faithfully done, the hope grows that future actions will be done yet more faithfully. We trust to your love, however, that your fidelity may not fall short of our hope, since from the fidelity of none of the kingdom's princes do we hope for greater things than from yours. Thus until this very time, we have rejoiced not only in what past affairs reveal but also in your promise of things still to be hoped for.

Let your good will stand by us, therefore, together with your power at this opportune time, the good will for which not only our need is earnestly longing, but also that of all your fellow bishops and brethren, nay rather, that of the whole oppressed Church. Certainly, you are not ignorant of this oppression. Only see to it that you do not withdraw assistance from the oppressed Church, but rather that you give your sympathy to the kingship and to the priesthood. Just as hitherto the Church was exalted by each of these offices, so now, alas, it is laid low, bereft of each; since one man has arrogated both for himself, he has injured both, and he who has neither wanted nor was able to be of benefit in either has been useless in each.

To keep you in suspense no longer as to the name of the man under discussion, learn of whom we speak: it is the monk Hildebrand (a monk indeed in habit), so-called pope who, as you yourself know clearly, presides in the Apostolic See not with the care of a pastor but with the violence of a usurper and from the throne of peace dissolves the bond of the one catholic peace. To cite a few things among many: without God's knowledge he has usurped for himself the kingship and the priesthood. In this deed he held in contempt the pious ordinance of God, which especially commanded these two—namely, the kingship and the priesthood—should remain, not as one entity, but as two. In his Passion, the Savior Himself meant the figurative sufficiency of the two swords to be understood in this way: When it was said to him, "Lord, behold there are two swords here," He answered, "It is enough," signifying by this sufficient duality, that the spiritual and the carnal swords are to be used in the Church and that by them every hurtful thing is to be cut off. That is to say, He was teaching that every man is constrained by the priestly sword to obey the king as the representative of God but by the kingly sword both to repel enemies of Christ outside and to obey the priesthood within. So in charity the province of one extends into the other, as long as neither the kingship is deprived of honor by the priesthood nor the priesthood is deprived of honor by the kingship. You yourself have found out, if you have wanted to discover it, how the Hildebrandine madness has confounded this ordinance of God; for in his judgment, no one may be a priest unless he begs that [honor] from his arrogance. He has also striven to deprive me of the kingship—me whom God has called to the kingship (God, however, has not called him to the priesthood)—since he saw that I wished to hold my royal power from God and not from him and since he himself had not constituted me as king. And further, he threatened to deprive me of kingship and life, neither of which he had bestowed.

Although he often contrived these outrages against us, and others like them, as you yourself know, nonetheless he was not satisfied unless from day to day he cast new and coarse sorts of affliction upon us, as he recently showed in dealing with our envoys. This paper is not sufficiently long to set forth how he handled those messengers of ours; how demeaningly he afflicted them; how cruelly he imprisoned them; and when they had been imprisoned, how he harmed them with nakedness, cold, hunger and thirst, and blows. Finally, he ordered them to be led about through the middle of the city to offer a spectacle to all, after the example of the martyrs. So you may believe and say that in common with the tyrant Decius he rages and torments the saints.

Wherefore, be not ashamed, most cherished friend, be not ashamed to satisfy the petition we make in common with your fellow bishops: that you come to Worms at Pentecost and hear many things there with the other princes, a few of which this letter mentions, and advise us what is to be done. For you are besought by the love of your fellow bishops, admonished through the advantage of the Church, and bound by the honor of our life and of the whole kingdom.

The Promise of Henry IV to Gregory VII (Promissio Oppenheimensis, 1076)

Admonished by the counsel of our vassals, I promise to maintain a due obedience in all things to the Apostolic See and to you, Pope Gregory.[4] I shall take care to emend with dutiful reparation whatever diminution of the honor of that See or of your own honor is seen to have arisen through us.

Since certain rather serious schemes which I am supposed to have against that same See and Your Reverence are now at issue, at a fitting time, either I shall clear them away through the prayer of innocence or through the help of God or at that very time I shall gladly undertake suitable penance for them.

It is also altogether fitting, however, for Your Sanctity not to ignore those things which have been spread abroad about you and which bear scandal to the Church. But after this scruple has also been removed from the public conscience, it is fitting that the universal tranquility of the Church as well as that of the kingdom be made firm through your wisdom.

Henry declares to his princes that he wishes to obey and to render satisfaction to Pope Gregory; he exhorts them to follow his example and to obtain release from excommunication (1076).

Henry, King by the grace of God, sends the glorious esteem of his good will to archbishops, bishops, dukes, margraves, counts, and to every order of dignity:

We have learned by the assertion of our vassals that on behalf of Our Mercy some men have detracted from the Apostolic See and its venerable pontiff, the Lord Pope Gregory. For this reason, it has pleased us, on beneficial counsel, to change our former position and after the fashion of our predecessors and ancestors to reserve in all respects due obedience to that same sacrosanct See and to the Lord Pope Gregory, who is known to serve as its head. It has also pleased us to make amends with fitting reparation if anything serious has been done against him.

We wish that you also admonished by the example of Our Serenity, like us, will not refuse to show solemn [obedience] to Saint Peter and to his vicar. And may whosoever know that they are bound by his ban strive to be absolved formally by this same Lord Pope Gregory.

Henry informs his mother, the Empress-dowager Agnes, that at a recent Diet he was persuaded to allow the case of the bishops who had deserted him to be discussed at another assembly in the near future. He grants her petition (1074-1076).

To the mother of blessing and well-being, Henry, King by the grace of God, sends love from his whole heart and whatever is better and beyond:

Since it is right for you to know well how we progress, we want to send you word, inasmuch as you are our dearest mother, of what this Curia and assembly has ordered and ratified. After much consideration of our case, we were finally overcome by the apostolic legation and by the counsel and persuasion of all our vassals, many of whom were present, and we granted and permitted the restitution of the deserter-bishops. Nonetheless, we did this in such a fashion that in whatever manner we wish, we may continue warily to watch these men in the interests of our side until the day we have set to consider their case. Know that those same legates of the pope are awaiting that day and time here.

But for the sake of that good faith which we have in you, ask earnestly of God that our cause may receive its long-expected outcome. As for that, however, which you have asked of us, most certainly you will receive it on that condition which you wish and of which you have notified us. In addition [you will receive] whatever we can grant to your love.

The Vow of Henry IV to Gregory VII at Canossa (1077).

Oath of Henry, King of the Germans.

Before the date the Lord Pope Gregory is to set, I, King Henry, shall bring about justice according to his judgment or harmony according to his counsel with regard to the complaint and objection now being made against me by archbishops, bishops, dukes, counts, the other princes in the realm of the Germans, and those who follow them by reason of the same objection. If a concrete obstacle hinder me or him, I shall be ready to do the same when that hindrance has been overcome. Also, if the same Lord Pope Gregory should wish to go beyond the mountains to other lands, he, those who are among his retainers or guards, and those who are sent by him or come to him from any region, will be safe in coming, staying, and going thence, from any harm to life and limb and from capture by me and by those whom I can control. Moreover, no other difficulty prejudicial to his honor will occur with my assent; and should any person create one for him, I shall help him [Gregory] in good faith, according to my ability.

Done at Canossa, 28 January, the fifteenth Indiction.

Decree of the Synod of Brixen (1080)

In the year of the incarnation of the Lord 1080,

with the most serene King Henry IV as modera-
tor, in the twenty-sixth year of his reign, on the
seventh day before the Kalends of July, on the
fifth day of the week, in the third indiction, when
an assembly of thirty bishops and of the leaders
of the army, not only of Italy but also of Germany,
was gathered at Brixen in Bavaria by royal order,
of one accord a voice came forth as though from
the mouth of all complaining terribly against the
cruel madness of one false monk, Hildebrand,
also called Pope Gregory VII. It complained that
the ever-unconquered King suffered this madness to rage untouched for so long, when Paul,
the vessel of election, witnesses that the prince
does not carry a sword without cause and Peter,
the first of the Apostles, cries out that the king not
only is supreme but that governors are to be sent
by him specifically for the punishment of evildo-
ers and for the praise of the good. In fulfillment
of these sayings it seemed just to this most glorious King and to his princes that the judgment of
the bishops with the sentence of divine censure
ought to issue against this Hildebrand before the
material sword went forth against him, with the
consequence that the royal power might resolve
to prosecute him with greater freedom after the
prelates of the Church had first deposed him
from his proud prelacy.

Which of the Faithful knowing him would fear
to let fly the shaft of damnation against him?
From the time he entered the world, this man
strove to procure position for himself[5] over men
through vain glory, without the support of any
merits; to set dreams and divinations, his own
and those of others, ahead of divine dispensation;
to appear a monk in habit and not to be one by
profession; to judge himself exempt from ecclesiastical discipline, subject to no master; to devote
himself more than laymen to obscene theatrical
shows; publicly for the sake of filthy lucre, to
attend to the tables of the money changers on the
porch of them who do business? And so from
these pursuits, he garnered his money and, sup-
planting the abbot, usurped the abbacy of Saint
Paul.

Thereafter, seizing the archdiaconate, he led a
certain man named Mancius astray by guile so
that man sold him his own office. And against the
will of Pope Nicholas, a popular tumult attend-

ing his action, he forced his advancement to the
stewardship of Saint Peter's. Finally, he is convicted of having murdered four Roman pontiffs
with violent deaths. His instrument was poison
administered at the hands of one of his intimates,
namely, John Braciutus. Although he repented
too late, while others still kept silent this minis-
trant of death himself bore witness to these deeds
with dire cries, pressed by the nearness of his
own death. And then, on the same night in which
the funeral rites of Pope Alexander were lovingly
performed in the basilica of the Savior, this oft-
mentioned plague-bearer fortified the gates of
the Roman city and the bridges, the towers and
the triumphal arches, with detachments of armed
men. When a military force had been brought
together, like an enemy he occupied the Lateran
Palace. And lest the clergy should dare oppose
him, since no one wished to elect him, he terrified
them by threatening them with death upon the
unsheathed swords of his followers. He sprang
upon the long-occupied throne before the body
of the dead man reached its tomb. But when certain of the clergy wanted to remind him of the
decree of Pope Nicholas (which was promulgated with the threat of anathema by one hundred
twenty-five bishops and with the approval of this
same Hildebrand and which stated that if anyone
presumed to be pope without the assent of the
Roman prince, he should be considered by all not
pope, but an apostate), he denied that he knew
there was a king anywhere, and he asserted that
he could adjudge the decrees of his predecessors
void.

What more? Not only Rome, indeed, but the
Roman world itself, bears witness that he has not
been elected by God but that he has most impu-
dently thrust himself upward through force,
fraud, and money. His fruits reveal his root; his
words show his intent. He it was who subverted
ecclesiastical order, who threw the rule of the
Christian empire into turmoil, who plotted death
of body and soul for the catholic and pacific King,
who defended a king who was a breaker of vows
and a traitor, who sowed discord among those in
concord, strife among the peaceful, scandals
among brothers, divorce among the married, and
who shook whatever was seen to stand in quiet
amidst those who lived piously.

Wherefore, as was said before, we who have been gathered together through the agency of God, supported by the legates and letters of the nineteen bishops who assembled at Mainz on the holy day of last Pentecost, pass judgment against that same most insolent Hildebrand: for he preaches acts of sacrilege and arson; he defends perjuries and murders; long a disciple of the heretic Berenger, he places in question the catholic and apostolic Faith in regard to the Body and Blood of the Lord; he is an open devotee of divinations and dreams, and a necromancer working with an oracular spirit;[6] and therefore he wanders beyond the limits of the true Faith. We judge that canonically he must be deposed and expelled and that, unless he descends from this See after hearing these words, he is forever damned.

I, Hugh Candidus,[7] cardinal priest of the holy Roman Church, from the Title of Saint Clement in the third district of the city, have assented to this decree promulgated by us, and I have subscribed it in the name of all the Roman cardinals.

I, Diepold, archbishop of Milan, have subscribed.

I, Kuono, bishop of Brescia, have subscribed.

I, Otto, bishop-elect of Tortona, have subscribed.

I, William, bishop of Pavia, have subscribed.

I, Reginald, bishop of Belluno, have subscribed.

I, Sigebod, bishop of Verona, have subscribed.

I, Dionysius, bishop of Piacenza, have subscribed.

Udo, bishop of Asti. I have subscribed.

I, Hugh, bishop-elect of Firmo, have subscribed.

Milo of Padua has subscribed.

I, Conrad, bishop of Utrecht, have subscribed.

Henry, the patriarch [of Aquileia], has subscribed.

Didald, bishop of Vicenza, has subscribed.

Regenger, bishop of Vercelli, has subscribed.

Rupert, bishop of Bamberg, has subscribed.

Norbert, bishop of Chur, has subscribed.

Eberhard, bishop of Parma, has subscribed.

Roland, by the grace of God, bishop of Treviso, most willingly has subscribed.

Arnold, bishop of Cremona, has subscribed.

Arnold, bishop of Bergamo, has subscribed.

I, Diedo, bishop of Brandenburg, have subscribed.

Leomar, archbishop of the holy church of Hamburg.

I, Werner, by the grace of God, bishop of Bobbio, have subscribed.

I, Altwin, bishop of Brixen, have subscribed.

I, Meginward, bishop of Freising, have subscribed.

I, Burchard, bishop of Lausanne, have subscribed.

I, Conrad, bishop of Genoa, have subscribed.

Henry, King by the grace of God. I have subscribed.

Henry praises the constancy of the clergy and people of Rome and announces his imminent arrival at Rome to assume his hereditary dignity (the Imperial office), to remove the conflicts of kingship and priesthood and to restore all things to peace and unity (1081).[8]

Henry, King by the grace of God, sends to the clergy and the Roman people, to the greater and lesser [feudatories], his affection in the most sincere expression of his favor and best wishes:

From many accounts of the elder nobles of our empire we have learned with what great fidelity and benevolence you honored our father of sacrosanct memory and with what great acts of honor he advanced publicly and privately both the dignity of your church and the universal grandeur of the Roman name. Nor, indeed, after his death did you cherish us in our infancy with less love and reverence. On all counts you stood beside us with faithful constancy as far as was possible in the face of the wickedness of certain pestilential and proud men. The helplessness of our youth was at first our plea for not responding to your enduring love with due requital by granting you our favor. And after we put on the man, so great a madness of tyrannical perfidy swelled up against us that supreme necessity forced us to direct the entire concern of our effort toward crushing it.

But now since we have cut off with the sword both the life and the pride of those most bitter enemies, not by our power but by that of God, and in large part have set in order the members of the disrupted and sundered Empire, we intend to come to you. Our specific aim is to receive from you, by the common assent and favor of you all, our due and hereditary dignity and to bestow with every kind of honor the thanks which you deserve. We are surprised, however, that when our approach became better known, no legation from you came to us in the customary manner. For that reason we have refrained from sending our envoys to you. You yourselves know with what infamous abuse our envoys, honored and venerable men, were afflicted in the last year by him from whom such conduct was least fitting, in a manner exceeding the inhumanity of all barbarians.

This is the very thing with which those disturbers of peace and concord charge us. They scatter word among you that we come meaning to diminish the honor of Saint Peter, the prince of the apostles, and through our own power to overturn the commonwealth of you all. Indeed, these tactics accord with their usual conduct. But we tell the truth to you in good faith, for it is altogether our will and resolve to visit you peacefully, as far as is within us, and then, having considered the advice of all of you especially, and of our other vassals, to remove from our midst the long-lasting discord of the kingship and the priesthood, and to recall all things to peace and unity in the name of Christ.

Notes

1   In December, 1075, almost six months to the day after Henry's great victory on the Unstrut over the Saxons, Gregory, prosecuting the policy he had begun at his Lenten Synod earlier in 1075, threatened to excommunicate Henry should he not shun the company of the bishops excommunicated at the Synod, obey the synodal edict against lay investiture, and conform to Papal orders in regard to Imperial churches in Italy. Henry received Gregory's letters early in 1076 and vigorously accepted their implicit challenge, dispatching at once the first four letters reprinted here and summoning the Synod of Brixen, where the majority of German bishops joined him in pronouncing Gregory's deposition.

2   The Latin original is *fidelis*, a word which appears

frequently throughout Henry IV's letters. At the risk of imprecision, the requirements of translation have forced a rendering as either "vassal" or "subject." The reader should not be misled, however, by the modern meaning of "vassal": *Fidelis* denoted no servile status, but, to the contrary, indicated a man who had taken an oath of "fealty" (*fidelitas*) to an overlord—and invariably, therefore, a *fidelis* was a person of high station within feudal political society.

3   A reference to Gregory's denial of Henry's right to name Tedald archbishop of Milan and to fill the sees of Fermo and Spoleto.

4   In joining battle with Gregory, Henry severely miscalculated his strength. While most of the German bishops supported him against Gregory, a great number of temporal princes led by his old enemies Welf of Bavaria, Rudolf of Swabia, and Berthold of Carinthia took the opportunity to rebel against their excommunicate King. The threat of revolt in Saxony also revived immediately. In October, 1076, Henry's army gathered at Oppenheim, facing the rebel army at Tribur just opposite them across the Rhine. Fearing the results of open battle, Henry offered this promise to the Papal legates who were with his enemies; it was accepted and, with the understanding that points at issue between Henry and Gregory's partisans would be settled at a future meeting, both armies disbanded. In the 1076 letter to the princes reprinted here, Henry declared his altered policy to his supporters and urged them to conform themselves to it. For their part, the rebellious princes sent a legation to Gregory, asking him to go to Germany the next February to arbitrate the conflict between them and their King. Gregory accepted these proposals and was making his way toward Germany when Henry intercepted him at Canossa and, after making his submission, was released from excommunication.

5   "Se commendare," in the feudal sense of commending oneself to a lord in order to gain lands and position.

6   Probably a reference to the prophecy Gregory made at the Lenten Synod of 1080, after he had excommunicated Henry for the second time: "Be it known to all of you, that if he does not repent before the feast of St. Peter, he will be killed or deposed. If it does not happen thus, no one need believe me ever again." Bonizo, *Liber ad Amicum*, chap. 9, *MGH Ldl.*, I, 616. Sigebert of Gembloux (*Chronicon, MGH SS.*, VI, 369) reports, "Pope Hildebrand predicted, as though it had been

divinely revealed to him, that the false king was to die in this year. Indeed, he predicted the truth; but the conjecture about the false king deceived him, since, according to his construction, the prediction referred to King Henry." Sigebert refers to the death of Rudolf of Rheinfelden.

7   At first a supporter of Gregory, he turned to the royalists within a year of Gregory's election, charging that it was uncanonical, and became a leader of the Synod of Worms (1076).

8   Between Canossa and Gregory's Lenten Synod of 1080, the Papacy took no major part in German affairs. Toward the end of this period, however, Gregory gave his support openly to the antiking Rudolf of Rheinfelden, whom Henry defeated and killed in battle in January, 1080. This defeat and Henry's steadfast refusal to obey Gregory's edicts against lay investiture led to Gregory's sec-

ond excommunication of the King at his Lenten Synod two months after Rudolf's death. Henry's position in Germany was then quite strong, and, in addition, the greater part of the German and Lombard bishops declared for him in this new crisis, rejecting Gregory as pope at the Synods of Bamberg and Mainz and electing Archbishop Wibert of Ravenna as his successor at the Synod of Brixen. With ample forces, Henry entered Italy early in 1080 to execute the judgments of his bishops; he then sent this letter to the people of Rome. Armed resistance to his march through the lands of his cousin, Mathilda of Tuscany, a stanch supporter of the reformed Papacy, kept him from Rome almost a year. Late in 1082 he withdrew from Tuscany, and in 1083 he began his brief and victorious siege of Rome.

THE CONCORDAT OF WORMS

THE FIRST PHASE OF THE INVESTITURE CONTROVERSY ENDED IN
September 1122 with a compromise between Calixtus II and Henry V—the
Concordat of Worms of September, 1122.

Source: Henry Bettenson, ed. *Documents of the Christian Church* (London: Oxford University Press, 1963).

Agreement of Pope Calixtus II.

I, Calixtus, Bishop, servant of the servants of God, do grant to thee, beloved son, Henry—by the grace of God Emperor of the Romans, Augustus—that the elections of bishops and abbots of the German kingdom, who belong to that kingdom, shall take place in thy presence, without simony or any violence; so that if any dispute shall arise between the parties concerned, thou, with the counsel or judgement of the metropolitan and the co-provincial bishops, shalt give consent and aid to the party which has the more right. The one elected shall receive the regalia from thee by the sceptre and shall perform his lawful duties to thee on that account. But he who is consecrated in the other parts of thy empire [i.e. Burgundy and Italy] shall, within six months, and without any exaction, receive the regalia from thee by the sceptre, and shall perform his lawful duties to thee on that account (saving all rights which are known to belong to the Roman church). Concerning matters in which thou shalt make complaint to me, and ask aid—I, according to the duty of my office, will furnish aid to thee. I give unto thee true peace, and to all who are or have been of thy party in this conflict.

Edict of the Emperor Henry V

In the name of the holy and indivisible Trinity I, Henry, by the grace of God Emperor of the Romans, Augustus, for the love of God and of the holy Roman church and of our lord Pope Calixtus, and for the salvation of my soul, do surrender to God, and to the holy apostles of God, Peter and Paul, and to the Holy Catholic Church, all investiture through ring and staff; and do grant that in all the churches that are in my kingdom or empire there may be canonical election and free consecration. All the possessions and regalia of St. Peter which, from the beginning of this discord unto this day, whether in the time of my father or in mine have been seized, and which I hold, I restore to that same Holy Roman Church. And I will faithfully aid in the restoration of those things which I do not hold. The possessions also of all other churches and princes, and of all other persons lay and clerical which have been lost in that war: according to the counsel of the princes, or according to justice, I will restore, as far as I hold them; and I will faithfully aid in the restoration of those things which I do not hold. And I grant true peace to our lord Pope Calixtus, and to the Holy Roman Church, and to all those who are or have been on its side. And in matters where the Holy Roman Church shall ask aid I will grant it; and in matters concerning which it shall make complaint to me I will duly grant to it justice. All these things have been done by the consent and counsel of the princes. Whose names are here adjoined: Adalbert archbishop of Mainz; F. archbishop of Cologne; H. bishop of Ratisbon; O. bishop of Bamberg; B. bishop of Spires; H. of Augsburg; G. of Utrecht; Ou. of Constance; E. abbot of Fulda; Henry, duke; Frederick, duke; S. duke; Pertolf, duke; Margrave Teipold; Margrave Engelbert; Godfrey, count Palatine; Otto, count Palatine; Berengar, count.

I, Frederick, archbishop of Cologne and archchancellor, have ratified this.

OTTO OF FREISING

The Deeds of Frederick Barbarossa

OTTO OF FREISING (1115-1158) WAS THE UNCLE OF FREDERICK Barbarossa. After studying in Paris with Abelard, Hugh of St. Victor and others, he entered the Cistercian Order and became Bishop of Freising in 1138. His greatest work is *Two Cities*, a world chronicle to 1146 which combines his philosophical and historical interests. His *Deeds of Frederick Barbarossa* presents a glorified vision of the reign of his nephew as a period of peace. The selection below describes his election, his disposition of internal German affairs, and the beginnings of his first campaign against Milan and the Lombard League.

Source: C.C. Mierow, *The Deeds of Frederick Barbarossa* (New York: W.W. Norton, 1953).

Here Begins the Prologue of the Book that Follows

I am not unaware, O paragon of emperors and kings, that while I am attempting to portray the magnificence of your exploits, my pen will prove unequal to the material, as your victories increase. Yet of the two evils, so to speak, I have thought it better that my work should be surpassed by the subject (through my deficiency in expression) than that your glorious deeds should be veiled in silence and perish, were I to say nothing of them.

But because I brought my previous little book to an end with the beginning of your rule as king and emperor, at the death of your most glorious uncle, King Conrad, may this second book, that is to vie with the glory of your principate, now, with God's favor, take its beginning.

Here Ends the Prologue.

Here Begins the Second Book.

i.   In the year 1800 since the founding of the City,[1] but 1154 [1152] from the incarnation of the Lord, the most pious King Conrad departed this life in the springtime, on the fifteenth day before the Kalends of March—that is, on the Friday following Ash Wednesday—in the city of Bamberg, as has been said. Wonderful to relate, it was possible to bring together the entire company of the princes, as into a single body, in the town of Frankfort, from the immense extent of the transalpine kingdom (as well as certain barons from Italy), by the third [fourth] day before the Nones of March [March 4]—that is, on Tuesday after *Oculi mei semper*. When the chief men took counsel together there concerning the choice of a prince—for this is the very apex of the law of the Roman empire, namely, that kings are chosen not by lineal descent but through election by the princes (this right it claims for itself as though by unique prerogative)—finally Frederick, duke of the Swabians, the son of Duke Frederick, was sought by all. By the favor of all he was raised to the rank of king.

ii.   The explanation of this support, the reason for so unanimous an agreement upon that person, was, as I recall, as follows. There have been hitherto in the Roman world, within the borders of Gaul and Germany, two renowned families: one that of the Henrys of Waiblingen,[2] the other that of the Welfs of Altdorf. The one was wont to produce emperors, the other great dukes. These families, eager for glory as is usually the case with great men, were frequently envious of each other and often disturbed the peace of the state. But by the will of God (as men believe), providing for the peace of his people in time to come, it came about that Duke Frederick, the father of this Frederick, who was a descendant of one of the two families (that is, of the family of the kings), took to wife a member of the other, namely, the daughter of Henry, duke of the Bavarians, and by her became the father of the Frederick who rules at the present time.

The princes, therefore, considering not merely the achievements and the valour of the youth already so frequently mentioned, but also this fact, that being a member of both families, he might—like a cornerstone—link these two separate walls, decided to select him as head of the realm. They foresaw that it would greatly benefit the state if so grave and so long-continued a rivalry between the greatest men of the empire for their own private advantage might by this opportunity and with God's help be finally lulled to rest. So it was not because of dislike for King Conrad, but (as has been said) in the interest of a universal advantage that they preferred to place this Frederick ahead of Conrad's son (likewise named Frederick), who was still a little child. By reason of such considerations and in this way the election of Frederick was celebrated.

iii.   When, therefore, all the princes who had thronged to that place had been bound by oath of fealty and homage, the king with a few men whom he considered suitable for the purpose, having dismissed the rest in peace, took ship, amid great rejoicing, on the fifth day of the week. He sailed by the Main and the Rhine, and disembarked at the royal seat at Sinzig. There taking horse, he came the next Saturday to Aachen. On the following day, that is, on that Sunday on which *Laetare Ierusalem* is sung, he was escorted by the bishops from the palace to the church of the blessed Mary ever virgin. With the greatest applause of all who were present, he was crowned by Arnold, archbishop of Cologne, the others assisting, and was seated on the throne of the realm of the Franks that was placed in that same church by Charles the Great. Not a few marveled that in so short a space of time not only had so great a throng of princes and of nobles of the kingdom flocked together, but that some also had arrived from western Gaul, whither the report of this event was supposed not yet to have arrived.

I think I ought not to omit the fact that while the diadem was being placed on Frederick's head, after the completion of the sacramental anointing, one of his retainers, from whom for certain grave offenses he had withdrawn his favor before he was king, cast himself at his feet in the center of the church, hoping to turn the latter's spirit from the rigour of justice on so happy an occasion. But Frederick maintained his previous severity and remained unmoved and thus gave to all of us not small proof of his firmness, declaring that it was not from hatred but out of regard for justice that this man had been excluded from his patronage. Nor did this fail to win the admiration of many, that pride could not dissuade the young man (already, as it were, in possession of an old man's judgment) from virtuous firmness to the fault of laxity. What more need be said? Neither the intercession of the princes, nor the favor of smiling fortune, nor the present joy of so great a festival could help that poor wretch. He departed from the inexorable prince unheard.

But this, too, should not be veiled in silence, that on the same day and in the same church the bishop-elect of Münster (also named Frederick) was consecrated by those same bishops who consecrated the king. So it was believed that the Highest King and Priest was actually participating in the present rejoicing: and this was the sign, that in one church one day beheld the anointing of the two persons who alone are sacramentally anointed according to the ordinance of the New and of the Old Testament, and are rightly called the anointed of Christ the Lord.

iv.   When all that pertains to the dignity of the crown had been duly performed, the prince retired to the private apartments of the palace and summoned the more prudent and powerful of the assembled nobles. After consulting them concerning the condition of the state, he arranged to have ambassadors sent to the Roman pontiff, Eugenius, to the City, and to all Italy, to carry the tidings of his elevation to the rank of king. Therefore, Hillin, archbishop-elect of Trier, and Eberhard, bishop of Bamberg, prudent and learned men, were sent. Then the prince advanced upon the lower regions of the Rhine, to punish the people of Utrecht for the arrogance which, as has previously been related, they had shown toward his uncle Conrad. After he had punished them by the imposition of a fine and confirmed Herman as bishop, moving back up the Rhine he celebrated holy Easter at Cologne. Thence he passed through Westphalia and entered Saxony.

v. In the kingdom of the Danes there arose at that time a serious controversy concerning the rule, between the two kinsmen Peter (who is also called Svein) and Knut. The king summoned them before him and held a great assembly in *Martinopolis*, a city of Saxony which is also called Merseburg, with a large number of princes. The aforesaid young men came there and humbly yielded themselves to his command. Their case is said finally to have been settled by the judgment or advice of the chief men as follows: that Knut (to whom certain provinces were left) should abdicate the royal title by surrendering his sword—for it is the custom of the court that kingdoms are bestowed by the prince or taken back again by the sword, provinces by the military standard—but that Peter, receiving the royal power at the sovereign's hand, should be bound to him by fealty and homage. So the crown of the realm was placed on his head by the hand of the prince, on Whitsunday, and he himself, wearing the crown, bore the sword of the king who marched in state wearing his crown. Waldemar, also, who was a member of the same family, received a certain duchy of Denmark.[3]

vi. At about the same time the church of Magdeburg (which is known to be the metropolis of Saxony), being bereft of its shepherd, determined to hold an election. And since some were for choosing Gerhard, the provost of that church, and others the dean, individuals being divided on this side and on that, they decided to approach the king, who was still tarrying in Saxony. The prince endeavored in many ways to lead them back to unity and the bond of peace. As he could not accomplish this, he persuaded one party—that is, the dean and his followers—to choose Wichmann, the bishop of Zeitz, a man still young but of noble blood, and having summoned him, invested him with the regalia of that church. For the court holds and declares that when the controversy between the empire and the papacy concerning the investiture of bishops was settled, under Henry V,[4] it was granted by the Church that when bishops died, if there happened to be a division in the choice of a successor, it should be the prerogative of the prince to appoint as bishop whomsoever he might please, with the advice of his chief men; and that no bishop-elect should receive consecration before having obtained the regalia from the prince's hand through the sceptre.

The king, having brought all matters in Saxony into good order and inclined to his own will all the princes of that province, entered Bavaria and wore his crown in Regensburg, the metropolis of that duchy, at the festival of the apostles,[5] in the monastery of St. Emmeram; for the cathedral had burned down, together with certain quarters of the city. The ambassadors sent to the City, to Pope Eugenius, and to the other cities of Italy returned to that same diet with glad tidings. There indeed did the prince, having displayed a strong will in arranging all to his satisfaction within the confines of his empire, think to display abroad a stout arm. He wished to declare war on the Hungarians and to bring them under the might of the monarchy. But being for certain obscure reasons unable to secure the assent of the princes in this matter, and thus being powerless to put his plans into effect, he postponed them until a more opportune time.

vii. However, though all was prospering in his kingdom, the most serene prince was indeed very anxious to end without bloodshed that dispute over the duchy of Bavaria between his own relatives, that is, Duke Henry, his paternal uncle, and Duke Henry, his maternal uncle's son.[6] (For the latter was the son of the former Duke Henry of Bavaria, whom King Conrad had compelled to remain in Saxony after he had been outlawed, as has been told elsewhere. His duchy he had bestowed first upon Leopold, the son of Margrave Leopold, and then upon this Henry, the younger Leopold's brother.) The king, therefore, to decide the aforesaid strife by judicial decree or by his counsel, appointed for them a diet at the city of Würzburg in autumn, during the month of October. Inasmuch as the one (that is, the son of

Duke Henry) appeared there and the other absented himself, the latter was summoned again and again.

At that same diet exiles from Apulia, whom Roger had driven out from their native land, made tearful lament and cast themselves pitifully at the feet of the prince. Both because of the affliction of these people and that he might receive the crown of empire, it was solemnly agreed that an expedition into Italy should be undertaken within a little less than two years.

viii. Next, the provost Gerhard hastened to Rome and applied to Pope Eugenius. Setting forth the case of the church of Magdeburg, he charged Wichmann (who, as has been narrated above, had been installed in office by the prince after his election by the second party) with usurpation, on many counts. How greatly disturbed the Roman pontiff was by this matter we have learned both from the letter he sent (in reply to certain bishops who had written to the Roman Church on his [Wichmann's] behalf, out of love for the king) and by word of mouth from the cardinals who were afterward sent across the Alps. Now the content of the letter was as follows:

"Bishop Eugenius, the servant of the servants of God, to his venerable brothers, the archbishops Eberhard of Salzburg, Hartwig of Bremen, and Hillin of Trier, and the bishops Eberhard of Bamberg, Herman of Constance, Henry of Regensburg, Otto of Freising, Conrad of Passau, Daniel of Prague, Anselm of Havelberg, and Burchard of Eichstädt, greeting and apostolic benediction.

"The letter which Your Prudence dispatched on behalf of the church of Magdeburg we received in all due kindness. But in reading it and learning its contents we were filled with great surprise and amazement, because we perceived them to be far other than beseems you, in consideration of your office of bishop. For though you have by Divine Providence been set at the head of the Church, to remove from its midst such things as are harmful and to preserve with zealous care the things that are useful, in the present case (as has become known to us from the contents of your letter)

you have heeded not what is expedient for the Church of God, what is in accord with the sanction of the sacred canons, what accordingly would be approved by the will of heaven, but rather that which is pleasing to earthly princes. And you, who ought to turn aside their hearts from their unrighteous intent and show where the way of the Lord is, have not advised them what is right, nor stood as a wall before the house of Israel. Nay even, as the prophet says, when men were building a wall you 'daubed it with untempered mortar'; a thing that we can scarcely say without great bitterness of spirit. Not so did the prince of the apostles judge, who in consequence of the confession of his faith obtained the promise that he should be the foundation of the whole Church; but when the sons of this world menaced the apostles and threatened destruction and death if they preached in the name of Jesus, he made answer: 'We ought to obey God rather than men.'

"But you, lest you should appear to disagree with earthly princes, bestow your favor upon that cause to which both the authority of ecclesiastical enactment and the test of the will of heaven is surely believed to be opposed. For whereas the expression of divine law does not permit the transferring of bishops without a proof of evident advantage and necessity, and whereas also a far greater harmony of clergy and people should precede [in such a transfer] than in other elections, in the transfer of our venerable brother Wichmann, bishop of Zeitz, we find none of these circumstances, but only the anticipated favor of the prince. Without investigating the needs of the Church, or considering the usefulness of the person, the clergy unwilling—nay more, with the majority of them, it is said, protesting it—you declare that he must be moved to the church of Magdeburg.

"We marvel the more at this, as we know from past experience how much weight and wisdom that person [Frederick] has, and likewise are not entirely ignorant of how useful he is to that church. Now whoever else may be moved by the breezes of temporal favor, we who are founded upon the stability of that rock which was worthy to be established as the foundation of the Church, both should not and desire not to be tossed about by 'every wind of doctrine,' or to wander because of some impulse from the right way of the sacred canons. We charge you, therefore, by this present writing that you no longer lend your favor to that cause, and that you endeavor by your exhortations so to influence our very dear son Frederick (whom God has exalted at this time to the eminence of royal authority to preserve the liberty of the Church) that he himself desist from his purpose in this matter, and no longer bestow his favor upon that same cause in opposition to God, in opposition to the sacred canons, in opposition to demands of his royal dignity; but that he relinquish to the church of Magdeburg—as also to the other churches of the realm entrusted to him by God—the free privilege of choosing whomsoever it wishes, in accordance with God's will, and sustain that same election thereafter by his favor, as is seemly for royal majesty. For if we could see that what he is endeavoring to do concerning our aforesaid brother is supported by reason, we would not think that either his will or your request should at all be opposed. But there is no petition whatever to which we can grant our consent in opposition to God and the sanctions of the sacred canons.

"Given at Segni, on the sixteenth day before the Kalends of September [August 17, 1152]."

ix.   Now the king, when he wore the crown in Bamberg the following Easter, had with him two cardinals, namely, the priest Bernard and the deacon Gregory, sent by the apostolic see for the deposing of certain bishops. So, while celebrating the next Whitsunday at Worms, he deposed through the instrumentality of the same cardinals Henry, archbishop of the see of Mainz (a man often reproved for weakening his Church, but never improved)[7] and replaced him by his chancellor, Arnold,[8] through election by certain of the clergy and people who had come thither. To the aforesaid court came the dukes previously mentioned, the two Henrys, contending for the duchy of Bavaria, as has been said. But as the one alleged that he had not been summoned in prop-

er form, the matter could not there reach a due conclusion. Moreover, the same cardinals with the permission of the prince likewise removed Burchard of Eichstädt, a man weighed down by years, giving as their reason his inefficiency. And when, after this, they were thinking of passing sentence upon the archbishop of Magdeburg and certain others, they were prevented by the prince and bidden to return home (ad propria redire).

x.   At that time Pope Eugenius, a just man and notable for his piety, departed this life [July 8, 1153] and left the see to Anastasius, who was of advanced age and experienced in the customs of the court.[9] When a certain cardinal, Gerard by name, had been sent by him to end the case of the archbishop-elect of Magdeburg, he had approached the prince in that same city while he was celebrating the Lord's Birthday.[10] As he tried to do certain things there against the will of the prince, he incurred the latter's anger and was compelled by stern command to return ingloriously, leaving unfinished the business for which he had come; indeed, he died on the road. But the prince sent messengers to Anastasius, together with Wichmann, and secured not only the ratification of his action but also the pallium for Wichmann, not without offending certain persons who had heard (from their own lips) that the Romans were immovably determined that this should never happen. Since that time the authority of the prince has very greatly increased in the administration not only of secular but also of ecclesiastical affairs.

xi.   At about the same time, in the month of September [1153], the princes and the leading men of Bavaria were called together by the king at Regensburg. But nothing could be settled there with reference to the blessing of peace in that province, on account of the strife between the two dukes. Now the king, because he had been separated from his wife by legates of the apostolic see not long before, on the ground of consanguinity, was negotiating for another marriage. Both on this account and for the overthrow of William of Sicily, who had recently succeeded his deceased father, Roger, the enemy of both empires, he arranged to send ambassadors to

Manuel, emperor of the Greeks. And so, by the advice of his chief men, that mission was undertaken by Anselm, bishop of Havelberg, and Alexander, once count of Apulia, but expelled by Roger with other nobles of that same province under suspicion of seeking the throne.

Then, in the following month of December [1153], both the dukes (Henry and the other Henry) attended the prince's judgment seat in the city of Speyer. But the case was postponed, because the one for the second time claimed that he had not been summoned in due legal form. Frederick had now striven for almost two years to terminate the strife between the two princes so close to him, as has been said, by blood relationship. Therefore, being at length moved by the insistence of the one who desired to return to the land he had inherited from his father, from which he had long been debarred, Frederick was compelled to make an end of the matter because of the imminent task of the expedition in which he needed that same youth as a knight and companion of his journey. Accordingly, holding court at Goslar, a town of Saxony, he summoned both dukes by issuing edicts. Since the one came and the other absented himself, the duchy of Bavaria was there by decision of the princes, adjudged to the former, that is, to Duke Henry of Saxony. After this the prince, betaking himself from Saxony into Bavaria and thence proceeding through Swabia, in the third year of his reign assembled a military force on the plains of the river Lech, the boundary of Bavaria, opposite the city of Augsburg, in order to enter Italy. This was at about the beginning of the month of October, almost two years having elapsed since the expedition had first been vowed. Nor, by the judgment recently proclaimed against so great a prince of the empire and the no little murmuring of other princes arising therefrom, was it possible to distract the illustrious spirit from so great a deed, but disregarding all those things that were behind, and entrusting himself to God, he pressed on to the things that were before. Therefore after crossing the passes of the Alps and passing through Brixen and the valley of the Trent, he encamped on the plains of Verona, near Lake Garda. When he was there taking counsel with his princes concerning their further advance, he determined he must first of all win the favor of the Prince of Heaven. In short, the army, being unable on its passage through the mountain barriers to find things necessary for the support of life, on account of the barrenness of the country, while suffering great want (a thing that is always very grievous for troops) had violated certain holy places. To atone for this—although they seemed to have the aforesaid excuse of necessity—the king ordered a collection to be taken from the entire army. He decided that the not inconsiderable sum of money thus amassed should be taken back by certain holy men to the two bishops (of Trent, that is, and of Brixen) and divided among the various places of the saints which had suffered loss. Thus he provided nobly for the common good, fulfilling nobly a leader's task. For being about to enter upon very great undertakings, he decided that before all else he must placate the Ruler and Creator of all, without Whom nothing is well begun, nothing successfully completed, and that His wrath must be averted from his people.

xii. Then, breaking camp, Frederick halted in the month of November on the plain of Roncaglia, on the Po, not far from Piacenza. Now it is the custom of the kings of the Franks (who are also called kings of the Germans), that as often as they have assembled a military force to cross the Alps in order to assume the crown of the Roman empire, they make a halt on the aforesaid plain. There a shield is suspended on a wooden beam that is raised aloft, and all the knights that are his vassals are summoned by the herald of the court to stand watch over their prince the ensuing night. Accordingly the princes who are in his company each likewise calls out his own feudatories, by heralds. The next day anyone discovered to have absented himself from the night watch is again summoned into the presence of the king and the other princes and illustrious men. Thus all the vassals, both of the sovereign and of the princes, who have remained at home without the full consent of their lords are punished [by confiscation of] their fiefs. The prince followed this custom, and not only the fiefs of some laymen but also the regalia of certain bishops (namely, Hartwig of Bremen and Ulrich of

Halberstadt) were taken away from them: only from these individuals, however, because they were bestowed in perpetuity by the princes upon the churches but not upon individuals.

Now since mention has been made of this country, I shall say a few words concerning its location and customs, and by whom it was previously inhabited, by what name it was called, by whom it was afterward possessed, by what appellation it was distinguished.

xiii. This land, shut in on this side and on that by the Pyrenees [Alps] and the Apennines, very high and rugged mountains that extend for a long distance, like the navel of these mountains—or rather of this range of mountains—extends as a very garden of delights from the Tyrrhenian Sea to the shore of the Adriatic Sea. It has to the north the Pyrenees mountains (as has been said); on the sough the Apennines which presently, changing their name, are commonly called the Mount of Bardo; on the west the Tyrrhenian; on the east the Adriatic Sea. It is watered by the course of the Po, or *Eridanus* River, which topographers rate as one of the three most famous rivers of Europe,[11] and of other streams, and by reason of the pleasantness of the soil and the moderate climate it is productive of wine and oil, to such a degree, indeed, that it brings forth fruit-bearing trees, especially chestnuts, figs, and olives, like forest groves.

The colony of the Romans, once called Farther Italy, was separated into three provinces: Venetia, Aemilia, and Liguria. Aquileia was the metropolis of the first, Ravenna of the second, and Milan of the third. The district in the Apennines themselves—where the city of Rome also is known to be situated—which is now called Tuscany, was quite properly termed Inner Italy because, being surrounded by the Apennines, it holds in its lap the City itself as well. But that plain which succeeds when the mountains run out, and is for this reason still customarily called Campania, was once termed Hither Italy or Greater Greece; now it is named Apulia and Calabria. It extends to Faro di Messina, an arm of the sea unfavorable for ships on account of the sandbanks; for Sicily, the boundary of Europe, is counted with Sardinia and the other islands of Italy. But some, who count this and mid-Italy as one, have preferred to call Hither Italy and Greater Greece "Italy," enumerating not three (as aforesaid) but only two Italies: Farther and Hither.

Some, indeed, hold that the aforesaid mountains, the Apennines and the Pyrenees, are one mountain range. For approximately where the city of Genoa (well versed in naval warfare) is situated, on the Tyrrhenian Sea, they enclose the aforesaid province by drawing close together. As a proof of their statement they declare that, according to Isidore, Pannonia received its name from being enclosed by the Apennines; however, not the Apennines (now called the Mount of Bardo) but the Pyrenees Mountains touch it. It is evident, I think, why I have previously called this land the navel of two ranges or of the one range.

But as it began to be subject to the invasions and the domination of the barbarians who, coming from the island of Scandza [Scandinavia] with their leader Alboin, first inhabited the Pannonias, from them it began to be called Lombardy. For to increase their army [by the drafting of women] they twisted the women's hair about the chin in such a way as to imitate a manly and bearded face, and for that reason they were called Lombards (*Longobardi*), from their long beards. Hence it came to pass that as the ancient inhabitants of that province were crowded together around the exarchate of Ravenna, that part of Italy (which was formerly called Aemilia) is commonly called even today *Romaniola*, which is known to be a diminutive, derived from "Rome."

But [the Lombards] having put aside crude, barbarous ferocity, perhaps from the fact that when united in marriage with the natives they begat sons who inherited something of the Roman gentleness and keenness from their mothers' blood, and from the very quality of the country and climate, retain the refinement of the Latin speech and their elegance of manners. In the governing of their cities, also, and in the conduct of public affairs, they still imitate the wisdom of the ancient Romans. Finally, they are so desirous of liberty that, avoiding the insolence of power, they are governed by the will of consuls rather than rulers. There are known to be three orders among them: captains, vavasors, and commoners.[12] And in order to suppress arrogance, the aforesaid consuls are chosen not from one but from each of the classes. And lest they should exceed bounds by lust for power, they are changed almost every year. The consequence is that, as practically that entire land is divided among the cities, each of them requires its bishops to live in the cities, and scarcely any noble or great man can be found in all the surrounding territory who does not acknowledge the authority of his city. And from this power to force all elements together they are wont to call the several lands of each [noble, or magnate] their contado (*comitatus*).[13] Also, that they may not lack the means of subduing their neighbors, they do not disdain to give the girdle of knighthood or the grades of distinction to young men of inferior station and even some workers of the vile mechanical arts, whom other peoples bar like the pest from the more respected and honorable pursuits. From this it has resulted that they far surpass all other states of the world in riches and in power. They are aided in this not only, as has been said, by their characteristic industry, but also by the absence of their princes,[14] who are accustomed to remain on the far side of the Alps. In this, however, forgetful of their ancient nobility, they retain traces of their barbaric imperfection, because while boasting that they live in accordance with law, they are not obedient to the laws. For they scarcely if ever respect the prince to whom they should display the voluntary deference of obedience or willingly perform that which they have sworn by the integrity of their laws, unless they sense his authority in the power of his great army. Therefore it often happens that although a citizen must be humbled by the laws and an adversary subdued by arms in accordance with the laws, yet they very frequently receive in hostile fashion him whom they ought to accept as their own gentle prince, when he demands what is rightfully his own. From this arises a twofold loss to the common weal: the prince is obliged to assemble an army for the subjugation of his people, and the people (not without great loss of their own possessions) are forced to obey their prince. Accordingly, by the same process of reasoning whereby impetuosity accuses the people for this situation, so should necessity excuse the prince in the sight of God and men.

xiv.   Among all the cities of this people Milan now holds chief place. It is situated between the Po and the Pyrenees, and between the Ticino and the Adda, which take their source from the same Pyrenees and drain into the Po, thereby creating a certain very fertile valley, like an island. Located midway, it is rightly called *Mediolanum*, although some think it was named *Mediolanum* by its founders from a certain portentous sow that had bristles on one side and wool on the other. Now this city is considered (as has been said) more famous than others not only because of its size and its abundance of brave men, but also from the fact that it has extended its authority over two neighboring cities situated within the same valley, Como and Lodi. Furthermore— as usually happens in our transitory lot when favoring fortune smiles—Milan, elated by prosperity, became puffed up to such audacious exaltation that not only did it not shrink from molesting its neighbors, but recently even dared incur the anger of the prince, standing in no awe of his majesty. From what causes this situation arose I shall afterward briefly set forth.

xv.   Meanwhile, it seems necessary to say a few words concerning the jurisdiction over the realm. For it is an old custom, maintained from the time that the Roman empire passed over to the Franks even down to our own day, that as often as the kings have decided to enter Italy they send ahead certain qualified men of their retinue to go about among the individual cities and towns to demand what pertains to the royal treasury and is called by the natives *fodrum*. Hence it comes about that, on the prince's arrival, most of the cities, towns, and strongholds that attempt to oppose this right by absolute refusal or by not making full payment are razed to the ground to give evidence of their impudence to posterity. Likewise, another right is said to have found its source in ancient custom. When the prince enters Italy all dignities and magistracies must be vacated and everything administered by his nod, in accordance with legal decrees and the judgment of those versed in the law. The judges are said also to accord him so great authority over the land that they think it just to supply for the use of the king as much as he needs from all that the land customarily produces that is essential for his use and may be of advantage to the army, only excepting the cattle and the seed devoted to the cultivation of the soil.

xvi.   Now the king abode, it is said, for five days [November 30-December 6, 1154] at Roncaglia and held a diet, with the princes, consuls, and elders of almost all the cities assembled there, and diverse things became known from the complaints of this party or of that. Among them were William, marchese of Montferrat, a noble and great man, and practically the only one of the barons of Italy who could escape from the authority of the cities, and also the bishop of Asti. They made serious charges: one, concerning the insolence of the people of Asti; the other (that is, the marchese), concerning that of the inhabitants of Chieri.

(But we do not think that, in comparison with his other valiant exploits, it contributes much to the prince's claim to glory if, while hastening on to more important things, we speak of the fortified places, rocky strongholds, towns, and great estates destroyed since his coming, not only by those of knightly order but even by the assault of the unbridled sergeants.)[15]

There were present also the consuls of Como and of Lodi, making mournful lament over the arrogance of the people of Milan. They bewailed their long-continued misery of mistreatment in the presence of two consuls of that very city, Oberto de Orto and Gerardo Negri. Therefore, as the prince was about to visit the upper regions of Italy and wished to pass through the Milanese territory he kept the aforesaid consuls with him to guide his way and to make arrangements for suitable places for encampments.

There came also to the same court ambassadors of the people of Genoa, who not long before this time had captured Almeria and Lisbon,[16] renowned cities in Spain, very famous for their workmanship of silk cloths, and returned laden with spoils of the Saracens. They presented the prince with lions, ostriches, parrots, and other valuable gifts.

xvii (xiii b).   Frederick, therefore, being (as has been said) about to set out for the upper regions

of Farther Italy, led his forces from Roncaglia and pitched camp in the territory of the Milanese. And as he was conducted by the aforesaid consuls through wastelands where provisions (*stipendia*) could neither be found nor secured by purchase, he was moved to anger and turned his arms against the people of Milan, having first ordered the consuls to return home. Another circumstance aggravated his wrath. The whole army is said to have been so exasperated by a heavy downpour of rain that in consequence of this double annoyance—hunger and the inclement weather—all aroused the prince against the consuls as much as they could. There was likewise another by no means trivial cause for this high feeling. The prince had already perceived their swollen insolence in the fact that they were not only unwilling to rebuild the cities which they had destroyed, but were even trying to bribe and to corrupt his noble and hitherto untarnished spirit to acquiesce in their iniquity. The king, moving his camp from the barren region, betook himself to fertile places of this land, not far from the city, and refreshed his weary soldiers.

Notes

1   Otto dated the birth of Christ in the year 752 from the founding of the City (*Two Cities* 111.vi), or 2 B.C., so that this date should read 1904 rather than 1800.

2   That is, the Hohenstaufen, so-called from the village of Waiblingen in Swabia; the Italians turned Waiblingen into "Ghibelline."

3   The emperors enjoyed a rather shadowy control over the states to the north and east: Denmark, Poland, Bohemia, Hungary. Though Otto's account leaves the impression that this settlement of the Danish throne was definitive, its actual effect seems to have been negligible. The struggle between Svein and Knut continued, and the former (Frederick's candidate) was driven into exile within two years. Svein had Knut killed in 1157, but the result was to put on the throne his cousin Waldemar, whom Otto had just mentioned.

4   The Concordat of Worms, 1122.

5   The apostles Peter and Paul, June 29.

6   Henry Jasomirgott, brother of Bishop Otto, half brother of Conrad III, and paternal uncle of Frederick, who had received the duchy of Bavaria

from Conrad, and Henry the Lion, son of Henry the Proud (Frederick's mother, Judith, was the latter's sister).

7   Archbishop Henry seems to have raised the only dissenting voice at Frederick's election as king, and this is probably the reason for his removal.

8   Arnold of Selenhofen, later murdered in a communal uprising at Mainz in 1160, and afterward canonized.

9   Anastasius IV, elected in July, 1153, and died December 3, 1154.

10   Frederick celebrated Christmas of 1153 at Speyer; the meeting with the cardinal seems to have occurred at Magdeburg on the following Easter (April 4, 1154); see Simonsfeld, *Jahrb cher des deutschen Reiches unter Friedrich I*, I, 215.

11   The others being the Danube and the Rhone; see below II.xliii, xlvi.

12   This is a sketchy attempt by Otto to indicate the class structure of the northern Italian towns. The captains are the great nobles.

13   Otto is here trying to describe the north Italian city state, with its extensive control over the surrounding territories. See *Cambridge Economic History*, I, 323-43, and Plesner, *L'Émigration de la campagne ... la ville libre de Florence au XIIIe siècle*.

14   That is, the emperors.

15   This paragraph, seemingly out of place here, may be a later addition to the text.

16   A Genoese fleet had operated in Spanish waters in 1147-48, and had assisted in the capture of Almeria and Tortosa. Lisbon also fell to the Christians in 1147, but the Genoese played no part in that enterprise. For the capture of Lisbon, see C.W. David, *De expugnatione Lyxbonensi: The Conquest of Lisbon* "Records of Civilization," No. 34 (New York, 1926).

CHARLES IV

Autobiography

IN THE FOURTEENTH CENTURY THE LUXEMBURG EMPEROR CHARLES IV [1355-78] made his kingdom of Bohemia an artistic and intellectual center. Charles himself took an active role in the cultivation of both Latin and Czech letters. His autobiography which describes the life of the pan-European aristocracy during his time, is one of the first true autobiographies of a lay person in the West.

Source: Bede Jarrett, O.P., *The Emperor Charles IV* (New York: Sheed & Ward, 1935).

II

Henry VII, Emperor of the Romans, begat my father, John by name, by Margaret, daughter of Wenceslaus II of Bohemia, and succeeded to the kingdom with her because of failure in the royal house of the Bohemians. He expelled Henry Duke of Carinthia, who had married the elder sister of his wife (who died later without children), who on account of his wife had obtained the kingdom of Bohemia before him, as can be seen in chronicles of the Bohemians. John, King of Bohemia, begat of Elizabeth the queen his first-born Wenzel,[1] 1316, on May 14, at one in the morning in Prague. Then another son, Ottokar, who died in childhood. Then a third son, John. The above king had two marriageable sisters; one he gave to Charles I, King of the Hungarians. She died without children. The other he gave to Charles IV, King of the Franks, reigning in France, 1323. My said father sent me to the same King of France in the seventh year of my boyhood. The said king had me confirmed by the Pope and imposed on me his own name of Charles, and gave me to wife the daughter of his uncle, Charles of Valois, Margaret by name, called Blanche. That year, his wife, my father's sister, died without children; the king then married again.

He loved me very much, and ordered my chaplain to teach me letters a little, though he himself was ignorant of letters. Thus I learned to read the hours of the glorious Virgin the Blessed Mary, and, understanding them a little every day, I gladly read all through my boyhood, because my guardians were told by the king to impel me to do this. The king was no avaricious lover of gold, he had good counsellors, and his court shone with a group of elder statesmen, spiritual and secular.

But soon a great dissension came between the King of England and the King of France. The King of England, Edward II, had as his wife the sister of the King of France, Isabella, and expelled her from England together with her son Edward. She came to France to her brother, and remained there with her first-born. But the King of France, indignant at the expulsion of his sister and his nephew, asked my father-in-law, his uncle, that he should avenge the insult offered to one of his family. He led an army into Aquitaine, and took all of it except Bordeaux and some strongholds of castles. Then Charles, coming back in triumph to France, gave his daughter's daughter, Philippa, the Countess of Hainault, niece of my wife, in marriage to the son of the King of England, Edward, then in exile. Further, giving him a company of men, he sent him into England. He prevailed against his father, captured him, deprived him of his kingdom, and took his crown. The same year his father was murdered in prison [1327].

In the very same year [1325][2] Charles my father-in-law died, and left an eldest son, Philip. Also the same year [1328] died King Charles, on the feast of the Purification, leaving his wife with child, a daughter. And because it is not the custom of the kingdom of France for daughters to succeed, Philip, the son of my father-in-law, was made King of the Franks, because he was the nearest of the male line. Philip continued the same counsellors as the late king, but agreed little with their counsels and took greedily to wealth. One of these counsellors, a most prudent man, was Peter, Abbot of Fécamp, a native of Limoges, gracious and literary, endowed with all moral virtues, who on Ash Wednesday in the first year of Philip during the celebration of mass preached with such studied care that he was commended by all. At that time I was at the Court of Philip, whose sister I had married (it was after the death of King Charles, with whom I was for five years). The abbot's facility of speech or eloquence so pleased me that day, and seeing him and hearing him gave me such devout and peaceful prayerfulness, that I began to think "Why is it that so much grace is poured into me from that man?" At once I acquainted myself with him, and he treated me kindly and fatherly, often teaching me the sacred Scriptures.

I remained at the Court of Philip two years after the death of King Charles. After these two years the king sent me and my wife (his sister Blanche) to my father, John, King of Bohemia, to the city of Luxemburg, which earldom my father inherited by succession from his father, Henry the Emperor of holy memory, who, being Count of Luxemburg, was elected King of the Romans, as is to be found more fully in the chronicles; also how and for how long he reigned.

Having come back from France [1330], I found my father in Luxemburg, Lewis of Bavaria being then emperor, styling himself "Lewis IV," who after the death of my grandfather, Henry VII, was (in a disputed election) chosen King of the Romans against Frederick, Duke of Austria. These whose names follow elected him and stood by him till his triumph when he captured his rival Frederick, Duke of Austria; namely John, King of Bohemia, my father, the archbishops of Mainz and Treves, and Wildemar, the last Brandenburger: on Frederick's side were the Archbishop of Cologne, the Duke of Saxony, and the Count Palatine. Lewis afterwards went to Rome and received his crown and consecration from a bishop of the Venetians against the will of Pope John XXII. Afterwards he created an antipope,

Nicholas by name, a Franciscan, who was later handed over to the Pope and died in penance.

Already Lewis had returned to Germany, as is clear from the chronicles of the Romans.

When I got back from France at that time and had found my father [1330], Duke Frederick of Austria was besieging Colmar in Alsace, and Lewis could not relieve it. My father went to them and made the two come into concord. Then he went to the County of Tyrol to the Duke of Carinthia, whom he had expelled from Bohemia. His first wife, my mother's sister, was dead. However, he had married a second wife, the sister of the Duke of Brunswick, by whom he had one daughter, Margaret [Maultasch]. Her he joined in marriage to my brother John. At his death he bequeathed to her the rule of the principality. Then my father went to Trent; at that time [Sept. 28] my mother died in Prague on the feast of B. Wenceslaus the martyr. While he was staying in Trent these Lombard cities offered themselves to him, Brescia, Bergamo, Cremona, Pavia, Parma, Reggio, Modena. Also Lucca in Tuscany with all the districts belonging to it gave itself to him. Drawing near to them, my father took up his abode in Parma [March 1331], and Azzo Visconti took them over from him as Vicar, accepting his Vicariate from my father.

It was then my father sent for me to Luxemburg. I came through the city of Metz, the dukedom of the Lorraine, through Burgundy and Savoy to the city of Lausanne on its lake. Then I crossed the mountains of Brega and came to the territory of Novara, and thence on Good Friday to the city of Pavia, which my father held. On Easter day, the third day after my arrival, my family were poisoned—which hurt, by divine grace, I escaped. For the high Mass was so prolonged and I wanted to go to communion at it so that I did not wish to eat before Mass was over. When at last I sat down to dinner, I was told that my family had suddenly been taken ill, and precisely those who had eaten the dinner. Sitting down at table, I did not wish to eat, so frightened was I. Then, looking about, I saw a beautiful man, very agile, whom I did not know, who walked by the table, pretending to be dumb. In my suspicion I had him seized. After three days of torture he confessed that he had put poison in the food by the order of Azzo Visconti of Milan. From that poison died John Lord of Berge, master of my Court, John of Hokrm, Simon of Kail, who waited on my table, and many others. But I remained there in Pavia in the monastery of St. Augustine, where his body lay, from which monastery Lewis of Bavaria had expelled the abbot and the canons regular. I recalled them and installed them in the abbey, which after the death of these brethren [1349], Pope John gave to the Augustinians who now have it; it was during my father's rule that I gave them possession of it. Then I went to my father at Parma; I was sixteen years old.

My father gave the rule of all these cities and my guardianship to Ludovico of Savoy, who was father-in-law of Azzo Visconti and governor of Milan. Leaving Parma, he went to France, and gave his second daughter, my sister, Guta [Bona] by name, to John, the eldest son of Philip of France. The eldest Margaret was already married to Henry Duke of Bavaria. At the time that I remained with the said Lord Ludovico of Savoy in Italy, there were secretly leagued against my father and me, Robert King of Apulia [Naples], the Florentines, Lord Azzo, governor of Milan, the Lord of Verona, who then held Padua, Trevico, Vicenza, Feltre and Belluno, the governor of Mantua, who had already sworn fealty to us, and the governor of Ferrara. Secretly they divided between them the cities I held. To Verona were to go Brescia and Parma, to Mantua Reggio, to Ferrara Modena, to Milan Pavia, Bergamo and Cremona, to Florence Lucca. Thus suddenly revolting, before we knew they had all broken faith with us, they attacked us who were in no wise expecting this, since they had vowed loyalty to us and had sworn to us and had confirmed in writing that they would faithfully assist my father and me.

Verona entered Brescia, Milan besieged Bergamo and took it suddenly. The Pavians, in whom I had greater confidence than in any other of the cities, rebelled against us, and accepted Beccaria as their tyrant. All these joined together to make a violent war against me. But the Lord Ludovico of Savoy, my vicar and guardian, though he had already foreseen some of these dangers, put no remedy to them, and moved I do not know by what (but perhaps by love of his son-in-law

Azzo), the said Lord withdrew from the country, leaving me to face the trouble. But the leading citizens of Parma, the Rossi, and the Fogliani and Manfredi of Reggio, and the Pii of Modena, and the Ponzoni, and Siena, and Cremona, and the Lord Simone Filippi of Pistoja, captain of Lucca, took my side and gave all the help and advice they could, as the following pages will make clear.

Then the allies above named gathered a strong army before our own city of Modena and stayed there six weeks, to wit, men from Milan, Verona, Ferrara and Mantua. After six weeks, when they had devastated the districts and countries of Modena and Reggio, they retired and stationed their forces and arms before the Castle of San Felice. And when they had been there a long time they made an agreement with the garrison that if I did not succour them within a month, namely by the feast of St. Catherine, which expired in a month's time, they would surrender the castle. But the men of Parma, Cremona, Modena and Reggio, hearing this, gathered their forces and sent to me, saying, "Sir, we must destroy before we are destroyed." Then, taking counsel, I went out into the country, and I fortified the castles, and on the feast of St. Catherine I came from the city of Parma to the castle which was on that day to surrender. And at nine o'clock with 1200 armed knights and 6000 foot I attacked the enemy, who were as numerous or more numerous than we. The battle lasted till sunset. Almost all the horses were killed on both sides and we were almost defeated, even the horse on which I sat was killed under me. Held up by my men, and standing and looking about and seeing we were almost destroyed, I was well aware how desperate was our state. But at that very moment the enemy began to fly with their standards, first those of Mantua and then the rest. So only by the grace of God we obtained the victory, capturing eighty armed knights in flight and killing 5000(?) foot. By this victory our castle of San Felice was freed. In this battle, along with 200 others, I received the dignity of knighthood. The next day we returned with great joy to Modena with booty and captives. Dismissing my people, I returned to Parma, where I then held my court. Afterwards I passed through to Lucca in Tuscany, and marshalled the war against the Florentines. There I built a fine castle with a fortified wall around it on the crest of a hill, ten miles from Lucca towards the Val de Nievole, and called it Monte Carlo. After this I returned to Parma, leaving its rule to the Lord Simone Pistoja, who had previously ruled well for us and had won the city of Barga from the enemy and had done many other good things in his rule. When I reached Parma, our enemies were gathered from everywhere strongly against us. But the severity of the winter helped us, for it was so fierce that no one could stay in their camps.

At the same time a treaty was made between Verona and our enemies on one side and on the other by Marsiglio dei Rossi, Gilbert dei Fogliani and the Manfredi of Reggio, who were nobles respectively of Parma, Reggio and Modena, and were almost rulers of their own cities. They went with very strong forces to a little church in the diocese of Reggio and agreed to unite together against me and destroy me, and they had Mass said, wishing to swear on the Eucharist to hold firm their agreements. But it happened that when the priest had consecrated, darkness came over the church and a high wind, so that all were terrified. And when it grew light again the priest could not find the host on the altar before him. Then, standing amazed, and looking at one another in distress, they saw the host lying at the feet of Marsiglio dei Rossi, who was the head and leader of the treaty. Then all said together: "What we have determined to do does not please God." So the council broke up and each went home. Then the priest who had said the Mass went to the city of Reggio and told the bishop what had happened. The bishop sent him to the Cardinal of Ostia [Bertrand de Poiet, nephew of John XXII], then legate in Lombardy, who was in Bologna at the time. The legate and bishop told it to my vicar, Egidio de Berlario Francigene, in the city of Reggio, that he should warn me of the conspiracy, so as to put me on my guard against them. However, these who had tried to conspire against me were so moved by contrition that they came to me and gave me every possible aid, keeping my cause in their hearts. One day Gilberto Septimo Fogliani said to me, "I should always have been distressed if the Body of Christ had been

found before my feet as It was before the feet of Marsiglio dei Rossi, and well hath God saved us from doing those things which we should rather have died than done." But I kept silence, as though I knew nothing at all.

In those days my father, hearing how hard beset I was, made arrangements with many in France, chief of whom were the Bishop of Beauvais, Count of Eu, Constable of the kingdom of France, Count St. Cesar, and many other counts and barons. They came from France into Savoy, thence through the Alps to the marquisate of Montserrat, and from thence to Lombardy up to Cremona, and from Cremona to Parma. There were about 600 armed knights in all who came to our aid. Thus our father with this assembled army came to succour the castle of Pavia, which still held out in my name against the city. We joined our camp with them and besieged the city of Pavia; then we were fully 3000 armed knights. We destroyed the suburbs and the monasteries of the suburbs and we filled the castle, to the aid of which we had come, with provisions and food. But we could not capture the city from the castle, because the citizens placed trenches and ramparts between the castle and the city so that we could not get in. They had 1000 armed knights from Milan to aid them. After ten days I left them, turning towards Milan and ravaging the country and district of Milan. Then I went to Bergamo, where I had an agreement with some friends of ours that they should open a gate to us. It was arranged that at dawn some of our people should enter and that a great regiment should follow them in and hold the city, till my father and I with all his army should arrive, which we promised to do that same day. It happened as we had agreed; our friends, the conspirators, opened the gates, and the first company of our men went in. But for some reason that I do not know the main force would not follow them. So the first comers had to retreat again, as they could not fight the whole city by themselves. Many of our friends in the city managed to escape with them. But the rest who remained were captured and hanged on the walls, more than fifty of them. When my father and I arrived and saw what had been done and what not done, we were frightened, and after some days we crossed the river Ada with our whole army and returned through the territory of Cremona to the city of Parma.

After this [1334] my father went to Bologna to the Cardinal of Ostia, Bertrand of Poiet, then legate-a-latere in the Lombardy, who ruled Bologna and other places, Piacenza, Ravenna, the Romagna and the march of Ancona, and discussed matters with him, for he was in treaty with us, and was thus the enemy of our enemies. But even already he was in enmity with the Lord of Ferrara for the sake of Holy Church and his own sake, for the Lord of Ferrara was allied with his enemies, each undertaking to support the other. The cardinal gave us men and money, and he put a force and built a tower against the enemy in the suburbs of Ferrara, the captain of which was later Count of Armagnac.

That same summer after Pentecost my father gathered a great army and sent me on ahead to Cremona from Parma beyond Padua, with 500 armed knights, whom he sent to the city of Pizzighetone, which had revolted from us and was being helped by Pavia and Milan. We remained with scarcely twenty armed knights at Cremona. Suddenly our enemies strengthened themselves and grew in such force that I began to look about for help. At the same time from Mantua and Ferrara they sent ships through Padua to Cremona, and sank all our ships, so that my father and his troops could neither help us nor send us word what to do. Thus in Cremona we were in great peril of destruction, being so few. Hence I was disheartened, for neither could my father aid me nor I him.

Happily, however, our enemies, who were besieging us on the river Po, quarrelled amongst themselves. Hearing this, my father came from Parma to the river, ordered the ships to be recovered from the river, and with a few crossed over to Cremona. Joining forces next day with us, we went to help those who were besieging Pizzighetone. By the grace of God we were now so strengthened as to be stronger than all our enemies, for we had 3000 armed knights. When, however, I saw that nothing could be done against the fort, I wished to proceed to Pavia. Knowing this, the enemy sent councillors who deceitfully treated with my father and made a league with him: they gave all sorts of undertak-

ings, under which we promised to withdraw. We did so, but they never kept their promises, and so we lost Pavia and, winter coming on, we could do no more. Thus was the proverb exemplified, delays are dangerous.

At that time the men of Ferrara, Verona, Mantua and Milan captured the captain of the Legate [the Count of Armagnac] in the suburbs of Ferrara and killed many of his army and drowned others in the Po, so that the legate could not recover his position.

Then my father, at last seeing that his resources were failing and that the war was making no progress, determined to return home and to leave his cities to their inhabitants and tyrants, Parma to the Rossi, Reggio to the Fogliani, Modena to the Pii, Cremona to the Ponzoni, who had given these cities to my father and to whom he wished to give them again. Lucca he wished to sell to Florence, but prevented by our advice and that of his councillors, he handed it over to the Rossi who ruled Parma.

At that time when I was in Lucca, the devil, who always seeks whom he may devour and offers men honey in which gall lurks, then tempted me, but by the grace of God I was not vanquished. For he instigated wicked men (since he could not do it himself), the councillors of my father, by bribery to lead me from the right way to the snares of impurity, so that with the perverse I might be perverse. Then my father not long after took me towards Parma, where I stayed at a village called Tarenzo in the diocese of Parma, on a Sunday which was the feast of the Assumption of Our Lady. Here I had a vision at night. An angel appeared to strike me on the left side and say, "Arise and come with us." I answered, "Lord, I know neither whither nor how to go with you." Taken by my hair through the air, I saw a great force of horsemen drawn up in front of a castle ready to fight. Holding me in the air over them, the angel said, "Look and see." Another angel with a flaming sword then appeared, and struck the leader of the host on the thigh. In great agony with the wound he still sat his horse. The angel asked me, "Do you know who he is who is struck by the angel and wounded to death?" "Lord," said I, "I neither know him nor the place where he is." "Know, then," answered he, "this is the Dauphin of Vienne, who on account of his sins of impurity is stricken by God. Beware, then, and tell your father that he too should beware of the same sin, or worse will befall him and you." I was sorry for that Dauphin of Vienne called Bigon [Guiges, 1318-1333], whose grandmother was the sister of our grandfather, and who was the son of the sister of King Charles I of Hungary. I asked the angel, "Shall he be able to confess before he dies?" so sad was I. "He will confess and live a few days," was the answer. Then I saw on my left a group of many in white, men of great reverence and holiness, talking to each other, looking at the horseman, and I noted them well. However, I had not the grace to ask, nor did the angel tell me who or what they were. Suddenly I found myself back, and dawn was breaking as I woke. Thomas of Villeneuve, the chamberlain of my father, a knight of Liege, came and woke me, saying: "Sir, why do you not get up? Your father is up and ready on horseback." Then I got up, and found I was quite tired out, as though after a great labor. I said to him, "Where shall I go, for this night I have suffered much, and I do not know what I ought to do?" "Why, Sir?" said he. I answered, "The dauphin is dead; now my father wants to gather an army and go to the dauphin's support, who is at war with the Count of Savoy: our aid will not profit him, for he is dead." But he laughed at me, and when we got to Parma told my father what I had said. Then my father called me and asked if it were true. To whom I answered, "Yes, sir, I know for sure that the dauphin is dead." My father upbraided me, saying, "Never believe in dreams." To these two I had not told all that I had seen, but only that the dauphin was dead. After some days news arrived that as the dauphin was besieging a castle of the Count of Savoy he was hit by a great arrow in the thigh, and after some time confessed and died. My father was astonished and said so. But no one spoke of my vision to those who brought the news.

My father, seeing that he was losing money and making no headway against the said lords of Lombardy, determined to go away and leave me in charge of the cities and the war. But I refused, because I could not honorably accept the charge. Then, giving me leave to go, he sent me ahead of him to Bohemia. So, making treaties with all our enemies, I went through the territory of Mantua to Verona, and thence to the county of Tyrol, where I found my brother John, whom my father had married to the daughter of the Duke of Carinthia and Count of Tyrol. This duke, father-in-law to my brother, had, as we have said, as his first wife Anna, the sister of my mother. After her death he had Adelaide as wife, the sister of the Duke of Brunswick, by whom he had a daughter, Margaret Maultasch. With her, since he had no male heirs, he undertook to bequeath Carinthia and Tyrol to my brother. So peace was made between him and my father, for there had been trouble between them since my father expelled him from Bohemia, as I have already said. From the Tyrol I went through Bavaria, where I found my eldest sister Margaret, who had one son, John, by Henry Duke of Bavaria. Then I came to Bohemia after an absence of eleven years.

I found that my mother, Elizabeth, had died some years before. While she yet lived, my second sister Guta [Bona] was sent to France and married to John, the eldest son of Philip, King of France, whose sister named Blanche was my wife. My third and last sister, Anne, was with her sister in France. So when I came to Bohemia I found neither father nor mother nor brother nor sister nor any one I knew. Also I had completely forgotten Bohemian, which later I relearnt, so that I now speak and understand it like any other Bohemian. By divine grace not only can I speak and read and write Bohemian, but French, Lombard, German and Latin. I am equally apt in all. Then my father went to Luxemburg on account of a war he had with the Duke of Brabant, he and his partners, the Bishop of Liege, the Marquis of Juliers, the Graf von Geldern and others. He gave me therefore a commission over Bohemia in his absence. I found that kingdom desolate. Not a castle free that was not pledged, so I had nowhere to lodge except in houses in cities like any other citizen. Prague had been desolated and destroyed since the days of King Ottokar. So I decided to build a new palace which should be large and handsome. It was built at a high cost, as is evident today to whoever looks at it. I then sent for my wife, who was still in Luxemburg. After she came she had her first daughter, Margaret. At that time my father, out of love for me, gave me the title of Margrave of Moravia, and that title I always used. But when the great council of Bohemia remembered that I belonged to the ancient house of Bohemia, they gave me help to recover the castles and royal possessions. With much labor and cost I repaired the castles of Burglitz, Tyrzow, Lichtenburg, Luze, Greiz, Piesek, Nechanic, Zbirow, Tachau and Trautenau in Bohemia, but in Moravia Luckow, Telcz, Weverzy, Olmuzc, Brünn, Znoymo, I recovered all sorts of other pawned goods, alienated from the kingdom. I had many knights serving me, and the kingdom prospered from day to day, and the great council was devoted to me. Evil was afraid and desisted from evil. Justice only in part prevailed in the kingdom, for the barons were often tyrannous and did not fear the king as they should have done, and the kingdom was thus divided. But for two years we held the captaincy of the kingdom, and things improved daily. I gave my sister Anne to Otto, Duke of Austria, as wife.

In those days died the Duke of Carinthia [April 2, 1335], my brother's father-in-law. Though my brother ought to have taken possession of the dukedom of Carinthia and the county of Tyrol, Lewis, who called himself emperor, made league secretly with the Dukes of Austria [to wit Albert and Otto] to divide my brother's lordship falsely and secretly between them. Thus was Louis forgetful and ungrateful to my father, who had supported him for the empire, as I have already said. The Duke of Austria, though he had my sister to wife, immediately after the death of the Duke of Carinthia, by a conspiracy with the Lord of Aufstein, who on the duke's behalf was captain of all Carinthia, took possession of it with his brother. It was fully made over to him by the same Aufstein. Thus my brother lost Carinthia. But the Tyrolese did not want to have Lewis, and remained loyal to my brother. Meanwhile, my father came to Bohemia with Beatrice, his second queen, the daughter of the Duke of Bourbon, of the race of the kings of France, by whom he begat Wenzel, the only son of this marriage.

At this time false and wicked counsellors prevailed against me with my father, thinking to secure their own good, both Bohemians and Lux-

emburgers. They went to my father saying: "Look you, Sire, your son has many castles in your kingdom and a large following of your people. Hence if he holds sway for long, he will be able to expel you when he wants to, for he is heir and of the blood royal of Bohemia, and much loved by the Bohemians, whereas you are a stranger." This they said to get profit and place by getting him to give them the said castles and goods. So far my father gave way as to lose confidence in me, and he took away all the castles and administration in Bohemia from me and the March of Moravia, so I had only the title of Margrave of Moravia, but not the powers.

At that time I went on horseback one day from Burglitz to Prague, wishing to visit my father, who was then in Moravia, and so we came late to the city of Prague, to an old burgh-house, where we stayed for some time before the great palace was built. At night we went to bed. Buscho of Willhartiscz the elder lay in another bed at the end of my bed. A big fire burnt in the room because it was winter, and many candles were also alight in the room, so that there was a good light in it. The windows and doors were shut. When we began to sleep we both heard something or other walking across the room, so that we both woke, and I made Buscho get up to see what it was. Getting up, he went round the room and saw nothing and could find nothing. Then he made the fire larger and lit even more candles and went to the jugs that were full of wine and stood on benches. He drank from one and replaced it near a great burning candle. When he had finished his drink he returned to bed. I sat up with my cloak around me, and could still hear someone walking round my bed, but could see no one. As I looked with Buscho at the jugs and the candles, we both saw the jug he had used thrown by some one or other beyond the bed of Buscho from one corner of the room to the opposite wall, hitting the wall and falling broken into the middle of the room. Seeing this, we were both terrified. All the while we heard some one ceaselessly walking, yet could see no one. Making the sign of the cross and calling on the name of Christ, we slept till morning. In the morning we found the jug lying broken in the middle of the room and showed it to our servants.

My father then sent me to the Duke of Silesia, Polcon by name, lord of Munsterberg, with a fine army. For that duke was not an independent prince but the vassal of my father and of the kingdom of Bohemia. My father had acquired the city of Warsaw through Lord Henry VII, Duke of Warsaw, who had no heirs. The same duke accepted Glaz for his life in exchange for its sovereignty; the duke preferred that it should go to my father and the kingdom of Bohemia rather than to his brother Bodeslaus, with whom he was at enmity. But after my father acquired Warsaw, all the Dukes of Silesia and Oppeln subjected themselves for ever to his rule and to the crown of Bohemia, to the end that they should be defended by the kings of Bohemia except the Lord of Schweidnitz and Polcon of Munsterberg. We devastated Polcon's territory, as you can read in the chronicles. So badly was it devastated that he had to surrender to my father and to the crown of Bohemia like the other dukes.

This done, I set out for Hungary to my father, whom I found at Blindenburg on the Danube with King Charles I, whose first wife was my father's sister, and who after her death had married the sister of King Casimir of Cracow, by whom he had three sons, Lewis the first-born, Andrew, and Stephen the third. King Charles made peace between my father and the King of Cracow, so that my father renounced his rights in Lower Poland—to wit, Gnesen and Kalisz and the other provinces of Poland. The King of Cracow in his turn renounced to my father and the crown of Bohemia for himself and his successors, for ever, the kingdoms of Lower Poland, the dukedoms of Silesia and Oppeln and the city of Warsaw. For before there was strife between them, since my grandfather, Wenzel II, King of Bohemia, possessed Lower Poland with the kingdoms of Cracow and Sandomierz through the sole heiress, daughter of Premysl, King of Lower Poland, and Duke of Cracow and Sandomierz, whom he had for wife. Premysl gave to my father and the crown of Bohemia for ever both the kingdom and the dukedom. But Casimir was uncle of the girl, and said he had rights over Lower Poland, since a woman could not inherit the kingdom. Hence war for a long time was waged between the kings of Bohemia, and Casimir and

his father Ladislaus, once kings of Lower Poland and Cracow. Peace was made by the King of Hungary, who in return for this promised to ally himself with my father and help him against the Duke of Austria, who had taken Carinthia from my brother, and against Lewis. These were, then, in the league: my father, the King of Hungary and Duke Henry of Bavaria, who had married my sister. At the same time, my father sent me to the Tyrol to govern it, as my brother and his wife were children. So I went there at my father's bidding and took part in every thing, and was admitted to rule over the place by the inhabitants of the said county.

On the day after Easter [April 1336] I gathered an army from the Tyrol and entered the valley of Pusterthal in the diocese of Brixen against the Count of Gorz [he had fiefs in Friuli and possessed Pusterthal in the valley of the Drave], and took the castle of Mount St. Lambert, and I went further against the same count, and devastated his land up to the fortress which is called Lienz. There I stayed three weeks, ravaging because he was an ally of the Dukes of Austria, our enemies. The day after the feast of St. George [April 23] my father drove Duke Otto beyond the Danube and took many castles in Austria. Lewis who called himself emperor was helping the Dukes of Austria, so too was all Germany, and the governors of the cities of Lombardy, and specially Mastino della Scala, Lord of Verona, Vicenza, Padua, Treviso, Brescia, Parma and Lucca. All these invaded us and the county of Tyrol; so that Trent and the whole valley of Etschthal was in great danger from the Lombards, and the valley of the Inn was threatened by the Swabians and Bavarians. Hence the Tyrol was in much danger on every side. Then I made Nicholas Brünn our chancellor Bishop of Trent, and Mathew, my brother's chaplain, Bishop of Brixen, for both bishoprics were vacant.

The same summer Lewis led a great army with all the princes of Germany against Henry Duke of Bavaria, my brother-in-law, who was with us. The Duke of Austria came through Passau to help the same Lewis: my father came to Henry's aid, and they pitched camp near a stream close to Landau. Lewis and the Duke of Austria came against them with a big army, but since they could not cross the river, they ravaged Bavaria for a month: and though Henry's army was smaller, Lewis and Austria were not able to work their will, and returned home. At the same time, I wished to come to my father's aid and Henry's with a large army of foot and horse from the Tyrol, but I could not get any further than Kuffstein, where Lewis' son was, whom we besieged with all his forces during the whole time that the princes lay opposite each other's camp. When they separated I returned to the Tyrol.

After this, about the feast of St. Michael, peace was made between my father and the Duke of Austria, who gave back the city of Znoymo, which my father had given as dowry with his daughter. Also a large sum of money was paid him, and some castles on the Drave were given to the county of Tyrol for my brother. But he, Otto, was allowed to keep the Dukedom of Carinthia.

That winter my father and I went to Prussia against the Lithuanians. With us were the young William of Holland, de Monte, young de Lo and many other earls and barons. The winter was so mild that there was no ice: so we could not cross the river to attack the Lithuanians, so each returned home.

Since a great war had broken out amongst the Lombards (which I had prepared for before I left the Tyrol) on account of the league made between Venice, Florence, Milan, Ferrara, Mantua, Bologna, etc., against Mastino della Scala, governor of Verona and Padua, who was our enemy, as will have been already seen, in April I went through Moravia to Austria, wanting to enter Lombardy, but the Duke of Austria would not give me leave. So, going on board ship, I went to the King of Hungary, who gave me leave to go through Croatia and Dalmatia, to the city of Zengg on the sea-shore, where we embarked. The Venetian captains, knowing this through their friends, wanted to capture us. So they surrounded our galley with their galleys in such a way that our galley could not escape. So when on the ninth day we came to their city of Grado, agreeing to the counsel given me by Bartholomew, Count of Veglia and Zengg, who was with us in the galley, I ordered that one of my men should say, "Behold, my lords, we see that we cannot escape your hands, so please go ahead of us to the city,

and treat with them so that they may be willing to receive us." Then secretly, while he spoke these friendly words, I climbed down from the prow of the galley into a little fishing-smack with Bartie and John de Lipa; and so, hidden by sacks and nets, we went through their galleys and came to the harbour amongst the reeds, and so, escaping their hands, walked to Aquileia. But they captured our galley and all my family, whom they held captive a few days and then set free.

When I was in Aquileia I notified my host who I was. He took the news to the Patriarch. He came at once to the city and to the ringing of bells, with great pomp of clergy and people, took us into his palace, and so for four weeks I and my family (when they had been set free) received his hospitality. He safeguarded us, taking us through Cadore to the Tyrol, which then I ruled for my brother, who was little more than a boy.

In June the Venetians, Florentines, Milanese, Mantuans, people of Ferrara and their other accomplices besieged Padua with enormous forces, about 10,000 armed knights and an infinite number of foot, and some part of them besieged also the city of Feltre with the Bishop Siccone de Caldinacio, the Earls of Siena and the Lords of the house of Camino.[3] For a long while they held to the siege with 500 armed knights and foot, because the city of Padua belonged to Mastino della Scala, Lord of Verona, who also owned the other city named above. Already the Venetians had got hold of Tinglam, Saravalle and Bassano, which were part of Mastino's dominions; moreover, Count Collalto, advocate of Treviso, and a number of others had also revolted from Mastino and made cause with Venice. On this account a certain citizen of the city of Belluno, named Sudracio de Bongagio, fearing lest in this way Feltre would be lost and fall into the hands of Venice, which especially he hated, and seeing it surrounded on every side, bethought himself of Jacopo Anoschano, who with certain castles and some mountains belonging to Belluno had put himself under my rule, and came to me secretly in a little boat, so that neither the Venetians nor Mastino should know, since he was acting against both of them, and said to us, "If you can put to flight the enemies round the city of Feltre, one door of the city shall be opened to you by me, for I would rather that you had the city than any one else at all." I listened to what he said and proposed a day on which I would come secretly as he asked. I was able to collect a force of men prudently because of a duel between two noblemen in the diocese of Neumarkt (between Bozen and Trent). On this excuse I gathered many nobles round me, pretending that their friends were causing a dissension, and this that none should know the reason for my having so many forces with me and yet that I should be able to go near Feltre secretly. As a matter of fact, we knighted the victor who killed his adversary. Then I asked the troops present if they would follow me where I wished. They agreed to come with me. We rode our horses through the Val di Fieme all night. The next day I rode through the desolate mountain ranges near Castrozza, where men are not wont to ride. When we came to a grove between Castrozza and Primiero I could not find any road on account of the fallen trees. My army was in despair. Then on foot with the other foot-soldiers I scouted till I found a way down sheer cliffs and broken roads, and till at last we got beyond the forest. Happily the forest wardens had gone at sunset, not expecting any trouble that night. Thus we got through the hills. With my following I came to Primiero, which was also besieged by the Venetians, and setting them to flight I captured it. These routed enemies went to their allies at Feltre and said that a huge army under someone or other whom they did not know had overwhelmed them. Hearing this they fled during the night. Passing the castle next day from Primiero to Agordo, we hurried to Belluno. I sent word to Sudracio that we had come with a large army. He at once got hold of the captains and magistrates and told them that he had received news that the Counts of Clermont, allies of Mastino della Scala, had come to their aid and scattered their foe. These joyously opened their gates, thinking us to be friends. I entered on the feast of St. Procopius, the 4th of July. When we had all entered I unfurled the banner of the King of Bohemia and the Count of Tyrol. When they saw we were enemies, they were amazed, and knew not how to resist our power. So by the grace of God I obtained the city, though the castle held out against us a few days; but when we had laid

mines to the castle, those in it surrendered it to us. Then we encamped before Feltre. But because the Lord of Verona was busy with the Venetians and they with him, neither was able to do us harm. Indeed, both entered into treaty with us, desiring to have us as allies. When we had sat in front of Feltre six weeks, we made a treaty with the Venetians. They agreed to help us by every means in their power against Mastino. At their own expense they sent us 700 armed knights and many foot.

Leaving my brother with the army, I went to Venice, where I was received with much honour and reverence, and I confirmed the treaty. Thence returning, we captured Feltre by starvation. Also the Carrara, Lords of Padua, treated with us and took Padua and captured Alberto, the elder brother of Mastino, whom they gave to the Venetians to imprison; and remaining our subjects, held Padua. But we, scattering our followers, installed them in the cities of Belluno and Feltre and in their castles as captains; Volcmar de Burchstal, a noble of the Tyrol, in Feltre, Sudracio de Bongagio in Belluno, and as captain against Verona John de Lipa, who died seven days after his appointment. In his place I named Lepor.

So I returned to the Tyrol by the valley of Inn and thence into the kingdom of Bohemia. I made an alliance with the Dukes of Austria (with whom before I was not friends). That winter in Septuagesima I gave my eldest daughter, Margaret, to the eldest son of Charles the Great, King of Hungary, named Lewis; and I made a treaty with him against all comers. Next day I had invited my brother-in-law to dine with me, but one of the servants woke me at dawn saying: "The last day has come; get up, the world is covered with locusts." So, getting up and going on my horse, I rode hurriedly out, wishing to see where they were. They were as far as Pultava, where they stretched seven miles long, but the width of them I could not gauge at all. Their noise was like a riot. Their wings seemed covered with black letters. They were in such numbers that the sun's light was obscured. A terrible stench preceded them. They divided, some to Bavaria, some to Lombardy, some in every direction all over the world. They were prolific: in a night two became twenty. At first they were very small, but grew very big. They were to be found for three years after. Within two months both our sister and her husband, the Duke of Austria, died. We never saw the locusts again from that time.

When we had come to Bohemia, we happened to reach Tauschim in Bunzlau, and when we were asleep we had by chance in a dream a picture of the gospel which says, "The kingdom of Heaven is like to a treasure hidden in a field," which is read on the feast of St. Limila.[4] And so beginning to picture it I began in my sleep the exposition of the Gospel. Waking, I remembered the opening concept of the first part of the Gospel, and so by divine help I learnt its meaning: Dear Brethren: no one can understand the words of the Holy Gospels ...

[Here for four chapters of the *Vita*, Charles gives in detail a commentary on the parables of the Kingdom from Matthew chapter XIII ...]

That same summer, coming to Muta, I broke the castle of Chocyn and many other castles of the Lord of Pottenstein, as I was at that time at war with him. Afterwards we came to terms. At the same time a silver mine was found in Vresnik.

I left Bohemia with my barons, wishing to go to Luxemburg to my father, who had sent for me. From Frankfurt I came back again, and coming back I inaugurated the college of All Saints in the royal Chapel of the Castle of Prague.

I went on then to the King of Hungary, who was sick. Before I got back to Bohemia, as I was leaving Hungary, my father went to Lewis who acted as emperor to make peace with him. Now, Lewis had promised me that he would make no treaties with my father without me, but that, thanks to my advice, he would deal kindly with my father. But Lewis, unmindful of his promises and of his plighted word, deceived my father into making terms with him by saying that he had already made a treaty with me. Thus he occasioned a difference between us; and because of this treaty and the one he said he had made with me, my father agreed to hold his territories from him as emperor. Also he came to terms with him and agreed to many things that he would not have done had he known that I had no treaty with him. Knowing nothing of this, I hurried to

Miltenburg in the diocese of Mainz to meet him, and told him that the whole affair that he had negotiated with the same Lewis of Bavaria was fraudulently reached, and so I with the barons of Bohemia refused to seal or confirm the treaty he had made, and held it to be null and void.

Then I went to Presburg on the frontiers of Hungary and Austria and persuaded the King of Hungary and the Duke of Austria to come to peace. Then my father went towards Moravia, wishing to destroy Nicholas, Duke of Troppau and Ratibor, whom with difficulty I reconciled to my father. Then we went to the siege of the castle of Pottenstein, which had rebelled against me and the King of Bohemia and had done much damage; and although it seemed inaccessible, within nine weeks I captured it and had thrown to the ground both the tower and the baron whose castle it was. I also razed the walls and the whole castle all by myself. Then I went with my father to Warsaw. The bishop of it was disobedient to my father because my father, in anger, had taken away from him the castle of Militsch. For this reason he excommunicated my father. This trouble between my father and the said cleric lasted two years.

Thence my father went to Budweis; and so to France to the aid of the King of France, because the war between the Kings of France and England was then beginning. He sent me in his place into his kingdom. But in my place I put Peter von Rosinberk and followed him into Bavaria. There I found that Henry, Duke of Bavaria, my sister's husband, was dead and had left an only son by my sister Margaret as his heir, aged ten years old, whose guardian and the guardian of the land Lewis, the supposed emperor, made himself, on the grounds of a treaty he had previously made with the boy's father. He repudiated the daughter of Rudolph I, Duke of Bavaria, and Count Palatine, the son of his brother, who had been promised and vowed to the said boy, and gave him instead his own daughter, who could not speak yet, saying that he would promise her for her till she could speak. By the permission of God she remained dumb all her life.

Thence passing through Bavaria I came to my father in the county of Luxembourg. There I wished to go to the aid of the King of France, for the English king was besieging the city of Cambrai before his enemy had time to collect his forces. Then he went to the city of St. Quentin, then to Ribemont, and finally to Laon. Then he returned to the county of Hainault, whither the French king followed him to its frontiers. Both pitched their camps on the frontiers of Hainault. But after the French king had waited for him a whole day and had his troops all in line, the King of England retreated, leaving his camp to the French king, although he had many German princes with him, the Duke of Brabant, the Marquis of Juliers and de Monti and the Earl of Flanders from Lower Germany, while from Upper Germany he had the Margrave of Meissen, the Margrave of Brandenburg, the son of the Bavarian, and many other of Lewis' forces: for Lewis had nominated the King of England his Vicar Imperial through Germany.

In those days, since for a long while my father had already lost the sight of one eye, the other eye began to get affected. He went to Montpellier secretly to doctors to see if he could get cured. From that time, however, he went completely blind. Meanwhile I intended to go to the King of Spain to his aid against the King of Granada, Yussuf I [1333-1354], and so sent forward my people and my siege engine to Montauban. But my father held me secretly at Montpellier and would not let me go beyond the passes. Since he could not get cured, I went with him to Pope Benedict XII at Avignon to treat with him about the Peter's pence which had been given by the diocese of Warsaw. But we made no settlement with the Bishop of Warsaw at the time, and affairs were left at variance. However, later on peace was made between us and the Church of Rome and the diocese of Warsaw over the money. When I was there I told the Pope my vision of the death of the dauphin as I have written it above. But I still at the time judged it better to keep from telling my father the whole story, for various reasons. But while we were with the Pope we found that Peter, late Abbot of Fécamp, of the diocese of Limoges, had meanwhile become Bishop of Orleans, then Archbishop of Sens, after that Archbishop of Rouen, and at that time was actually Cardinal Priest of the title of SS. Nereo and Achilleo. I have already spoken of him, saying

that he was a councillor of King Philip, and had said Mass in his presence one Ash Wednesday. At Avignon he took me to his house, I being then Margrave of Moravia and visiting Pope Benedict. One day when I was in his house he said to me, "You will yet be king of the Romans." I answered him, "Before that happens you will be Pope." Both of these things came to pass.

After that I returned with my father to France. Then my father sent me to my sister [Margaret], the relict of Henry, Duke of Bavaria, who was oppressed by Lewis, in order to give her counsel and aid. When I got there, I found she had made peace with him. So I turned to go through the archbishopric of Salzburg by the Alps that are called Hohen Tauern. As at day I came through the Valley of Gerlostal, I remembered the miracle or vision which had come to me on the Assumption of Our Lady in Tarenzo in the Parma diocese. From that moment I got the idea of ordering the hours of the glorious Virgin Mary to be sung daily in her honour in the Church of Prague, and that her life and miracles and the account of her should be proclaimed in new lessons in the office. This took place as I shall describe below. Then I went to visit my brother at Innsbrück, sending the Duke of Trent to act as captain in the county of the Tyrol; my brother came with me to Bohemia, thence to the King of Cracow, and thence to Charles of Hungary, with whom and his son Lewis, my son-in-law, he bound himself firmly by a treaty and league.

When he was there, news reached him that his wife with the barons of his county of the Tyrol had conspired against him. So he had to return post haste through Bavaria and Bohemia to the Tyrol. In a short while I followed him into the same county into the valley of the Inn. There I learnt secretly that Albert, the natural brother of his wife, and a certain baron who was master of the court to my brother, had, with her consent and that of the other barons of the county, decided to divorce my brother and marry her to Lewis, son of the Bavarian, the alleged emperor, and that the barons wanted to have him for their lord, and that she wanted to be his wife. Anxious to be certain of this, I laid a trap for Albert through Buschko the Younger, and captured him and took him through a wood to the castle which is called

Sonnenburg, south of Innsbrück. Under torture he confirmed everything that had already been told me. After that I tried to capture my brother's master of the court, but he then escaped me: but his castle I destroyed. Later on his friends gave him to me with leave to do whatever I liked to him so long as I spared his life. I told my brother all this, who was grateful to me and followed my advice in this campaign. We besieged his wife in a castle of the Tyrol.

Then I went to my sister in Bavaria, who needed me; thence I returned through Salzburg and the bishopric of Brixen to the castle of Taufers. Thence I went to the valley of Cordevole to Belluno, and by night went to the suburbs of the strong castle of Zumelles on the vigil of the feast of St. Wenceslaus. I besieged and possessed it from Count Czenench, who was lord of Camerino, a city of the Venetians, who were then my enemies. It remained in my hands after the peace. Then I came to Trent. Coming into the county of Tyrol I was there till the vigil of St. Catherine. I besieged the castle Penede on Lake Garda, defended by the Milanese and the Lord of Arco. This army after a secret treaty with the Bishop of Trent I put to flight; and on the feast of St. Catherine the castle was put into my hands. I gave it to the church of Trent. Then I came to the castle of Belvicino, in the diocese of Vicenza, which city with all the county was held by Mastino. I had to go to the bishop secretly by night with great danger to defend him from his people. Thence I went on to Trent, and from Trent to Belluno. When I was there, the Patriarch of Aquileia, who was overpowered by the Duke of Austria and the Lord of Verona near Frejus, whom he could not resist, sent me this letter:—

"To you, illustrious Prince Charles, of the royal house of Bohemia, Margrave of Moravia, and to your army I notify that the House of the Queen of queens and Virgin of virgins at Aquileia is grievously oppressed by her enemies. These knightly princes who are pledged to defend maidens and women should rather have defended it. But I ask you and all your princes that by the love of this Maiden of maidens you do not allow her house and property to be violated."

When we got this letter, we marched with our troops of nearly 200 armed knights and 1000 foot over mountains which have seldom been crossed. Thus the Lord prepared our way over Serravalle, south of Belluno, near Ceneda, and after much difficulty we got to Aquileia, and the next day to the Patriarch. He had collected his people and had pitched his camp near a river opposite the enemy, who lay on the farther side of it. They learnt that night of our arrival and fled, and their army broke up. We followed them and besieged part of them in a castle. There we halted some time and often attacked the castle but lost many men wounded.

[5]A little after [June 1341] King John and Charles returned to Bohemia; and King John gave the administration of the whole kingdom to Charles, on this condition that Charles on the one side should undertake to give the king 5000 pounds of money, and that King John on the other should promise not to come to Bohemia for two years nor within that time ask any money from Bohemia. The money was speedily collected for Charles and given to King John, who left for France. Once he had gone, Charles happily and with great diligence ruled the kingdom, and by recovering what had been dissipated, reduced the debt and administered the wealth of the kingdom well.

After the two years were over King John returned to Bohemia and persuaded Charles to march with him against the Lithuanians in Prussia. Quickly getting together what was necessary for their journey, they went to Warsaw, where were also the King of Hungary, the Count of Holland, and many other princes, dukes and notables come for the same purpose from all over Christendom. While these were waiting at Warsaw, amongst other pastimes which the kings used for their amusement, they played at the evil and foolish game of dice. The King of Hungary and the Count of Holland played the game so eagerly against each other that the count won 600 florins from the king. When he saw the king was angry and furious, he shouted with arrogance: "O Lord King, it is a wonderful thing that a prince so magnificent as you, whose land abounds in gold, should be so irritated by the loss of so small a sum and should be so disturbed in mind. That you all may see clearly that I do not want money so obtained and shall not use it for myself, I freely let it slip." So saying he threw it amongst the people. This made the king even more furious, but he was wise enough to hide it. Not long after all these princes and great men left Warsaw for Prussia. And when they had remained there a long time, waiting for the frost, the winter was so warm and mild that they could not cross the ice as they had done in other years. Thus these great men failed of their purpose, and lost their labours and at much expense too to themselves. The said Lords went back, each to his own place.

But the King of Cracow and the Duke Polco made a deceitful agreement to capture King John and Charles on their return from Prussia, and after much hurt to squeeze the last farthing out of them. Ignorant of these wiles, King John, taking passage by the March of Brandenburg and Lusatz, went to Luxemburg. But Charles could not help going through the territory of the King of Cracow towards Warsaw. Thus he came to Kalisch, where the King of Cracow had him caught, not openly like a public enemy, but by having the city gates shut once he was within the city. This Charles saw, but he pretended not to notice it, and asked to stay there a few days. However, he managed to send out a messenger on foot to the captain of Warsaw to explain what had happened. At once he came with 300 horsemen to within a mile of Kalisch and stationed a fine horse outside the city gate. Charles, instructed by the messenger whom he had sent, very cleverly managed to have the horse brought to him to show to the magistrates. At the open gate as the horse was led in he got on it and scampered off to join his men from Warsaw. When the King of Cracow saw that Charles had escaped, he imprisoned his whole family; but after a while he let them all go.

After this the said King Casimir besieged and took the city of Skiernienice, near the Warsaw territory, when he committed many enormities, dishonouring maidens and wives. When King John of Bohemia, who then was waiting on the banks of the Rhine, heard this, he at once returned to Bohemia and gathering an army besieged Schweidnitz and butchered its suburbs and devastated its lands; he attacked and took the city of

Landshut. Moreover, because they knew that the Duke of Schweidnitz had arranged the trap whereby Charles had been held at Kalisch, King John and Charles remained seven weeks there in his land, doing damage in revenge for the crime, and then returned to Bohemia. Not long after Lewis the Bavarian, who called himself emperor, with the King of Hungary, the Duke of Austria, the King of Cracow, the Margrave of Meissen and the Duke of Schweidnitz, all made a lasting treaty against King John of Bohemia and Charles Margrave of Moravia, in one week calling all their forces, intending to invade these two and pursue them to death. Frightened by this news, King John sent a solemn embassy, to wit, Lord Nicholas of Luxemburg, his intimate councillor, and Lord Henry the treasurer, his protonotary in Neuenberg, to Lewis to draw up some treaty or concord with him. Lewis refused absolutely to have anything to do with drawing up any treaty or truce with him. John, hearing this, said, "In the Lord's name, the larger the host of enemies we have, the more the loot and booty will there be. I swear by the Lord Jesus Christ that whoever first invades me I shall so root up as to terrify all the rest."

Not long after this Casimir, King of Cracow, attacked the city of Nicholas, Duke of Troppau, Sohr by name, and besieged it, who straightway sent the news to John at Prague, asking that he should send him sufficient armed men to save him from King Casimir, who had surrounded him. King John, hearing this, answered gladly that he would not send him men, but that within four days he would come himself with a huge army. At once King John, having called together all the barons of Bohemia, addressed them thus: "Behold, nobles, faithful, loyal and beloved, we must defend our country against those who insult us with swords and arms. And since Casimir, King of Cracow, has held us and our kingdom of Bohemia in such despite as to attack Nicholas, Duke of Troppau, our vassal and prince, he thus has offended our majesty gravely, for we cannot bear it lightly that those who submit to our peace and grace should suffer trouble. Lest this should be ascribed to our laziness and drowsy lethargy, we wish and order that each and all of you should at once take arms and follow us to war without delay to lower his pride who has presumed to invade our prince and vassal. Aided by our power he shall rejoice in peace and tranquillity." The barons, however, answered the king: "Lord King: it is our oath, and has been inviolably observed from ancient times, that outside the limits of the kingdom we should not set forth armed, but that within the limits of the kingdom we should defend the kingdom from all aggression." So the king answered them: "The duchy of Troppau, like the other duchies of Poland, is within the kingdom, since it is known to belong to the King of Bohemia and to the crown of the kingdom. Hence I will go to this war, and I shall see which of you will be bold enough or presumptuous enough to remain behind." So that night King John with 500 armed knights came down from Mount Kutno, where he had made this speech to his barons, and hurried off to Nicholas, Duke of Troppau, in a day and a night. Immediately all the barons and notables of the kingdom followed him, and before they reached the duke they numbered 2000 armed knights, besides archers and others heavily armed. These Zdenko de Lipa quickly despatched with 300 armed men, and attacked fiercely the Hungarians and others whom King Casimir had ordered to besiege the city of the duke. These they pursued in flight to the walls of Cracow. In this flight 300 Hungarians were killed and sixty nobles captured. But the rest he pursued with such fury that he and most of his men burst into the city. The portcullis was instantly lowered and they were caught in the city. King John was furious at not being present at the fight, as he believed he could have captured the city with a single blow. However, he advanced to Cracow and besieged it with a large army and devastated all its suburbs and county round. Then King Casimir of Cracow sent word that to avoid useless slaughter they should engage in single combat, and whoever won should have his will. But since King John was quite blind, he sent word that if Casimir would first blind himself he would very gladly give him combat with equal arms. After this Casimir asked and got a seven weeks' treaty. During it the whole cause of the trouble was settled, so that Charles went to the March of Moravia free and at peace, having received 10,000 marks from Casimir. The cause of the trouble ended, there was peace between them. In which peace all these princes who had first opposed King John and Charles Margrave of Moravia were included.

After this Lewis the Bavarian sent an embassy to King John and Charles asking anxiously that they should have a talk with him, for he said that he wanted to indemnify the king and his son John for all that the latter had suffered in the taking away of his wife Margaret and the county of Tyrol, and to make complete amends. This was arranged to take place on a certain day at Treves before the Archbishop of Treves, who was the uncle of King John. To it came many lords and magnificent princes on behalf of King John, because of the greatness of the injury done him by the wicked and execrable crime of the divorce. For it had not been heard of for a century that a great and generous prince and lord, by the evil of his own councillors and by their betrayal, should be deprived of his land and wife. After much discussion it was publicly agreed that John, who had been deceitfully ejected and expelled from the Tyrol and other lordships, could not honorably be indemnified by the restoration of the Tyrol, nor could he honorably take back his wife, whom, because of her adultery, he could no longer caress or love again. It came, however, to this, that Lewis of Bavaria should give instead to King John and to his son, who had both been deprived of their lordships, the land of Lusatz (*i.e.* Gorlitz and Budweis), and that these and all their lordships should be incorporated in the kingdom of Bohemia for ever; moreover, that 20,000 marks of pure silver should be given to King John and his son John; and that they should hold Berlin, Brandenburg and Stendal with all profits and fines until the money should be paid. This King John accepted. But when he had shown this to his sons, Charles Margrave of Moravia and John, they refused to agree to it: "If our father gets that money he will spend it amongst his Rhine troopers, and so we shall remain deceived and betrayed." When Lewis understood that the sons of King John would not accept the arrangement nor confirm it, the whole treaty stood null and void. At this Lewis the Bavarian was amazed and stupefied; and thought it an evil that the treaty made after mature counsel by great princes and with much wisdom should be fiercely and proudly rejected by the sons of King John.

After this King John went to the Court at Avignon to Pope Benedict, and with him made arrangements that he should persuade all the electors that Lewis of Bavaria was not the emperor, since he was opposed to the Holy Roman Church, the mother of Christendom, and had created a pope to crown him, namely, a certain friar minor. And so at once the electors proceeded to a new election and chose Charles, Margrave of Moravia, as King of the Romans, with most happy auguries.

Notes

1   This is himself, to whom, as he says, the name Charles was subsequently given instead of Wenzel.

2   It will be seen that these dates given by Charles are often not exact.

3   The Camini were Lords Treviso, Feltre and Belluno earlier in the century.

4   St. Limila, Patroness of Bohemia, was Charles' great-grandmother. Her feast is kept on Sept. 16.

5   From this point onwards the narrative is not in the first person and would appear therefore not to be Charles' own account but an account nevertheless by an eye-witness. The style of the Latin is different now from Charles' usual style.

THE GOLDEN BULL

THE GOLDEN BULL OF EMPEROR CHARLES IV ESTABLISHED THE process by which emperors would be selected and confirmed the autonomy of the German princes. The provisions largely formalized the structure that the Empire had taken on its own by the fourteenth century, a form characterized by extreme fragmentation and a lack of universally accepted principles of legitimacy.

Source: E. F. Henderson, *Select Historical Documents*. (London: George Bell, 1894).

The Golden Bull of the Emperor Charles IV. 1356 A.D.

Eternal, omnipotent God, in whom the sole
  hope of the world is,
Of Heaven the Maker Thou, of earth, too,
  the lofty Creator:
Consider, we pray Thee, Thy people, and
  gently, from out Thy high dwelling,
Look down lest they turn their steps to the
  place where Erinis is ruler;
There where Allecto commands, Megaera
  dictating the measures.
But rather by virtue of him, this emperor
  Charles whom Thou lovest,
O most beneficent God, may'st Thou
  graciously please to ordain it,
That, through the pleasant glades of forests
  ever in flower,
And through the realms of the bless'd, their
  pious leader may bring them
Into the holy shades, where the heavenly
  waters will quicken
The seeds that were sown in the life, and
  where the ripe crops are made glorious,
Cleansed in supernal founts from all of the
  thorns they have gathered.
Thus may the harvest be God's, and great
  may its worth be in future,
Heaping a hundred fold the corn in the
  barns overflowing.

In the name of the holy and indivisible Trinity felicitously amen. Charles the Fourth, by favor of the divine mercy emperor of the Romans, always august, and king of Bohemia; as a perpetual memorial of this matter. Every kingdom divided against itself shall be desolated. For its princes have become the companions of thieves. Wherefore God has mingled among them the spirit of dizziness, that they may grope in midday as if in darkness; and He has removed their candlestick from out of His place, that they may be blind and leaders of the blind. And those who walk in darkness stumble; and the blind commit crimes in their hearts which come to pass in time of discord. Tell us, pride, how would'st thou have reigned over Lucifer if thou had'st not had discord to aid thee? Tell us, hateful Satan, how would'st thou have cast Adam out of Paradise if thou had'st not divided him from his obedience? Tell us, luxury, how would'st thou have destroyed Troy, if thou had'st not divided Helen from her husband? Tell us, wrath, how would'st thou have destroyed the Roman republic had'st thou not, by means of discord, spurred on Pompey and Caesar with raging swords to internal conflict? Thou, indeed, oh envy, hast, with impious wickedness, spued with the ancient poison against the Christian empire which is fortified by God, like to the holy and indivisible Trinity, with the theological virtues of faith, hope, and charity; whose foundation is happily established above in the very kingdom of Christ. Thou hast done this, like a serpent, against the branches of the empire and its nearer members; so that, the columns being shaken, thou mightest subject the whole edifice to ruin. Thou hast often spread discord among the seven electors of the holy empire, through whom, as through seven candlesticks throwing light in the unity of a septiform spirit, the holy empire ought to be illuminated.

Inasmuch as we, through the office by which we possess the imperial dignity, are doubly—both as emperor and by the electoral right which we enjoy—bound to put an end to future danger of discords among the electors themselves, to whose number we, as king of Bohemia are known to belong: we have promulgated, decreed and recommended for ratification, the subjoined laws for the purpose of cherishing unity among the electors, and of bringing about a unanimous election, and of closing all approach to the aforesaid detestable discord and to the various dangers which arise from it. This we have done in our solemn court at Nuremberg, in session with all the electoral princes, ecclesiastical and secular, and amid a numerous multitude of other princes, counts, barons, magnates, nobles and citizens; after mature deliberation, from the fullness of our imperial power; sitting on the throne of our imperial majesty, adorned with the imperial bands, insignia and diadem; in the year of our Lord 1356, in the 9th Indiction, on the 4th day before the Ides of January, in the 10th year of our reign as king, the 1st as emperor.

1. What sort of escort the electors should have, and by whom furnished.

1   We decree, and, by the present imperial and ever valid edict, do sanction of certain knowledge and from the plenitude of the imperial power: that whenever, and so often as in future, necessity or occasion shall arise for the election of a king of the Romans and prospective emperor, and the prince electors, according to ancient and laudable custom, are obliged to journey to such election,—each prince elector, if, and whenever, he is called upon to do this, shall be bound to escort any of his fellow prince electors or the envoys whom they shall send to this election, through his lands, territories and districts, and even as much beyond them as he shall be able; and to lend them escort without guile on their way to the city in which such election is to be held, and also in returning from it. This he shall do under pain of perjury and the loss, for that time only, of the vote which he was about to have in such election; which penalty, indeed, we decree that he or they who shall prove rebellious

or negligent in furnishing the aforesaid escort shall, by the very act, incur.

2   We furthermore decree, and we command all other princes holding fiefs from the holy Roman empire, whatever the service they have to perform,—also all counts, barons, knights, noble and common followers, citizens and communities of castles, cities and districts of the holy empire: that at this same time—when, namely, an election is to take place of king of the Romans and prospective emperor—they shall, without guile, in the manner aforesaid, escort through their territories and as far beyond as they can, any prince elector demanding from them, or any one of them, help of this kind, or the envoys whom, as has been explained before, he shall have sent to that election. But if any persons shall presume to run counter to this our decree they shall, by the act itself, incur the following penalties: all princes and counts, barons, noble knights and followers, and all nobles acting counter to it, shall be considered guilty of perjury and deprived of all the fiefs which they hold of the holy Roman empire and of any lords whatever, and also of all their possessions no matter from whom they hold them. All cities and guilds, moreover, presuming to act counter to the foregoing, shall similarly be considered guilty of perjury, and likewise shall be altogether deprived of all their rights, liberties, privileges and favours obtained from the holy empire, and both in their persons and in all their possessions shall incur the imperial bann and proscription. And any man, on his own authority and without trial or the calling in of any magistrate, may henceforth with impunity attack those whom we, by the act itself, deprive, from now or from a past time on, of all their rights. And, in attacking them, he need fear no punishment on this account from the empire or any one else; inasmuch as they, rashly negligent in so great a matter, are convicted of acting faithlessly and perversely, as disobedient and perfidious persons and rebels against the state, and against the majesty and dignity of the holy empire, and even against their own honour and safety.

3   We decree, moreover, and command, that the citizens and guilds of all cities shall be compelled

to sell or cause to be sold to the aforesaid prince electors, or to any one of them who demands it, and to their envoys, when they are going to said city for the sake of holding said election, and even when they are returning from it: victuals at the common and current price for the needs of themselves or the said envoys and their followers. And in no way shall they act fraudulently with regard to the foregoing. We will that those who do otherwise shall, by the act itself, incur those penalties which we, in the foregoing, have seen fit to decree against citizens and guilds. Whoever, moreover, of the princes, counts, barons, knights, noble or common followers, citizens or guilds of cities shall presume to erect hostile barriers or to prepare ambushes for a prince elector going to hold the election of a king of the Romans or returning from it,—or to attack or disturb them or any one of them in their persons or in their property, or in the persons of said envoys sent by them or any one of them, whether they have sought escort or have not considered it worth while to demand it: we decree that he, together with all the accomplices of his iniquity, shall, by the act itself, have incurred the above penalties; in such wise, namely, that each person shall incur the penalty or penalties which, according to what precedes, we have thought best, relatively to the rank of those persons, to inflict.

4   But if any prince elector should be at enmity with any one of his co-electors, and any contention, controversy, or dissension should be going on between them;—notwithstanding this, one shall be bound, under penalty of perjury and loss, for this one time, of his vote in the election, as has been stated above, to escort in said manner the other, or the envoys of the other who shall be sent in said manner to such election.

5   But if any princes, counts, barons, knights, noble or common followers, citizens, or guilds of cities, should bear ill-will to one or more of the prince electors, or any mutual discord, or war, or dissension should be going on between them: nevertheless, all opposition and fraud being laid aside, they ought to furnish such escort to this or to these prince electors, or to his or their envoys

dispatched to or returning from such election, according as they each and all desire to avoid the said punishments declared by us against them; punishments which those who act counter shall, we decree, by the act itself incur. Moreover, for the ampler security and certitude of all the above, we command and we will that all the prince electors and other princes, also the counts, barons, nobles, cities or guilds of the same, shall confirm all the aforesaid through their writings and through their oaths, and shall efficaciously bind themselves to fulfill them with good faith and without guile. But whoever shall refuse to give writings of this kind, shall, by the act itself, incur such punishment as we, by the above, have seen fit to inflict on each person according to his rank.

6   But if any prince elector or other prince of whatever condition or standing, or any count, baron, or noble, or the successors or heirs of such, holding a fief or fiefs from the holy empire, be not willing to fulfill our imperial constitutions and laws above and below laid down, or shall presume to act counter to them: if such a one, indeed, be an elector prince, his co-electors shall, from that time on, exclude him from association with themselves, and he shall lose both his vote in the election and the position, dignity and privileges possessed by the other electors; nor shall he be invested with the fiefs which he shall obtain from the holy empire or from any one otherwise, and shall, in addition, incur by the act itself all the aforesaid penalties concerning his person.

7   Although, indeed, we have willed and decreed in general terms that all princes, counts, barons, nobles, knights, followers, and also cities and guilds of the same, are bound, as has been said, to furnish the aforesaid escort to any prince elector or his envoys: nevertheless, we have thought best to designate for each one of them special escorts and conductors who will be best suited for them according to the nearness of their lands and districts, as will directly be made clearer from what follows.

8   For first the king of Bohemia, the arch-cup-bearer of the holy empire, shall be escorted by the

archbishop of Mainz, the bishops of Bamberg and Wurzburg, the burgraves of Nuremburg; likewise by those of Hohenlohe, of Wertheim, of Bruneck and of Hohenau; likewise by the cities of Nuremburg, Rothenburg, and Windesheim.

9   Then the archbishop of Cologne, the arch-chancellor of the holy empire for Italy, shall be escorted—they being bound to furnish such escort—by the archbishops of Mainz and Treves, the count palatine of the Rhine, the landgrave of Hesse; likewise by the counts of Katzenellenbogen, of Nassau, of Dietz; likewise of Ysenburg, of Westerburg, of Runkel, of Limburg and Falkenstein; likewise by the cities of Wetzlar, Gelnhausen and Friedberg.

10   In like manner the archbishop of Treves, arch-chancellor of the holy empire for the Gallic provinces and for the kingdom of Arles, shall be escorted by the archbishop of Mainz, the count palatine of the Rhine; likewise the counts of Sponheim, of Veldenz; likewise the Raugraves and Wiltgraves of Nassau, of Ysenburg, of Westerburg, of Runkel, of Dietz, of Katzenellenbogen, of Eppenstein, of Falkenstein; likewise the city of Mainz.

11   Then the count palatine of the Rhine, arch-steward of the holy empire, ought to be escorted by the archbishop of Mainz.

12   But the duke of Saxony, the arch-marshall of the holy empire, shall, by right, be escorted by the king of Bohemia, the archbishops of Mainz and Magdeburg; likewise by the bishops of Bamberg and Wurzburg, the margrave of Meissen, the landgrave of Hesse; likewise the abbots of Fulda and Hersfeld, the burgraves of Nuremburg; likewise those of Hohenlohe, of Wertheim, of Bruneck, of Hohenau, of Falkenstein; likewise the cities of Erfurt, Mülhausen, Nuremburg, Rothenburg and Windesheim. And all of these last named shall likewise be bound to escort the margrave of Brandenburg, arch-chamberlain of the holy empire.

13   We will, moreover, and do expressly decree that each prince elector who shall wish to have

such escort shall make known this fact and the way by which he is to pass, and shall demand this escort in such good time that those who have been deputed to furnish such escort, and from whom it shall thus have been demanded, may be able to prepare themselves for this in good time and conveniently.

14   We declare, moreover, that the foregoing decrees promulgated concerning the matter of escort shall, indeed, be so understood that each person named above—or perhaps not expressed—from whom, in the aforesaid case, escort may happen to be demanded, shall be bound to furnish it at least through his lands and territories, and as far beyond as he can, without fraud, under the penalties contained above.

15   Moreover we decree, and also ordain, that he who shall be archbishop of Mainz at the time shall intimate this same election to the different princes, ecclesiastical and secular, his co-electors, by letters patent, through his envoys. In which letters, indeed, the day and the term shall be expressed within which those letters may probably reach each of those princes. And letters of this sort shall state that, within three successive months from the day expressed in the letters themselves, each and all of the prince electors ought to be settled at Frankfort on the Main, or to send their lawful envoys, at that time and to that place, with full and diverse power, and with their letters patent, signed with the great seal of each of them, to elect a king of the Romans and prospective emperor. How, moreover, and under what form such letters ought to be drawn up, and what formality ought to be immutably observed with regard to them, and in what form and manner the prince electors should arrange what envoys are to be sent to such election, and the power, mandate, or right of procuration that they are to have: all this will be found clearly and expressly written at the end of the present document. And we command and decree, through the plenitude of the imperial power, that the form there established be preserved unto all time.

16   Moreover we ordain and decree that when the death of the emperor or king of the Romans

shall come to be known for certain in the diocese of Mainz,—within one month of that time, counting continuously from the day of the notice of such death, the death itself and the summons of which we have spoken shall be announced by the archbishop of Mainz through his letters patent. But if this same archbishop should chance to be negligent or remiss in carrying out this and in sending the summons,—thereupon those same princes of their own accord shall, even without summons, by virtue of the fealty which they owe to the holy empire, come together in the oft-mentioned city of Frankfort within three months after this, as is contained in the decree immediately preceding, being about to elect a king of the Romans and future emperor.

17 Moreover any one prince elector or his envoys should, at the time of the aforesaid election, enter the said city of Frankfort with not more than two hundred mounted followers, among which number he may be allowed to bring in with himself only fifty armed men or fewer, but not more.

18 But a prince elector, called and summoned to such election, and neither coming to it nor sending lawful envoys with letters patent, sealed with his greater seal and containing empowerment, full, free and of every kind, for the election of king of the Romans and prospective emperor; or one who comes, or perchance sends envoys, to the same, but who, afterwards, himself—or the aforesaid embassy—goes away from the place of election before a king of the Romans and prospective emperor, has been elected, and does not formally substitute a lawful procurator and leave him there: shall forfeit for that time the vote or right which he had in that election and which he abandoned in such a manner.

19 We command, moreover, and enjoin on the citizens of Frankfort, that they, by virtue of the oath which we decree they shall swear on the gospel concerning this, shall, with faithful zeal and anxious diligence, protect and defend all the prince electors in general and each one of them in particular from the invasion of the other, if any quarrel shall arise between them; and also from

the invasion of any other person. And the same with regard to all the followers whom they or any one of them shall have brought into the said city among the said number of two hundred horsemen. Otherwise they shall incur the guilt of perjury, and shall also lose all their rights, liberties, privileges, favours and grants which they are known to hold from the holy empire, and shall, by the act itself, fall under the bann of the empire as to their persons and all their goods. And, from that time on, every man on his own authority and without judicial sentence may, with impunity, invade as traitors and as disloyal persons and as rebels against the empire, those citizens whom we, in such a case, from now or from a former time on, deprive of all their rights. And such invaders need in no way fear any punishment from the holy empire or from any one else.

20 The said citizens of Frankfort, moreover, throughout all that time when the oft-mentioned election is being treated of and carried on, shall not admit, or in any way permit any one, of whatever dignity, condition or standing he may be, to enter the aforesaid city: the prince electors and their envoys and the aforesaid procurators alone being excepted; each of whom shall be admitted, as has been said, with two hundred horsemen. But if, after the entry of these same prince electors, or while they are present, any one shall chance to be found in the said city, the citizens themselves shall, effectually and without delay, straightway bring about his exit, under penalty of all that has above been promulgated against them, and also by virtue of the oath concerning this that those same citizens of Frankfort must, by the terms of this present decree, swear upon the gospel, as has been explained in the foregoing.

2. Concerning the election of a king of the Romans.

1 After, moreover, the oft-mentioned electors or their envoys shall have entered the city of Frankfort, they shall, straightway on the following day at dawn, in the church of St. Bartholomew the apostle, in the presence of all of them, cause a mass to be sung to the Holy Spirit, that the Holy Spirit himself may illumine their hearts and

infuse the light of his virtue into their senses; so that they, armed with his protection, may be able to elect a just, good and useful man as king of the Romans and future emperor, and as a safeguard for the people of Christ. After such mass has been performed all those electors or their envoys shall approach the altar on which that mass has been celebrated, and there the ecclesiastical prince electors, before the gospel of St. John: "In the beginning was the word," which must there be placed before them, shall place their hands with reverence upon their breasts. But the secular prince electors shall actually touch the said gospel with their hands. And all of them, with all their followers, shall stand there unarmed. And the archbishop of Mainz shall give to them the form of the oath, and he together with them, and they, or the envoys of the absent ones, together with him, shall take the oath in common as follows:

2 "I, archbishop of Mainz, arch-chancellor of the holy empire throughout Germany, and prince elector, do swear on this holy gospel of God here actually placed before me, that I, through the faith which binds me to God and to the holy Roman empire, do intend by the help of God, to the utmost extent of my discretion and intelligence, and in accordance with the said faith, to elect one who will be suitable, as far as my discretion and discernment can tell, for a temporal head of the Christian people,—that is, a king of the Romans and prospective emperor. And my voice and vote, or said election, I will give without any pact, payment, price, or promise, or whatever such things may be called. So help me God and all the saints."

3 Such oath having been taken by the electors or their envoys in the aforesaid form and manner, they shall then proceed to the election. And from now on they shall not disperse from the said city of Frankfort until the majority of them shall have elected a temporal head for the world and for the Christian people; a king, namely, of the Romans and prospective emperor. But if they shall fail to do this within thirty days, counting continuously from the day when they took the aforesaid oath: when those thirty days are over, from that time

on they shall live on bread and water, and by no means leave the aforesaid city unless first through them, or the majority of them, a ruler or temporal head of the faithful shall have been elected, as was said before.

4 Moreover after they, or the majority of them, shall have made their choice in that place, such election shall in future be considered and looked upon as if it had been unanimously carried through by all of them, no one dissenting. And if any one of the electors or their aforesaid envoys should happen for a time to be detained and to be absent or late, provided he arrive before the said election has been consummated, we decree that he shall be admitted to the election in the stage at which it was at the actual time of his coming. And since by ancient approved and laudable custom what follows has always been observed inviolately, therefore we also do establish and decree by the plenitude of the imperial power that he who shall have, in the aforesaid manner, been elected king of the Romans, shall, directly after such election shall have been held, and before he shall attend to any other cases or matters by virtue of his imperial office, without delay or contradiction, confirm and approve, by his letters and seals, to each and all of the elector princes, ecclesiastical and secular, who are known to be the nearer members of the holy empire, all their privileges, charters, rights, liberties, ancient customs, and also their dignities and whatever they shall have obtained and possessed from the empire before the day of the election. And he shall renew to them all the above after he shall have been crowned with the imperial adornments. Moreover, the elected king shall make such confirmation to each prince elector in particular, first as king, then, renewing it, under his title as emperor; and, in these matters, he shall be bound by no means to impede either those same princes in general or any one of them in particular, but rather to promote them with his favour and without guile.

5 In a case, finally, where three prince electors in person, or the envoys of the absent ones, shall elect as king of the Romans a fourth from among themselves or from among their whole number—

an elector prince, namely, who is either present or absent:—we decree that the vote of that person who has been elected, if he shall be present, or of his envoys if he shall chance to be absent, shall have full vigour and shall increase the number of those electing, and shall constitute a majority like that of the other prince electors.

3. Concerning the seating of the bishops of Treves, Cologne and Mainz.

In the name of the holy and indivisible Trinity felicitously amen. Charles the Fourth, by favour of the divine mercy emperor of the Romans, always august, and king of Bohemia. As a perpetual memorial of this matter. The splendour and glory of the holy Roman empire, and the imperial honour, and the cherished advantage of the state are fostered by the concordant will of the venerable and illustrious prince electors, who, being the chief columns as it were, sustain the holy edifice by the vigilant piety of circumspect prudence; by whose protection the right hand of the imperial power is strengthened. And the more they are bound together by an ampler benignity of mutual favour, so much more abundantly will the blessings of peace and tranquillity happily flow for the people of Christ. In order, therefore, that between the venerable archbishops of Mainz, Cologne and Treves, prince electors of the holy empire, all causes of strife and suspicion which might arise in future concerning the priority or dignity of their seats in the imperial and royal courts may be for all time removed, and that they, remaining in a quiet state of heart and soul, may be able, with concordant favour and the zeal of virtuous love, to meditate more conveniently concerning the affairs of the holy empire, to the consolation of the Christian people: we, having deliberated with all the prince electors, ecclesiastical as well as secular, do decree from the plenitude of the imperial power, by this law, in the form of an edict, to be forever valid,—that the aforesaid venerable archbishops can, may, and ought to sit as follows in all public transactions pertaining to the empire; namely, in courts, while conferring fiefs, when regaling themselves at table, and also in councils and in all other business on account of which they happen

or shall happen to come together to treat of the honor or utility of the empire. He of Treves, namely, shall sit directly opposite and facing the emperor. But at the right hand of the emperor of the Romans shall sit he of Mainz when in his own diocese and province; and also, outside of his province, throughout his whole arch-chancellorship of Germany, excepting alone the province of Cologne. And he of Cologne, finally, shall sit there when in his own diocese and province, and, outside of his province, throughout all of Italy and Gaul. And we will that this form of seating, in the same order as is above expressed, be extended forever to the successors of the aforesaid archbishops of Cologne, Treves and Mainz; so that at no time shall any doubt whatever arise concerning these matters.

4. Concerning the prince electors in common.

We decree, moreover, that, as often as an imperial court shall henceforth chance to be held, in every assembly,—in council, namely, at table or in any place whatsoever where the emperor or king of the Romans shall happen to sit with the prince electors, on the right side of the emperor or king of the Romans there shall sit immediately after the archbishop of Mainz or the archbishop of Cologne—whichever, namely, shall happen at that time, according to the place or province, following the tenor of his privilege, to sit at the right hand of the emperor—first, the king of Bohemia, as he is a crowned and anointed prince, and secondly, the count palatine of the Rhine. But on the left side, immediately after whichever of the aforesaid archbishops shall happen to sit on the left, the duke of Saxony shall have the first, and, after him, the margrave of Brandenburg the second place.

But so often and whenever the holy empire shall hereafter happen to be vacant, the archbishop of Mainz shall then have the right, which he is known from of old to have had, of convoking the other princes, his aforesaid companions in the said election. And when all of them, or those who can will be present, are assembled together at the term of the election, it shall pertain to the said archbishop of Mainz and to no other to call for the votes of these his co-electors, one by one in the following order. First, indeed, he shall interrogate the archbishop of Treves, to whom we declare that the first vote belongs, and to whom, as we find, it hitherto has belonged. Secondly, the archbishop of Cologne, to whom belongs the dignity and also the duty of first imposing the royal diadem on the king of the Romans. Thirdly, the king of Bohemia, who, rightly and duly, on account of the prestige of his royal dignity, has the first place among the lay electors. Fourthly, the count palatine of the Rhine. Fifthly, the duke of Saxony. Sixthly, the margrave of Brandenburg. Of all these the said archbishop of Mainz shall call for the votes in the aforesaid order. This being done, the aforesaid princes his companions, shall, in their turn, call on him to express his own intention and to make known to them his vote. Moreover, when an imperial court is held, the margrave of Brandenburg shall present the water for washing the hands of the emperor or king of the Romans. And the king of Bohemia shall be the first to offer drink; but, according to the tenor of the privileges of his kingdom, he shall not be bound to offer it with his royal crown on, except of his own free will. The count palatine of the Rhine, moreover, shall be obliged to offer food, and the duke of Saxony shall perform the office of marshal, as has been the custom from of old.

5. Concerning the right of the count palatine and also of the duke of Saxony.

Whenever, moreover, as has been said before, the throne of the holy empire shall happen to be vacant, the illustrious count palatine of the Rhine, arch-steward of the holy empire, the right hand of the future king of the Romans in the districts of the Rhine and of Swabia and in the limits of Franconia, ought, by reason of his principality or by privilege of the county palatine, to be the administrator of the empire itself, with the power of passing judgments, of presenting to ecclesiastical benefices, of collecting returns and revenues and investing with fiefs, of receiving oaths of fealty for and in the name of the holy empire. All of these acts, however, shall, in due time, be renewed by the king of the Romans who is afterwards elected, and the oaths shall be sworn to him anew. The fiefs of princes are alone excepted,

and those which are commonly called banner-fiefs: the conferring of which, and the investing, we reserve especially for the emperor or king of the Romans alone. The count palatine must know, nevertheless, that every kind of alienation or obligation of imperial possessions, in the time of such administration, is expressly forbidden to him. And we will that the illustrious king of Saxony, arch-marshal of the holy empire, shall enjoy the same right of administration in those places where the Saxon jurisdiction prevails, under all the modes and conditions that have been expressed above.

And although the emperor or king of the Romans, in matters concerning which he is called to account, has to answer before the count palatine of the Rhine and prince elector—as is said to have been introduced by custom:—nevertheless the count palatine shall not be able to exercise that right of judging otherwise than in the imperial court, where the emperor or king of the Romans shall be present.

6. Concerning the comparison of prince electors with other, ordinary princes.

We decree that, in holding an imperial court, whenever in future one shall chance to be held, the aforesaid prince electors, ecclesiastical and secular, shall immutably hold their positions on the right and on the left—according to the prescribed order and manner. And no other prince, of whatever standing, dignity, pre-eminence or condition he may be, shall in any way be preferred to them or anyone of them, in any acts relating to that court; in going there, while sitting or while standing. And it is distinctly declared that especially the king of Bohemia shall, in the holding of such courts, in each and every place and act aforesaid, immutably precede any other king, with whatsoever special prerogative of dignity he may be adorned, no matter what the occasion or cause for which he may happen to come or to be present.

7. Concerning the successors of the princes.

Among those innumerable cares for the well-being of the holy empire over which we, by

God's grace, do happily reign—cares which daily try our heart,—our thoughts are chiefly directed to this: that union, desirable and always healthful, may continually flourish among the prince electors of the holy empire, and that the hearts of those men may be preserved in the concord of sincere charity, by whose timely care the disturbances of the world are the more easily and quickly allayed, the less error creeps in among them, and the more purely charity is observed, obscurity being removed and the rights of each one being clearly defined. It is, indeed, commonly known far and wide, and clearly manifest, as it were, throughout the whole world, that those illustrious men the king of Bohemia and the count palatine of the Rhine, the duke of Saxony and the margrave of Brandenburg, have—the one by reason of his kingdom, the others of their principalities,—together with the ecclesiastical princes their co-electors, their right, vote and place in the election of the king of the Romans and prospective emperor. And, together with the spiritual princes, they are considered and are the true and lawful prince electors of the holy empire. Lest, in future, among the sons of these same secular prince electors, matter for scandal and dissension should arise concerning the above right, vote and power, and the common welfare be thus jeopardized by dangerous delays, we, wishing by God's help to wholesomely obviate future dangers, do establish with imperial authority and decree, by the present ever-to-be-valid law, that when these same secular prince electors, or any of them, shall die, the right, vote and power of thus electing shall, freely and without the contradiction of any one, devolve on his first born, legitimate, lay son; but, if he be not living, on the son of this same first born son, if he be a layman. If, however, such first born son shall have departed from this world without leaving male legitimate lay heirs,—by virtue of the present imperial edict, the right, vote and aforesaid power of electing shall devolve upon the elder lay brother descended by the true paternal line, and thence upon his first born lay son. And such succession of the first born sons, and of the heirs of these same princes, to their right, vote and power, shall be observed in all future time; under such rule and condition, however, that if a prince

elector, or his first born or eldest lay son, should happen to die leaving male, legitimate, lay heirs who are minors, then the eldest of the brothers of that elector, or of his first born son, shall be their tutor and administrator until the eldest of them shall have attained legitimate age. Which age we wish to have considered, and we decree that it shall be considered, eighteen full years in the case of prince electors; and, when they shall have attained this, the guardian shall straightway be obliged to resign to them completely, together with his office, the right, vote and power, and all that these involve. But if any such principality should happen to revert to the holy empire, the then emperor or king of the Romans should and may so dispose of it as of a possession which has lawfully devolved upon himself and the empire. Saving always the privileges, rights and customs of our kingdom of Bohemia concerning the election, through its subjects, of a king in case of a vacancy. For they have the right of electing the king of Bohemia; such election to be made according to the contents of those privileges obtained from the illustrious emperors or kings of the Romans, and according to long observed custom; to which privileges we wish to do no violence by an imperial edict of this kind. On the contrary we decree that, now and in all future time, they shall have undoubted power and validity as to all their import and as to their form.

8. Concerning the immunity of the king of Bohemia and his subjects.

Inasmuch as, through our predecessors the divine emperors and kings of the Romans, it was formerly graciously conceded and allowed to our progenitors and predecessors the illustrious kings of Bohemia, also to the kingdom of Bohemia and to the crown of that same kingdom; and was introduced, without hindrance of contradiction or interruption, into that kingdom at a time to which memory does not reach back, by a laudable custom preserved unshaken by length of time, and called for by the character of those who enjoy it; that no prince, baron, noble, knight, follower, burgher, citizen—in a word no person belonging to that kingdom and its dependencies wherever they may be, no matter what his standing, dignity, pre-eminence, or condition—might, or in all future time may, be cited, or dragged or summoned, at the instance of any plaintiff whatsoever, before any tribunal beyond that kingdom itself other than that of the king of Bohemia and of the judges of his royal court: therefore of certain knowledge, by the imperial authority and from the plenitude of imperial power, we renew and also confirm such privilege, custom and favour; and by this our imperial forever-to-be-valid edict do decree that if, contrary to the said privilege, custom, or favour, any one of the foregoing—namely, any prince, baron, noble, knight, follower, citizen, burgher, or rustic, or any aforementioned person whatever—at any time be cited in any civil, criminal, or mixed case, or concerning any matter, before the tribunal of any one outside the said kingdom of Bohemia, he shall not at all be bound to appear when summoned, or to answer before the court. But if it shall chance that, against any such person or persons not appearing, by any judge outside of that kingdom of Bohemia, no matter what his authority, judicial proceedings are instituted, a trial is carried on, or one or more intermediate or final sentences are passed and promulgated: by the aforesaid authority, and also from the plenitude of the aforesaid imperial power, we declare utterly vain, and do annul such citations, commands, proceedings and sentences, also the carrying out of them and everything which may in any way be attempted or done in consequence of them or any one of them. And we expressly add and, by the same authority and from the fullness of the aforesaid power, do decree by an ever-to-be-valid imperial edict that, just as it has been continually observed from time immemorial in the aforesaid kingdom of Bohemia, so, henceforth, no prince, baron, noble, knight, follower, citizen, burgher, or rustic—in short no person or inhabitant of the oft-mentioned kingdom of Bohemia, whatever be his standing, pre-eminence, dignity, or condition—may be allowed to appeal to any other tribunal from any proceedings, provisional or final sentences, or ordinances of the king of Bohemia or of his judges, instituted or promulgated, or henceforth to be instituted or promulgated against him, in the royal court or before tribunals of the king, the

kingdom or the aforesaid judges. Nor may he appeal against the putting into execution of the same Provocations or appeals of this kind, moreover, if any, contrary to this edict, should chance to be brought, shall of their own accord be invalid; and those appealing shall know that, by the act itself, they have incurred the penalty of loss of their case.

9. Concerning mines of gold, silver and other specie.

We establish by this ever-to-be-valid decree, and of certain knowledge do declare that our successors the kings of Bohemia, also each and all future prince electors, ecclesiastical and secular, may justly hold and lawfully possess—with all their rights without exception, according as such things can be, or usually have been possessed—all the gold and silver mines and mines of tin, copper, lead, iron and any other kind of metal, and also of salt: the king, those which have been found, and which shall at any future time be found, in the aforesaid kingdom and the lands and dependencies of that kingdom,—and the aforesaid electors in their principalities, lands, domains and dependencies. And they may also have the Jew taxes and enjoy the tolls which have been decreed and assigned to them in the past, and whatever our progenitors the kings of Bohemia of blessed memory, and these same prince electors and their progenitors and predecessors shall have legally possessed until now; as is known to have been observed by ancient custom, laudable and approved, and sanctioned by the lapse of a very long period of time.

10. Concerning money.

(1) We decree, moreover, that our successor, the king for the time being of Bohemia, shall have the same right which our predecessors the kings of Bohemia of blessed memory are known to have had, and in the continuous peaceful possession of which they remained: the right, namely, in every place and part of their kingdom, and of the lands subject to them, and of all their dependencies—wherever the king himself may have decreed and

shall please—of coining gold and silver money and of circulating it in every way and manner observed up to this time in this same kingdom of Bohemia in such matters. (2) And, by this our imperial ever-to-be-valid decree and favor we establish, that all future kings of Bohemia forever shall have the right of buying or purchasing, or of receiving in gift or donation for any reason, or in bond, from any princes, magnates, counts or other persons, any lands, castles, possessions, estates or goods, under the usual conditions with regard to such lands, castles, possessions, estates, or goods: that, namely, alods shall be bought or received as alods, freeholds as freeholds; that holdings in feudal dependency shall be bought as fiefs, and shall be held as such when bought. In such wise, however, that the kings of Bohemia shall themselves be bound to regard and to render to the holy empire its pristine and customary rights over these things (lands, etc.) which they shall, in this way, have bought or received, and have seen fit to add to the kingdom of Bohemia. (3) We will, moreover, that the present decree and favour, by virtue of this our present imperial law, be fully extended to all the elector princes, ecclesiastical as well as secular, and to their successors and lawful heirs, under all the foregoing forms and conditions.

11. Concerning the immunity of the prince electors.

We also decree that no counts, barons, nobles, feudal vassals, knights of castles, followers, citizens, burghers—indeed, no male or female subjects at all of the Cologne, Mainz and Treves churches, whatever their standing, condition or dignity—could in past times, or may or can in future be summoned at the instance of any plaintiff whatsoever, beyond the territory and boundaries and limits of these same churches and their dependencies, to any other tribunal or the court of any other person than the archbishops of Mainz, Treves and Cologne and their judges. And this we find was the observance in the past. But if, contrary to our present edict, one or more of the aforesaid subjects of the Treves, Mainz or Cologne churches should chance to be summoned, at the instance of any one whatever, to

the tribunal of any one beyond the territory, limits or bounds of the said churches or of any one of them, for any criminal, civil or mixed case, or in any matter at all; they shall not in the least be compelled to appear or respond. And we decree that the summons, and the proceedings, and the provisional and final sentences already sent or passed, or in future to be sent or passed against those not appearing, by such extraneous judges,—furthermore their ordinances, and the carrying out of the above measures, and all things which might come to pass, be attempted or be done through them or any one of them, shall be void of their own accord. And we expressly add that no count, baron, noble, feudal vassal, knight of a castle, citizen, peasant—no person, in short, subject to such churches or inhabiting the lands of the same, whatever be his standing, dignity or condition—shall be allowed to appeal to any other tribunal from the proceedings, the provisional and final sentences, or the ordinances—or the putting into effect of the same—of such archbishops and their churches, or of their temporal officials, when such proceedings, sentences or ordinances shall have been, or shall in future be held, passed or made against him in the court of the archbishops or of the aforesaid officials. Provided that justice has not been denied to those bringing plaint in the courts of the aforesaid archbishops and their officials. But appeals against this statute shall not, we decree, be received; we declare them null and void. In case of defect of justice, however, it is allowed to all the aforementioned persons to appeal, but only to the imperial court and tribunal or directly to the presence of the judge presiding at the time in the imperial court. And, even in case of such defect, those to whom justice has been denied may not appeal to any other judge, whether ordinary or delegated. And whatever shall have been done contrary to the above shall be void of its own accord. And, by virtue of this our present imperial law, we will that this statute be fully extended, under all the preceding forms and conditions, to those illustrious men the count palatine of the Rhine, the duke of Saxony, the margrave of Brandenburg,—the secular or lay prince electors, their heirs, successors and subjects.

12. Concerning the coming together of the princes.

In view of the manifold cares of state with which our mind is constantly distracted, after much consideration our sublimity has found that it will be necessary for the prince electors of the holy empire to come together more frequently than has been their custom, to treat of the safety of that same empire and of the world. For they, the solid bases and immovable columns of the empire, according as they reside at long distances from each other, just so are able to report and confer concerning the impending defects of the districts known to them, and are not ignorant how, by the wise counsels of their providence, they may aid in the necessary reformation of the same. Hence it is that, in the solemn court held by our highness at Nuremburg together with the venerable ecclesiastical and illustrious secular prince electors, and many other princes and nobles, we, having deliberated with those same prince electors and followed their advice, have seen fit to ordain, together with the said prince electors, ecclesiastical as well as secular, for the common good and safety: that these same prince electors, once every year, when four weeks, counting continuously from the Easter feast of the Lord's resurrection, are past, shall personally congregate in some city of the holy empire; and that when next that date shall come round, namely, in the present year, a colloquium, or court, or assembly of this kind, shall be held by us and these same princes in our imperial city of Metz. And then, and henceforth on any day of an assembly of this kind, the place where they shall meet the following year shall be fixed upon by us with their counsel. And this our ordinance is to endure just so long as it may be our and their good pleasure. And, so long as it shall endure, we take them under our imperial safe conduct when going to, remaining at, and also returning from said court. Moreover, lest the transactions for the common safety and peace be retarded, as is sometimes the case, by the delay and hindrance of diversion or the excessive frequenting of feasts, we have thought best to ordain, by concordant desire, that henceforth, while the said court or congregation shall last, no one may be allowed to give general entertainments for all the princes. Special ones, however, which do not impede the transaction of business, may be permitted in moderation.

13. Concerning the revocation of privileges.

Moreover we establish, and by this perpetual imperial edict do decree, that no privileges or charters concerning any rights, favors, immunities, customs or other things conceded, of our own accord or otherwise, under any form of words, by us or our predecessors of blessed memory the divine emperors or kings of the Romans, or about to be conceded in future by us or our successors the Roman emperors and kings, to any persons of whatever standing, pre-eminence or dignity, or to the corporation of cities, towns, or any places: shall or may, in any way at all, derogate from the liberties, jurisdictions, rights, honors or dominions of the ecclesiastical and secular prince electors; even if in such privileges and charters of any persons, whatever their pre-eminence, dignity or standing, as has been said, or of corporations of this kind, it shall have been, or shall be in future, expressly cautioned that they shall not be revokable unless, concerning these very points and the whole tenor included in them, special mention word for word and in due order shall be made in such revocation. For such privileges and charters, if, and in as far as, they are considered to derogate in any way from the liberties, jurisdictions, rights, honours or dominions of the said prince electors, or any one of them, in so far we revoke them of certain knowledge and cancel them, and decree, from the plenitude of our imperial power, that they shall be considered and held to be revoked.

14. Concerning those from whom, as being unworthy, their feudal possessions are taken away.

In very many places the vassals and feudatories of lords unseasonably renounce or resign, verbally and fraudulently, fiefs or benefices which they hold from those same lords. And, having made such resignation, they maliciously challenge those same lords, and declare enmity against them, subsequently inflicting grave harm upon them. And, under pretext of war or hostility, they again invade and occupy benefices and fiefs which they had thus renounced, and hold possession of them. Therefore we establish, by the present ever-to-be-valid decree, that such renunciation or resignation shall be considered as not having taken place, unless it shall have been freely and actually made by them in such way that possession of such benefices and fiefs shall be personally and actually given over to those same lords so fully that, at no future time, shall they, either through themselves or through others, by sending challenges, trouble those same lords as to the goods, fiefs or benefices resigned; nor shall they lend counsel, aid or favor to this end. He who acts otherwise, and in any way invades his lords as to benefices and fiefs, resigned or not resigned, or disturbs them, or brings harm upon them, or furnishes counsel, aid or favor to those doing this: shall, by the act itself, lose such fiefs and benefices, shall be dishonoured and shall underlie the bann of the empire; and no approach or return to such fiefs or benefices shall be open to him at any time in future, nor may the same be granted to him anew under any conditions; and a concession of them, or an investiture which takes place contrary to this, shall have no force. Finally, by virtue of this present edict, we decree that he or they who, not having made such resignation as we have described, acting fraudulently against his or their lords, shall knowingly invade them—whether a challenge has previously been sent or has been omitted,—shall, by the act itself, incur all the aforesaid punishments.

15. Concerning conspiracies.

Furthermore we reprobate, condemn, and of certain knowledge declare void, all conspiracies, detestable and frowned upon by the sacred laws and conventicles, or unlawful assemblies in the cities and out of them, and associations between city and city, between person and person or between a person and a city, under pretext of clientship, or reception among the citizens, or of any other reason; furthermore the confederations and pacts—and the usage which has been introduced with regard to such things, which we consider to be corruption rather than any thing else—which cities or persons, of whatever dignity, condition or standing, shall have thus far made and shall presume to make in future, whether among themselves or with others, without the authority of the lords whose subjects or serving-men they are, those same lords being expressly excluded. And it is clear that such are prohibited and declared void by the sacred laws of the divine emperors our predecessors. Excepting alone those confederations and leagues which princes, cities and others are known to have formed among themselves for the sake of the general peace of the provinces and lands. Reserving these for our special declaration, we ordain that they shall remain in full vigor until we shall decide to ordain otherwise concerning them. And we decree that, henceforth, each individual person who, contrary to the tenor of the present decree, and of the ancient law issued regarding this, shall presume to enter into such confederations, leagues, conspiracies and pacts, shall incur, besides the penalty of that law, a mark of infamy and a penalty of ten pounds of gold. But a city or community similarly breaking this our law shall, we decree, by the act itself incur the penalty of a hundred pounds of gold, and also the loss and privation of the imperial liberties and privileges; one half of such pecuniary penalty to go to the imperial fisc, the other to the territorial lord to whose detriment the conspiracies, etc., were formed.

16. Concerning pfalburgers.

Moreover since some citizens and subjects of princes, barons and other men—as frequent complaint has shown us,—seeking to cast off the yoke of their original subjection, nay, with bold daring despising it, manage, and frequently in the past have managed to be received among the citizens of other cities; and, nevertheless, actually residing in the lands, cities, towns and estates of the former lords whom they so fraudulently presume or have presumed to desert, succeed in enjoying the liberties of the cities to which they thus transfer themselves and in being protected by them—being what is usually called in common language in Germany "pfalburgers": therefore, since fraud and deceit ought not to shelter any one, from the plenitude of the imperial power and by the wholesome advice of all the ecclesiastical and secular prince electors, we establish of certain knowledge, and, by the present ever-to-be-valid law do decree, that in all territories, places, and provinces of the holy empire, from the present day on, the aforesaid citizens and subjects thus eluding those under whom they are, shall in no way possess the rights and liberties of those cities among whose citizens they contrive, or have contrived, by such fraudulent means to be received; unless, bodily and actually going over to such cities and there taking up their domicile, making a continued, true and not fictitious stay, they submit to their due burdens and municipal functions in the same. But if any, contrary to the tenor of our present law, have been, or shall in future be received as citizens, their reception shall lack all validity, and the persons received, of whatever condition, dignity or standing they may be, shall, in no case or matter whatever, in any way exercise or enjoy the rights and liberties of the cities into which they contrive to be received. Any rights, privileges, or observed customs, at whatever time obtained, to the contrary notwithstanding; all of which, in so far as they are contrary to our present law, we, by these presents, revoke of certain knowledge, decreeing from the plenitude of the aforesaid imperial power that they lack all force and validity. For in all the aforesaid respects, the rights of the princes, lords and other men who chance, and shall in future chance, to be thus deserted, over the persons and goods of any subjects deserting them in the oft-mentioned manner, shall always be regarded. We decree, moreover, that those who, against the ordering of our present law, shall presume, or shall in the past have presumed, to receive the oft-mentioned citizens and subjects of other men, if they do not altogether dismiss them within a month after the present intimation has been made to them, shall, for such transgression, as often as they shall hereafter commit it, incur a fine of a hundred marks of pure gold, of which one half shall be applied without fail to our imperial fisc, and the rest to the lords of those who have been received as citizens.

17. Concerning challenges of defiance.

We declare that those who, in future, feigning to have just cause of defiance against any person, unseasonably challenge them in places where they do not have their domicile, or which they do not inhabit in common, cannot with honour inflict any harm through fire, spoliation or rapine, on the challenged ones. And, since fraud and deceit should not shelter any one, we establish by the present ever-to-be-valid decree that challenges of this kind, thus made, or in future to be made by any one against any lords or persons to whom they were previously bound by companionship, familiarity or any honest friendship, shall not be valid; nor is it lawful, under pretext of any kind of challenge, to invade any one through fire, spoliation or rapine, unless the challenge, three natural days before, shall have been intimated personally to the challenged man himself, or publicly in the place where he has been accustomed to reside, where full credibility can be given, through suitable witnesses, to such an intimation. Whoever shall presume otherwise to challenge any one and to invade him in the aforesaid manner, shall incur, by the very act, the same infamy as if no challenge had been made; and we decree that he be punished as a traitor by his judges, whoever they are, with the lawful punishments.

We prohibit also each and every unjust war and feud, and all unjust burnings, spoliations and rapines, unlawful and unusual tolls and escorts, and the exactions usually extorted for such escorts, under the penalties by which the sacred laws prescribe that the foregoing offences, and any one of them, are to be punished.

18. Letter of intimation.

To you, illustrious and magnificent prince, lord margrave of Brandenburg, arch-chamberlain of the holy empire, our co-elector and most dear friend, we intimate by these presents the election of the king of the Romans, which is about to take place on account of rational causes. And, as a duty of our office, we duly summon you to said election, bidding you within three months, counting continuously, from such and such a day, yourself, or in the person of one or more envoys or procurators having sufficient mandates, to be careful and come to the rightful place, according to the form of the holy laws issued concerning this, ready to deliberate, negotiate and come to an agreement with the other princes, yours and our co-electors, concerning the election of a future king of the Romans and, by God's favor, future emperor. And be ready to remain there until the full consummation of such election, and otherwise to act and proceed as is found expressed in the sacred laws carefully promulgated concerning this. Otherwise, notwithstanding your or your envoys' absence, we, together with our other co-princes and co-electors, shall take final measures in the aforesaid matters, according as the authority of those same laws has sanctioned.

19. Formula of representation sent by that prince elector who shall decide to send his envoys to carry on an election.

We ... such a one by the grace of God, etc., of the holy empire, etc., do make known to all men by the tenor of these presents, that since, from rational causes, an election of a king of the Romans is about to be made, we, desiring to watch with due care over the honor and condition of the holy empire, lest it be dangerously subjected to so grave harm, inasmuch as we have the great confidence, as it were of an undoubted presumption, in the faith and circumspect zeal of our beloved ... and ..., faithful subjects of ours: do make, constitute and ordain them and each one of them, completely, in every right, manner and form in which we can or may do it most efficaciously and effectually, our true and lawful procurators and special envoys—so fully that the condition of him who is acting at the time shall not be better than that of the other, but that what has been begun by one may be finished and lawfully terminated by the other. And we empower them to treat wherever they please with the others, our co-princes and co-electors, ecclesiastical as well as secular, and to agree, decide and settle upon some person fit and suitable to be elected king of the Romans, and to be present, treat and deliberate in the transactions to be carried on concerning the election of such a person, for us and in our place and

name; also, in our stead and name, to nominate such a person, and to consent to him, and also to raise him to be king of the Romans, to elect him to the holy empire, and to take, upon our soul, with regard to the foregoing or any one of the foregoing, whatever oath shall be necessary, requisite or customary. And we empower them to substitute altogether, as well as to recall, one or more other procurators who shall perform each and every act, included in and concerning the foregoing matters, that may be needful, useful, or even in any way convenient, even to the consummation of such negotiations, nomination, deliberation and impending election. Even if the said matters, or any one of them, shall require a special mandate; even if they shall turn out to be greater or more especial than the above mentioned; provided that we could have performed them ourselves had we been present personally at the carrying on of such negotiations, deliberation, nomination and eventual election. And we consider, and wish to consider, and firmly promise that we always will consider satisfactory and valid any thing done, transacted or accomplished, or in any way ordained, in the aforesaid matters or in any one of them, by our aforesaid procurators or envoys, or their substitutes, or by those whom the latter shall substitute.

20. Concerning the unity of the electoral principalities and of the rights connected with them.

Since each and all the principalities, by virtue of which the secular prince electors are known to hold their right and vote in the election of the king of the Romans and prospective emperor, are so joined and inseparably united with such right of election, also with the offices, dignities and other rights connected with each and every such principality and dependent from it, that the right, vote, office and dignity, and all other privileges belonging to each of these same principalities may not devolve upon any other than upon him who is recognized as possessing that principality itself, with all its lands, vassalages, fiefs and domains, and all its appurtenances: we decree, by the present ever-to-be-valid imperial edict, that each of the said principalities, with the right and vote and duty of election, and with all other dignities, rights and appurtenances concerning the same, ought so to continue and to be, indivisibly and for all time, united and joined together, that the possessor of any principality ought also to rejoice in the quiet and free possession of its right, vote and office, and dignity, and all the appurtenances that go with it, and to be considered prince elector by all. And he himself, and no one else, ought at all times to be called in and admitted by the other prince electors, without any contradiction whatever, to the election and to all other transactions to be carried on for the honor or welfare of the holy empire. Nor, since they are and ought to be inseparable, may any one of the said rights, etc., be divided from the other, or at any time be separated, or be separately demanded back, in court or out of it, or distrained, or, even by a decision of the courts, be separated; nor shall any one obtain a hearing who claims one without the other. But if, through error or otherwise, any one shall have obtained a hearing, or proceedings, judgment, sentence or any thing of the kind shall have taken place, or shall chance in any way to have been attempted, contrary to this our present decree: all this, and all consequences of such proceedings, etc., and of any one of them, shall be void of their own accord.

21. Concerning the order of marching, as regards the archbishops.

Inasmuch as we saw fit above, at the beginning of our present decrees, fully to provide for the order of seating of the ecclesiastical prince electors in council, and at table and elsewhere, whenever, in future, an imperial court should chance to be held, or the prince electors to assemble together with the emperor or king of the Romans—as to which order of seating we have heard that in former times discussions often arose: so, also, do we find it expedient to fix, with regard to them, the order of marching and walking. Therefore, by this perpetual imperial edict, we decree that, as often as, in an assembly of the emperor or king of the Romans and of the aforesaid princes, the emperor or king of the Romans shall be walking, and it shall happen that the insignia are carried in front of him, the archbishop of Treves shall walk

in a direct diametrical line in front of the emperor or king, and those alone shall walk in the middle space between them, who shall happen to carry the imperial or royal insignia. When, however, the emperor or king shall advance without those same insignia, then that same archbishop shall precede the emperor or king in the aforesaid manner, but so that no one at all shall be in the middle between them; the other two archiepiscopal electors always keeping their places—as with regard to the seating above explained, so with regard to walking—according to the privilege of their provinces.

22. Concerning the order of proceeding of the prince electors, and by whom the insignia shall be carried.

In order to fix the order of proceeding, which we mentioned above, of the prince electors in the presence of the emperor or king of the Romans when he is walking, we decree that, so often as, while holding an imperial court, the prince electors shall, in the performance of any functions or solemnities, chance to walk in procession with the emperor or king of the Romans, and the imperial or royal insignia are to be carried: the duke of Saxony, carrying the imperial or royal sword, shall directly precede the emperor or king, and shall place himself in the middle, between him and the archbishop of Treves. But the count palatine, carrying the imperial orb, shall march in the same line on the right side, and the margrave of Brandenburg, bearing the sceptre, on the left side of the same duke of Saxony. But the king of Bohemia shall directly follow the emperor or king himself, no one intervening.

23. Concerning the benedictions of the archbishops in the presence of the emperor.

Furthermore, so often as it shall come to pass that the ceremony of the mass is celebrated in the presence of the emperor or king of the Romans and that the archbishops of Mainz, Treves and Cologne, or two of them, are present,—in the confession which is usually said before the mass, and in the presenting of the gospel to be kissed, and in the blessing to be said after the "Agnus

Dei," also in the benedictions to be said after the end of the mass, and also in those said before meals, and in the thanks to be offered after the food has been partaken of, the following order shall be observed among them, as we have seen fit to ordain by their own advice: namely, on the first day each and all of these shall be done by the first of the archbishops, on the second, by the second, on the third, by the third. But we will that first, second and third shall be understood in this case, according as each one of them was consecrated at an earlier or later date. And, in order that they may mutually make advances to each other with worthy and becoming honour, and may give an example to others of mutual respect, he whose turn it is according to the aforesaid, shall, without regard to that fact, and with charitable intent, invite the other to officiate; and, not till he has done this, shall he proceed to perform the above, or any of the above functions.

24.

(1) If any one, together with princes, knights or privates, or also any plebian persons, shall enter into an unhallowed conspiracy, or shall take the oath of such conspiracy, concerning the death of our and the holy Roman empire's venerable and illustrious prince electors, ecclesiastical as well as secular, or of any one of them—for they also are part of our body; and the laws have decided that the intention of a crime is to be punished with the same severity as the carrying out of it:—he, indeed, shall die by the sword as a traitor, all his goods being handled over to our fisc. (2) But his sons, to whom, by special imperial lenity, we grant their life—for those ought to perish by the same punishment as their father, whose portion is the example of a paternal, that is of a hereditary crime—shall be without share in any inheritance or succession from the mother or grandparents, or even from relatives; they shall receive nothing from other people's wills, and shall be always poor and in want; the infamy of their father shall always follow them, and they shall never achieve any honor or be allowed to take any oath at all; in a word they shall be such that to them, grovelling in perpetual misery, death shall be a solace and life a punishment. (3) Finally we command that

those shall be made notorious, and shall be without pardon, who shall ever try to intervene with us for such persons. (4) But to the daughters, as many of them as there are, of such conspirators, we will that there shall go only the "falcidia"—the fourth part of the property of the mother if she die intestate; so that they may rather have the moderate alimony of a daughter, than the entire emolument or name of an heir;—for the sentence ought to be milder in the case of those who, as we trust, on account of the infirmity of their sex, are less likely to make daring attempts. (5) Deeds of gift, moreover, made out to either sons or daughters by the aforesaid persons, after the passing of this law, shall not be valid. (6) Dotations and donations of any possessions; likewise, in a word, all transfers which shall prove to have been made, by any fraud or by right, after the time when first the aforesaid people conceived the idea of entering into a conspiracy or union, shall, we decree, be of no account. (7) But the wives of the aforesaid conspirators, having recovered their dowry—if they shall be in a condition to reserve for their children that which they shall have received from their husbands under the name of a gift,—shall know that, from the time when their usufruct ceases, they are to leave to our fisc all that which, according to the usual law, was due to their children. (8) And the fourth part of such property shall be put aside for the daughters alone, not also for the sons. (9) That which we have provided concerning the aforesaid conspirators and their children, we also decree, with like severity, concerning their followers, accomplices and aiders, and the children of these. (10) But if any one of these, at the beginning of the formation of a conspiracy, inflamed by zeal for the right kind of glory, shall himself betray the conspiracy, he shall be enriched by us with reward and honor; he, moreover, who shall have been active in the conspiracy, if, even late, he disclose secret plans which were, indeed, hitherto unknown,—shall nevertheless be deemed worthy of absolution and pardon. (11) We decree, moreover, that if anything be said to have been committed against the aforesaid prince electors, ecclesiastical or secular,—even after the death of the accused that charge can be instituted.[1] (12) Likewise in such a charge, which regards high treason against his prince electors, slaves shall be tortured even in a case concerning the life of their master. (13) We will, furthermore, and do decree by the present imperial edict, that even after the death of the guilty persons this charge can be instituted,[2] and, if some one already convicted die, his memory shall be condemned and his goods taken away from his heirs. (14) For from the time when any one conceived so wicked a plot, from then on he has to some extent been punished mentally; but from the time when any one drew down upon himself such a charge, we decree that he may neither alienate nor release, nor may any debtor lawfully make payment to him. (15) For in this case we decree that slaves may be tortured in a matter involving the life of their master; that is, in the case of a damnable conspiracy against the prince electors, ecclesiastical and secular, as has been said before. (16) And if any one should die, on account of the uncertain person of his successor his goods shall be held, if he be proved to have died in a case of this kind.

25.

If it is fitting that other principalities be preserved in their entirety, in order that justice may be enforced and faithful subjects rejoice in peace and quiet: much more ought the magnificent principalities, dominions, honors and rights of the elector princes to be kept intact—for where greater danger is imminent a stronger remedy should be applied,—lest, if the columns fall, the support of the whole edifice be destroyed. We decree, therefore, and sanction, by this edict to be perpetually valid, that from now on unto all future time the distinguished and magnificent principalities, viz.: the kingdom of Bohemia, the county palatine of the Rhine, the duchy of Saxony and the margravate of Brandenburg, their lands, territories, homages or vassalages, and any other things pertaining to them, may not be cut, divided, or under any condition dismembered, but shall remain forever in their perfect entirety. The first born son shall succeed to them, and to him alone shall jurisdiction and dominion belong; unless he chance to be of unsound mind, or idiotic, or have some other marked and known defect on account

of which he could not or should not rule over men. In which case, he being prevented from succeeding, we will that the second born, if there should be one in that family, or another elder brother or lay relative, the nearest on the father's side in a straight line of descent, shall have the succession. He, however, shall always show himself clement and gracious to the others, his brothers and sisters, according to the favor shown him by God, and according to his best judgment and the amount of his patrimony,—division, partition or dismemberment of the principality and its appurtenances being in every way forbidden to him.

26.

On the day upon which a solemn imperial or royal court is to be held, the ecclesiastical and secular prince electors shall, about the first hour, come to the imperial or royal place of abode, and there the emperor or king shall be clothed in all the imperial insignia; and, mounting their horses, all shall go with the emperor or king to the place fitted up for the session, and each one of them shall go in the order and manner fully defined above in the law concerning the order of marching of those same prince electors. The arch-chancellor, moreover, in whose arch-chancellorship this takes place, shall carry, besides the silver staff, all the imperial or royal seals and signets. But the secular prince electors, according to what has above been explained, shall carry the sceptre, orb and sword. And immediately before the archbishop of Treves, marching in his proper place, shall be carried first the crown of Aix and second that of Milan: and this directly in front of the emperor already resplendent with the imperial adornments; and these crowns shall be carried by some lesser princes, to be chosen for this by the emperor according to his will. The empress, moreover, or queen of the Romans, clad in her imperial insignia, joined by her nobles and escorted by her maids of honor, shall proceed to the place of session after the king or emperor of the Romans, and also, at a sufficient interval of space, after the king of Bohemia, who immediately follows the emperor.

27. Concerning the offices of the prince electors in the solemn courts of the emperors or kings of the Romans.

We decree that whenever the emperor or king of the Romans shall hold his solemn courts, in which the prince electors ought to serve or to perform their offices, the following order shall be observed in these matters. First, then, the emperor or king having placed himself on the royal seat or imperial throne, the duke of Saxony shall fulfil his office in this manner: before the building where the imperial or royal session is being held, shall be placed a heap of oats so high that it shall reach to the breast or girth of the horse on which the duke himself shall sit; and he shall have in his hand a silver staff and a silver measure, which, together, shall weigh 12 marks of silver; and, sitting upon his horse, he shall first fill that measure with oats, and shall offer it to the first slave who appears. This being done, fixing his staff in the oats, he shall retire; and his vice-marshal, namely, he of Pappenheim, approaching—or, in his absence, the marshall of the court,—shall further distribute the oats. But when the emperor or king shall have gone into table, the ecclesiastical prince electors—namely the archbishops,—standing before the table with the other prelates, shall bless the same according to the order above prescribed; and, the benediction over, all those same archbishops if they are present, otherwise two or one, shall receive from the chancellor of the court the imperial or royal seals and signets, and he in whose arch-chancellorship this court happens to be held advancing in the middle, and the other two joining him on either side, shall carry those seals and signets—all touching with their hands the staff on which they have been suspended—and shall reverently place them on the table before the emperor or king. The emperor or king, however, shall straightway restore the same to them, and he in whose arch-chancellorate this takes place, as has been said, shall carry the great seal appended to his neck until the end of the meal, and after that until, riding from the imperial or royal court, he shall come to his dwelling place. The staff, moreover, that we spoke of shall be of silver, equal in weight to twelve marks of silver; of which silver, and of

which price, each of those same archbishops shall pay one third; and that staff afterwards, together with the seals and signets, shall be assigned to the chancellor of the imperial court to be put to what use he pleases. But after he whose turn it has been, carrying the great seal, shall, as described, have returned from the imperial court to his dwelling place, he shall straightway send that seal to the said chancellor of the imperial court. This he shall do through one of his servants riding on such a horse as, according to what is becoming to his own dignity, and according to the love which he shall bear to the chancellor of the court, he shall be bound to present to that chancellor.

Then the margrave of Brandenburg, the arch-chamberlain, shall approach on horseback, having in his hands silver basins with water, of the weight of twelve marks of silver, and a beautiful towel; and, descending from his horse, he shall present the water to the lord emperor or king of the Romans to wash his hands.

The count palatine of the Rhine shall likewise enter on horseback, having in his hands four silver dishes filled with food, of which each one shall be worth three marks; and, descending from his horse, he shall carry them and place them on the table before the emperor or king.

After this, likewise on horseback, shall come the king of Bohemia, the arch-cupbearer, carrying in his hands a silver cup or goblet of the weight of twelve marks, covered, filled with a mixture of wine and water; and, descending from his horse, he shall offer that cup to the emperor or king of the Romans to drink from.

Moreover, as we learn it to have hitherto been observed, so we decree, that, after their aforesaid offices have been performed by the secular prince electors, he of Falkenstein, the sub-chamberlain, shall receive for himself the horse and basins of the margrave of Brandenburg; he of Northemburg, master of the kitchen, the horse and dishes of the count palatine; he of Limburg, the vice-cupbearer, the horse and cup of the king of Bohemia; he of Pappenheim, the vice-marshal, the horse, staff and aforesaid measure of the duke of Saxony. That is, if these be present at such imperial or royal court, and if each one of them minister in his proper office. But if they, or any one of them, should see fit to absent themselves from the said court, then those who daily minister at the imperial or royal court shall, in place of the absent ones,—each one, namely, in place of that absent one with whom he has his name and office in common,—enjoy the fruits with regard to the aforesaid functions, inasmuch as they perform the duties.

28.

Moreover the imperial or royal table ought so to be arranged that it shall be elevated above the other tables in the hall by a height of six feet. And at it, on the day of a solemn court, shall sit no one at all except alone the emperor or king of the Romans.

But the seat and table of the empress or queen shall be prepared to one side in the hall, so that that table shall be three feet lower than the imperial or royal table, and as many feet higher than the seats of the prince electors; which princes shall have their seats and tables at one and the same altitude among themselves.

Within the imperial place of session tables shall be prepared for the seven prince electors, ecclesiastical and secular,—three, namely, on the right, and three others on the left, and the seventh directly opposite the face of the emperor or king, as has above been more clearly defined by us in the chapter concerning the seating and precedence of the prince electors; in such wise, also, that no one else, of whatever dignity or standing he may be, shall sit among them or at their table.

Moreover it shall not be allowed to any one of the aforesaid secular prince electors, when the duty of his office has been performed, to place himself at the table prepared for him so long as any one of his fellow prince electors has still to perform his office. But when one or more of them shall have finished their ministry, they shall pass to the tables prepared for them, and, standing before them, shall wait until the others have fulfilled the aforesaid duties; and then, at length, one and all shall place themselves at the same time before the tables prepared for them.

29.

We find, moreover, from the most renowned accounts and traditions of the ancients that, from time immemorial, it has been continuously observed, by those who have felicitously preceded us, that the election of the king of the Romans and future emperor should be held in the city of Frankfort, and the first coronation in Aix, and that his first imperial court should be celebrated in the town of Nuremburg. Wherefore, on sure grounds, we declare that the said usages should also be observed in future, unless a lawful impediment should stand in the way of them or any one of them. Whenever, furthermore, any prince elector, ecclesiastical or secular, detained by a just impediment, and not able to come when summoned to the imperial court, shall send an envoy or procurator, of whatever dignity or standing,—that envoy, although, according to the mandate given him by his master, he ought to be admitted in the place of him who sends him, shall, nevertheless, not sit at the table or in the seat intended for him who sent him.

Moreover, when those matters shall have been settled which were at that time to be disposed of in any imperial or royal court, the master of the court shall receive for himself the whole structure or wooden apparatus of the imperial or royal place of session, where the emperor or king of the Romans shall have sat with the prince electors to hold his solemn court, or, as has been said, to confer fiefs on the princes.

30. Concerning the rights of the officials when princes receive their fiefs from the emperor or king of the Romans.

We decree by this imperial edict that the prince electors, ecclesiastical and secular, when they receive their fiefs or regalia from the emperor or king, shall not at all be bound to give or pay anything to anybody. For the money which is paid under such a pretext is due to the officials; but since, indeed, the prince electors themselves are at the head of all the offices of the imperial court, having also their substitutes in such offices, furnished for this by the Roman princes, and paid,—

it would seem absurd if substituted officials, under cover of any excuse whatever, should demand presents from their superiors; unless, perchance, those same prince electors, freely and of their own will, should give them something.

On the other hand, the other princes of the empire, ecclesiastical or secular,—when, in the aforesaid manner, any one of them receives his fiefs from the emperor or king of the Romans,—shall give to the officials of the imperial or royal court 63 marks of silver and a quarter, unless any one of them can protect himself by an imperial or royal privilege or grant, and can prove that he has paid or is exempt from such, or also from any other, payments usually made when receiving such fiefs. Moreover the master of the imperial or royal court shall make division of the 63-1/4 marks as follows: first reserving, indeed, 10 marks for himself, he shall give to the chancellor of the imperial or royal court 10 marks; to the masters, notaries, copyists, 3 marks; and to the sealer, for wax and parchment, one quarter. This with the understanding that the chancellor and notaries shall not be bound to do more than to give the prince receiving the fief a testimonial to the effect that he has received it, or a simple charter of investiture.

Likewise, from the aforesaid money, the master of the court shall give to the cupbearer, him of Limburg, 10 marks; to the master of the kitchen, him of Northemburg, 10 marks; to the vice-marshall, him of Pappenheim, 10 marks; and to the chamberlain, him of Falkenstein, 10 marks: under the condition, however, that they and each one of them are present and perform their offices in solemn courts of this kind. But if they or any one of them shall have been absent, then the officials of the imperial or royal court who perform these same offices, shall carry off the reward and the perquisites of those whose absence they make good, individual for individual, according as they fill their place, and bear their name, and perform their task.

When, moreover, any prince, sitting on a horse or other beast, shall receive his fiefs from the emperor or king, that horse or beast, of whatever kind he be, shall be the due of the highest marshal—that is, of the duke of Saxony if he shall be present; otherwise of him of Pappenheim, his vice-marshall; or, in his absence, of the marshall of the imperial or royal court.

31.

Inasmuch as the majesty of the holy Roman empire has to wield the laws and the government of diverse nations distinct in customs, manner of life, and in language, it is considered fitting, and, in the judgment of all wise men, expedient, that the prince electors, the columns and sides of that empire, should be instructed in the varieties of the different dialects and languages: so that they who assist the imperial sublimity in relieving the wants of very many people, and who are constituted for the sake of keeping watch, should understand, and be understood by, as many as possible. Wherefore we decree that the sons, or heirs and successors of the illustrious prince electors, namely of the king of Bohemia, the count palatine of the Rhine, the duke of Saxony and the margrave of Brandenburg—since they are expected in all likelihood to have naturally acquired the German language, and to have been taught it from their infancy,—shall be instructed in the grammar of the Italian and Slavic tongues, beginning with the seventh year of their age; so that, before the fourteenth year of their age, they may be learned in the same according to the grace granted them by God. For this is considered not only useful, but also, from the aforementioned causes, highly necessary, since those languages are wont to be very much employed in the service and for the needs of the holy empire, and in them the more arduous affairs of the empire are discussed. And, with regard to the above, we lay down the following mode of procedure to be observed: it shall be left to the option of the parents to send their sons, if they have any—or their relatives whom they consider as likely to succeed themselves in their principalities,—to places where they can be taught such languages, or, in their own homes, to give them teachers, instructors, and fellow youths skilled in the same, by whose conversation and teaching alike they may become versed in those languages.

JOINVILLE

Life of St. Louis

UNDER KING LOUIS IX (1226-1270) THE FRENCH MONARCHY perfected not only truly sovereign powers but an efficient bureaucracy which made the king's presence felt throughout the kingdom. Louis was an extraordinary figure: a saint, a crusader, and a king sincerely concerned with justice. Jean, Sire de Joinville (ca. 1227-1317) was seneschal of Champagne and close companion and advisor to Louis. He wrote his life of Louis when he was in his eighties, both as a tribute to the memory of Louis and as a lesson for Louis' grandson, King Philip IV. Thus it can be compared with Einhard's life of Charlemagne.

Source: Frank Marziais (trans.), *Memoirs of the Crusades by Villehardhouin and de Joinville* (London: J.M. Dent, 1908).

Beginning of The First Book: Principal Virtues of St. Louis

In the name of God Almighty, I, John, Lord of Joinville, seneschal of Champagne, dictate the life of our holy King Louis; that which I saw and heard by the space of six years that I was in his company on pilgrimage oversea, and that which I saw and heard after we returned. And before I tell you of his great deeds, and of his prowess, I will tell you what I saw and heard of his good teachings and of his holy words, so that these may be found here set in order for the edifying of those who shall hear thereof.

This holy man loved God with all his heart, and followed Him in His acts; and this appeared in that, as God died for the love He bore His people, so did the king put his body in peril, and that several times, for the love He bore to his people; and such peril he might well have avoided, as you shall be told hereafter.

The great love that he bore to his people appeared in what he said during a very sore sickness that he had at Fountainebleau, unto my Lord Louis, his eldest son. "Fair son," he said, "I pray thee to make thyself beloved of the people of thy kingdom; for truly I would rather that a Scot should come out of Scotland and govern the people of the kingdom well and equitably than that thou shouldest govern it ill in the sight of all

men." The holy king so loved truth, that, as you shall hear hereafter, he would never consent to lie to the Saracens as to any covenant that he had made with them.

Of his mouth he was so sober, that on no day of my life did I ever hear him order special meats, as many rich men are wont to do; but he ate patiently whatever his cooks had made ready, and was set before him. In his words he was temperate; for on no day of my life did I ever hear him speak evil of any one; nor did I ever hear him name the Devil—which name is very commonly spoken throughout the kingdom, whereby God, as I believe, is not well pleased.

He put water into his wine by measure, according as he saw that the strength of the wine would suffer it. At Cyprus he asked me why I put no water into my wine; and I said this was by order of the physicians, who told me I had a large head and a cold stomach, so that I could not get drunk. And he answered that they deceived me; for if I did not learn to put water into my wine in my youth, and wished to do so in my old age, gout and diseases of the stomach would take hold upon me, and I should never be in health; and if I drank pure wine in my old age, I should get drunk every night, and that it was too foul a thing for a brave man to get drunk.

He asked me if I wished to be honoured in this world, and to go into paradise at my death? And

I said "Yes." And he said: "Keep yourself then from knowingly doing or saying anything which, if the whole world heard thereof, you would be ashamed to acknowledge, saying 'I did this,' or 'I said that'." He told me to beware not to contradict or impugn anything that was said before me—unless indeed silence would be a sin or to my own hurt—because hard words often move to quarrelling, wherein men by the thousand have found death.

He said that men ought to clothe and arm their bodies in such wise that men of worth and age would never say, this man has done too much, nor young men say, this man has done too little. And I repeated this saying to the father of the king that now is, when speaking of the embroidered coats of arms that are made nowadays; and I told him that never, during our voyage oversea, had I seen embroidered coats, either belonging to the king or to any one else. And the king that now is told me that he had such suits, with arms embroidered, as he had cost him eight hundred pounds parisis. And I told him he would have employed the money to better purpose if he had given it to God, and had had his suits made of good taffeta (satin) ornamented with his arms, as his father had done.

St. Louis's Horror of Sin—His Love For The Poor

He called me once to him and said: "Because of the subtle mind that is in you I dare not speak to you of the things relating to God; so I have summoned these two monks that are here, as I want to ask you a question." Now the question was this: "Seneschal," said he, "what manner of thing is God?" And I said: "Sire, it is so good a thing that there cannot be better." "Of a truth," said he, "you have answered well; for the answer that you have given is written in this book that I hold in my hand."

"Now I ask you," said he, "which you would the better like, either to be a leper, or to have committed a mortal sin?" And I, who never lied to him, made answer that I would rather have committed thirty mortal sins than be a leper. And when the monks had departed, he called me to him alone, and made me sit at his feet, and said,

"How came you to say that to me yesterday?" And I told him that I said it again. And he answered, "You spoke hastily and as a fool. For you should know that there is no leprosy so hideous as the being in mortal sin, inasmuch as the soul that is in mortal sin is like unto the Devil; wherefore no leprosy can be so hideous. And sooth it is that, when a man dies, he is healed of the leprosy in his body; but when a man who has committed mortal sin dies, he cannot know of a certainty that he has, during his lifetime, repented in such sort that God has forgiven him; wherefore he must stand in great fear lest that leprosy of sin should last as long as God is in paradise. So I pray you," said he, "as strongly as I can, for the love of God, and for the love of me, so to set your heart that you prefer any evil that can happen to the body, whether it be leprosy, or any other sickness, rather than that mortal sin should enter into your soul."

He asked me if I washed the feet of the poor on Holy Thursday "Sire," said I, "it would make me sick! The feet of these villains will I not wash." "In truth," said he, "that was ill said; for you should never disdain what God did for our teaching. So I pray you, for the love of God first, and then for the love of me, that you accustom yourself to wash the feet of the poor."

Regard of St. Louis for Worth and Uprightness

He so loved all manner of people who had faith in God and loved Him, that he gave the constableship of France to my Lord Giles Le Brun, who was not of the kingdom of France, because men held him in so great repute for his faith and for love to God. And verily I believe that his good repute was well deserved.

He caused Master Robert of Sorbon to eat at his table, because of the great repute in which he was held as a man of uprightness and worth. One day it chanced that Master Robert was eating at my side, and we were talking to one another. The king took us up, and said: "Speak out, for your companions think you are speaking ill of them. If you talk at table of things that can give us pleasure, speak out, and, if not, hold your peace."

When the king would be mirthful he would say to me: "Seneschal, tell me the reasons why a man of uprightness and worth (prud'-homme) is better than a friar?" Then would begin a discussion between me and Master Robert. When we had disputed for a long while, the king would give sentence and speak thus: "Master Robert, willingly would I bear the title of upright and worthy (prud'-homme) provided I were such in reality—and all the rest you might have. For uprightness and worth are such great things and such good things that even to name them fills the mouth pleasantly."

On the contrary, he said it was an evil thing to take other people's goods. "For," he said, "to restore is a thing so grievous, that even in the speaking the word restore scratches the throat by reason of the rs that are in it, and these rs are like so many rakes with which the Devil would draw to himself those who wish to 'restore' what they have taken from others. And very subtly does the Devil do this; for he works on great usurers and great robbers in such sort that they give to God what they ought to 'restore' to men."

He told me to warn King Thibaut, from him, to beware of the house of the Preachers of Provins, which he was building, lest he should encumber his soul on account of the great sums he was spending thereon. "For wise men," said he, "should, while they live, deal with their possessions as executors ought to do. Now the first thing a good executor does is to satisfy all the claims upon the dead, and pay back to others what is due to them, and it is only after having done this that he should spend in alms what remains of the dead man's possessions."

How St. Louis Thought Men Ought to Clothe Themselves

The holy king was at Corbeil one Pentecost day, and there were there eighty knights. The king came down after dinner into the court below the chapel, and was talking, at the entrance of the door, to the Count of Brittany, the father of the count that now is—whom may God preserve!— when Master Robert of Sorbon came to fetch me thither, and took me by the skirt of my mantle and led me to the king; and all the other knights came after us. Then I said to Master Robert, "Master Robert, what do you want with me?" He

said, "I wish to ask you whether, if the king were seated in this court, and you were to seat yourself on his bench, and at a higher place than he, ought you to be greatly blamed?" And I said, "Yes." And he said, "Then are you to be blamed when you go more nobly apparelled than the king, for you dress yourself in fur and green cloth, and the king does not do so." And I replied: "Master Robert, saving your grace, I do nothing blameworthy when I clothe myself in green cloth and fur, for this garment was left to me by my father and mother. But you are to blame, for you are the son of a common man and a common woman, and you have abandoned the vesture worn by your father and mother, and wear richer woollen cloth than the king himself." Then I took the skirt of his surcoat, and of the surcoat of the king, and said, "See if I am not speaking sooth." Then the king set himself to defend Master Robert and all his power.

After this my lord the king called my Lord Philip, his son, the father of the king that now is, and King Thibaut, and sat himself at the entrance to his oratory, and put his hand to the ground and said: "Sit yourselves down here, quite close to me, so that we be not overheard," "Ah! Sire," they replied, "we should not dare to sit so close to you." And he said to me, "Seneschal, sit you here." And I did so—so close that my robe touched his. And he made them sit after me, and said to them: "You have done very ill, seeing you are my sons, and have not, at the first word, done what I commanded you. See, I pray you, that this does not happen again." And they said it should not so happen. Then he said to me that he had so called us together to confess that he had wrongly defended Master Robert against me. "But," said he, "I saw that he was so discouraged that he had great need of my help. Nevertheless, you must not attach import to anything I may have said to defend Master Robert; for, as the seneschal says, you ought to clothe yourselves well and suitably, so that your wives may love you the better, and your people hold you in the greater honour. For, as the sage tells us, our garments should be of such fashion as neither to cause the aged and worthy to say that too much has been spent upon them, nor the young to say that too little has been spent."

The Warnings of God—How They Are to be Turned to Advantage

You shall be told here of one of the lessons he taught me at sea, when we were returning from the lands oversea. It chanced that our ship struck before the island of Cyprus, when a wind was blowing which is called *garban*; and this wind is not one of the four great winds. And at the shock that our ship received, the mariners so despaired that they rent their garments and tore their beards. The king sprang from his bed, barefoot, for it was night, and having on no more than his tunic, and went and placed himself cross-wise before the body of our Lord, as one who expected nothing but death. The day after this happened, the king called me to him alone, and said: "Seneschal, God has just showed us a portion of His great power; for one of these little winds, a wind so little that one can scarcely give it a name, came near to drown the King of France, his children, his wife, and his men. Now St. Anselm says that such are warnings from our Lord, as if God meant to say to us, 'See how easily I could have compassed your death, had it been my will.' 'Lord God,' says the saint, 'why dost Thou thus threaten us? For when Thou dost threaten us, it is not for Thine own profit, nor for Thine advantage—seeing that if Thou hadst caused us all to be lost, Thou wouldst have been none the poorer, and if Thou hadst caused us all to be saved, Thou wouldst have been none the richer. Therefore, this Thy warning is not for Thine own advantage, but for ours, if so be that we suffer it do its work.' Let us therefore take the warning that God has given us in such sort that, if we feel that we have, in our hearts or bodies, anything displeasing to God, we shall remove it hastily, and if there by anything we think will please Him, let us try hastily to do it. If we so act, then our Lord will give us blessings in this world, and in the next blessings greater than we can tell. And if we do not act thus, He will deal with us as the good lord deals with his wicked servant; for if the wicked servant will not amend after warning given the lord punishes him with death, or with other great troubles that are worse than death."

Let the king that now is beware; for he has escaped from peril as great as that in which we then were, or greater. Therefore let him amend from his evil deeds in such sort that God smite him not grievously, either in himself or in his possessions.

What St. Louis Thought About Faith

The holy king endeavoured with all his power—as you shall here be told—to make me believe firmly in the Christian law, which God has given us. He said that we ought to believe so firmly the articles of faith that neither from fear of death, nor for any mischief that might happen to the body, should we be willing to go against them in word or deed. And he said that the Enemy is so subtle that, when people are dying, he labours all he can to make them die doubting as to some points of the faith. For he knows that he can in no wise deprive a man of the good works he has done; and he knows also that the man is lost to him if he dies in the faith.

Wherefore we should so guard and defend ourselves from this snare, as to say to the Enemy, when he sends such a temptation: "Away!" Yes, "Away!" must one say to the Enemy. "Thou shalt not tempt me so that I cease to believe firmly all the articles of the faith. Even if thou didst cause all my members to be cut off, yet would I live and die in the faith." And whosoever acts thus, overcomes the Enemy with the very club and sword that the Enemy desired to murder him withal.

He said that the Christian faith and creed were things in which we ought to believe firmly, even though we might not be certain of them except by hearsay. On this point he asked me what was my father's name? And I told him his name was Simon. And he asked how I knew it. And I said I thought I was certain of it, and believed it firmly, because my mother had borne witness thereto. Then he said, "So ought you to believe all the articles of the faith, to which the Apostles have borne witness, as also you chant of a Sunday in the Creed."

William, Bishop Of Paris, Comforts a Certain Theologian

He told me that the bishop, William of Paris, had related how a great master of divinity had come

to him and told him he desired to speak with
him. And the bishop said to him: "Master, say
on" And when the master thought to speak to the
bishop, he began to weep bitterly. And the bishop
said: "Master, say on; be not discomfited; no one
can sin so much but that God can forgive him
more." "And yet I tell you," said the master, "that
I cannot choose but weep; for I fear me I am a
miscreant, inasmuch as I cannot so command my
heart as to believe in the sacrifice of the altar, like
as holy Church teaches; and yet I know well that
this is a temptation of the Enemy."

"Master," said the bishop, "pray tell me, when
the Enemy sends you this temptation, does it
give you pleasure?" And the master said: "Sir far
from it; it troubles me as much as anything can
trouble me." "Now," said the bishop, "I will ask
you whether, for gold or silver you would utter
anything out of your mouth that was against the
sacrament of the altar, or the other holy sacraments of the Church?" "Sir!" said the master, "be
it known to you that there is nothing in the world
that would induce me so to do; I would much
rather that every member were torn from my
body than that I should say such a thing."

"Now I will say something more," said the
bishop. "You know that the King of France is at
war with the King of England, and you know
too that the castle that lies most exposed in the
border-land between the two is the castle of la
Rochelle in Poitou. Now I will ask you a question: If the king had set you to guard la
Rochelle, which is in the dangerous border-
land, and had set me to guard the castle of
Montlhéri, which is in the heart of France,
where the land is at peace, to whom, think you,
would the king owe most at the end of the
war—to you who had guarded la Rochelle
without loss, or to me, who had guarded the
castle of Montlhéri without loss?" "In God's
name, sir," said the master, "to me, who had
guarded la Rochelle without losing it."

"Master," said the bishop, "my heart is like the
castle of Montlhéri; for I have neither temptation
nor doubt as to the sacrament of the altar. For
which thing I tell you that for the grace that God
owes to me because I hold this firmly, and in
peace, He owes to you four-fold, because you
have guarded your heart in the war of tribula-

tion, and have such good-will towards Him that
for no earthly good, nor for any harm done to the
body, would you relinquish that faith. Therefore I
tell you, be of good comfort, for in this your state
is better pleasing to our Lord than mine." When
the master heard this, he knelt before the bishop,
and held himself for well appeased.

Faith of the Count of Montfort—One Must Not Enter Into Controversy with Jews

The sainted king told me that several people
among the Albigenses came to the Count of
Montfort, who was then guarding the land of the
Albigenses for the king, and asked him to come
and look at the body of our Lord, which had
become Blood and flesh in the hands of the priest.
And the Count of Montfort said, "Go and look at
it yourselves, you who do not believe it. As for
me, I believe it firmly, holding as holy Church
teaches of the sacrament of the altar. And do you
know what I shall gain," said the count, "in that
during this mortal life I have believed as holy
Church teaches? I shall have a crown in the heavens, above the angels, for the angels cannot but
believe, inasmuch as they see God face to face."

He told me that there was once a great disputation between clergy and Jews at the monastery
of Cluny. And there was at Cluny a poor knight
to whom the abbot gave bread at that place for
the love of God; and this knight asked the abbot
to suffer him to speak the first words, and they
suffered him, not without doubt. So he rose, and
leant upon his crutch, and asked that they should
bring to him the greatest clerk and most learned
master among the Jews; and they did so. Then he
asked the Jew a question, which was this: "Master," said the knight, "I ask you if you believe that
the Virgin Mary, who bore God in her body and
in her arms, was a virgin mother, and is the mother of God?"

And the Jew replied that of all this he believed
nothing. Then the knight answered that the Jew
had acted like a fool when—neither believing in
her, nor loving her—he had yet entered into her
monastery and house. "And verily," said the
knight, "you shall pay for it!" Whereupon he lifted his crutch and smote the Jew near the ear, and
beat him to the earth. Then the Jews turned to

flight, and bore away their master, sore wounded. And so ended the disputation.

The abbot came to the knight and told him he had committed a deed of very great folly. But the knight replied that the abbot had committed a deed of greater folly in gathering people together for such a disputation; for there were a great many good Christians there who, before the disputation came to an end, would have gone away misbelievers through not fully understanding the Jews. "And I tell you," said the king, "that no one, unless he be a very learned clerk, should dispute with them; but a layman, when he hears the Christian law mis-said, should not defend the Christian law, unless it be with his sword, and with that he should pierce the mis-sayer in the midriff, so far as the sword will enter."

The Devotions of St. Louis—How He Did Justice In His Land

The rule of his land was so arranged that every day he heard the hours sung, and a *Requiem* mass without song; and then, if it was convenient, the mass of the day, or of the saint, with song. Every day he rested in his bed after having eaten, and when he had slept and rested, he said, privily in his chamber—he and one of his chaplains together—the office for the dead; and after he heard vespers. At night he heard complines.

A gray-friar (Franciscan) came to him at the castle of Hyères, there where we disembarked; and said in his sermon, for the king's instruction, that he had read the Bible, and the books pertaining to heathen princes, and that he had never found, either among believers or misbelievers, that a kingdom had been lost, or had changed lords, save there had first been failure of justice. "Therefore let the king, who is going into France, take good heed," said he, "that he do justice well and speedily among his people, so that our Lord suffer his kingdom to remain in peace all the days of his life." It is said that the right worthy man who thus instructed the king, lies buried at Marseilles, where our Lord, for his sake, performs many a fine miracle. He would never consent to remain with the king, however much the king might urge it, for more than a single day.

The king forgot not the teaching of the friar,

but ruled his land very loyally and godly, as you shall hear. He had so arranged that my Lord of Nesle, and the good Count of Soissons, and all of us who were about him, should go, after we had heard our masses, and hear the pleadings at the gate which is now called the gate of Requests.

And when he came back from church, he would send for us and sit at the foot of his bed, and make us all sit round him, and ask if there were any whose cases could not be settled save by himself in person. And we named the litigants; and he would then send for such and ask: "Why do you not accept what our people offer?" And they would make reply, "Sire, because they offer us very little." Then would he say, "You would do well to accept what is proposed, as our people desire." And the saintly man endeavoured thus, with all his power, to bring them into a straight path and a reasonable.

Ofttimes it happened that he would go, after his mass, and seat himself in the wood of Vincennes, and lean against an oak, and make us sit round him. And all of those who had any cause in hand came and spoke to him, without hindrance of usher, or of any other person. Then would he ask, out of his own mouth, "Is there any one who has a cause in hand?" And those who had a cause in hand stood up. Then would he say, "Keep silence all, and you shall be heard in turn, one after the other." Then he would call my Lord Peter of Fontaines and my Lord Geoffry of Villette, and say to one of them, "Settle me this cause."

And when he saw that there was anything to amend in the words of those who spoke on his behalf, or in the words of those who spoke on behalf of any other person, he would himself, out of his own mouth, amend what they had said. Sometimes have I seen him, in summer, go to do justice among his people in the garden of Paris, clothed in a tunic of camlet, a surcoat of tartan without sleeves, and a mantle of black taffeta about his neck, his hair well combed, no cap, and a hat of white peacock's feathers upon his head. And he would cause a carpet to be laid down, so that we might sit round him, and all the people who had any cause to bring before him stood around. And then would he have their causes settled, as I have told you afore he was wont to do in the wood of Vincennes.

St. Louis Refuses An Unjust Demand Made By the Bishops

I saw him, yet another time, in Paris, when all the prelates of France had asked to speak with him, and the king went to the palace to give them audience. And there was present Guy of Auxerre, the son of my Lord William of Mello, and he spoke to the king on behalf of all the prelates, after this manner: "Sire, the lords who are here present, archbishops and bishops, have directed me to tell you that Christendom, which ought to be guarded and preserved by you, is perishing in your hands." The king crossed himself when he heard that word, and he said, "Tell me how that may be."

"Sire," said Guy of Auxerre, "it is because excommunications are at the present day so lightly thought of that people suffer themselves to die before seeking absolution, and will not give satisfaction to the Church. These lords require you therefore, for the sake of God, and because it is your duty, to command your provosts and bailiffs to seek out all such as suffer themselves to remain excommunicated for a year and day, and constrain them, by seizure of their goods, to have themselves absolved."

And the king replied that he would issue such commands willingly whensoever it could be shown to him that the excommunicate persons were in the wrong. The bishops said they would accept this condition at no price whatever, as they contested his jurisdiction in their causes. Then the king told them he would do no other; for it would be against God and reason if he constrained people to seek absolution when the clergy were doing them wrong. "And of this," said the king, "I will give you an example, viz., that of the Count of Brittany, who, for seven years long, being excommunicated pleaded against the prelates of Britanny, and carried his cause so far that the Apostle (the Pope) condemned them all. Wherefore, if I had constrained the Count of Brittany, at the end of the first year, to get himself absolved, I should have sinned against God and against him." Then the prelates resigned themselves; nor did I ever hear tell that any further steps were taken in the aforesaid matters.

The Uprightness of St. Louis

The peace that he made with the King of England was made against the advice of his council, for the council said to him: "Sire, it seems to us that you are giving away the land that you make over to the King of England; for he has no right thereto, seeing that his father lost it justly." To this the king replied that he knew well that the King of England had no right to the land, but that there was a reason why he should give it to him, "for," said he, "we have two sisters to wife, and our children are cousins-german; wherefore it is fitting that there should be peace between us. Moreover a very great honour accrues to me through the peace that I have made with the King of England, seeing that he is now my liegeman, which he was not aforetime."

The uprightness of the king may be seen in the case of my Lord Renaud of Trie, who brought to the saintly man a charter stating that the king had given to the heirs of the Countess of Boulogne, lately deceased, the county of Dammartin in Gouelle. The seal on the charter was broken, so that naught remained save half the legs of the image on the king's seal, and the stool on which the king set his feet. And the king showed the seal to all those who were of his council, and asked us to help him to come to a decision. We all said, without a dissentient, that he was not bound to give effect to the charter. Then he told John Sarrasin, his chamberlain, to give him a charter which he had asked him to obtain. When he held this charter in his hands, he said: "Lords, this is the seal I used before I went overseas, and you can see clearly from this seal that the impression on the broken seal is like unto that of the seal that is whole; wherefore I should not dare, in good conscience, to keep the said county." So he called to him my lord Renaud of Trie, and said, "I give you back the county."

Second Book

Birth and Coronation of St. Louis

In the name of God Almighty, we have, hereinbefore, written out a part of the good words and of the good teachings of our saintly King Louis, so that those who read may find them set in order, the one after the other, and thus derive more profit therefrom than if they were set forth among his deeds. And from this point we begin, in the name of God and in his own name, to speak of his deeds.

As I have heard tell he was born on the day of St. Mark the Evangelist, after Easter (25th April 1214). On that day crosses are, in many places, carried in procession, and, in France, these are called black crosses; and this was as it were a prophecy of the great number of people who were to die in the two Crusades, viz., that of Egypt, and the other, in which he himself died, at Carthage, whereby there were great mournings in this world, and many great rejoicings in paradise for such as in these two pilgrimages died true Crusaders.

He was crowned on the first Sunday in Advent (29th November 1226). The beginning of the mass for that Sunday runs: *Ad te levavi animam meam* and what follows after; and this means, "Fair Lord God, I shall lift up my soul to thee, I put my confidence in thee." In God had he great confidence from his childhood to his death; for when he died, in his last words, he called upon God and His saints, and specially upon my lord St. James and my lady St. Genevieve.

First Troubles In The Reign Of St. Louis

God, in whom he put his trust, kept him all his days from childhood unto the end; and specially, in his youth, did he keep him, when great need was, as you shall shortly hear.

As to his soul, God kept it through the good teachings of his mother, who taught him to believe in God and to love Him, and to gather round himself all good people of religion. And, child as he was, she made him recite all the Hours, and listen to the sermons on festival days. He recorded that his mother had sometimes given him to understand that she would rather he were dead than have committed a mortal sin.

Good need had he of God's help in his youth, for his mother, who came from Spain, had neither relations nor friends in all the kingdom of France. And because the barons of France saw that the king was but a child, and the queen, his mother, a foreign woman, they made the Count of Boulogne, who was uncle to the king, their chief, and held him as their lord. After the king was crowned, there were certain barons who demanded of the queen that she should give them great lands, and because she would none of it, all the barons assembled at Corbeil.

And the saintly king told me that neither he, nor his mother, who were at Montlhéri, dared return to Paris till those in Paris came in arms to fetch them. And he told me that all the way, from Montlhéri to Paris, was filled with people, armed and unarmed, and that all cried to our Saviour to give him a good life and a long, and to defend and guard him from his enemies. And this God did, as you shall presently hear.

In this parliament which the barons held at Corbeil, the barons there present decided, so it is said, that the good knight, the Count Peter of Brittany, should rebel against the king, and they agreed besides that they would each in person, and with two knights only, attend the count when he obeyed the summons which the king would address to him. And this they did to see if the Count of Brittany would be able to master the queen, who was a foreign woman, as you have heard. And many people say that the count would have mastered the queen and the king too, if God had not helped the king in this his hour of need, as He never failed to do.

The help God gave him was such that Count Thibaut of Champagne, who was afterwards the King of Navarre, came there to serve the king with three hundred knights; and through the help that the count gave to the king, the Count of Britanny had to yield to the king's mercy, and when making that peace, as it is said, to surrender to the king the county of Anjou and the county of the Perche.

Crusade of Richard Coeur-de-lion—Rights of Alice, Queen of Cyprus, Over Champagne

Inasmuch as there are certain things of which you should have knowledge, I hold it fitting here to depart somewhat from my subject. We will tell you here, therefore, that the good Count Henry the Large had by the Countess Mary—who was sister to the King of France and sister to King Richard of England—two sons, of whom the elder was called Henry and the other Thibaut. This Henry, the elder, went as a Crusader on pilgrimage to the Holy Land at the time when King Philip and King Richard besieged Acre and took it.

So soon as Acre was taken, King Philip returned to France, for which he was greatly blamed; but King Richard remained in the Holy Land, and did there such mighty deeds that the Saracens stood in great fear of him; so much so, as it is written in the book of the Holy Land, that when the Saracen children cried, their mothers called out, "Wisht! here is King Richard," in order to keep them quiet. And when the horses of the Saracens and Bedouins started at tree or bush, their masters said to the horses, "Do you think that is King Richard?"

This King Richard wrought to such effect that he gave for wife to Count Henry of Champagne, who had remained with him, the Queen of Jerusalem, who was direct heiress to the kingdom. By the said queen Count Henry had two daughters of whom the first was Queen of Cyprus, and the other did my Lord Everard of Brienne have to wife, and from them sprang a great lineage, as is known in France and Champagne. Of the wife of my Lord Everard of Brienne I will say nothing to you at this present; but I will speak to you of the Queen of Cypress, seeing she is related to the matter I have in hand; and I speak, therefore, as follows.

The Barons Attack Thibaut IV, Count of Champagne

After the king had foiled Count Peter of Brittany, all the barons of France were so wroth with Count Thibaut of Champagne that they settled to send for the Queen of Cyprus, who was the daughter of the eldest son of Champagne, so as to disinherit Count Thibaut, who was the son of the second son of Champagne.

But some took steps to reconcile Count Peter with Count Thibaut, and the matter was discussed to such effect that Count Thibaut promised to take to wife the daughter of Count Peter of Brittany. A day was fixed on which the Count of Champagne should espouse the damsel; and she was to be taken, for the marriage, to an abbey of Premontre near Chateau-Thierry, and called as I believe, Val-Secret. The barons of France, who were nearly all related to Count Peter, undertook this duty, and conducted the damsel to Val-Secret to be married, and advised thereof the Count of Champagne, who was at Chateau-Thierry.

And while the Count of Champagne was coming for the marriage, my Lord Geoffry of la Chapelle came to him on the part of the king, with a letter of credence, and spoke thus: "My Lord Count of Champagne, the king has heard that you have covenanted with Count Peter of Brittany to take his daughter in marriage. Now the king warns you that, unless you wish to lose everything you possess in the kingdom of France, you will not do this thing, for you know that the Count of Brittany has done more evil to the king than any man living." Then the Count of Champagne, by the advice of those he had with him, returned to Chateau-Thierry.

When Count Peter and the barons of France, who were expecting him at Val-Secret, heard this, they were all like men distraught, with anger at what he had done to them, and they at once sent to fetch the Queen of Cyprus. And as soon as she was come, they entered into a common agreement to gather together as many men-at-arms as they could, and enter into Brie and Champagne, from the side of France; and the Duke of Burgundy, who had to wife the daughter of Count Robert of Dreux, was to enter into Champagne from the side of Burgundy. And they fixed a day on which they should assemble before the city of Troyes, to take the city of Troyes if they could accomplish it.

The duke collected all the people he could, and the barons also. The barons came burning and wasting everything on one side, and the Duke of Burgundy on another, and the King of France came on yet another side to fight against them. The evil plight of the Count of Champagne was such that he himself burned his cities before the arrival of the barons, so that they might not find supplies therein. Among the other cities that the Count of Champagne burned, he burned Epernay, and Vertus, and Sézanne.

Simon of Joinville Defends Troyes—Peace Between The Count of Champagne And The Queen of Cyprus

The citizens of Troyes, when they perceived that they had lost the help of their lord, asked Simon, lord of Joinville, and father of the lord of Joinville that now is, to come to their help. And he, who had gathered together all his men-at-arms, moved from Joinville by night, so soon as the tidings were brought to him, and came to Troyes before it was day. And thus were the barons foiled of their intent to take the said city; wherefor the barons passed before Troyes without doing aught, and went and encamped in the meadow of l'Isle—there where the Duke of Burgundy already was.

The King of France, who knew they were there, at once addressed himself to go thither and attack them; and the barons sent and begged him to withdraw in person from the field, and then they would go and fight against the Count of Champagne and the Duke of Lorraine and the rest of the king's people, with three hundred knights less than the count and duke had in their force. But the king told them they should not so fight without him, for he would remain with his people in person. Then the barons sent back to the king and said that, if it so pleased him, they would willingly incline the Queen of Cyprus to make peace. The king replied that he would agree to no peace, nor suffer the Count of Champagne to agree to any peace, till they had retired from the county of Champagne.

They retired in such sort that from Isle, where they were, they went and encamped before Jully, and the king encamped at Isle, from which he had driven them. And when they knew that the king had come to Isle, they went and encamped at Chaource, and not daring to wait for the king, they went and encamped at Laignes, which belonged to the Count of Nevers, who was of their party. So the king caused the Count of Champagne and the Queen of Cyprus to come to terms, and peace was made in such sort that the Count of Champagne gave to the Queen of Cyprus about two thousand livres (yearly) in land, and forty thousand livres, which latter sum the king paid for the Count of Champagne. And

the Count of Champagne sold to the king, for the said forty thousand livres, the fiefs hereinafter names, viz.—the fief of the county of Blois, the fief of the county of Chartres, the fief of the county of Sancerre, the fief of the county of Châteaudun. Now there are certain people who say that the king only holds the said fiefs in pledge; but this is not so, for I asked our saintly king of it when we were oversea.

The land that Count Thibaut gave to the Queen of Cyprus is held by the Count of Brienne that now is, and by the Count of Joigny, because the great-grandmother of the Count of Brienne was daughter to the Queen of Cyprus and wife to the great Count Walter of Brienne.

Of Henry I, Called The Large-hearted, Count of Champagne

In order that you may learn whence came the fiefs that the Count of Champagne sold to the king, you must know that the great Count Thibaut, who lies buried at Lagny, had three sons. The first was called Henry, the second Thibaut, and the third Stephen. The aforesaid Henry was Count of Champagne and of Brie, and was called Count Henry the Large-hearted; and rightly was he so called, for he was large-hearted both in his dealings with God and the world: large-hearted towards God as appears in the Church of St. Stephen of Troyes and the other fair churches which he founded in Champagne, and large-hearted towards the world as appeared in the case of Artaud of Nogent, and on many other occasions, of which I would tell you if I did not fear to interrupt my story.

This Artaud of Nogent was the citizen of all the world in whom the count had the greatest faith; and he became so rich that he built the castle of Nogent L'Artaud with his moneys. Now it happened that Count Henry was coming down from his halls at Troyes to go and hear mass at St. Stephen's on the day of Pentecost. At the foot of the steps there came before him a poor knight and knelt down before him and spoke thus: "Sire, I pray you, for the love of God, to give me of what is yours, so that I may marry my two daughters whom you see here." Artaud, who went behind him, said to the poor knight: "Sir knight, it is not courteous on your part to beg of my lord, for he has given away so much that he has nothing left to give." The large-hearted count turned towards Artaud and said: "Sir villain, you speak not sooth when you say I have nothing left to give; I have you left. There, take him, sir knight, for I give him to you, and moreover, I pledge myself for him." The knight was not abashed, but took hold of Artaud's cloak, and said he would not leave him till they had done business together. And before he escaped, Artaud had done business with him to the tune of five hundred livres.

The second brother of Count Henry was called Thibaut and was Count of Blois. The third brother was called Stephen, and was Count of Sancerre. And these two brothers held from Count Henry all their heritages, and their counties, and the appurtenances thereof; and they held them afterwards from the heirs of Count Henry who held the county of Champagne, until such time as Count Thibaut sold them to the King of France, as has been related above.

St. Louis Holds A Full Court at Saumur in 1241

Now let us return to our subject and tell how, after these things, the king held a full court at Saumur in Anjou, and I was there and can testify that it was the best-ordered court that ever I saw. For at the king's table ate, after him, the Count of Poitiers, whom he had newly made knight at the feast of St. John; and after the Count of Poitiers, ate the Count of Dreux, whom he had also newly made knight; and after the Count of Dreux the Count of la Marche; and after the Count of la Marche the good Count Peter of Brittany; and before the king's table, opposite the Count of Dreux, ate my lord and the King of Navarre, in tunic and mantle of samite well bedight with a belt and a clasp, and a cap of gold; and I carved before him.

Before the king the Count of Artois, his brother, served the meat, and before the king the good Count John of Soissons carved with the knife. In order to guard the king's table there were there my Lord Imbert of Beaujeau, who was afterwards Constable of France, and my Lord Enguerrand of Coucy, and my Lord Archamband of Bourbon. Behind these three barons stood some thirty of their knights, in tunics of silken cloth, to keep guard over them; and behind these knights there were a great quantity of sergeants bearing on their clothing the arms of the Count of Poitiers embroidered in taffeta. The king was clothed in a tunic of blue satin, and surcoat and mantle of vermeil samite lined with ermine, and he had a cotton cap upon his head, which suited him very badly, because he was at that time a young man.

The king held these banquets in the halls of Saumur which had been built, so it was said, by the great King Henry of England (Henry II.) in order that he might hold his great banquets therein; and this hall is built after the fashion of the cloisters of the white monks of the Cistercian order. But I think there is none other hall so large, and by a great deal. And I will tell you why I think so—it is because by the wall of the cloister, where the king ate, surrounded by his knights and sergeants who occupied a great space, there was also room for a table where ate twenty bishops and archbishops, and yet again, besides the bishops and archbishops, the Queen Blanche, the king's mother, ate near the table, at the head of the cloister, on the other side from the king.

And to serve the queen there was the Count of Boulogne, who afterwards became King of Portugal, and the good Count Hugh of St. Paul, and a German of the age of eighteen years, who was said to be the son of St. Elizabeth of Thuringia, for which cause it was told that Queen Blanche kissed him on the forehead, as an act of devotion, because she thought that his mother must ofttimes have kissed him there.

At the end of the cloister, on the other side, were the kitchens, the cellars, the pantries and the butteries; from this end were served to the king and to the queen meats, and wine, and bread. And in the wings and in the central court ate the knights, in such numbers, that I knew not how to count them. And many said they had never, at any feast, seen together so many surcoats and other garments, of cloth of gold and of silk; and it was said also that no less than three thousand knights were there present.

Battle of Taillebourg in 1242

After this feast the king led the Count of Poitiers to Poitiers, so that his vassals might do homage for his fiefs. And when the king came to Poitiers, he would gladly have been back in Paris, for he found that the Count of la Marche, who had eaten at his table on St. John's day, had assembled as many men-at-arms as he could collect, at Lusignan near Poitiers. The king remained at Poitiers nearly a fortnight, nor did he dare to depart therefrom till he had come to terms—how, I know not—with the Count of la Marche.

Ofttimes I saw the Count of la Marche come from Lusignan to speak to the king at Poitiers, and always he brought with him the Queen of England, his wife, who was mother to the King of England. And many people said that the king and the Count of Poitiers had made an evil peace with the Count of la Marche.

No long time after the king had returned from Poitiers, the King of England came into Gascony to wage war against the King of France. Our saintly king rode forth to fight against him with as many people as he could collect. Then came the King of England and the Count of la Marche to do battle before a castle called Taillebourg, seated on an evil river called La Charente, at a point where one cannot pass except over a stone bridge, very narrow.

So soon as the king came to Taillebourg, and the hosts came in sight of one another, our people, who had the castle behind them, bestirred themselves mightily and passed over the stream with great peril, in boats, and on pontoons, and fell upon the English. Then began a battle grim and fierce. When the king saw this, he put himself in peril, with the others; and for every man that the king had with him when he passed the stream, the English had, on their side, at least twenty. Nevertheless, as God willed, it so befell that when the English saw the king pass over, they fled, and took refuge in the city of Saintes, and several of our people entered into the city, mingled with them, and were taken prisoners.

Those of our people who were taken at Saintes reported that they heard great discord arise between the King of England and the Count of la Marche; and the King of England said that the Count of la Marche had sent for him on the plea that he would find great help in France. That very night the King of England had left Saintes and went away into Gascony.

Submission of the Count of La Marche

The Count of la Marche, as one who could do no better for himself, came to the king's prison, and brought with him to the prison his wife and his children; and the king, in making peace with the count, obtained a great deal of his land, but how much I know not, for I had nothing to do with that matter, seeing I had never then worn a hauberk (i.e. was not yet a knight). But I heard tell that besides the land which the king thus gained, the Count of la Marche made over to him ten thousand livres *parisis*, which were in the king's coffers, and the same sum every year.

When we were at Poitiers I saw a knight, my Lord Geoffry of Rancon by name, who, for some great wrong that the Count of la Marche had done him, so it was said, had sworn on holy relics that he would never have his head shorn, as knights are wont, but would wear his hair in woman's tresses until such time as he should see vengeance done on the Count of la Marche, either by himself or by some other. And when my lord Geoffry saw the Count of la Marche, his wife, and his children, kneeling before the king and crying for mercy, he caused a trestle to be brought, and his tresses cut off, and had himself immediately shorn in the presence of the king, of the Count of la Marche, and of all those there present.

In this expedition against the King of England, and against the barons, the king gave great gifts, as I have heard tell by those who returned thence. But neither on account of such gifts, nor of the expenses incurred in this expedition, nor in other expeditions, whether beyond the seas or this side of the seas, did he ever demand, or take, any (money) aid from his barons, or his knights, or his men, or his good cities, in such sort as to cause complaint. Nor is this to be wondered at; for he ruled himself by the advice of the good mother who was with him—and whose counsel he took—and of the right worthy men who had remained by him from the time of his father and of his grandfather.

St. Louis Falls Ill, and Takes the Cross in 1244

After the things related above, it happened, as God so willed, that a very grievous sickness came upon the king in Paris, and brought him to such extremity, so it was said, that one of the ladies who were tending him wished to draw the cloth over his face, saying he was dead; but another lady, who was on the other side of the bed, would not suffer it, and said the soul was still in his body.

And as he listened to the debate between these two ladies, our Lord wrought within him, and soon sent him health, for before that he had been dumb and could not speak. And as soon as he was in case to speak, he asked that they should give him the cross, and they did so. When the queen, his mother, heard say that speech had come back to him, she made as great joy thereof as ever she could. But when she knew that he had taken the cross—as also he himself told her—she made as great mourning as if she had seen him dead.

After he had taken the cross, so also took the cross, Robert, Count of Artois, Alfonse, Count of Poitiers, Charles, Count of Anjou, who afterwards was King of Sicily—all three brothers of the king;—and there also took the cross, Hugh, Duke of Burgundy, William, Count of Flanders, and brother of Count Guy of Flanders lately deceased, the good Hugh, Count of St. Paul, and my Lord Gaucher, his nephew, who did right well oversea, and would have done much good service if he had lived.

With them also took the cross, the Count of la Marche and my Lord Hugh LeBrun, his son, the Count of Sarrebruck and my Lord Gobert of Apremont, his brother—in whose company I, John, Lord of Joinville, passed over the sea in a ship which we hired because we were cousins—and we passed over with twenty knights, of whom he was over ten, and I over ten.

Joinville Prepares to Join the Crusade

At Easter, in the year of grace that stood at 1248, I summoned my men, and all who held fiefs from me, to Joinville, and on the vigil of the said Easter, when all the people that I had summoned were assembled, was born my son John, Lord of Ancerville, by my first wife, the sister of the Count of Grandpre. All that week we feasted and danced, and my brother, the Lord of Vaucouleurs, and the other rich men who were there, gave feasts on the Monday, the Tuesday, the Wednesday and the Thursday.

On the Friday I said to them: "Lords, I am going oversea, and I know not whether I shall ever return. Now come forward; if I have done you any wrong, I will make it good, as I have been used to do, dealing, each in turn, with such as have any claim to make against me, or my people." So I dealt with each, according to the opinions of the men on my lands; and in order that I might not weigh upon their debate, I retired from the council, and agreed, without objection raised, to what they recommended.

Because I did not wish to take away with me any penny wrongfully gotten, therefore I went to Metz, in Lorraine, and placed in pawn the greater part of my land. And you must know that on the day when I left our country to go to the Holy Land, I did not hold more than one thousand livres a year in land, for my lady mother was still alive; and yet I went, taking with me nine knights and being the first of three knights-banneret. And I bring these things to your notice, so that you may understand that if God, who never yet failed me, had not come to my help, I should hardly have maintained myself for so long a space as the six years that I remained in the Holy Land.

As I was preparing to depart, John, Lord of Apremont and Count of Sarrebruck in his wife's right, sent to tell me he had settled matters to go oversea, taking ten knights, and proposed, if I so willed, that we should hire a ship between him and me; and I consented. His people and mine hired a ship at Marseilles.

Of a Clerk Who Killed Three of The King's Sergeants

The King summoned all his barons to Paris, and made them take oath that, if anything happened to him while away, they would give faith and loyalty to his children. He asked me to do the same; but I would not take the oath, because I was not his liegeman.

While I was on my way to Paris, I found three men dead upon a cart, whom a clerk had killed; and I was told they were being taken to the king. When I heard this, I sent one of my squires after, to know what befell. And my squire, whom I had sent, told me that the king, when he came out of his chapel, went to the entrance steps to look at the dead, and inquired of the provost of Paris how this thing had happened.

And the provost told him that the dead men were three of his sergeants of the Chatelet, who had gone into unfrequented streets to rob people. "And they found," said he to the king, "this clerk, whom you see here, and robbed him of all his clothes. The clerk, being only in his shirt, went to his lodging, and took his crossbow, and caused a child to bring his falchion. Then when he saw them again he cried out upon them, and said they should die. So the clerk drew his crossbow, and shot, and pierced one of the men through the heart. The two other made off flying. And the clerk took the falchion which the child handed to him, and followed them in the moonlight, which was fine and clear. The one man thought to pass through a hedge into a garden, and the clerk struck him with his falchion," said the provost, "and cut right through his leg, in such sort that it only holds to the boot, as you may see here. The clerk then followed the other, who thought to go down into a strange house, where the people were still awake; but the clerk struck him in the middle of the head with his falchion, so that he clove his head to the teeth, as you may see here," said the provost to the king. "Sire," continued he, "the clerk showed what he had done to the neighbours in the street, and then came and made himself your prisoner. And now sire, I have brought him to you to do with him what you will. Here he is."

"Sir clerk," said the king, "you have forfeited your priesthood by your prowess; and for your prowess I take you into my service, and you shall go with me overseas. And this thing I do for you, because I would have my men to fully understand that I will uphold them in none of their wickedness."

When the people there assembled heard this, they cried out to our Saviour, and prayed God to give the king a good and a long life, and bring him back in joy and health.

Joinville Leaves His Castle

After these things I returned to our county, and we agreed, the Count of Sarrebruck and I, that we should send our baggage in carts to Ausonne, thence to be borne on the river Saone, and to Arles by the Saone and the Rhone.

How The King Reformed His Bailiffs, Provosts, and Mayors—And How He Instituted New Ordinances—and How Stephen Boileau Was His Provost of Paris

After King Louis had returned to France from overseas, he bore himself very devoutly towards our Saviour, and very justly towards his subjects; wherefore he considered and thought it would be a fair thing, and a good, to reform the realm of France. First he established a general ordinance for all his subjects throughout the realm of France, in the manner following:

"We, Louis, by the grace of God King of France, ordain that Our bailiffs, viscounts, provosts, mayors, and all others, in whatever matter it may be, and whatever office they may hold, shall make oath that, so long as they hold the said office, or perform the functions of bailiffs, they shall do justice to all, without acceptation of persons, as well to the poor as to the rich, and to strangers as to those who are native-born; and that they shall observe such uses and customs as are good and have been approved.

"And if it happens that the bailiffs, or viscounts, or others, as the sergeants or foresters, do aught contrary to their oaths, and are convicted thereof, we order that they be punished in their goods, or in their persons, if the misfeasance so require; and the bailiffs shall be punished by Ourselves, and others by the bailiffs.

"Henceforward the other provosts, the bailiffs and the sergeants shall make oath to loyally keep and uphold Our rents and Our rights, and not to suffer Our rights to lapse or to be suppressed or diminished; and with this they shall swear not to take or receive, by themselves or through others, gold, nor silver, nor any indirect benefit, nor any other thing, save fruit, or bread, or wine, or other present, to the value of ten sous, the said sum not being exceeded.

"And besides this they shall make oath not to take, or cause to be taken, any gift, of whatever kind, through their wives, or their children, or their brothers, or their sisters, or any other persons connected with them; and so soon as they have knowledge that any such gifts have been received, they will cause them to be returned as soon as may be possible. And, besides this, they shall make oath not to receive any gift, of whatever kind, from any man belonging to their bailiwicks, nor from any others who have a suit or may plead before them.

"Henceforth they shall make oath not to bestow any gift upon any men who are of Our council, nor upon their wives, or children, or any person belonging to them; nor upon those who shall receive the said officers' accounts on Our behalf, nor to any persons who we may send to their bailiwicks, or to their provostships, to enquire into their doings. And with this they shall swear to take no profit out of any sale that may be made of Our rents, Our bailiwicks, Our coinage, or aught else to Us belonging.

"And they shall swear and promise, that if they have knowledge of any official, sergeant, or provost, serving under them, who is unfaithful, given to robbery and usury, or addicted to other vices whereby he ought to vacate Our service, then they will not uphold him for any gift, or promise, or private affection, or any other cause, but punish and judge him in all good faith.

"Henceforward Our provosts, Our viscounts, Our mayors, Our foresters, and Our other sergeants, mounted and dismounted, shall make oath not to bestow any gift upon their superiors, nor upon their superiors' wives, nor children, nor upon any one belonging to them.

"And because We desire that these oaths be fairly established, We order that they be taken in full assize, before all men, by clerks and laymen, knights and sergeants, notwithstanding that any such may have already made oath before Us; and this We ordain so that those who take the oaths may avoid the guilt and the sin of perjury, not only from the fear of God and of Ourselves, but also for shame before the world.

"We will and ordain that all Our provosts and bailiffs abstain from saying any word that would bring into contempt God, or our Lady, or the saints; and also that they abstain from the game of dice and keep away from taverns. We ordain that the making of dice be forbidden throughout Our realm, and that lewd women be turned out of every house; and whosoever shall rent a house to a lewd woman shall forfeit to the provost, or the bailiff, the rent of the said house for a year.

"Moreover, We forbid Our bailiffs to purchase wrongfully, or to cause to be purchased, either directly, or through others, any possession or lands that may be in their bailiwick, or in any other, so long as they remain in Our service, and without Our express permission; and if any such purchases are made, We ordain that the lands in question be, and remain, in Our hands.

"We forbid Our bailiffs, so long as they shall be in Our service, to marry any sons or daughters that they may have, or any other person belonging to them, to any other person in their bailiwick, without Our special sanction; and moreover We forbid that they put any such into a religious house in their bailiwick, or purvey them with any benefice of holy Church, or any other possession; and moreover We forbid that they obtain provisions or lodgings from any religious house, or nearby, at the expense of the religious. This prohibition as concerns marriages and the acquisition of goods, as stated above, does not apply to provosts, or mayors, nor to others holding minor offices.

"We order that no bailiff, provost, or any other, shall keep too many sergeants or beadles, to the burdening of our people; and We ordain that the beadles be appointed in full assize, or else be not regarded as beadles. When sergeants are sent to a distant place, or to a strange county, We ordain that they be not received without letters from their superiors.

"We order that no bailiff or provost in Our service shall burden the good people in his jurisdiction beyond what is lawful and right; and that none of Our subjects be put in prison for any debt save in so far as such debt may be due to Ourselves only.

"We ordain that no bailiff levy a fine for a debt due by any of Our subjects, or for any offence, save in full and open court, where the amount of such fine may be adjudged and estimated, with the advice of worthy and competent persons, even when the fine has already been considered by them (informally? passage obscure). And if it happens that the accused will not wait for the judgment of Our court, which is offered him, but offers for the fine a certain sum of money, such as has been commonly received aforetime, we ordain that the court accept such sum of money if it be reasonable and convenient; and, if not, we ordain that the fine be adjudicated upon, as aforesaid, even though the delinquent place himself in the hands of the court. We forbid that the bailiffs, or the mayors, or the provosts, should compel Our subjects, either by threats, or intimidation, or any chicanery, to pay a fine in secret or in public or accuse any save for reasonable cause.

"And We ordain that those who hold the office of provost, viscount, or any other office, do not sell such office to others without Our consent; and if several persons buy jointly any of the said offices, We order that one of the purchasers shall perform the duties of the office for all the rest, and alone enjoy such of its privileges in respect of journeyings, taxes, and common charges, as have been customary aforetime.

"And We forbid that they sell the said offices to their brothers, nephews, or cousins, after they have bought them from Us; and that they claim any debts that may be due to themselves, save such debts as appertain to their office. As regards their own personal debts, they will recover them by authority of the bailiff, just as if they were not in Our service.

"We forbid Our bailiffs and provosts to weary our subjects, in the causes brought before them, by moving the venue from place to place. They shall hear the matters brought before them in the place where they have been wont to hear them, so that Our subjects may not be induced to forego their just rights for fear of trouble and expense.

"From henceforth we command that Our provosts and bailiffs dispossess no man from the seisin which he holds, without full enquiry, or Own own especial order; and that they impose upon Our people no new exactions, taxes and imposts; and that they compel no one to come forth to do service in arms, for the purpose of exacting money from him; for We order that none who owes Us service in arms shall be summoned to join the host without sufficient cause, and that those who would desire to come to the host in person should not be compelled to purchase exemption by money payment.

"Moreover, we forbid Our bailiffs and provosts to prevent corn, wine and other merchandise from being taken out of Our Kingdom, save for sufficient cause; and when it is convenient that these goods should not be taken out of the kingdom, the ordinance shall be made publicly, in the council of worthy and competent elders, and without suspicion of fraud or misdoing.

"Similarly We ordain that all bailiffs, viscounts, provosts, and mayors do remain, after they have left office, for the space of forty days in the land where such office has been exercised—remaining there in person or by deputy—so that they may answer to the new bailiffs in respect of any wrong done to such as may wish to bring a complaint against them."

By these ordinances the king did much to improve the condition of the kingdom.

Reform of The Provostship of Paris

The provostship of Paris was at that time sold to the citizens of Paris, or indeed any one; and those who bought the office upheld their children and nephews in wrongdoing; and the young folk relied in their misdoings on those who occupied the provostship. For which reason the mean people were greatly downtrodden; nor could they obtain justice against the rich, because of the great presents and gifts that the latter made to the provosts.

Whenever at that time any one spoke the truth before the provost, and wished to keep his oath, refusing to perjure himself regarding any debt, or other matter on which he was bound to give evidence, then the provost levied a fine upon that person, and he was punished. And because of the great injustice that was done, and the great robberies perpetrated in the provostship, the mean people did not dare to sojourn in the king's land, but went and sojourned in other provostships and other lordships. And the king's land was so deserted that when the provost held his court, no more than ten or twelve people came thereto.

With all this there were so many malefactors and thieves in Paris and the country adjoining that all the land was full of them. The king, who was very diligent to enquire how the mean people were governed and protected, soon knew the truth of this matter. So he forbade that the office of provost in Paris should be sold; and he gave great and good wages to those who henceforward should hold the said office. And he abolished all the evil customs harmful to the people; and he caused enquiry to be made throughout the kingdom to find men who would execute good and strict justice, and not spare the rich any more than the poor.

Then was brought to his notice Stephen Boileau, who so maintained and upheld the office of provost that no malefactor, no thief, nor murderer dared to remain in Paris, seeing that if he did, he was soon hung or exterminated: neither parentage, or lineage, nor gold, nor silver could save him. So the king's land began to amend, and people resorted thither for the good justice that prevailed. And the people so multiplied, and things so amended, that sales, seisines, purchases, and other matters were doubled in value, as compared with what the king had received aforetime.

A further ordinance issued by the king did much to bring about a better state of things in the Kingdom of France, as many wise and venerable persons have testified. It ran as follows:

"In all these matters which We have ordained for the advantage of Our subjects, and of Our realm, we reserve to Ourselves the right to elucidate, amend, adjust, or diminish, according as We may determine."

By this ordinance also the king did much to reform the kingdom of France, as many wise and ancient persons bear witness.

Love of St. Louis for the Poor—of his Alms and Pious Foundations

From the time of his childhood, the king had pity on the poor suffering; and the custom was that, wherever the king went, six score poor persons were always fed every day, in his house, with bread and wine, and meat or fish. In Lent and Advent the number of the poor was increased; and ofttimes it happened that the king served them, and set their food before them, and carved the meat before them, and gave them money with his own hand at their departing.

Particularly at the great vigils, before the solemn festivals, he served the poor in all matters as aforesaid, before he himself either ate or drank. Besides all this he had, every day, to dine or sup near him, old and broken men, and caused them to be fed with the same meats of which he himself partook; and when they had eaten they took away a certain sum of money.

Besides all this the king gave, day by day, large and great alms to the poor religious, to the poor in hospitals, to the poor sick, and to poor communities, also to poor gentlemen and ladies, and girls, and to fallen women, and to poor widows and to women who were lying in, and to poor workmen, who through age or sickness could no longer work at their crafts; so that hardly would it be possible to number his alms. Therefore may it well be said that he was more fortunate than Titus, the Emperor of Rome of whom old writings tell that he was sad and discomforted for any day on which he had not been able to confer some benefit.

From the first that he came to his kingdom and knew where he stood he began to erect churches, and many religious houses, among which the abbey of Royaumont bears the palm for honour and magnificence. He caused many almshouses to be erected: the almshouse for Paris, that of Pontoise, that of Compiegne and of Vernon, and assigned to them large rents. He founded the abbey of St. Matthew at Rouen, where he set women of the order of the Preaching Brothers; and he founded that of Longchamp, where he set women of the order of the Minorist Brothers, and assigned to them large rents for their livelihood.

And he allowed his mother to found the abbey of the Lis near Melun-sur-Seine, and the abbey near Pontoise, which is called Maubuisson, and there assigned to them large rents and possessions. And he caused to be built the House of the Blind, near Paris, for the reception of the poor blind of the city; and caused a chapel to be built for them, so that they might hear the service of God. And the good king caused the house of the Carthusians, which is called Vauvert, to be built outside Paris, and assigned sufficient rents to the monks who there served our Saviour.

Pretty soon after he caused another house to be built outside Paris, on the way to St. Denis, and it was called the house of Filles-Dieu; and he caused to be placed there a great multitude of women, who, through poverty, had lapsed into the sin of incontinence; and he gave them, for their maintenance, four hundred livres a year. And in many places of his kingdom he instituted houses for beguines, and gave them rents for their livelihood, and commanded that any should be received therein who were minded to live in chastity.

There were some of his familiars who murmured at his giving such large alms, and because he expended so much; and he would say: "I like better that the great and excessive expenditure which I incur should be incurred in almsgiving for the love of God, than in pomp and splendour and for the vainglory of this world." Yet, notwithstanding that the king spent so largely in almsgiving, he did not forbear to incur daily great expenditure in his household. Largely and liberally did the king behave to the parliaments and assemblies of his barons and knights; and he caused his court to be served courteously, and largely, and without stint, and in more liberal fashion than aforetime in the court of his predecessors.

Of The Religious Orders That The King Established in France

The king loved all people who set themselves to serve God, and took on them the religious habit; nor did any come to him but he gave them what they needed for a living. He provided for the brothers of Carmel, and bought them land on the Seine, towards Charenton, and caused a house to be built for them, and purchased for them vestments, chalices, and such other things as are needful for the service of our Saviour. And after he provided for the brothers of St. Augustine, and bought them the grange of a citizen of Paris, and all its appurtenances, and caused a church to be built for them outside the gate of Montmartre.

The brothers of the "Sacks" he provided for, and he gave them a site on the Seine, towards Saint-Germain des Pres, where they established themselves; but they remained there no long time, for they were shortly suppressed. After the brothers of the "Sacks" had been lodged came another kind of brothers, who were called the order of the "White Mantles," and they begged the king to give them help so that they might remain in Paris. The king bought them a house and certain old buildings lying round where they might lodge near the old gate of the Temple of Paris, rather near to the Weavers' house. These "White Mantles" were suppressed at the Council of Lyons, held by Gregory X.

Afterward came yet another kind of brothers, who had themselves called brothers of the Holy Cross, and wore a cross upon their breasts; and they asked the king to help them. The king did so willingly, and lodged them into a street called the Cross-roads of the Temple, and now called the street of the Holy Cross.

Thus did the good king surround the city of Paris with people of religion.

ENQUÊTS OF KING LOUIS

THE *Querimoniae Normanorum* WERE COLLECTED WHEN LOUIS IX (Saint Louis, 1226-1270) sought to reform royal administration in thirteenth-century France on the eve of a crusade. The conquest of Normandy in 1204 by Philip Augustus brought a large territory under French rule. Wishing to impose his personal standards of justice and piety on a growing administration, Saint Louis dispatched special judges (*enquêteurs*) in 1247 to hear the complaints (*querimoniae*) of his Norman subjects against royal officers. The 64 cases in this selection are drawn from the diocese of Séez in the viscounty of Falaise (an administrative district). The cases form a unified group. Very long or repetitive examples have been excluded. A few terms recur throughout the cases. *Baillis* were the most important royal officials in Normandy; they served as judges in lawsuits involving the King's rights, and were responsible for the King's revenues. Subordinate to them were *firmarii*, the revenue farmers or collectors of rents. Awarded a particular region after a successful bid, a *firmarius* was permitted to "farm" a certain source of revenue in the region for a specified term, usually one year. Income that exceeded his bid constituted his profit. The currency prevalent in thirteenth-century Normandy and France was the pound, either the *livre* (l.) *parisis* or *livre* (l.) *tournois*; smaller amounts were expressed in shillings (*solidii*), abbreviated as s. and pennies (*denarii*), abbreviated as d. References to pounds alone are assumed to be to *livres parisis*.

Source: L. Delisle ed. *Recueil des historiens des Gaules et de la France* (Paris, 1904) vol. 4, pp. 1-73, translated by Jonathan M. Elukin, with the assistance of Professor William Chester Jordan.

Querimoniae Normanorum de Domino Rege in Vicecomitati Falesiae in Dyocesi Sagiensi

[Complaints of the Normans concerning the Lord King in the Viscounty of Falaise in the Diocese of Séez]

355. R ... de Clerdoit, Richard Flori, ... Herberti, Hugues Herberti, Guillaume, son of Hugh de Clerdoit, of Saint Jacques de ... t, complain that both they and all others from the said parish for whom they similarly complain, were forced by the *baillis* and revenue farmers of the Lord King to pay a customs duty on all things they sell and purchase, wherever they sell or purchase them, just as they had been accustomed to do when there was a market at Montpinçon ... on the Tuesday of each week, at the time when Raoul de Grandvilliers, knight and baron, held peaceful possession of his land before he went to England with King John; at which time he forfeited the land. And they say that they paid the said customs duty unjustly because, from the time when the land of the said baron came to the hand of King Philip, there has been no market in the village of Montpinçon, as there had been at the aforesaid time; and nevertheless, they have paid the said customs duty from that time till the present and are still compelled to pay it.

356. Robert, called "the Passionate," of Le Renouard ..., complains that Girard de La Boiste wrested from him a certain mill, found in the aforesaid parish, which he used to hold in fief from the Lord King for 2 measures of oats and 6 hens, because he [Robert] did not wish to provide all the components of the said mill; and although he was only supposed to provide the millstone

and the iron implements that hold the millstone, he has not been able to recover the said mill for the past 6 years.

358. Geoffroy *de Ponte Malveisin*, of the parish of Saint-Pierre-de-Chapelle, complains that the Lord King keeps in his hand his mother's marriage portion, which, located in the parish of *Roonnai* of the diocese of Séez, is currently worth 4-1/2 l. *tournois* annually to the Lord King, because her husband had crossed over to England at the time of the conquest of Normandy and did not come to the peace of Philip, King of France, of illustrious memory. Geoffroy's mother had died before the death of her husband, who died beyond the sea as a Hospitaller. The said husband had neither sons nor daughters from the said woman, so [Geoffroy] says, for he was not Geoffroy's father but his stepfather.

359. Mabel, widow of Richard, son of Fulk, the knight, of Vieuxpont-en-Auge, complains that Girard de La Boiste acquired for the Lord King land lying in the parish of Castillon, of the diocese of Lisieux, and worth approximately 100s. annually, because the brother of the said woman, a lay person, after the death of his brother the priest, also died in England. It is the priest who had given the said land to Mabel, on the condition that he peacefully and with no interference hold the aforesaid land at farm from Mabel and her heirs throughout his lifetime for one pair of gloves worth 6d. The land was acquired by the Lord King last year on the previous Nativity of the Lord.

361. Agnes, a minor, daughter of Raoul Taquel of Saint-Georges-en-Auge, complains that about 12 years ago, the revenue farmers of the Lord King acquired for him 6 acres of land, consisting of pasturage, wood, and cultivated fields, found in the parish of Le Tilleul. [They took the land], worth 20s., 2 loaves, 2 hens, and 20 eggs annually to the Lord King, on account of Agnes' youth and helplessness. However, she was supposed to hold it in fief from the Lord King for the aforesaid rent, namely the specified moneys, eggs, hens, and breads.

362. Robin *de Ripparia*, of Saint-Martin-de-Fresnay, complains that 24 years ago, Renaud de Ville-Thierri acquired for the Lord King in the aforesaid parish 1 acre of wood, which is next to the wood of the Lord King, upon the single statement of Robert Hirauth, a sergeant of the King, who said such things because he did not wish to lose the 1 pound of pepper which [Robinus] used to pay him annually.

364. Gilbert de Vaudeloges, *de Tot Ysembert*, complains that Pierre du Thillai, a *bailli* of the Lord King, seized from his father a certain sergeanty [consisting] of a plot, which is between La Dive and La Vie, and placed it in the hand of the Lord King 28 years ago; for he claimed that his father was not an enfeoffed sergeant, because he was not able to show [Pierre] a written charter to this effect. [Gilbert claims the charter] had been burned in a certain house, and he is prepared to seek an investigation by a jury[1] about this. And [Gilbert complains], the said Pierre, about 15 years ago, seized the patronage of the church of Heurtevent from his mother after the death of his father, and placed it in the hand of the Lord King, because his mother did not want to give the church[2] according to Pierre's wish.

366. Emeline, daughter of Alain of Bretteville-sur-Dive complains that the revenue farmers of the Lord King acquired for the King 1-1/2 acres of land, which lie in the aforesaid parish. She was not able to recover them after the death of her father, who used to hold them from the said Lord King in fief for 3 capons, 3 hens, and 3 loaves to be paid annually; and the land was taken into the King's hand approximately 12 years ago. Nor in this matter was the Lord King injured.

367. Guillaume Pipart, a knight, of Escoz, complains that 4 years ago Jean de Vignes extracted 100l. *tournois*, which went to the Lord King as [Jean] acknowledged before the said Lord King. He was not supposed to extract [the money] unless [Guillaume] went to England, as was acknowledged before the King. Therefore, since he did not cross over to England at that time, Guillaume moves that the aforesaid money be returned to him.

368. Hugues d'Abbeville, of Vendeuvre, complains that King Philip, of good memory, ordered the land of Robert Louvel, of Morteaux-Couliboeuf, to be seized, land which the said Robert had given in pledge to Hugues for 22l. *tournois*, because Robert had gone to England and did not come to [the King's] peace. Hugues has since extracted nothing from the said land in the parish of Vendeuvre, nor was he able to recover afterwards the said money, which he had given to Robert. The land was taken into the Lord King's possession at the time of the conquest of Normandy, so [Hugues] says.

369. Robert *de Senonis*, a clerk, of Condé-sur-Laison, complains that the servants or revenue farmers of the Lord King of France, at the time of the conquest of Normandy, wrested from his uncle, his father, and from himself 3 measures of oats, customarily worth 15s., beyond the rent that his ancestors were accustomed to pay to the King of England, before the said conquest, from a certain piece of land, in the said parish, which he holds in fief from the Lord King. The aforesaid ancestors used to pay only 2s. annually from the land, so he says.

370. Richard, called "the Englishman" of Saint-Pierre-sur-Dive, complains that Guillaume [*de Oilleio*], archdeacon of Angers, whose land came into the possession of the Lord King 16 years ago, owed him 100s., which he has not been able to recover; for the said land came to the hand of the said Lord King because his [Guillaume's] heirs remained in England.

371. Adam, son of Beatrice, of Saint-Pierre-sur-Dive, complains that Guillaume, archdeacon of Angers, whose land came into the possession of the Lord King 16 years ago because his heirs remained in England, owed her 17l. from his accounts, which he has not been able to recover since the death of that individual.

372. Robert *de Fel*, of Saint-Pierre-sur-Dive, complains that Lord King Philip, at the time of the conquest of Normandy, took the land of Robert Louvel of Cesny-aux-Vignes, a knight; which land [Louvel] has handed over to [De Fel] in

pledge for 8l. *tournois*, which money he has not been able to recover.

374. Robert, called "the Blockhead" of Eraines, complains on behalf of his wife, since she is ill, saying that 20 years ago the Lord King retained in his possession the 3 quarts of barley that his wife used to collect in a certain land lying in the parish of Aubigny; for the *baillis* of the King did not wish to return the land to his wife's mother nor to her after the year and a day that it had been held in the hand of the King. [It was held] because of the outlawry of one of her men, who had been holding that land from [his wife's] mother; although it ought to have been returned after a year and a day.

377. Hugues, the priest, rector of the church of Saint-Loup-Canivet, complains that Pierre du Thillai, formerly a *bailli* of the Lord King, 30 years ago disseized him of 2 sheaves of the tithe of the said parish, which are worth 3 measures of barley at the Falaise measure annually to Lord King, in whose hand they have been held unjustly from that time; for [Pierre] disseized him without cause, as was discovered through 2 investigations [by jury] made about this matter, so he says. The first one, conducted by the venerable father in Christ, the Bishop of Séez, was made known before the Lord King, and the other one was made by Girard de La Boiste, who was then *bailli*.

378. Raoul Viethe and Robert *de Porta*, Nicholas le Fornier, Laurence Belebarbe, Etienne *de Furno* and Robert le Daneis, of Epaney, complain that the service of a wagon is being exacted from them to carry the timber of the mill of Jort, which they and their ancestors never did of old. And they have fallen into this evil custom because they used to give a little something every year to the servants of the King who had demanded the aforesaid service from them, so they would be quit from the said service. They have fallen into performing that service for 2 years.

382. Guillaume des Loges, squire, of the parish of Aubigny, complains that at the time of the conquest of Normandy, King Philip, of illustrious

memory acquired land, worth 18l. a year and lying in the parishes of Martigny, Pierrepont, Tassilly, and Les Loges-Saulces, which Guillaume, called "the Blockhead," the knight, had wrested from his father. [The King received the said land] with all the land of the aforesaid knight, who, on account of his forfeiture by going to England and not coming to the King's peace, had given up his land. And it now remains in the hands of the present King. And although [Guillaume des Loges] works the land for the Lord King and has the homage of the men, he is still not able to recover the aforesaid rents. And his mother, by inquiry, has a third portion from the said land in dower, which goes to the King after her death.

385. Leceline, widow of G. Ferant, and Guillaume, her son, of the parish of Saint-Loup-Canivet, complain that they are not able to recover 4 acres of land, lying next to a certain field, which they hold from the Lord King, and which the Lord King gave 8 years ago to the aforesaid Leceline to hold for herself and her heirs in return for 20s. to be paid annually for the said acres and the said field. And Girard de La Boiste was commanded to transfer the property to her, but he refused even though Jean de Vignes had commanded him to do it.

388. Giroth *de Treperel*, of the parish of Martigny, complains that Girard de La Boiste acquired for the Lord King 1 acre of land that Morel [de Falaise] the Jew had purchased in his fief during the life of his father [but] without the assent and permission of the said father. Giroth is not able to recover [the land] for the price that the Jew had given for the land.

390. Robert Hultauth, of Bernieres-sur-Dive, complains that about 15 years ago Jean de Vignes wrested from his father and received for the Lord King a certain piece of land, lying in the aforesaid parish and worth 11 quarts of barley at the measure of Saint-Pierre-sur-Dive, because a certain brother, a clerk, of the said father had died in England before the aforesaid time, where he had been staying because he had an ecclesiastical benefice there.

391. Heudeart, widow of Michel *de Bohon*, of the same parish, complains that her husband died in the service of the Lord King 5 years ago at Saint-Jean-d'Angely in Acquitaine. He died before payment was made to the King's workers, for which reason he was not able to have 40s., which were owed to him from his wages. And therefore she seeks that they be given to her.

392. Matthieu de Bu, of the parish of Sainte-Trinité-de-Falaise, complains that 22 years ago Jean le Guerrier acquired for the Lord King 7 acres of land, lying in the parish of Saint-Pierre-du-Bu and 1 acre of wood also found in the same parish, [the whole] worth 7 measures of barley. Matthew was supposed to receive the land after the death of his nephew, who was the son of an illegitimate sister, as he says. And let it be known that the said Jean received the said land because Matthew was born from a legitimate union, but his sister was born out of the fornication of concubinage. But Matthew seeks the land because his nephew was born from a legitimate marriage. Jean [also] wrested land worth 1 measure of oats and 1 goose from his wife's father, asserting that a certain brother of his had died in England; nor was an investigation [by jury], which [Matthew] sought, made about this. The land lies in the parish of Saint-Pierre-du-Bu, nor is there another heir except his wife.

393. Pierre le Peletier of Saint-Philbert-sur-Orne complains that Jean de Vignes acquired for the Lord King 1 acre of garden, lying in the parish of Saint-Philbert-sur-Orne and worth 20s. annually, which Enguerrand de Saint-Philbert-sur-Orne, a knight, had wrested from [Pierre]. All of Enguerrand's land along with the said garden returned to the King because Enguerrand did not wish to appear before the justice of the King. [The King] gave the garden to Simon le Cornu, castellan of Falaise, in whose hand it is held. And likewise, the Lord King gave another garden, worth 30s. annually, which the said Enguerrand had wrested from Pierre's brother, to the same castellan, and [Pierre] seeks on behalf of Raoul, son of Ami and W., his brother, and his three other brothers, and his nephews, that it be returned to them.

394. Robert Tison and Hugues, his brother, of Damblainville, complain that the revenue farmers of the Lord King, out of greed, acquired for the Lord King 3 virgates of land lying in the aforesaid parish and worth 1 quart of oats yearly, and they are now retained in the possession of the Lord King; for [the revenue farmers] arranged for an oath to be made [concerning the royal] demesne, without the viscount[3] or *bailli*, they being absent and uninformed.

395. Nicholas, rector of the church of Ussy, and Jean de Soulangy, priest, and Hugues, called "the Englishman," a clerk of the Lord King, complain for themselves and for all parsons and vicars of the churches of the deanery of Aubigny, saying that the *prévôts*[4] of Falaise exact a duty from them on those things, pertaining to [their] livelihood, which they buy for their own use—if they exceed the price of 5 pennies; briefly, on all the things that they purchase for their use and the use of their churches, just as from lay dues payers, so they say. The dean of Falaise and Thomas of Morteaux-Couliboeuf, a priest, make a similar complaint for all the priests of the aforesaid deanery.

396. Robert l'Ardant, of Crocy, complains that Jean le Guerrier acquired for the King land valued at 15s. per year lying in the aforesaid parish [Aubigny], which was supposed to come into his wife's possession by hereditary right and to a certain blood relative of hers by the name of Erremborch, wife of Auberic le Brun. And he took the land 22 years ago, after the death of Renaud Bordon, because a certain son of the said Renaud, 6 years before the death of his father, went to England as a pilgrim and there, after 2 years, entered the Cistercian order.

399. W. d'Olendon complains that Guillaume le Cras (the "Blockhead"), in the year before he left for England during the conquest of Normandy, seized by his brute force a *vavassoria*[5] of land, containing about 30 acres, which Robert d'Olendon used to hold from [Le Cras]. And there was no fault or forfeiture on the part of the said Robert, whose closest heir the said W. says he is; but the Lord King retained the said land from

that time and still keeps it, with other lands and rents of the said Guillaume le Cras.

402. Jean Sapience, of Evesqueville, complains that the King retains in his possession a certain piece of land at Evesqueville, worth 1 quart of oats valued at 2s., which he and the ancestors of his line had possessed 10 years ago, and up to this time he pays the rent of the said land with all his other lands, although a certain man from the said village received it from the revenue farmers of the King because Jean did not cultivate it.

403. Guillaume de Falaise, of Saint-Pierre-Canivet, complains that Pierre du Thillai, *bailli* of the Lord King disseized him of a certain rent, which he used to collect for 15 years in the *prévôté* of Falaise, for the guard of the gate of the castle of Falaise. Renaud de Ville-Thierri had given the rent to him by the command of the Lord King Louis. Nor did [Pierre] command that the said money that he was supposed to collect in the said *prévôté* be returned to him—for each year he would have had 61s. and would have them till now, as he says—as a result of which he was injured to the value of 45l. and 15s. And John, King of England, when he farmed the castle, did not render to him 21l. of annual rent, which he was supposed to have from the site of the said castle of Falaise, nor did he give anything in exchange for it, because at the time he was supposed to make an exchange for it, [John] lost the land of Normandy. [Guillaume] was not able to recover anything later from any King of France for the said rent, which he used to collect at the site of the moat-battlements of the castle.

404. Jean *de Mool*, knight, of Barberry, of the diocese of Bayeux, complains that at the time of the conquest of Normandy, a certain man who was holding a *vavassoria* from his father went to England. On account of which he lost the land and it fell into the King's possession, and at that time the said father was not able to obtain the services owed from the aforesaid *vavassoria*, such as the reliefs, the [military] services, the pleas, and the three aids of Normandy. The said Jean, after the death of his father, is till now not able to recover the said *vavassoria*—which lies in the parish of

Fourches near Vignats—from the prioress of Parthenon Sainte-Marguerite de Vignats, of the diocese of Séez, to whom the Lord King had given it, as a result of which, he and his father had been injured to the value of 10l.

407. Robert Guillaume, of the parish of Morteaux-Couliboeuf, complains that the Lord King at the time of the conquest of Normandy acquired 15 acres of land that the father of his wife had handed over, as a result of coercion and violence, to Guillaume le Cras, to whom [the father] used to make an annual payment because he held it from [him] in fief. The acres lie in the parish of Saint-Loup-Canivet and are worth annually more than the rent that the said father used to pay, to the value of 60s.

409. Raoul Garnier and Pierre *de Ponte Oilleii*, Jean his brother, a cleric, and their mother, the widow of Jean *de Ponte Oilleii*, and Bienvenue, widow of Pierre le Petit, *de Ponte Oilleii*, and his four sons and a certain daughter of his complain that Jean de Vignes threw Raoul, and the said Jean and Pierre [Le Petit], now dead, into prison because Pierre *de Ponte Oilleii* had said that they had had him arrested by Richard Suarth, a knight, (the castellan of Caen, at the time of the war in Brittany), and he was prepared to prove this. And they were not able to get out of prison until they had promised to pay the Lord King 1800l. *tournois*, which they did and afterward were freed from the prison. And of the 1800l., the said Raoul paid 600l., Jean, 900l., and Pierre le Petit, 300l. And although the ones noted above who had been put in prison had sought an investigation [by jury] about this, they were not able to procure it.

411. Agnes *de Veilleio*, of Falaise, complains that King Philip, of illustrious memory, 2 years after the conquest of Normandy acquired possession of 2 plots, worth 48s. annually, and there fortified the castle of Falaise with moat-battlements and other structures; nor did he exchange [anything for them] with her, although the said plots had been given to her as a marriage portion.

414. Robert Ansere, of Sainte-Marguerite-de-

Viette, of the diocese of Lisieux, complains that 22 years ago Renaud de Ville-Thierri acquired for the Lord King a certain virgate of land lying in the parish of Bretteville-sur-Laize near Saint-Pierre-sur-Dive and worth 10s. annually to the Lord King, on account of the poverty and helplessness of the said Robert. And the Lord King was in no way injured by this, since he only paid 3s. for that [land], so [Robert] says, and 2 hens.

415. Acelin le Telier, of the parish of Aubigny, complains that 28 years ago, Pierre du Thillai took his son, W. Acelini into the King's hand, on account of land lying in the aforesaid parish and worth to the Lord King 5 bushels of barley at the Falaise measure to the Lord King. Pierre claimed that a certain cousin of [Acelin's], whose land it had been, had gone into Poitou against the King, but [in fact] before he had left his province to set out for Poitou, the said cousin had sold the land to Acelin, so he says.

416. Raoul *de Cantepie* and Pierre, his brother, of Beaumais, complain that 40 years ago, Jean le Guerrier acquired for the King 20 acres of land and 1 fishpond, lying in the aforesaid parish and worth 40s. per year to the King, by asserting that their father owed one-third of 18l. to Morel [de Falaise] the Jew. However, King Philip, of illustrious memory, had quit him of that third part and had returned to him that land which he had handed over to Morellus in pledge, so they say.

417. Raoul *de Fago*, of the parish of Sainte-Trinité-de-Falaise, complains that Richard Clerc, a revenue farmer of the King, acquired for the said Lord King 7 acres of land lying in the parish of Le Mesnil-Hermier and worth 5s. annually to the Lord King—[land] which his father had granted in fief to a certain female blood relative of his for 2s.—because the said Raoul was not in the country, but on pilgrimage when the said relative died; and he might have had the said land if Jean de Vignes, who was conducting an investigation into this matter through his viscount, had not died so quickly. And the land was kept in the hand of the Lord King about 9 years.

419. Jeanne la Porcelle, of the parish of Saint-Ger-

vais-de-Falaise, complains that King Philip, of illustrious memory, caused her orchard to be destroyed 40 years ago when he had a large tower made at the castle of Falaise, and he did not offer anything to her or to her husband in exchange, and it was worth a full 12s. each year.

420. Andre *de Plessiaco*, of the parish of Sainte-Trinité-de-Falaise, complains that King Philip took into his own hand 2 plots, lying in the aforesaid parish and worth 32s. annually, when he constructed the moat-battlement next to the "Aaliz" gate of the castle of Falaise 42 years ago. [The land] had been given as a marriage portion to Bienvenue, his wife, and he had nothing in exchange for them, so he says.

421. Robert Caffrei, of Olendon, complains that 6 years ago, Girard de La Boiste took in the Lord King's hand a certain *vavassoria* lying in the aforesaid parish and worth 10s. annually to [Robert], after the death of a certain man who was holding the said *vavassoria* from him [Robert]—because the son of that man had acknowledged the lordship of the King after the death of [his] father; however, through an investigation [by jury] made about this it was discovered that the said *vavassoria* should have been held from the said Robert. And the said Girard had [collected] for the relief, 32s., for the aid of the host, 13s., and 10s. from [Robert] for bailing himself out of jail— in which [Girard] had put him for claiming the said *vavassoria*.

423. Guillaume Martin, cleric, Guillaume de Villeray, Geoffroy *de Hamello*, Nicolas Chaperon, Roger Tustain, and Elnaud *de Fonte*, of Beaumais, complain that the revenue farmers of the Lord King refuse to help them pay the 36s. of aid for the host, which they were accustomed to pay for the demesne of the King. And they make the complaint for themselves and for their fellows. For the revenue farmers have not paid the said money for 3 years, although they [Guillaume Martin and company] have paid the aid for the host each year.

425. Nicolas *de Hamello*, of Cordey, Guillaume Fuchier, [and] Guillaume Eemelench complain

on behalf of the entire parish, saying that they were accustomed to have a certain quittance, such that they did not pay the duty in Falaise on either wood or fields, for 1 penny, which each bordar of those [aforesaid] men used to pay to the *prévôt* of Falaise annually at the Circumcision of the Lord. Nevertheless, for the past 9 years the duty on forests and fields is demanded from them, although they are quit from the said rent.

430. Hugues le Boeuf, of Olendon, and Guillaume *de Long Prato*, of Aubigny, complain that King Philip, of illustrious memory, acquired possession of land lying in the parish of Soulangy— namely 3 acres of land worth 4 measures of barley a year to the King—which had belonged to the father of Hugues' wife and the father of the said Guillaume [*de Long Prato*], and which Guillaume le Cras had wrested from the said fathers. [Philip acquired] all the land of the aforesaid knight [Guillaume le Cras] on account of his forfeit. [Guillaume le Cras] had wrested the said land from the fathers, when a certain bastard brother of theirs gave [him] the portion [this brother] used to have in that land. But since he was a bastard, he was supposed to have no part of that land. It was received into the King's hand at the time of the conquest of Normandy, so they say.

432. W. Sibille de Soulangy, complains about 7-1/2 acres of land, which is found in the parish of Saint-Loup-Canivet and is worth 7 measures (*sextarii*) and 1 measure (*mina*) of oats at the Falaise measure to the Lord King. Guillaume, called "the Blockhead" had wrested [the land] from his [W.'s] wife's father, accusing him of poorly caring for his pigs, because they died; when he had, in fact, taken good care of them. At the conquest of Normandy, King Philip, of illustrious memory, took possession of all the land of the aforesaid knight [Guillaume].

436. Guillaume *de Cerez*, Robert Guiart and Guillaume de Breuil, of Bellou-en-Houlme, complain on behalf of the whole parish that the Lady of La Ferté, at the time when King Philip, of illustrious memory, fought at the bridge of Bouvines, exacted from them payment for the right to pasture—

worth 60s. annually to the Lord King—which they had never paid and yet had had the right to pasture their flocks. After the death of the said lady, whose land came into the King's possession two years after the said battle, the revenue farmers of the Lord King demanded the said payment for pasturage from the same men. And for 22 years, they have not had the full pasturage because, since the aforesaid time, the revenue farmers of the Lord King had put the land in which they used to have pasturage partially under cultivation. Nor however did they reduce the rent of pasturage; and the revenue farmers demand from the men each year 13s. and 4d. as a payment of wethers, but they still do not receive the dead wood that they used to have in the forest of Bellou in return for the payment, which they used to pay to the Lord of Ferté, whose land came to the King completely after the death of the aforesaid lady. And they demand from the men a dry multure [duty] worth 40s. annually in case the mills stop on account of the failure of water or anything else. But they are not responsible for the repair of the mills because the *seneschals* of the said Lord of Ferté imposed on them such a milling due without the knowledge of the lord, who then was staying in England, nor did he come to the King's peace at the time of the conquest of Normandy, for which reason his land went to the King's hand.

437. Pierre *de Hamello*, and Guillaume, his brother, of Bellou-en-Houlme, complain concerning a certain piece of land, which their mother had gained in the court of the Lord King through a jury of the country. After the death of the mother, revenue farmers of the Lord King, 22 years ago, wrested away 10 acres from them, which they then placed in the possession of the Lord King. And the said acres are found in the aforesaid parish and are worth 10s. annually to the Lord King. [The acres] were placed under the hand of the Lord King on account of the default of the said brothers.

439. Sybil, widow of Enguerrand de Saint-Philbert-sur-Orne, the knight, complains that Jean de Vignes, at the time of the war at Saint-James-de-Beuvron, had claimed that her husband

had harboured the enemies of the King [and] that he was aware of the capture of Pierre *de Ponte*, mayor of Falaise, whom Richard Suarth, brother of the said Sybil, had taken. He [Enguerrand] sought an investigation [by jury] about this through the abbot *de Fonteneto* and through many others, but was not able to procure one: for Engerrand did not dare to appear before him [Jean] lest he be imprisoned, because he was old, infirm and ill; and because he did not appear, his land was taken into the King's possession, and the Lord King then gave [it] to Simon le Cornu, the castellan of Falaise, for an annual rent of 31l. and 8s., which the same Simon holds till now because the said Enguerrand, not daring to appear, as was said above, went to England and there he died. Thus, the said Sybil petitions the King, if it should so please him, to act compassionately and benignly to her sons, the children of the said Enguerrand.

442. Robert Guiart, of Bellou-en-Houlme, complains that the revenue farmers of the Lord King, 25 years ago, exacted 36s. every year both from his father as well as from himself from 3 *vavassoriae*, which he holds from the Lord King and which his ancestors held before him, for which the said ancestors made payment both to the Lord of La Ferté and to King Philip amounting to 18s. for three mounted sergeants;[6] and they complain that King Philip acquired at the time of the conquest of Normandy 1-1/2 acres of field, which the Lord of La Ferté—by the oath of three men whom he made swear to his lordship, although a fourth did not agree with the others—had wrested from his father, together with the land of the aforesaid knight, and still he [Robert] pays the rent for the land to the Lord King.

443. Thomas Faber, of Bellou-en-Houlme, complains that Bertrand de Fresnay, knight, and revenue farmer of the Lord King has not rendered to him for the past 16 years his supply of firewood and coal for his forge, and his quittance, which he had concerning the forest of Bellou and the other forests of the Lord of La Ferté such that he would be allowed to pasture pigs in these woods; and regarding his duty to provide hospitality, he was quit from providing food if the said lord were

present in the aforesaid village of Bellou, on the condition that he would shoe all the lord's horses, as well as those of his knights, squires, and other servants. And nevertheless, [Bertrand] demanded from him that he shoe all of his horses and those of his servants since the time specified; as a result of which he was damaged for every year of the 16 years to the amount of 50s., since beyond the aforesaid rent he was supposed to have a squire's robe, which he [Bertrand] has not rendered to him since the aforesaid time, so he says.

445. The lepers of Moulin Seranz, of Saint-Andre-de-Messei, complain that the sergeants of the Lord King acquired for the King 2 acres of land lying in the parish of Bellou-en-Houlme. They have been retained since the time of the conquest of Normandy despite the fact that they were seized of them at the time of said conquest, and they fell into the hand of the Lord King on account of their helplessness and ...

447. Hugues de Saint André, of Briouze-Saint-Gervais, complains [for the sons] of Richard *de Plessiaco*, namely Rob[ert] ... that 21 years ago, the Lord King retained in his hand land of the said Richard, worth 100s. annually to the Lord King and lying in the aforesaid parish of Briouze-Saint-Gervais, because Renaud de Ville-Thierri, by the act of certain knights, had the said Richard hanged unjustly, on the charge of theft. He was not found in possession of anything nor has Hugues been able to secure an investigation by a jury, which he was seeking.

450. Guillaume, called "the King," of Les Rotours, complains that about 35 years ago, Pierre du Thilai acquired for the King the land of a certain man, who used to render annually to his father 5s., which he has not been able to recover since from the said Pierre or from any other *baillis*, and the land remains in the hand of the King.

451. Robert, called "the Strong," of Écouché, a cleric, complains that 4 years ago, Jean de Vignes caused a millstream to be made through the field of the said Robert for the King's mill, which is called the "Choisel," at Tanquiez. He promised to make an exchange [with regard to] the said field, which he did not do; whence he reckons to have been damaged to the amount of 30s. annual rent for the aforesaid millstream of the King.

452. Richard Corneth and two of his brothers, of Falaise, complain that 10 years after the conquest, Pierre du Thillai acquired for the King land, worth approximately 7l. *tournois* annually to the King and lying in the parish of Aubigny, which their father had handed over in pledge to Guillaume le Cras, and which King Philip, of illustrious memory, returned to the said brothers after the conquest of Normandy. Pierre du Thillai claimed that the said land had not been given in pledge to Guillaume but had been sold; nevertheless, it was discovered through an investigation [by jury] that it had been pledged, so they say.

453. Jean L'esveille, of Briouze-Saint-Gervais, complains that Raoul le Cordoanier, who 30 years ago was a revenue farmer of the Lord King in Briouze-Saint-Gervais, imposed on his fief 10s. of annual rent, which his ancestors had never paid before and Robert *de Poteria*, a knight, who was the revenue farmer 10 years ago, imposed another 10s. on the same fief. Jean himself and his brother have paid the 20s., unjustly, to other revenue farmers from then on.

455. Gautier, son of Guillaume, called "the Old Man," of Ifs-sur-Laizon, complains that King Philip acquired a certain house and 3 acres of land lying in the said parish—and worth 6s. annually and 3 measures of oats at the Falaise measure—which Guillaume le Cras had wrested from his father before the conquest of Normandy on account of the father's helplessness. King Philip took the land at the time of the conquest along with the land of the said knight [Guillaume le Cras], because he did not wish to come to the Lord King's peace.

456. Guillaume Poucin, of Saint Ouen, complains that 20 years ago Jean de La Porte acquired for the Lord King land belonging to his man, lying in the said parish, and in which he used to collect annually 5s. and services worth another 5s. Jean claimed that the said man, who died without heirs, had

died in England, but no investigation [by jury] was begun into this matter, and the said Guillaume was not able to recover the rent from the sergeants of the Lord King since the aforesaid time.

457. Richard Gronneit, of the parish of Sainte-Trinité-de-Falaise, complains that before the conquest of Normandy, John, King of England, took the land of his father—worth 100s. annually to him—so that he could build the moat-battlements of the castle of Falaise on it, for which he did not give him anything in return, because at the time he was supposed to make restitution, he lost the land of Normandy, nor did the father have any recompense from any King of France, nor he himself after the death of his father.

458. Robert Louvel, of Bellou-en-Houlme, complains that about 14 years ago, Elnaud le Flamench acquired for the King 3 virgates of land, which lie in the aforesaid parish next to the woods of the Lord King, because the said woods had overgrown that land; before the seizure, he [Robert] used to take his firewood from that land, which he has not been able to recover since the aforesaid time.

461. Guillaume le Batard and Hugues *de Fonte* and Jean *de Capella*, of Habloville, complain for themselves and their fellows, saying that Jean de Vignes and Girard de La Boiste forced them to rebuild the mill of Habloville, which they were not responsible to repair, for they had never done it before in the time of the Lord and Lady of Ferté, from whom the mill had come into the possession of the Lord King; by which they were injured to the amount of 9l. Nor did the said Jean, 3 years ago, wish to have an investigation [by jury] made about this matter although he had received a command from the court of the Lord King that he should do so, so they say.

462. Alexander le Testu and Richard le Testu, of Ifs-sur-Laizon, complain that 15 acres of land lying in the aforesaid parish, which Guillaume le Cras had wrested from their fathers by his own power, were taken by King Philip, of illustrious memory, with the land of the aforesaid knight [Guillaume le Cras] at the time of the conquest of

Normandy because he did not come to [the King's] peace; and afterwards those lands were given as a gift of the Lord King to Simon le Cornu, who is now the castellan of Falaise; and they are worth annually 7-1/2 measures of oats at the Falaise measure, and 7s., 2 capons, 1 hen, 30 eggs, and 12d. Still the said fathers, who used to hold the land in fief from the said Guillaume, only made payment of 4s., 3 capons, and 30 eggs.

464. Baudouin *de Montibus*, a knight, complains that when compelled, he had gone to the Albigensian regions in the King's pay, [but] the clerks who were responsible for paying out on behalf of the King had kept out from his wages 100s., because of the debt that Thomas *de Colunchis*, a knight, owed to them. Baudouin was not of his retinue, nor did he act as pledge on Thomas' behalf, nor was he present at the lending or at the receiving of the aforesaid debt 4 years ago when Lord Imbert de Beaujeu, right after Jean de Beaumont, left for the aforesaid regions.

465. The abbot and convent of Silli-en-Gouffern complain that the King exacts the *tiers*[7] from the sale of [wood from] the forests of Blanefosse in the parishes of Saint-Martin-sur-Vivre and of Belhotel. [The abbey] used to sell [this wood] without the said *tiers* at the time of King Philip, of illustrious memory, and at the time of the father, of illustrious memory, of [the present] King. In addition, they seek the patronage of the church of Marigny, which Nicolas *de Sancto Lothario*, a clerk, had granted to them, and which Jean de La Porte acquired for the Lord King; for through an investigation [by jury] made about the said patronage, he [Jean] found out that the Lord of Marigny had presented the last [parson]; yet he did not wish to inquire nor hear from the jurors how the said Lord had presented the said parson. But if he had done it, they would have acquired the said patronage, since the said clerk had received the patronage in the court of the Lord King against the [claim of the] aforesaid lord, after the presentation of the last parson.

Notes

1 Latin: *Inquisitio patriae*; literally, the investigation

of the country. Under Norman law, this meant the sworn testimony of local men. In several cases below, *inquisitio* appears alone but also refers to a jury.

2 Latin: *dare ecclesiam;* appoint the parson, or parish priest.

3 A royal official immediately subordinate to the *baillis* with important duties in supervising commerce and routine judicial work.

4 Subordinate royal officials, with duties roughly equivalent to the viscounts, who were usually active in urban areas.

5 The amount of land comprising a subordinate type of fief and not carrying the full spectrum of feudal obligations.

6 [?] Latin: *pro tribus servitiis equi.*

7 A payment made to the King by landowners for the privilege of selling timber from their own forests.

JEAN FROISSART

Chronicles

JEAN FROISSART (1337-CA. 1410) IS THE PRINCIPAL CHRONICLER OF
the first phase of the series of campaigns between England and France known
as the Hundred Years' War. Froissart served in the entourage of Edward III,
in the household of the Counts of Flanders, Wenceslas of Bohemia, the Count
of Blois, and others. For the earlier parts of his *Chronicle* he depended on the
writings of Jean Le Bel who had been a participant in much of the early fighting. Most of his later material was collected orally, by being present at important events, by talking with principal participants, and by talking with participants on both sides.

The following selections describe the Campaign of Crécy, (1356) and the
near anarchy in the aftermath of the capture of the French king John II at
Poitiers in 1356 which included the communal revolt of Étienne Marcel and
the peasant uprising known as the Jacquerie.

Source: Geffrey Brerenton, *Froissart: Chronicles* (Harmondsworth: Penguin, 1968).

The Campaign of Crécy (1346)

*Edward formally terminates the truce with Philip,
alleging French violations. He sends one of his commanders, Thomas Dagworth, to Brittany, where the
local struggle is still raging. At the request of the pro-
English Gascon nobles, he sends a larger force to Bordeaux, under Henry of Derby, to repel French
encroachments in Aquitaine. (The duchy had already
been declared confiscate by Philip VI, after Edward's
retraction of his homage.) Derby is at first highly successful, but in 1346 a powerful French army under the
Duke of Normandy wipes out many of his gains and
lays siege to the English-held castle of Aiguillon.*

*Froissart's statement that Edward's campaign in
Northern France which followed, and led to Crécy and
the acquisition of Calais, was originally planned as a
relief expedition to Gascony, is not discounted by
responsible historians and has documentary support
(Rymer, Foedera).*

When the King of England heard how hard
pressed his men were in the Castle of Aiguillon
and learnt that his cousin, the Earl of Derby, who
was at Bordeaux, was not strong enough to take
the field and raise the siege, he decided to assemble a large army and lead it to Gascony. He gave
orders for full preparations to be made, mobi-

lized men from his own kingdom and engaged
mercenaries in other countries where they could
be found.

At that time Sir Godfrey of Harcourt, having
been banished from France, arrived in England.
He went straight to the King and Queen, who
were than at Chertsey, a town on the Thames
some fifteen miles from London. He was received
with open arms and was immediately made a
member of the King's household and council. A
large estate was assigned to him in England to
enable him to maintain himself and his followers
on a lavish scale. Soon after this the King completed the first stage of his preparations. A large
fleet was brought together in Southampton harbor, and all kinds of men-at-arms and archers
were assembled there.

At about midsummer 1346 the King took leave
of the Queen, whom he left in the care of his
cousin, the Earl of Kent. He appointed Lord
Percy and Lord Neville to be guardians of his
kingdom together with four prelates, the Archbishops of Canterbury and York and the Bishops
of Lincoln and Durham. He left sufficient forces
in England to defend it if need be, then rode
down to Southampton to wait for a favorable
wind. When it came, he boarded his ship, as did

his son the Prince of Wales, Sir Godfrey of Harcourt, and the other lords, earls and barons, according to the order of embarkment. There must have been four thousand men-at-arms and ten thousand archers, without counting the Irish and Welsh who followed his army on foot....

They set sail in accordance with the will of God, the wind and the sailors, and made a good start towards Gascony, where the King intended to go. But on the third day the wind changed and drove them back to the coasts of Cornwall, where they lay at anchor for six days. At this point the King held a new council at the suggestion of Sir Godfrey, whose advice was that it would be a better venture to make a landing in Normandy. 'Normandy,' said Sir Godfrey, 'is one of the richest countries in the world. I promise you, on my life, that once you reach it, it will be easy to land there. There will be no serious resistance, for the inhabitants have no experience of arms and the whole cream of the Norman knights are at the siege of Aiguillon with the Duke. You will find large towns and fortresses completely undefended, in which your men will win enough wealth to make them rich for twenty years to come. Your fleet will be able to follow you almost as far as Caen. If you see fit to take my advice, you and all of us will profit by it. We shall have gold, silver, food supplies and everything else in abundance.'

The King of England, who was then in his prime and desired nothing better than to meet the enemy and see action, readily agreed with Sir Godfrey, whom he called his cousin. He ordered his seamen to change course for Normandy and, taking the admiral's flag from the Earl of Warwick, made himself admiral and led the fleet for that voyage. With the wind now in their favor, they sailed to the port of La Hogue in the Cotentin Peninsula. The news that the English had arrived soon spread and the townships of Cotentin sent messengers at all speed to the King of France in Paris. King Philip already knew that the English King had been assembling a large army and that his fleet had been seen passing the coasts of Normandy and Brittany, but it was not known where he was making for. So as soon as he received the news of the landing in Normandy, he summoned his Commander-in-Chief, the Count of Guines, and the Count of Tancarville,

who had both recently arrived from Gascony, and ordered them to go to Caen to be ready to defend the town and its approaches against the English. They promised to do their utmost and set out from Paris accompanied by a large force of men-at-arms, whose ranks were constantly swollen by new arrivals. Reaching Caen, they were greeted with joy by the citizens and the people from the surrounding country who had taken refuge there. They began to put the town in a state of defence (it was not walled at that period) and to see that the inhabitants were armed and equipped each according to his standing.

To return to the English fleet which had entered La Hogue: when it was drawn up and anchored on the shore, the King came off his ship. But as his foot touched the ground, he stumbled and fell so heavily that the blood gushed from his nose. The knights who were round him took this for a bad omen and begged him to go back on board for that day. 'Why?' retorted the King without hesitation. 'It's a very good sign for me. It shows that this land is longing to embrace me.' They were all greatly cheered by this answer. So the King encamped on the beach for that day and night and the whole of the next.

Meanwhile the horses were unloaded from the ships with all their gear and a council was held to decide how they should proceed. The King appointed Sir Godfrey of Harcourt and the Earl of Warwick to be Marshals of the army, with the Earl of Arundel as Commander-in-Chief. The Earl of Huntingdon was directed to remain with the fleet with a hundred men-at-arms and four hundred archers. At a second council they decided their order of march. The men were divided into three columns, one to take the right flank and follow the coast, another the left, while the third marched in the centre under the King and the Prince of Wales. Each night the flanking columns led by the two Marshals were to join up again with the King.

Following this plan, the English army began its advance. The fleet sailed along the coast, seizing every vessel, large or small, that they fell in with. Archers and foot-soldiers marched near them within sight of the sea, robbing, pillaging and carrying off everything they came across. They moved forward by land and sea until they reached Barfleur, a seaport and fortified town which they took immediately because the inhabitants surrendered in the hope of saving their lives, though this did not prevent the town from being emptied of its gold, silver and jewelry. They found so much of it there that the very servants in the army turned up their noses at fur-lined gowns. All the men in the town were taken and put on board the ships so that there should be no danger of their rallying afterwards and harassing them in the rear.

After capturing and plundering Barfleur, though without burning it, they spread out over the country, though they still kept near the coast. They did whatever they pleased, for no one resisted them. They came in time to a large wealthy town and port called Cherbourg. They sacked and burnt part of it, but found the citadel too strongly defended to be taken, so they went on towards Montbourg and Valogne. This last they sacked completely and then set fire to it. They did the same to a number of other towns in the region, taking so much valuable booty that it would have been an impossible task to count it.

Continuing from Valogne, the Earl of Warwick's column takes and sacks the fortified town of Carentan. The other two columns meet with similar success, amassing huge quantities of plunder in the form of household possessions and the livestock in which Normandy abounds.

So was the good, fat land of Normandy ravaged and burnt, plundered and pillaged by the English, until news of the havoc they were wreaking reached the King of France in Paris. When he heard of it, King Philip swore that they should not go home without being brought to battle and made to pay dearly for the misery and destruction they were inflicting on his subjects. He immediately caused a number of letters to be written. The first were to his friends in the Empire because they were the most distant from him: to the good King of Bohemia, who was very dear to him, and also to his son Charles of Bohemia, who at that time styled himself King of Germany, and by general consent was its king thanks to the influence and support of his father

and of the King of France. Indeed, he had already assumed the arms of the Empire.

King Philip urgently requested them to join him with all their available forces in the campaign he was preparing against the English who were ravaging his country. They made no excuses, but assembled men from Germany, Bohemia and Luxemburg and came to France in strength to aid its king. The latter also wrote to the Duke of Lorraine, who brought more than four hundred lances to serve him. The Count of Salm, the Count of Saarbrück, the Count of Flanders and Count William of Namur came also, each with a very handsome company. King Philip sent another letter with a special summons to Sir John of Hainault[1] who had recently become his ally through the influence of his son-in-law, Count Louis of Blois, and of the Lord of Fagnolle. Sir John responded by bringing a large and splendidly equipped force of good knights from Hainault and elsewhere. His arrival so delighted the King that he attached him to his personal service and made him a member of his inner council. In this way the King of France summoned fighting men from every possible quarter and assembled one of the largest forces of great lords, dukes, counts, barons and knights that had been seen in France for a hundred years. But he had to bring them from such distant countries that it took a long time to collect them; and meanwhile the King of England had devastated the whole region of Cotentin and Normandy.

The tale of plunder continues. The inhabitants, who have never experienced war, flee at the mere mention of the English, leaving their houses and barns filled with provisions for the taking. The army find an abundance of everything they need except wine, and there are reasonable stocks even of that. They capture Saint-Lô, where they acquire such quantities of cloth that 'they would have let it go cheap if they had had anyone to sell it to.'

When the King of England and his men had done as they pleased with the town of Saint-Lô, they marched on towards Caen, which was three times larger and full of wealth in the form of cloth and other goods, with rich citizens, noble ladies and very fine churches. In particular, there are two big and extremely wealthy abbeys, that of St Stephen and that of the Trinity, situated at either end of the town. One of them housed a hundred and twenty nuns, all fully endowed. Besides this, one of the strongest and finest castles in Normandy lies on one side of the town. Its captain at that time was a gallant Norman knight called Sir Robert de Wargnies, commanding a garrison of three hundred Genoese.

In the town itself were the Count of Eu and Guines, Constable of France, and the Count of Tancarville with a large number of good fighting men. The King of England advanced cautiously towards them, ordered his columns to join up, and encamped that night in open country five miles from the town. His fleet kept constantly near him and came to a port called Ouistreham, some six miles from Caen on the River Orne, which flows through Caen. The Constable of France and the other lords with him kept good watch over the town that night and were not over concerned about the English. The next morning they armed themselves, ordering their men and all the townspeople to do the same, and then held a council to decide their plan of action. The Constable and the Count of Tancarville wished to keep all their forces in the town to hold the gates, the bridge and the river, and to abandon the outskirts to the English because they were not fortified. It would be difficult enough to hold the main part of the town, since the river was its only line of defence.

The townspeople refused to agree and insisted on marching out to the fields to meet the English there, saying that they were numerous and strong enough to fight them. When the Constable heard their decision, he replied: 'So be it then, and God be with us. If you fight, I and my men will fight with you.' They marched out of the town in good enough order at the beginning. They seemed ready to risk their lives courageously and to put up a good defence.

On that day the English rose very early and made ready to advance. The King heard mass before sunrise, then mounted his horse, as did his son the Prince and Sir Godfrey of Harcourt, on whose advice the King largely relied. They moved forward in perfect order, with the Marshals' banner-bearers in the van, until they came

close to the town of Caen and its defenders. These were waiting drawn up in the fields, apparently in excellent shape. But no sooner did the townsmen see the English advancing upon them in three solid, close-ordered divisions and catch sight of the banners and the innumerable pennons waving and fluttering in the wind and hear the shouting of the archers—all things of which they had had no previous experience— than they were so filled with dismay that nothing in the world could have stopped them taking to their heels. They turned and fled in confusion, in spite of everything the Constable could do. In a few moments their whole order of battle had broken up and they were rushing in terror to reach the safety of the town. Many of them stumbled and fell in the struggle to escape, while others piled on top of them in their panic.

The Constable and the Count of Tancarville with a few knights reached a gate at the entry to the bridge in safety. Since their men had broken, they could see that the battle was already lost. The English were now among them, killing as they liked without mercy. A few knights and squires and others who knew the way managed to reach the castle, where they were admitted by Sir Robert de Wargnies, who had plenty of room and provisions. There they were out of danger. Meanwhile the English, men-at-arms and archers, were continuing the slaughter of the fugitives, sparing none. Looking out from the gate-tower where they had taken refuge and seeing the truly horrible carnage which was taking place in the street, the Constable and the Count began to fear that they themselves might be drawn into it and fall into the hands of archers who did not know who they were. While they were watching the massacre in dismay, they caught sight of a gallant English knight with only one eye, called Sir Thomas Holland, and five or six other knights with him. They recognized him because they had campaigned together in Granada and Prussia and on other expeditions, in the way in which knights do meet each other. They were much relieved when they saw him and called out to him as he passed: 'Sir Thomas, come and speak to us.' On hearing his own name the knight stopped dead and asked: 'Who are you, sirs, who seem to know me?' They gave their names, saying: 'We are so-and-so. Come to us in this gate-tower and make us your prisoners.'

When he heard this Sir Thomas was delighted, not only because he could save their lives but also because their capture meant an excellent day's work and a fine haul of valuable prisoners, enough to bring in a hundred thousand gold *moutons*. So he brought the whole of his troop to the spot as quickly as possible and went up with sixteen of his men into the gate-tower, where he found the lords who had called to him and at least twenty-five knights with them, all looking very uneasy at the slaughter they could see in the town. They surrendered immediately and pledged themselves to be Sir Thomas' prisoners. Leaving sufficient of his men to guard them, the knight rode on through the streets. He was able that day to prevent many cruel and horrible acts which would otherwise have been committed, thus giving proof of his kind and noble heart. Several gallant English knights who were with him also prevented a number of evil deeds and rescued many a pretty townswoman and many a nun from rape.

Fortunately for the English, the river which flows through Caen and which can float large ships was so low and sluggish that they could easily pass it without troubling about the bridge.

In this way the King of England became master of Caen, though at a heavy price in men. For some of the inhabitants went up to the garrets overhanging the narrow streets and flung down stones and beams and masonry, killing and injuring several hundred of the English. The King was enraged when this was reported to him in the evening and gave orders for the whole population to be put to the sword on the next day and the town to be set on fire. Sir Godfrey of Harcourt forestalled this order by saying to him:

'Beloved sire, be a little less impetuous and content yourself with what you have done. You still have a long way to go before you reach Calais, as you intend. There are large numbers of people in this town who will defend themselves from house to house if they are attacked. To destroy the place might cost you dear and cripple your expedition. Remember that your enemy King Philip is certain to march against you in full strength and engage you, for good or ill, so there is still plenty of fighting before you, for which you will need all the forces you have and more. We can be masters of this town without further killing. Both men and women will be quite ready to give up everything they have to us.'

Sir Godfrey sent his banner through all the streets and had it proclaimed, in the King's name, that none should dare, on pain of the gallows, to start a fire, kill a man or rape a woman.

This proclamation reassured the townspeople and they allowed some of the English into their homes, without attempting to harm them. Some opened their chests and strong-boxes and gave up all they had, on condition that their lives were spared. But notwithstanding this and the orders of the King and the Marshal, there were many ugly cases of murder and pillage, of arson and robbery, for in an army such as the King of England was leading it was impossible that there should not be plenty of bad characters and criminals without conscience.

For three days the English remained in possession of Caen, where they won an amazing quantity of wealth for themselves. They used the time to put their affairs in order and sent boats and barges laden with their gains—clothes, jewelry, gold and silver plate and many other valuable things—down the river to Ouistreham where their main fleet lay. They decided after long deliberation to send the fleet back to England with the booty and the prisoners. The Earl of Huntingdon remained in command of it, with two hundred men-at-arms and four hundred archers. The King of England bought the Count of Guines, Constable of France, and the Count of Tancarville from Sir Thomas Holland and his companions for twenty thousand nobles in cash.

So the King sent back his fleet full of conquered spoils and of good prisoners, including more than sixty knights and three hundred wealthy citizens, with a host of loving greetings to his wife, my lady Philippa, the gracious Queen of England.

The English ravage the country west of the Seine, but without attacking the fortified places, 'because the King wished to husband his men and artillery (i.e., siege-engines).' They follow the left bank of the river as far as Poissy, some twenty miles from the capital.

They found all the bridges over the Seine destroyed, so went on until they came to Poissy. Here the bridge had also been broken down, but the piles and cross-beams were still in the river. The King halted there for five days until the bridge had been rebuilt strongly enough for his army to cross with ease and safety. His Marshals made forays nearly to Paris, burning Saint-Germain-en-Laye and La Montjoie, Saint-Cloud, Boulogne and Bourg-le-Reine. At this the people of Paris grew alarmed, for the city was not fortified at that time and they were afraid that the English would come right into it.

King Philip bestirred himself and had all the penthouses in Paris removed to make it easier for his men to ride through the streets. Then he prepared to leave for Saint-Denis, where the King of Bohemia, Sir John of Hainault, the Duke of Lorraine, the Counts of Flanders and Blois and many barons and knights were waiting.

When the people of Paris saw that their King was leaving, they were more alarmed than ever. They came and knelt before him, saying: 'Beloved sire and noble king, what are you about to do? Will you abandon your good city of Paris in this way? The enemy are only five miles from us. When they hear that you have gone they will be here in an instant, and we shall have no one to defend us against them. Sire, we beg you to stay and help protect your loyal city.'

The King answered: 'My good people, you have nothing to fear. The English will come no nearer. I am going to Saint-Denis to be with my soldiers, for I mean to march against the English and fight them, whatever the outcome.'

In this way the King of France calmed the people of Paris, who were in great fear of being attacked and destroyed, so suffering the same fate as Caen. But the King of England lodged in the Abbey of Poissy-les-Dames and held his solemn state on the Feast of the Assumption, in the middle of August. He sat at table in a sleeveless scarlet gown trimmed with ermine.

The English leave Poissy on 16 August and move rapidly north. They skirt Beauvais, burning the suburbs, and take several smaller places before they reach Vimeu, the district west of Amiens and Abbeville. King Philip is now in close pursuit with a much superior army. On his orders the bridges over the Somme have either been destroyed or are so strongly defended that the English probe in vain to find a way across. They are in danger of being hemmed in against the river. At this point in the narrative, the French are at Amiens and the English have just decamped from the neighboring town of Airaines to move to Oisemont, a few miles farther on. King Philip has sent a detachment under Sir Godemar du Fay to guard the last remaining crossing of the Somme, the ford of Blanchetaque, below Abbeville.

Having given these orders, King Philip, who was eager to come up with the English and engage them, left Amiens with his whole force. At about noon he reached Airaines, which the King of England had quitted in the early morning. The French found that large quantities of provisions had been left behind. There was meat on the spits, there were loaves and pies in the ovens, barrels and kegs of wine, and many tables ready laid, for the English had left in great haste.

At Airaines King Philip's advisers said to him: 'Sire, you should halt here and wait for the rest of your army. It is certain now that the English cannot escape you.' So the King took up his quarters in the town and, as the various lords arrived, they were lodged there also.

To return to the King of England, who was in the town of Oisemont and well aware that the King of France was following him in full strength thirsting for battle. He would have given much to be across the River Somme with his men. When his two Marshals returned in the evening, after ranging the country as far as the gates of Abbeville and reaching Saint-Valery-sur-Somme, where there had been a sharp skirmish, he called together his council and, sending for some prisoners from Vimeu and Ponthieu, he said to them in a kindly voice:

'Do any of you know of a crossing—it must be below Abbeville—by which we and our army can pass safely? If anyone can guide us to it, we will set him free with twenty of his comrades.'

There was a certain groom called Gobin Agace who knew the ford of La Blanchetaque as well as any man, having been born and bred near it and having crossed over it several times that year. This man came forward and said:

'Yes indeed, sire. I promise you on my life that I can take you to a place where you can cross quite safely. There are some shallows wide enough for twelve men to walk over abreast, with the water no higher than their knees. When the tide is in, the river is too deep to ford. But when it goes out, which happens twice a day, it is low enough to be crossed on horseback or on foot. That is the only place where it can be done, except by the bridge at Abbeville, but that is a fortified town with a strong garrison. The ford I am telling you about, my lord, has a firm bottom of white gravel which will bear the weight of carts. That is why it is called Blanchetaque.'

When the King heard this, he was as pleased as if he had won a fortune, and he said: 'Well, friend, if what you tell me proves to be true, I will set you free with all your comrades and give you a hundred gold nobles.'

'On my life I swear it,' said Gobin Agace. 'But make your arrangements now to be on the bank before sunrise.'

'Certainly,' said the King. He gave orders for the whole army to be armed and ready to move on again at the sound of the trumpets.

He slept little that night, but rose at midnight and had the trumpeters sound the signal to strike camp. Soon everything was ready, the pack-horses loaded and the wagons filled. Leaving Oisement at first light, they made such good progress guided by the groom that by sunrise they were near to the ford. But the tide was in and they could not cross, so the King was obliged to wait for the rest of his men to catch up with him. When the tide had gone out it was mid-morning and by that time Sir Godemar du Fay, the knight whom King Philip had sent to guard the crossing, had appeared with a large force on the opposite bank.

King Philip had given him a thousand men-at-arms and five thousand foot-soldiers, including the Genoese, and he had been joined on the way by large numbers of local men, so that they were at least twelve thousand strong when they drew up along the bank to dispute the crossing.

This brought no change to the King of England's plans. He ordered his Marshals to strike at once into the water and his archers to shoot steadily at the French opposite. The two Marshals of England sent their banner-bearers forward, in the name of God and St George, and followed closely themselves. The bravest knights hurled their horses into the water, with the best mounted in the lead. There were many jousts in the river and many unhorsings on both sides, for Sir Godemar and his men defended the crossing bravely. A number of his knights, with others from Artois and Picardy, had decided not to wait on the bank but to ride into the ford and fight there in order to win greater distinction. So there was, as I have said, many a joust and many a skilled piece of fighting, for the knights sent to defend the shallows were picked men who stood in good order at the neck of the crossing and clashed fiercely with the English as these came up out of the water. The Genoese also did much damage with their cross-bows, but the English archers shot so well together that it was an amazing sight to see. And while they were harassing the French, the mounted men got through.

When the English were finally across, though not without considerable losses, they spread out over the fields, with the King, the Prince of Wales and all their nobles. After this, the French order was broken and those who could get away from the ford made off like defeated men. Some went towards Abbeville, others towards Saint-Riquier. There was great slaughter among them because those on foot had no means of escape. The pursuit went on for more than three miles and many from Abbeville, Montreuil, Rue and Saint-Riquier were killed or captured. On the other hand, some of the English were attacked before they could get over the river by squires from the French army who had come out looking for a fight. These belonged in particular to the Empire, to the King of Bohemia and to Sir John of Hainault. They captured some horses and equipment and killed or wounded a number in the English rear who were still trying to cross.

King Philip had left Airaines that morning and was riding rapidly forward when news was brought him of the English crossing and Sir Godemar's defeat. He was extremely angry, for he had been expecting to find the English on the bank of the Somme and fight them there. He halted in open country and asked his Marshals what was the best thing to do. They replied: 'Sire, you cannot cross the river yourself because the tide is in again now.' So the King turned back in fury and took up his quarters in Abbeville with all his people.

When the English had scattered the enemy and cleared the ground, they formed up in excellent order, assembled their supply-train and moved off in their habitual way. Knowing that the Somme was behind them they were full of confidence. The King of England thanked and praised God many times that day for bringing him safely over the water and making him overcome his enemies in battle. He then sent for the groom who had guided him to the ford, set him free with all his comrades, and gave him a hundred gold nobles and a good horse. I do not know what became of him afterwards.

As the King and his army rode slowly and joyfully along, they thought of quartering for the night in the nearby town of Noyelle. But when they learnt that it belonged to the Countess of Aumale, the sister of the late Robert of Artois, they spared the town and the lady's lands for his sake—an act of friendship for which she thanked them warmly. The King halted instead in open country near La Broye, while the Marshals made an incursion to Crotoy, on the coast, which they took and burnt to the ground. In the harbor they found a number of ships and barges laden with Poitou wines which belonged to merchants from Saintonge and La Rochelle. They quickly bought up the lot and the Marshals had some of the best of them sent to the King's army encamped a few miles away.

Early the next day the King struck camp and moved towards Crécy in Ponthieu. The Marshals led their forces on either side of him. One pushed forward as far as the gates of Abbeville, then turned away towards Saint-Riquier, burning and devastating the country. The other kept near the coast and reached the town of Rue. Then at noon on that Friday the three divisions joined up again and the whole army came to halt not far from Crécy.

Knowing that the King of France was close behind him and eager for battle, King Edward said to his men:

'I will take up my position here and go no further until I have a sight of the enemy. I have good reason to wait for him, for I am on the land I have lawfully inherited from my royal mother, which was given to her as her marriage portion. I am ready to defend my claim to it against my adversary Philip of Valois.'

The King encamped in the open fields with his army and, since he was willing to risk the fortunes of battle with numbers which he knew were only an eighth of those of the King of France, he had to give urgent thought to his dispositions. He ordered his Marshals, the Earl of Warwick and Sir Godfrey of Harcourt, and with them that stout and gallant knight Sir Reginald Cobham, to consider the best place in which to draw up their forces. The three commanders rode round the fields and carefully studied the terrain to find the most advantageous position. Then they brought the King to it, with many others as well. Meanwhile, scouts had been sent out towards Abbeville, where they knew the King of France would cross the Somme, to discover if he was leaving that day to take the field. They reported that there was no sign of this.

So King Edward stood down his men for the day, with orders to assemble early next morning at the sound of the trumpets, in readiness to fight at once on the chosen positions. They all went to their quarters and busied themselves in checking and polishing their arms and armour.

The King of France spends the same day (Friday, 25 August) in Abbeville, also preparing for battle. His scouts have reconnoitered the position of the English and reported that they are evidently waiting for him. He moves some troops out of the town in readiness to march the next day. In the evening he gives a supper for the principal nobles, at which they pledge themselves to behave as brothers-in-arms. King Edward also gives a supper for his commanders and then retires to his oratory. Froissart continues:

He knelt before his altar, devoutly praying God to grant that, if he fought the next day, he should come through the business with honour. He rose fairly early in the morning and heard mass with his son the Prince of Wales. They took communion and most of their men also confessed and put themselves in a state of grace.

The King then gave orders for every man to go to the positions decided upon the day before. Close to a wood in the rear he had a large park set up, in which all the wagons and carts were put. All the horses were led into this park, leaving every man-at-arms and archer on foot. The park had only one entrance.

He caused his Constable and his Marshals to divide the army into three bodies. In the first was his son the young prince, and to fight beside him he chose the Earl of Warwick, the Earl of Oxford, Sir Godfrey of Harcourt, Sir Reginald Cobham, Sir Thomas Holland, Sir Richard Stafford, the Lord of Man, the Lord Delawar, Sir John Chandos, Sir Bartholomew Burghersh, Sir Robert Neville, Sir Thomas Clifford, the Lord Bourchier, the Lord Latimer and many other brave knights and squires, whom I cannot name in full. In the Prince's division there would have been about eight hundred men-at-arms, two thousand archers and a thousand light infantry including the Welsh. This body moved on to its positions in good order, each knight marching beneath his banner or pennon, or among his men.

In the second division were the Earls of Northampton and Arundel, the Lord Ros, the Lord Lucy, the Lord Willoughby, the Lord Basset, the Lord St Aubin, Sir Lewis Tufton, the Lord Multon, the Lord Alasselle and a number of others. This body consisted of about five hundred men-at-arms and twelve hundred archers.

The third division was the King's and was made up, as was fitting, of numerous good knights and squires, amounting to seven hundred men-at-arms and two thousand archers. When the three divisions had taken up their positions and each earl, knight and squire knew what he had to do, the King mounted a small riding-horse and, holding a white baton in his hand, rode slowly round the ranks escorted by his Marshals, encouraging his men and asking them to stand up for his honor and help defend his rights. He spoke to them in such a smiling, cheerful way that the most disheartened would have plucked up courage on hearing him. When he had gone round the whole army it was about midday. Returning to his own division, he gave orders for

all the men to stand down and eat and drink at their ease. Having done this and packed up the pots, kegs and provisions in the carts again, they went back to their battle-positions. They sat down on the ground with their helmets and bows in front of them, so as to be fresh and rested when the enemy arrived.

That Saturday morning the King of France rose early and heard mass in the Abbey of St Peter in Abbeville, where he had his quarters. All the great lords and commanders who were in Abbeville, the King of Bohemia, the Count of Alençon, the Count of Blois, the Count of Flanders and others followed his example. It should be said that not all had been quartered in Abbeville, for there would not have been room for them. Some had lodged in the surrounding villages and a large number at Saint-Riquier, which is a fortified town. The King moved out of Abbeville after sunrise with such a great force of fighting men as has been rarely seen. Accompanied by the King of Bohemia and Sir John of Hainault, he rode very slowly to allow his men to catch up with him. When he had advanced about six miles in the direction of the enemy, his officers said to him:

'Sire, it would be advisable to put your divisions in order and to let all the foot-soldiers go forward to avoid being trampled down by the horsemen. And you should send some of your knights ahead to reconnoiter the enemy's position.'

The King readily agreed and sent forward four gallant knights, Le Moine de Bazeilles, the Lord of Noyers, the Lord of Beaujeu and the Lord of Aubigny, who approached so near to the English that they obtained a very good view of their disposition. The English saw clearly what they were doing, but they made no move and let them ride off unmolested.

The four returned towards the King of France and his commanders, who had been walking their horses until they came back and halted when they saw them. The knights pushed through the crowd to reach the King, who called to them: 'Well, my lords, what news?' They looked at each other without answering, for none of them wished to be the first to speak, as a matter of courtesy towards his companions. At last the King turned to Le Moine de Bazeilles, who was esteemed as one of the bravest and most chivalrous of knights and one of the most experienced in war, and formally commanded him to give his opinion. This knight was a dependent of the King of Bohemia, who always felt more secure when he had him with him.

'Sire,' said Le Moine de Bazeilles, 'I will speak since it is your wish, subject to correction by my companions. We rode forward. We viewed the English lines. I have to report that they are drawn up in three divisions, very prettily disposed, and show no sign of intending to retreat. They are obviously waiting for you. So my advice— always subject to a better opinion—is that you should halt all your men now and encamp in the open for today. Before the rear can come up with you and you can put your divisions in some order, it will be getting late. Your men will be tired and in no sort of shape and you will find that the enemy are fresh and rested and in no doubt of the way they plan to fight. In the morning you will be able to give more thought to your battle-order and make a closer study of the enemy's position to see which is the best line of attack. You can be sure that they will still be there.'

The King fully approved this advice and ordered his Marshals to put it into execution. One of them rode forward and the other back, shouting to the standard-bearers: 'Halt banners on the King's orders, in the name of God and St Denis!' At this command the leaders halted, but those behind continued to advance, saying that they would not stop until they had caught up with the front ranks. And when the leaders saw the others coming they went on also. So pride and vanity took charge of events. Each wanted to outshine his companions, regardless of the advice of the gallant Le Moine and with the disastrous consequences of which you shall shortly hear. Neither the King nor his Marshals could restrain them any longer, for there were too many great lords among them, all determined to show their power.

They rode on in this way, in no order or formation, until they came within sight of the enemy. For what they did then the leaders were much to blame. As soon as they saw the English they reined back like one man, in such disorder that those behind were taken by surprise and imagined they had already been engaged and were retreating. Yet they still had room to advance if they wished to. Some did, while others stopped where they were.

The countryside was also covered with countless volunteers from the district. They crowded the roads between Abbeville and Crécy, and when they came within ten miles of the enemy they drew their swords and shouted: 'Kill! Kill!' Yet they hadn't seen a soul.

There is no one, even among those present on that day, who has been able to understand and relate the whole truth of the matter. This was especially so on the French side, where such confusion reigned. What I know about it comes chiefly from the English, who had a good understanding of their own battle-plan, and also from some of Sir John of Hainault's men, who were never far from the King of France.

The English, who were drawn up in their three divisions and sitting quietly on the ground, got up with perfect discipline when they saw the French approaching and formed their ranks, with the archers in harrow-formation[2] and the men-at-arms behind. The Prince of Wales's division was in front. The second, commanded by the Earls of Northampton and Arundel, was on the wing, ready to support the Prince if the need arose.[3]

It must be stressed that the French lords— kings, dukes, counts and barons—did not reach the spot together, but arrived one after another, in no kind of order. When King Philip came near the place where the English were and saw them, his blood boiled, for he hated them. Nothing could now stop him from giving battle. He said to his Marshals: 'Send forward our Genoese and begin the battle, in the name of God and St Denis.'

He had with him about fifteen thousand[4] Genoese bowmen who would sooner have gone to the devil than fight at that moment, for they had just marched over eighteen miles, in armour and carrying their crossbows. They told their commanders that they were not in a state to fight much of a battle just then. These words came to the ears of the Count of Alençon, who grew very angry and said: 'What is the use of burdening ourselves with this rabble who give up just when they are needed!'

While this argument was going on and the Genoese were hanging back, a heavy storm of rain came on and there were loud claps of thunder, with lightning. Before the rain, huge flocks of crows had flown over both armies, making a deafening sound in the air. Some experienced knights said that this portended a great and murderous battle.

Then the sky began to clear and the sun shone out brightly. But the French had it straight in their eyes and the English at their backs. The Genoese, having been marshalled into proper order and made to advance, began to utter loud whoops to frighten the English. The English waited in silence and did not stir.[5] The Genoese hulloa'd a second time and advanced a little farther, but the English still made no move. Then they raised a third shout, very loud and clear, levelled their crossbows and began to shoot.

At this the English archers took one pace forward and poured out their arrows on the Genoese so thickly and evenly that they fell like snow. When they felt those arrows piercing their arms, their heads, their faces, the Genoese, who had never met such archers before, were thrown into confusion. Many cut their bowstrings and some threw down their crossbows. They began to fall back.

Between them and the main body of the French there was a hedge of knights, splendidly mounted and armed, who had been watching their discomfiture and now cut off their retreat. For the King of France, seeing how miserably they had performed, called out in great anger: 'Quick now, kill all that rabble. They are only getting in our way!' Thereupon the mounted men began to strike out at them on all sides and many staggered and fell, never to rise again. The English continued to shoot into the thickest part of the crowd, wasting none of their arrows. They impaled or wounded horses and riders, who fell to the ground in great distress, unable to get up again without the help of several men.

So began the battle between La Broye and Crécy in Ponthieu at four o'clock on that Saturday afternoon.

The noble and gallant King of Bohemia, also known as John of Luxemburg because he was the son of the Emperor Henry of Luxemburg, was told by his people that the battle had begun. Although he was in full armour and equipped for combat, he could see nothing because he was blind. He asked his knights what the situation was and they described the rout of the Genoese and the confusion which followed King Philip's order to kill them. 'Ha,' replied the King of Bohemia. 'That is a signal for us.' He then asked for news of his son Charles, King of Germany, and was told: 'My lord, we have none. We believe he must be fighting on some other part of the field.' Then the King said a very brave thing to his knights: 'My lords, you are my men, my friends and my companions-in-arms. Today I have a special request to make of you. Take me far enough forward for me to strike a blow with my sword.'

Because they cherished his honor and their own prowess, his knights consented. Among them was Le Moine de Bazeilles, who rode beside him and would never willingly have left him, and there were several other good knights from the County of Luxemburg. In order to acquit themselves well and not lose the King in the press, they tied all their horses together by the bridles, set their king in front so that he might fulfil his wish, and rode towards the enemy.

It is true that too few great feats of arms were performed that day, considering the vast number of fine soldiers and excellent knights who were with the King of France. But the battle began late and the French had had a long and heavy day before they arrived. Yet they still went forward and preferred death to a dishonorable flight. There present were the Count of Alençon, the Count of Blois, the Count of Flanders, the Duke of Lorraine, the Count of Harcourt,[6] the Count of Saint-Pol, the Count of Namur, the Count of Auxerre, the Count of Aumale, the Count of Sancerre, the Count of Saarbrück and many other lords, barons and knights.

There also was Lord Charles of Bohemia, who bore the title and arms of King of Germany, and who brought his men in good order to the battlefield. But when he saw that things were going badly for his side, he turned and left. I do not know which way he went.

Not so the good King his father, for he came so close to the enemy that he was able to use his sword several times and fought most bravely, as did the knights with him. They advanced so far forward that they all remained on the field, not one escaping alive. They were found the next day lying round their leader, with their horses still fastened together.

The King of France was in great distress when he saw his army being destroyed piecemeal by such a handful of men as the English were. He asked the opinion of Sir John of Hainault, who was at his side. 'Well, sire,' Sir John answered, 'the only advice I can give you now is to withdraw to some place of safety, for I see no hope of recovery. Also, it will soon be dark and you might just as easily fall in with your enemies and meet disaster as find yourself among friends.'

The King, shaking with anger and vexation, made no immediate reply, but rode on a little farther as though to reach his brother the Count of Alençon, whose banners he could see at the top of a small rise. The Count was launching a very well-ordered attack on the English, as was the Count of Flanders from another quarter. They moved their forces along the flank of the archers and reached the Prince of Wales's division, which they engaged fiercely for a long time. King Philip would gladly have joined them had it been possible, but there was such a throng of archers and men-at-arms in front of him that he could not get through. The farther he advanced, the smaller his numbers grew....

The lateness of the hour harmed the French cause as much as anything, for in the dark many of the men-at-arms lost their leaders and wandered about the field in disorder only to fall in with the English, who quickly overwhelmed and killed them. They took no prisoners and asked no ransoms, acting as they had decided among themselves in the morning when they were aware of the huge numbers of the enemy.

Yet some French knights and squires, and with them Germans and Savoyards, succeeded in breaking through the Prince of Wales's archers and engaging the men-at-arms in hand-to-hand combat with swords. There was much brave and skilful fighting. On the English side, Sir Reginald

Cobham and Sir John Chandos distinguished themselves, as well as others too numerous to be named, for all the flower of the English knighthood was there with the Prince. At that point the Earls of Northampton and Arundel, commanding the second division on the wing, sent support over to the Prince's division. It was high time, for otherwise it would have had its hands full. And because of the danger in which those responsible for the Prince found themselves, they sent a knight to King Edward, who had his position higher up on the mound of a windmill, to ask for help.

When he reached the King, the knight said: 'Sire, the Earls of Warwick and Oxford and Sir Reginald Cobham, who are with the Prince, are meeting a very fierce attack by the French. So they ask you to bring your division to their support, because if the attack grows any heavier, they fear it will be about as much as your son can deal with.' The King asked the knight, whose name was Sir Thomas of Norwich: 'Is my son dead or stunned, or so seriously wounded that he cannot go on fighting?' 'No, thank God,' replied the knight, 'but he is very hard pressed and needs your help badly.'

'Sir Thomas,' the King answered, 'go back to him and to those who have sent you and tell them not to send for me again today, as long as my son is alive. Give them my command to let the boy win his spurs, for if God has so ordained it, I wish the day to be his and the honor to go to him and to those in whose charge I have placed him.'

The knight went back to his commanders and gave them the King's message. It heartened them greatly and they privately regretted having sent him. They fought better than ever and must have performed great feats of arms, for they remained in possession of the ground with honor.

Late in the evening, as it was growing dark, King Philip left the field in despair, accompanied by five lords only. These were Sir John of Hainault, the first and nearest to him, and the Lords of Montmorency, Beaujeu, Aubigny, and Montsault. The King rode lamenting and mourning for his men until he came to the castle of La Broye. He found the gate shut and the drawbridge up, for it was now fully night and pitch-dark. He called for the captain of the castle, who came to the look-out turret and shouted down: 'Who comes knocking at this hour?' 'Open your gate, captain,' King Philip answered. 'It is the unfortunate King of France.'

The captain came out at once, recognizing the King's voice and having already heard of the defeat from fugitives who had passed the castle. The drawbridge was lowered and the King entered with his whole troop, but he was warned that it would be unwise to stay shut up inside there. So he and his men took a drink and left the castle again at about midnight, taking guides with them who knew the country. They rode so hard that by daybreak they reached Amiens, where the King stopped and lodged in an abbey, saying he would go no farther until he had news of the fate of all his army.

It must be said that fearful losses had been inflicted on the French and that the kingdom of France was greatly weakened by the death of so many of her brave nobility. If the English had mounted a pursuit, as they did at Poitiers, they would have accounted for many more, including the King himself. But this did not happen. On the Saturday they never once left their lines to pursue the enemy, but stayed on their positions to defend themselves against attack.

Froissart insists again on the part played by the English archers, and repeats that a decisive factor was the discomfiture of the Genoese crossbowmen at the beginning, with the confusion into which this threw the French horsemen. He says his last word on the actual battle:

However, among the English there were pillagers and irregulars, Welsh and Cornishmen armed with long knives, who went out after the French (their own men-at-arms and archers making way for them) and, when they found any in difficulty, whether they were counts, barons, knights or squires, they killed them without mercy. Because of this, many were slaughtered that evening, regardless of their rank. It was a great misfortune and the King of England was afterwards very angry that none had been taken for ransom, for the number of dead lords was very great.

When night had fully come and no more shouting or whooping or rallying-cries could be heard, the English concluded that the enemy were routed and the field was theirs. So they lit great numbers of lanterns and torches because it was very dark. King Edward, who had not put on his battle-helmet all that day, came down with his whole division to his son the Prince. He embraced him and said: 'Dear son, God grant that you may long go on in this way. You are indeed my son, for you have done your duty most loyally this day. You have proved yourself worthy to rule a land.' The Prince bowed very low and humbly did honor to his father, as was right.

It was natural that the English should be filled with joy when they realized that they had won the day. They hailed it as a glorious victory and were full of praise for their leaders and veteran captains. And several times that night they gave thanks to God for showing them such great mercies.

On the King's orders there were no noisy celebrations, and the night passed quietly. When Sunday morning dawned there was a heavy mist, making it impossible to see farther than about fifty yards. So the King and his Marshals sent out a force of some five hundred men-at-arms and two thousand archers, who were to ride round and see if any of the French had reassembled. Levies of townsmen from Rouen and Beauvais had set out that morning from Abbeville and Saint-Riquier, knowing nothing of the previous day's defeat. To their misfortune they fell in with the English and went right up to them, thinking they were their own people. When the English recognized them, they charged down on them fiercely. There was a sharp engagement and the French were soon fleeing in disorder. More than seven thousand of them were killed in the open fields or under hedges and bushes. If the weather had been clear not a man would have escaped.

Not long after, the English ran into a force led by the Archbishop of Rouen and the Grand Prior of France, who also knew nothing of the defeat and had heard that the King of France would not fight until that Sunday. These also mistook the English for their own side and went towards them, and once again the English attacked lustily.

There was another fierce engagement, for the two French lords had some good men-at-arms with them. But they could not hold out long and soon nearly all were killed, including the two leaders. No prisoners were taken for ransom.

So the English rode about that morning looking for adventures. They came across a good many French who had lost touch with their leaders the day before and had slept out in the open. These met with short shrift at their hands, being all put to the sword. I was told that the number of levies from the cities and towns who were killed on that Sunday morning was over four times greater than the number who died in the main battle on the Saturday.

The King of England was just coming away from mass when his horsemen and archers returned from their reconnaissance. They reported all they had seen and done and said that there was no sign that the French were re-forming. The King therefore decided to have the dead examined to find out what nobles had fallen. Two gallant knights, Sir Reginald Cobham and Sir Richard Stafford, were instructed to go out, taking with them three heralds to identify the dead by their arms and two clerks to write down their names. They were amazed at the number they found. They searched all the fields as thoroughly as they could, working on until late evening. Returning just as the King was about to go to supper, they gave him an exact report of what they had seen. Eleven princes lay dead on the field, eighty bannerets, twelve hundred ordinary knights and about thirty thousand other men....[7]

The English remained there for that night and prepared to leave on the Monday morning. As an act of grace the King caused the bodies of all the chief nobles to be taken up and buried in consecrated ground in the nearby church at Maintenay. He accorded the people of the district a three days' truce to go over the battlefield and bury the other dead. He then made for Montreuil-sur-mer, while his Marshals went towards Hesdin and burnt Waben and Beaurain. But the castle at the last place was too strong for them to do any damage to it. They camped that Monday by the river which runs through Hesdin, on the Blangy side, and went on towards Boulogne the next day. On

their way they burnt Saint-Josse and Neufchâtel, and then Étables and Rue and the country round Boulogne. They passed between the woods of Boulogne and the Forest of Hardelot until they came to the large town of Wissant. There the King, the Prince and the whole army took up their quarters and rested for one day. On the Thursday they left it and came before the fortified town of Calais.

Consequences of Poitiers

The Three Estates; The Free Companies

If the English and their allies were jubilant at the capture of King John, the kingdom of France was deeply disturbed by it. There was cause enough, for it brought loss and suffering to people of all conditions, and the wiser heads predicted that greater evils were to come. Their sovereign was a prisoner and all the best of their knights were also in prison or dead, and the three princes who had escaped, Charles, Louis and John, were very young in age and experience, so there was little chance of recovery through them.

In addition, those knights and squires who had returned from the battle were so blamed and detested by the commons that they were reluctant to go into the big towns. There was much intriguing and mutual recrimination, until some of the wiser ones realized that things could not be allowed to go on in this way, but that something must be done about it. There was a force of English and Navarrese in the Cotentin, under Sir Godfrey of Harcourt, which was ranging over the whole region and laying it waste.

So all the prelates of the Church, bishops and abbots, all the nobility, lords and knights, the Provost of the merchants of Paris[8] and the burgesses, and the councillors of the French towns, met together in Paris to consider how the realm should be governed until their King should be set free. They also wanted to find out what had happened to the vast sums which had been raised in the past through tithes, levies on capital, forced loans, coinings of new money and all the other extortionate measures by which the population had been tormented and oppressed while the soldiers remained underpaid and the country inadequately protected. But of these matters no one was able to give an account.

It was therefore agreed that the prelates should elect twelve good men from among them, with powers, as representatives of the clergy, to devise suitable means of dealing with the situation described. The barons and knights also elected twelve of the wisest and shrewdest of their number to attend to the same matters, and the burgesses twelve in the same way. It was then decided by common consent that these thirty-six persons should meet frequently in Paris to discuss the affairs of the realm and put them in order. Questions of all kinds were to be referred to these Three Estates. Their acts and ordinances were to be binding on all the other prelates, nobles and common people of the cities and towns. Nevertheless, even at the beginning, several of those elected were viewed unfavorably by the Duke of Normandy[9] and his council.

As a first measure, the Three Estates stopped the coining of the money then being minted and took possession of the dies. Secondly, they required the Duke to arrest his father's Chancellor, with Sir Robert de Lorris, Sir Simon de Bucy, Jean Poillevilain [Master of the Mint] and the other financial officers and former counsellors of the King, in order that they should render a true account of all the funds which had been levied and collected on their advice. When these high officials heard of this, they completely disappeared and were wise to do so. They left the kingdom of France as quickly as they could and went to live in other countries until the situation should have changed.

Next, they appointed on their own authority officials with the duty of raising and collecting all the levies, taxes, tithes, loans and other duties payable to the crown and they had new coinage of fine gold minted, called *moutons*.[10] They would also have liked to have the King of Navarre[11] released from the castle of Arleux in the Cambrésis, where he was held prisoner, for many of them felt that, provided he was willing to be loyal and cooperative, the kingdom would be strengthened by such a measure, since after the defeat of Poitiers there were very few great lords who could act as leaders. They therefore requested the Duke of Normandy to set him free, saying that he appeared to have been greatly wronged and they did not know why he was held in prison. The Duke very prudently replied that he dared not release him nor advocate doing so, since it was his father the King who had put him there for reasons which he did not know. The King of Navarre was consequently not released just then.

At that time a knight called Sir Regnault de Cervoles, commonly known as the Archpriest, took command of a large company of men-at-arms assembled from many countries. These found that their pay had ceased with the capture of King John and could see no way of making a living in France. They therefore went towards Provence, where they took a number of fortified towns and castles by assault and plundered the whole country as far as Avignon under the sole leadership of Sir Regnault. Pope Innocent VI and his cardinals who were at Avignon at that date were in such fear of them that they hardly knew where to turn and they kept their household servants armed day and night. After the Archpriest and his men had pillaged the whole region, the Pope and his College opened negotiations with him. He entered Avignon with most of his followers by friendly agreement, was received with as much respect as if he had been the King of France's son, and dined several times at the palace with the Pope and the cardinals. All his sins were remitted him and when he left he was given forty thousand crowns to distribute among his companions. The company left the district but still remained under the command of the Archpriest.

At that time also there arose another company of men-at-arms and irregulars from various countries, who subdued and plundered the whole region between the Seine and the Loire. As a result, no one dared to travel between Paris and Vendôme, or Paris and Orléans, or Paris and Montargis, and no one dared to remain there. All the inhabitants of the country districts fled to Paris or Orléans. This company had a Welsh captain called Ruffin,[12] who had himself made a knight and became so powerful and rich that his wealth was uncountable. These companions often carried their raids almost to Paris, or at other times towards Orléans or Chartres. No place was safe from being attacked and pillaged unless it was very strongly defended.... They ranged the country in troops of twenty, thirty or forty and they met no one capable of putting up a resistance to them. Elsewhere, along the coast of Normandy, there was a larger company of English and Navarrese pillagers and marauders commanded by Sir Robert Knollys, who conquered towns and castles in the same way and also found no one to oppose them. This Sir Robert Knollys had been following this practice for a long time and had acquired at least a hundred thousand crowns. He had a large number of mercenaries at his command and paid them so well that they followed him eagerly.

These activities of what were known as the Free Companies, who attacked all travellers carrying valuables, began under the administration of the Three Estates. The nobles and the prelates began to grow tired of the institution of the Estates and left the Provost of the Merchants and some of the burgesses of Paris to go their own way, finding that these were interfering more than they liked with the conduct of affairs.

It happened one day, when the Duke of Normandy was at the palace with a large company of nobles, knights and prelates, that the Provost of the Merchants also assembled a great crowd of the common people of Paris who supported him, all wearing similar caps by which they could recognize each other. He went to the palace surrounded by his men and entered the Duke's room, where he asked him very sharply to shoulder responsibility for the affairs of the realm and give some thought to them, so that the kingdom—which would eventually be his—should be properly protected from the depredations of the Free Companies. The Duke replied that he would be quite ready to do so if he had the means at his disposal, but that it should be done by whoever collected the revenue and taxes belonging to the realm.

I do not know exactly how it happened, but such an angry argument arose that there, in the presence of the Duke of Normandy, three of the chief members of his council were killed, so close to him that his robe was splashed with blood and

he himself was in great danger. But he was given one of the people's caps to put on his head and was forced to pardon the murder of his three knights, two of them soldiers and the third a legal officer. The first were Sir Robert de Clermont, a nobleman of high standing, and the Lord of Conflans. The lawyer was Master Regnault d'Acy, the Advocate General.

On the initiative of the Provost, the King of Navarre is released from prison and brought to Paris. (Although Froissart places this after the killings just described, it occurred in fact some three months before them.)

When the King of Navarre had been in Paris for a short time, he called together a variety of people, prelates, knights, clerks of the University of Paris and any others who wished to attend, and delivered a speech to them. Speaking at first in Latin, with the Duke of Normandy present, he complained very temperately and reasonably of the wrongs and violence which had been done to him without good cause. He said that no one should feel any fear of him, since he was ready to live and die defending the kingdom of France— as indeed he was bound to, for he was descended in the direct line on both his father's and his mother's side. And he let it be understood clearly enough that, if he ever wished to lay claim to the French crown, he could show that he had a better right to it than the King of England. His speech and his arguments were listened to with approval, and in such ways he gradually acquired great popularity among the Parisians, until they came to prefer him to the Regent, the Duke of Normandy. The same thing happened in a number of other French cities and towns.

The Jacquerie (1358)

Not long after the King of Navarre had been set free, there were very strange and terrible happenings in several parts of the kingdom of France. They occurred in the region of Beauvais, in Brie and on the Marne, in Valois, in Laonnais, in the fief of Coucy and round Soissons. They began when some of the men from the country towns came together in the Beauvais region. They had no leaders and at first they numbered scarcely a hundred. One of them got up and said that the nobility of France, knights and squires, were disgracing and betraying the realm, and that it would be a good thing if they were all destroyed. At this they all shouted: 'He's right! He's right! Shame on any man who saves the gentry from being wiped out!'

They banded together and went off, without further deliberation and unarmed except for pikes and knives, to the house of a knight who lived near by. They broke in and killed the knight, with his lady and his children, big and small, and set fire to the house. Next they went to another castle and did much worse; for, having seized the knight and bound him securely to a post, several of them violated his wife and daughter before his eyes. They killed the wife, who was pregnant, and the daughter and all the other children, and finally put the knight to death with great cruelty and burned and razed the castle.

They did similar things in a number of castles and big houses, and their ranks swelled until there were a good six thousand of them. Wherever they went their numbers grew, for all the men of the same sort joined them. The knights and squires fled before them with their families. They took their wives and daughters many miles away to put them in safety, leaving their houses open with their possessions inside. And those evil men, who had come together without leaders or arms, pillaged and burned everything and violated and killed all the ladies and girls without mercy, like mad dogs. Their barbarous acts were worse than anything that ever took place between Christians and Saracens. Never did men commit such vile deeds. They were such that no living creature ought to see, or even imagine or think of, and the men who committed the most were admired and had the highest places among them. I could never bring myself to write down the horrible and shameful things which they did to the ladies. But, among other brutal excesses, they killed a knight, put him on a spit, and turned him at the fire and roasted him before the lady and her children. After about a dozen of them had violated the lady, they tried to force her and the children to eat the knight's flesh before putting them cruelly to death.

They had chosen a king from among them who came, it was said, from Clermont in Beauvaisis; and they elected the worst of the bad. This king was called Jack Goodman. Those evil men burned more than sixty big houses and castles in the Beauvais region round Corbie and Amiens and Montdidier. If God had not set things right by His grace, the mischief would have spread until every community had been destroyed and Holy Church afterwards and all wealthy people throughout the land, for men of the same kind committed similar acts in Brie and in Pertois. All the ladies of the region, with their daughters, and the knights and squires, were forced to flee one after another to Meaux in Brie as best they could, in no more than their tunics. This happened to the Duchess of Normandy and the Duchess of Orléans and to a number of other great ladies, like the humbler ones, as their only alternative to being violated and then murdered.

Other wicked men behaved in just the same way between Paris and Noyon, and between Paris and Soissons and Ham in Vermandois, and throughout the district of Coucy. That was where the worst violators and evil-doers were. In that region they pillaged and destroyed more than a hundred castles and houses belonging to knights and squires, killing and robbing wherever they went. But God by His grace provided a remedy— for which He is devoutly to be thanked—in the manner of which you shall now hear.

When the gentry of the Beauvaisis and of the other districts where those wicked men assembled and committed their barbarous deeds saw their houses destroyed and their friends killed, they sent to their friends in Flanders, Hainault, Brabant and Hesbaye to ask for help. Soon they arrived in considerable numbers from all sides. The foreign noblemen joined forces with those of the country who guided and led them, and they began to kill those evil men and to cut them to pieces without mercy. Sometimes they hanged them on the trees under which they found them. Similarly the King of Navarre put an end to more than three thousand of them in one day, not far from Clermont in Beauvaisis. But by then they had increased so fast that, all taken together, they easily amounted to a hundred thousand men. When they were asked why they did these things, they replied that they did not know; it was because they saw others doing them and they copied them. They thought that by such means they could destroy all the nobles and gentry in the world, so that there would be no more of them....

At the time when these evil men were plaguing the country, the Count of Foix and his cousin the Captal de Buch came back from Prussia. On the road, when they were about to enter France, they heard of the dreadful calamities which had overtaken the nobility, and were filled with horror. They rode on so fast that they reached Châlons in Champagne in a single day. Here there were no troubles from the villeins, for they were kept out from there. They learnt in that city that the Duchess of Normandy and the Duchess of Orléans and at least three hundred other ladies and their daughters, as well as the Duke of Orléans, were waiting at Meaux in a state of great anxiety because of the *Jacquerie*. The two gallant knights decided to visit the ladies and take them whatever support they could, although the Captal de Buch was English. But at that time there was a truce between the Kingdoms of France and of England, so that the Captal was free to go wherever he wished. Also he wanted to give proof of his knightly qualities, in company with the Count of Foix. Their force was made up of about forty lances and no more, for they were on their way back from a journey abroad, as I said.

They rode on until they came to Meaux in Brie. There they went to pay their respects to the Duchess of Normandy and the ladies, who were overjoyed to see them arrive, for they were in constant danger from the Jacks and villeins of Brie, and no less from the inhabitants of the town, as it soon became plain. When those evil people heard that there were a large number of ladies and children of noble birth in the town, they came together and advanced on Meaux, and were joined by others from the County of Valois. In addition, those of Paris, hearing of this assembly, set out one day in flocks and herds and added their numbers to the others. There were fully nine thousand of them altogether, all filled with the most evil intentions. They were constantly reinforced by men from other places who joined them along the various roads which converged on Meaux. When they reached that town, the wicked people inside did not prevent them from entering, but opened the gates and let them in. Such multitudes passed through that all the streets were filled with them as far as the market-place.

Now let me tell you of the great mercy which God showed to the ladies, for they would certainly have been violated and massacred, great ladies though they were, but for the knights who were in the town, and especially the Count of Foix and the Captal de Buch. It was these two who made the plan by which the villeins were put to flight and destroyed.

When these noble ladies, who were lodged in the marketplace—which is quite strong, provided it is properly defended, for the River Marne runs round it—saw such vast crowds thronging towards them, they were distracted with fear. But the Count of Foix and the Captal de Buch and their men, who were ready armed, formed up in the market-place and then moved to the gates of the market and flung them open. There they faced the villeins, small and dark and very poorly armed, confronting them with the banners of the Count of Foix and the Duke of Orléans and the pennon of the Captal de Buch, and holding lances and swords in their hands, fully prepared to defend themselves and to protect the market-place.

When those evil men saw them drawn up in this warlike order—although their numbers were comparatively small—they became less resolute than before. The foremost began to fall back and the noblemen to come after them, striking at them with their lances and swords and beating them down. Those who felt the blows, or feared to feel them, turned back in such panic that they fell over each other. Then men-at-arms of every kind burst out of the gates and ran into the square to attack those evil men. They mowed them down in heaps and slaughtered them like cattle; and they drove all the rest out of the town, for none of the villeins attempted to take up any sort of fighting order. They went on killing until they were stiff and weary and they flung many into the River Marne.

In all, they exterminated more than seven thousand Jacks on that day. Not one would have escaped if they had not grown tired of pursuing them. When the noblemen returned, they set fire to the mutinous town of Meaux and burnt it to ashes, together with all the villeins of the town whom they could pen up inside.

After that rout at Meaux, there were no more assemblies of the Jacks, for the young Lord de Coucy, whose name was Sir Enguerrand, placed himself at the head of a large company of knights and squires who wiped them out wherever they found them, without pity or mercy.

The Last Days of Étienne Marcel (1358)

Meanwhile the burghers of Paris under Étienne Marcel have acquired control of the city and completed its fortifications. They are virtually besieged by the Regent, who has withdrawn to the outskirts from which he harries the capital with a strong force of mercenaries. The King of Navarre also leaves the capital and installs himself at Saint-Denis with his own army of mercenaries. These are ostensibly maintained for the protection of the Parisians, who are providing their pay. But, while pretending to support the burghers, the King enters into a secret pact with the Regent.

The Provost of the Merchants and his faction, knowing that they had incurred the resentment and hatred of their sovereign lord the Duke of Normandy, began to feel uneasy. They often visited the King of Navarre at Saint-Denis, pointing out to him gently but plainly that he was the cause of the danger in which they found themselves; for they had freed him from prison and brought him to Paris and would gladly have made him their lord and king had they been able to, and had indeed connived at the killing of the three councillors in the palace because they were opposed to him. They entreated him not to fail them or to place too much trust in the Duke of Normandy and his council. The King of Navarre, realizing that the Provost and his supporters were growing anxious and reassured them as well as he could by saying: 'My dear sirs and friends, you will never suffer any harm from me. Now, while you are in control of Paris with no one daring to thwart you, I would advise you to make provision for the future by building up a fund of gold and silver in some place where you

can lay hands on it in case of need. If you send it here to Saint-Denis and entrust it to me, I will keep it for you and use it secretly to maintain a force of men-at-arms with whom you can fight your enemies if necessary.' The Provost of the Merchants agreed to this. Twice a week from then on he sent two pack-horses laden with florins to Saint-Denis to the King of Navarre, who received them with jubilation.

Now it happened that inside Paris itself there had remained a large number of English and Navarrese mercenaries who had been retained by the Provost and the commons to help defend them against the Duke of Normandy. As long as the fighting lasted these men had behaved loyally and well. When peace was made between them and the Duke, some of them left, but not all. Those who left went to the King of Navarre, who took them on his strength, but more than three hundred stayed on in Paris, enjoying themselves and spending their money freely, as soldiers do in such towns. A disturbance arose between them and the Parisians, in which more than sixty of the soldiers were killed, either in the streets or in their lodgings. The Provost of the Merchants was highly incensed by this and blamed the Parisians bitterly. But nevertheless, to appease the people, he took some hundred and fifty of the soldiers and imprisoned them in the Louvre, telling the citizens, who were clamouring to kill them, that he would punish them according to their crimes. This quietened the Parisians and after nightfall the Provost, who wished to propitiate those English mercenaries, released them from prison and sent them on their way. They all joined the King of Navarre at Saint Denis....

When they were all assembled at Saint-Denis, they decided to avenge their comrades and the treatment inflicted on themselves. They sent a declaration of war to the Parisians and began to rove about outside the city killing and hacking to pieces any of the inhabitants who were bold enough to venture out. These were in such fear of the English that soon no one dared to go outside the gates. For this the Provost was held responsible and, afterwards, openly accused.

When the people of Paris found themselves harried like this by the English soldiers, they were frantic with rage and demanded that the

Provost should arm some of their community and send them out to fight. He agreed and said he would go with them, so one day they set out, over two thousand strong. Hearing that the English were somewhere near Saint-Cloud, they decided to divide into two bodies and take two separate roads, so as to make sure that the enemy should not escape them. They were to meet again at a certain spot not far from Saint-Cloud. So the two forces parted company, the Provost taking the smaller one, and spent most of the day circling around Montmartre[13] and finding no trace of what they were looking for.

About mid-afternoon the Provost, having accomplished nothing and growing tired of wandering about the country, returned to Paris by the Porte Saint-Denis. The other body knew nothing of this and stayed out longer; if they had known, they would have gone back also. In the evening they did make for home, marching without order, like men who had no expectation of meeting the enemy. They moved along in groups, looking thoroughly sick and tired of the whole business. Some carried their helmets in their hands or let them hang from their necks, some, through weariness and apathy, trailed their swords along the ground or wore them slung from their shoulders. Slouching along in this way, they took the road leading into Paris through the Porte Saint-Honoré. Suddenly at a turning of the road they were attacked by the English soldiers, who were at least four hundred strong and all of one sort and one mind. They dashed in shouting among the French, striking out at them lustily. Over two hundred were accounted for at the first onslaught.

Taken completely by surprise, the French were too shaken to attempt an organized resistance. They took to flight and let themselves be cut to pieces like cattle. Those who could fled back into Paris, but over seven hundred were killed in the pursuit which continued as far as the barriers of the city. The Provost was fiercely blamed for this occurrence, many saying that he had betrayed them.

The next morning, the relatives and friends of those who had been killed went out with carts and wagons to fetch their bodies and give them burial. But on the way they were ambushed by the English and over a hundred more of them were killed or wounded. The people of Paris fell into such distress and confusion that they no longer knew whom to trust. They began to murmur and be suspicious of everyone. The King of Navarre was growing cool towards them, both because of the pact with his brother-in-law the Duke of Normandy and because of the way they had attacked the English mercenaries who had remained in Paris. He was quite willing for them to be punished and so pay more dearly for that evil deed. The Duke of Normandy for his part would not intervene as long as the Parisians were still ruled by the Provost of the Merchants. He sent them a public notification in writing that he would not make peace with them unless twelve of the citizens, to be chosen by himself, were surrendered to him at discretion. It is easy to understand why the Provost and others who knew that they were inculpated were filled with alarm. They saw clearly enough, on considering the situation, that things could not continue as they were for long, for the people of Paris were beginning to cool in their enthusiasm for them and their party. They spoke of them contemptuously, and this was known to them.

Finally they concluded that if the choice lay between remaining alive and prosperous and being destroyed, it would be better for them to kill than to be killed. On that conclusion they based their whole plan of action and entered into secret negotiations with the English soldiers who were harrying Paris. A pact was made between the two parties, according to which the Provost and his supporters were to seize possession of the Porte Saint-Honoré and the Porte Sainte-Antoine and to open those two gates at midnight to a combined force of English and Navarrese, who would come ready armed to ravage and destroy Paris. These plunderers were to spare neither man nor woman, of high or low degree, but to put everyone to the sword, except for some who would be recognized by marks on their doors and windows.[14]

On the very night when this was to happen, an inspiration from God awoke some of the citizens who had an understanding with the Duke of Normandy and whose leaders were Sir Pepin des

Essarts and Sir Jean de Charny. These by divine inspiration—for so it must be supposed—learnt that Paris was to be plundered and destroyed. They immediately armed themselves and all their friends and caused the news to be whispered around secretly, so as to gain more supporters.

Pepin des Essarts and others, well armed and numerous, raised the banner of France to the cry of: 'Up with the King and the Duke!' and were followed by the people. They went to the Porte Saint-Antoine, where they found the Provost of the Merchants with the keys of the gate in his hands. There they met Jean Maillart, who had had a quarrel earlier that day with the Provost and with Josseran de Maçon[15] and had come over to the Duke of Normandy's party. Bitter accusations were hurled at the Provost and he was attacked and forced back. The people were in a tumult, clamouring and hooting. They shouted: 'Death to the Provost and his friends! They have betrayed us! Kill them!'

In the midst of the commotion the Provost, who was standing on the steps of the Saint-Antoine blockhouse, would gladly have escaped had he been able to, but was so close-pressed that he could not. Sir Jean de Charny hit him on the head with an axe and stretched him on the ground. There he was struck by Master Pierre de Fouace and others, who did not leave off until he was dead, together with six others of his faction, including Philippe Guiffart, Jean de Lille, Jean Poiret, Simon Le Paonnier and Gilles Marcel. Several other traitors were caught and put in prison. A search was made through the streets and the city was put in a state of defence and strong guards posted over it for the remainder of the night.

As soon as the Provost and his supporters had been killed or caught, which took place on the evening of Tuesday, 31 July 1358, messengers were sent in haste with the news to the Duke of Normandy, who was at Meaux. He was naturally delighted and prepared to come to Paris. But before his arrival, the King of Navarre's Treasurer, Josseran de Maçon, and Charles Toussac, an alderman of Paris, were executed as traitors on the Place de Grève. The bodies of the Provost and the others killed with him were dragged to the courtyard of St Catherine's Church in the Val des Écoliers. Gashed and naked as they were, they were laid in front of the cross in the courtyard and left there for a long time, so that any who wished to see them could do so. Afterwards they were thrown into the Seine.

Brigandry, Warfare and Predictions

Acclaimed by his supporters, the Duke of Normandy re-enters Paris and takes up residence in the Louvre. For a time Charles of Navarre continues his campaign of brigandage round Paris, but finally makes peace with the Regent. His brother Philip, however, continues to pillage the country, in connivance with the English. Elsewhere also English, or so-called English, bands maintain a reign of terror, virtually paralysing trade and agriculture.

The kingdom of France was plundered and pillaged in every direction, so that it became impossible to ride anywhere without being attacked. Sir Eustace d'Aubrecicourt maintained himself in Champagne, of which he was the virtual master. Whenever he liked he could assemble at a day's notice seven hundred to a thousand fighting men. He or his men made raids almost daily, sometimes towards Troyes, sometimes towards Provins, or as far as Château-Thierry or Châlons. The whole of the low country was at their mercy, on both sides of the Seine and the Marne. This Sir Eustace performed many fine feats of arms and no one could stand up to him, for he was young and deeply in love and full of enterprise. He won great wealth for himself through ransoms, through the sale of towns and castles, and also through the redemption of estates and houses and the safe-conducts which he provided. No one was able to travel, either merchants or others, or venture out from the cities and towns without his authority. He had a thousand soldiers in his pay and held ten or twelve fortresses.

Sir Eustace at that time was very sincerely in love with a young lady of high breeding, and she with him. There is no harm in giving her name, since she later became his lawful wife. She was Madame Isabel de Juliers, daughter of the Count of Juliers by one of the daughters of the Count of Hainault. The Queen of England was her aunt, and as a girl she had been married in England to the Earl of Kent, but he died young. This lady was still young and she had fallen in love with Sir Eustace for his great exploits as a knight, of which accounts were brought to her every day. While he was in Champagne, she sent him several hackneys and chargers, with love-letters and other tokens of great affection, by which the knight was inspired to still greater feats of bravery and accomplished such deeds that everyone talked of him.

Sir Eustace d'Aubrecicourt is defeated and captured in a skirmish, to be ransomed later. As a result, the English evacuate a number of castles, but still hold others.

Sir Peter Audley remained none the less at Beaufort and Jean de Ségur at Nogent and Albrecht at Gyé-sur-Seine. At that time there departed this life in rather strange circumstances, in the castle of La Hérelle which he held, ten miles from Amiens, Sir Jean de Picquigny, strangled, it was said, by his chamberlain. One of his most trusted knights, called Sir Lus de Bethisi, also died in the same way. May God have mercy on their souls and forgive them their misdeeds.

A very strange thing happened at about the same time to an English squire belonging to the troop of Sir Peter Audley and Albrecht. They had gone raiding one day to a village called Ronay and began plundering it just as the priest was chanting high mass. This squire entered the church and went up to the altar and, seizing the chalice in which the priest was about to consecrate the blood of Our Lord, he spilt the wine on the ground. When the priest protested, he gave him a back-hand blow with his gauntlet, so hard that the blood spurted on to the altar. After this, they all left the village and, while they were riding across the country, with the robber who had committed the outrage carrying the chalice, the plate and the communion cloth against his breast, this thing suddenly happened which I will relate; it was a true example of God's anger and vengeance and a warning to all other pillagers. His horse and he on it began whirling madly about in the fields and raising such an outcry that none dared to go near them; until at last they fell in a heap with their necks broken and were

immediately turned to dust and ashes. All this was witnessed by the comrades who were present and who were so terrified that they swore before God and Our Lady that they would never again violate a church, or rob one. I do not know whether they kept their promise.

In the autumn of 1359 Edward III led an expedition from Calais through north-eastern France with the object of bringing the Regent to heel and enforcing a peace treaty which would consolidate the gains of Poitiers. He besieged Rheims unsuccessfully before finally reaching Chartres.

While Rheims was being besieged, the English nobles were dispersed about the neighboring country, where they could live more easily and could guard the roads to stop supplies from entering the city. That fine soldier and great English baron, Lord Bartholomew Burghersh, had his quarters with his whole contingent of men-at-arms and archers in the town of Cormicy, where there was an excellent castle belonging to the Archbishop of Rheims. The Archbishop had entrusted its defence to a knight from Champagne called Sir Henry de Vaulx, who had a number of good soldiers with him. The castle seemed safe from all assaults, having a great square tower with thick walls and strong battlements.

When Lord Burghersh, having invested the castle and considered its strong construction, had seen that he could not take it by assault, he summoned a band of miners whom he had in his service and ordered them to do their work of mining the fortress, adding that they would be well paid for it. 'Right,' they said. They started their mine and by digging continually night and day they made such progress that they came right under the great tower. All the time they were mining they were putting in props, but the men in the castle did not know they were working. When the tower was directly over the mine, so that it could be brought down at any moment, the miners went to Lord Burghersh and said: 'Sir, we've pushed on so far with the job that the big tower can be dropped whenever you give the word.' 'That's good,' said the knight, 'but do nothing more until you have my orders.' 'Right,' they said.

Lord Burghersh mounted his horse and, taking one of his companions, Jean de Ghistelles, with him, he rode up to the castle and signalled that he wished to speak with the men inside. Sir Henry came on to the battlements and asked him what he wanted. 'What I want,' said Lord Burghersh, 'is for you to surrender. If not, you will all be dead men before long.' 'What?' said the French knight, beginning to laugh. 'We are all safe and sound in here and well supplied with everything we need, and you ask us to surrender like that! No sir, never.' 'Come, Sir Henry,' said the English knight, 'if you knew what a mess you were in, you would surrender at once without arguing.' 'And what mess are we in, sir?' asked the French commander. 'Just come outside and I'll show you,' said Lord Burghersh, 'on condition that if you want to go back into your tower I'll let you. You have my promise of that.'

Sir Henry took the English knight at his word and accepted the offer. He came out of his fortress with only three companions and joined Lord Burghersh and Sir Jean de Ghistelles outside. They took him at once to their mine and let him see that the great tower was only supported by wooden props. When the French knight realized the danger they were in, he said to Lord Burghersh: 'Certainly, sir, you were quite right and it was a really gentlemanly act to do what you did. We put ourselves at your disposal with everything we have with us.'

Lord Burghersh accepted them as his prisoners and brought all their men out of the tower together with their possessions. Then he had fire set to the mine. When the props burnt through, the huge square tower split down the middle and collapsed. 'Look at that,' said Lord Burghersh to Sir Henry de Vaulx and the rest of the garrison. 'Didn't I tell you?' 'Yes, sir,' they replied. 'We will remain prisoners at your discretion and we are grateful for your courteous dealing. If the Jack Goodmans who were once uppermost in this district had got the better of us as you did just now, they would never have treated us in this generous way.'

That was how the garrison of Cormicy was captured and the castle demolished.

You may like to know that on this campaign the great English lords and men of substance took with them tents of various sizes, mills for grinding corn, ovens for baking, forges for shoeing the horses and all other necessities. To carry all this, they had fully eight thousand wagons, each drawn by four good, strong rounseys which they had brought over from England. They also carried on the wagons a number of skiffs and other small boats so skillfully made from leather that they were a sight worth seeing. Each could take three men over the biggest lake or pond to fish whatever part of it they liked. This was a great standby for them at all seasons, including Lent, at least for the lords and the royal household, but the common soldiers had to manage with what they found. In addition, the King had for his personal use thirty mounted falconers and their loads of birds and sixty couples of big hounds and as many coursing-dogs, with which he went either hunting or wild-fowling every day. Many of the nobles and wealthy men also had their hounds and hawks like the King. Their army was always divided into three bodies, each moving independently with its own vanguard and rear-guard and halting for the night three miles behind the preceding one. The Prince commanded one division, the Duke of Lancaster another, and the King the third and largest. They kept this formation the whole way from Calais until they reached the city of Chartres.

In those days there was a Franciscan friar at Avignon, a very learned and intelligent man, called Brother Jean de la Rochetaillade. He was kept imprisoned by Pope Innocent VI in the castle of Bagnols because of the extraordinary misfortunes which he predicted, firstly for the prelates and princes of the Church, on account of the excessive luxury and pomp in which they lived; and also for the Kingdom of France and the great lords of Christendom, because of the way in which they oppressed the common people. This Friar John claimed to prove his utterances by the Apocalypse and the ancient books of the holy prophets, whose sense was made clear to him, he said, by the grace of the Holy Spirit. Many of his predictions were hard to believe, yet some came true within the period in which he placed them. He did not speak as a prophet, but knew about them through the old Scriptures and by the grace of the Holy Spirit—as one says—who had granted him understanding to make clear all those ancient prophecies and writings, so as to announce to all Christians the year and the date when the troubles were to come. He composed several books, well written and based on sound theological knowledge, one of which appeared in the year 1356. In it he described so many strange events for the years 1356 to 1360 that they seemed incredible, although several of them in fact occurred. And when he was asked about the war between the French and the English he replied that what had been seen so far was nothing beside what was to come, and that there would be no peace nor end before the realm of France had been wasted and destroyed in every district and region. That came true, for France was indeed ravaged, wasted and destroyed, and in particular during the time which the friar predicted, in '56, '57, '58 and '59, in all its regions, so savagely that none of the princes or nobles dared to show his face before those people of low degree, drawn from many different countries, coming one after another, with no highly placed leaders at all. And the realm was defenseless before them, as you have already heard.

Notes

1   The same man who had assisted Queen Isabella and the young Edward III in 1326-7.
2   The most plausible interpretation of this phrase, *en manière de herse*, is that the archers formed hollow wedges pointed towards the enemy, at each end of a body of foot-soldiers and positioned slightly in advance of these.
3   The King's division remained in reserve and, according to Froissart's account, took no part in the battle, as appears later.
4   Modern authorities put their numbers at six thousand at most, and perhaps much fewer.
5   In one manuscript this sentence runs: 'And the English kept quite still and fired off some cannons which they had in their battle-formation, to frighten the Genoese.' The *Chroniques Abrégées*, an abridgement of the *Chronicles* of late date attributed to Froissart, also mentions the firing of 'two or three bombards.'
6   Brother of the English commander, Sir Godfrey of Harcourt. Froissart later records that he was killed in the battle, as were nearly all the other nobles listed here.
7   Froissart's total of 1,291 for the dead nobility is reasonably close to the figure of '1,541 good men-at-arms' given by an English eye-witness, Michael de Northburgh, in a letter written a few days after the battle. Northburgh gives no figure for what he calls 'the commons and foot-soldiers,' but Froissart's 'thirty thousand' for these other ranks is usually considered to be at least three times too high. In the Amiens MS he has: 'fifteen to sixteen thousand.'
8   Étienne Marcel.
9   King John's eldest son, later Charles V. He assumed the powers of Regent within a fortnight of the defeat of Poitiers.
10 So called because one side represented the 'Lamb of God'. The coin had been current in earlier reigns.
11 Charles 'the Bad,' King of Navarre, had been seized and imprisoned by King John a few months before Poitiers.
12 Also known as 'Griffon,' so perhaps 'Griffith' or 'Gruffydd.'
13 The apparent illogicality of looking for the enemy in the wrong direction—Montmartre was north of Paris, Saint-Cloud west—seems explained by the fact, not recorded by Froissart, that the King of Navarre helped to lead the expedition and had no desire to clash with the English mercenaries.
14 In Froissart's account the villain of the piece is Étienne Marcel, and too little is made of the dubious part played by the King of Navarre in these events. In spite of his secret understanding with the Regent, he seems to have been anxious to gain possession of Paris for himself and was at least rumoured to have intended pressing on with his claim to the French throne, to the exclusion both of the Regent and of the captive King John.
15 The King of Navarre's Treasurer. According to another source, the *Grandes Chroniques de France*, Étienne Marcel had ordered the keys of one of the gates to be handed over to him, but Jean Maillart, the captain of the guard, had refused.

THE TRIAL OF JOAN OF ARC

JOAN OF ARC 1412-1431, WAS THIRTEEN YEARS OLD WHEN SHE BEGAN to hear voices urging her to help the Dauphin, Later Charles VII of France, defeat the English and claim the crown. In 1429 she convinced the Dauphin and a board of theologians of the veracity of her mission. Given an army, she decisively defeated the English and paved the way for Charles' coronation at Rheims. Subsequently, she continued to fight the English and their Burgundian allies and in 1430 was captured at the battle of Compiegne. Tried in the English-held city of Rouen by clerical allies of the English, she was condemned as a heretic for wearing masculine clothing and claiming that she was directly responsible to God. She signed a confession but was tricked into again dressing in men's clothing, upon which she was retried as a lapsed heretic and burned at the stake on May 30, 1431. Twenty-five years later the church retried the case and found her innocent. The following excerpts from the transcript from her first trial cover questions of her childhood and early experiences of the voices and visions that led her on her extraordinary mission.

Source: *The Trial of Joan of Arc*: Being the verbatim report of the proceedings from the Orleans Manuscript, translated with an Introduction and Notes by W.S. Scott (Associated Booksellers: Westport, Conn., no date [1956]). First published in 1956 by The Folio Society, London.

FIRST PUBLIC SESSION

The following day, which was Wednesday the twenty-first day of February, in the chapel royal of the castle of Rouen, in the presence of the bishop and of my lords and masters, my lord Gilles, Abbot of Fécamp, Jean Beaupère, Jean de Châtillon, Jacques le Tessier, Nicolas Midi, Gerard Feuillet, Guillaume Haiton, Thomas de Courcelles and Maître Richard Praty, were read the letters of the King of England wherein he commanded the ordinary judges of Rouen to hand over and deliver the Pucelle to the bishop to be tried; the letters of the Chapter of Rouen showing that they had given permission to the bishop to hold the trial within the territory of Rouen; and the citation to the Pucelle to appear before him, together with the account of him who had cited her.

These being read, Maître Jean Estivet, appointed promoter at the trial by the bishop, required the Pucelle to be brought and questioned in accordance with law. Which was granted by the bishop.

And since Jeanne had made a supplication that she might be allowed to hear Mass, the bishop said that he had consulted with several wise and notable persons, on whose advice he had come to the conclusion that, in view of the crimes of which she was accused, and of the fact that she wore man's dress, they ought to defer this request: and thus he declared it.

Very soon after, Jeanne was led in to the presence of the bishop and the assessors afore-mentioned.

She being present, the judge spoke to her and explained that she had been taken within the boundaries of his diocese. And since there was common report of a number of her deeds which were contrary to our faith, not only within the realm of France but in all the States in which they were known and published, and since she was accused of heresy, she had been handed over to him to be tried in a matter of faith.

After these words, the promoter showed how at his request she had been cited and convened to answer in a matter of faith, as appeared from the letters and acts which he then exhibited, begging that she should be adjured to speak the truth, and then questioned upon the accusations that he would deliver.

This was granted by the bishop and the court.

This request being granted, as has been said, the bishop caused Jeanne to come before him, and charitably admonished her.

And told her that she should tell the truth concerning the things which would be asked her, as much for the shortening of her trial as for the unburdening of her conscience, without subterfuge or craft; and that she should swear on the Holy Gospels to tell the truth concerning everything she should be asked.

Jeanne answered: I do not know on what you may wish to question me. Perhaps you may ask such things as I will not answer.

Whereupon the bishop said to her:

You will swear to tell the truth about whatever you are asked concerning the Catholic Faith, and all else that you may know.

To which Jeanne answered that concerning her father and mother, and concerning everything she had done since she took the road for France,[1] she would willingly swear. But as for revelations sent her from God, never had she told or revealed them save to Charles, who she said was her king. And if they cut her head off, she would not reveal them; for she knew from her visions that she must keep them secret. But within eight days she would know if she ought to reveal them.

After these words the bishop admonished her, and asked her to take the oath to tell the truth concerning the faith.

Jeanne knelt down, her two hands on the book, that is to say a missal, and swore that she would tell the truth in all matters asked her concerning the Faith. But that, about the aforesaid revelations, she would not tell anyone.

The same day, after several questions had been put to her concerning the name of her father and mother, the place where she was born, and her age, Jeanne complained of the fetters which she had on her legs.

She was told by the bishop that several times she had endeavoured to escape from her prisons, wherefore, in order that she might be kept the more securely, he had ordered that she should be fettered.

To which Jeanne answered that it was true that on these previous occasions she would have much liked to escape from prison, as was lawful for every prisoner. She said further that if she had been able to escape, no one could have said that she had broken faith, for she had never given her parole to anyone.

On account of this answer, the bishop ordered John Rice, John Bernard, and William Talbot,[2] to whom the guardianship of Jeanne was committed, that they should guard her strictly, and that they should not allow anyone to speak to her unless they had his express permission; and made the guards place their hands on the missal, upon which they took a solemn oath to do all that they had been ordered.

The same day, Jeanne, being questioned as to her name and surname,

Answered that, in the place where she was born, she was called Jeannette, and in France, Jeanne; of a surname she knew nothing.

Questioned as to the place of her birth,

She answered that she was born in a village called Domremy de Greux, and in Greux is the principal church.

Questioned as to the name of her father and mother,

She answered that her father was named Jacques Tart and her mother Ysabeau.

Questioned as to where she had been baptised,

She answered that it was in the church of Domremy.

Questioned as to who were her godfathers and godmothers,

She answered that they were a woman named Agnes and another called Jeanne; and a man called Jean Bavent was her godfather. She said also that she had heard her mother say that she had other godfathers and godmothers as well as these.

Questioned as to who was the priest who baptised her,

She answered that he was called Messire Jean Nynet [Minet], to the best of her belief.

Questioned as to whether the said Nynet was still alive,

She answered yes, to the best of her belief.

Questioned as to how old she was,

She answered that she was nineteen or thereabouts. She said also that her mother taught her the *Pater Noster*, *Ave Maria* and *Credo*; and that no one else save her mother taught her her faith.

Being required to repeat the *Pater Noster* and *Ave Maria*,

She answered that she would say it willingly, provided that my lord Bishop of Beauvais, who was present, would hear her confession. And although she was several times required to say the *Pater Noster* and *Ave Maria*, she answered that she would not say them unless the bishop would hear her in confession.

And then the bishop said: I will give you one or two notable persons of this company to whom you will say your *Pater Noster* and *Ave Maria*,

To which she answered: I will not say them at all, if they do not hear me in confession.

SECOND SESSION

The year one thousand four hundred and thirty, the twenty-second day of February. The bishop showed how he had summoned and required Le Maître, as general Inquisitor of the Faith, to join in the trial of Jeanne, offering to communicate to him everything that had been done at the trial.

To which Le Maître answered that he was only commissioned in the city and diocese of Rouen; and since the trial was held before the bishop, not as Ordinary of the diocese of Rouen, but as of borrowed jurisdiction, he was doubtful of joining in the matter. And although he had been doubtful as to joining in the trial, nevertheless, as much in order that the trial should not be null and void, as for the unburdening of his conscience, he was content to be present at the trial since he had inquisitorial powers.

This offer being made, Jeanne was first admonished and required to take the oath that she had taken the day before to tell the truth concerning all that would be asked her of the crimes and evils of which she was accused,

To which Jeanne answered that she had already taken the oath, and this should suffice.

And she was again ordered to swear to tell the absolute truth concerning everything that would

be asked her; assuring her that there was not a prince who could or should refuse to take the oath to tell the truth in a matter of faith.

To which she answered: I did so yesterday. You are burdening me too much.

Finally she took the oath in the form in which she had taken it the day before.

The oath being taken, the bishop ordered Maître Jean Beaupère to question her. In obedience to his orders Beaupère questioned her as follows:

Firstly he asked her if she would tell the truth.

To which she replied: You may well ask me such things that as to some I shall tell the truth, as to others, not. She said further: If you are well informed about me, you would wish that I were out of your hands. I have done nothing save by revelation.

Questioned as to what age she was when she left her father's house,

She said that she did not know the answer.

Questioned as to whether she had learned any craft or trade,

She said yes; and that her mother had taught her to sew; and that she did not believe there was any woman in Rouen who could teach her anything in this matter.

She said also that she had left her father's house partly for fear of the Burgundians; and that she went to Neufchâteau with a woman named La Rousse;[3] where she stayed a fortnight. In this house she did the household tasks, and did not go into the fields to keep the sheep or other animals.

Asked whether she made her confession every year,

She said yes, to her own curé. And if he were prevented, she confessed to another priest, with her curé's leave. And she also said that she had confessed two or three times to mendicant friars. And that she received the Body of Our Lord every year at Easter.

Asked whether she had not received the Body of Our Lord at other feasts than Easter,

She answered: Go to the next question. And she said that, from the age of thirteen, she received revelation from Our Lord by a voice which taught her how to behave. And the first time she was greatly afraid. And she said that the voice came that time at noon, on a summer's day, a fast day, when she was in her father's garden, and that the voice came on her right side, in the direction of the church. And she said that the voice was hardly ever without a light, which was always in the direction of the voice.

She said further that, after she had heard it three times, she knew that it was the voice of an angel.

She said also that this voice had always taken good care of her.

Questioned as to what teaching this voice gave her as to the salvation of her soul,

She answered that it taught her how to behave. And it said to her that she ought to go often to church. And later it said to her that it was necessary that she should go into France.

And it said to her two or three times a week that she must leave and go into France. And that her father knew nothing of her going.

And with this, it said to her that she must hurry and go and raise the siege of Orleans; and that she should go to Robert de Baudricourt, captain of Vaucouleurs; and that he would give her men to accompany her.

To which she answered that she was only a poor woman, who knew nothing of riding or of making war.

And after these words, she went to an uncle's house, where she stayed a week, after which her uncle brought her to Robert de Baudricourt, whom she recognized, although she had never seen him before.

And she said that she recognized him by her voices, which had told her that it was he.

She said further that de Baudricourt refused her twice. The third time he received her, and gave her people to conduct her to France, as the voice had told her.

[She said also that before she received her king's commands, the Duke of Lorraine asked for her to be sent to him. She went, and told him that she wished to be sent into France. He questioned her concerning his health, of which she told him she knew nothing. She said to him little about her journey, but asked him to lend her his son and some others to conduct her to France, and then she would pray God for his restoration to health.

She went to him with a safe conduct, and returned to the town of Vaucouleurs.]

She said further that when she left Vaucouleurs, she took man's dress, and also a sword which de Baudricourt gave her, but no other armour. And she said she was accompanied by a knight and four other men; and that day they spent the night in the town of Saint Urbain, where she slept in the Abbey.[4]

She said also that as for her route, she passed through Auxerre, where she heard Mass in the great church; and that she often had her voices with her.

Questioned as to who advised her to take male dress,

[To this question I have found in one book that her voices had commanded her to take man's dress; and in the other I found that, although she was several times asked, she never made any other reply than `I charge nobody.' And I found in this book that several times she answered variously.]

She said further that Robert de Baudricourt made her escort swear that they would conduct her well and safely.

She also said that when they left, de Baudricourt said to her: Go, and let come what may.

She said that she was well assured that God greatly loved the Duke of Orleans, and that she had more revelations concerning him than any man in France, except her king.

She said further that it was absolutely essential for her to change her dress.

Questioned as to what letters she sent the English and what they contained,

She said that she sent letters to the English, who were before Orleans, wherein she wrote to them that they must leave. And she said that in these letters, as she had heard it said, they have altered two or three words; for example, Render to the Pucelle, where it should be Render to the king; and where there is Body for body, and Chieftain of war; this was not in the letters.

She said also that she went to her king without hindrance.

Further, she said that she found her king at

Chinon, where she arrived about noon, and lodged at an inn, and after dinner went to the king who was in the castle.

She said that she went right into the room where the king was; whom she recognized among many others by the advice of the voice.

She said that she told the king that she wished to make war on the English.

Questioned whether, when the voice pointed the king out to her, there was any light,

She answered: Go on to the next question.

Questioned if she saw an angel above the king,

She answered: Forgive me. Pass on to the next.

She said also that before the king set her to work, he had several apparitions and glorious revelations.

Questioned as to what revelations,

She answered: I shall not tell you yet; go to the king and he will tell you.

She said further that the voice promised her that very soon after she arrived the king would receive her.

She said also that those of her party well knew that the voice came from God; and that they saw and knew the voice; and that she knows this well.

She said that the king and several members of his Council heard and saw the voices who came to her; and amongst others, Charles, Duke of Bourbon.

She said also that she never asked anything of the voice save at the last the salvation of her soul.

She said further that the voice told her that she should stay at Saint Denis in France; and there she wished to remain. But the lords were not willing to leave her there, because she was wounded; otherwise she would not have left. And she said that she was wounded in the moat of Paris; of which wound she was cured within five days.

She said that she had made a great assault on Paris.

Asked whether the day she made this assault were a feast day,

She answered, after being questioned several times, that she believed it was a feast.

Asked if she thought it a good thing to make an assault on a feast day,

She replied: Go on to the next question.

These questions and answers being done, the Bishop of Beauvais postponed the matter until the following Saturday.

THIRD SESSION

The following Saturday, which was the twenty-fourth of February, those who were there the previous day were convoked and called together by the Dean of the Christendom of Rouen.

The Bishop of Beauvais directed and admonished Jeanne to swear absolutely and without condition to tell the truth. Three times she was thus admonished and required.

To which she answered: Give me leave to speak.

And then said: By my faith, you might ask me such things as I will not tell you.

She further said: It could be that there are many things you might ask me of which I would not tell you the truth, especially concerning the revelations; for you would perhaps force me to say by mistake something that I have sworn not to say. Thus I should be perjured, which you ought not to wish.

Addressing my lord of Beauvais, she said: Beware of saying that you are my judge. For you take upon yourself great responsibility, and you overburden me.

She also stated that she thought it was enough to have taken the oath twice.

Questioned again and again as to whether she would take the oath simply and absolutely,

She answered: You can well do without it. I have sworn twice; that is enough. And I believe that all the clergy of Rouen and Paris would not condemn me save in error.

And she added that she would not have told all in a week.

She said also that, of her coming into France she will willingly tell the truth, but not everything.

As to what was told her, that she should take the advice of those present as to whether or no she should take the oath,

She answered that she would willingly tell the truth as to her coming, but nothing more. And that she should not be spoken to any more concerning the matter.

And being admonished and told that she would make herself suspect by her unwillingness to take the oath,

She answered as before.

The bishop ordering and requiring her to swear precisely and absolutely,

She answered: I shall willingly tell you what I know, but not all.

She also said that she came from God, and ought not to be here; and said that they should remit her into the hands of God, from Whom she came.

After being again and again ordered and required to take the oath and admonished to do so on pain of being found guilty of the acts imputed to her,

She answered: I have sworn enough. Leave the matter.

And when time and again she was admonished to tell the truth in what concerned her trial, it being explained to her that she was endangering herself,

She answered: I am ready to swear and to say all that I know concerning my trial. But I will not say all that I know.

After saying which, she took the oath.

These things being done, she was questioned by Maître Jean Beaupère. Firstly he asked her when she had last eaten or drunk,

To which she answered: yesterday afternoon.

Questioned since when had she heard her voice,

She answered that she had heard it both yesterday and to-day.

Questioned at what time she had heard it yesterday,

She said that she had heard it three times; once in the morning; again at the hour of Vespers; and yet again at the hour of the Ave Maria; sometimes she heard it more often than [this], she said.

Questioned as to what she was doing yesterday morning when she heard this voice,

She answered that she was asleep, and that the voice awoke her.

Asked whether the voice woke her by its sound, or by touching her on the arms or elsewhere,

She answered that she was wakened by the voice without being touched.

Questioned as to whether the voice was still in her room,

She replied that she thought not, but that it was in the castle.

Asked if she did not thank the voice, and kneel down,

She answered that she thanked it, being seated on her bed. And she said that she joined her hands together, and begged and prayed that it might help and advise her in what she had to do.

To which the voice told her to answer boldly.

Asked what the voice told her when she was awake,

She answered that it said that she must ask advice from Our Lord.

Asked whether it had said anything before she questioned it,

She said that before she was awake, the voice had said several words to her that she did not understand. But when she had wakened, she understood that the voice had told her that she must answer boldly.

She said several times to the bishop, You say that you are my judge; consider well what you do; for in truth I am sent from God, and you are putting yourself in great peril.

Asked if this voice had ever varied in its advice,

She answered that she had never found in it two contradictory words.

Asked whether it were an angel coming direct from God,[5] or if it were a saint,

She answered that it came from God.

And added, I am not telling you all I know, for I am greatly afraid of saying something displeasing to it in my answers to you.

And she said further: In this questioning I beg you that I may be allowed a delay.

Asked if she believed that God would be displeased if she told the truth,

She answered my lord of Beauvais that the voices had told her to say some things to the king and not to him.

She also said that the voice told her that night things concerning the king's good; things that she wished the king to know immediately; and that she would drink no wine till Easter, wherefore he would be happier when he dined.

Asked if she could make this heavenly voice obey her and carry a message to her king,

She answered that she did not know whether it would be willing to obey her, unless it were the will of God, and that Our Lord agreed.

And that, if it pleased God, it would be able to reveal it to the king; if so [she added] I would be very happy.

Questioned as to why she cannot now speak with her king, as she used to do in his presence,

She said that she did not know if it were God's will.

She said further that if she were not in the grace of God she could do nothing.

Asked if her counsel [her voices] had not revealed to her that she should escape,

She answered: I have [yet] to tell you this.

Asked if this voice has not now given her advice and counsel as to what she should answer,

She replied that if it had revealed or said anything to her [about this], she had not well understood it.

Questioned as to whether, on the last two days that she heard her voices, a light had appeared,

She answered that the light comes before the voice.

Asked if with the voice she sees something,

She answered: I am not going to tell you everything, for I have not permission; and also my oath does not touch that; but I do say to you that it is a beautiful voice, righteous and worthy; otherwise I am not bound to answer you.

For this reason she asked to see in writing the points upon which they desired to question her.

Asked if the voice could see; that is to say, whether it had eyes,

She answered: You may not know that yet.

She said also that there is a saying among little children that people are often hanged for telling the truth.

Asked if she knew whether she were in the grace of God,

She answered: If I am not, may God put me there; if I am, may He keep me there.

She said further that if she knew she were not in the grace of God, she would be the most miserable person in the world. She said also that if

she were in mortal sin, the voice would not come to her. And she would that everyone might hear them as well as she did.

She also said that she thought she was thirteen years of age when the voice came to her the first time.

Asked whether in her childhood she used to go and play in the fields with the others,

She said she did so sometimes. But she did not know at what age.

Asked if the people of Domremy sided with the Burgundians or the Armagnacs,

She answered that she only knew one Burgundian, whose head she would like to see chopped off, that is if it had pleased God.

Asked whether at Maxey they were Burgundians or Armagnacs,

She said they were Burgundians.

Questioned as to whether her voice told her in her childhood to hate the Burgundians,

She answered that ever since she learned that the voices were for the King of France, she did not love the Burgundians.

She added that the Burgundians would have war, if they did not do as they ought; she knew this from the voice.

Asked if the voice told her in her childhood that the English should come into France,

She said they were already in France when the voice first spoke to her.

Asked if she were ever with the other children when they played at fights between English and French,

She said no, as far as she could remember. But she had often seen those of her village fighting against those of Maxey, and sometimes coming back wounded and bleeding.

Asked if in her youth she had a great desire to defeat the Burgundians,

She answered that she had a great desire that the king should have his kingdom.

Asked if she had wanted to be a man when she knew that she had to come [into France],

She said that she had answered elsewhere.

Asked if she ever used to lead the animals to pasture,

She replied that she had already answered; and that, since she had grown up and reached years of understanding, she did not look after them;

but she did help to drive them to the meadows, and to a castle called de I'Ile, for fear of the soldiers; but as to whether she looked after them or not in her childhood, she did not remember.

Questioned concerning the tree,

She answered that quite close to Domremy there was a tree which was called the Ladies' tree; others called it the Fairies' tree; and near it there was a spring; and she had heard it said that persons suffering from fever drank of it; and she has seen them going to it to be cured. But she did not know whether they were cured or not.

She said also that she had heard that the sick, when they could get up, went to the tree to walk about; and she said it was a large tree called a beech, from whence comes the *beau mai*;[6] and it belonged to Messire Pierre de Bourlémont.[7]

She said that she sometimes went there with the other girls in summer time, and made wreaths for Notre Dame de Domremy.

She had heard several old folk say, not of her family, that the fairies frequented it; and she had heard her godmother Jeanne, wife [of the mayor of the village of Domremy], say that she had seen them there. Whether this was true, she does not know.

She said that she herself had never seen a fairy, as far as she knew, either at the tree or anywhere else.

She said further that she had seen garlands hung on the branches of the tree by the girls; and she herself had hung them there with the other girls. Sometimes they took them away, and sometimes they left them.

She also said that ever since she learned that she must come into France, she played very little, the least that she could. And she did not know whether, since she had reached years of discretion, she had danced near the tree. Sometimes she may have danced there with the children, but she more often sang than danced.

She also said that there was a wood called the Bois Chesnu that one could see from her father's house, not more than a league away; but she was unaware and had never heard it said that the fairies frequented it.

She had heard from her brother that it was said in the neighbourhood that she received her revelations at the tree and from the fairies. But she had not. And she told him quite the contrary.

She said further that when she came before the king, many people asked whether in her country there was not a wood called the *Bois Chesnu*, for there was a prophecy saying that from the Bois Chesnu should come a maiden who would perform marvellous acts; but she put no faith in it.[8]

Questioned as to whether she wanted a woman's dress.

She answered: If you give me permission, give me one, and I will take it and go. Otherwise no. I am content with this one, since it is God's will that I wear it.

After these questions were done, the following Tuesday was appointed, at eight o'clock. And the assessors were requested to assemble on that day at the said hour, under pain of displeasure.

FOURTH SESSION

The following Tuesday, which was the twenty-seventh day of the month of February, following the Sunday of Reminiscere, in the year one thousand four hundred and thirty, for the fifth session.[9]

Firstly the assessors were convoked; and in their presence Jeanne was required by my lord the Bishop of Beauvais to swear and take the oath concerning what touched her trial.

To which she answered that she would willingly swear as to what touched her trial, but not as to everything she knew.

Many times she was requested by the bishop to answer the truth concerning everything that would be asked her,

To which she answered as before: It seems to me you ought to be satisfied; I have sworn enough.

By order of my lord of Beauvais, Maître Jean Beaupère began to interrogate Jeanne, and asked her how she had been since Saturday.

She answered: You can see that I am as well as I can be.

Questioned as to whether she fasted every day of this Lent,

She replied: What has that to do with your trial?

To which Beaupère said: Yes, indeed, it belongs to the trial.

She replied: Yes, certainly, I have fasted the whole time.

Asked whether she had heard her voice since Saturday,

She answered: Yes, indeed, many times.

Questioned as to whether she heard it in this hall on Saturday,

She answered: That has nothing to do with your trial; and afterwards said, yes.

Asked what it said to her on Saturday,

She answered: I did not well understand it; I understood nothing that I could tell you until my return to my room.

Asked what it said to her when she was back in her room,

She replied: That I should answer you boldly.

And she said further that she asked advice concerning the things that were asked her.

She said also that when she has leave of Our Lord to reveal it, she will tell it willingly; but touching the revelations concerning the King of France, she will not tell without permission from her voice.

Asked if the voice forbade her to tell everything,

She answered that she had still not quite understood.

Asked what the voice said to her,

She said that she asked advice from it as to certain questions that had been asked her.

Asked whether the voice had given her advice as to these matters, She replied that on certain points she had received advice.

She said also that as to certain questions, they might demand an answer, but she would not give it without leave; and if by chance she answered without permission, she would not have them for warrant. But [she said] when I have Our Lord's leave, then I shall not be afraid to answer, for I shall have a good warrant.

Questioned as to whether it were the voice of an angel, or of a saint, or directly from God,

She answered that the voices were those of Saint Catherine and of Saint Margaret. And their heads are crowned with beautiful crowns, most richly and preciously. And [she said] for [telling you] this I have leave from Our Lord. If you

doubt it, send to Poitiers where I have been previously examined.

Asked how she knew that it was these two saints, and if she could tell the one from the other,

She answered that she was certain that it was these; and that she well knew the one from the other.

Asked how she knew the one from the other,

She replied that she knew them by the greeting they gave her.

She also said that it was seven years since they first began to guide her.

She also said she knows them because they tell her their names.

Asked whether they are dressed in the same cloth,

She answered: I shall not now tell you anything else. She also said that she had not leave to reveal it. And if you do not believe me [she added], go to Poitiers.

She said further: there are some revelations which were intended for the King of France, and not for those who question me.

Asked if they are of the same age,

She said: I have not leave to tell you that.

Asked if they talked at the same time, or one after the other,

She replied: I have not leave to tell you that; nevertheless I always receive advice from both of them.

Asked which [appeared] first,

She answered: I do not recognize them at once. I used to know well enough, but now I have forgotten. If she has leave, she will willingly say; and it is in the register of Poitiers.

She said also that she received counsel from Saint Michael.

Questioned which came first,

She said it was Saint Michael.

Asked if it were long ago,

She answered: I do not speak of Saint Michael's voice, but of the great comfort [he brought me].

Asked which was the first voice that came to her when she was thirteen,

She said it was Saint Michael whom she saw before her eyes; and he was not alone, but was accompanied by angels from heaven.

She said also that she would not have come into France had it not been for God's command.

Asked if she saw Saint Michael and the angels corporeally and in reality,

She answered: I saw them with my bodily eyes, as well as I am seeing you.

And when they left her, she wept and greatly longed that they should have taken her with them.

Asked in what form was Saint Michael,

I have not yet answered you this; and have not yet leave to tell it.

Questioned as to what Saint Michael said to her the first time,

She answered: You will not have any other answer.

[She also said that the voices told her to answer boldly.]

She said further that she had not yet leave to reveal what Saint Michael told her; and greatly wished that her examiner had a copy of the book which is at Poitiers, provided that was pleasing to God.

Asked whether Saint Michael and the other saints had told her not to tell her revelations without their permission,

She answered: I will not answer you further about that. And, concerning what I have leave to tell you, I will gladly answer. And [she added] that if they had forbidden her, she did not so understand it.

Asked what sign she gives whereby it might be known that they come from God, and that they are Saint Catherine and Saint Margaret,

She replied: I have told you often enough that they are Saint Catherine and Saint Margaret. Believe me if you will.

Asked how she is able to make a distinction between answering certain points, and not others,

She replied that on some points she had asked leave, and on some, she had obtained it.

She said furthermore that she would rather be torn asunder by horses than come into France without God's leave.

Asked if the voice ordered her to wear a man's dress,

She answered that the dress is but a small matter; and that she had not taken it by the advice of any living man; and that she did not take this dress nor do anything at all save by the command of Our Lord and the angels.

Questioned as to whether it seemed to her that this command to take male dress was a lawful one,

She answered that everything she had done was at Our Lord's command, and if He had ordered Jeanne to take a different dress, she would have done so, since it would have been at God's command. Nor had she ever taken this dress at the order of Robert [de Baudricourt].

Asked if she had done well to take man's dress,

She said that everything she had done at our Lord's command she considered well done, and from it she expected good surety and good support.

She said also that she had a sword which she obtained at Vaucouleurs.

Questioned as to whether in this particular case of taking male dress she considered she had done rightly,

She answered that without God's command she had not done so; and that she had done nothing in the world save by His command.

Asked whether, when she saw the voice, there was a light with it,

She said that there was a great deal of light on all sides as was fitting.

Asked whether there was an angel over her king's head when first she saw him,

She answered: By Saint Mary, if there were any, I did not know, nor did I see one.

Asked whether there was a light there,

She said that there were more than three hundred knights and fifty torches, not counting the spiritual light; and that she rarely received revelations without there being a light.

Asked how her king gave credence to her words,

She replied that he had good signs; and through the clergy.

Asked what revelations the king had,

She answered: You will not learn them from me, this year.

She said also that the ecclesiastics of her party were of this opinion, that there seemed to be nothing but good in her.

Asked whether she had been to Saint Catherine de Fierbois,

She answered yes. And there she heard three

masses in one day, and then went to the town of Chinon.

She said that she told her king on one occasion that it had been revealed to her that she should go to him.

She said also that she had sent letters to her king, saying that she was writing to know whether she should enter the town where he was, and that she had already travelled a good hundred and fifty leagues to come to his aid, and that she had much good news for him; and she thought that the letter also said that she would be able to recognize him amongst all others.

She said further that she had a sword, which, when she was in Tours or in Chinon, she sent to be looked for at Saint Catherine de Fierbois. This sword was in the ground, behind the altar of Saint Catherine, and it was immediately found there, all rusted.

Asked how she knew the sword was there,

She said it was in the ground, all rusted, and upon it were five crosses. This she knew from her voices, saying that she never saw the man who was sent to look for the sword. She wrote to the clergy of the place asking that it might please them to let her have the sword, which they sent her. It was not deep in the ground behind the altar, so she thought, although in truth she was not certain whether it were in front of it or behind, but she believed that she wrote that it was behind [the altar].

She added that as soon as the sword was found, the clergy of the place rubbed it, and the rust fell off without any effort; and that it was an armourer of Tours who went to find the sword.[10] And the clergy of Saint Catherine and the citizens of Tours both gave her sheaths for it. They made two sheaths, one of crimson velvet and the other of cloth of gold. She herself had another made of very strong leather.

She also stated that when she was taken prisoner she no longer had this sword; but that she had always worn it until her departure from Saint Denis.

Asked whether she had ever said or caused to be said a blessing upon this sword,

She said no, nor would she have known how to do so.

She said also that she greatly prized this sword, since it was found in the church of Saint Catherine, whom she much loved.

Asked whether she had placed her sword upon any altar,

She said no, as far as she knew, nor had she done so in order that it might have better fortune.

Asked if she had her sword when she was taken prisoner,

She said no, but that she had one which was taken from a Burgundian.

She added that she had this sword at Lagny, and from Lagny to Compiègne she wore the Burgundian's sword, because it was a good sword for war, useful for giving hard clouts.

She said also that as to where she lost this sword, this had nothing to do with the trial, and she would not reply now.

Asked whether, when she was before the city of Orleans, she had a standard, and of what colour it was,

She replied that it had a field sown with fleurs-de-lis, and showed a world with an angel on either side, white in colour, of linen or *boucassin*; and she thought that the names JESUS MARIA were written on it; and it had a silk fringe.

Asked if these names JESUS MARIA were written at the top or the bottom, or along the side,

She answered that she thought they were along the side.

Asked which she preferred, her sword or her standard,

She replied that she was forty times fonder of her standard than she was of her sword.

Asked who persuaded her to have this design on her standard,

She said: I have told you often enough that I have done nothing save by God's command.

She said moreover that she herself bore her standard during an attack, in order to avoid killing anyone. And she added that she had never killed anyone at all.

Asked what forces her king gave her when he set her to work,

She answered, ten or twelve thousand men; and that at Orleans she went first to the fort of Saint Loup and then to that at the bridge [the Tourelles].

Asked at which fort she ordered her men to retire,

She said that she did not remember.

She said also that, through the revelation made to her, she was quite certain that she would relieve Orleans; adding that she had so informed her king before she went there.

Asked whether, in launching her attack before Orleans, she told her men that she would receive arrows, missiles and stones from the bombards,

She said no; there were a good hundred wounded, and maybe more. But she had told her men to have no fear, and they would raise the siege.

She also said that during the attack on the fort at the bridge she was wounded in the neck by an arrow, but she was greatly comforted by Saint Catherine, and was well again in a fortnight; nor did she give up either riding or her military command on account of this wound.

Asked whether she knew beforehand that she would be wounded,

She said that she well knew it, and had informed her king of it; but that notwithstanding she would not give up her work. And this was revealed to her by the voices of Saint Catherine and Saint Margaret.

She said also that she herself was the first to plant the ladder against the fort at the bridge; and it was while she was raising it that she was wounded in the neck by an arrow.

Asked why she had not concluded a treaty with the captain of Jargeau,

She said that the lords of her party had told the English that they would not have the delay of a fortnight for which they had asked, but that they must go away immediately, and take their horses with them. And for her own part, she told them that they might go if they wished, in their doublets and tunics, safe and sound; if they did not, they would be taken by assault.

Asked whether she had any conversation with her counsel, that is to say her voices, as to whether or no to grant a delay,

She answered that she did not remember.

FIFTH SESSION

Asked whether she had letters from the Comte d'Armagnac, asking her which of the three claimants to the Papacy should be obeyed,[11]

She answered that the count wrote a letter to this effect, to which she replied, amongst other matters, that when she was in Paris or anywhere else, when she had some time [to spare], she would give him a reply. She was just about to mount her horse when she gave this answer.

After this the letters from the count and from Jeanne were read, and she was asked whether it was her own letter in reply,

To which she said that she thought she had given such an answer, at any rate in part, if not the whole.

Questioned as to whether she said that she knew by the counsel of the King of kings what he ought to believe in this matter,

She answered that she knew nothing about it.

Asked if she were in any doubt as to whom the count should obey,

She said she did not know what to tell him as to whom he ought to obey, for he desired to know whom Our Lord wished him to obey. But as for herself, she held and believed that one ought to obey our lord the Pope at Rome.

She added that she had said other things to the messenger than what is contained in the letter. If he had not gone away so hurriedly he would have been thrown into the water, though not through her.

She said also that with reference to his inquiry as to whom it pleased God that he should obey, she answered that she did not know, but sent him many messages which were not put into writing. As for herself, she believed in the Pope at Rome.

Asked why she had written that she would give him a further answer, since she believed in the Pope at Rome,

She replied that the answer she had given referred to another matter than the three Popes.

Asked if she had ever said she would have counsel concerning the three Popes,

She said that she had never written or caused to be written anything concerning the three Popes. And she swore on oath that on this subject she had neither written nor caused to be written anything at all.

She said also that before seven years are past the English will have lost a greater stake than they did before the town of Orleans, for they will have lost all they hold in France.

She added, as before, that she knew this by revelation, as well as she knew that we, the Bishop of Beauvais, were there present before her, saying in the French tongue: *Je le sçay aussi bien comme vous estes ici.*[12]

And this she knew by the revelation given her; and that it would come to pass before seven years are past; and she was much grieved that it should be so long delayed.

Asked in what year,

She answered: You will not yet learn this; but I hope it may be before Saint John's Day.

Asked whether she had said it would come to pass before Saint Martin's Day in winter,

She replied that she had said that many events would be seen before Saint Martin's Day; and it might be that the English would be overthrown.

Asked what she had said to John Grey, her gaoler in the prison, concerning Saint Martin's Day,

She answered: I have already told you.

Questioned as to through whom she knew that this would come to pass,

She replied that it was through Saint Catherine and Saint Margaret.

Asked whether, since the previous Tuesday, she had often spoken with Saint Catherine and Saint Margaret,

She said yes, both yesterday and to-day; but she does not know at what time; and there is no day when she does not hear them.

Asked whether the saints always appeared to her in the same dress,

She answered that she [always sees them] in the same form; and their heads are richly crowned; of their other clothing she does not speak, and of their robes she knows nothing.

Asked how she knows whether it is a man or woman who appears to her,

She answered that she was certain it was those saints by their voices, and by what they told her.

Asked what part of them she saw,

She answered, the face.

Asked whether they had hair,

She replied: Assuredly; in the French tongue, *Il est bon a savoir.*

Asked if there was anything between their crowns and their hair,

She answered, no.

Asked if their hair were long and hung down,

She replied: I do not know.

She added that she did not know if they had anything in the nature of arms or other members.

She said moreover that they spoke most excellently and beautifully; and that she understood them perfectly.

Asked how they spoke, when they had no other members,

She answered: I leave that to God.

She said that the voice was lovely, sweet and low in tone, and spoke in French.

Asked if that voice, that is to say Saint Margaret, spoke English,

She answered: Why should she speak English? She is not on the side of the English.

Asked who gave her the ring which the Burgundians have,

She answered, her father or mother; and she thought that JESUS MARIA was written on it. But she did not know who had had this written; she did not think there was any stone in it; and it was given to her at Domremy.

She said also that her brother had given her a ring which we, the bishop, now have; and she requested us to give it to the church.

She said further that she had never cured anyone with any of her rings.

Asked whether Saint Catherine and Saint Margaret had spoken to her beneath the tree,

She answered: I do not know.

Being repeatedly asked if the saints had spoken to her at the aforementioned spring,

She replied yes; and she had heard them there. But what they then said to her she does not know.

Being again asked if they had made any promises to her there or elsewhere,

She replied that they did not make any promise to her, except by leave of Our Lord.

Asked what promises Saint Catherine and Saint Margaret made her,

She answered: This does not concern your trial at all.

Amongst other things, they told her that her king would be reestablished in his kingdom, whether his enemies wished it or no.

She said also that the saints promised to bring her to Paradise, as she had asked them.

Asked whether they had promised her anything else, as well as to bring her to Paradise,

She replied that they had made her other promises, but she will not tell them. She said this did not concern her trial.

She said further that within three months she will reveal another promise.

Asked whether the saints had told her that within three months she would be freed from prison,

She answered: That is not in your trial. But she does not know when she will be freed.

She said also that those who wished to remove her from this world might well themselves go first.

Asked whether her counsel had told her that she would be freed from prison,

She answered: Ask me in three months' time, and I will then give you my reply.

She also requested that the assessors should give their opinions on oath as to whether this concerns the trial.

And afterwards, when the assessors had deliberated and come to the conclusion that it did concern the trial,

She said: I have always told you that you cannot know all.

And she added: One day I must be freed. And I wish to have leave to tell you [when]. And for this she begged a delay.

Asked if the saints forbade her to tell the truth,

She answered: Do you wish me to tell you the affairs of the King of France?

She said that there were many matters which did not concern the trial.

She said also that she was well assured that her king would regain his kingdom; this she knows as well as she knows us [the bishop] to be present here.

She said also that she would be dead, were it not for the revelation which comforts her each day.

Asked what she has done with her mandrake,[13]

She answered that she never had one; but that she had heard it said that there was one near her village; but that she had never seen it.

She had heard it said that it was a dangerous and evil thing to him who keeps it; but she does not know its purpose.

Asked where is the place where this thing of which she has heard [is to be found],

She replied that she had heard that it is in the ground near the tree, but she does not know the spot. But she has heard it said that over the place grows a tree called a hazel.

Asked what purpose this mandrake serves,

She answered that she had heard it said that it attracts money, but she does not believe it, and on this matter her voices have never told her anything at all.

Asked in what form Saint Michael appeared,

She answered that she did not see his crown; and as to his clothing, she knew nothing.

Asked if he were naked,

She answered: Do you think that Our Lord has not wherewithal to clothe him?

Questioned as to whether Saint Michael had his scales,[14]

She replied: I do not know.

She said that she had great joy when she saw him; and said also that he told her, when she saw him, that she was not in a state of mortal sin.

She said further that Saint Catherine and Saint Margaret gladly heard her confession, each in turn.

She also said that if she is in mortal sin, she is not aware of it.

Asked whether, when she made her confession, she ever thought she was in mortal sin,

She replied that she did not know if she were, but she did not believe that she had ever committed such sins. And please God [she added], I never did so, nor will I act in such a way that my soul should be guilty of mortal sin.

Asked what sign she gave her king to show him that she came from God,

She answered: I have always told you that you will not drag that out of me. Go and ask him.

A pair of scales is the emblem of the Archangel.

Asked whether she has sworn not to reveal what has been asked her touching the trial,

She said: I have told you before that I will not tell you anything concerning the king: but that which concerns the trial and the faith, I will tell you.

Asked if she did not know the sign,

She answered: You will not know that from me.

Being told that this concerns the trial,

She said: I will willingly tell you [other matters]; but the things I have promised to keep secret, I will not tell you.

And I have promised, so I cannot tell you without being forsworn.

Asked to whom she made this promise,

She said, to Saint Catherine and Saint Margaret; and it [the sign] was shown to the king.

She said also that she promised them without them asking her, and at her own request; and she said that too many people would have asked her if she had not promised.

Questioned whether, when she showed the sign, there was anyone present save the king,

She answered: I think there was no one but he, although there were a number of people fairly near.

Asked if she saw any crown on the king's head, when she showed him the sign,

She answered: I cannot tell you without perjuring myself.

Asked if he had a crown at Rheims,

She answered that she thinks that the one he found at Rheims he took with pleasure. But a very rich one was brought later. And he did so to hasten [his coronation] at the request of the citizens of the town, to avoid the cost of the men-at-arms; and if he had waited, he would have been crowned with one a thousand times richer.

Asked whether she had seen this richer crown,

She answered: I cannot tell you without being forsworn; and although I have not seen it, I have heard that it was so rich.

And after these questions were done, the following Saturday was appointed, at the hour of eight in the morning. And the assessors were requested to assemble on this day at the said hour under certain penalties.

Notes

1 France here refers to the parts of the country owing allegiance to Charles II.

2 The officer in command of the guard was John Gray, a gentleman in the Household of the Duke of Bedford, who was afterwards knighted. He was assisted by John Berwoit and William Talbot. Four soldiers were engaged in the actual work of surveillance, Nicholas Bertin, Julian Flocquet, William Mouton, and another whose name is not known.

3 The widow of one Jean Waldaires. She was nicknamed La Rousse on account of her red hair.

4   Women were allowed to stay in the guest-house of the monastery, which stood beside the great gateway. This gateway is the only portion of the original buildings to remain standing.

5 *Interrogée si c'est un angèle de Dieu, sans moyen.* Courcelles writes: *Sit unus angelus, velutrum sit a Deo, immediate.*

6 The *beau mai* was a branch from a beech tree, traditionally used for decoration.

7 The family of de Bourlémont were seigneurs of Domremy. The château of Bourlémont still stands not far from the village.

8 This refers to a prophecy attributed to Merlin, current in the courntryside. It was to the effect that a marvellous Maid should come from the *Nemus Canutum* (*bois chesnu*) for the healing of nations.

9 The Orleans manuscript puts the fourth and fifth sessions into one, by reason of its omission of a long passage of interrogation [here supplied from d'Estivet]. This Sunday was the second Sunday in Lent. (P.D.)

10 This probably refers to the armourer from Tours who made Jeanne's armour, Colin de Montbazon.

11 Martin V was then Pope; there were also two anti-Popes. Armagnac was a supporter of one of these, for which he had been excommunicated by Pope Martin.

12 The whole of this passage, being taken from d'Estivet, was originally in Latin.

13 A mandrake (*mandragora officinarum*) is a plant of the potato family. Little images made of this root, which often looked like the lower limbs of a man, were cherished as oracles, and used in witchcraft and enchantments. The mandrake was believed to shriek when torn out of the earth.

14 A pair of scales is the emblem of the Archangel.

DOMESDAY BOOK

IN 1085 WILLIAM THE CONQUEROR ORDERED A SURVEY OF HIS KING-
dom in order to provide him with an exact record of the local contributions to
royal taxation. In addition, the inquest was designed to inform him of the
manner that England had been divided among his vassals and to settle issues
of land disputes which had been continuing since the conquest twenty years
before. The result was an extraordinarily rich and detailed survey which is an
invaluable source for understanding English social, economic, and political
structures in the eleventh century.

The survey of Huntingdonshire is fairly typical of the entries. In general,
each entry describes the assessment of the manor in hides to the geld. These
"hides" are not actual units of land but units of tax assessment. It then states
the number of "ploughs," that is, the amount of arable land that can be
ploughed each year by a team of 8 oxen. Finally, it states the number of
ploughs on the demesne of the manor and the number in the peasant tenures.
Finally, it may add miscellaneous information about other resources and its
value at the death of Edward the Confessor in 1066 (T.R.E. tempore Regis
Edwardi) and in 1086.

Source: David Douglas and G. W. Greenaway (ed.) *English Historical Documents*
vol. II (Oxford: Oxford University Press 1953).

Huntingdonshire

In the borough of Huntingdon there are 4 quarters.

In 2 quarters there were *T.R.E.*, and are now,
116 burgesses rendering all customs and the
king's geld, and under them there are 100 bordars
who help them to pay the geld. Of these burgesses St. Benedict of Ramsey had 10 with sake and
soke and every custom except that they paid geld
T.R.E. Eustace took them away wrongfully from
the abbey and they are, with the others, in the
king's hand. Ulf Fenisc had 18 burgesses, now
Gilbert of Ghent has them with sake and soke
except for the king's geld.

The abbot of Ely has 1 toft with sake and soke
except for the king's geld.

The bishop of Lincoln had in the site of the castle a messuage with sake and soke which has
now disappeared.

Earl Siward had a messuage with a house with
sake and soke, quit from all custom, which the
Countess Judith has now.

In the site of the castle there were 20 messuages

assessed to all customs, and rendering yearly 16
shillings and 8 pence to the king's 'farm'. These
do not exist now.

In addition to these, there were and are 60
waste messuages within these quarters. These
gave and give their customs. And in addition to
these there are 8 waste messuages which *T.R.E.*
were fully occupied. These gave all customs.

In the other 2 quarters there were and are 140
burgesses, less half a house, assessed to all customs and the king's geld, and these had 80 haws
for which they gave and give all customs. Of
these St. Benedict of Ramsey had 22 burgesses
T.R.E. Two of these were quit of all customs, and
30 rendered 10 pence yearly each. All other customs belonged to the abbot, apart from the king's
geld.

In these quarters Aluric the sheriff *T.R.E.* had 1
messuage which King William afterwards granted to his wife and sons. Eustace has it now, and
the poor man, with his mother, is claiming it. In
these 2 quarters there were and are 44 waste messuages which gave and give their customs. And
in these 2 quarters Borred and Turchil *T.R.E.* had

1 church with 2 hides of land and 22 burgesses with houses belonging to the same church with sake and soke; Eustace has all this now. Wherefore these men claim the king's mercy; nevertheless these 22 burgesses give every custom to the king.

Geoffrey the bishop has 1 church and 1 house from the aforesaid which Eustace took away from St. Benedict, and the same saint is still claiming them.

In this borough Gos and Hunef had 16 houses *T.R.E.* with sake and soke and toll and team. The Countess Judith has them now.

The borough of Huntingdonshire used to defend itself towards the king's geld for 50 hides as the fourth part of Hurstingstone hundred, but now it does not so pay geld in that hundred, after the king set a geld of money on the borough. From this whole borough 10 pounds came out *T.R.E.* by way of 'Landgable' of which the earl had the third part, and the king two-thirds. Of this rent 16 shillings and 8 pence, divided between the earl and the king, now remain upon 20 messuages where the castle is. In addition to these payments the king had 20 pounds and the earl 10 pounds from the 'farm' of the borough more or less according as each could make disposition of his part. One mill rendered 40 shillings to the king and 20 shillings to the earl. To this borough there belong 2 ploughlands and 40 acres of land and 10 acres of meadow, of which the king with two parts, and the earl with the third part, divide the rent. The burgesses cultivate this land and take it on lease through the servants of the king and the earl. Within the aforesaid rent there are 3 fishermen rendering 3 shillings. In this borough there were 3 moneyers paying 40 shillings between the king and the earl, but now they are not there. *T.R.E.* it rendered 30 pounds; now the same.

In Hurstingstone hundred demesne ploughlands are quit of the king's geld. Villeins and sokemen pay geld according to the hides written in the return, apart from Broughton where the abbot of Ramsey pays geld for 1 hide with the others.

Here are noted those holding lands in Huntingdonshire

1. King William.
2. The bishop of Lincoln.
3. The bishop of Coutances.
4. The abbey of Ely.
5. The abbey of Crowland.
6. The abbey of Ramsey.
7. The abbey of Thorney.
8. The abbey of Peterborough.
9. Count Eustace.
10. The count of Eu.
11. Earl Hugh.
12. Walter Giffard.
13. William of Warenne.
14. Hugh of Bolbec.
15. Eudo, son of Hubert.
16. Sweyn of Essex.
17. Roger of Ivry.
18. Arnulf of Hesdins.
19. Eustace the sheriff.
20. The Countess Judith.
21. Gilbert of Ghent.
22. Aubrey 'de Vere'.
23. William, son of Ansculf.
24. Rannulf, the brother of Ilger.
25. Robert Fafiton.
26. William 'Ingania'.
27. Ralph, son of Osmund.
28. Rohais, the wife of Richard.
29. The king's thegns.

1. The land of the king

Hurstingstone hundred

A manor. In Hartford King Edward had 15 hides assessed to the geld. There is land for 17 ploughs. Rannulf the brother of Ilger keeps it now. There are 4 ploughs now on the demesne; and 30 villeins and 3 bordars have 8 ploughs. There is a priest; 2 churches; 2 mills rendering 4 pounds; and 40 acres of meadow. Woodland for pannage, 1 league in length and half a league in breadth. *T.R.E.* it was worth 24 pounds; now 15 pounds.

Normancross hundred

A manor. In Bottlebridge King Edward had 5 hides assessed to the geld. There is land for 8 ploughs. The king has 1 plough now on the demesne; and 15 villeins have 5 ploughs. There is a priest and a church; 60 acres of meadow and 12 acres of woodland for pannage in Northampton-shire. *T.R.E.* it was worth 100 shillings; now 8 pounds. Rannulf keeps it.

In this manor belonging to the king, and in other manors, the enclosure of the abbot of Thorney is doing harm to 300 acres of meadow.

In Stilton the king's sokemen of Normancross have 3 virgates of land assessed to the geld. There is land for 2 ploughs, and there are 5 ploughing oxen.

In Orton the king has soke over 3-1/2 hides of land in the land of the abbot of Peterborough which was Godwine's.

Toseland hundred

A manor. In Gransden Earl Alfgar had 8 hides of land assessed to the geld. There is land for 15 ploughs. There are 7 ploughs now on the demesne; and 24 villeins and 8 bordars have 8 ploughs. There is a priest and a church; 50 acres of meadow; 12 acres of underwood. From the pasture come 5 shillings and 4 pence. *T.R.E.* it was worth 40 pounds; now 30 pounds. Rannulf keeps it.

Leightonstone hundred

A manor. In Alconbury, and in Gidding, which is an outlying estate, there were 10 hides assessed to the geld. There is land for 20 ploughs. There are now 5 ploughs belonging to the hall on 2 hides of this land; and 35 villeins have 13 ploughs there; 80 acres of meadow. *T.R.E.* it was worth 12 pounds; now the same. Rannulf, the brother of Ilger, keeps it.

A manor. In Keyston King Edward had 4 hides of land assessed to the geld. There is land for 12 ploughs. There are 2 ploughs now on the demesne; and 24 villeins and 8 bordars have 10 ploughs; 86 acres of meadow. Scattered wood-land for pannage 5 furlongs in length and 1-1/2 furlongs in breadth. *T.R.E.* it was worth 10 pounds; now the same. Rannulf, the brother of Ilger, keeps it.

A manor. In Brampton King Edward had 15 hides assessed to the geld. There is land for 15

ploughs. There are 3 ploughs now on the demesne; and 36 villeins and 2 bordars have 14 ploughs. There is a church and a priest; 100 acres of meadow. Woodland for pannage half a league in length and 2 furlongs in breadth. Two mills rendering 100 shillings. *T.R.E.* it was worth 20 pounds; now the same. Rannulf, the brother of Ilger, keeps it.

Soke.[1] In Graffham there are 5 hides assessed to the geld. There is land for 8 ploughs. The soke is in Leightonstone hundred. There 7 sokemen and 17 villeins have 6 ploughs now and 6 acres of meadow. Woodland for pannage 1 league in length and 1 league in breadth. *T.R.E.* it was worth 5 pounds; now 10 shillings less.

A manor. In Godmanchester King Edward had 14 hides assessed to the geld. There is land for 57 ploughs. There are 2 ploughs now on the king's demesne on 2 hides of this land; and 80 villeins and 16 bordars have 24 ploughs. There is a priest and a church; 3 mills rendering 100 shillings; 160 acres of meadow; and 50 acres of woodland for pannage. From the pasture come 20 shillings. From the meadows come 70 shillings. *T.R.E.* it was worth 40 pounds; now it is worth the same 'by tale'.

2. The land of the bishop of Lincoln

Toseland hundred

A manor. In 'Cotes' the bishop of Lincoln had 2 hides assessed to the geld. There is land for 3 ploughs. There are 2 ploughs now on the demesne; and 3 villeins have 2 oxen; 20 acres of meadow. *T.R.E.* it was worth 40 shillings; now the same. Thurstan holds it of the bishop.

A manor. In Staughton the bishop of Lincoln had 6 hides assessed to the geld. There is land for 15 ploughs. There are 2-1/2 ploughs on the demesne; and 16 villeins and 4 bordars have 8 ploughs. There is a priest and a church; 24 acres of meadow; 100 acres of underwood. *T.R.E.* it was worth 10 pounds; now the same. Eustace holds it of the bishop. The abbot of Ramsey claims this manor against the bishop.

A manor. In Diddington the bishop of Lincoln had 2-1/2 hides assessed to the geld. There is land for 2 ploughs. There are now 2 ploughs on the demesne and 5 villeins have 2 ploughs. A church, and 18 acres of meadow. Woodland for pannage half a league in length and half in breadth. *T.R.E.* it was worth 60 shillings; now 70 shillings. William holds it of the bishop.

A manor. In Buckden the bishop of Lincoln had 20 hides assessed to the geld. There is land for 20 ploughs. There are now 5 ploughs on the demesne; and 37 villeins and 20 bordars have 14 ploughs. There is a church and a priest; 1 mill worth 30 shillings; 84 acres of meadow. Woodland for pannage 1 league in length and 1 league in breadth. *T.R.E.* it was worth 20 pounds; now 16 pounds and 10 shillings.

Normancross hundred

A manor. In Denton Godric had 5 hides assessed to the geld. There is land for 2 ploughs. There is 1 plough on the demesne; and 10 villeins and 2 bordars have 5 ploughs. There is a church and a priest; 24 acres of meadow and 24 acres of underwood. *T.R.E.* it was worth 100 shillings; now 4 pounds. Thurstan holds it of the bishop.

A manor. In Orton Leuric had 3 hides and 1 virgate of land assessed to the geld. There is land for 2 ploughs and 1 ox. There is now 1 plough on the demesne; and 2 villeins and 9 acres of meadow. *T.R.E.* it was worth 20 shillings; now 10 shillings. John holds it of the bishop. The king claims the soke of this land.

A manor. In Stilton Tovi had 2 hides assessed to the geld. There is land for 2 ploughs and 7 oxen. There is now 1 plough on the demesne; and 6 villeins have 3 ploughs; 16 acres of meadow and 5 acres of underwood. *T.R.E.* it was worth 40 shillings; now the same. John holds it of the bishop. This land was given to Bishop Wulfwig *T.R.E.*

Leightonstone hundred

A manor. In Leighton Bromswold Turchil the Dane had 15 hides assessed to the geld. There is land for 17 ploughs. There are now 6 ploughs on the demesne; and 33 villeins and 3 bordars have 10 ploughs. One mill rendering 3 shillings; 3 knights hold 3 hides less 1 virgate of this land: they have 3 ploughs and 3 villeins with half a plough. There are 30 acres of meadow and 10

acres of underwood. *T.R.E.* the bishop's demesne was worth 20 pounds and it is worth the same now. The land of the knights is worth 60 shillings. Earl Waltheof gave this manor in alms to St. Mary of Lincoln.

In Pertenhall Alwin had 1 virgate of land assessed to the geld. There is land for half a plough. This land is situated in Bedfordshire but renders geld and service in Huntingdonshire. The king's servants claim this land for his use. *T.R.E.* it was worth 5 shillings; now the same. William holds it of Bishop Remigius and ploughs it with his own demesne.

3. The land of the bishop of Coutances

In Hargrave Semar had 1 virgate of land assessed to the geld. There is land for 2 oxen. The soke belongs to Leightonstone hundred. The same man himself holds it of the bishop of Coutances and ploughs there with 2 oxen and has 2 acres of meadow. *T.R.E.* it was worth 5 shillings; now the same.

4. The land of the abbey of Ely

Hurstingstone hundred

A manor. In Colne the abbey of Ely had 6 hides assessed to the geld. There is land for 6 ploughs and in demesne the abbey has land for 2 ploughs apart from the 6 hides. There are now 2 ploughs on the demesne, and 13 villeins and 5 bordars have 5 ploughs; 10 acres of meadow. Woodland for pannage 1 league in length and half a league in breadth; marsh of the same extent. *T.R.E.* it was worth 6 pounds; now 100 shillings.

A manor. In Bluntisham the abbey of Ely had 6-1/2 hides assessed to the geld. There is land for 8 ploughs, and, apart from these hides, the abbey has land for 2 ploughs in demesne. There are now 2 ploughs on the demesne; and 10 villeins and 3 bordars have 3 ploughs. There is a priest and a church; 20 acres of meadow. Woodland for pannage 1 league in length and 4 furlongs in breadth. *T.R.E.* it was worth 100 shillings; now the same.

A manor. In Somersham the abbey of Ely had 8 hides assessed to the geld. There is land for 12 ploughs, and, apart from these hides, the abbey had land for 2 ploughs in demesne. There are now 2 ploughs on the demesne; and 32 villeins and 9 bordars have 9 ploughs. There are 3 fisheries rendering 8 shillings, and 20 acres of meadow. Woodland for pannage 1 league in length and 7 furlongs in breadth. *T.R.E.* it was worth 7 pounds; now 8 pounds.

A manor. In Spaldwick the abbey of Ely had 15 hides assessed to the geld. There is land for 15 ploughs. There are now 4 ploughs on the demesne on 5 hides of this land; and 50 villeins and 10 bordars have 25 ploughs. There is 1 mill rendering 2 shillings; and 160 acres of meadow; and 60 acres of woodland for pannage. *T.R.E.* it was worth 16 pounds; now 22 pounds.

A manor. In Little Catworth, outlying estate of Spaldwick, there are 4 hides assessed to the geld. Land for 4 ploughs; 7 villeins have 2 ploughs there now.

5. The land of the abbey of Crowland

A manor. In Morborne the abbey of Crowland has 5 hides assessed to the geld. There is land for 9 ploughs. There are now 2 ploughs on the demesne on 1 hide of this land; and 16 villeins and 3 bordars have 7 ploughs. There is a church and a priest; 40 acres of meadow; 1 acre of underwood. *T.R.E.* it was worth 100 shillings; now the same.

In Thurning there are 1-1/2 hides assessed to the geld. There is land for 1-1/2 ploughs. The soke belongs to the king's manor of Alconbury. Eustace holds it now from the abbot of Crowland, and had 1 plough there and 1 villein with half a plough and 6 acres of meadow. *T.R.E.* it was worth 20 shillings; now the same.

6. The land of St. Benedict of Ramsey

[This is similarly described as lying in Stukeley; Abbot's Ripton; Broughton; Wistow; Upwood; Holywell; St. Ives; Houghton; Wyton; Warboys; Sawtry; Elton; Lutton; Yelling; Hemingford Abbots; Offord; Dillington; Gidding; Bythorn; Bringtin; Old Weston; Ellington.]

7. The land of St. Mary of Thorney

[This is similarly described as lying in Yaxley;

Stanground; Woodstone; Haddon; Water Newton; Sibson; Stibbington.]

8. The land of St. Peter of Peterborough

[This is similarly described as lying at Fletton; Alwalton; Orton Waterville.]

9. The land of Count Eustace

[This is similarly described as lying at Glatton; Chesterton; Sibson.]

10. The land of the Count of Eu

[This is similarly described as lying at Buckworth.]

11. The land of Earl Hugh

[This is similarly described as lying in Upton; Coppingford.]

12. The land of Walter Giffard

[This is similarly described as lying at Folksworth.]

13. The land of William of Warenne

[This is similarly described as lying at Kimbolton; Keysoe; Catworth.]

14. The land of Hugh of Bolbec

[This is similarly described as lying at Wood Walton.]

15. The land of Eudo, son of Hubert

[This is similarly described as lying at Hamerton.]

16. The land of Sweyn of Essex

[This is similarly described as lying at Waresley.]

17. The land of Roger of Ivry

[This is similarly described as lying at Covington.]

18. The land of Arnulf of Hesdins

[This is similarly described as lying in Offord Cluny.]

19. The land of Eustace the sheriff

[This is similarly described as lying in Sawtry; Caldecot; Washingley; Orton Longueville; Stilton; Chesterton; Bottlebridge; Swineshead; Catworth; Hargrave; Gidding; Winwick; Thurning; Luddington; Weston; Wooley; Hemingford; Offord; Waresley; Hail Weston; Southoe; Perry; Catworth.]

20. The land of the Countess Judith

[This is similarly described as lying in Conington; Sawtry; Stukeley; Molesworth; 'Cotes'; Eynesbury; Offord; Diddington; Paxton.]

21. The land of Gilbert of Ghent

[This is similarly described as lying in Fen Stanton.]

22. The land of Aubrey 'de Vere'

[This is similarly described as lying in Yelling; Hemingford.]

23. The land of William, son of Ansculf

[This is similarly described as lying in Waresley.]

24. The land of Rannulf, brother of Ilger

[This is similarly described as lying in Everton.]

25. The land of Robert Fafiton

[This is similarly described as lying in Hail Weston; Southhoe.]

26. The land of William 'Ingania'

[This is similarly described as lying in Gidding.]

27. The land of Ralph, son of Osmund

[This is similarly described as lying in Hemingford.]

28. The land of Rohais, wife of Richard fitz Gilbert

Toseland hundred

A manor. In Eynesbury Robert, son of Wimarc, had 15 hides assessed to the geld. There is land for 27 ploughs. Rohais, the wife of Richard, has 7 ploughs on the demesne there now. In the same place St. Neot has from her 3 ploughs on the demesne, and in the same village 19 villeins and 5 bordars have 7 ploughs. There is 1 mill worth 23 shillings, and 1 fishery which is valued with the manor; 65-1/2 acres of meadow. *T.R.E.* it was worth 24 pounds; now it is worth 21 pounds apart from that which is assigned to the food of the monks, which is valued at 4 pounds. William 'Brito' holds 2 hides and 1 virgate of this land from Rohais and has half a plough on the demesne; and 3 villeins and 4 bordars have 1 plough. It is worth 30 shillings.

29. The land of the king's thegns

A manor. In Washingley, Chetelebert had 2-1/2 hides assessed to the geld. There is land for 4 ploughs. He himself holds from the king and has 1 plough there; and 10 villeins have 4 ploughs. There is a church and a priest; 12 acres of meadow. Woodland for pannage 7 furlongs in length and 10-1/2 furlongs in breadth. *T.R.E.* it was worth 10 shillings; now the same.

Leightonstone hundred

In Keysoe Alwine had 1 virgate of land assessed to the geld with sake and soke. There is land for 2 oxen. It belongs to Bedfordshire, but gives geld in Huntingdonshire. He himself holds now of the king and has 1 villein there with 2 oxen in a plough. *T.R.E.* it was worth 16 pence; now the same.

A manor. In Catworth Avic had 3 hides assessed to the geld. There is land for 4 ploughs. Eric holds it now of the king. And the same man has under the king 1 hide assessed to the geld. There is land for 1 plough. He has 2 villeins there, and 6 acres of meadow. *T.R.E.* it was worth 40 shillings; now 20 shillings.

In Brampton Elric has 1 hide and 1 virgate of land assessed to the geld. There is land for 10 oxen. There are 3 bordars and 1 plough. It is worth 30 shillings.

A manor. In Wooley Golde and Uluric, his son, had 3 hides assessed to the geld. There is land for 6 ploughs. They themselves now have it from the king. There is 1 plough on the demesne; and 14 villeins have 5 ploughs; 20 acres of meadow. *T.R.E.* it was worth 60 shillings; now the same.

In Sawtry Alwine had half a carucate assessed to the geld. There is land for 6 oxen. His wife holds it now of the king, and has 1 plough there and 2 acres. *T.R.E.* it was worth 10 shillings; now the same.

[Claims]

The jurors of Huntingdon say that the church of St. Mary of the borough and the land which is annexed to it belonged to the church of Thorney, but the abbot gave it in pledge to the burgesses. Moreover, King Edward gave it to Vitalis and Bernard, his priests, and they sold it to Hugh, chamberlain to King Edward. Moreover, Hugh sold it to two priests of Huntingdon, and in respect of this they have the seal of King Edward. Eustace has it now without livery, without writ, and without seisin.

Eustace took away wrongfully the house of Leveve and gave it to Oger of London.

They bear witness that the land of Hunef and Gos was under the hand of King Edward on the day when he was alive and dead and that they held of him and not of the earl. But the jurors say that they heard that King William was said to have given it to Waltheof.

Touching the 5 hides of Broughton the jurors say that it was the land of sokemen *T.R.E.*, but that the same king gave the land and the soke

over the men to St. Benedict of Ramsey in return for a service which Abbot Alwin did for him in Saxony, and ever afterwards the saint had it.

The shire bears witness that the land of Bricmer 'Belehorne' was 'reeveland' *T.R.E.* and belonged to the king's 'farm'.

They bear witness that the land of Alwin the priest was to the abbot....

They bear witness that Aluric's land of Yelling and Hemingford belonged to St. Benedict and that it was granted to Aluric for the term of his life on the condition that after his death it ought to return to the church, and 'Bocstede' with it. But this same Aluric was killed in the battle of Hastings, and the abbot took back his lands and held them until Aubrey 'de Vere' deprived him of possession.

Touching 2 hides which Ralph, son of Osmund, holds in Hemingford, they say that one of them belonged to the demesne of the church of Ramsey in King Edward's day, and that Ralph holds it against the abbot's will. Touching the other hide, they say that Godric held it from the abbot, but when the abbot was in Denmark, Osmund, Ralph's father, seized it from Sawin the fowler, to whom the abbot had given it for love of the king.

Touching Summerlede they say that he held his land from Turulf who gave it to him, and afterwards from the sons of Turulf, and they had sake and soke over him.

The jurors say that the land of Wulwine Chit of Weston was a manor by itself, and did not belong to Kimbolton, but that nevertheless he was a man of Earl Harold.

Touching a hide and a half of land which was Ælget's, the jurors say that this Ælget held them from Earl Tosti with sake and soke and afterwards of Waltheof.

Godric the priest likewise held 1 hide of land from Earl Waltheof *T.R.E.*, and Eustace holds it now.

They say that the land of Godwine of Weston in no way belonged to Saxi, Fafiton's predecessor.

The men of the shire bear witness that King Edward gave Swineshead to Earl Siward with sake and soke, and so Earl Harold had it, except that the men paid geld in the hundred, and performed military service with them.

Touching the land of Fursa, the soke was the king's. King Edward had soke over 1 virgate of land of Alwin Deule in Pertenhall.

The jurors say that the hide of land which Wulwine Chit had in Catworth was in the king's soke and that Earl Harold did not have it.

In Little Catworth the same Wulwine had 1 hide over which King Edward always had sake and soke. But Wulwine could give and sell the land to whom he wished. But the men of the countess say that the king gave the land to Earl Waltheof.

The shire bears witness that the third part of half a hide which lies in Easton and pays geld in Bedfordshire belongs to the abbot of Ely's manor of Spaldwick. The abbot of Ely thus held it *T.R.E.*, and for five years after the coming of King William. Eustace seized this land wrongfully from the church, and kept it.

The jurors say that Keystone was and is of the 'farm' of King Edward, and although Aluric the sheriff resided in that village, he nevertheless always paid the king's 'farm' therefrom, and his sons after him, until Eustace took the sheriffdom. They have never seen or heard of a seal of King Edward that he put it outside his 'farm'.

Alwold and his brother claim that Eustace took away their land from them, and the men of the shire deny that they have ever seen a seal, or seen anyone who gave Eustace seisin of it.

On the day when King Edward was alive and dead, Gidding was an outlying estate of Alconbury in the king's 'farm'.

The men of the shire bear witness that Buckworth was an outlying estate of Paxton *T.R.E.*

They say that 36 hides of land in Brampton which Richard 'Ingania' claims to belong to the forest were of the king's demesne 'farm', and did not belong to the forest.

They say that Graffham was and is the king's sokeland, and that they have not seen the writ, or anyone who gave legal possession of this to Eustace.

Touching 6 hides in Conington they said they had heard that these formerly belonged to the church of Thorney, and that they were granted to Turchill on condition that after [his] death they ought to return to the church with the other 3 hides in the same village. The jurors said that they had heard this, but they had not seen evidence of it, nor were they present when the arrangement was made.

Touching the land of Tosti of Sawtry, they say that Eric, his brother, bequeathed it to the church of Ramsey after his death and after the death of his brother and sister.

Touching Fletton the jurors say that *T.R.E.* the whole belonged to the church of Peterborough, and so it should.

Touching Leuric's land the jurors say that it was in the king's soke, but Bishop Remigius shows the writ of King Edward by which he gave Leuric with all his land to the bishopric of Lincoln with sake and soke.

Notes

1 This term prefixed to estates in this survey indicates "a group of tenements—united to some manor by the ties of rent, the homage of the peasant landholders, and in most cases their suit of court to the manorial centre".

RICHARD FITZ NIGEL

Dialogue of the Exchequer

THE *Dialogue of the Exchequer*, WRITTEN BETWEEN 1177 AND 1179, presents in dialogue form the system by which the accounts of sheriffs were audited and enrolled by royal officials. This accounting system gave the English kings the most efficient form of financial control and hence ready wealth in Europe.

Source: E. F. Henderson, *Select Historical Documents* (London, George Bell, 1894); David C. Douglas and George W. Greenaway, *English Historical Documents 1042-1189* (New York: Oxford University Press, 1953).

First Book

In the twenty-third year of the reign of King Henry II, while I was sitting at the window of a tower next to the River Thames, a man spoke to me impetuously, saying: "master, hast thou not read that there is no use in science or in a treasure that is hidden?" when I replied to him, "I have read so," straightway he said: "why, therefore, dost thou not teach others the knowledge concerning the exchequer which is said to be thine to such an extent, and commit it to writing lest it die with thee?" I answered: "lo, brother, thou hast now for a long time sat at the exchequer, and nothing is hidden from thee, for thou art painstaking. And the same is probably the case with the others who have seats there." But he, "just as those who walk in darkness and grope with their hands frequently stumble,—so many sit there who seeing do not perceive, and hearing do not understand." Then I, "thou speakest irreverently, for neither is the knowledge so great nor does it concern such great things; but perchance those who are occupied with important matters have hearts like the claws of an eagle, which do not retain small things, but which great ones do not escape." And he, "so be it: but although eagles fly very high, nevertheless they rest and refresh themselves in humble places; and therefore we beg thee to explain humble things which will be of profit to the eagles themselves." Then I; "I have feared to put together a work concerning these things because they lie open to the bodily senses and grow common by daily use; nor is there, nor can there be in them a description of subtile things, or a pleasing invention of the imagination." And he, "those who rejoice in imaginings, who seek the flight of subtile things, have Aristotle and the books of Plato; to them let them listen. Do thou write not subtile but useful things." Then I; "of those things which thou demandest it is impossible to speak except in common discourse and in ordinary words." "But," said he, as if aroused to ire,—for to a mind filled with desire nothing goes quickly enough,— "writers on arts, lest they might seem to know too little about many things, and in order that art might less easily become known, have sought to appropriate many things, and have concealed them under unknown words: but thou dost not undertake to write about an art, but about certain customs and laws of the exchequer; and since these ought to be common, common words must necessarily be employed, so that the style may have relation to the things of which we are speaking. Moreover, although it is very often allowable to invent new words, I beg, nevertheless, if it please thee, that thou may'st not be ashamed to use the customary names of the things themselves which readily occur to the mind, so that no new difficulty from using unfamiliar words may arise to disturb us." Then I; "I see that thou art angry; but be calmer; I will do what thou dost urge. Rise, therefore, and sit opposite to me; and ask me concerning those things that occur to thee. But if thou shalt propound something unheard of, I shall not blush to say 'I do not know.' But let us both, like discreet beings, come to an agreement." And he; "thou respondest to my wish. Moreover, although an elementary old man is a disgraceful and ridiculous thing, I will nevertheless begin with the very elements."

I. What the Exchequer is, and what is the reason of this name.

Disciple. What is the exchequer?

Master. The exchequer is a quadrangular surface about ten feet in length, five in breadth, placed before those who sit around it in the manner of a table, and all around it it has an edge about the height of one's four fingers, lest any thing placed upon it should fall off. There is placed over the top of the exchequer, moreover, a cloth bought at the Easter term, not an ordinary one but a black one marked with stripes, the stripes being distant from each other the space of a foot or the breadth of a hand. In the spaces moreover are counters placed according to their values; about these we shall speak below. Although, moreover, such a surface is called exchequer, nevertheless this name is so changed about that the court itself which sits when the exchequer does is called exchequer; so that if at any time through a decree any thing is established by common counsel, it is said to have been done at the exchequer of this or that year. As, moreover, one says today "at the exchequer," so one formerly said "at the tallies."

D   What is the reason of this name?

M   No truer one occurs to me at present than that it has a shape similar to that of a chess board.

D   Would the prudence of the ancients ever have called it so for its shape alone, when it might for a similar reason be called a table (tabularium)?

M   I was right in calling thee painstaking. There is another, but a more hidden reason. For just as, in a game of chess, there are certain grades of combatants and they proceed or stand still by certain laws or limitations, some presiding and others advancing: so, in this, some preside, some assist by reason of their office, and no one is free to exceed the fixed laws; as will be manifest from what is to follow. Moreover, as in chess the battle is fought between kings, so in this it is chiefly between two that the conflict takes place and the war is waged,—the treasurer, namely, and the sheriff who sits there to render account; the others sitting by as judges, to see and to judge.

D   Will the accounts be received then by the treasurer, although there are many there who, by reason of their power, are greater?

M   That the treasurer ought to receive the account from the sheriff is manifest from this, that the same is required from him whenever it pleases the king: nor could that be required of him which he had not received. Some say, nevertheless, that the treasurer and the chamberlains should be bounden alone for what is written in the rolls in the treasury, and that for this an account should be demanded of them. But it is believed with more truth that they should be responsible for the whole writing of the roll, as will be readily understood from what is to follow.

II. That there is a lower one and an upper one; both have the same origin however.

D   Is that exchequer, in which such a conflict goes on, the only one?

M   No. For there is a lower exchequer which is also called the Receipt, where the money is handed over to be counted, and is put down in writing and on tallies, so that afterwards, at the upper exchequer, an account may be rendered of them; both have the same origin however, for whatever is declared payable at the greater one is here paid; and whatever has been paid here is accounted for there.

III. As to the nature or arrangement of the lower one according to the separate offices.

D   What is the nature or arrangement of the lower exchequer?

M   As I see, thou canst not bear to be ignorant of any of these things. Know then that that lower exchequer has its persons, distinct from each other by reason of their offices, but with one intent devoted to the interests of the king, due regard, nevertheless, being paid to equity; all serving, moreover, not in their own names but in the names of their masters; with the exception of two knights, he, namely, who conducts the assays, and the melter. Their offices depend on the will of our king; hence they seem to belong rather to the upper than to the lower exchequer, as will be explained below. The clerk of the treasurer is there with his seal. There are also two knights of the chamberlains. There is also a certain knight who may be called the silverer, for, by reason of his office, he presides at the testing of silver. There are also four tellers to count the money. There is also the usher of the treasury and the watchman. These, moreover, are their offices: The clerk of the treasurer, when the money has been counted and put in boxes by the hundred pounds, affixes his seal and puts down in writing how much he has received, and from whom, and for what cause; he registers also the tallies which have been made by the chamberlains concerning that receipt. Not only, moreover, does he place his seal on the sacks of money, but also, if he wishes, on the chests and on the separate boxes in which the rolls and tallies are placed, and he diligently supervises all the offices which are under him, and nothing is hidden from him. The office of the knights, who are also called chamberlains because they serve in the name of the chamberlains, is this: they carry the keys of the chests; for each chest has two locks of a different kind, that is, to neither of which the key of the other can be fitted; and they carry the keys of them. Each chest, moreover, is girded with a certain immovable strap, on which, in addition, when the locks are closed the seal of the treasurer is placed; so that neither of the chamberlains can have access except by common consent. Likewise it is their duty to weigh the money which has been counted and placed by the hundred shillings in wooden receptacles, so that there be no error in the amount; and then, at length, to put them in boxes by the hundred pounds as has been said. But if a receptacle is found to have any deficiency, that

which is thought to be lacking is not made good by calculation, but straightway the doubtful one is thrown back into the heap which is to be counted. And take note that certain counties from the time of king Henry I and in the time of king Henry II could lawfully offer for payment coins of any kind of money provided they were of silver and did not differ from the lawful weight; because indeed, by ancient customs, not themselves having moneyers, they sought their coins from on all sides; such are Northumberland and Cumberland. Coins thus received, moreover, although they came from a farm, were nevertheless set apart from the others with some marks placed on them. But the remaining counties were accustomed to bring only the usual and lawful coin of the present money as well from farms as from pleas. But after the illustrious king whose renown shines the brighter in great matters, did, in his reign, institute one weight and one money for the whole kingdom, each county began to be bound by one necessity of law and to be constrained by the manner of payment of a general commerce. All, therefore, in whatever manner they are bounden, pay the same kind of money; but nevertheless all do not sustain the loss which comes from the testing by combustion. The chamberlains likewise make the tallies of receipts, and have in common with the clerk of the treasurer to disburse the treasure received when required by writs of the king or an order of the barons; not, however, without consulting their masters. These three, all together or by turns, are sent with treasure when it is necessary. These three have the principal care of all that is done in the lower exchequer.

D   Therefore, as I perceive, these men are allowed to disburse the treasure received, in consequence of a royal writ or of an order from those who preside—after consultation with their masters, however.

M   They are allowed, I say; in so far as they are entrusted with the payment of the servants of the lower exchequer, and with buying the small necessaries of the exchequer, such as the wooden receptacles, and other things which will be mentioned below; but not otherwise. When any one brings a writ or order of the king for money, by command of their masters that sum which is expressly named in the writ may be paid, with the understanding that, before he go out, he shall count the money received. But if anything be lacking, he who received it shall return to the exchequer and shall give an oath to this effect: that he has brought back as much as he received, adding this, *upon his conscience*, as is done in other things; and this being done the rest shall be paid him, it being first counted in the presence of all by the regular tellers. But if, the conditions being known to him, he shall have gone out of the door of the treasury, whoever the person, or however great the loss, no heed shall be paid to him. The offices of the knight silverer and of the melter are conjoined and belong rather to the upper exchequer, and therefore will be explained there with the other offices. The office of the four tellers is the following: When the money is sent to the exchequer to be counted, one of them diligently mixes the whole together, so that the better pieces may not be by themselves and the worse by themselves, but mixed, in order that they may correspond in weight; this being done, the chamberlain weighs in a scale as much as is necessary to make a pound of the exchequer. But if the number shall exceed 20 shillings by more than six pence in a pound, it is considered unfit to be received; but if it shall restrict itself to six pence or less, it is received, and is counted diligently by the tellers by the hundred shillings as has been said. But if the coins are from a farm and are to be tested, 44 shillings from the heap, being mixed together, are placed in a compartment by themselves, and on this the sheriff puts a mark; so that there may be afterwards a testing, which is commonly called assaying, of them, as will be made clear further on. It shall, moreover, be the care of those who preside over the Receipt by virtue of their masters—that is of the clerks of the treasurer and of the chamberlains—when the money is received, to put aside weights of the tested silver and coins from a farm, placing certain marks on the bags that contain them, so that, if the king wishes silver vessels to be made for the uses of the house of God, or for the service of his own palace, or perchance money for beyond seas, it may be made from this.

D There is something in what thou hast said that strikes me.

M Speak then.

D Thou said'st, if I remember rightly, that sometimes money is brought to be paid into the exchequer which is judged unfit to be received, if, indeed, being weighed against a pound weight of the exchequer, a deficiency is found of more than six pence. Inasmuch, then, as all money of this kingdom ought to have the stamped image of the king, and all moneyers are bound to work according to the same weight, how can it happen that all their work is not of one weight?

M That is a great question which thou askest, and one which requires further investigation; but it can happen through forgers and clippers or cutters of coin. Thou knowest, moreover, that the money of England can be found false in three ways: false, namely, in weight, false in quality, false in the stamping. But these kinds of falsification are not visited by an equal punishment. But of this elsewhere.

D If it please thee, continue concerning the offices as thou hast begun.

M It is the duty of the usher to exclude or admit as is necessary, and to be diligent in guarding every thing which is shut in by the door; wherefore, as door-money, he shall have two pence from each writ of exit. He furnishes the boxes to put the money in, and the rolls and the tallies, and the other things which become necessary during the year; and for each box he has two pence. He furnishes the whole Receipt with wood suitable for the tallies of receipts and of accounts, and once, that is at the Michaelmas term, he receives five shillings for the wood of the tallies. He furnishes the wooden receptacles, the knives, the compartments, and the straps and the other minute necessaries of the fisc. At that same term are due two shillings for furnishing the ink of the whole year to both exchequers, and this amount, by ancient right, the sacristan of the greater church of Westminster claims for himself. The office of the watchman is the same there as elsewhere; most diligent guarding, namely, at night, chiefly of the treasure and of all those things which are placed in the treasury building. Thus thou hast the various offices of those who serve in the lower exchequer. And they have fixed payments while the exchequer is in progress, that is from the day on which they are called together, to the day on which there is a general departure. The clerk of the treasurer who is below, has five pence a day. The scribe of the same treasurer in the upper exchequer has likewise five. The scribe of the chancellor, five. The two knights who bear the keys have each eight, by reason of their knighthood. For they claim that they are bound to be ready with the necessary horses and weapons, so that when they are sent with the treasure they may thus more readily execute what pertains to their office. The knight-silverer has twelve pence a day. The melter, five. The usher of the greater exchequer, five. The four tellers, each three pence, if they are at London; if at Winchester each one has two, since they are generally taken from there. The watchman has one penny. For the light of each night at the treasury one halfpenny.

D   For what reason does the usher of the treasury alone receive no pay?

M   I do not exactly know. But, however, perhaps he does not receive any pay because he is seen to receive something as door-money, and for furnishing the boxes and tallies; or perchance because he seems to serve, not the king, but the treasurer and the chamberlains in guarding the door of their building. In this way, then, has the arrangement of the lower exchequer or Receipt been made.

D   I have been so well satisfied in this regard that nothing seems to be wanting. Proceed now, if it please thee, concerning the greater exchequer.

IV. What is the competency of the Upper Exchequer, and whence it takes its origin.

M   Although the offices of those who have seats at the greater exchequer seem to differ in certain functions, the purpose, nevertheless, of all the offices is the same, to look out for the king's advantage; with due regard for equity, however, according to the fixed laws of the exchequer. The arrangement or ordering of the latter is confirmed by its antiquity and by the authority of the nobles who have their seats there. It is said to have begun with the very conquest of the kingdom made by king William, the arrangement being taken, however, from the exchequer across the seas; but they differ in very many and almost the most important points. Some believe it to have existed under the Anglo-Saxon kings, taking their argument in this matter from the fact that the peasants and already decrepit old men of those estates which are called of the crown, whose memory is gray in these matters, knew very well, having been taught by their fathers, how much extra money they are bound to pay on the pound for the blanching of their farm. But this argument applies to the payment of the farm, not to the session of the exchequer. The fact also seems to be against those who say that the blanching of the farm began in the time of the Anglo-Saxon kings, that in the Domesday book, in which a diligent description of the whole kingdom is contained, and in which the value is expressed of the different estates as well of the time of king Edward as of the time of king William, under whom it was made,—there is no mention at all of the blanching of the farm: from which it seems probable that, after the time when that survey was made in the reign of the aforementioned king, the blanching of the farm was fixed upon by his investigators on account of causes which are noted below. But at whatever time it came into use, it is certain that the exchequer is confirmed by the authority of the great, so that it is allowed to no one to infringe its statutes or to resist them by any kind of rashness. For it has this in common with the Court itself of the lord king (Curia Regis), in which he in his own person administers the law, that no one is allowed to contradict a record or a sentence passed in it. The authority, moreover, of this court is so great, as well on account of the pre-eminence of the royal image, which, by a special prerogative, is kept on his seal of the treasury, as on account of those who have their seats there, as has been said; by whose watchfulness the condition of the whole kingdom is kept safe. For there sits the Chief Justice of the lord king by reason of his judicial dignity, as well as the greatest men of the kingdom, who share familiarly in the royal secrets; so that whatever has been established or determined in the presence of such great men subsists by an inviolable right. In the first place, there sits, nay also presides, by reason of his office, the first man in the kingdom,—namely, the Chief Justice. With him sit, solely by command of the sovereign, with momentary and varying authority, indeed, certain of the greatest and most discreet men in the kingdom, who may belong either to the clergy or to the court. They sit there, I say, to interpret the law and to decide upon the doubtful points which frequently arise from incidental questions. For not in its reckonings, but in its manifold judgments, does the superior science of the exchequer consist. For it is easy when the sum required has been put down, and the sums which have been handed in are placed under it for comparison, to tell by subtraction if the demands have been satisfied or if anything remains. But when one begins to make a many-sided investigation of those things which come into the fisc in varying ways, and are required under different conditions, and are not collected by the sheriffs in the same way,—to be able to tell if the latter have acted otherwise than they should, is in many ways a grave task. Therefore the greater science of the exchequer is said to consist in these matters. But the judgments on doubtful or doubted points which frequently come up can not be comprehended under one form of treatment; for all kinds of doubts have not yet come to light. Certain, however, of the matters which we know to have been brought up and settled, we shall note below in their proper place.

ACCOUNTS OF THE EXCHEQUER: AN EXAMPLE

The accounts of the Exchequer were recorded in the Pipe rolls. The following brief example is that of Henry II for Staffordshire from 1186.

Source: *English Historical Documents II.*

Thomas Noel[1] accounts for the 'farm' of Staffordshire. He has paid in the Treasury 88 pounds and 6 pence 'blanch'.

He has disbursed:

In fixed alms 1 mark to the knights of the Temple. In fixed liveries half a mark to the canons of Llanthony for the keeping of the king's houses at Cannock.
In lands granted to the monks of Bordesley 10 pounds 'blanch' in Tardebigg. And in Trentham 30 pounds 'blanch' concerning which Geoffrey Savage accounts below. And in Meertown 8 pounds 'blanch' concerning which Roger Muisson accounts below. And to William 'de Herovilla' 60 shillings 'blanch' in Wednesbury.
And he is quit.

Concerning purprestures and escheats

The same sheriff accounts for 33 shillings and 4 pence for the 'farm' of Broom; and for 1 mark for the 'farm' of Rowley Regis. He has made payment in the Treasury by means of 2 tallies. And he is quit.
Geoffrey Savage accounts for 30 pounds 'blanch' in respect of the 'farm' of Trentham. He has paid into the Treasury 14 pounds and 23 pence 'blanch'.
He has disbursed:
In lands given to the knights of the Temple in Keele, 43 shillings and 7 pence.
To John the chaplain, 100 shillings.
In fixed liveries to ten serjeants, 9 pounds, 2 shillings and 6 pence.
In pasture which the king granted to John

Lestrange, 8 shillings and 8 pence. And he is quit.

The same Geoffrey renders account for 8 pounds 'blanch' for the 'farm' of Meretown. He has paid into the Treasury. And he is quit.

Robert 'de Broc' accounts for 3 marks in respect of rent for the forest of Cannock for the third year. He has paid this in the Treasury. And he is quit.

The same Robert accounts for 6 pounds, 13 shillings and 4 pence for rent for the same forest of Cannock for this year. He has paid in the Treasury. And he is quit.

The same Robert accounts for 116 shillings and 3 pence in respect of the pannage of the forest of Cannock. He has paid in the Treasury. And he is quit.

[The same sheriff] accounts for 6 pounds in respect of the increase of Walsall. And for 3 shillings and 6 pence in respect of the house of Walter the reeve in the cemetery of Stafford. He has paid in the Treasury by means of 2 tallies. And he is quit.

The same sheriff accounts for 3 shillings in respect of the profits of the mill at Cradley. And for 13 shillings and 4 pence for the prebend of Penkridge. He has made payment in the Treasury by means of 2 tallies. And he is quit.

[William], son of Guy, owes 2 war-horses in respect of the amercement of the king in connexion with the forest.

[Gervase] Paynel accounts for 14 pounds, 13 shillings and 4 pence that he may be quit of the pledge made by the earl of Leicester to Aaron the Jew, and that he may not be distrained for that pledge. He has paid 5 marks in the Treasury. And he owes 11 pounds, 6 shillings and 8 pence.

The same sheriff owes 21 shillings in respect of the wastes, the assarts, the purprestures and the pleas of the forest of Staffordshire through Thomas, son of Bernard.

Ernald the priest owes 1 mark for false pleading.

Richard Miles the forester owes half a mark for default.

Robert of Beaumais accounts for 1 mark for the sale of wood in the forest. He has paid half a mark into the Treasury. And he owes half a mark.

Concerning pleas of the court

Alice who was the wife of Robert of Bec accounts for 10 pounds for the recognition of 1 knight's fee against Robert of Stafford by the pledge of Geoffrey Savage. She has paid 6 pounds in the Treasury. And she owes 4 pounds.

Alina of Darlaston owes 2 marks in respect of the right given her in the king's court against Walter of Caverswall concerning the land of Olnea. But she has not yet had right.

[Geoffrey] Savage accounts for 100 pounds for goods distrained by the sheriff. By writ of the king the said Geoffrey has been pardoned 100 pounds. And he is quit.

[Robert] 'Pulerefice' owes half a mark for making a false charge.

Concerning the offerings of the court

[William, son of] Turkill, owes 20 shillings for right in respect of 10 marks which he claims against the prior of Staines.

William of Sandford owes 1 mark for right concerning 5 marks against Robert of Tamhorn by the pledge of John of Sandford. But he has not yet had right.

New pleas and new agreements through Robert Marmion, Ralph of Arden, Hugh Pantulf, William, son of Stephen, and Thomas Noel

The same sheriff[2] accounts for 1 mark from Totmonslow for murder.[3]

And for 1 mark from Eitroph Hasting because he first denied what he afterwards admitted.

And for 40 shillings from William of Birmingham because he did not have what he had pledged. He has made payment in the Treasury by means of 3 tallies. And he is quit.

The same sheriff accounts for 2 marks from Gerard of Stafford in respect of the pledge of Robert the Frenchman. And for 1 mark from William the Frenchman for the same. And for 1 mark from Margaret 'de la Barre' for false accusation.

And for 1 mark from Hereward of 'Huneswurth' for false witness.

The king has granted by his writ 5 marks from the amercements of the above to the brethren of the Hospital of Jerusalem.

And he is quit.

The same sheriff accounts for 20 shillings from 'Pirhulle' hundred for murder. He has paid 18 shillings in the Treasury. And he owes 2 shillings. The same sheriff accounts for 1 mark from Cuttleston hundred for murder. He has paid 12 shillings and 8 pence in the Treasury. And he owes 8 pence.

Hugh of Comberford accounts for 10 marks for 'novel disseisin'. He has paid 44 shillings and 4 pence in the Treasury. And he owes 4 pounds and 9 shillings.

Simon, son of Ailwin, accounts for 2 marks for the same. He has paid half a mark into the Treasury. And he owes 20 shillings.

Concerning those who have paid in full

The same sheriff accounts for 10 pounds and 3 shillings and 4 pence in respect of petty amercements from those men whose names and debts and delinquencies are noted in the roll of the aforesaid, and which they have paid in the Treasury. He has made payment in the Treasury by means of 30 tallies. And he is quit.

Gamel of 'Deruereslawa' owes half a mark because he did not have 'Suanhilda' whom he had pledged.

Godwin, son of Chilla, owes half a mark for 'novel disseisin'.

Richard Wagtail accounts for half a mark because he withdrew from his appeal. He has paid 12 pence in the Treasury. And he owes 5 shillings and 8 pence.

Concerning the pleas of the forest through Robert 'de Broc', William of Stanton and Robert of 'Haselea'

John of Perton accounts for 20 shillings for keeping dogs in the forest without a warrant. He has paid this in the Treasury. And he is quit.

Concerning those who have paid in full in respect of pleas of the forest

The same sheriff accounts for 66 shillings in respect of petty amercements for the forest. He has paid in the Treasury, and he is quit.

Robert of Walton owes 2 shillings for new purpresture.

The same sheriff accounts for 63 shillings and 4 pence in respect of petty amercements for the forest. He has paid in the Treasury by means of 9 tallies. And he is quit.

The same sheriff accounts for 4 pounds, 2 shillings and 3 pence in respect of the assarts of Staffordshire. He has paid in the Treasury 40 shillings and 9 pence. And he owes 41 shillings and 6 pence.

Concerning the pleas of the court

Guy of Swinfen renders account for 1 mark for making his complaint against Henry of Perry in the king's court instead of in the shire court. He has paid in the Treasury. And he is quit.

Concerning the tallage of the demesne lands of the king and of those lands which were then in the king's hands; through Robert Marmion and his associates as aforesaid

The same sheriff accounts as follows:

For 15 pounds, 4 shillings and 8 pence for the gift of Newcastle.[4] He has paid 8 pounds and 10 shillings in the Treasury. And he owes 6 pounds, 13 shillings and 8 pence.

For 13 pounds for the gift of the borough of Stafford. He has paid 6 pounds and 10 shillings in the Treasury. And he owes 6 pounds and 10 shillings.

For 55 shillings in respect of the gift of Meretown. He has paid 53 shillings. And he owes 2 shillings.

For 103 shillings and 8 pence for the gift of Penkridge. He has paid 52 shillings in the Treasury. And he owes 51 shillings and 8 pence.

For 46 shillings and 8 pence for the gift of Cannock. He has paid 23 shillings and 4 pence in the Treasury. And he owes 23 shillings and 4 pence.

For 4 pounds and 17 shillings for the gift of Kinver. He has paid this in the Treasury. And he is quit.

For 71 shillings for the gift of Rugeley. He has paid 35 shillings and 6 pence into the Treasury. And he owes 35 shillings and 6 pence.

For 58 shillings and 4 pence for the gift of Clent.

He has paid 29 shillings and 2 pence in the Treasury. And he owes 29 shillings and 2 pence.

For 34 shillings for the gift of Wolverhampton. He has paid 17 shillings in the Treasury. And he owes 17 shillings.

For 36 shillings for the gift of Bilston. He has paid 18 shillings in the Treasury. And he owes 18 shillings.

For 17 shillings for the gift of Willenhall. He has paid this into the Treasury. And he is quit.

For 63 shillings and 8 pence for the gift of Tettenhall. He has paid 31 shillings and 10 pence in the Treasury. And he owes 31 shillings and 10 pence.

For 40 shillings for the gift of Bromley. He has paid 20 shillings in the Treasury. And he owes 20 shillings.

For 42 shillings for the gift of Walsall. He has paid 21 shillings in the Treasury. And he owes 21 shillings.

For 74 shillings for the gift of Swinford. He has paid 37 shillings in the Treasury. And he owes 37 shillings.

For 24 shillings and 8 pence for the gift of Penkhull. He has paid in the Treasury. And he is quit.

For 43 shillings and 4 pence for the gift of Tamworth. He has paid 28 shillings and 4 pence in the Treasury. And he owes 15 shillings.

For 100 shillings for the gift of Wigginton. He has paid 60 shillings in the Treasury. And he owes 40 shillings.

For 4 pounds, 7 shillings and 4 pence for the gift of Aldridge. He has paid 44 shillings in the Treasury. And he owes 43 shillings and 4 pence.

For 20 shillings for the gift of 'Lench'. He has paid 10 shillings in the Treasury. And he owes 10 shillings.

The same sheriff owes 40 shillings for the gift of Arley.

Concerning the chattels of outlaws

The same sheriff accounts as follows:

For 6 shillings and 9 pence for the chattels of Richard of Great Barr for the same.

For 8 shillings and 2 pence for the chattels of Ordric of Great Barr for the same.

For 11 pence for the chattels of William Prutel for the same.

For 19 shillings and 3 pence for the chattels of William of Featherstone.

For 5 shillings for the chattels of Anschill of Madeley.

For 17 shillings and 8 pence for the chattels of Ralph of Himley.

For 14 pence for the chattels of William the clerk of Swinford.

For 12 shillings for the chattels of Aldred of Ketley.

For half a mark for the chattels of Adam and Robert of Pipe. The sum is 4 pounds, 12 shillings and 7 pence. He has paid this in the Treasury by means of 10 tallies. And he is quit.

The same sheriff renders account for 43 shillings and 5 pence for the profit of the land of Simon 'le Sage', which his of the fee of the bishop of Chester. He has paid this into the Treasury. And he is quit.

The same sheriff renders account for 28 shillings and 9 pence for the profit of Coton, which was in the possession of William, son of Alan, for a whole year and for a quarter of a year. He has paid this into the Treasury. And he is quit.

The same sheriff renders account for 8 shillings and 1 penny for the profit of the land of Ralph of Himley for three-quarters of a year. He has paid this into the Treasury. And he is quit.

Concerning the scutage of the knights of Staffordshire who did not go with the king on the expedition to Galloway

The bishop of Chester renders account for 15 pounds of the scutage of his knights. He has paid 14 pounds in the Treasury. And he owes 20 shillings.

Bertram of Verdun renders account for 20 shillings of the scutage of 1 knight. He has paid this into the Treasury, and he is quit.

Robert 'de Broc' and William of Stanton and Robert of 'Haselea' render account for 6 pounds and 4 shillings and 2 pence in respect of the pannage of Herefordshire in Wales. And for 110 shillings and 9 pence of the pannage of Gloucestershire. And for 6 shillings for the pannage of Bushley in Worcestershire. And for 48 shillings and 2 pence for the pannage of Shropshire. The sum is 14 pounds and 9 shillings and 1 penny. They have made payment for this in the Treasury by means of 4 tallies. And they are quit.

Notes

1 The sheriff.
2 Thomas Noel; see above.
3 The *murdrum* or murder-fine.
4 Newcastle-under-Lyme.

MAGNA CARTA

Magna carta, THE CONSERVATIVE BARONIAL REACTION TO KING John's policies and to his defeat at the hands of the French, took final form only over the course of several years. The following documents allow one to trace this evolution. The *Articles of the barons* was the draft of terms demanded by the barons at Runnymede. The second is the form of *Magna carta* issued by the royal chancery shortly after Runnymede. Within the year, John's nominal lord, Pope Innocent III declared the document, radical by ecclesiastical standards, null and void (third document). The final is the altered version reissued by Henry III in 1216.

Source: *English Historical Documents*, vol. 3, edited by Harry Rothwell

The articles of the barons, 15 June 1215

These are the articles which the barons ask for and the lord king grants

1   After the death of their predecessors, heirs who are of full age shall have their inheritance on payment of the old relief, which is to be stated in the charter.

2   Heirs who are under age and are wards shall have their inheritance when they come of age without paying relief and without making fine.

3   The guardian of the land of an heir shall take reasonable revenues, customary dues and services without destruction and waste of his men and goods, and if the guardian of the land causes destruction and waste, he shall lose the wardship; and the guardian shall keep in repair the houses, parks, preserves, ponds, mills and other things pertaining to the land out of the revenue from it; and that heirs shall be so married that they are not disparaged and on the advice of those nearest in blood to them.

4   That a widow shall not pay anything to have her dower or marriage portion after the death of her husband, but shall remain in his house for forty days after his death, and within that term the dower shall be assigned to her; the marriage portion and her inheritance she shall have forthwith.

5   King or bailiff shall not seize any land for debt while the chattels of the debtor suffice; nor shall those who have gone surety for the debtor be distrained while the principal debtor is himself able to pay; if however the principal debtor fails to pay, the sureties shall, if they wish, have the lands of the debtor until that debt is fully paid, unless the principal debtor can show that he has discharged his obligation in the matter to the sureties.

6   The king shall not grant any baron the right to take an aid from his free men, except for ransoming his person, for making his eldest son a knight and for once marrying his eldest daughter, and this he shall do by a reasonable aid.

7   That no one shall do greater service for a knight's fee than is due from it.

8   That common pleas shall not follow the court of the lord king, but shall be assigned in some fixed place; and that recognitions be held in the counties to which they relate, in this manner— that the king shall send two justices four times a year, who with four knights of the same county chosen by the county shall hold assizes of *novel disseisin, mort d'ancestor* and *darrein presentment*, nor shall anyone be summoned on account of this save the jurors and the two parties.

9   That a free man shall be amerced for a trivial offence in accordance with the degree of the

offence, and for a grave offence in accordance with its gravity, yet saving his way of living; a villein also shall be amerced in the same way, saving his means of livelihood; and a merchant in the same way, saving his stock-in-trade; by the oath of good men of the neighborhood.

10   That a clerk shall be amerced in respect of his lay fief after the manner of the others aforesaid and not according to his ecclesiastical benefice.

11   That no vill shall be amerced for the purpose of making bridges at river banks save where they used to be legally and of old.

12   That the measure for wine, corn and widths of cloths and other things be improved; and so with weights.

13   That assizes of *novel disseisin* and of *mort d'ancestor* be shortened; and similarly with other assizes.

14   That no sheriff shall concern himself with pleas pertaining to the crown without coroners; and that counties and hundreds be at the old rents without any additional payment, except the king's demesne manors.

15   If anyone holding of the king dies, it shall be lawful for the sheriff or other bailiff of the king to seize and make a list of his chattels under the supervision of lawworthy men, provided that none of the chattels shall be removed until it is more fully known whether he owes any manifest debt to the lord king and then the debt to the king is paid in full; the residue however shall be left to the executors for carrying out the will of the deceased. And if nothing is owing to the king, all the chattels shall accrue to the deceased.

16   If any free man dies without leaving a will, his goods shall be distributed by his nearest kinfolk and friends and under the supervision of the church.

17   That widows shall not be forced to marry, so long as they wish to live without a husband, provided that they give security not to marry without the consent of the king, if they hold of the king, or of the lords of whom they hold.

18   That no constable or other bailiff shall take corn or other chattels unless he pays on the spot in cash for them, unless he can delay payment by arrangement with the seller.

19   That no constable shall be able to compel any knight to give money instead of castle-guard if he is willing to do the guard himself or through another good man, if for some good reason he cannot do it himself; and if the king leads him on military service, let him be excused guard in proportion to the time.

20   That no sheriff or king's bailiff or anyone else shall take the horses or carts of any free man for transport work save with his agreement.

21   That neither the king nor his bailiff shall take another man's timber for castles or other works of his, except with the agreement of him whose timber it is.

22   That the king shall not hold for more than a year and a day the land of those convicted of felony, but then it shall be handed over to the lord of the fief.

23   That all fish-weirs be henceforth cleared completely from the Thames and Medway and throughout all England.

24   That the writ called *Praecipe* be not in future issued to anyone in respect of any holding whereby a free man may lose his court.

25   If any one has been disseised of or kept out of his lands, franchises and his right by the king without a judgment, let it be immediately restored to him; and if a dispute arises over this, then let it be decided by the judgment of the twenty-five barons; and that those who were disseised by the father or the brother of the king get justice without delay by the judgment of their peers in the king's court; and let the archbishop and bishops by a certain date give their decision, which shall be final, whether the king

should have the respite allowed to other crusaders.

26 That nothing be given for the writ of inquisition of life or limbs, but that instead it be freely granted without charge and not refused.

27 If anyone holds of the king by fee-farm, by socage, or by burgage, and of another by knight service, the lord king shall not, by reason of the burgage or socage, have the wardship of the knights of the fief of the other, nor ought he to have custody of the burgage, socage or fee-farm; and that a free man shall not lose his knight service by reason of petty serjeanties, such as those who hold any holding by rendering knives or arrows or the like for it.

28 That no bailiff be able to put anyone to trial[1] upon his own bare word without reliable witnesses.

29 That the body of a free man be not arrested or imprisoned or disseised or outlawed or exiled or in any way victimised, nor shall the king attack or send anyone to attack him with force, except by the judgment of his social equals or by the law of the land.

30 That right be not sold or delayed or forbidden to be done.

31 That merchants be able to go and come safely for buying or selling by the ancient and right customs, free from all evil tolls.

32 That no scutage or aid be imposed in the kingdom unless by common counsel of the kingdom, except for ransoming the king's person, for making his eldest son a knight, and for once marrying his eldest daughter; and for this a reasonable aid shall be levied. Be it done in like manner concerning tallages and aids from the city of London and from other cities which have liberties in respect thereof, and that the city of London have in full its ancient liberties and free customs as well by water as by land.

33 That it be lawful for any one, without prejudicing the allegiance due to the lord king, to leave the kingdom and return, save, in the public interest, for a short period in time of war.

34 If anyone who has borrowed from the Jews any sum, great or small, dies before it is repaid, the debt shall not bear interest as long as the heir is under age, of whomsoever he holds; and if the debt falls into the hand of the king, the king shall not take anything except the principal which is mentioned in the bond.

35 If anyone dies indebted to the Jews, his wife shall have her dower; and if children are left, they shall be provided with necessities befitting the holding; and the debt shall be paid out of the residue, reserving, however, service due to lords of the land; other debts shall be dealt with in like manner; and that the guardian of the land shall restore to the heir when he comes of full age his land stocked, according to what he can reasonably bear from the revenues of the land, with ploughs and the means of husbandry.

36 If anyone who holds of some escheat such as the honour of Wallingford, Nottingham, Boulogne, and Lancaster or of other escheats which are in the king's hands and are baronies, dies, his heir shall give no other relief or do no other service to the king than he would have done to the baron; and that the king hold it in the same manner in which the baron held it.

37 That fines made for dowers, marriage portions, inheritances and amercements unjustly and against the law be entirely remitted, or else let them be settled by the judgment of the twenty-five barons, or by the judgment of the majority of the same, along with the archbishop and such others as he may wish to associate with himself, provided that if any one or more of the twenty-five are in a like suit they be removed and others put in their place by the rest of the twenty-five.

38 That hostages and charters given to the king as security be returned.

39 That those who were outside the forest need not come before justices of the forest upon a gen-

eral summons, unless they are impleaded or are sureties; and that wicked customs connected with forests and with foresters and warrens and sheriffs and river-banks be amended by twelve knights of every county who are to be chosen by good men of the same county.

40 That the king remove completely from office the relations and all the following of Gerard d'Athée so that they have no office in future, namely Engeland, Andrew, Peter and Guy de Chanceaux, Guy de Cigogné, Matthew de Martigny and his brothers and his nephew Geoffrey and Philip Marc.

41 And that the king remove foreign knights, mercenaries, cross-bowmen, routiers and serjeants, who come with horses and arms to the detriment of the kingdom.

42 That the king make justices, constables, sheriffs and bailiffs of such as know the law of the land and mean to observe it well.

43 That barons who have founded abbeys, for which they have royal charters or ancient tenure, have the custody of them during vacancies.

44 If the king has disseised or kept out Welshmen from lands or liberties or from other things in England or in Wales they shall be immediately restored to them without a lawsuit; and if they were disseised or kept out of their holdings in England by the king's father or brother without the judgment of their peers, the king shall without delay do justice to them in the way that he does justice to the English, for their holdings in England according to the law of England, and for holdings in Wales according to the law of Wales, and for holdings in the March according to the law of the March; Welshmen shall do the same to the king and his men.

45 That the king give back the son of Llywelyn and, besides, all the hostages from Wales and the charters that were handed over to him as security for peace (unless, in the judgment of the archbishop and of such others as he may wish to asso-ciate with himself, it ought to be otherwise by the charters which the king has).

46 That the king act towards the king of the Scots concerning the return of hostages and concerning his franchises and his right in the same manner in which he acts towards the barons of England (unless, in the judgment of the archbishop and of such others as he may wish to associate with himself, it ought to be otherwise by the charters which the king has).

47 And let all forests that have been made forest by the king in his time be dis-afforested, and so be it done with river-banks that have been made preserves[2] by the king himself.

48 All these customs and liberties which the king has granted to be observed in the kingdom as far as it pertains to him towards his men, all of the kingdom, clerks as well as laymen, shall observe as far as it pertains to them towards their men.

[A space in the manuscript between [48] and [49].]

49 This is the form of security for the observance of the peace and liberties between the king and the kingdom. The barons shall choose any twenty-five barons of the kingdom they wish, who must with all their might observe, hold and cause to be observed, the peace and liberties which the lord king has granted and confirmed to them by his charter; so that if the king or the justiciar or the king's bailiffs or any one of his servants offends in any way against any one or transgresses any of the articles of the peace or the security and the offence be notified to four of the aforesaid twenty-five barons, those four barons shall come to the lord king, or to his justiciar if the king is out of the kingdom, and, laying the transgression before him, shall petition him to have that transgression corrected without delay; and if the king or his justiciar does not correct it, if the king is out of the kingdom, within a reasonable time to be determined in the charter, the aforesaid four shall refer that case to the rest of the twenty-five barons and those twenty-five

together with the community of the whole land shall distrain and distress the king in every way they can, namely, by seizing castles, lands, possessions, and in such other ways as they can, saving the person of the lord king and the persons of the queen and his children, until, in their opinion, amends have been made; and when amends have been made they shall obey the lord king as before. And anyone in the land who wishes shall take an oath to obey the orders of the said twenty-five barons for the execution of the aforesaid matters, and with them to distress the king as much as he can, and the king shall publicly and freely give anyone leave to take the oath who wishes to take it and he shall never prohibit anyone from taking it. Indeed, all those in the land who are unwilling of their own accord and of themselves to take an oath to the twenty-five barons to help them to distrain and distress the king, the king shall make them take the oath as aforesaid at his command. Also, if any of the said twenty-five barons dies or leaves the country or is in any other way prevented from carrying out the things aforesaid, the rest of the twenty-five shall choose as they think fit another one in his place, and he shall take the oath like the rest. In all matters the execution of which is committed to these twenty-five barons, if it should happen that these twenty-five are present yet disagree among themselves about anything, or if some of those summoned will not or cannot be present, that shall be held, as fixed and established which the majority of them ordained or commanded, exactly as if all the twenty-five had consented to it; and the said twenty-five shall swear that they will faithfully observe all the things aforesaid and will do all they can to get them observed. Furthermore, the king shall give them security by charters of the archbishop and bishops and master Pandulf that he will procure nothing from the lord pope whereby any of the things here agreed might be revoked or diminished, and if he does procure any such thing, let it be reckoned void and null and let him never use it.

Magna Carta, 1215

John, by the grace of God, king of England, lord of Ireland, duke of Normandy and Aquitaine, and count of Anjou, to the archbishops, bishops, abbots, earls, barons, justiciars, foresters, sheriffs, stewards, servants, and to all his bailiffs and faithful subjects, greeting. Know that we, out of reverence for God and for the salvation of our soul and those of all our ancestors and heirs, for the honor of God and the exaltation of holy church, and for the reform of our realm, on the advice of our venerable fathers, Stephen, archbishop of Canterbury, primate of all England and cardinal of the holy Roman church, Henry archbishop of Dublin, William of London, Peter of Winchester, Jocelyn of Bath and Glastonbury, Hugh of Lincoln, Walter of Worcester, William of Coventry and Benedict of Rochester, bishops, of master Pandulf, subdeacon and member of the household of the lord pope, of brother Aymeric, master of the order of Knights Templar in England, and of the noble men William Marshal earl of Pembroke, William earl of Salisbury, William earl of Warenne, William earl of Arundel, Alan of Galloway constable of Scotland, Warin fitz Gerold, Peter fitz Herbert, Hubert de Burgh seneschal of Poitou, Hugh de Neville, Matthew fitz Herbert, Thomas Basset, Alan Basset, Philip de Aubeney, Robert of Ropsley, John Marshal, John fitz Hugh, and others, our faithful subjects:

1   In the first place have granted to God, and by this our present charter confirmed for us and our heirs for ever that the English church shall be free, and shall have its rights undiminished and its liberties unimpaired; and it is our will that it be thus observed; which is evident from the fact that, before the quarrel between us and our barons began, we willingly and spontaneously granted and by our charter confirmed the freedom of elections which is reckoned most important and very essential to the English church, and obtained confirmation of it from the lord pope Innocent III; the which we will observe and we wish our heirs to observe it in good faith for ever. We have also granted to all free men of our kingdom, for ourselves and our heirs for ever, all the liberties written below, to be had and held by them and their heirs of us and our heirs.

2   If any of our earls or barons or others holding

of us in chief by knight service dies, and at his death his heir be of full age and owe relief he shall have his inheritance on payment of the old relief, namely the heir or heirs of an earl £100 for a whole earl's barony, the heir or heirs of a baron £100 for a whole barony, the heir or heirs of a knight 100s, at most, for a whole knight's fee; and he who owes less shall give less according to the ancient usage of fiefs.

3   If, however, the heir of any such be under age and a ward, he shall have his inheritance when he comes of age without paying relief and without making fine.

4   The guardian of the land of such an heir who is under age shall take from the land of the heir no more than reasonable revenues, reasonable customary dues and reasonable services, and that without destruction and waste of men or goods; and if we commit the wardship of the land of any such to a sheriff, or to any other who is answerable to us for its revenues, and he destroys or wastes what he has wardship of, we will take compensation from him and the land shall be committed to two lawful and discreet men of that fief, who shall be answerable for the revenues to us or to him to whom we have assigned them; and if we give or sell to anyone the wardship of any such land and he causes destruction or waste therein, he shall lose that wardship, and it shall be transferred to two lawful and discreet men of that fief, who shall similarly be answerable to us as is aforesaid.

5   Moreover, so long as he has the wardship of the land, the guardian shall keep in repair the houses, parks, preserves, ponds, mills and other things pertaining to the land out of the revenues from it; and he shall restore to the heir when he comes of age his land fully stocked with ploughs and the means of husbandry according to what the season of husbandry requires and the revenues of the land can reasonably bear.

6   Heirs shall be married without disparagement, yet so that before the marriage is contracted those nearest in blood to the heir shall have notice.

7   A widow shall have her marriage portion and inheritance forthwith and without difficulty after the death of her husband; nor shall she pay anything to have her dower or her marriage portion or the inheritance which she and her husband held on the day of her husband's death; and she may remain in her husband's house for forty days after his death, within which time her dower shall be assigned to her.

8   No widow shall be forced to marry so long as she wishes to live without a husband, provided that she gives security not to marry without our consent if she holds of us, or without the consent of her lord of whom she holds, if she holds of another.

9   Neither we nor our bailiffs will seize for any debt any land or rent, so long as the chattels of the debtor are sufficient to repay the debt; nor will those who have gone surety for the debtor be distrained so long as the principal debtor is himself able to pay the debt; and if the principal debtor fails to pay the debt, having nothing wherewith to pay it, then shall the sureties answer for the debt; and they shall, if they wish, have the lands and rents of the debtor until they are reimbursed for the debt which they have paid for him, unless the principal debtor can show that he has discharged his obligation in the matter to the said sureties.

10   If anyone who has borrowed from the Jews any sum, great or small, dies before it is repaid, the debt shall not bear interest as long as the heir is under age, of whomsoever he holds; and if the debt falls into our hands, we will not take anything except the principal mentioned in the bond.

11   And if anyone dies indebted to the Jews, his wife shall have her dower and pay nothing of that debt; and if the dead man leaves children who are under age, they shall be provided with necessaries befitting the holding of the deceased; and the debt shall be paid out of the residue, reserving, however, service due to lords of the land; debts owing to others than Jews shall be dealt with in like manner.

12   No scutage or aid shall be imposed in our kingdom unless by common counsel of our kingdom, except for ransoming our person, for making our eldest son a knight, and for once marrying our eldest daughter; and for these only a reasonable aid shall be levied. Be it done in like manner concerning aids from the city of London.

13   And the city of London shall have all its ancient liberties and free customs as well by land as by water. Furthermore, we will and grant that all other cities, boroughs, towns, and ports shall have all their liberties and free customs.

14   And to obtain the common counsel of the kingdom about the assessing of an aid (except in the three cases aforesaid) or of a scutage, we will cause to be summoned the archbishops, bishops, abbots, earls and greater barons, individually by our letters—and, in addition, we will cause to be summoned generally through our sheriffs and bailiffs all those holding of us in chief—for a fixed date, namely, after the expiry of at least forty days, and to a fixed place; and in all letters of such summons we will specify the reason for the summons. And when the summons has thus been made, the business shall proceed on the day appointed, according to the counsel of those present, though not all have come who were summoned.

15   We will not in future grant any one the right to take an aid from his free men, except for ransoming his person, for making his eldest son a knight and for once marrying his eldest daughter, and for these only a reasonable aid shall be levied.

16   No one shall be compelled to do greater service for a knight's fee or for any other free holding than is due from it.

17   Common pleas shall not follow our court, but shall be held in some fixed place.

18   Recognitions of *novel disseisin*, of *mort d'ancester*, and of *darrein presentment*, shall not be held elsewhere than in the counties to which they relate, and in this manner—we, or, if we should be out of the realm, our chief justiciar, will send two justices through each county four times a year, who, with four knights of each county chosen by the county, shall hold the said assizes in the county and on the day and in the place of meeting of the county court.

19   And if the said assizes cannot all be held on the day of the county court, there shall stay behind as many of the knights and freeholders who were present at the county court on that day as are necessary for the sufficient making of judgments, according to the amount of business to be done.

20   A free man shall not be amerced for a trivial offence except in accordance with the degree of the offence, and for a grave offence he shall be amerced in accordance with its gravity, yet saving his way of living; and a merchant in the same way, saving his stock-in-trade; and a villein shall be amerced in the same way, saving his means of livelihood—if they have fallen into our mercy: and none of the aforesaid amercements shall be imposed except by the oath of good men of the neighborhood.

21   Earls and barons shall not be amerced except by their peers, and only in accordance with the degree of the offence.

22   No clerk shall be amerced in respect of his lay holding except after the manner of the others aforesaid and not according to the amount of his ecclesiastical benefice.

23   No vill or individual shall be compelled to make bridges at river banks, except those who from of old are legally bound to do so.

24   No sheriff, constable, coroners, or others of our bailiffs, shall hold pleas of our crown.

25   All counties, hundreds, wapentakes and trithings³ shall be at the old rents without any additional payment, except our demesne manors.

26   If anyone holding a lay fief of us dies and our sheriff or bailiff shows our letters patent of

summons for a debt that the deceased owed us, it shall be lawful for our sheriff or bailiff to attach and make a list of chattels of the deceased found upon the lay fief to the value of that debt under the supervision of law-worthy men, provided that none of the chattels shall be removed until the debt which is manifest has been paid to us in full; and the residue shall be left to the executors for carrying out the will of the deceased. And if nothing is owing to us from him, all the chattels shall accrue to the deceased, saving to his wife and children their reasonable shares.

27   If any free man dies without leaving a will, his chattels shall be distributed by his nearest kinfolk and friends under the supervision of the church, saving to every one the debts which the deceased owed him.

28   No constable or other bailiff of ours shall take anyone's corn or other chattels unless he pays on the spot in cash for them or can delay payment by arrangement with the seller.

29   No constable shall compel any knight to give money instead of castle-guard if he is willing to do the guard himself or through another good man, if for some good reason he cannot do it himself; and if we lead or send him on military service, he shall be excused guard in proportion to the time that because of us he has been on service.

30   No sheriff, or bailiff of ours, or anyone else shall take the horses or carts of any free man for transport work save with the agreement of that freeman.

31   Neither we nor our bailiffs will take, for castles or other works of ours, timber which is not ours, except with the agreement of him whose timber it is.

32   We will not hold for more than a year and a day the lands of those convicted of felony, and then the lands shall be handed over to the lords of the fiefs.

33   Henceforth all fish-weirs shall be cleared completely from the Thames and the Medway and throughout all England, except along the sea coast.

34   The writ called *Praecipe* shall not in future be issued to anyone in respect of any holding whereby a freeman may lose his court.

35   Let there be one measure for wine throughout our kingdom, and one measure for ale, and one measure for corn, namely "the London quarter"; and one width for cloths whether dyed, russet or halberget, namely two ells within the selvedges. Let it be the same with weights as with measures.

36   Nothing shall be given or taken in future for the writ of inquisition of life or limbs; instead it shall be granted free of charge and not refused.

37   If anyone holds of us by fee-farm, by socage, or by burgage, and holds land of another by knight service, we will not, by reason of that fee-farm, socage, or burgage, have the wardship of his heir or of land of his that is of the fief of the other; nor will we have custody of the fee-farm, socage, or burgage, unless such fee-farm owes knight service. We will not have custody of anyone's heir or land which he holds of another by knight service by reason of any petty serjeanty which he holds of us by the service of rendering to us knives or arrows or the like.

38   No bailiff shall in future put anyone to trial[4] upon his own bare word, without reliable witnesses produced for this purpose.

39   No free man shall be arrested or imprisoned or disseised or outlawed or exiled or in any way victimised, neither will we attack him or send anyone to attack him, except by the lawful judgment of his peers or by the law of the land.

40   To no one will we sell, to no one will we refuse or delay right or justice.

41   All merchants shall be able to go out of and come into England safely and securely and stay and travel throughout England, as well by land

as by water, for buying and selling by the ancient and right customs free from all evil tolls, except in time of war and if they are of the land that is at war with us. And if such are found in our land at the beginning of a war, they shall be attached, without injury to their persons or goods, until we, or our chief justiciar, know how merchants of our land are treated who were found in the land at war with us when war broke out; and if ours are safe there, the others shall be safe in our land.

42   It shall be lawful in future for anyone, without prejudicing the allegiance due to us, to leave our kingdom and return safely and securely by land and water, save, in the public interest, for a short period in time of war—except for those imprisoned or outlawed in accordance with the law of the kingdom and natives of a land that is at war with us and merchants (who shall be treated as aforesaid).

43   If anyone who holds of some escheat such as the honor of Wallingford, Nottingham, Boulogne, Lancaster, or of other escheats which are in our hands and are baronies dies, his heir shall give no other relief and do no other service to us than he would have done to the baron if that barony had been in the baron's hands; and we will hold it in the same manner in which the baron held it.

44   Men who live outside the forest need not henceforth come before our justices of the forest upon a general summons, unless they are impleaded or are sureties for any person or persons who are attached for forest offences.

45   We will not make justices, constables, sheriffs or bailiffs save of such as know the law of the kingdom and mean to observe it well.

46   All barons who have founded abbeys for which they have charters of the kings of England or ancient tenure shall have the custody of them during vacancies, as they ought to have.

47   All forests that have been made forest in our time shall be immediately dis-afforested; and so be it done with river-banks that have been made preserves[5] by us in our time.

48   All evil customs connected with forests and warrens, foresters and warreners, sheriffs and their officials, river-banks and their wardens shall immediately be inquired into in each county by twelve sworn knights of the same county who are to be chosen by good men of the same county, and within forty days of the completion of the inquiry shall be utterly abolished by them so as never to be restored, provided that we, or our justiciar if we are not in England, know of it first.

49   We will immediately return all hostages and charters given to us by Englishmen, as security for peace or faithful service.

50   We will remove completely from office the relations of Gerard de Athée so that in future they shall have no office in England, namely Engelard de Cigogné, Peter and Guy and Andrew de Chanceaux, Guy de Cigogné, Geoffrey de Martigny and his brothers, Philip Mark and his brothers and his nephew Geoffrey, and all their following.

51   As soon as peace is restored, we will remove from the kingdom all foreign knights, cross-bowmen, serjeants, and mercenaries, who have come with horses and arms to the detriment of the kingdom.

52   If anyone has been disseised of or kept out of his lands, castles, franchises or his right by us without the legal judgment of his peers, we will immediately restore them to him: and if a dispute arises over this, then let it be decided by the judgment of the twenty-five barons who are mentioned below in the clause for securing the peace: for all the things, however, which anyone has been disseised or kept out of without the lawful judgment of his peers by king Henry, our father, or by king Richard, our brother, which we have in our hand or are held by others, to whom we are bound to warrant them, we will have the usual period of respite of crusaders, excepting those things about which a plea was started or an inquest made by our command before we took the cross; when however we return from our pilgrimage, or if by any chance we do not go on it, we will at once do full justice therein.

53 We will have the same respite, and in the same manner, in the doing of justice in the matter of the disafforesting or retaining of the forests which Henry our father or Richard our brother afforested, and in the matter of the wardship of the lands which are of the fief of another, wardships of which sort we have hitherto had by reason of a fief which anyone held of us by knight service, and in the matter of abbeys founded on the fief of another, not on a fief of our own, in which the lord of the fief claims he has a right; and when we have returned, or if we do not set out on our pilgrimage, we will at once do full justice to those who complain of these things.

54 No one shall be arrested or imprisoned upon the appeal of a woman for the death of anyone except her husband.

55 All fines made with us unjustly and against the law of the land, and all amercements imposed unjustly and against the law of the land, shall be entirely remitted, or else let them be settled by the judgment of the twenty-five barons who are mentioned below in the clause for securing the peace, or by the judgment of the majority of the same, along with the aforesaid Stephen, archbishop of Canterbury, if he can be present, and such others as he may wish to associate with himself for this purpose, and if he cannot be present the business shall nevertheless proceed without him, provided that if any one or more of the aforesaid twenty-five barons are in a like suit, they shall be removed from the judgment of the case in question, and others chosen, sworn and put in their place by the rest of the same twenty-five for this case only.

56 If we have disseised or kept out Welshmen from lands or liberties or other things without the legal judgment of their peers in England or in Wales, they shall be immediately restored to them; and if a dispute arises over this, then let it be decided in the March by the judgment of their peers—for holdings in England according to the law of England, for holdings in Wales according to the law of Wales, and for holdings in the March according to the law of the March. Welshmen shall do the same to us and ours.

57 For all the things, however, which any Welshman was disseised of or kept out of without the lawful judgment of his peers by king Henry, our father, or king Richard, our brother, which we have in our hand or which are held by others, to whom we are bound to warrant them, we will have the usual period of respite of crusaders, excepting those things about which a plea was started or an inquest made by our command before we took the cross; when however we return, or if by any chance we do not set out on our pilgrimage, we will at once do full justice to them in accordance with the laws of the Welsh and the foresaid regions.

58 We will give back at once the son of Llywelyn and all the hostages from Wales and the charters that were handed over to us as security for peace.

59 We will act toward Alexander, king of the Scots, concerning the return of his sisters and hostages and concerning his franchises and his right in the same manner in which we act towards our other barons of England, unless it ought to be otherwise by the charters which we have from William his father, formerly king of the Scots, and this shall be determined by the judgment of his peers in our court.

60 All these aforesaid customs and liberties which we have granted to be observed in our kingdom as far as it pertains to us towards our men, all of our kingdom, clerks as well as laymen, shall observe as far as it pertains to them towards their men.

61 Since, moreover, for God and the betterment of our kingdom and for the better allaying of the discord that has arisen between us and our barons we have granted all these things aforesaid, wishing them to enjoy the use of them unimpaired and unshaken for ever, we give and grant them the under-written security, namely, that the barons shall choose any twenty-five barons of the kingdom they wish, who must with all their might observe, hold and cause to be observed, the peace and liberties which we have granted and confirmed to them by this present

charter of ours, so that if we, or our justiciar, or our bailiffs or any one of our servants offend in any way against anyone or transgress any of the articles of the peace or the security and the offence be notified to four of the aforesaid twenty-five barons, those four barons shall come to us, or to our justiciar if we are out of the kingdom, and, laying the transgression before us, shall petition us to have that transgression corrected without delay. And if we do not correct the transgression, or if we are out of the kingdom, if our justiciar does not correct it, within forty days, reckoning from the time it was brought to our notice or to that of our justiciar if we were out of the kingdom, the aforesaid four barons shall refer that case to the rest of the twenty-five barons and those twenty-five barons together with the community of the whole land shall distrain and distress us in every way they can, namely, by seizing castles, lands, possessions, and in such other ways as they can, saving our person and the persons of our queen and our children, until, in their opinion, amends have been made; and when amends have been made, they shall obey us as they did before. And let anyone in the land who wishes take an oath to obey the orders of the said twenty-five barons for the execution of all the aforesaid matters, and with them to distress us as much as he can, and we publicly and freely give anyone leave to take the oath who wishes to take it and we will never prohibit anyone from taking it. Indeed, all those in the land who are unwilling of themselves and of their own accord to take an oath to the twenty-five barons to help them to distrain and distress us, we will make them take the oath as aforesaid at our command. And if any of the twenty-five barons dies or leaves the country or is in any other way prevented from carrying out the things aforesaid, the rest of the aforesaid twenty-five barons shall choose as they think fit another one in his place, and he shall take the oath like the rest. In all matters the execution of which is committed to these twenty-five barons, if it should happen that these twenty-five are present yet disagree among themselves about anything, or if some of those summoned will not or cannot be present, that shall be held as fixed and established which the majority of those present ordained or commanded, exactly as if all the

twenty-five had consented to it; and the said twenty-five shall swear that they will faithfully observe all the things aforesaid and will do all they can to get them observed. And we will procure nothing from anyone, either personally or through anyone else, whereby any of these concessions and liberties might be revoked or diminished; and if any such thing is procured, let it be void and null, and we will never use it either personally or through another.

62   And we have fully remitted and pardoned to everyone all the ill-will, indignation and rancor that have arisen between us and our men, clergy and laity, from the time of the quarrel. Furthermore, we have fully remitted to all, clergy and laity, and as far as pertains to us have completely forgiven, all trespasses occasioned by the same quarrel between Easter in the sixteenth year of our reign and the restoration of peace. And, besides, we have caused to be made for them letters testimonial patent of the lord Stephen archbishop of Canterbury, of the lord Henry archbishop of Dublin and of the aforementioned bishops and of master Pandulf about this security and the aforementioned concessions.

63   Wherefore we wish and firmly enjoin that the English church shall be free, and that the men in our kingdom shall have and hold all the aforesaid liberties, rights and concessions well and peacefully, freely and quietly, fully and completely, for themselves and their heirs from us and our heirs, in all matters and in all places for ever, as is aforesaid. An oath, moreover, has been taken, as well on our part as on the part of the barons, that all these things aforesaid shall be observed in good faith and without evil disposition. Witness the above-mentioned and many others. Given by our hand in the meadow which is called Runnymede between Windsor and Staines on the fifteenth day of June, in the seventeenth year of our reign.

Pope Innocent III declares Magna Carta null and void, 24 August 1215

Innocent, Bishop, Servant of the Servants of God,

to all the faithful of Christ who will see this document, greeting and apostolic benediction.

Although our well-beloved son in Christ, John illustrious king of the English, grievously offended God and the church—in consequence of which we excommunicated him and put his kingdom under ecclesiastical interdict—yet, by the merciful inspiration of Him who desireth not the death of a sinner but rather that he should turn from his wickedness and live, the king at length returned to his senses, and humbly made to God and the church such complete amends that he not only paid compensation for losses and restored property wrongfully seized, but also conferred full liberty on the English church: and further, on the relaxation of the two sentences, he yielded his kingdom of England and of Ireland to St Peter and the Roman church, and received it from us again as fief under an annual payment of one thousand marks, having sworn an oath of fealty to us, as is clearly stated in his privilege furnished with a golden seal; and desiring still further to please Almighty God, he reverently assumed the badge of the life-giving Cross, intending to go to the relief of the Holy Land—a project for which he was splendidly preparing. But the enemy of the human race, who always hates good impulses, by his cunning wiles stirred up against him the barons of England so that, with a wicked inconsistency, the men who supported him when injuring the church rebelled against him when he turned from his sin and made amends to the church. A matter of dispute had arisen between them: several days had been fixed for the parties to discuss a settlement: meanwhile, formal envoys had been sent to us: with them we conferred diligently, and after full deliberation we sent letters by them to the archbishop and the English bishops, charging and commanding them to devote earnest attention and effective effort to restoring a genuine and full agreement between the two sides; by apostolic authority they were to denounce as void any leagues and conspiracies which might have been formed after the outbreak of trouble between the kingdom and the priesthood: they were to prohibit, under sentence of excommunication, any attempt to form such leagues in future: and they were prudently to admonish the magnates and

nobles of England, and strongly to enjoin on them, to strive to conciliate the king by manifest proofs of loyalty and submission; and then, if they should decide to make a demand of him, to implore it respectfully and not arrogantly, maintaining his royal honor and rendering the customary services which they and their predecessors paid to him and his predecessors (since the king ought not to lose these services without a judicial decision), that in this way they might the more easily gain their object. For we in our letters, and equally through the archbishop and bishops, have asked and advised the king, enjoining it on him as he hopes to have his sins remitted, to treat these magnates and nobles kindly and to hear their just petitions graciously, so that they too might recognise with gladness how by divine grace he had had a change of heart, and that thereby they and their heirs should serve him and his heirs readily and loyally; and we also asked him to grant them full safeconduct for the outward and homeward journey and the time between, so that if they could not arrive at agreement the dispute might be decided in his court by their peers according to the laws and customs of the kingdom. But before the envoys bearing this wise and just mandate had reached England, the barons threw over their oath of fealty; and though, even if the king had wrongfully oppressed them they should not have proceeded against him by constituting themselves both judges and executors of the judgment in their own suit, yet, openly conspiring as vassals against their lord and as knights against their own king, they leagued themselves with his acknowledged enemies as well as with others, and dared to make war on him, occupying and devastating his territory and even seizing the city of London, the capital of the kingdom, which had been treacherously surrendered to them. Meantime the aforesaid envoys returned to England and the king offered, in accordance with the terms of our mandate, to grant the barons full justice. This they altogether rejected and began to stretch forth their hands to deeds still worse. So the king, appealing to our tribunal, offered to grant them justice before us to whom the decision of this suit belonged by reason of our lordship: but this they utterly rejected. Then he offered that four discreet men chosen by him and four more chosen by themselves should, together with us, end the dispute, and he promised that, first in his reforms, he would repeal all abuses introduced into England in his reign: but this also they contemptuously refused. Finally, the king declared to them that, since the lordship of the kingdom belonged to the Roman church, he neither could nor should, without our special mandate, make any change in it to our prejudice: and so he again appealed to our tribunal, placing under apostolic protection both himself and his kingdom with all his honor and rights. But making no progress by any method, he asked the archbishop and the bishops to execute our mandate, to defend the rights of the Roman church, and to protect himself in accordance with the form of the privilege granted to crusaders. When the archbishop and bishops would not take any action, seeing himself bereft of almost all counsel and help, he did not dare to refuse what the barons had dared to demand. And so by such violence and fear as might affect the most courageous of men he was forced to accept an agreement which is not only shameful and demeaning but also illegal and unjust, thereby lessening unduly and impairing his royal rights and dignity.

But because the Lord has said to us by the prophet Jeremiah, "I have set thee over the nations and over the kingdoms, to root out, and to destroy, to build and to plant," and also by Isaiah, "Loose the bands of wickedness, undo the heavy burdens," we refuse to ignore such shameless presumption, for thereby the apostolic see would be dishonored, the king's rights injured, the English nation shamed, and the whole plan for a crusade seriously endangered; and as this danger would be imminent if concessions, thus extorted from a great prince who has taken the Cross, were not cancelled by our authority, even though he himself should prefer them to be upheld, on behalf of Almighty God, Father, Son, and Holy Spirit, and by the authority of SS Peter and Paul His apostles, and by our own authority, acting on the general advice of our brethren, we utterly reject and condemn this settlement, and under threat of excommunication we order that the king should not dare to observe it and that the barons and their associates should not require

it to be observed: the charter, with all undertakings and guarantees whether confirming it or resulting from it, we declare to be null, and void of all validity for ever. Wherefore, let no man deem it lawful to infringe this document of our annulment and prohibition, or presume to oppose it. If anyone should presume to do so, let him know that he will incur the anger of Almighty God and of SS Peter and Paul His apostles.

Anagni, the 24th of August, in the eighteenth year of our pontificate.

Magna Carta, 1216

Henry, by the grace of God king of England, lord of Ireland, duke of Normandy and Aquitaine, and count of Anjou, to the archbishops, bishops, abbots, earls, barons, justiciars, foresters, sheriffs, stewards, servants, bailiffs and to all his faithful subjects, greeting. Know that we, out of reverence for God and for the salvation of our soul and those of all our ancestors and *successors*, for the honour of God and the exaltation of holy church, and for the reform of our realm, on the advice of our venerable fathers, *the lord Gualo, cardinal priest of St Martin, legate of the apostolic see, Peter of Winchester, R. of St Asaph, J. of Bath and Glastonbury, S. of Exeter, R. of Chichester, W. of Coventry, B. of Rochester, H. of Llandaff,—of St David's,—of Bangor and S. of Worcester, bishops*, and of the noble men *William Marshal earl of Pembroke, Ranulf earl of Chester, William de Ferrers earl of Derby, William count of Aumale, Hubert de Burgh our justiciar, Savari de Mauléon, William Brewer the father, William Brewer the son, Robert de Courtenay, Fawkes de Breauté, Reynold de Vautort, Walter de Lacy, Hugh de Mortimer, John of Monmouth, Walter de Beauchamp, Walter de Clifford, Roger de Clifford, Robert de Mortimer, William de Cantilupe, Matthew fitz Herbert, John Marshal, Alan Basset, Philip de Aubeney, John Lestrange* and others, our faithful subjects:

1   In the first place have granted to God, and by this our present charter confirmed for us and our heirs for ever, that the English church shall be free, and shall have its rights undiminished and

its liberties unimpaired. We have also granted to all free men of our kingdom, for ourselves and our heirs for ever, all the liberties written below, to be had and held by them and their heirs of us and our heirs. [1215, c.1]

2   If any of our earls or barons or others holding of us in chief by knight service dies, and at his death his heir be of full age and owe relief he shall have his inheritance on payment of the old relief, namely the heir or heirs of an earl £100 for a whole earl's barony, the heir or heirs of a baron £100 for a whole barony, the heir or heirs of a knight 100s, at most, for a whole knight's fee; and he who owes less shall give less according to the ancient usage of fiefs. [1215, c.2]

3   If, however, the heir of any such be under age, *his lord shall not have wardship of him, nor of his land, before he has received his homage; and after being a ward such an heir* shall have his inheritance when he comes of age, *that is of twenty-one years,* without paying relief and without making fine, *so, however, that if he is made a knight while still under age, the land nevertheless shall remain in his lord's wardship for the full term.* [1215, c. 3]

4   The guardian of the land of such an heir who is under age shall take from the land of the heir no more than reasonable revenues, reasonable customary dues and reasonable services, and that without destruction and waste of men or goods; and if we commit the wardship of the land of any such to a sheriff, or to any other who is answerable to us for the revenues *of that land,* and he destroys or wastes what he has wardship of, we will take compensation from him and the land shall be committed to two lawful and discreet men of that fief, who shall be answerable for the revenues to us or to him to whom we have assigned them; and if we give or sell to anyone the wardship of any such land and he causes destruction or waste therein, he shall lose that wardship and it shall be transferred to two lawful and discreet men of that fief, who shall similarly be answerable to us as is aforesaid. [1215, c. 4]

5   Moreover, so long as he has the wardship of

the land, the guardian shall keep in repair the houses, parks, preserves, ponds, mills and other things pertaining to the land out of the revenues from it; and he shall restore to the heir when he comes of age his land fully stocked with ploughs and *all other things in at least the measure he has received. All these things shall be observed in the case of wardships of vacant archbishoprics, bishoprics, abbeys, priories, churches and dignities except that wardships of this kind may not be sold.* [1215, c. 5]

6   Heirs shall be married without disparagement. [1215, c.6]

7   A widow shall have her marriage portion and inheritance forthwith and without *any* difficulty after the death of her husband; nor shall she pay anything to have her dower or her marriage portion or the inheritance which she and her husband held on the day of her husband's death; and she may remain in her husband's house for forty days after his death, within which time her dower shall be assigned to her, *unless it has already been assigned to her or unless the house is a castle; and if she leaves the castle, a suitable house shall be immediately provided for her in which she can stay honorably until her dower is assigned to her in accordance with what is aforesaid.* [1215, c.7]

8   No widow shall be forced to marry so long as she wishes to live without a husband, provided that she gives security not to marry without our consent if she holds of us, or without the consent of her lord if she holds of another. [1215, c.8]

9   *We or our bailiffs will not* seize for any debt any land or rent, so long as the *available* chattels of the debtor are sufficient to repay the debt *and the debtor himself is prepared to have it paid therefrom;* nor will those who have gone surety for the debtor be distrained so long as the principal debtor is himself able to pay the debt; and if the principal debtor fails to pay the debt, having nothing wherewith to pay it *or is able but unwilling to pay,* then shall the sureties answer for the debt; and they shall, if they wish, have the lands and rents of the debtor until they are reimbursed for the debt which they have paid for him, unless the principal debtor can show that he has dis-

charged his obligation in the matter to the said sureties. [1215, c.9]

10 The city of London shall have all its ancient liberties and free customs. Furthermore, we will and grant that all other cities, boroughs, towns, *the barons of the Cinque Ports*, and *all* ports shall have all their liberties and free customs. [1215, c.13]

11 No one shall be compelled to do greater service for a knight's fee or for any other free holding than is due from it. [1215, c.16]

12 Common pleas shall not follow our court, but shall be held in some fixed place. [1215, c.17]

13 Recognitions of novel disseisin, of mort d'ancestor, and of darrein presentment, shall not be held elsewhere than in the counties to which they relate, and in this manner—we, or, if we should be out of the realm, our chief justiciar, will send two justices through each county four times a year, who, with four knights of each county chosen by the county, shall hold the said assizes in the county and on the day and in the place of meeting of the county court. [1215, c.18]

14 And if the said assizes cannot all be held on the day of the county court, there shall stay behind as many of the knights and freeholders who were present at the county court on that day as are necessary for the sufficient making of judgments, according to the amount of business to be done. [1215, c.19]

15 A free man shall not be amerced for a trivial offence except in accordance with the degree of the offence, and for a grave offence in accordance with its gravity, yet saving his way of living; and a merchant in the same way, saving his stock-in-trade; and a villein shall be amerced in the same way, saving his means of livelihood; if *he has* fallen into our mercy: and none of the aforesaid amercements shall be imposed except by the oath of good *and law-worthy* men of the neighborhood. [1215, c.20]

16 Earls and barons shall not be amerced except by their peers, and only in accordance with the degree of the offence. [1215, c.21]

17 No clerk shall be amerced except after the fashion of the aforesaid and not according to the amount of his ecclesiastical benefice. [1215, c. 22]

18 No vill or individual shall be compelled to make bridges at river banks, except *one* who from of old *is* legally bound to do so. [1215, c.23]

19 No sheriff, constable, coroners, or others of our bailiffs shall hold pleas of our crown. [1215, c.24]

20 If anyone holding a lay fief of us dies and our sheriff or bailiff shows our letters patent of summons for a debt that the deceased owed us, it shall be lawful for our sheriff or bailiff to attach and make a list of chattels of the deceased found upon the lay fief to the value of that debt under the supervision of law-worthy men, provided that none of the chattels shall be removed until the debt which is manifest has been paid to us in full; and the residue shall be left to the executors for carrying out the will of the deceased. And if nothing is owing to us from him, all the chattels shall accrue to the deceased, saving to his wife and *his* children their reasonable shares. [1215, c.26]

21 No constable *or his bailiff* shall take the corn or other chattels of anyone *who is not of the vill where the castle is situated* unless he pays on the spot in cash for them or can delay payment by arrangement with the seller; *if the seller is of the vill, he shall be bound to pay within three weeks.* [1215, c.28]

22 No constable shall compel any knight to give money instead of castle-guard if he is willing to do *it* himself or through another good man, if for some good reason he cannot do it himself; and if we lead or send him on military service, he shall be excused guard in proportion to the time that because of us he has been on service. [1215, c.29]

23 No sheriff, or bailiff of ours, or *other person* shall take *anyone's* horses or carts for transport

work unless *he pays for them at the old-established rates, namely at ten pence a day for a cart with two horses and fourteen pence a day for a cart with three horses.* [1215, c.30]

24   Neither we nor our bailiffs will take, for castles or other works of ours, timber which is not ours, except with the agreement of him whose timber it is. [1215, c.31]

25   We will not hold for more than a year and a day the lands of those convicted of felony, and then the lands shall be handed over to the lords of the fiefs. [1215, c.32]

26   Henceforth all fish-weirs shall be cleared completely from the Thames and the Medway and throughout all England, except along the sea coast. [1215, c.33]

27   The writ called Praecipe shall not in future be issued to anyone in respect of any holding whereby a free man may lose his court. [1215, c.34]

28   Let there be one measure for wine throughout our kingdom, and one measure for ale, and one measure for corn, namely "the London quarter"; and one width for cloths whether dyed, russet or halberget, namely two ells within the selvedges. Let it be the same with weights as with measures. [1215, c.35]

29   Nothing shall be given in future for the writ of inquisition of life or limbs: instead, it shall be granted free of charge and not refused. [1215, c.36]

30   If anyone holds of us by fee-farm, by socage, or by burgage, and holds land of another by knight service, we will not, by reason of that fee-farm, socage or burgage, have the wardship of his heir or of land of his that is of the fief of the other; nor will we have custody of the fee-farm, socage, or burgage, unless such fee-farm owes knight service. We will not have custody of anyone's heir or land which he holds of another by knight service by reason of any petty serjeanty which he holds of us by the service of rendering to us knives or arrows or the like. [1215, c.37]

31   No bailiff shall in future put anyone to trial upon his own bare word without reliable witnesses produced for this purpose. [1215, c.38]

32   No free man shall be arrested or imprisoned or disseised or outlawed or exiled or victimised in any *other* way, neither will we attack him or send anyone to attack him, except by the lawful judgment of his peers or by the law of the land. [1215, c.39]

33   To no one will we sell, to no one will we refuse or delay right or justice. [1215, c.40]

34   All merchants, *unless they have been publicly prohibited beforehand*, shall be able to go out of and come into England safely and securely and stay and travel throughout England, as well by land as by water, for buying and selling by the ancient and right customs free from all evil tolls, except in time of war and if they are of the land that is at war with us. And if such are found in our land at the beginning of a war, they shall be attached, without injury to their persons or goods, until we, or our chief justiciar, know how merchants of our land are treated who were found in the land at war with us when war broke out; and if ours are safe there, the others shall be safe in our land. [1215, c.41]

35   If anyone who holds of some escheat such as the honor of Wallingford, Nottingham, Boulogne, Lancaster, or of other escheats which are in our hands and are baronies dies, his heir shall give no other relief and do no other service to us than he would have done to the baron if that *land* had been in the baron's hands; and we will hold it in the same manner in which the barons held it. [1215, c.43]

36   Men who live outside the forest need not henceforth come before our justices of the forest upon a general summons, unless they are impleaded or are sureties for any person or persons who are attached for forest offences. [1215, c.44]

37   All barons who have founded abbeys for which they have charters of the kings of England

or ancient tenure shall have the custody of them during vacancies, as they ought to have *and as it is made clear above.* [1215, c.46]

38   All forests that were made forest in the time *of king John, our father,* shall be immediately disafforested; and so be it done with river-banks that were made preserves by *the same J. in his* time. [1215, c.47]

39   No one shall be arrested or imprisoned upon the appeal of a woman for the death of anyone except her husband. [1215, c.54]

40   *And if king J. our father* disseised or kept out Welshmen from lands or liberties or other things without the legal judgment of their peers in England or in Wales, they shall be immediately restored to them; and if a dispute arises over this, then let it be decided in the March by the judgment of their peers—for holdings in England according to the law of England, for holdings in Wales according to the law of Wales, and for holdings in the March according to the law of the March. Welshmen shall do the same to us and ours. [1215, c.56]

41   All these aforesaid customs and liberties which we have granted to be observed in our kingdom as far as it pertains to us towards our men, all of our kingdoms, clerks as well as laymen, shall observe as far as it pertains to them towards their men. [1215, c.60]

42   *However, because there were certain articles contained in the former charter which seemed important yet doubtful, namely On the assessing of scutage and aids, On debts of Jews and others, On freedom to leave and return to our kingdom, On forests and foresters, warrens and warreners, On the customs of counties, and On river-banks and their wardens, the above-mentioned prelates and magnates have agreed to these being deferred until we have fuller counsel, when we will, most fully in these as well as other matters that have to be amended, do what is for the common good and the peace and estate of ourselves and our kingdom. Because we have not yet a seal, we have had the present charter sealed with the seals of our venerable father, the lord Gualo cardinal priest of St Martin, legate of the apostolic see, and William Marshal earl of Pembroke, ruler of us and of our kingdom. Witness all the aforementioned and many others. Given by the hands of the aforesaid lord, the legate, and William Marshal earl of Pembroke at Bristol on the twelfth day of November in the first year of our reign.*

Notes

1   *lex* (here a technical term for a trial, such as compurgation, ordeal or combat)
2   literally, "are 'in defence'"
3   i.e. ridings
4   *lex* (see n. 1)
5   literally, "put 'in defence'"

ROYAL COURTS OF ENGLAND

The Huntingdonshire Eyre of 1286

THE RECORDS OF ROYAL COURTS ARE A MAJOR SOURCE OF INFORMATION
on the social, legal, and economic structures of England in the thirteenth century. The following excerpts from the Huntingdonshire Eyre of 1286 show
typical types of actions brought before the royal justices.

Source: Anne Reiber De Windt and Edwin Brezette DeWindt, *Royal Justice and the
Medieval English Countryside* vol. 2, (Toronto: Pontifical Institute of Medieval Studies,
1981).

Action of Right

The Abbot of Crowland claims against Emma,
who was the wife of Berenger le Moyne, one messuage and half of one virgate of land with appurtenances in Thurning as the right of his church of
Crowland by *precipe in capite*, whereupon he says
that a certain Henry of Longchamp, former abbot
of Crowland, his predecessor, was seised of the
aforesaid tenements with appurtenances in his
demesne as of fee and right of his church of Saint
Guthlac of Crowland in a time of peace, the time
of the lord King Richard, kinsman of the present
lord king, taking esplees[1] therein to the value of
[*unspecified*]. And he offers to prove that such is
the right of his church.

Emma comes, and on another occasion she
said that the aforesaid tenements with appurte-
nance were given to Berenger, her late husband,
and to her in free marriage, and of them were
born Rose, wife of Geoffrey of Southorpe, Emma,
wife of Richard of Carlby, and Margaret, wife of
John Peche, whereupon she said that she could
not answer therein without Geoffrey and Rose,
Richard and Emma, [and] John and Margaret, so
that the sheriff was ordered to summon them to
be here on this day, namely on Monday, three
weeks after Michaelmas, to answer together.
They have not come, and they were summoned.
Therefore, it is adjudged that the aforesaid Emma
will answer without them.

Emma denies the right of the abbot and his
church and the seisin of that Henry, predecessor
of this abbot, of whose seisin, etc., as the right of

his church of Saint Guthlac of Crowland, and
everything, etc. And she puts herself on a jury of
the country in place of the Grand Assize of the
lord king and seeks that acknowledgment be
made whether she has greater right in those tenements with appurtenances as her right and marriage gift, or the aforesaid abbot.

John Russel, John of Drayton, John Mowyn
and Richard of Bevil, four knights summoned to
elect both knights and other free and lawful men,
came and elected these, namely: John of Drayton
(sworn), John Mowyn (sworn), Richard of Bevil
(sworn), Guy of Waterville (sworn), Robert of
Beaumes (sworn), knights. Richard of Catworth
(sworn), William Engayne (sworn), Richard of
Hotot (sworn), Richard Marshall (sworn) of
Stoneley, John of Cantelou (sworn), William of
Hampton (sworn), (and) Geoffrey of Haddon
(sworn), who say on their oath that the aforesaid
abbot has greater right in the aforesaid tenements
as the right of his church of Saint Guthlac of
Crowland than the aforesaid Emma. Therefore, it
is adjudged that the abbot recover his seisin of
those tenements with appurtenances, to be held
by him and his successors and his church, quit,
from this Emma and her heirs in perpetuity. And
Emma is in mercy.

Action of Dower

Agnes, who was the wife of John Gate of Offord
Darcy, claims against the prior of Huntingdon the
third part of one messuage and a half-virgate of
land with appurtenances in Offord Darcy as her

dower, *unde nichil habet*, etc.

The prior comes and says that Agnes ought not to have dower from that, for he says that John, former husband of Agnes, neither on the day he married her nor afterward was ever seised of those tenements as of fee so that he could give her dower therein. For he says that those tenements were at one time a certain Reginald le Moyne's, of Offord, who gave those tenements, along with his body, to the church of Saint Mary of Huntingdon and to the canons serving there, in free, pure and perpetual alms, together with a certain Richard Gate, grandfather of this John, at that time a villein of this Reginald, with his entire family of that Richard [who were] at that time holding those tenements in villeinage, whereupon he says that the ancestors of this John always held those tenements in villeinage. And concerning this he puts himself on the country, and Agnes does the same. Therefore, let there be a jury.

Concerning this, a certain Geoffrey Gate, brother of the aforesaid John, comes and says that he is a villein on the prior and his church and holds those tenements from him in villeinage, and that his ancestors, from the time of the enfeoffment of that Reginald le Moyne, have been villeins of the predecessors of the prior and his church, and that they have held those tenements from him in villeinage. And the prior seeks that this jury consider the evidence mentioned above.

The jurors say on their oath that the aforesaid John, neither on the day that he married Agnes nor afterwards, was ever seised of those tenements as of fee so that he could give her dower therein. Therefore, it is adjudged that the prior go without a day and that Agnes take nothing by this jury but is in mercy for a false claim.

Action of Entry

Agnes, widow of Roger Knight, claims against Robert of Bedford and Juliana, his wife, two acres of land and three acres of meadow with appurtenances in Little Paxton; and against John, son of Roger Webster, one rod of meadow with appurtenances in the same vill; and against Roger of Daventry and Cecilia, his wife, one acre and one rod of land with appurtenances in that vill, as her

right and inheritance, and in which Robert and Juliana, John, Roger and Cecilia do not have entry except after the surrender that Roger Knight, her late husband, whom she, in his lifetime, could not contradict, made to Hugh de la Mare.

Robert, Juliana, John, Roger and Cecilia come and deny Agnes' right. And Roger and Cecilia, concerning the judgment claimed against them, say that they are not obliged to answer her, for they say that they have nothing in the aforesaid tenements except only a tenancy at the will of a certain John of Offord, without whom they cannot bring those tenements into judgement. And Agnes cannot deny this. Therefore, Roger and Cecilia go without a day, and Agnes takes nothing against them by this writ but is in mercy for a false claim.

Robert and Juliana, concerning the tenements claimed against them, say that they cannot answer Agnes, for they say that they do not hold those tenements entirely, but that a certain Stephen of Dalham holds one rod of land therein and held it on the day Agnes sought her writ, namely: 16 May, the fourteenth year of the present king. And concerning this they put themselves on the country, and Agnes does the same. Therefore, let there be a jury.

The jurors, elected by consent of the parties, say on their oath that Robert and Juliana do not hold those tenements entirely nor did they on the day she [Agnes] sought her writ, for a certain Stephen of Dalham holds one rod therein, as Robert and Juliana say. Therefore, it is adjudged that Robert and Juliana go without a day and that Agnes take nothing by this writ but is in mercy for a false claim.

John, son of Roger Webster, concerning the tenements claimed against him, says that Roger, late husband of this Agnes, was never in seisin of that rod of meadow so that he could have surrendered it to Hugh or to anyone else. And concerning this he puts himself on the country, and Agnes does the same. Therefore, let there be a jury.

The jurors, elected by consent of the parties, say on their oath that Roger, late husband of Agnes, was never in seisin of that rod of meadow so that he could have released it to anyone, as

John says. Therefore, it is adjudged that John go without a day and that Agnes take nothing by this writ but is in mercy for a false claim.

Action of Novel Disseisin

An assize comes to declare whether William le Moyne Sr. of Raveley, John of Raveley and Alan le Kew unjustly disseised William, son of William le Moyne, and Eleanor of Lovetot of their free tenement in Sawtry le Moyne, whereupon they complain that they disseised them of one messuage and three carucates of land with appurtenances.

The same assize comes to declare whether William le Moyne Sr., John of Raveley and Alan le Kew unjustly disseised William, son of William le Moyne, of his free tenement in Gidding and Loddington, whereupon he complains that they disseised him of one messuage and one carucate of land with appurtenances in Gidding and of one messuage and two carucates of land with appurtenances in Loddington.

William le Moyne Sr. comes and answers for himself as tenant and for John and Alan as their bailiff, and he says nothing to stay the assize except only that William and Eleanor were never in seisin of the aforesaid tenements in Sawtry as of a free tenement so that they could be disseised therein. Nor was that William, son of William, in seisin of the aforesaid tenements in Gidding and Loddington as of his free tenement so that he could be disseised. And concerning this, he puts himself on the assize. Therefore, let the assize be taken.

The jurors say on their oath, regarding the tenements in Sawtry, that the aforesaid William Sr. and the others unjustly disseised William, son of William, and Eleanor, as they complain; and regarding the tenements in Gidding and Loddington, they say on the same oath that William Sr. and the others unjustly disseised William, son of William, as he complains. Therefore, it is adjudged that William, son of William, and Eleanor recover their seisin of the aforesaid tenements in Sawtry by view of the recognitors, and that William, son of William, recover his seisin of the aforesaid tenements in Gidding and Loddington by view of the aforesaid recognitors.

And William le Moyne Sr. and the others are in mercy.

Damages, regarding the first assize: 10s.; and regarding the second assize, concerning the tenements in Loddington: a half-mark; and concerning the tenements in Gidding: 40d., all to the clerks.

Later, the fine is excused at the request of John of Lovetot.

Damages to the clerks.

Action of Mort d'Ancestor

An assize comes to declare whether Ellen of Folksworth, the mother of Henry, son of Robert of Blymhill, was seised in her demesne as of fee of a half-virgate with appurtenances in Folksworth on the day that [she died], which Richard, son of Thomas of Wennington, holds.

Richard comes and vouches Geoffrey de la Hose to warrant. He is present and warrants him, and he says that Ellen did not die seised of the aforesaid tenements in her demesne as of fee. He says further that Ellen had nothing in this, except for the term of her life, from the surrender of Thomas de la Hose. And concerning this, he puts himself on the assize.

The jurors say on their oath that Ellen, concerning whose death [the assize is brought] died seised of the aforesaid tenement in her demesne as of fee and after the term, and that Henry is her closest heir. Therefore, it is adjudged that Henry recover his seisin of the tenements with appurtenances by view of the recognitors against Richard and that Richard have land from that of Geoffrey in a suitable place of the same value. And Geoffrey is in mercy.

Damages: 20s., to the clerks, etc.

Appeal of Felony

Unidentified malefactors, at night, encountered Simon Chyne in the fields of Hemingford and wounded him, so that three days later he died. Afterwards they fled, and it is not known who they were nor where they went.

Later it was determined by the coroners' rolls that Agnes, widow of the aforesaid Simon of Chyne, appealed in the county court Laurence, son of Robert Fenner of Saint Ives of the death of Simon, her husband. She also appealed Adam, son of Robert Fenner, brother of the aforesaid Laurence, as an accomplice. And it is determined by the coroners' rolls that Agnes brought suit against them up to the fourth county court, at which Laurence and Adam appeared and were arrested and delivered to Thomas of Belhus, the sheriff at that time.

Later, before William Musket, John Russel and his associates, justices assigned to gaol delivery, they were delivered, having been accused by the county without a separate warrant. Therefore, the sheriff is ordered to make the aforesaid William and John, with their associates who were involved, come with the rolls and warrant. And the jurors attest that the aforesaid Laurence killed Simon. Therefore, the sheriff is ordered to arrest him if, etc., and saving, etc. And Geoffrey Fenner and John Aylmer, who were attached because they were present, come and are not suspected. Therefore, they are acquitted. Nothing is known of Laurence's chattels. He was not in tithing because he was a cleric.

Indictment of Felony

The jurors present that Margery Mouner of Keyston and William Mercer of Keyston were indicted by Robert Scochere of Oundle, and afterwards, because of that, they fled. William was later captured at Lincoln and hanged there. His chattels: 10s., for which the sheriff will answer. He had chattels in the county of Northampton at Islip worth 10s., for which William of Soule will answer. And because he took those chattels without warrant, he is in mercy. Margery's chattels, 2 s. 6 d., for which the sheriff will answer. And the twelve jurors concealed those chattels in their presentment. Therefore, they are in mercy. And because Margery is suspected, let her be exacted and waived. She was not in tithing because she is a woman.

Presentment of Felony by Jury

The jurors present that William, son of Thomas Beadle, put himself in the church of Warboys and acknowledged that he was a thief and abjured the realm before the coroner. He had no chattels. He was not in tithing because he is a free man, but he was of the household of the aforesaid Thomas, his father, who now does not have him to stand trial. Therefore, he is in mercy. And because the vill of Warboys did not capture him, it is in mercy. And the twelve jurors did not mention in their verdict before which coroner this abjuration was made. Therefore, they are in mercy.

Presentment of Death by Misadventure

Margery daughter of William Springolf was struck in the head by a kicking mare, so that three days later she died. The first-finder and four neighbors come and are not suspected, nor is anyone else. Judgment: misadventure. Price of the mare: 3s., for which the sheriff will answer. And the vills of Somersham and Earith falsely appraised that deodand. Therefore, they are in mercy. And the twelve jurors concealed a part of that deodand. Therefore, they are in mercy.

Note

1   enjoyment

A MEDIEVAL ENGLISH VILLAGE

Wharram Percy

The best preserved and studied abandoned village in England is Wharram Percy, Yorkshire East Riding. Excavations there have uncovered successive habitations from the iron age until its destruction in the early sixteenth century.

Throughout the medieval period, all houses were long houses except for a courtyard farm in the manorial enclosure. Prior to the thirteenth century, the houses were timber. After that time, they were constructed of chalk quarried on individual tofts. In the thirteenth century, houses were constructed at right angles with the gable to the street.

The site of the manor changed across time. The Anglo-Saxon manor was probably near the church. In the twelfth century, it was moved onto the hill at the north end of the village, and in the thirteenth century it was again moved several hundred yards further north.

The village church shows the changes in the village. Its first period may be pre-Danish. Massive rebuilding took place in the Norman Period. In the twelfth and thirteenth centuries, aisles and chapels were demolished and the chancel halved.

Source: Maurice Beresford and John G. Hurst, eds. *Deserted Medieval Villages* (St. Martin's Press: New York, 1971).

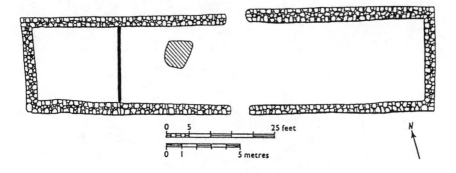

Plan, three-roomed long-house, Wharram Percy.

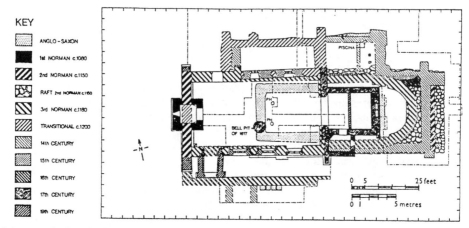

KEY

- ▨ ANGLO - SAXON
- ▨ 1st NORMAN c.1080
- ▨ 2nd NORMAN c.1150
- ▨ RAFT 2nd NORMAN c.1160
- ▨ 3rd NORMAN c.1180
- ▨ TRANSITIONAL c.1200
- ▨ 14th CENTURY
- ▨ 15th CENTURY
- ▨ 16th CENTURY
- ▨ 17th CENTURY
- ▨ 9th CENTURY

Plan of the parish church showing the expansion from the small Saxon church to the large medieval church with nave, chancel, north and south aisles, and chapels at the peak of the prosperity of the village in the fourteenth century. In the fifteenth and sixteenth centuries the aisles and chapels were pulled down and in the seventeenth century the chancel was halved in size after the desertion of four of the five townships in the parish.

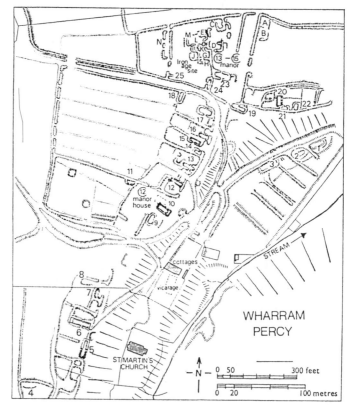

Plan of the village showing the early extent of the settlement (4-8) with the twelfth century manor house and boundary bank; to the north the thirteenth-century planned extension of the village (12-18) with the new site for the manorial complex (A-N and 19-25).

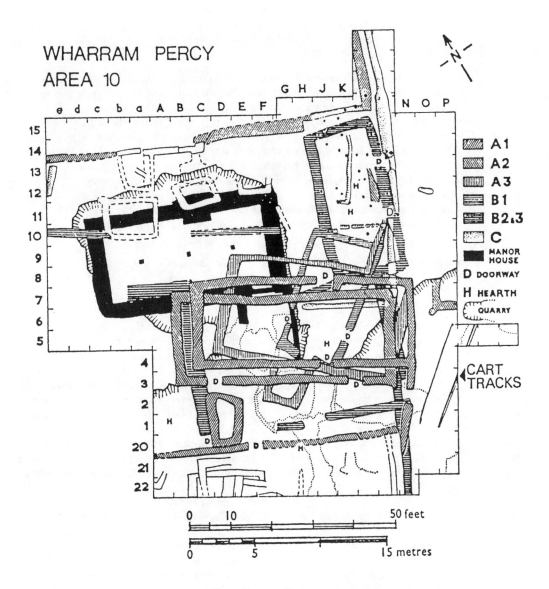

Plan of Area 10 showing the complex sequence-of superimposed periods on different alignments. The late twelfth-century Percy Manor house and chalk quarries were replaced by two thirteenth-century houses oriented north-south (B2-3). In the fourteenth century these were replaced by a single house (B1) while in the fifteenth century the long-houses were built east-west on quite a different alignment (A1-3).

GIOVANNI SCRIBA

Notary Book

THE FOLLOWING CONTRACTS MAKE IT POSSIBLE TO FOLLOW THE business dealings of the Genovese merchant Oliverius Nivetelle in the sixties of the twelfth century. They were recorded in the Notary book of Giovanni Scriba, the earliest extant notary book from Genoa. Most of the contracts are a form of bilateral commenda contract termed in Genoa *societas*. Traditionally, the investor who stays home contributed two thirds of the capital and the traveling partner one third plus his labor. The profits were divided by half according to the amount of the original investment and losses are proportionally borne by both.

One text records a land transaction and can be compared with the text of the Theodosian code above to see the influence of Roman law in twelfth century Italy.

Source: M. Chiaudano and M. Moresco, eds. *Il cartolare di Giovanni Scriba II*, (Turin: 1935).

---

654 Witnesses Oliverii Nivetele and Iohanis Cirbini Witnesses Ogerius Spion, Ioffredus the pelterer de Clavica and Iohannes de Doda. Oliverius Nivetella and Iohannes Cirbinus contracted a societas in which Oliverius brought 30 pounds and Iohannes Cirbinus 15 pounds. This same Iohannes must transact the business in Palermo and through Sicily and must come to Genoa and dissolve this societas into the hands of this Oliverus or his agent, the profits being equally divided. Done in the house of this same Oliverius, 1160, May 12, 7th indiction.

655 Oliverius Nivetelle and Oliverius de Reco.

Same witnesses, place and time and Iohannes Cirbinus and Ansaldinus Testa. Oliverius Nivetella and Oliverius de Reco contracted a societas in which Oliverius Nivetella invested 20 pounds 4-1/2 shillings and the above mentioned Oliverius invested 11 pounds. Oliverius must take the work of this societas to Palermo and through Sicily and then must settle accounts with Oliverius or his agent, and after the capital is returned the profits will be divided equally.

656 Oliverius Nivetelle and Oliverius Ferretus The same witnesses, day and place as above.

Oliverius Nivetella and Oliverius Ferretus on the directive and authority of their lord Oto Dormacagar contracted a societas in which this Oliverius Nivetella states that he contributed 25 pounds and Oliverius Ferrerius and his lord and the same Oliverius contributed 17-1/2 pounds. Oliverius must take this societas to Palermo and then Sicily and from there this ship and its crew will return without exception and after the capital has been divided he will divide the profits of this venture equally with Oliverius or his agent.

878 Oliverius Nivetelle

Witnesses Bonus Vassallus Salsa, Bombellus the banker, Lanfrancus de Albario, Jordanus de Isa and Nicolosus de domo. We Otobonus master and Druda his spouse have taken from you, Oliverius Nivetella, 60 pounds in Genovese pennies as full price for a house and a parcel of land of our hereditary right which is in Clavica. Its boundaries are on two sides the public road, and on two others your house.

We sell you the above-mentioned purchaser everything within these boundaries with its entrance and exit and all of its rights for you and your heirs or to whomever you may wish to give it to do whatever you wish as proprietor. We further promise not to hinder you and to defend you against everyone else under penalty of a double payment according to its present or future increased value, in order to make good our pledge that we have sold to you all that we have or should have and we promise that without your authority and advice we shall not make any evaluation or claims on it in for sale. We give you possession and lordship of this house. I Druda made this with the advice and authority of my kinsman Iordanus de Isa and Nicolosus de domo renouncing my rights in this case according to the senatusconsult of Velleianus[1] on the law of mortgages and the law of Julia on non appraised values.[2] Done in the church of Saint Laurence, 17 August, in the 8th indiction.

1125   Oliverius Nivetelle and Ferretus

Witnesses Bonus Vassallus Salsa, Aimericus, Master Bernardus, Oto Painardus and Enricus Nivetella. Oliverius Nivetella and Oliver Ferretus have contracted a societas in which they both state that Oliverius Nivetella invested 40 pounds and Oliverius Ferretus 20 pounds. Oliverius Ferretus must take this societas in the ship of Enrici Gagina and on his return must divide principal and interest with Oliverii Nivetelle. After the capital has been separated, the profits are to be divided equally. Oliverius Ferretus further swears that he has promised 20 pounds in this societas and that he will execute and will make every effort to advance this societas in good faith and legally according to the tenor of the contract of the societas and that he will return it as stipulated above and that as long as he is doing business with this Oliverius and had his property and this societas in his power he will keep faith and

will restore to him or to his agent without fraud nor will he deprive him of more than 10 shillings per year which he expects in good faith unless he receives permission to do so by him or by his reliable agent. Done in the house of Iohannis the scribe, 1163, 25 September, the 11th indiction.

1126   Oliverius Nivetella and Enricus Gagina

Witnesses Bonus Vassallus Salsa, Oto Rainardus, Donatus de Sancto Donato and Enricus Nivetella. Oliverius Nivetella and Enricus Gagina state that they have divided all of the societas which they had previously shared and that each has taken his share. Done before lord Bernardus the magistrate, in the same day as above.

1127   Oliverius Nivetella and Enricus Gagina

The above witnesses in the preceding document and on the same day and place. Oliverius Nivetella and Enricus Gagina have formed a societas in which Oliverius contributes 102 pounds and Enricus 51. Enricus undertakes this societas in a ship which is to depart and return and when the capital has been removed, the profits are to be divided in halves. In addition Enricus will carry 49 pounds of his own which he should spend and from which he should freely profit and which will be his own profit.

Notes

1   In Roman Law, the Senatusconsult Velleianum forbad/forbade surety by women.
2   The Julian law protected the alienation of a woman's dowry by her husband or guardian. See above, Theodosian code 3,1,3.

DIALOGUES OF CATHERINE OF SIENA

Catherine of Siena (1347-1380) was born Caterina Benincasa to a family of modest means in the city of Siena. From childhood she had visions and after entering the Third Order of St. Dominic at sixteen she became famous for her austerity, contemplation, and work with the poor. She dictated letters and discussions of spiritual matters in a trance-like state to her confessor and spiritual director who, after 1374 was Raymond of Capua, future master general of the Dominican order. Among the most significant were her Dialogues, a treatise in four books dedicated respectively to Divine Providence, Discretion, Prayer, and Obedience. The following passage from the second book deals with the nature of love. It is followed by an eyewitness account of her death by Barduccio di Piero Canigiani.

Source: *The Dialogue of the Seraphic Virgin Catherine of Siena* (DICTATAED BY HER, WHILE IN A STATE OF ECSTASY, TO HER SECRETARIES, AND COMPLETED IN THE YEAR OF OUR LORD 1370 TOGETHER WITH AN ACCOUNT OF HER DEATH BY AN EYE-WITNESS.) Trans. Algar Thorold (Westminster, Maryland: The Newman Bookshop, 1944).

Of the imperfection of those who love GOD for their own profit, delight, and consolation.

"Some there are who have become faithful servants, serving Me with fidelity without servile fear of punishment, but rather with love. This very love, however, if they serve Me with a view to their own profit, or the delight and pleasure which they find in Me, is imperfect. Dost thou know what proves the imperfection of this love? The withdrawal of the consolations which they found in Me, and the insufficiency and short duration of their love for their neighbour, which grows weak by degrees, and ofttimes disappears. Towards Me their love grows weak when, on occasion, in order to exercise them in virtue and raise them above their imperfection, I withdraw from their minds My consolation and allow them to fall into battles and perplexities. This I do so that, coming to perfect self-knowledge, they may know that of themselves they are nothing and have no grace, and accordingly in time of battle fly to Me, as their Benefactor, seeking Me alone, with true humility, for which purpose I treat them thus, without drawing from them consolation indeed, but not grace. At such a time these weak ones, of whom I speak, relax their energy, impatiently turning backwards, and sometimes abandon, under colour of virtue, many of their exercises, saying to themselves, *This labour does not profit me*. All this they do, because they feel themselves deprived of mental consolation. Such a soul acts imperfectly, for she has not yet unwound the bandage of spiritual self-love, for, had she unwound it she would see that, in truth, everything proceeds from Me, that no leaf of a tree falls to the ground without My providence, and that what I give and promise to My creatures, I give and promise to them for their sanctification, which is the good and the end for which I created them. My creatures should see and know that I wish nothing but their good, through the Blood of My only-begotten Son, in which they are washed from their iniquities. By this Blood they are enabled to know My Truth, how, in order to give them eternal life, I created them in My image and likeness and re-created them to grace with the Blood of My Son, making them sons of adoption. But, since they are imperfect, they make use of Me only for their own profit, relaxing their love for their neighbour. Thus, those in the first state come to nought through the fear of enduring pain, and those in the second, because they slacken their pace, ceasing to render service to their neighbour, and withdrawing their charity if they see their own profit or consolation withdrawn from them: this happens because their love was originally impure, for they gave to their neighbour the same imperfect love which they gave to Me, that is to say, a love based only on desire of their own advantage. If, through a desire for perfection, they do not recognise this imperfection of theirs, it is impossible that they should not turn back. For those who desire Eternal Life, a pure love, prescinding from themselves, is necessary, for it is not enough for eternal life to fly sin from fear of punishment, or to embrace virtue from the motive of one's own advantage. Sin should be abandoned because it is displeasing to Me, and virtue should be loved for My sake. It is true that, generally speaking, every person is first called in this way, but this is because the soul herself is at first imperfect, from which imperfection she must advance to perfection, either while she lives, by a generous love to Me with a pure and virtuous heart that takes no thought for herself, or, at least, in the moment of death, recognising her own imperfection, with the purpose, had she but time, of serving Me, irrespectively of herself. It was with this imperfect love that S. Peter loved the sweet and good Jesus, My only-begotten Son, enjoying most pleasantly His sweet conversation, but, when the time of trouble came, he failed, and so disgraceful was his fall, that, not only could he not bear any pain himself, but his terror of the very approach of pain caused him to fall, and deny the Lord, with the words, '*I have never known Him.*' The soul who has climbed this step with servile fear and mercenary love alone, falls into many troubles. Such souls should arise and become sons, and serve Me, irrespective of themselves, for I, who am the Rewarder of every labour, render to each man according to his state and his labour; wherefore, if these souls do not abandon the exercise of holy prayer and their other good works, but go on, with perseverance, to increase their virtues, they will arrive at the state of filial love, because I respond to them with the same love, with which they love Me, so that, if they love Me, as a servant does his master, I pay them their wages according to their deserts, but I do not reveal Myself to them, because secrets are revealed to a friend, who has become one thing with his friend, and not to a servant. Yet it is true, that a servant may so advance by the virtuous love, which he bears to his master, as to become a very dear friend, and so do some of these of whom I have spoken, but while they remain in the state of mercenary love, I do not manifest Myself to them. If they, through displeasure at their imperfection, and love of virtue, dig up, with hatred, the root of spiritual self-love, and mount to the throne of conscience, reasoning with themselves, so as to quell the motions of servile fear in their heart, and to correct mercenary love by the light of the holy faith, they will be so pleasing to Me, that they will attain to the love of the friend. And I will manifest Myself to them, as My Truth said in these words: '*He who loves Me shall be one thing with Me and I with him, and I will manifest Myself to him and we will dwell together.*' This is the state of two dear friends, for though they are two in body, yet they are one in soul through the affection of love, because love transforms the lover into the object loved, and where two friends have one soul, there can be no secret between them, wherefore My Truth said: 'I will come and we will dwell together,' and this is the truth ."

Of the way in which GOD manifests Himself to the soul who loves Him.

"Knowest thou how I manifest Myself to the soul who loves Me in truth, and follows the doctrine of My sweet and amorous Word? In many is My virtue manifested in the soul in proportion to her desire, but I make three special manifestations. The first manifestation of My virtue, that is to say, of My love and charity in the soul, is made through the Word of My Son, and shown in the Blood, which He spilled with such fire of love. Now this charity is manifested in two ways; first, in general, to ordinary people, that is to those who live in the ordinary grace of God. It is manifested to them by the many and diverse benefits which they receive from Me. The second mode of manifestation, which is developed from the first, is peculiar to those who have become My friends in the way mentioned above, and is known through a sentiment of the soul, by which they taste, know, prove, and feel it. This second manifestation, however, is in men themselves; they manifesting Me, through the affection of their love. For though I am no Acceptor of creatures, I am an Acceptor of holy desires, and Myself in the soul in that precise degree of perfection which she seeks in Me. Sometimes I manifest Myself (and this is also a part of the second manifestation) by endowing men with the spirit of prophecy, showing them the things of the future. This I do in many and diverse ways, according as I see need in the soul herself and in other creatures. At other times the third manifestation takes place. I then form in the mind the presence of the Truth, My only-begotten Son, in many ways, according to the will and the desire of the soul. Sometimes she seeks Me in prayer, wishing to know My power, and I satisfy her by causing her to taste and see My virtue. Sometimes she seeks Me in the wisdom of My Son, and I satisfy her by placing His wisdom before the eye of her intellect, sometimes in the clemency of the Holy Spirit and then My Goodness causes her to taste the fire of Divine charity, and to conceive the true and royal virtues, which are founded on the pure love of her neighbour."

Why Christ did not say " I will manifest My Father," but "I will manifest Myself."

"Thou seest now how truly My Word spoke, when He said: *'He who loves Me shall be one thing with Me.'* Because, by following His doctrine with the affection of love, you are united with Him, and, being united with Him, you are united with Me, because We are one thing together. And so it is that I manifest Myself to you, because We are one and the same thing together. Wherefore if My Truth said, *'I will manifest Myself to you,'* He said the truth, because, in manifesting Himself, He manifested Me, and, in manifesting Me, He manifested Himself. But why did He not say, *'I will manifest My Father to you'*? For three reasons in particular. First, because He wished to show that He and I are not separate from each other, on which account He also made the following reply to S. Philip, when he said to Him, *'Show us the Father, and it is enough for us.'* My Word said, *'Who sees Me sees the Father, and who sees the Father sees Me.'* This He said because He was one thing with Me, and that which He had, He had from Me, I having nothing from Him; wherefore, again, He

said to Judas, *'My doctrine is not Mine, but My Father's who sent Me,'* because My Son proceeds from Me, not I from Him, though I with Him and He with Me are but one thing. For this reason He did not say *'I will manifest the Father,'* but *'I will manifest Myself'* being one thing with the Father. The second reason was because, in manifesting Himself to you, He did not present to you anything He had not received from Me, the Father. These words, then, mean, the Father has manifested Himself to Me, because I am one thing with Him, and I will manifest to you, by means of Myself, Me and Him. The third reason was, because I, being invisible, could not be seen by you, until you should be separated from your bodies. Then, indeed, will you see Me, your GOD, and My Son, the Word, face to face. From now until after the general Resurrection, when your humanity will be conformed with the humanity of the Eternal Word, according to what I told thee in the treatise of the Resurrection, you can see Me, with the eye of the intellect alone, for, as I am, you cannot see Me now. Wherefore I veiled the Divine nature with your humanity, so that you might see Me through that medium. I, the Invisible, made Myself, as it were, visible by sending you the Word, My Son, veiled in the flesh of your humanity. He manifested Me to you. Therefore it was that He did not say *'I will manifest the Father to you,'* but rather, *'I will manifest Myself to you,'* as if He should say, *'According as My Father manifests Himself to Me, will I manifest Myself to you, for, in this manifestation of Himself, He manifests Me.'* Now therefore thou understandest why He did not say *'I will manifest the Father to you.'* Both, because such a vision is impossible for you, while yet in the mortal body, and because He is one thing with Me."

How the soul, after having mounted the first step of the Bridge, should proceed to mount the second.

"Thou hast now seen how excellent is the state of him who has attained to the love of a friend; climbing with the foot of affection, he has reached the secret of the Heart, which is the second of the three steps figured in the Body of My Son. I have told thee what was meant by the three powers of the soul, and now I will show thee how they signify the three states, through which the soul passes. Before treating of the third state, I wish to show thee how a man becomes a friend and how, from a friend, he grows into a son, attaining to filial love, and how a man may know if he has become a friend. And first of how a man arrives at being a friend. In the beginning, a man serves Me imperfectly through servile fear, but, by exercise and perseverance, he arrives at the love of delight, finding his own delight and profit in Me. This is a necessary stage, by which he must pass, who would attain to perfect love, to the love that is of friend and son. I call filial love perfect, because thereby, a man receives his inheritance from Me, the Eternal Father, and because a son's love includes that of a friend, which is why I told thee that a friend grows into a son. What means does he take to arrive thereat? I will tell thee. Every perfection and every virtue proceeds from charity, and charity is nourished by humility, which results from the knowledge and holy hatred of self, that is, sensuality. To arrive thereat, a man must persevere, and remain in the cellar of self-knowledge in which he will learn My mercy, in the Blood of My only begotten Son, drawing to Himself, with this love, My divine charity, exercising himself in the extirpation of his perverse self-will, both spiritual and temporal, hiding himself in his own house, as did Peter, who, after the sin of denying My Son, began to weep. Yet his lamentations were imperfect and remained so, until after the forty days, that is until after the Ascension. But when My Truth returned to Me, in His humanity, Peter and the others concealed themselves in the house, awaiting the coming of the Holy Spirit, which My Truth had promised them. They remained barred in from fear, because the soul always fears until she arrives at true love. But when they had persevered in fasting and in humble and continual prayer, until they had received the abundance of the Holy Spirit, they lost their fear, and followed and preached Christ crucified. So also the soul, who wishes to arrive at this perfection, after she has risen from the guilt of mortal sin, recognising it for what it is, begins to weep from fear of the penalty, whence she rises to the consideration of My mercy, in which contemplation, she finds her own pleasure and profit. This is an imperfect state, and I, in order to develop perfection in the soul, after the forty days, that is after these two states, withdraw Myself from time to time, not in grace but in feeling. My Truth showed you this when He said to the disciples 'I will go and will return to you.'

"Everything that He said was said primarily, and in particular, to the disciples, but referred in general to the whole present and future, to those, that is to say, who should come after. He said ' I will go and will return to you;' and so it was, for, when the Holy Spirit returned upon the disciples, He also returned, as I told you above, for the Holy Spirit did not return alone, but came with My power, and the wisdom of the Son, who is one thing with Me, and with His own clemency, which proceeds from Me the Father, and from the Son. Now, as I told thee, in order to raise the soul from imperfection, I withdraw Myself from her sentiment, depriving her of former consolations. When she was in the guilt of mortal sin, she had separated herself from Me, and I deprived her of grace through her own guilt, because that guilt had barred the door of her desires. Wherefore the sun of grace did not shine, not through its own defect, but through the defect of the creature, who bars the door of desire. When she knows herself and her darkness, she opens the window and vomits her filth, by holy confession. Then I, having returned to the soul by grace, withdraw Myself from her by sentiment, which I do in order to humiliate her, and cause her to seek Me in truth, and to prove her in the light of faith, so that she come to prudence. Then, if she love Me without thought of self, and with lively faith and with hatred of her own sensuality, she rejoices in the time of trouble, deeming herself unworthy of peace and quietness of mind. Now comes the second of the three things of which I told thee, that is to say: how the soul arrives at perfection, and what she does when she is perfect. This is what she does. Though she perceives that I have withdrawn Myself, she does not, on that account, look back, but perseveres with humility in her exercises, remaining barred in the house of self-knowledge, and, continuing to dwell therein, awaits, with lively faith, the coming of the Holy Spirit, that is of Me, who am the fire of charity. How does she await me? Not in idleness, but in watching and continued prayer, and not only with physical, but also with intellectual watching, that is, with the eye of her mind alert, and, watching with the light of faith, she extirpates, with hatred, the wandering thoughts of her heart, looking for the affection of My charity, and knowing that I desire nothing but her sanctification, which is certified to her in the Blood of My Son. As long as her eye thus watches, illumined by the knowledge of Me and of herself, she continues to pray with the prayer of holy desire, which is a continued prayer, and also with actual prayer, which she practises at the appointed times, according to the orders of Holy Church. This is what the soul does in order to rise from imperfection and arrive at perfection, and it is to this end, namely that she may arrive at perfection, that I withdraw from her, not by grace but by sentiment. Once more do I leave her, so that she may see and know her defects, so that, feeling herself deprived of consolation and afflicted by pain, she may recognise her own weakness, and learn how incapable she is of stability or perseverance, thus cutting down to the very root of spiritual self-love, for this should be the end and purpose of all her self-knowledge, to rise above herself, mounting the throne of conscience, and not permitting the sentiment of imperfect love to turn again in its death-struggle, but, with correction and reproof, digging up the root of self-love, with the knife of self-hatred and the love of virtue."

How an imperfect lover of GOD loves his neighbour also imperfectly, and of the signs of this imperfect love.

"And I would have thee know that just as every imperfection and perfection is acquired from Me, so is it manifested by means of the neighbour. And simple souls, who often love creatures with spiritual love, know this well, for, if they have received My love sincerely without any self-regarding considerations, they satisfy the thirst of their love for their neighbour equally sincerely. If a man carry away the vessel which he has filled at the fountain and then drink of it, the vessel becomes empty, but if he keep his vessel standing in the fountain, while he drinks, it always remains full. So the love of the neighbour,

whether spiritual or temporal, should be drunk in Me, without any self-regarding considerations. I require that you should love Me with the same love with which I love you. This indeed you cannot do, because I loved you without being loved. All the love which you have for Me you owe to Me, so that it is not of grace that you love Me, but because you ought to do so. While I love you of grace, and not because I owe you My love. Therefore to Me, in person, you cannot repay the love which I require of you, and I have placed you in the midst of your fellows, that you may do to them that which you cannot do to Me, that is to say, that you may love your neighbour of free grace, without expecting any return from him, and what you do to him, I count as done to Me, which My Truth showed forth when He said to Paul, My persecutor—'*Saul, Saul, why persecutest thou Me?*' This He said, judging that Paul persecuted Him in His faithful. This love must be sincere, because it is with the same love with which you love Me, that you must love your neighbour. Dost thou know how the imperfection of spiritual love for the creature is shown? It is shown when the lover feels pain if it appear to him that the object of his love does not satisfy or return his love, or when he sees the beloved one's conversation turned aside from him, or himself deprived of consolation, or another loved more than he. In these and in many other ways can it be seen that his neighbourly love is still imperfect, and that, though his love was originally drawn from Me, the Fountain of all love, he took the vessel out of the water, in order to drink from it. It is because his love for Me is still imperfect, that his neighbourly love is so weak, and because the root of self-love has not been properly dug out. Wherefore I often permit such a love to exist, so that the soul may in this way come to the knowledge of her own imperfection, and for the same reason do I withdraw myself from the soul by sentiment, that she may be thus led to enclose herself in the house of self-knowledge, where is acquired every perfection. After which I return into her with more light and with more knowledge of My Truth in proportion to the degree in which she refers to grace the power of slaying her own will. And she never ceases to cultivate the vine of her soul, and to root out the thorns of evil thoughts, replacing them with the stones of virtues, cemented together in the Blood of Christ crucified, which she has found on her journey across the Bridge of Christ, My only-begotten Son. For I told thee, if thou remember, that upon the Bridge, that is, upon the doctrine of My Truth, were built up the stones, based upon the virtue of His Blood, for it is in virtue of this Blood that the virtues give life."

Trinity, I have known in Thy light, which Thou hast given me with the light of holy faith, the many and wonderful things Thou hast declared to me, explaining to me the path of supreme perfection, so that I may no longer serve Thee in darkness, but with light, and that I may be the mirror of a good and holy life, and arise from my miserable sins, for through them I have hitherto served Thee in darkness. I have not known Thy truth and have not loved it. Why did I not know Thee? Because I did not see Thee with the glorious light of the holy faith; because the cloud of self-love darkened the eye of my intellect, and Thou, the Eternal Trinity, hast dissipated the darkness with Thy light. Who can attain to Thy Greatness, and give Thee thanks for such immeasurable gifts and benefits as Thou hast given me in this doctrine of truth, which has been a special grace over and above the ordinary graces which Thou givest also to Thy other creatures? Thou hast been willing to condescend to my need and to that of Thy creatures—the need of introspection. Having first given the grace to ask the question, Thou repliest to it, and satisfiest Thy servant, penetrating me with a ray of grace, so that in that light I may give Thee thanks. Clothe me, clothe me with Thee, oh! Eternal Truth, that I may run my mortal course with true obedience and the light of holy faith, with which light I feel that my soul is about to become inebriated afresh."

A Letter of Ser Barduccio di Piero Canigiani, containing the Transit of the Seraphic Virgin, Saint Catherine of Siena, to Sister Catherine Petriboni in the Monastery of San Piero a Monticelli near Florence. In the Name of Jesus Christ.

Dearest Mother in Christ Jesus, and Sister in the holy memory of our blessed mother Catherine, I, Barduccio, a wretched and guilty sinner, recommend myself to your holy prayers as a feeble infant, orphaned by the death of so great a mother. I received your letter and read it with much pleasure, and communicated it to my afflicted mothers here, who, supremely grateful for your great charity and tender love towards them, recommend themselves greatly, for their part, to your prayers, and beg you to recommend them to the Prioress and all the sisters that they may be ready to do all that may be pleasing to God concerning themselves and you. But since you, as a beloved and faithful daughter, desire to know the end of our common mother, I am constrained to satisfy your desire; and although I know myself to be but little fitted to give such a narration, I will write in any case what my feeble eyes have seen, and what the dull senses of my soul have been able to comprehend.

This blessed virgin and mother of thousands of souls, about the feast of the Circumcision, began to feel so great a change both in soul and body, that she was obliged to alter her mode of life, the action of taking food for her sustenance becoming so loathsome to her, that it was only with the greatest difficulty that she could force herself to take any, and, when she did so, she swallowed nothing of the substance of the food, but had the habit of rejecting it. Moreover, not one drop of water could she swallow for refreshment, whence came to her a most violent and tedious thirst, and so great an inflammation of her throat that her breath seemed to be fire, with all which, however, she remained in very good health, robust and fresh as usual. In these conditions we reached Sexagesima Sunday, when, about the hour of vespers, at the time of her prayer, she had so violent a stroke that from that day onwards she was no longer in health. Towards the night of the following Monday, just after I had written a letter, she had another stroke so terrific, that we all mourned her as dead, remaining under it for a long time without giving any sign of life. Then, rising, she stood for an equal space of time, and did not seem the same person as she who had fallen.

From that hour began new travail and bitter pains in her body, and, Lent having arrived, she began, in spite of her infirmity, to give herself with such application of mind to prayer that the frequency of the humble sighs and sorrowful plaints which she exhaled from the depth of her heart appeared to us a miracle. I think, too, that you know that her prayers were so fervent that one hour spent in prayer by her reduced that dear tender frame to greater weakness than would be suffered by one who should persist for two whole days in prayer. Meanwhile, every morning, after communion, she arose from the earth in such a state that any one who had seen her would have thought her dead, and was thus carried back to bed. Thence, after an hour or two, she would arise afresh, and we would go to St. Peter's, although a good mile distant, where she would place herself in prayer, so remaining until vespers, finally returning to the house so worn out that she seemed a corpse.

These were her exercises up till the third Sunday in Lent, when she finally succumbed, conquered by the innumerable sufferings, which daily increased, and consumed her body, and the infinite afflictions of the soul which she derived from the consideration of the sins which she saw being committed against God, and from the dangers ever more grave to which she knew the Holy Church to be exposed, on account of which she remained greatly overcome, and both internally and externally tormented. She lay in this state for eight weeks, unable to lift her head, and full of intolerable pains, from the soles of her feet to the crown of her head, to such an extent that she would often say: "These pains are truly physical, but not natural; for it seems that God has given permission to the devils to torment this body at their pleasure." And, in truth, it evidently was so; for, if I were to attempt to explain the patience which she practised, under this terrible and unheard-of agony, I should fear to injure, by my explanations, facts which cannot be explained. This only will I say, that, every time that a new torment came upon her, she would joyously raise her eyes and her heart to God and say: "Thanks to Thee, oh eternal Spouse, for granting such graces afresh every day to me, Thy miserable and most unworthy handmaid!"

In this way her body continued to consume itself until the Sunday before the Ascension; but by that time it was reduced to such a state that it seemed like a corpse in a picture, though I speak not of the face, which remained ever angelical and breathed forth devotion, but of the bosom and limbs, in which nothing could be seen but the bones, covered by the thinnest skin, and so feeble was she from the waist downwards that she could not move herself, even a little, from one side to another. In the night preceding the aforesaid Sunday, about two hours or more before dawn, a great change was produced in her, and we thought that she was approaching the end. The whole family was then called around her, and she, with singular humility and devotion, made signs to those who were standing near that she desired to receive Holy Absolution for her faults and the pains due to them, and so it was done. After which she became gradually reduced to such a state that we could observe no other movement than her breathing, continuous, sad, and feeble. On account of this it seemed right to give her extreme unction, which our abbot of Sant' Antimo did, while she lay as it were deprived of feeling.

After this unction she began altogether to change, and to make various signs with her head and her arms as if to show that she was suffering from grave assaults of demons, and remained in this calamitous state for an hour and a half, half of which time having been passed in silence, she began to say: "I have sinned! Oh Lord, have mercy on me!" And this, as I believe, she repeated more than sixty times, raising each time her right arm, and then letting it fall and strike the bed. Then, changing her words, she said as many times again, but without moving her arms, "Holy God, have mercy on me!" Finally she employed the remainder of the above-mentioned time with many other formulas of prayer both humble and devout, expressing various acts of virtue, after which her face suddenly changed from gloom to angelic light, and her tearful and clouded eyes became serene and joyous, in such a manner that I could not doubt that, like one saved from a deep sea, she was restored to herself, which circumstance greatly mitigated the grief of her sons and daughters who were standing around in the affliction you can imagine.

Catherine had been lying on the bosom of Mother Alessia and now succeeded in rising, and with a little help began to sit up, leaning against the same mother. In the meantime we had put before her eyes a pious picture, containing many relics and various pictures of the saints. She, however, fixed her eyes on the image of the cross set in it, and began to adore it, explaining, in words, certain of her most profound feelings of the goodness of God, and while she prayed, she accused herself in general of all her sins in the sight of God, and, in particular, said: "It is my fault, oh eternal Trinity, that I have offended Thee so miserably with my negligence, ignorance, ingratitude, and disobedience, and many other defects. Wretch that I am! for I have not observed Thy commandments, either those which are given in general to all, or those which Thy goodness laid upon me in particular! Oh mean creature that I am!" Saying which, she struck her breast, repeating her confession, and continued: "I have not observed Thy precept, with which Thou didst command me to seek always to give Thee honour, and to spend myself in labours for my neighbour, while I, on the contrary, have fled from labours, especially where they were necessary. Didst Thou not command me, oh, my God! to abandon all thought of myself and to consider solely the praise and glory of Thy Name in the salvation of souls, and with this food alone, taken from the table of the most holy Cross, to comfort myself? But I have sought my own consolation. Thou didst ever invite me to bind myself to Thee alone by sweet, loving, and fervent desires, by tears and humble and continuous prayers for the salvation of the whole world and for the reformation of the holy Church, promising me that, on account of them, Thou wouldst use mercy with the world, and give new beauty to Thy Spouse; but I, wretched one, have not corresponded with Thy desire, but have remained asleep in the bed of negligence.

"Oh, unhappy that I am! Thou hast placed me in charge of souls, assigning to me so many beloved sons, that I should love them with singular love and direct them to Thee by the way of Life, but I have been to them nothing but a mirror of human weakness; I have had no care of them; I have not helped them with continuous and humble prayer in Thy presence, nor have I given them sufficient examples of the good life or the warnings of salutary doctrine. Oh, mean creature that I am! with how little reverence have I received Thy innumerable gifts, the graces of such sweet torments and labours which it pleased Thee to accumulate on this fragile body, nor have I endured them with that burning desire and ardent love with which Thou didst send them to me. Alas! oh, my Love, through Thy excessive goodness Thou didst choose me for Thy spouse, from the beginning of my childhood, but I was not faithful enough; in fact, I was unfaithful to Thee, because I did not keep my memory faithful to Thee alone and to Thy most high benefits; nor have I fixed my intelligence on the thought of them only or disposed my will to love Thee immediately with all its strength."

Of these and many other similar things did that pure dove accuse herself, rather, as I think, for our example than for her own need, and then, turning to the priest, said: "For the love of Christ crucified, absolve me of all these sins which I have confessed in the presence of God, and of all the others which I cannot remember." That done, she asked again for the plenary indulgence, saying that it had been granted her by Pope Gregory and Pope Urban, saying this as one an hungered for the Blood of Christ. So I did what she asked, and she, keeping her eyes ever fixed on the crucifix, began afresh to adore it with the greatest devotion, and to say certain very profound things which I, for my sins, was not worthy to understand, and also on account of the grief with which I was labouring and the anguish with which her throat was oppressed, which was so great that she could hardly utter her words, while we, placing our ears to her mouth, were able to catch one or two now or again, passing them on from one to the other. After this she turned to certain of her sons, who had not been present at a memorable discourse which, many days previously, she had made to the whole family, showing us the way of salvation and perfection, and laying upon each of us the particular task which he was to perform after her death. She now did the same to these others, begging most humbly pardon of all for the slight care which she seemed to have had of our salvation. Then she said certain things to Lucio and to another, and finally to me, and then turned herself straightway to prayer.

Oh! had you seen with what humility and reverence she begged and received many times the blessing of her most sorrowful mother, all that I can say is that it was a bitter sweet to her. How full of tender affection was the spectacle of the mother, recommending herself to her blessed child, and begging her to obtain a particular grace from God—namely, that in these melancholy circumstances she might not offend Him. But all these things did not distract the holy virgin from the fervour of her prayer; and, approaching her end, she began to pray especially for the Catholic Church, for which she declared she was giving her life. She prayed again for Pope Urban VI., whom she resolutely confessed to be the true Pontiff, and strengthened her sons never to hesitate to give their life for that truth. Then, with the greatest fervour, she besought all her beloved children whom the Lord had given her, to love Him alone, repeating many of the words which our Saviour used, when He recommended the disciples to the Father, praying with such affection, that, at hearing her, not only our hearts, but the very stones might have been broken. Finally, making the sign of the cross, she blessed us all, and thus continued in prayer to the end of her life for which she had so longed, saying: "Thou, oh Lord, callest me, and I come to Thee, not through my merits, but through Thy mercy alone, which I ask of Thee, in virtue of Thy Blood!" and many times she called out: "Blood, Blood!" Finally, after the example of the Saviour, she said: "Father, into Thy Hands I commend my soul and my Spirit," and thus sweetly, with a face all shining and angelical, she bent her head, and gave up the ghost.

Her transit occurred on the Sunday at the hour of Sext, but we kept her unburied until the hour of Compline on Tuesday, without any odour being perceptible, her body remaining so pure, intact, and fragrant, that her arms, her neck and her legs remained as flexible as if she were still alive. During those three days the body was visited by crowds of people, and lucky he thought himself who was able to touch it. Almighty God also worked many miracles in that time, which in my hurry I omit. Her tomb is visited devoutly by the faithful, like those of the other holy bodies which are in Rome, and Almighty God is granting many graces in the name of His blessed spouse, and I doubt not that there will be many more, and we are made great by hearing of them. I say no more. Recommend me to the Prioress and all the sisters, for I have, at present, the greatest need of the help of prayer. May Almighty God preserve you and help you to grow in His grace.

FLORENCE: CATASTO OF 1427

THE CATASTO SURVEY OF 1427-30 IS ONE OF THE EARLIEST ATTEMPTS to compile a precise record of a city's population and its wealth. This record is a unique source for exploring social and economic questions about types of households, role of women, business ties, financial and kin networks, household composition, and social responsibilities.

The particular examples below all describe members of the important Alberti family of Florence. Previously, the adult male members of the family had been exiled from the city and therefore the reports are all made by their wives, widows, or minor children.

Source: ASF, Catasto 35, ff. 1337r-1341v and Cat. 72, f. 413r. Translation: Susannah Foster Baxendale for this volume.

Portata for the 'Heirs of Albertaccio'

In the Name of God

Before you, Sirs, Officials of the Catasto of the people and Commune of Florence, this relates to the property and taxes that on this the 19th of January 1427 [1428] one finds of the estate of Albertaccio degli Alberti taxed in the quarter of Santa Croce, gonfalone of Leon Nero and to report the holdings of Monna Ginevra wife of the late Albertaccio degli Alberti. And [the estate] has a prestanzone rating of ƒ18 which according to the testament of the said Monna Ginevra 3/4 is to be paid by the said heirs and 1/2 by whoever gets the other estate. The said estate belongs to Piero di Bartolomeo degli Alberti during his life and after his life to his sons. And their property is this, that is:

A house with a courtyard, loggia, arcade, well and kitchen garden, situated in the parish of San Romeo of Florence, at the foot of the Rubaconte Bridge in the place called 'of the Alberti's house.' [It is bounded] on the first, second, third and fourth [sides], [by] the street. Monna Caterina wife of the late Piero di Messer Filippo Corsini lives in this house and Monna Sandra her aunt by hereditary privilege. Beneath this house are the following places, used as rented-out shops, as we will now state:

One shop for use as silk dyeing,

under this house along the Arno, which is rented by Tommaso di Domenico, knifemaker, for his son and he owes a yearly rent of ƒ16.   ƒ16

One shop for use of a blacksmith, situated under the said house on the corner, which is rented by Aveduto Malischalcho and he owes a yearly rent of ƒ14.   ƒ14

One shop for use of a construction worker, situated under the said house. It is rented by Zanobi di Michele, construction worker, and he owes a yearly rent of L.48 fp.   ƒ12

One shop for use of a cooper, situated under the said house which is rented by Andrea di Niccolo, old clothes dealer, and he owes a yearly rent of ƒ14. [Added in a later hand: This shop belongs to Daniello de Piero himself.]   ƒ14

Also facing the said house, seven little shops, one after the other, with arcades, [bounded] on the first [side], the street; the second, the Via Lungharno; third, Antonio degli Alberti; fourth, the *piazzuola* of the said Alberti. The following renters are in the said shops:

In the shop on the corner facing Santa Maria delle Gratie and the blacksmith, is Andrea di Niccolo, flax-dresser, and he owes a yearly rent of ƒ13.

ƒ13

A shop next to the said one is rented by Lorenzo di Cristofano [son of] the late Naviolo and he owes a yearly rent of ƒ6.

ƒ6

A shop next to the said one is rented by Antonio di Piero, cooper, and he owes a yearly rent of ƒ6.

ƒ6

A shop next to the said one is renated by Filippo di Giovanni Gangaliardi, lasagna-maker, and he owes a yearly rent of ƒ6.

ƒ6

A shop next to the said one rented by Antonio di Loso, driver, and he owes a yearly rent of ƒ6.

ƒ6

A shop next to the said one rented by 'il Calamanza' and he owes a yearly rent of ƒ6.

ƒ6

A shop next to the said one rented by Lazaro di Zanobi, the 'barber' and he owes a yearly rent of ƒ8.

ƒ8

A house with stalls and land for use of silk dyeing, situated on the *piazzuola* in the place called 'of the Alberti's house,' [bounded] on the first, the said *piazzuola*; second, Antonio degli Alberti; third, the via Lungharno; fourth [left blank]. Of this, a half belongs to Daniello di Piero degli Alberti himself. Agniolo di Ser Giovanni, dyer, rents it and owes a yearly rent of ƒ14.

ƒ14

The fourth part, indivisible, of the Palagietto, situated on the corner of Corso de'Tintori under which there is a shop for use of a barber, of which 1/4 belongs to us and the other 3/4 to Filippo degli Alberti and the Otto di Guardia. [Bounded] on the first, the street, that is, Corso de'Tintori; on the second, the street which goes to the Ponte Rubacconte; third, Luigi degli Alberti; on the fourth, the Parte Guelfa. The said Palagietto is rented by Francesco di Betto Busini for ƒ6 a year for the 1/4 and the barber shop is rented by Bartolo di Luigi, barber, and he owes ƒ1 for the 1/4 a year. In all, ƒ7-1/4.

ƒ7-1/4

A half house, situated on Corso de'Tintori over the entrance to the Fungha; the other half is held by the Otto di Guardia. [Bounded] on the first, the street of Corso de'Tintori; second, Fabiano d'Antonio Martini; on the third, the bake-house of the late Betto Busini; on the fourth, the Piazza of the Fungha. Benedetto di Michele, doublet-maker, rents this half-house and owes a yearly rent of L.9 fp.

ƒ2-1/4

A house situated in the Fungha of Corso de'Tintori, [bounded] on the first, the Piazza of the said Fungha; second, us ourselves; third, Bucello di Francesco; fourth, the cap-dyeing shop. There are 2 renters in this house, that is: Gualente di Tommaso, a dye worker, and he owes a yearly rent of L.6 fp. for the half.

ƒ1-1/2

Piero of Ravenna, dye worker, and he owes a yearly rent of L.6 fp. for half.

ƒ1-1/2

A house situated in the Fungha of Corso de'Tintori, next to the above-mentioned [house, bounded] on the first, the Piazza of the said Fungha; on the second, us ourselves; on the third, the Otto di Guardia; on the fourth, Bucello di Francesco. There are 2 renters in this house, that is: Giovanni d'Orlanduccio, called Monteuchi, and he owes a yearly rent of L.7 fp.

ƒ1-3/4

Giusto and Benedetto di Piero, por-
ters, and they owe a yearly rent of
L.6 fp.   *f*1-1/2

Also there are several houses in the Fungha held
by the Otto di Guardia which we claim to be ours
and of our ownership but [because of] the inability to re-enter the homeland, we have not been
able to demonstrate to the Otto that they [the
houses] are in our ownership. We are seeking [to
recover] our accounts and if we acquire anything,
you will be notified. And we are giving you this
notice so as to not prejudice our accounts.

[The 'heirs' go on to list possessions outside
the city: an abandoned house and three attached
farms worth *f*69; a farm worth *f*33; a farm worth
*f*22; one worth *f*15; a house and three attached
farms worth *f*50; a farm worth *f*50; a farm worth
*f*40; and two farms with payments in kind.]

And further we find ourselves inscribed in the
Monte Comune of Florence in the quarter of
Santa Croce:

In the Monte Comune *f*898 *s*12 *d*9
with payments from 1423 til now,
inscribed in [the name of] Monna
Caterina wife of the late Piero di
Messer Filippo Corsini and previously in [the name of] Monna Ginevra the wife of the late Albertaccio
degli Alberti.   *f*898 *s*12 *d*9

In the Monte di Pisa *f*212 inscribed
in [the name of] the said Monna
Caterina and previously in the
said Monna Ginevra.   *f*212

In the Monte Comune *f* [left blank]
with all the payments from then on,
inscribed in Cherubino d'Albertaccio
degli Alberti and as of now it has not
been possible for us to claim them.
We mention it to you for the record
so as to not prejudice our accounts
and when they see we are right, you
will be notified.   *f* [blank]

*f*9 *s*3 *d*9 of payments received from
Monte Commune [credits] from 1415
to 1416 inscribed in Monna Caterina
wife of the late Piero di Messer Filippo
Corsini.   *f*9 *s*3 *d*9

*f*57 *s*10 of payments in the said
Monte inscribed in the same [Caterina]
from 1415 to 1419 at 20,000   *f*57 *s*10

*f*62 *s*13 of said payments from
1419 to 1423 inscribed in the same
[Caterina] at 120,000.   *f*62 *s*13

*f*21 *s*4 of payments made from the
Monte of Pisa from 1415 to 1419,
at 126,000, inscribed in the said Monna
Caterina.   *f*21 *s*4

All the above-named monies were previously in
the name of Monna Ginevra d'Albertaccio.

Further we are owed the following by Carlo
Macinghi and others:

*f*275 of Monte di 5 complete, which
the said Carlo had inscribed in his
son Niccolò and which belong to us.   *f*275

*f*511 di Monte di 8, of which we retain 1/4 and which begin to accrue
the first of January 1427 [1428] and
are inscribed in the said Niccolò.   *f*511

*f*37 of the said Monte which were invested in the Monte on 1 July
1427 and are inscribed in the said
Niccolò.   *f*37

*f*18-1/2 for one *prestanzone* paid by
Antonio di Bernardo di Luigi in his
name which were invested in the
Monte in July 1427.   *f*18-1/2

*f*93 *s*17 *d*4 of Monte Commune
inscribed in Francesco di Piero
degli Alberti, quarter of Santa Croce.   *f*93 *s*17 *d*4

*f*9 *s*6 of payments received from the
said [credits].   *f*9 *s*6

Debtors

Zanobi di Michele, construction
worker, owes   *f*24

Andrea di Niccolò, flax-worker   *f*20

Tommaso di Domenico, knife-
maker   *f*15

Bartolo di Pagnio of Terina   *f*9

Monna Telda, wife of the late
Zanobi, barber   *f*3

Filippo di Giovanni, lasagna-
maker   *f*20

Aveduto Malischalco   *f*20

Agniolo di Ser Giovanni, dyer   *f*10

'Il Chalamanza'   *f*3

Antonio di Loso   *f*3

Antonio di Piero, cooper   *f*4

Lorenzo di Cristofano, rope-maker   *f*6

Niccolo and Domenico di Giovanni
del Calice   *f*49

Bernaba di Giovanni, called
Necha   *f*21

Berto di Monna Maddalena   *f*20

Pagholo di Masotto   *f*10

Andrea di Michele   *f*10

Piero di Ciecco, Baker   *f*30

                                             *f*277

[Written to the side of the last of debtors]
A total of 18 debtors who owe *f*277; these are
old monies and one could retrieve them only

with great effort and lots of time [at a rate of] *s*10
to the lire or less. They [the debts] are all lost....

Creditors

We owe the following creditors, that is:
Carlo di Niccolò Macinghi is owed
*f*850, *f*500 of which are for a be-
quest which Cherubino made to
Mona Albiera his [Carlo's] wife, and
the remainder is for monies used by
the estate for *prestanze* and other
things.   *f*850

Monna Caterina wife of the late Piero
di Messer Filippo Corsini is owed   *f*150

Messer Iacopo di Totto of Modena
is owed 50 ducats for cloths received
from him for clothes for Piero and his
household [famiglia] a while ago.
They [the ducats] are   *f*55

Bartolomeo di Giovanni Chalora is
still owed for rent of the house we
rent from him in Modena and
other things received from him a
while ago. 30 ducats.   *f*33

Giovanni Charandini, druggist, in
Modena is owed for medicine receiv-
ed for Piero and for the funeral of
Iacopo's children. 15 ducats   *f*16*s*10

Valets and other servants are still
owed 20 ducats by Piero.   *f*22

Bivigliano degli Alberti is owed 100
ducats which he paid for us on 6
August 1425 to Francesco di
Guidalotto of Bologna, which we
owed. They are   *f*110

Antonio di Ricciardo degli Alberti
is owed 300 ducats which Ricciardo
lent [us] on 12 October 1418 and
because of inability they have not
yet been repaid.   *f*330

Roberto Poggio of Lechlade [delle Ceclade], English, is owed *l*123 *s*12 *d*6 sterling by Daniello himself. They are, at 40 pounds sterling to the florin,   *f*742

Ulichoccho, a draper of Cirencester [Sirisestri] in England is owed *l*53 *s*15 sterling by Daniello himself. They are, at 40 pounds sterling to the florin,   *f*322 *s*10

Dominico Villani of London is still owed for Daniello's living expenses from a while ago. *l*sterling are, at 40 pounds sterling to the florin,   *f*144

Monna Ginevra wife of the late Albertaccio degli Alberti for the loss of 4 *accatti* sold at a bad loss, that is, *f*16 *s*19, and we list them here because the said Monna Ginevra lists the *accatti*   *f*16 *s*13

Obligations

It costs us for yearly rent of the house we maintain in Modena 12 ducats which are   *f*13

Daniello has yearly expenses in England, 20 crowns, for his return over his living [costs]   *f*21

It costs us a year to maintain the houses and shops in Florence which are 18 or so sites, *f*1-1/2 a year, site for site, and more besides. In all *f*27   *f*27

It costs us every year the loan of oxen to work our possessions and maintain the houses of the said possessions, which are 16 or so houses. In all, yearly   *f*30

It costs us a year for planting and clearing of three farms in Monte Chucchi al'Angella around *f*20 and often more.   *f*20

And we cite to you the obligation of *f*13 for rent in Modena and *f*21 for the return of Daniello to England and, notwithstanding ours is one single family, one can't do less since Daniello is exiled and the limits of his exile are 100 miles and he cannot, according to the limits, live in Modena. And wanting to observe them [the limits], the said Daniello has taken London in England for his place of habitation such that one can do no less than the obligation of the rent in Modena and in London.

Mouths

Piero di Bartolomeo degli Alberti, ill, stricken
with gout.

He is aged	73 years
Iacopo his son, aged	42 years
Daniello his son, aged	33 years
Benedetto, son of the said Iacopo, aged	2-1/2 years
Caterina, daughter of Daniello, aged	3 years
	5 mouths
	are *f*1000

property	*f*7198 *s*9
obligations	*f*3441 *s*13
remainder	*f*3756 *s*16

Portata for Caterina, wife of the late Piero Corsini

To you, the wise and prudent officials of the Catasto, empowered by the Commune of Florence, I, Caterina, daughter of the late Albertaccio degli Alberti and wife of the late Piero di Messer Filippo Corsini, reveal my property and my obligations:

Lorenzo di Messer Palla di Nofri degli Strozzi and partners have *f*500 of mine at their discretion.

Antonio di Salvestro di Ser Ristoro and partners have *f*300 of mine similarly.

Andrea Borghognoni and Ser Pagholo di Ser Lando and partners have *f*200 similarly.

Antonio di Bernardo di Luigi has *f*200 of mine in the above-said manner.

Francesco di Filippo di Messer Castellano and partners have ƒ100 of mine.

Bernardo di Messer Biagio Guasconi owes me around ƒ25 which are the remainder of ƒ300 which he had of mine when he defaulted and went bankrupt at less than 16 soldi to the lira. And for all that I do not think I will get this remainder.

The Commune of Florence owes me ƒ600 and they are in the Monte Commune account inscribed for the quarter of Santa Croce.

The abovementioned Commune owes me ƒ11 for 4 *accatti* inscribed for the quarter of Santa Croce.

The estate of Monna Ginevra wife of the late Albertaccio degli Alberti owes me ƒ150. Concerning these monies: when I recover them, it is agreed that I will use them to buy furnishings since the household furnishings I have been using until now will revert to the heirs of Albertaccio degli Alberti. And because of this, I entreat you [the officials] that it please you to not tax these 150 florins.

These are my obligations; and two servants with a salary enough to keep them; and I cannot manage with less.

And I am taxed in the *gonfalone* of Leon Nero and have as a *prestanze* rate ƒ2 s17 and I was not previously given any tax relief.

And I, the abovementioned Caterina, who lives in the house which was Albertaccio's, by right of inheritance as he left me the [privilege of] return to the house upon being widowed. The said house is in the parish of San Romeo [bounded] on the first and second and third [sides], the street; on the fourth, Daniello degli Alberti. To you, the abovementioned officials, I am sending this declaration which I have written in my own hand.

I Niccolò di Carlo Macinghi have carried this [to the officials] with the approval of the said Monna Caterina.

10 July 1428

Portata for wife and heirs of Adovardo d'Alberto di Luigi degli Alberti

+ In the name of God on the [blank] day of July 1427

Before you, Sirs, officials of the Catasto, Piero Cambini, as manager of the property which one finds belonging to the heirs of Adovardo d'Alberto di Luigi degli Alberti. There remain his wife whose name is Monna Caterina, aged 36, with four children, three feminine and one masculine, whom I will describe below. And they [the heirs] are not of age and are in exile and are staying in Bologna. And they live pretty meagerly because they have little; and they are taxed in Leon Nero, the quarter of Santa Croce, and have as a *prestanzone* rate ƒ [left blank]. And the goods they have are these. And I advise you that they have little income and wouldn't manage too well were it not that their mother stays with the children in the house of her brother who is Antonio di Lionardo [*sic*] degli Alberti. This is the utter truth.

A *palazzo* fronting on Via Mastia with a tower on the corner, and, on the Borgo Santa Croce [a part] like a house, all situated in the parish of San Iacopo tralle Fosse in the place called 'of the Albertis' house' [bounded] first is the big street which goes to the Rubaconte Bridge; second, Borgo Santa Croce; third, Tommaso di Francesco Davizzi and partly the heirs of Bernardo d'Iacopo degli Alberti; fourth, Monna Catelana daughter of the late Alberto di Bernardo degli Alberti. The said *palazzo* facing [the street] with the tower is rented by Luca di Giovanni of Cortona for ƒ20 a year. The part on Borgo Santa Croce is rented by Asino di Bongianni for ƒ20-1/2 a year.

Five parts of nine parts, that is, 5/9 of a farm situated in the *contado* of Florence in the place called 'at the waters of Rinfusa' in the parish of Sanminiato al Monte; and Monna Aura, wife of Tommaso Corsi, holds 4/9 for life. It has workers' houses, hay-threshing floor and oven ... rent of ƒ28-1/4 for all, of which ƒ15 l3 s8 d4 fp. belongs to the 5/9th belonging to the heirs of Adovardo.

Five parts of nine parts, that is, 5/9 of a *casetta* of which the other 4/9 is held for life by the said Monna Aura, wife of Tommaso Corsi ... rent ƒ3-1/2 a year; our part is l7 s16 fp.

[He lists a farm, a *casetta*, a parcel of land, and 4 farms]

You [the officials] need to take off for the loan of oxen ...

You need to take off for the maintenance of the houses in Florence and in the *contado*.

You need to take off for the factor who manages their affairs. Before he didn't want to be paid while in service; Piero Cambini, no price given.

The woman to account for, Monna Caterina aged 36, stays in Bologna in exile with her children for the sake of the male child who cannot stay here [in Florence]; she has three girl children and one boy child.

One named Costanza aged	12 or 13
Another named Margherita aged	9 or 10
Adovarda aged	4 or 5
Alberto the boy is aged	8 or 9

[The debtors are listed for a total worth of about *f*150]

These people [the heirs] don't have cash because Alessio degli Alberti ruined his brother Adovardo, father of these children while he was in Barbery. And he lost his own and that of others in such a manner that they were left debtors for a goodly amount to their kin [*consorti*], an amount I don't see that they can ever pay any of it, but like good relatives [*parenti*], they help them [the heirs] with expenses.

They have these monies in the Monte, as we will write:

*f*41 in the Monte Comune, inscribed in Monna Margherita wife of the late Alberto di Luigi degli Alberti ...

*f*52 inscribed in the Monte Comune in the name of Adovardo d'Alberto di Luigi degli Alberti ...

property	*f*1737 *s*9 *d*4
obligations	*f*1028
remainder	*f*711 *s*9 *d*4

Portata of Antonia wife of Piero Dini

+ In the name of God on the 31st day of July 1427

To you, the esteemed citizens elected to do the catasto of the property of every citizen of the parishes of Florence. Monna Antonia, daughter of the late Alberto degli Alberti and wife of Piero di Giovanni Dini living in the city of Venice declares here following all of her moveable and immoveable property piece by piece and every obligation. First:

A half house [held] in common indivisibly with Monna Catalana, her sister and wife of the late Francesco Davizzi, situated in the gonfalone of Leon Nero in the street called Borgo Santa Croce, bounded on the first, the said street; second, the heirs of Adovardo degli Alberti; third, Tommaso Davizzi and Nerozzo degli Alberti; fourth, Francesco d'Altobianco degli Alberti. The said Monna Catelana lives in this [the house] by virtue of the testament of the said Alberto their father who bequeathed the return to and use of the said house should any of his daughters be left widowed. Documented by the hand of Ser Antonio di Ser chello. And for this reason, the said Monna Catelana has always held it and lived in it, because she is a widow, without paying anything; therefore this is not taxable [literally: is accounted valueless].

A half small farm [held] indivisibly in common with the said Monna Catelana ...

A half piece of land in the same place [held] indivisibly with the abovementioned [Catelana] ...

A piece [of land] in the same place, indivisible as above ...

All the abovementioned lands are worked by Mane di Lapo Bugli and his son Meo. My part of the return, that is, the half is ...

12 staia of corn
3 *staia* of grain
9 or 10 barrels of wine
1/2 barrel of oil
30 pounds of pork

Further I find myself [owed] for the remainder of 200 florins of withheld costs for him, Tommaso di Francesco Davizzi, from the heirs of Filippo Macinghi	. *f*150
Further she is owed for 24 ordinary payments of Monte Comune on *f*268	*f*25
Further she is owed by Tomasso Davizzi and by Monna Catelana his mother, around	*f*55

Further she is owed the payments sustained from the said *f*268 of Monte Comune from 1415 to 1419 and from 1419 to 1423. I believe she received [the payments] for 1411 to 1415 since she's not aware if there were any more. Her account is neither counted nor settled. *f* [blank]

The said Monna Antonia lives in Venice, aged [blank] *f*200

property	*f*464 *s*10	
obligations	*f*200	
remainder	*f*264 *s*10	

Portata of Tomasso di Francesco Davizzi and his mother

Tommaso di Francesco Davizzi and Monna Catelana his mother in the quarter of Santa Croce, *gonfalone* of Leon Nero; they have a *prestanzone* rate of *f*7.

To you, revered citizens, elected officials to do the Catasto of the property of every citizen of the city of Florence. I Tommaso di Francesco Davizzi report to you all moveable and immoveable goods, debtors and creditors of mine and of Monna Catelana my mother here in every detail and, following, all our obligations. First:

A half house, indivisible, where we presently live, situated in the *gonfalone* of Leon Nero in the parish of Sant'Iacopo tralle fosse in Borgo Santa Croce. [Bounded] first, the said street; second, the heirs of Adovardo degli Alberti; third, Tommaso Davizzi and Nerozzo degli Alberti; fourth, Francesco d'Altobianco degli Alberti. Further, household furnishings for our use in the said house and in the summer house.

5 or 6 parts, indivisible, of a house situated in the said parish in the street called 'of the Alberti's house.' Bounded first, the street; second, the heirs of Adovardo degli Alberti; third, the above-named house of Monna Catelana and Monna Antonia d'Alberto degli Alberti; fourth, Francesco d'Altobianco degli Alberti. This [house] is rented by Tommaso Busini; he gives me *f*20 yearly; I get, for my part, *f*16 *s*13 *d*10 a year.

[He goes on to list 5/6 of a farm; 5/6 of a farm with one parcel of land; and a half farm]

I find myself in the partnership which I have with Tommaso and Simone Corsi, a base capital of *f*1500

We have not yet settled the accounts; we are overextended rather than settled; I will have to report to you what I have in the shop.

I find myself, next, bankrupt in the new company, current account *f*270
[He lists some small Monte credits]

Here next I will write all the debtors I find, those whom I reckon to be good for payment ultimately.

The heirs of Cipriano and Ser Luigi di Simone Guiduccini	*f*60
Nastagio di Simone Guiduccini	*f*35
Niccolò di Sanminiato de'Ricci	*f*55
Antonio, priest, of Sant'Angelo	*f*65
The Commune of Assissi for 10 *accatti*	*f*28
Benedetto da Panzano	*f*8 *s*15
Pagolo Quaratesi	*f*9 *s*17
Rosso di Strozza	*f*6 *s*11
	*f*267 *s*20

Here next I will write all the credits to be recovered:

Cosimo and Lorenzo de'Medici and heirs	*f*430
Monna Vaggia di Bindo Guasconi	*f*150
Giovanni di Bartolo Morelli	*f*500
Ilarione di Lipanno de'Bardi	*f*42

Antonio di Salvestro and partners ƒ20

Monna Antonia, wife of Piero Dini ƒ50 +

The old company of Tommaso and
Simone Corsi and with the remainder, I should have ƒ450

ƒ1542

Here below I will record the many debtors I find
which are no-account, from whom I have not
been able, in times past, to collect, nor do I expect
to [ever]. These debtors are, that is:

Tommaso di Filippo di Michele ƒ4-1/2

Lorenzo and Giovanni di Scholai
degli Pini; I paid for them to their
syndic ƒ555

Santi Pisiro ƒ1

The heirs and estate of Bernardo degli
Alberti, for the remainder of a finding I got against them; and for money
I paid to the gonfalone for them. They
don't have their property, so one must
let it [the debt] ride. ƒ765

Bartolo di Maschio ƒ765

Giovanni Manini ƒ10

| Monna Catelana is aged | 44 |
| Tommaso aged | 26 |

Checca is a girl who Monna Catelana vowed to
raise for the love of God since she has neither
daddy nor mama to raise her aged 4 or 6

[He is not given credit for Checca]

property	ƒ3361 s4 d8
obligations	ƒ2042
remainder	ƒ1319 s4 d8

Portata of Messer Alberto di Giovanni degli Alberti

Jesus

Before you, the wise and prudent officials of
the Catasto, reported for me, Messer Alberto di
Giovanni degli Alberti, quarter of Santa Croce,
gonfalone [left blank], parish of San Iacopo tralle
Fosse, who has a prestanzione rate of [left blank]
that in this [my portata] I will mention to you of
my little houses, my furniture and obligations.
And first:

A farm situated in the Valdarno di Sopra ... the
farm is worked by Bartolomeo di Mariotto and
his brothers and they have rented it a long time.
It yields 100 staia of grain a year, sequestered by
the official; and it isn't run with oxen nor [has it]
prestanza.

Another farm without a house ... For many
years rented by Ghezo di Giunta da Marrano. It
yields 100 staia of grain a year.

With [the following] obligations, first:

I Messer Alberto, aged	48
Mariotto di Duccio my blood cousin, aged	30
Luigi and Antonio di Niccolo di Luigi, my second cousins,	45 and 35

[I am] omitting the other household members
whom I know you won't accept.

I owe the Commune [blank], all that is posted
in this last venture and even perhaps some old
prestanze.

The present document done in the name of
Messer Alberto was written by the hand of me,
Valorino di Barna, at his behest and according to
how he directed that I set it out and record it by
me myself. I know that the abovesaid matters are
true, and because I am still weak from a long illness, I can't come to depose [the portata], but my
son Lapozzo will come or Piero Cambini.

Portata of Caterina wife of the late Messer Cipriano degli Alberti

Before you, Sirs, honorable and prudent officials of the Catasto of the city,

contado and territory of Florence, I am producing my *portata* done by me, Madonna Caterina, wife of the late Messer Cipriano degli Alberti, of moveable and immoveable property, debts and credits and obligations taxed in the *gonfalone* of Leon Nero in the quarter of S. Croce in the parish of San Iacopo tralle Fosse of Firenze. And the said Madonna Caterina has a *prestaze* rating of 1 florin 3 soldi, that is, *f*1 *s*3

Property, that is:

[She then lists a farm with 10 parcels of land worth *f*20; a farm with 16 parcels worth *f*25; a farm with 7 parcels worth *f*20; a farm with 8 parcels worth *f*28; four small parcels rented for payment in kind]

A house in Empoli in which house I live myself and keep my crops, bounded [left blank]. I am obliged to keep an animal to carry me and to efficiently carry my farm goods and I can manage with no less.

Debts and obligations:

I spend 12 florins a year for the house in Florence, used for my habitation, which house I rent from Domenico di Gherardino, on Borgo Santa Croce. Bounded by first, the street; second, Bartolino Bisarnesi and partly the said Domenico; third, Antonio di Salvestro di Ser Ristoro; fourth, Francesdo d'Altobianco [degli Alberti; it is] in the [area known as the] Fungha *f*12

I owe Piero Cambini 18 florins, for cloth for me from the warehouse of the Alexandri *f*18

Also I owe the said warehouse for cloth I got for my servant who I keep in the house *f*7

And further I owe Messer Guiliano Davanzati those monies still owing for my *prestanze* *f*6

[The following entry was cancelled: And further I owe the heirs of Giovanni degli Peruzzi *f*30 which they lent me to pay my debts and dues *f*30]

I still must pay Lucia her dowry, when she will be of age; she lives with me in the house and I pay those expenses of hers which pertain to me [blank]

I keep a servant for 12 florins a year and pay his expenses *f*12

Heads

Madonna Caterina, wife of the late Messer Cipriano degli Alberti, aged 60
Mariotto di Duccio, grandson of the said Madonna Caterina, aged 27

The said Mariotto doesn't live in Florence. I am obligated to support and pay his expenses in such amounts that he is in my [household, as opposed to anyone else's]

[in the left margin of the official copy, next to Mariotto's name, was written: Give him to Messer Alberto for his 'mouth', written on page 253 of this (volume)].

I Lodovico di Cheroso di Bartoli di Ser Segna filled out this *portata* at the will of the said Madonna Caterina abovesaid, and I have undersigned for me in my own hand.

property	*f*1808 *s*5 *do*
obligations	*f*402 *s*8 *do*
remainder	*f*1405 *s*17

Portata of Maria wife of the late Ricciardo degli Alberti

(Source: ASF, Cat. 35, ff. 1048r-v and Cat. 72, f. 357v)

Before you, Sirs, officials of the Catasto, I Piero Cambini of Santa Felice in Piazza report to you as a factor of this property of Monna Maria wife of the late Ricciardo degli Alberti and daughter of Messer Mainardo Cavalcanti. And today she is a widow and lives in Bologna with her daughters of whom one is a widow. And she [Maria] is ill and has a lot of difficulty making ends meet, such that she is recommended to your consideration such as it can be. And this is the property that she holds between her dowry and bequests and monies.

[He lists two farms left to her by her mother]

This Monna Maria has not had *prestanze* nor do I find her taxed with *prestanze*. She is ill and somehow she must live as a woman of substance.

I Piero Cambini attest to these things I have written at the request of Monna Maria and I have never asked anything ever for my pains. However, I am here [in Florence] or in Venice, such that it will be necessary [to find] another factor to serve her. And I salute you.

Portata of Tommasa wife of Bivigliano degli Alberti

The property of Monna Tommasa, wife of Bivigliano degli Alberti, who [the Alberti] were consigned [to exile] and daughter of Noffo Ridolfi. And taxed in prestanze in the quarter of Santa Croce in the *gonfalone* of Leon Nero.   *f*1 *s*12 *d*5

A 'noble house' with a kitchen garden in the place called 'in the woods' in the parish of San Piero a Ema.

Below I will write her debtors:

Piero di Nofri dell'Antella   *f*33

Giovanni di [blank] who tends the vines [in the garden mentioned] holds a little farm which he rents from the commune. And because he works the farm and the said vineyard, I lent him *f*40   [blank]

Below I will write her creditors:

Schiatta Ridolfi and Giovanni Giugni   *f*20

I am here in his house [Schiatta's?] and I am about to take a rental [place]. Thus, use your discretion [as to how to tax me].

[In the official version, this portion is written: I am in the house of others and am about to take a house. Therefore take into account what is my [tax] responsibility.]

Monna Tommasa, aged	60
Bivigliano, her husband, aged	69
Francesco, her son, aged	42
Bertoldo, her son, aged	26
Monna Isabella, wife of Francesco her son, aged	24
Marco, son of the said Francesco, aged	6
Diamante, son of the said Francesco, aged	2-1/2
Bartolomea, daughter of the said Francesco, aged	3
Nera, daughter of the said Francesco, aged in months	18
Altobiancho, son of the said Francesco, aged in months	3

submitted 12 July 1427

[She is given only her 'mouth'.]

property	*f*841
obligations	*f*220
remainder	*f*621

Portata of Selvaggia wife of the late Filippo Magalotti

[From the outside of the *portata*]
12 July

Leon Nero. Monna Vaggia wife of the late Messer Filippo Magalotti *f*1 *s*12 *d*5

The said document for Monna Vaggia wife of the late Messer Filippo Magalotti. Fetched by me Folco Portinari with her consent.

[From the inside]

+ In the name of God on the 10th day of July 1427

Before you, Sirs, officials of the Catasto, here following are written all the property and obligations of Monna Vaggia wife of the late Messer Filippo Magalotti of the quarter of Santa Croce, *gonfalone* of Leon Nero at the *prestanze* rate of *f*1 *s*12 *d*5.

In the Monte Comune, inscribed in Monna Vaggia in the quarter of Santa Croce, *f*2038 *s*10 *d*10 with payments from 1419 to 1423, *f*100 at 9/67

And for her lifetime, inscribed in the Hospital of Santa Maria Nuova in the same quarter, *f*172 of Monte Comune [credit].

[She rents out two small houses and a shop one right next to the other]

All the said rents are mine for life.

A half farm, indivisible, [with nine parcels of land]. This farm is held in common with the heirs of Andrea di Messer Bindo de'Bardi. It is worked by Scuosino, called Tasso....

A farm ...

Both farms are held for my lifetime.

Here following I will give the obligations of the abovementioned Monna Vaggia, aged 60 years.

Caterina, her granddaughter, daughter of the late Bernardo Magalotti.

Luca, her grandson, son of the late said Bernardo, aged 11; he is not legitimate.

And with a house rented from Piero Cambini which belongs to the grandsons of Messer Niccolaio degli Alberti. I pay yearly *f*11.

And expenses to maintain my little houses which I rent out, *f*2-1/2 a year.

And to maintain the Valdarno property, *f*2 a year.

Here following are the debts:

And to give to Piero Cambini for the rental of the house   *f*11

And to him for wine I had [of him] for the year gone by   *f*11

And to give for [the love of] God for the soul of Bernardo my son *f*15 a day

[sic] and I will give proof why it is as it is   *f*15

And to give, in accordance with a vow I made, to a girl who married   *f*10

And to give to Monna Dianora who stays with me, for her salary   *f*8

And to give to a girl who stayed with me a while, *l*50 fp.   *f*12-1/2

And to give to Tommaso di Lapo Corsi for velvet gotten from them [his company?] for one of my girls when I remarried her off   *f*4

And to give Antonio di Piero   *f*1 *l*3

And to give to Giovanni Charadori for furnishings   *f*1

And to pay for 4 *prestanzoni*, *f*2 *s*16 fp.   *f*2 *s*16

Also to give for the farm of San Marcellino in Bisano, the *decima* to X, that is, 5 half barrels of wine and 5 half *staia* of grain.

To give to Maestro di Baldano who repairs the house of the farm for me, for my part,   *f*2-1/2

property	*f*1543 *s*10	
obligations	*f*639	
remainder	*f*904 *s*10	

GREGORIO DATI

Diary

GREGORIO DATI WAS AN IMPORTANT BUSINESSMAN ACTIVE PRIMARILY
in the manufacture and sale of silk cloth. His private diary, kept to record his
business dealings, provides a view into the private life of a successful Florentine merchant at the beginning of the fifteenth century.

Source: *Two memoirs of Renaissance Florence; The Diaries of Buonaccorso Pitti and Gregorio Dati.* Tr. Julia Martinas. Ed. Gene Brecker. (New York: Harper and Row 1967).

In the name of God, his Mother and all the Saints
of Paradise, I shall begin this book wherein I shall
set forth an account of our activities so as to have
a record of them, and wherein having once more
and always invoked the name of God, I shall
record the secret affairs of our company and their
progress from year to year. This ledger belongs to
Goro [Gregorio], son of Stagio Dati, and I shall
call it the secret ledger. In the name of God,
Father, Son, and Holy Ghost, I shall here record
some particular things known to myself. God
grant they meet with the approval of whoever
learns of them when I am gone.

I learn from old registers that Dato and Pero di
Bencivenni were purse-vendors on the Ponte Vecchio next to the fishmongers, and that their shop
was destroyed by the flood of 1333. It appears
from there that Dato had a number of sons, the
eldest of whom, Stagio, was born on 9 March
1317. His mother's name was Monna Filippa.
According to Stagio's registers he married our
mother, Monna Ghita, in the year ..., giving her
the ring on 5 August and celebrating the wedding on 4 November.

I find that Stagio went into partnership with
Vanni di Ser Lotto [Castellani]. The company was
set up on 1 January 1353 with a capital of one
thousand gold florins. This appears on page 3 of
Register A.

I was born on 15 April 1362. This is recorded in
a register marked with an asterisk on page 85
where the seventeen children he had by Monna
Ghita are listed in order of age.

Our father Stagio left this world for a better
one on 11 September 1374, when he was a Consul

of the Wool Guild and Treasurer of the Commission on the Salt Tax and Forced Loans. He had
been ill for several days before his death and, several days earlier, while still in health, had made a
will. He received all the sacraments of the church
as befits a devout Christian, and by the mercy of
God passed on to eternal life in a state of grace.

On 15 April 1375, when I had learned enough
arithmetic, I went to work in the silk merchant's
shop belonging to Giovanni di Giano and his
partners. I was thirteen years old and I won their
esteem.

We gave Madalena [Goro's sister] in marriage
in June 1380. This is recorded in register E, page
84.

I left Giovanni di Giano on 2 October 1380,
spent fifteen months with the Wool Guild and
returned to him on 1 January 1382.

Partnership Accounts – 1384

In the name of God, the Virgin Mary and all the
Saints—may they grant me health in soul and
body and prosperity in business—I shall record
here all my dealings with our company.

On 1 January 1385, Giovanni di Giano and his
partners made me a partner in their silk business
for as long as it may please God. I am to invest
300 gold florins which I have not got, being actually in debt to the business. However, with God's
help, I hope to have the money shortly and am to
receive two out of every twenty-four shares, in
other words, a twelfth of the total profit. We settled our accounts on 8 June 1387, on Giovanni di
Giano's death. May he rest in peace. My share of

the profits for the two years and five months I had been a partner came to 468 gold florins, 7 *soldi a fiorino*.[1] Thanks be to God. We formed a new partnership on the following terms: Buonaccorso Berardi is to invest 8,000 florins and have eleven shares; Michele di Ser Parente is to invest 3,500 florins and have eight shares; Goro, son of Stagio Dati, is to invest 500 florins and have three shares; Nardo di Lippo is to invest 500 and have two shares. Thus the capital of the company shall amount to 12,500 gold florins. And if any partner invests additional money in the company, that investment will earn one-half of the percentage of the profits earned by the regular shares.

On 1 January 1389, we settled our accounts, and my share of the profits for the nineteen months came to 552 gold florins, 6 *soldi a fiorino*. Praise and thanks be to God. On 1 January 1390, we reviewed our accounts for the year and my profit was 341 florins, 10 *soldi a fiorino*. Thanks be to God. I left for Valencia on the company's business on 1 September 1390 and got there on 26 October. I was back in Florence on 29 November 1392. The accounts I kept regarding our business there is entered in the white ledger on page ... in my name and Berardo's. The company did not pay any of our expenses for this trip. It is true that Giovanni left the business in a bad way and with a number of debts.

On 1 January 1393, we dissolved the company and Michele di Ser Parente withdrew all his investments. My profit was reckoned as 1,416 florins, 21 *soldi a fiorino*, and 60 florins were paid for Simone's salary. However this was assuming Giovanni Stefani's debt would be paid, which it has not been, and so it was decided instead that 954 florins, 25 *soldi a fiorino* cash should be deducted from my account corresponding to the debts outstanding, and that I should get back this money when the debts were paid. This was done in order to enable us to set up a new company with real money. Anyway, between cash and expectations my profits came to 1,476 florins, 21 *soldi a fiorino*.

Recommending ourselves to God and good fortune, we set up a new company for a year, starting on 1 January 1393 on the following terms: Buonaccorso Berardi shall invest 4,000 florins and receive eleven shares; Goro di Stagio

shall invest 1,000 florins and receive five shares; Nardo di Lippo shall invest 500 florins and receive three and one-half shares. The capital shall amount to 6,000 florins. May the Lord bless our enterprise.

In God's name I shall continue my review of the accounts written above on page two of our company's agreements, and of my shares, balance sheets and profits and shall record what followed and is yet to follow. As appears in these accounts, we renewed our partnership on 1 January 1393 when I undertook to invest 1,000 florins. I did not actually have the money but was about to get married—which I then did—and to receive the dowry which procured me a larger share and more consideration in our company. Yet we achieved little that year.

I set out for Valencia in September 1393 in order to wind up matters there but did not get beyond Genoa. When I reached the Riviera, I was set upon and robbed by a galley from Briganzone and returned to Florence on 14 December, having lost 250 florins' worth of pearls, merchandise and clothes belonging to myself, and 300 gold florins' worth of the company's property.

On 1 January 1394, we drew up our balance sheet and my profit came to 162 florins, 2 *soldi a fiorino*. We renewed our partnership for another year and made a few changes. Whereas Buonaccorso Berardi had previously invested 4,000 florins and received eleven shares, under the new arrangement he was to invest 4,000 florins and receive twelve shares, and whereas I had previously invested 1,000 florins and received five shares, I was now to invest 500 florins and receive four shares. The reason for this was that I had not got the money and Antonio di Segna put it up. (In this agreement "this year" is to be read as "last year" and "Buonaccorso Berardi" is to be understood as including Antonio di Segna, who is to be paid what is due to him by Buonaccorso at the latter's discretion.)

I went to Valencia on 20 April 1394 and returned on 24 January of the next year. On 1 February 1395, our company expired and we settled our accounts. My profit was 295 florins, and Simone's salary for the outgoing year was 30 florins. May God be thanked. That December I left Simone in Valencia with Andrea Lopis who was to invest 500 florins in Simone's name on the understanding that all profits on cloth, silks, and other matters were to be divided equally between them and that any goods they might order from me for their own use were to be paid for within the usual time, six months. Moreover, I was to send them goods of my own and they were to sell them for me and take a commission.

On January 1396, I found I had made 600 florins on my own, independently of any partnership, on goods sent to and received from Valencia and elsewhere. My expenditure, however, of which I have kept no account, came to about 250 florins, leaving a balance of 350. These sums, earned over three years in the three payments mentioned above, are entered like the others on page 2[2] above. Altogether I found myself in 1395 with little cash in hand, as a result of the great expenses to which I had gone in the hope that they would yield greater profits than they did. In addition, there were the expenses I was put to by our brother Don Jacopo,[3] my losses over Giovanni Stefani in Valencia, and the money which was stolen from me near Genoa. It is fitting to give praise to God for all things. Altogether, having reckoned my profits, the two dowries received and my outlay for the half-share in the farm in S. Andrea, bought from Monna Tita, I have about 200 florins in hand. God grant that henceforth we prosper in soul and body. This balance of 200 florins is entered on page 3 above under Receipt and Expenditure.

Memoranda, 1393

In God's name, I shall continue this record of my activities, which it is well to have in writing so as to recollect them, and which I began back on page 1. My beloved wife, Bandecca, went to Paradise after a nine-month illness started by a miscarriage in the fifth month of pregnancy. It was eleven o'clock at night on Friday, 15 July 1390, when she peacefully returned her soul to her Creator in Buonaccorso-Berardi's house. The next day I had her buried in S. Brancazio; she had received the last sacraments.

I went to Valencia on 1 September 1390. taking Bernardo with me. I came back on 30 November 1392, having suffered much hardship during my stay, both in mind and body. We were still owed 4,000 Barcelona pounds by Giovanni di Stefano, who acknowledged this debt in a notarized deed which I brought back with me to Florence. In Valancia I had an illegitimate male child by Margherita, a Tartar slave whom I had bought. He was born on 21 December 1391, in Valencia on St. Thomas's Day and I named him after that saint. I sent him to Florence in March on Felice del Pace's ship. God grant that he turn out well.

On the expiration of our partnership, on 1 January 1393, Michele di Ser Parente withdrew. Later, I made an agreement with him whereby he made over to me his share in Giovanni di Stefani's debt and a few other items which are entered on page 6.

I married my second wife, Isabetta, the daughter of Mari Vilanuzzi on Sunday, 22 June, as is recorded on the other side of this page.

On 10 September 1393, I left Florence for Catalonia and, while we were at sea in a small galley a little beyond Portovenere, a galley from Briganzone came after us, held us up, and robbed us and took our goods to Baldo Spinoli at Briganzone. We got some of them back later, although with great difficulty and at great expense. I came back here on 14 December. On 20 April, I went to Valencia on Felice's ship. I visited Majorca and Barcelona where Simone joined me, after which we both went to Valencia where I left him. I returned home by land and reached Florence on 24 January 1395. Thanks be to God. Our partnership expired on 1 February 1395, and that year I did business of my own and was very successful. Thanks be to God. I went into partnership once more with Michele di Ser Parente on 1 January 1396, and the terms and clauses are entered on page 6.

Our Simone, who had been in Valencia since December 1394, wanted to come to Florence. He arrived on 12 December 1396, and left to go back there on 3 January 1397. However, while he was at sea, a Neapolitan galley overtook him just outside Pisa and took him as a prisoner to Naples. On 3 April, he was released for ransom at Gaeta, from whence he made his way back to Valencia.

A general remission and acquittance was granted to us, to Michele di Ridolfo's sons, and to the Commune of Florence with regard to the matter concerning Dato by Andrea da Bologna, an inhabitant of Montpellier, on 14 February 1398. The notary was Giovanni da Pino. This is entered in my long Ledger A, page 131. It cost us 100 gold francs and I have the deed in my strong-box.[4]

My Wife Betta's Personal Accounts – 1393

In the name of God and the Virgin Mary, of Blessed Michael the Archangel, of SS. John the Baptist and John the Evangelist, of SS. Peter and Paul, of the holy scholars SS. Gregory and Jerome, and of St. Mary Magdalene and St. Elisabeth and all the blessed saints in heaven—may they ever intercede for us—I shall record here how I married my second wife, Isabetta, known as Betta, the daughter of Mari di Lorenzo Vilanuzzi and of Monna Veronica, daughter of Pagolo d'Arrigo Guglielmi, and I shall also record the promises which were made to me. May God and his Saints grant by their grace that they be kept.

On 31 March 1393, I was betrothed to her and on Easter Monday, 7 April, I gave her the ring. On 22 June, a Sunday, I became her husband in the name of God and good fortune. Her first cousins, Giovanni and Lionardo di Domenico Arrighi, promised that she should have a dowry of 900 gold florins and that, apart from the dowry, she should have the income on a farm in S. Fiore a Elsa, which had been left her as a legacy by her mother, Monna Veronica. It was not stated at the time how much this amounted to, but it was understood that she would receive the amounts. We arranged our match very simply indeed and with scarcely any discussion. God grant that nothing but good may come of it. On the 26th of that same June, I received a payment of 800 gold florins from the bank of Giacomino and Company. This was the dowry. I invested it in the shop of Buonaccorso Berardi and his partners, and it is recorded here, on page 2 among the profits. At the same time I received the trousseau which my wife's cousins valued at 106 florins, in the light of which they deducted six florins from another account, leaving me the equivalent of 100 gold florins. But from what I heard from her and what I saw myself, they had overestimated it by 30

florins or more. However, from politeness, I said nothing about this.

I have not declared this dowry nor insured it on account of their negligence and in order to put off paying the tax. They dare not urge me to do so since they are obligated towards me. Yet I must do so, and if by God's will something were to happen before I do, I want her to be as assured as can be of having her dowry, just as though it had been declared and insured. For the fault is not hers. It turns out that the income she is to receive comes from a farm in S. Fiore on the Elsa on the way to Pisa. It is a nice piece of property which apparently belonged to Pagolo Guglielmi. Giovanni and Lionardo bought it from Betta's mother, Monna Veronica, or rather bought a half-share in it for 500 gold florins and paid a tax on this sale. Later they sold back their share to Monna Veronica, paying another tax, for 575 florins. These transactions are recorded in the register of taxes on contracts in register 500, 40; 500, 41 and 500, 42. When Monna Veronica died in April 1391, she left the income from this farm to Betta and to her children after her.

On 26 September 1402, as Simone was in Florence for a while before leaving for Catalonia, and as the penalties for evading tax on contracts were remitted by law for those who paid that day, I and Simone declared the dowry of 900 gold florins received from Leonardo and Domenico. The notary was Ser Giunta Franceschi and on the 30th of the same September, I paid 30 gold florins, being 3-1/8 per cent, to the account of the taxes on contracts.

Our Lord God was pleased to call to himself the blessed soul of Isabetta, known as Betta, on Monday, 2 October, between four and five o'clock in the afternoon. The next day, Tuesday, at three in the afternoon, she was buried in our grave at S. Spirito. May God receive her soul in His glory. Amen.

Children, 1393

In praise, glory, honor and benediction of Almighty God, I shall record the fruits that His grace will grant us, and may He in His mercy vouchsafe that they be such as to console our souls eternally, amen. On Sunday morning, 17

May 1394, Betta gave birth to a girl whom we called Bandecca in memory of my first wife. Goro d'Andrea, Niccolaio di Bartolommeo Niccoli, and Berardo di Buonacorso were her sponsors.

On Friday evening, 17 March 1396, towards two o'clock in the morning, the Lord blessed our marriage with a male son whom we named Stagio and whom we had baptized in the love of God on Sunday morning by Fra Simone Bartoli of the Augustinian Hermits, my partner Nardo di Lippo, and Sandro di Jacopo, a pauper.

At two o'clock in the night of Monday, 12 March 1397, Betta gave birth to our third child, a girl. We called her after Betta's mother, giving her the names Veronica Gostanza, and Sandro di Jacopo baptized her in the love of God.

At midday on Saturday, 27 April 1398, Betta gave birth to our fourth child which was a boy. We called him Bernardo Agostino and he was baptized the same day in the love of God by Monna Agnola del Ciri and Monna Francesca Aldobrandino. God grant he turn out well.

At dawn on Tuesday, 1 July 1399, Betta had our fifth child and we baptized him in the love of God the same day, calling him Mari Piero. The sponsors were Master Lionardo[5] and Fra Zanobi.

On Tuesday evening, 22 June 1400, Betta gave birth for the sixth time. The child was a girl. We called her Filippa Giovanna and she was baptized on Friday morning in the love of God. Fra Simone Bartoli held her.

Our Lord God was pleased to take to Himself the fruits which He had lent us, and He took first our most beloved, Stagio, our darling and blessed first-born. He died of the plague on the morning of Friday, 30 July 1400, in Florence without my seeing him, for I was in the country. Master Lionardo and Monna Ghita were with him. May God bless him and grant that he pray for us.

On 22 August of the same year, the Divine bounty was pleased to desire a companion for that beloved soul. God called our son Mari to Himself and he died at eleven o'clock on Sunday, of the plague. God grant us the grace to find favor with Him and to bless and thank Him for all things.

On Wednesday, 13 July 1401, after midnight, the Lord lent us a seventh child. Betta had a son who we called Stagio Benedetto. The sponsors

were Nardo di Lippo and Domenico Benini. Divine providence was pleased to take him back and for this too may He be thanked and praised. The child suffered from a cough for a fortnight, and at midday on 29 September, St. Michael's Day and the Eve of St. Jerome's Day, passed away to Paradise. God grant that we, when we leave this mortal life, may follow him there.

On 5 July 1402, before the hour of terce, Betta gave birth to our eighth child. We had him baptized straight after terce in the love of God. His godparents were Nardo and blind Margherita, and we called him Piero Antonio because of Betta's special devotion to S. Antonio. God bless him and grant that he become a good man.

After that my wife Isabetta passed on to Paradise as is recorded on the opposite page, and I shall have no more children by her to list here. God be praised.

Our Creator was pleased to call to Himself the soul of our gentle and good son Antonio. He left this life, I think, on 2 August. For I was in great trouble and did not know it at the time. It was in Pisa where he is buried at S. Caterina's.

Betta and I had eight children, five boys and three girls.

Memo, 1394

I record that on 1 February I withdrew from the partnership with Buonacorso Berardi and did business on my own this year. I bought goods and sent them to Simone in Valencia, lent money to friends in Pisa and elsewhere, received goods from Valencia for sale here and continued like this for eight months until the beginning of October. I did very well during this period. I have not kept accounts but earned and spent on my own. Yet I can see that the transactions I carried out have been successful, and I hope those which are not yet concluded will be equally so. I may go through with them by myself or may go into partnership with someone.

And once more in God's name I have formed a partnership with Michele di Ser Parente from 1 October 1395. In our account books, it will be reckoned as beginning on 1 January 1396, when Mariotto di Lodovico is to withdraw. I am now beginning to do things for this new partnership. I shall record the terms and clauses of our agreements further on, on page 6, and may God bless our enterprise.

Going over my accounts, I find that when Michele di Ser Parente withdrew from our partnership on 1 January 1393, my total assets amounted to about 800 florins, which was all the actual money I would have possessed had I wished to withdraw in my turn. This meant I had made no profit. For I had to pay back about 950 florins which was the part of my profits corresponding to the debts owed us in Catalonia and elsewhere, which should not have been reckoned as recoverable for the moment. We realized this later when Antonio di Segna's guile made it seem advisable to check the various assets of the company. This was why I resolved to put up with anything for the next two years and to stay in their shop and suffer Antonio di Segna and everything else, as I was too short of money to try and do things my own way. I have been hoping that Matteo will help me to send Simone to Valencia where he will be very useful to me for my business here. I pray God that it may so turn out.

After that in 1393 I got the dowry which came to 800 florins, while my profits from our partnership were 162 florins, and for the year after were 325 florins which comes to a total of 1,287 florins. My expenditure, entered in folio 3 under "Expenditure," was in two amounts, totaling 1,425 florins. This includes my losses when I was robbed on the Riviera, about 275 florins paid for the farm and about 100 florins lent to Michele's heir. Whereas in 1392 I was owed 950 florins and owed about 150 florins, since then I find my debits exceeding my credits by about 140 florins, which makes a total debit of 290. I estimate that in the eight months I have been in business on my own, I have made good my losses and wiped out this debt, or will have done so when the ventures I embarked on then have been concluded. So now I can live within my capital. Would to God and the Virgin Mary that I were sure of continuing to do so from 1 January 1396, and were sure that my debits would not exceed my credits from the time I go into partnership with Michele. But God will grant us His grace as He has always done. I am not entering the 950 florins and 25 soldi a fiorino in my accounts since they cannot be put to any use.

After that year by God's grace I did better than I had expected, for the Valencia branch did well and paid up, and I have been able to transfer 200 florins from the credit side and deduct them from my debits as appears on Outgo, folio 3.

Account Book – 1395

May God and His gentle Mother bestow their grace upon us. In their name I shall note here the terms and clauses of the new partnership which I and others formed with Michele di Ser Parente and the sums of money involved. Michele di Ser Parente shall invest 8,000 florins and receive thirteen and three-quarter shares; I, Goro di Stagio, am to invest 1,000 florins and have four and one-half shares; Nardo di Lippo Nardi is to invest 400 florins and have two shares. The total capital is to amount to 9,600 florins and be divided in twenty-four shares.[6]

I engage to contribute 1,000 florins to the capital of our partnership so as to enjoy a substantial share and consideration in the firm. I have not got the cash at present but expect that Matteo di Tommaso will lend me 400 florins belonging to his stepmother, Monna Lorenza, plus some money of his own. I shall try to raise the rest somewhere else if I can and will debit it to the Valencia account until I have made enough either in my business here or with Simone in Valencia to pay it back.

I have agreed with Michele to send his son Giovanni to Valencia, where he is to form a business partnership with Simone for as long as we shall decide. We will supply the goods they require and our firm will put 1,000 florins cash at their disposal. One half of whatever profits they make will be ours, and the other half is to be divided between them so that each will have one quarter of the total profits. Giovanni went to Valencia in May 1396, but only stayed there a short time as he did not get on with Simone. Simone came to Florence on 12 December 1396 and reached an agreement with myself and Michele whereby they were to keep whatever profits, good or bad, they might manage to make in Valencia, without giving our firm any share in them, and to pay us whatever they owed us on the usual terms.

Simone left here for Valencia on 3 January and, having set sail from Pisa on the 8th, was captured by one of King Louis's[7] admirals, Messer Giovanni Gonsalvo of Seville, who took him as a prisoner to Naples. When he had been held there for three months, he was taken to Gaeta and released for a ransom of 200 florins. This was paid for him by Doffo Spini, whom we reimbursed, and debited to the Valencia account with a number of other expenses. On 3 April, he left for Majorca on the *nave dipungiata*.[8] May God grant he get there safely and that we recover our losses. Giovanni and Simone continued to wrangle and bicker even more than before, until finally Giovanni resolved to leave for Barcelona and settle there. They continued, however, to be partners. Then of their own accord they dissolved the partnership, agreeing that Simone should keep whatever profits he had made in Valencia and Giovanni should have what he had made in Barcelona. God grant His grace to each of them.

Shop Accounts, 1403

When the partnership with Michele di Ser Parente expired, I set up shop on my own under the name of Goro Stagio and company. My partners are Piero and Jacopo di Tommaso Lana who contribute 3,000 [florins] while I contribute 2,000, and Nardo di Lippo who contributes his services. The partnership is to start on 1 January 1403 and to last three years. The clauses and articles of agreement and the amounts invested by each partner will be entered in a secret ledger covered with white leather belonging to our partnership.

On my account and with my own money, I paid 75 florins to the heirs of Simone Vespucci and their representative, Lapo Vespucci, for the goodwill and licence to exercise my profession in one of the shops of Por Santa Maria.[9] The brokers were Andrea di Bonaventura and Niccolaio Niccoli. On 6 March 1403, Isau d'Agnolo and Antonio Manni, a silk merchant who was in the shop, received 25 florins from me. The broker was Meo d'Andrea del Benino. The fixtures and repairs cost me about 100 florins, so altogether, between the goodwill and the fixtures I paid 200 florins out of my own

pocket, in God's name, for myself and my heirs. The site of the shop belongs to the Carthusian monks, from whom I am to rent it on the usual terms for 35 gold florins a year. Ser Ludovico of the guild drew up the lease, which is to run for five years from the beginning of February 1403.

As already stated, I have undertaken to put up 2,000 florins. This is how I propose to raise them: 1,370 florins and 25 *soldi a fiorino* are still due to me from my old partnership with Michele di Ser Parente, as appears on page 118 of my ledger for stock and cash on hand. The rest I expect to obtain if I marry again this year, when I hope to find a woman with a dowry as large as God may be pleased to grant me. If I do not marry, I will find the money some other way.

The partnership with Piero was set up and formally notarized several months ago. Voluntarily and of his own accord, he asked me to see to the investments and the dividing into shares, leaving all this in my hands....

1 January 1404.

I know that in this wretched life our sins expose us to many tribulations of soul and passions of the body, that without God's grace and mercy which strengthens our weakness, enlightens our mind and supports our will, we would perish daily. I also see that since my birth forty years ago, I have given little heed to God's commandments. Distrusting my own power to reform, but hoping to advance by degrees along the path of virtue, I resolve from this day forward to refrain from going to the shop or conducting business on solemn Church holidays, or from permitting others to work for me or seek temporal gain on such days. Whenever I make exceptions in cases of extreme necessity, I promise, on the following day, to distribute alms of one gold florin to God's poor. I have written this down so that I may remember my promise and be ashamed if I should chance to break it.

Also, in memory of the passion of Our Lord Jesus Christ who freed and saved us by His merits, that He may, by His grace and mercy preserve us from guilty passions, I resolve from this very day and in perpetuity to keep Friday as a day of total chastity—with Friday I include the following night—when I must abstain from the enjoyment of all carnal pleasures. God give me grace to keep my promise, yet if I should break it through forgetfulness, I engage to give 20 *soldi* to the poor for each time, and to say twenty Paternosters and Avemarias.

I resolve this day to do a third thing while I am in health and able to, remembering that each day we need Almighty God to provide for us. Each day I wish to honor God by some giving of alms or by the recitation of prayers or some other pious act. If, by inadvertence, I fail to do so, that day or the next day I must give alms to God's poor of at least 5 *soldi*. These however are not vows but intentions by which I shall do my best to abide.[10]

3 May 1412. On 28 April, my name was drawn as Standard-bearer of the Militia Company.[11] Up until then I had not been sure whether my name was in the purses for that office, although I was eager that it should be both for my own honor and that of my heirs. I recalled that my father Stagio had held a number of appointments in the course of his life, being frequently a consul of the Guild of Por Santa Maria, a member of the Merchants' Court and one of the officials in charge of gabelles and the treasurers. Yet he was never drawn for any of the Colleges during his lifetime, though shortly after his death he was drawn as a prior. I recalled that I had aroused a great deal of animosity eight years ago because of my business in Catalonia, and that last year I only just escaped being arrested for debt by the Commune. On the very day my name was drawn for this office, only fifteen minutes before it was drawn, I had taken advantage of the reprieve granted by the new laws and finished paying off my debt to the Commune. That was a veritable inspiration from God, may His name be praised and blessed! Now that I can obtain other offices, it seems to me that, having had a great benefit, I should be content to know that I have sat once in the Colleges and should aspire no further. So, lest I should ungratefully give way to the insatiable appetites of those in whom success breeds renewed ambition, I have resolved and sworn to myself that I shall not henceforth invoke the aid of any or attempt to get myself elected to public offices or to have my name included in new purses. Rather,

I shall let things take their course without interfering. I shall abide by God's will, accepting those offices of the guilds or Commune for which my name shall be drawn, and not refusing the labor but serving and doing what good I may. In this way I shall restrain my own presumption and tendency towards ambition and shall live in freedom without demeaning myself by begging favors from any. And if I should depart from this resolve, I condemn myself each time to distribute two gold florins in alms within a month. I have taken this resolution in my fiftieth year.

Knowing my weakness in the face of sin, I make another resolve on the same day. In order to ensure the peace and good of my own conscience, I vowed that I would never accept any office, if my name should be drawn, wherein I would have power to wield the death penalty. If I should depart from this resolution, I condemn myself to give 25 gold florins in alms to the poor within three months for each such office that I have agreed to accept. And I shall in no way attempt to influence those who make up the purses for such offices, either asking them to put or not put in my name, but shall let them do as they think fit. If I should do otherwise, I condemn myself to distribute a gold florin.

Children – 1404

Glory, honor and praise be to Almighty God. Continuing from folio 5, I shall list the children which He shall in His grace bestow on me and my wife, Ginevra.

On Sunday morning at terce, 27 April of the same year, Ginevra gave birth to our first-born son. He was baptized at the hour of vespers on Monday the 28th in the church of S. Giovanni. We named him Manetto Domenico. His sponsors in God's love were Bartolo di Giovanni di Niccola, Giovanni di Michelozzo, a belt-maker, and Domenico di Deo, a goldsmith. God make him good.

At the third hour of Thursday, 19 March 1405, Ginevra gave birth to a female child of less than seven months. She had not realized she was pregnant, since for four months she had been ailing as though she were not, and in the end was unable to hold it. We baptized it at once in the church of S. Giovanni. The sponsors were Bartolo, Monna Buona, another lady, and the blind woman. Having thought at first that it was a boy, we named it Agnolo Giovanni. It died at dawn on Sunday morning, 22 March, and was buried before the sermon.

At terce on Tuesday morning, 8 June 1406, Ginevra had her third child, a fine full-term baby girl whom we had baptized on Friday morning, 9 June. We christened her Elisabetta Caterina and she will be called Lisabetta in memory of my dead wife, Betta. The sponsors were Fra Lorenzo, Bartolo, and the blind woman.

On 4 June 1407, a Saturday, Ginevra gave birth after a nine-month pregnancy to a little girl whom we had baptized on the evening of Tuesday the 7th. We named her Antonia Margherita and we shall call her Antonia. Her godfather was Nello di Ser Piero Nelli, a neighbor. God grant her good fortune.

At terce, Sunday, 31 July 1411, Ginevra gave birth to a very attractive baby boy whom we had baptized on 4 August. The sponsors were my colleagues among the Standard-bearers of the Militia Companies with the exception of two: Giorgio and Bartolomeo Fioravanti. We called the child Niccolò. God bless him. God was pleased to call the child very shortly to Himself. He died of dysentery on 22 October at terce. May he intercede with God for us.

At terce on Sunday, 1 October 1412, Ginevra had a son whom, from devotion to St. Jerome—since it was yesterday that her pains began—I called Girolamo Domenico. The sponsors were Master Bartolomeo del Carmine, Cristofano di Francesco di Ser Giovanni, and Lappuccio di Villa, and his son Bettino. God grant him and us health and make him a good man.

God willed that the blessed soul of our daughter Betta should return to Him after a long illness. She passed away during the night between Tuesday and the first Wednesday of Lent at four in the morning, 21 February 1414. She was seven years and seven months, and I was sorely grieved at her death. God grant she pray for us.

On 1 May 1415, at the hour of terce on a Wednesday, God granted us a fine little boy, and I had him baptized at four on Saturday morning. Jacopo di Francesco di Tura and Aringhieri di Jacopo, the wool merchant, were his godfathers. May God grant that he be healthy, wise, and good. We named him after the two holy apostles, Jacopo and Filippo, on whose feast day he was born and we shall call him Filippo.

At eleven o'clock on Friday, 24 April 1416, Ginevra gave birth to a baby girl after a painful and almost fatal labor. The child was baptized immediately on S. Marco's Day, the 25th. We called her Ghita in memory of our mother. Monna Mea di Franchino was her godmother.

Manetto died in Pisa in January 1418. He had been very sick and was buried in S. Martino. Pippo died on 2 August 1419 in Val di Pesa in a place called Polonia. This is recorded in notebook B.

At two o'clock on the night following Monday 17 July, Lisa was born. She was baptized by Master Pagolo from Montepulciano, a preaching friar,[12] on Wednesday at seven o'clock. God console us, amen. She later died.

Altogether Ginevra and I had eleven children: four boys and seven girls.

Memorandum – 1405

To take up my record of past years from folio 7, I served among the Ten on Liberty.[13] My term began on 1 April and ran four months. My colleagues were Arrigo Mazinghi, Niccoloso Cambi, Giraldo di Lorenzo, Piero Velluti, Nastagio di Benincasa, Uguccione Giandonati, Michele di Banco, two artisans, and myself. I pleased everyone and acted as rightly as I was able.

I was Guild Consul for the third time from 1 May of the same year. With me were Zanobi di Ser Gino, Agnolo di Ghezzo, Noze Manetti, and Agnolo di Filippo di Ser Giovanni [Pandolfini].

I began proceedings against Messer Giovanni Serristori and Company on the ... of September before the Merchants' Court. I was reluctant to do this but had no choice. I had suffered grievous harm in spirit and pocket and was likely to be ruined if I did not defend myself. God bring me safely out of this! The partnership with Piero and Jacopo Lana and Nardo di Lippo expired on 31 December 1406. We did not renew it because of the risks we had run in connection with what had happened in Spain. It is advisable for us to lie low for a while and wait and pay our creditors and put our trust in God. I have reached an agreement with Piero establishing the time and manner in which I must pay him. I am to do so through Bernardo who has a copy of the agreement.

I was a Guild Consul for the fourth time from 1 September 1408, in company with Lapo Corsi, Chimento di Stefano, Filippo di Ghezo, Francesco di Messer Jacopo Marchi, and Matteo di Lorenzo, the goldsmith.

On 11 November 1408, I set out for Valencia and Murcia, and reached Murcia on 30 December. I travelled overland in the company of Pagolo Mei and it was a difficult journey. I left Murcia in May 1410 and delayed in Valencia on account of the risks of both the sea and land route, due to the war between ourselves and the King[14] and the Genoese. In February I finally set out and took ship at Barcelona whence I sailed for Piombino which I reached on 12 March at terce on St. Gregory's Day and was in Florence on 15 March 1411.

In that year 1411, there was a plague, and Piero Lana died. That December I made an agreement with his brother and partner, Jacopo, who had been my partner too, and with Piero's sons through Dino di Messer Guccio and Bernardo and Pagolo di Vanni and Zanobi di Ser Benozzo, who acted as intermediaries.

Our Master Lionardo was elected Father General of the Dominican Order by the chapter, with great harmony and festivities and honor on 29 September, the Feast of the Angels, and the following day, the feast of S. Jerome, the holiday and procession were held. Praise be to God.

Mona Ghita, our beloved mother, departed this wretched life and returned her soul to her Creator before dawn on Monday morning, 29 January 1414. She received the last sacraments and passed away peacefully. May God receive her in his bosom. Amen.

Partnership with Pietro Lana, 1408

The accounts of the shop and company are written above on page 8. As a result of the adversity which overtook us in Barcelona, and of the lawsuit here which followed it, and of the suspicions concerning Simone's ventures and the calumnies that were spread about, we were very short of credit. So we were forced to withdraw from business and collect whatever we could to pay our creditors, borrowing from friends and using all our ingenuity, suffering losses, high interest and expense in order to avoid bankruptcy and shame. And although my partner was in favor of going bankrupt so as to avoid some losses and expenditure, I was resolved to face ruin rather than loss of honor. I held out so firmly and struggled to such purpose that in the end we managed to pay all our debts, and I satisfied all claims except those of my partners. May God be praised and blessed. I am sure too that if I had managed to send Simone the silk and gold which he was to sell the King, he would have brought his business to a successful conclusion. But I could not send it, and indeed had to abandon all business activity until 1405. Then the lawsuit began and I had to sell whatever goods I had here so as to pay my debts, and I was obliged to renege on my promises to send him what he needed for the King. Consequently, his business began to collapse and stagnate. Indeed, it sank into such confusion that it has been impossible to set it back on its feet, and it has gone ever since from bad to worse.

As Simone was doing badly himself, he was unable to send us the consignments and remittances we needed. My partner, who had grown very impatient, kept complaining in public and behaving in a way unfavorable to our common interest. While I was in Spain, Antonio di Ser Bartolomeo and two other powerful companies took proceedings against him in connection with a transaction they had concluded with me. He defended our interest very badly, did not produce our accounts as evidence, and merely tried to show that he himself was not liable. The judgement went against him and he was forced to pay. Of the 500 florins we had received from them, I had already paid back 300 florins to their agent in Spain, so that we only owed them a residue of 200. Yet they were awarded 2,000 silver florins. I do not think such a thing ever happened before or since. And I hope it may bring them bad luck. Yet we have to stand to the loss of it and the fault lies with my partner and his crooked ways.

Hearing that Pagolo Mei was going to Spain, I

decided to travel with him and see whether I could save something from the ruin of our branch there. We left Florence on 12 November 1408, travelled by land and, after a very wearisome journey in harsh wintry weather, reached Murcia[15] on 30 December. Simone came to meet us there and for a while we had good hopes of his business but these were later deceived because of the falsity of the Spaniards, and because, through no error of his, he was unfairly treated. I was back in Florence safe and sound on 15 March 1411, but all I brought with me was a great deal of sorrow and weariness.

My partner, Lana, kept tormenting me in every way he could and denounced me to the Merchant's Court as a bankrupt, asking them to have me publicly denounced by their herald. He did not succeed in getting them to pass sentence against me, for I had not gone bankrupt but had returned from abroad to settle my accounts with him and to do what I could towards satisfying him. In the middle of this dispute, he died of the plague in July 1411.

After that it was God's will to recall to Himself the blessed soul of my wife Ginevra. She died in childbirth after lengthy suffering, which she bore with remarkable strength and patience. She was perfectly lucid at the time of her death when she received all the sacraments: confession, communion, extreme unction, and a papal indulgence granting absolution for all her sins, which she received from Master Lionardo, who had been granted it by the Pope. It comforted her greatly, and she returned her soul to her Creator on 7 September, the Eve of the Feast of Our Lady, at nones: the hour when Our Blessed Lord Jesus Christ expired on the cross and yielded up his spirit to our Heavenly Father. On Friday the 8th she was honorably buried and on the 9th, masses were said for her soul. Her body lies in our plot at S. Spirito and her soul has gone to eternal life. God bless her and grant us fortitude. Her loss has sorely tried me. May He help me to bring up the unruly family which is left to me in the best way for their souls and bodies.

God who shows his wisdom in all things permitted the plague to strike our house. The first to succumb was our manservant Paccino at the end of June 1420. Three days later it was the turn of our slave-girl Marta, after her on 1 July my daughter Sandra and on 5 July my daughter Antonia. We left that house after that and went to live opposite, but a few days later Veronica died. Again we moved, this time to Via Chiara where Bandecca and Pippa fell ill and departed this life on 1 August. All of them bore the marks of the plague. It passed off after that and we returned to our own house. May God bless them all. Bandecca's will and her accounts appear on page ... of my ledger A.

I then took another wife, Caterina, the daughter of Dardano Guicciardini. She was thirty years of age, and came to our house on 30 March 1421. Her personal accounts are written in detail further on in folio 13. God grant us a good life together, amen.

My name was drawn to serve among the Twelve Good Men, and I began my term of office on 15 September 1421. My colleagues were Antonio d'Ubaldo di Fetto, Buonaccorso Corsellini, Antonio di Piero di Fronte, Piero di Buonaccorso di Vanni, Lapo di Giovanni Bucelli, Dino di Messer Guccio, Tomaso di Giacomo di Goggio, Guarente the goldsmith, Michele di Nardo Pagnini, Bencivenni di Cristoforo, and Puccino di Ser Andrea. No greater unanimity could be found than that which reigned amongst us. Thanks be to God.

My name was drawn to be Overseer for the Guild Hospital[16] for one year. I began to serve on 1 May 1422 with Bartolo Corsi, Giovanni di Deo, Salvi Lotti, Cione di Cecco Cioni, and Tommaso di Pazzino.

On 9 September 1422, the Signoria and Colleges elected me to serve among the Five Defenders of the County and District in lieu of Parigi Corbinelli who had been appointed Podestà. I took office on the 10th of the month and served during January with Giovanni di Messer Forese [Salviati], Salvestro Popoleschi, Giovanni Carradori, and Piero del Palagio. It is an onerous office, in which one may gain merit in the sight of God and acquire contempt for the world. We did a great deal to improve the lot of the unfortunate peasants.

My Fourth Wife's Personal Account

In the name of God and of the Virgin Mary, or SS.

Gregory and Catherine, I shall note down here matters relating to my fourth wife.

Memo that on Tuesday, 28 January 1421, I made an agreement with Niccolò d'Andrea del Benino to take his niece, Caterina, for my lawful wife. She is the daughter of the late Dardano di Niccolò Guicciardini and of Monna Tita, Andrea del Benino's daughter. We were betrothed on the morning of Monday, 3 February, the Eve of Carnival. I met Piero and Giovanni di Messer Luigi [Guicciardini] in the church of S. Maria sopra Porta, and Niccolò d'Andrea del Benino was our mediator. The dowry promised me was 600 florins, and the notary was Ser Niccolò di Ser Verdiano. I went to dine with her that evening in Piero's house and the Saturday after Easter—29 March 1421—Ser Niccolò drew up a public instrument, whereby I attested to the receipt of a dowry amounting to 615 florins from Giovanni di Messer Luigi. I then received it from him and her as appears in my ledger B on page 128, including a trousseau worth fifteen florins. Madalena and Bernardo and Michele di Manetto went surety for me. That day I gave her the ring and then on Sunday evening, 30 March, she came to live in our house simply and without ceremony. On 7 May 1421, I paid the tax on contracts. See Register A 72, page 56. It came to sixteen florins, four *soldi*, four *denari*. God be praised and thanked and may He grant us a peaceful and healthy life, amen.

Offspring – 1422

The following is a list of the children begotten by me.

I was single when my first son, Maso,[17] was born on 21 December 1391—this appears on the back of page 4. Before his birth I had got Bandecca with child but she had a miscarriage in her sixth month in July 1390. After that, as I have indicated on page 5, I had eight children by my second wife, Betta; five boys and three girls. Then, as I show on page 10, I had eleven children by my third wife, Ginevra: four boys and seven girls. Altogether, not counting the one that did not live to be baptized, I have had twenty children: ten boys and ten girls. Of these, Maso, Bernardo, Girolamo, Ghita and Betta are still alive. Praise be to God for all things, amen.

Caterina, my fourth wife, miscarried after four months and the child did not live long enough to receive baptism. That was in August 1421.

On 4 October 1422, at one o'clock on a Sunday night, Caterina gave birth to a daughter. We had Fra Aducci and Fra Giovanni Masi baptize her on Monday the 5th and christen her Ginevra Francesca. May God bless her.

At three o'clock on Friday, 7 January 1424, Caterina gave birth to a fine healthy boy whom we had baptized on the morning of Saturday the 8th.

The godparents were the Abbot Simone of S. Felice and Michele di Manetto. We christened the child Antonio Felice. God grant he turn out a good man.

Between eight and nine o'clock on the morning of Tuesday, 20 March 1425, Caterina had another healthy and attractive child who was baptized the following day—the 21st—which was the feast of St. Benedict. Fra Cristofano, Father Provincial of the monks of S. Maria Novella, the prior, Master Alessio, Master Girolamo, and Fra Benedetto were his sponsors. We christened him Lionardo Benedetto. God make him a good man.

At three in the morning of 26 July 1426, Caterina had a fine little girl whom we christened Anna Bandecca. The baptism was on the 27th and her sponsors were Antonina and Monna Lucia. God grant her His grace and that she be a comfort to us.

At two o'clock in the night of Monday, 28 August 1427, Caterina gave birth to a fine little girl. She was baptized on Wednesday morning the 22nd and christened Filippa Felice. The Abbot of S. Felice, Giovanni di Messer Forese Salviati, and Giuliano di Tommaso di Guccio, who had served in the same office with me, were her sponsors. God grant she be a source of consolation to us and fill her with His grace. Our Lord called her to Himself on 19 October 1430. This appears on page 30, notebook E. May God bless her.

At about eleven o'clock on Saturday, 2 June 1431, Caterina gave birth to a girl who was baptized on Monday the 4th in S. Giovanni's and christened Bartolomea Domenica. See notebook E, page 46.

Our Lord was pleased to call to Himself and to eternal life our two blessed children, Lionardo and Ginevra, on Saturday, 6 October 1431. This appears in notebook one, page 14. Lionardo had been in perfect health twenty-four hours before his death. God bless them and grant us the grace to bear their loss with fortitude.

Memoranda – 1422

Some items worth bearing in mind are noted above on page 12. I shall follow them up with an account of events which happen during the course of the current year or of years to come.

We received news that our brother, Simone di Stagio, who had lived for about twenty-eight years in Spain and Valencia, had passed from this life of tribulation at the hour of nones on Saturday, 23 May, after receiving the sacraments as befits a devout Christian. May Our Lord receive his soul in eternal life.

I bought the house next to my own house on the corner from Monna Mea through a third party to whom she had mortgaged it. The whole transaction is clearly described in my ledger B on page 132. It cost me 50 florins.

I was Guild Consul for the eighth time from the beginning of May 1423. With me served Francesco della Luna, Agnolo di Ghezo, Niccolò di Giovanni Carducci, Francesco Bartolelli, and Giovanni di Deo. Agnolo died during his term in office, and his place was taken by Lorenzo di Piero di Lenzo.

I agreed to serve as Podestà of Montale and Agliana in order to avoid the plague. My term of office was from 12 April to 12 October 1424. A great number of people accompanied me there and, by God's grace, none of us got sick. I was the first to stay in the residence at Montale and I saw to it that it was properly furnished and arranged. I acquired little wealth there but was highly esteemed by the inhabitants. Thanks be to God.

Our brother, Master Lionardo, General of the Preaching Friars, passed on from this life on Friday, 16 March 1425. He had been in very poor health. He received the sacraments and his funeral was honored by the Commune, the Parte Guelfa, the Merchant's Court, and the Guild Heads. His personal account is entered on page 116 of ledger B. I received a general acquittance from the friars and Chapter covering all transactions I had ever conducted with him. The instrument was drawn up by Ser Cristofano da Laterina on the advice of Messer Stefano Bonaccorsi on 3 March 1425 and I have it at home.

My name was drawn to serve among the Lord Priors of the city of Florence for a term of two months, starting on 1 July and finishing on the last day of August 1425. Serving with me were: Giovanni Grasso, Lapo Bucelli, Piero di Bonaccorso, Domenico di Tano, Giandonato di Cecco, Niccolò Valori, Cresci di Lorenzo, and Lorenzo di Piero di Lenzo, the Standard-bearer of Justice. The war[18] made our task extremely onerous but, by the grace of God, we left matters in a better way than we found them.

By the grace of God, I was Standard-bearer of Justice for two months from 1 March 1429. The priors serving with me were: Zanobi di Tommaso Bartoli, a feather-bed maker, Bianco d'Agnoli, a maker of wine glasses, as artisans of the quarter of S. Spirito; Riccardo di Niccolò Fagni and Berto di Lionardo Berti for S. Croce; Pierozzo di Francesco della Lana and Piero di Francesco Redditi for S. Maria Novella; Antonio di Ghezzo della Casa and Francesco di Piero Gherucci for S. Giovanni; and Ser Iacopo Salvestri, our notary. By God's grace we worked harmoniously together and accomplished a number of good things. I had a column placed in Piazza S. Felice; it was brought from the Mercato Vecchio, and the decision was taken by the priorate.

1428. Chronological notes concerning myself. The first, which appears on page 12, records how I was born on 15 April 1362. Further on, mention is made of the death of Stagio in 1374 and of how I began to work in the silk business in 1375 and of how Madalena got married in 1380. It is true that we owed Manetto more than 200 florins at that time, and that we owned nothing but the house and some old furniture. On 1 January 1385, I was made a partner in the business and was supposed to invest 300 florins in it. However, as appears on page 3, I was already in debt for even more than that, largely on account of expenses to which I had been put by Don Jacopo. I did well for several years after that as can be seen on page 2. In 1388 I got married and received a dowry and was able to pay off the debt that year, as well as furnishing the house decently and keeping almost within my capital. In 1390, my wife Bandecca died and I went to Valencia for the company. I returned in 1392. We had done well during this period, but due to the bad debt that Giovanni Stefani contracted with our company, I found myself rather short of money. In 1393 I married my second wife as is indicated on page 4. The dowry was substantial but I spent too much. In 1394 I was captured and robbed at sea and suffered considerable losses as is shown on page 4 of this diary. That year I bought a half share in the farm at Antella and neither made nor lost money. However, having left the company in 1395, I set up on my own and did well and made 300 or more florins. As appears on page 6, I bought Michele's share of Giovanni Stefani's debt from him for 600 florins with certain terms. I thought this to be a clever move, but it turned out not to be and I lost most of my investment. However I went into partnership with Michele in 1396, as is shown above on page 6. As I was short of money, I promised to put up 1,000 florins which, for as long as the company lasted, I was obliged to borrow on interest or raise in other ways, drawing money against Simone's account in Valencia by means of bills of exchange and other stratagems. And I did very well up to the year 1402, as appears on page 7. However, in 1400, I took refuge from the plague in Antella and spent more than 500 florins on the house and in planting vines. I had other expenses too, so that in 1402, when I parted company with Michele, I had about 1,000 florins. The entry indicates 1,370 [florins] but I owed the rest. That year, as is indicated earlier, I went into partnership with Piero Lana and engaged myself to invest 2,000 florins. I got married that same year for the third time and received over 600 florins cash as is shown on page 8. Thus I was able to invest that sum in the company, which meant that I still owed over 300 florins.

At this point, fortune turned against me. Simone had gone into business on his own account in Valencia and was involved in transactions with the King of Castile. I let him have great quantities of merchandise and bills of exchange for large sums of money. I had been against his engaging in this activity, but he was convinced that he was in trouble, litigation and losses so

that we went deeply into debt and were on the point of going bankrupt. I had to join him in Spain in 1408, and spent almost three years there and in Valencia, recovering only a tiny portion of our losses. As ill fortune would have it, the King, with whom Simone had dealt, died in 1406 and as a result of this Simone was unjustly treated and ruined. Our company lost over 10,000 florins in this affair, which swallowed up all our capital. Over and above these losses, Piero Lana was forced to pay further sums, and so was I, for I paid over 1,000 florins from Matteo's legacy. Piero brought a lawsuit against me which might have harmed me greatly and, in 1412, I reached a settlement with his heirs as appears on page 72 of Ledger B. I agreed to pay them 2,400 florins and, as also appears from the ledger, I finished paying off this debt in 1422. The interest I had to pay in this period amounted to over 600 florins. So one may say that in 1412, according to a rough estimate that I made of my losses and the interest I had to pay on account of them, I was in debt for over 3,000 florins. That same year 1412, my name was drawn to be Standard-bearer of Justice, and I served in that office. This was the beginning of my recovery. After that, in 1414, I married off Bandecca and gave her a dowry of 550 florins. That same year our brother Lionardo was made Father General of his Order. So our trust in God aided and comforted us.

After reaching the settlement with Piero Lana's heirs in 1412, I found myself in debt for about 3,000 florins. God came to my aid then with the promotion of my brother who, as Father General, was in a position to help me pay off the debt. The assistance he gave me from time to time and according to his means is recorded in ledger B, page 94. The sums he paid out to me and in my name up to the year 1420 amounted to 2,330 florins, and he made me a gift of them. There were still 700 florins to be paid off and, as my living expenses during that time amounted to more than that sum, my total debt was 1,500 florins. However, I had sold off various pieces of furniture, which brought in 200 florins; the sale of the Campi farm brought in 250 gold florins; Ginevra's communal bonds brought in interest amounting to 200 florins. When Pope John [XXIII] came, I made 150 Bologna florins from cloths I made for him, and in 1418 I made 200 florins as *Proveditore*19 in Pisa. All this amounted to 1,000 florins, so that I can say that in 1412 I only owed 500 florins.

I set up in business again, and in 1421 I remarried and my wife brought me 600 florins. In the course of 1421 and 1422, the Father General lent me 1,000 florins. Michele joined my company and I did well so that when we drew up our third balance sheet on 1 January 1424, my own profit came to 1,100 florins. This profit, together with my wife's dowry and what the Father General had lent me, came to 2,700. When I had subtracted the 500 florins for my debt and further sums for expenses, I had about 900 florins left in hand. In 1424 I got money from the Father General in Cosimo's20 name which he later turned into a gift, together with another sum which brought it to 500 florins, so that altogether I had 1,400 florins net. However, God called him to Himself that year and we did badly in the business. I don't know how this occurred, for I was at Montale and my losses amounted to 250 florins. Then the war started and we made very little while it lasted but had to bear heavy expenses. However, the greatest damage to me was the terrible tax burden imposed by the Commune, which cost me 1,200 florins. I had to pay back a dowry, for which I had gone surety, to Nardo di Lippo's wife. This cost me 300 florins, and I have entered this debt against the heir on page 2 of register D. I don't know whether I will be able to recover the money. So, in 1427, I was almost able to keep within my capital. I set up a new company with Michele and Giovanni di Ser Guido and, in my red account book, the capital and merchandise assessed at the cash value amounted to 1,000 florins, allowing 300 florins to pay for the furnishings and goodwill. But in my old white purchases book B, I have a debt of about 700 florins, so I have practically no liquid capital at all.21

Notes

1 The phrase *soldi a fiorino* refers to a money of account commonly used in Florentine monetary

calculation. Twenty-nine *soldi a fiorino* were equivalent to one gold florin.

2 These and other page references refer to pages in Dati's ledger.

3 Jacopo was a priest.

4 This was apparently an old business dispute involving Gregorio Dati's grandfather, Dato.

5 Gregorio's brother, Lionardo Dati, was a Dominican friar, who later was elected General of the Order.

6 The disparity between capital invested and shares held is due to the fact that some partners (e.g., Michele di Ser Parente) contributed capital and no labor, while others (Dati, Spinello, and Niccolaio del Bene) contributed their services as part of their investment in the company.

7 Louis of Anjou, claimant to the Kingdom of Naples.

8 *nave dipungiata*. The phrase should perhaps be translated: "the ship owned [or captained] by Pungiata."

9 Por Santa Maria was the guild of the silk manufacturers.

10 Dati meant that these obligations were not to be considered legally binding.

11 A member of one of the Signoria's advisory Colleges. Dati's district (*gonfalone*) was Ferze, in the quarter of S. Spirito.

12 A member of the Dominican Order.

13 The Ten on Liberty (*Dieci di Libertà*) was a magistracy whose primary function was to settle quarrels between citizens.

14 Florence's antagonist was King Ladislaus of Naples. This war is described in Pitti's diary.

15 Murcia is an inland town in southeastern Castile, some 100 miles south of the port city of Valencia.

16 The famous Spedale degli Innocenti, the Foundling Home in the Piazza SS. Annunziata. The construction of the building, for which Brunelleschi was architect, was begun two years earlier, in 1420.

17 Maso was the child born of the slave girl, Margherita, in Valencia.

18 Florence was then at war with Filippo Maria Visconti, ruler of Milan.

19 The *Proveditori*, a magistracy of five citizens with general responsibility for the government of Pisa and its contado.

20 The banker, Cosimo de' Medici.

21 Dati died on 17 September 1435; he did not keep his diary for the last eight years of his life.